JOHN DRYDEN

a reference guide

JAMES M. HALL

G.K.HALL &CO.

70 LINCOLN STREET, BOSTON, MASS.

Library of Congress Cataloging in Publication Data

Hall, James M.
  John Dryden, a reference guide.

  Bibliography
  Includes index.
  1. Dryden, John, 1631-1700—Bibliography. I. Title.
Z8244.H34 1984 [PR3423]   016.821'4   83-10753
ISBN 0-8161-8088-1

This publication is printed on permanent/durable acid-free paper
MANUFACTURED IN THE UNITED STATES OF AMERICA

Contents

The Author

James M. Hall is associate professor of English at the University of Cincinnati. He received his Ph.D. from Yale University in 1966, where he wrote a dissertation on Milton's prose under Professor Davis P. Harding. His current research interests include English Renaissance and Restoration Literature, especially lyric poetry, Milton, Dryden, and Samuel Pepys.

Preface

I have compiled this bibliography and research guide while sitting on giants' shoulders. I must especially mention David J. Latt and Samuel Holt Monk, whose John Dryden: A Survey and Bibliography (1976.30) provided the master list for the period 1895-1972. I have examined nearly every item in their list and can testify to its accuracy and completeness. Indeed many of their items do not appear here: it was obviously their intent to cast as wide a net as possible, and often works listed there, while interesting and significant in themselves, are truly tangential to Dryden studies. I have also benefited from the work of James M. Osborn, Hugh Macdonald, W.R. Keast, James and Helen Kinsley, Upali Amarasinghe, John A. Zamonski, and George Hammerbacher.

Aside from its coverage of periods not previously surveyed, the major innovation of this work is to provide full summaries of the contents of as many secondary works on Dryden as possible. Since this has not been done before, the duplication (at times, quadruplication) of surveys of recent scholarship seems justified. Much remains to be done, especially for the eighteenth and early nineteenth centuries, where periodical literature lies essentially unexamined. What appears here should be taken as only representative of what might have been listed, in a much longer survey, for the period 1700-1850. What such a listing would add to our understanding of the course of Dryden's reputation is unclear, but it is likely that my division of its history into phases would both be substantiated and complicated.

This work is essentially complete through 1980. I have added such entries for 1981 as I could find before the book had to go to press. Readers who wish to investigate more recent material should consult the annual bibliographies of the Modern Language Association and the Modern Humanities Research Association, checking items listed under general seventeenth-century categories as well as those under Dryden. An especially useful additional tool (for books) is the annual review of Restoration and eighteenth-century scholarship in the Summer issue of Studies in English Literature 1500-1900. The Eighteenth Century: A Current Bibliography, published by the AMS Press, also provides usefully wide coverage of Dryden and his period. I have included only those editions of collected or individual works which contain significant introductory material or notes: thus school texts, for example, do not appear. I have not, for the most part, annotated dissertations that did not originally appear in book format. Most of these are abstracted by their authors in DA or DAI. Entries I have not seen are marked with an asterisk: I have given such bibliographic information as I could find, together with the source of that information. Reprint information is selective: virtually every scholarly work that has passed out of copyright has been reprinted somewhere, often more than once. I have tended to avoid multiple listing, and with older material have given the standard modern edition.

Research for this bibliography was aided by a grant from the Charles Phelps Taft Memorial Foundation for the academic year 1977-78. A grant from the University Research Council of the University of Cincinnati supported the preparation of the manuscript. The staffs of the libraries of the University of Cincinnati (especially the Interlibrary Loan Department), Cambridge University, Wright State University, and Northern Kentucky University were invaluable early and late. Danny Miller, my research assistant in the Spring Quarter of 1980, performed some of the more tiresome parts of the work with good humor and efficiency, as did Debbie, Rachel, and John Hall. Elizabeth Sato and Kazuya Sato helped with Japanese titles. I would also like to thank three of my colleagues in the Department of English at the University of Cincinnati—Jill Rubenstein, Keith Stewart, and especially Sanford Golding—for advice, assistance, and encouragement at various stages of the project. Evelyn Schott facilitated matters with her customary skill; the manuscript was typed by Marilyn Schwiers, Janice Schwiers, and Barb Cassell. My family bore my long distraction with good grace.

Introduction

> More libels have been written against me, than almost
> any man now living, and I had reason on my side, to
> have defended my own innocence. I speak not of my
> poetry, which I have wholly given up to the critics;
> let them use it as they please; posterity, perhaps,
> may be more favourable to me, for interest and pas-
> sion will lie buried in another age, and partiality
> and prejudice be forgotten.

So Dryden wrote in 1693, in "Discourse Concerning the Original
and Progress of Satire." His immediate comment concerns the many partisan attacks on his morality, politics, and religion. These have indeed been largely forgotten, but his hope about the future treatment of
his work is even yet not completely fulfilled. This bibliography documents that treatment. It is not surprising that Dryden was often attacked during his lifetime: as a public writer he took many controversial positions in a contentious and articulate age. What is surprising is the extent to which the nature and quality of his work have
always been a matter of argument. To read through three hundred years
of Dryden criticism is to read a series of debates--on his personal
morality and the morality of his work; on the propriety (and, more recently, the causes) of his conversion to Roman Catholicism; on his
stature compared to Pope's; on his role in the "dissociation of sensibility"; on the question of his "Pyrrhonical skepticism" or lack of
it; on whether his poetry is poetry or prose; on the essential non-
seriousness of Restoration drama; on his relation to Shakespeare; on
how much worse a playwright he is than Shakespeare; on his debts to
French literature, to Spanish literature, to the classics; on the gap
(or continuity) between his theory and practice, between his declared
intent and realized effect. It is the nature of his work, and especially his habit of commenting on his work, to invite such arguments.

For Dryden is himself one of the great Dryden critics. This has
been both a boon and a hindrance to his reputation. Many of his students have found in his self-directed comments a convenient starting
point for analysis and evaluation, but on the other hand he has laid
himself open to discussions of consistency, sincerity, and authorial

intent which other writers have escaped. In the line of great English author-critics which runs from Sir Philip Sidney through Samuel Johnson to T.S. Eliot and Virginia Woolf he is unique in the extent and depth of his self-consciousness. The importance of this quality as a model for critics, authors, and students of literature has transcended the difficulties it may have caused his reputation. If the tradition of English criticism has a flexibility, grace, and vigor not to be found in neighboring countries (or across the Atlantic) Dryden is probably more responsible than anyone else.

Dryden's criticism covers more than thirty-five years, a longer span than that of all but a very few of the more than one thousand critics included in the present work. With the exception of the early Essay of Dramatic Poesy (1668), his critical work is occasional: much of the inconsistency with which he has been charged can be explained by reference to the pragmatic and shifting demands of local circumstances, including not only the nature of the play or poem involved (most of his critical pieces are in fact prefaces) but also the identity of his dedicatee and, sometimes, the tenor of someone's comment on another of his works. But in a general sense he is a transmitter of the classical tradition and what to him were its modern versions. Within that framework his position is basically Horatian, emphasizing as it does the obligation of art to teach and, especially, please. His classicism is sufficiently flexible, however, to note (as in "Heads of an Answer to Rymer," 1677) situations in which the "rules" seemed not to match the experience of his taste. This flexibility has contributed to his reputation for inconsistency. But while his failure to develop a system may have been criticized by some, his contributions to the vocabulary and techniques of criticism are crucial to the development of literary inquiry as a practicable occupation.

The history of Dryden's reputation has four phases. The first, that of his own lifetime, is characterized by much attack and some praise, in either case largely the product of personal (or political) animosity or friendship. Among these pieces there is little of permanent value or interest. The Duke of Buckingham's The Rehearsal (1671.1) is not only the most important piece of Dryden criticism in the period, it is the only extended example of it. Its satiric exposure of the excesses of the heroic play seems to have had little effect either on Dryden or on the popularity of the form, but it did establish many of the terms on which the genre is still attacked and defended. The other major piece of criticism during the seventeenth century was not directed primarily at Dryden, nor was it essentially literary in its concerns: Jeremy Collier's A Short View of the Profaneness and Immorality of the English Stage (1698.2). This piece, separated from The Rehearsal by a major shift in taste, attacks the morality of Restoration drama: Collier is particularly upset at the improper distribution of punishments and rewards at the plays' ends. In his disparaging comparison of the drama of his own time with that of earlier ages, Collier however shows himself (probably unwittingly) to be a disciple of Dryden: the concept of literary periods is one which Dryden recognized as early as the preface to <u>The Rival Ladies</u> (1664).

The second phase, which establishes the stature of Dryden as a monument, runs from his death in 1700 to Samuel Johnson's essay in <u>Lives of the Poets</u> (1779.2). Writers in this period may occasionally carp at Dryden's lapses in poetic decorum, but they see him as the progenitor of Augustan poetry, more responsible than any other influence for the refinement of English style. Johnson's oft-quoted tribute to Dryden's achievement may be taken as an epitome of the eighteenth-century attitude: "What was said of Rome, adorned by Augustus, may be applied . . . to English poetry embellished by Dryden, . . . he found it brick, and he left it marble."

When new views about the proper ends of art rose to the surface in the Romantic period, Dryden's reputation, now in its third phase, began to suffer, although Upali Amarasinghe has shown (in 1962.2) that "Augustan" points of view persisted, at least as a strong minority voice, well into the nineteenth century. Two contemporary comments on Sir Walter Scott's great edition of Dryden's complete works (1808.3) are perhaps typical: one reviewer deplores the "baneful industry of research" that has made Dryden available; another, the literary historian Henry Hallam, praises Dryden for writing well--in spite of his material (1813.1; 1808.1). These attitudes were to last well into the twentieth century. Dryden was widely seen as both inconsistent (in almost every way imaginable) and immoral. Macaulay's essay in the <u>Edinburgh Review</u> (1828.1), which attacks him for lack of realism as well as on these other grounds, was still being quoted a century later (although usually by Dryden's defenders). Another phenomenon of this phase is the relative neglect of the poetry (except for the <u>Fables</u> and the St. Cecilia's Day poems, which seem to have fit the taste of the period). The major satires and religious poems, although they are often mentioned, do not dominate commentary on Dryden, as they did in earlier and would do in later periods: most critics draw their examples largely from the plays.

At the same time, however, much important biographical and textual work was getting done. Edmond Malone's life (1800.1), as expanded and reworked by Scott (1808.3), provided a plausible chronology and explanation of the relatively few biographical detailes that were known. With the onset of scholarly journals in the second half of the century, and the editions of Robert Bell (1854.2), W.D. Christie (1870.1), George Saintsbury (1882.3--a revision and correction of Scott), and George R. Noyes (1909.4), the Dryden canon and text were basically established, so that detailed study of his works only needed the impetus of widespread approval.

The modern phase of Dryden studies may be said to begin with Mark Van Doren's <u>The Poetry of John Dryden</u> (1920.10). This study was the first comprehensive discussion and evaluation of the poetry (including the dramatic poetry). Van Doren's book in turn stimulated T.S. Eliot's

arguments for Dryden's significance and potential value for modern
poets "in the next revolution of taste" (1921.3). Furthermore, the
three-hundredth anniversary of Dryden's birth in 1931 brought forth a
large number of appreciations which solidified his position as a writer
of the first rank. Another development of the 1920s and 1930s, perhaps
even more significant, was the arrival of rigorous American historical
and textual scholarship in the work of such figures as Richard Foster
Jones, George Williamson, William S. Clark, Roswell G. Ham, Charles E.
Ward, and especially Louis I. Bredvold. These scholars did much to
open to view the literary, political, religious, and philosophical contexts of Dryden's work. Bredvold's The Intellectual Milieu of John
Dryden: Studies in Some Aspects of Seventeenth Century Thought
(1934.3), though its findings have since been rejected by most scholars,
was a particularly important book in that it established Dryden's knowledge and use of intellectual issues and documents of his own time.

Since the 1930s scholars, now aided by the ongoing University of
California Edition of The Works of John Dryden (in progress since 1956),
have been engaged in refining, with increasing sophistication and spe-
cialization, our views of the nature and significance of what Dryden
said and meant. With the proliferation of journals and graduate pro-
grams, especially in the United States, the output of work on Dryden
accelerated in the 1960s and 1970s. Fully half of all the material in
this bibliography has been published since 1960, although many of these
items are dissertations whose authors did not go on, or have not yet
gone on, to put their work into print. There is room for more: scholars have become narrower in focus and more limited in the works they
choose for scrutiny. While studies abound on Absalom and Achitophel,
MacFlecknoe, The Hind and the Panther (after a period of neglect), All
for Love, and Essay of Dramatic Poesy, on the other hand several major
poems and several plays are still almost undiscussed. A look at the
Dryden section of the index of this work will confirm that statement:
to cite one example, Don Sebastian, though it is often singled out for
very high praise, has only eight entries primarily devoted to it.
There is also the problem of scope: aside from an interesting but very
short book by William Myers (1973.63), and the major books of Earl Miner
on the poetry (1967.43) and Robert D. Hume on the criticism (1970.42),
few studies have been written which take a synoptic view of even a por-
tion of Dryden's total work. Miner's Dryden's Poetry, now more than
fifteen years old, is the most recent fully comprehensive study of the
poems, for instance. While more recent books have contributed much of
value, especially about the political and religious dimensions of individual works and groups of works, it is to be hoped that the contribution of the current generation of Dryden scholars will include at
least one broad study of this most important and influential writer.

A Chronology of Dryden's Life and Works

Dates are Old Style, but 1 January is used as the beginning of the year. Dates of plays are for the first performance.

1631   Born 9 August, Aldwinckle, Northants.

1646   Enters Westminster School.

1649   "Upon the Death of the Lord Hastings."

1650   Enters Trinity College, Cambridge.

1653   "To Honor Dryden."

1654   B.A., Cambridge.

1658   Death of Oliver Cromwell.

1659   Heroic Stanzas.

1660   "To My Honoured Friend Sir Robert Howard."

      Restoration of Charles II.

      Astraea Redux.

1661   To His Sacred Majesty.

1662   "To My Lord Chancellor."

1663   Elected to the Royal Society.

      "To My Honour'd Friend, Dr. Charleton."

      The Wild Gallant.

      Married 1 December to Lady Elizabeth Howard.

1664   The Rival Ladies.

      The Indian Queen (with Sir Robert Howard).

1665   The Indian Emperour.

1666   Son Charles born 27 August.

1667   Annus Mirabilis.

      Secret Love.

	Sir Martin Mar-All.
	The Tempest (with Sir William Davenant).
1668	Essay of Dramatic Poesy.
	"Defence of an Essay of Dramatic Poesy."
	Appointed Poet Laureate.
	Son John born.
	An Evening's Love.
1669	Son Erasmus-Henry born 2 May.
	Tyrannic Love.
1670	Appointed Historiographer Royal.
	The Conquest of Granada (Part 1).
1671	The Conquest of Granada (Part 2).
	Marriage a-la-Mode.
1672	"Of Heroic Plays: An Essay."
	"Defence of the Epilogue."
	The Assignation.
1673	Amboyna.
1674	Writes The State of Innocence (published 1677).
	The Mistaken Husband (authorship uncertain).
1675	Aureng-Zebe.
1677	"The Author's Apology for Heroic Poetry and Poetic Licence."
	The State of Innocence (written 1674).
	"Heads of an Answer to Rymer."
	All for Love.
1678	Mr. Limberham.
	Leaves King's Company for Duke's Company.
	MacFlecknoe (written?).
	Oedipus (with Nathaniel Lee).
1679	Troilus and Cressida.
	"The Grounds of Criticism in Tragedy."
	Exclusion Crises begin.
	Attacked and beaten in Rose Alley, 18 December.
1680	The Spanish Friar.
	Preface to Ovid's Epistles, Translated.

1681   His Majesties Declaration Defended.

        Absalom and Achitophel.

1682   The Medal.

        Religio Laici.

        The Duke of Guise (with Nathaniel Lee).

        The Second Part of Absalom and Achitophel (with Nahum Tate).

        MacFlecknoe (written c. 1678).

1683   The Vindication of the Duke of Guise.

        "Life of Plutarch."

1684   The History of the League (translation).

        Miscellany Poems.

        "To the Memory of Mr. Oldham."

1685   Preface to Sylvae.

        Death of Charles II; accession of James II.

        Threnodia Augustalis.

        Albion and Albianus.

        Conversion to Roman Catholicism?

        "To the Pious Memory of . . . Anne Killigrew."

1686   A Defence of the Papers Written by the Late King.

1687   The Hind and the Panther.

        Song for St. Cecilia's Day.

1688   The Life of St. Francis Xavier (translation).

        Britannia Rediviva.

        Deposition of James II.

1689   Accession of William III and Mary II.

        Removed as Poet Laureate and Historiographer Royal.

        Don Sebastian.

1690   Amphitryon.

1691   King Arthur (with Henry Purcell).

1692   Eleonora.

        Cleomenes.

1693   Satires of Juvenal and Persius (translations).

        "Discourse concerning the Original and Progress of Satire."

        Examen Poeticum (miscellany).

1694   Love Triumphant.

"To My Dear Friend Mr. Congreve."

"To Sir Godfrey Kneller."

Contracts with Jacob Tonson to translate Virgil.

1695   "A Parallel of Poetry and Painting."

1696   "Ode on the Death of Mr. Henry Purcell."

1697   The Works of Virgil (translation).

Alexander's Feast.

1698   Contracts with Jacob Tonson to produce Fables, Ancient and
Modern.

1700   Fables, Ancient and Modern (translations).

"The Secular Masque."

Dies 1 May; buried in Westminster Abbey.

Abbreviations

CE	College English
CL	Comparative Literature
CQ	The Cambridge Quarterly
DA	Dissertation Abstracts
DAI	Dissertation Abstracts International
DUJ	Durham University Journal
EA	Études anglaises
ECS	Eighteenth-Century Studies
EIC	Essays in Criticism
ELH	Journal of English Literary History
ELN	English Language Notes
ES	English Studies
Expl	Explicator
HLB	Harvard Library Bulletin
HLQ	Huntington Library Quarterly
JEGP	Journal of English and Germanic Philology
JWCI	Journal of the Warburg and Courtauld Institutes
Kinsley and Kinsley	Kinsley, James, and Helen Kinsley, eds. Dryden: The Critical Heritage. London: Routledge and Kegan Paul; New York: Barnes and Noble, 1971.

Lang&S   Language and Style

Latt and Monk   Latt, David J., and Samuel Holt Monk, John Dryden: A
                Survey and Bibliography of Critical Studies, 1895–
                1974. Minneapolis: University of Minnesota Press,
                1976.

MLA   Modern Language Association

MLN   Modern Language Notes

MLQ   Modern Language Quarterly

MLR   Modern Language Review

MP   Modern Philology

N&Q   Notes and Queries

OED   Oxford English Dictionary

PBSA   Papers of the Bibliographical Society of America

PLL   Papers on Language and Literature

PLPLS–LHS   Proceedings of the Leeds Philosophical and Literary
                    Society, Literary and Historical Section

PMLA   Publications of the Modern Language Association

PQ   Philological Quarterly

RECTR   Restoration and Eighteenth–Century Theatre Research

RES   Review of English Studies

RLC   Revue de littérature comparée

RLV   Revue des langues vivantes

SB   Studies in Bibliography

SCN   Seventeenth–Century News

SEL   Studies in English Literature, 1500–1900

SLitI   Studies in the Literary Imagination

SP   Studies in Philology

SQ   Shakespeare Quarterly

Abbreviations

SR	Sewanee Review
TLS	Times Literary Supplement
TN	Theatre Notebook
TSLL	Texas Studies in Literature and Language
UTQ	University of Toronto Quarterly
YES	Yearbook of English Studies

Writings about John Dryden

1668

1   F., R. [RICHARD FLECKNOE?]. A Letter from a Gentleman to the
    Honourable E. Howard, Esq.; Occasioned by a Civilized Epistle
    of Mr. Dryden's, Before his Second Edition of his Indian
    Emperour. London: printed by Thomas Newcomb, 14 pp.
        A point-by-point response to Dryden's response to Sir Robert
    Howard's quarrel with him over rhyme and verisimilitude. Accuses
    Dryden of literary (and political) inconsistency. Draws examples
    from Astraea Redux and The Indian Emperour to make Dryden seem
    foolish and incapable of applying his own theories. Reprinted:
    1975.15. See 1668.2.

2   HOWARD, Sir ROBERT. The Great Favourite, or, The Duke of Lerma.
    London: printed for Henry Herringman, 68 pp.
        The preface, "To the Reader," argues against Dryden's posi-
    tion in Essay of Dramatic Poesy that rhyme is more effective than
    blank verse in serious drama, it being less natural for a character
    to speak in rhyme than without it. Also attacks Dryden's qualified
    support for the unities of place and time. Concludes that authors
    should follow "Propositions" rather than "confident Lawes, or Rules
    made by Demonstration." Reprinted: 1975.15. See 1668.1.

1671

1   BUCKINGHAM, GEORGE VILLIERS, Duke of. The Rehearsal.
        A farce which burlesques Dryden ("Bayes") and his works,
    especially the heroic plays. Shows him to be libertine, mercenary,
    and silly; his plays to be hidebound by rules, mechanical, witless,
    and bombastic. First performed 1671. Printed: 1672.1; 1683.2.

1672

1   BUCKINGHAM, GEORGE VILLIERS, Duke of. The Rehearsal. London:
    printed for Thomas Dring.

Published version of 1671.1. The fourth edition (1683.2)
contains revisions and additions. Many times reprinted.

<u>1673</u>

1   ANON. <u>A Description of the Academy of the Athenian Virtuosi:</u>
    <u>With a Discourse held there in Vindication of Mr. Dryden's</u>
    <u>Conquest of Granada; Against the Author of the Censure of the</u>
    <u>Rota</u>. London.
         Defends Dryden's conception of Almanzor by appealing to
    "Heroick vertue" as the subject of the play. This subject demands
    mightiness of language and action. Compares the play with classi-
    cal epics to show Dryden's correctness. Reprinted: 1971.45;
    1975.15. See 1673.5.

2   ANON. <u>The Friendly Vindication of Mr. Dryden From the Censure</u>
    <u>of the Rota by His Cabal of Wits</u>. Cambridge, 17 pp.
         A supercilious "vindication" which in fact attacks Dryden
    for using incongruous and indecorous metaphors, for praising him-
    self in his dedications and prefaces, for verbal inconsistencies,
    for writing comedies which are bawdy rather than witty. Concen-
    trates on <u>The Conquest of Granada</u> and <u>Tyrannic Love</u>. Excerpted:
    1971.45; reprinted: 1975.15. See 1673.4-5.

3   [ARROWSMITH, JOSEPH.] <u>The Reformation</u>. London: printed for
    William Cademan, 80 pp.
         A brief passage (pp. 45-50) makes fun of Dryden's heroic
    drama (taking essentially the same line as <u>The Rehearsal</u>), and
    also mocks him for currying favor with influential people at Court.
    Excerpted: 1971.45.

4   [BLOUNT, CHARLES.] <u>Mr. Dreyden Vindicated, in a Reply to The</u>
    <u>Friendly Vindication of Mr. Dreyden. With Reflections on the</u>
    <u>Rota</u>. London.
         Defends Dryden, point by point, against <u>The Friendly</u>
    <u>Vindication</u> (1673.2); accuses the author of stealing his ideas
    from <u>The Censure of the Rota</u> (1673.5). Excerpted: 1971.45; re-
    printed: 1975.15.

5   [LEIGH, RICHARD.] <u>The Censure of the Rota. On Mr. Driden's</u>
    <u>Conquest of Granada</u>. Oxford: printed by H.H. for Fran. Oxlad
    junior, 21 pp.
         Relates a discussion by the "Athenian Vertuosi." The vari-
    ous speakers make good-humored fun of the play, criticizing the
    excesses of its heroic style, especially Dryden's use of incorrect
    or indecorous figures, and of paradox. Excerpted: 1971.45; re-
    printed: 1975.15. See 1673.1-2, 4.

1674

1 RYMER, THOMAS. <u>Reflections on Aristotle's Treatise of Poesie</u>
<u>. . . with Reflections on the Works of the Ancient and Modern</u>
<u>Poets, and their Faults noted</u>. London.
    Praises some lines from <u>The Indian Emperour</u> for their "vari-
ety of matter" and "choice thoughts." Is particularly interested
in Dryden's ability to condense meaning into a few words. Excerpted: 1971.45.

2 [SETTLE, ELKANAH.] <u>Notes and Observations on the Empress of</u>
<u>Morocco Revised</u>. London: printed for William Cademan, 98 pp.
    Answers the attacks of Crowne, Shadwell, and especially
Dryden upon Settle's <u>The Empress of Morocco</u>. Often points to similar or worse faults in Dryden's work, or to precedents in classical
authors. Mainly attacks on grounds of fact or sense. Reprinted:
1975.15.

1675

1 PHILLIPS, EDWARD. <u>Theatrum Poetarum, or a Compleat Collection</u>
<u>of the Poets</u>. London: printed for Charles Smith, 291 pp.
    A brief entry on Dryden's drama (pp. 107-8) criticizes his
"French way of continual Rime and interlarding of History with
factitious Love and Honour."

1680

1 MAIDWELL, LAWRENCE. <u>The Loving Enemies: a Comedy</u>. London.
    The prologue complains of the dangers of satire, alluding
to Dryden's beating in Rose Alley. Refers to Dryden's satire as
"witty" and "just."

2 ROCHESTER, JOHN WILMOT, Earl of. "An Allusion to Horace." In
<u>Poems on Several Occasions</u>. Antwerp, 151 pp.
    Finds Dryden's works "stoln, unequal, . . . dull," his per-
son lewd and arrogant. Credits him however with pleasing his audience. Many times reprinted. The standard modern edition of
Rochester's poetry is <u>The Complete Poetry of John Wilmot, Earl of</u>
<u>Rochester</u>, ed. David M. Vieth (New Haven: Yale University Press,
1968).

1681

1 ANON. "An Essay on Dramatick Poetry." In <u>Amaryllis to Tityrus</u>
<u>. . . [by] Monsieur Scudéry</u>. London: printed for William
Cademan.
    Praises Dryden as the greatest playwright of the time; claims

that he "has much exceeded any of his Predecessors, in the number of good Plays." Reprinted and discussed: 1964.22.

2   ANON. A Panegyrick on the Author of Absalom and Achitophel, occasioned by his former writing of an Elegy in praise of Oliver Cromwel. London: printed for Charles Leigh, 2 pp.
     A mock-panegyric on Dryden's mercenary and changeable nature. Reprinted: 1975.15.

3   ANON. Poetical Reflections on . . . Absalom and Achitophel. By a Person of Honour. London: printed for Richard Janeway, 15 pp.
     A partisan attack upon Dryden and his poem, accusing him of libel. Praises Shaftesbury. Does not imitate or parody Absalom and Achitophel. Reprinted: 1961.26; 1975.15; excerpted: 1971.45. See 1925.16.

4   HICKERINGHILL, EDMUND. The Mushroom: Or, a Satyr against Prelatical Tantivies; in Answer to a Satyr against Sedition, called the Meddal. London.
     A scurrilous poem attacking Dryden as man and poet, followed by a "Post-Script" in the same vein. Generally accuses Dryden of prostituting his talent. Reprinted: 1975.15.

1682

1   ANON. Absolon's IX Worthies: or, A Key to a late Book or Poem, entituled A.B. and A.C. London, 2 pp.
     Praise for "that incomparable POEM." Predicts that "a numerous mixed Croud/ Of seduc'd Patriots [will cry] aloud/ For Grace to Godlike David." The nine worthies are nine of the rebel party of Absalom and Achitophel, in procession (one quatrain each). Reprinted: 1975.15; excerpted: 1971.45.

2   ANON. The Tory Poets: A Satyr. London: printed by R. Johnson, 11 pp.
     Contains a vicious personal attack on Dryden. Also claims that anything pleasing in Dryden's plays is borrowed from Corneille. Reprinted: 1975.15; excerpted: 1971.45. See 1927.4.

3   [NESSE, CHRISTOPHER.] A Key (With the Whip) To open the Mystery and Iniquity of the Poem called, Absalom and Achitophel: shewing its Scurrilous Reflections upon both King and Kingdom. London: published by Richard Janeway, 24 pp.
     Claims that Dryden's biblical parallels do not fit their supposed modern equivalents, and that furthermore their implications are scandalous. Admits that Dryden's meter is good. Reprinted: 1975.15. See 1729.2.

4   PORDAGE, SAMUEL. Azaria and Hushai. London: printed for

Charles Lee, 40 pp.

A hostile imitation of <u>Absalom and Achitophel</u>. Azaria (Monmouth) and Hushai (Shaftesbury) are now the heroes of the Jews' resistance to the plots of the Canaanites. Sticks closely to Dryden's story line, but ends with Charles on the other side, acknowledging Monmouth and vowing that the people will no longer have to fear Papists. Shimei (Dryden) is briefly portrayed as a hireling poet who has debased his talent. Reprinted: 1961.26; 1975.15; excerpted: 1971.45.

5 _____. <u>The Medal Revers'd: A Satyre against Persecution</u>. London: printed for Charles Lee, 31 pp.

A political attack upon Dryden and the Tories. Does not comment upon <u>The Medal</u>, except to call it "a much slovenlier Beast" than <u>Absalom and Achitophel</u>. Reprinted: 1975.15.

6 SETTLE, ELKANAH. <u>Absalom Senior: or, Achitophel Transpos'd</u>. London: printed for S.E., 42 pp.

The prefatory "Epistle to the Tories" attacks <u>Absalom and Achitophel</u> as "more against a David, than an Achitophel," and the Tories for their dangerous disbelief in a Popish Plot. The poem is a parody of Dryden's poem, violently anti-Catholic. Casts Dryden as a changeable court poet who "A Pyramide to his Saint, <u>Int'rest</u>, rais'd." Reprinted: 1961.26; 1975.15; excerpted: 1971.45.

7 [SHADWELL, THOMAS.] <u>The Medal of John Bayes: A Satyr Against Folly and Knavery</u>. London: printed for Richard Janeway, 31 pp.

The "Preface to the Tories" attacks Dryden as a plagiarist, hireling, and ignoramus. The poem is scurrilous and <u>ad hominem</u>. Reprinted: 1975.15; excerpted: 1971.45.

8 _____. <u>Satyr to his Muse. By the Author of Absalom and Achitophel</u>. London: printed for D. Green, 18 pp.

In the guise of a "complaint" by Dryden to his muse. Attacks his political activities, especially the writing of <u>Absalom and Achitophel</u>. Sees the poem as dangerous scaremongering. Reprinted: 1975.15.

<u>1683</u>

1 ANON. <u>The True History of the Duke of Guise</u>. London: printed by R. Baldwin, 34 pp.

The preface attacks Dryden's <u>The Duke of Guise</u> as false and dangerous, and suggests that by reviving fears of a Popish Plot it defeats its own ends. The body of the work recounts the historical events from a Whig viewpoint, denying the justice of the play's parallels.

2 BUCKINGHAM, GEORGE VILLIERS, Duke of. <u>The Rehearsal: As it is now Acted at the Theatre-Royal</u>. 4th ed., "with Amendments and

large Additions by the Author." London: printed for R. Bentley
and S. Magnes, 56 pp.
   Published version of 1671.1. Many times reprinted.

3 HUNT, THOMAS. A Defence of the Charter, and Municipal Rights
   of the City of London. London: printed by Richard Baldwin,
   46 pp.
      Attacks The Duke of Guise (pp. 24-31) as a dangerous politi-
   cal influence, and goes on to attack Dryden as a dramatist whose
   "Hero's are commonly such Monsters as Theseus and Hercules are,
   renowned throughout all Ages for destroying." Urges the authori-
   ties to proceed against him: "Such publick Blasphemies against
   Religion, never went unpunished in any Country or Age but this."
   Reprinted: 1975.15.

4 [SHADWELL, THOMAS.] Some Reflections Upon the Pretended
   Parallel in the Play Called The Duke of Guise. London: printed
   for Francis Smith, 25 pp.
      Accuses Dryden of perverting Nathaniel Lee's original design
   by turning it against the Protestants. Attacks the legitimacy of
   Dryden's parallels between political situations in the Paris of the
   play and contemporary London, between the Duke of Guise and Monmouth,
   and between Henry III and Charles. Implies, however, that a parallel between Henry IV (in his apostacy) and the Duke of York would
   be pertinent. Reprinted: 1975.15.

1685

1 ANON. The Laurel, A Poem on the Poet-Laureat. London: printed
   for Benjamin Tooke, 39 pp.
      An occasionally pastoral poem which exalts Dryden and attacks
   his enemies (Hunt, Settle, Shaftesbury, and especially Shadwell).
   Praises Dryden for making history memorable (in his heroic plays)
   and for saving England during the Exclusion Crisis. Asserts that
   "verse fixt her Pillars [of Hercules] in thine Absolon." Places
   Dryden in the line of Spenser and Cowley. Reprinted: 1975.15.

1687

1 ANON. The Revolter. A Trage-Comedy Acted between the Hind and
   Panther, and Religio Laici, etc. London, 32 pp.
      Contains an introductory poem jeering at Dryden for choosing
   a ludicrous and unbelievable fable for his subject, some prose comment along the same lines, and a "dialogue" between "Mr. D. the
   Romanist" and "Mr. D. the Protestant." The speeches are quotations
   from The Hind and the Panther and Religio Laici respectively. Reprinted: 1975.15.

2 BURNET, GILBERT. A Defence of the Reflections On the Ninth

Book of the First Volume of Mr. Varilla's History of Heresies.
Being a Reply to his Answer. Amsterdam: printed for J.S.,
154 pp.
 Contains a harsh attack on Dryden (pp. 138-40): claims that
he is "the Author of the worst Poem [The Hind and the Panther],
become likewise the Translator of the worst History, that the Age
has produced." Mocks Dryden for having changed from no religion
to one of the worst, and for general immorality.

3 CLIFFORD, MARTIN. Notes upon Mr. Dryden's Poems in Four Letters,
 to which are annexed some Reflections upon the Hind and Panther.
 By another Hand. London, 35 pp.
 Attacks The Conquest of Granada: relates Almanzor to
Shakespeare's "fuming Achilles," Pistol. Accuses Dryden of plagiarism in the Essay of Dramatic Poetry. Finds his similes and
figures of speech senseless, and his style bombastic. Suggests
that he apply himself to "some honest Calling." The "Reflections"
upon The Hind and the Panther conclude that "this Poem [is] one of
the rankest pieces of Folly and Malice blended together . . . the
Town is at this time tired with." Reprinted: 1975.15; excerpted:
1971.45.

4 [HEYRICK, THOMAS.] The New Atlantis. A Poem, In Three Books.
 With Some Reflections upon the Hind and the Panther. London:
 printed for the Author, 68 pp.
 The Catholic church, having lost adherents because of its
debasement, hires a poet, Bavius (Dryden), to plead its cause.
Bavius's poem, to be called The Hind and the Panther, will attempt
to hide the Church's deviousness and wickedness. But unfortunately
for Bavius, the Church is suddenly reconciled to God, and Bavius
loses his job. Reprinted: 1975.15.

5 LANGBAINE, GERARD. Momus Triumphans: or, The Plagiaries of the
 English Stage. London: printed for Nicholas Cox, 32 pp.
 Lists English plays alphabetically by author, with footnotes
indicating sources. The preface contrasts the practices of modern
and ancient playwrights in using source materials: accuses the
moderns of continual plagiarism. Praises Dryden's artistic skill
but charges that he steals from others "almost in all the Plays he
writes." Reprinted: 1971.49.

6 PRIOR, MATTHEW, and CHARLES MONTAGU. The Hind and the Panther
 Transversed. London: printed for W. Davis.
 Adapts characters of The Rehearsal (Bays, Johnson, and Smith)
to burlesque Dryden's poem, through Bays's fable "The Country Mouse
and the City Mouse." Implies that Dryden's poem is pretentious and
unbelievable. Reprinted: 1975.15; excerpted: 1971.45.

1688

1   ANON. A Poem in Defence of the Church of England. London, 19 pp.
      An answer to The Hind and the Panther, attacking the Roman Catholic Church as a spiritual and political force. Makes occasional use, especially at the beginning, of Dryden's beast fable, and at several points criticizes its lack of verisimilitude. Reprinted: 1975.15.

2   BROWN, TOM. The Reasons of Mr. Bays Changing His Religion. London: printed for S.T., 32 pp.
      A burlesque of the Essay of Dramatic Poesy. Makes fun of Dryden's conversion, especially in the light of his other inconsistencies. Presents "Bays" as having changed his religion after two days' drunken debauch in Greenwich. Reprinted: 1975.15. See 1690.1-2.

3   [R., J.]. Religio Laici, or a Lay-mans Faith, Touching the Supream Head and Infallible Guide of the Church. London: printed for John Newton, 28 pp.
      Uses quotes from Dryden's Religio Laici to argue against the doctrine of Infallibility; swipes at Dryden for having changed his opinion. Reprinted: 1975.15.

1689

1   [GOULD, ROBERT.] The Murmurers. London: printed for R. Baldwin, 16 pp.
      The title alludes to Dryden's description of the "Jews" in Absalom and Achitophel. Attacks Dryden ("Balaam") for not using his gifts to support the government of William III. Echoes Dryden's poem to John Oldham: "But now thy Glory sleeps in Shades profound,/ By Fate and gloomy Death encompass'd round."

1690

1   BROWN, TOM. The Late Converts Exposed: or the Reasons of Mr. Bays's Changing his Religion: Part the Second. London: printed for Thomas Bennet, 73 pp.
      Includes a travesty of The Hind and the Panther called "The Fable of the Bat and the Birds." Reprinted: 1975.15. See 1688.2; 1690.2.

2   _____. The Reasons of Mr. Joseph Haines: The Player's Conversion and Re-conversion. Being the Third and Last Part to the Dialogue of Mr. Bays. London: printed for Richard Baldwin, 32 pp.
      A dialogue between "Bays" (Dryden) and Haines, a noted comic

actor. Haines reports on Europe's response to Bays's conversion, and gives the farcical circumstances of his own, which take up the bulk of the piece. Reprinted: 1975.15. See 1688.2; 1690.1.

1691

1 LANGBAINE, GERARD. An Account of the English Dramatick Poets. Oxford: printed for George West and Henry Clements, 556 pp.
Arranged alphabetically by author. The Dryden section (pp. 130-77) is almost entirely concerned with Dryden's borrowings from other writers, mostly French, Spanish, and Italian. Also implies that Dryden is disrespectful of earlier English playwrights, and prone to violent opinions in religion and politics. Reprinted: 1973.40; excerpted: 1909.7; 1971.45.

1693

1 ADDISON, JOSEPH. "To Mr. Dryden." In Examen Poeticum: Being the Third Part of Miscellany Poems . . . By the Most Eminent Hands. London.
Celebrates Dryden for having transcended old age. Compares him favorably in this to Ovid. Reprinted: 1971.45.

2 DENNIS, JOHN. The Impartial Critick. London.
Compares the Dryden-Lee Oedipus with Sophocles, noting Dryden's departures from Aristotelean norms. Reprinted: 1909.7; 1939.9; excerpted: 1971.45.

3 RYMER, THOMAS. A Short View of Tragedy. London: printed and are to be sold by Richard Baldwin, 194 pp.
Deals only implicitly with Dryden, but provoked his "Heads of an Answer to Rymer." Gives a critical history of poetry, emphasizing tragic drama. Suggests to Dryden a model for a play based on the Spanish Armada (pp. 13-17). Promotes strict imitation of classical Greek drama under Aristotelean principles. Praises Waller as the perfector of the English language. See 1956.40 for standard modern edition.

4 WRIGHT, JAMES. The Humours, and Conversations of the Town. London: printed for R. Bentley and J. Tonson, 139 pp.
Praises Dryden's company and conversation (p. 73); lists Essay of Dramatic Poesy among several works that will help would-be wits find "Critical Observations in the Greek Poets" (p. 107).

1695

1 B., A. An Ode Occasion'd by the Death of the Queen, with a Letter from the Author to Mr. Dryden. London: printed by Tho.

Warren for Francis Saunders, 4 pp.
The letter attacks Dryden for his silence at the death of Queen Mary. Compares him, in passing, to Virgil: "Virgil was a good Man and a clean Poet, all his Excellent Writings may be carried by a Child in one hand more easily, than all your Almanzors can be by a Porter upon both shoulders." Reprinted: 1975.15.

2 HOWARD, EDWARD. An Essay Upon Pastoral: As also an Elegy Dedicated to the Ever Blessed Memory of Her Most Serene Majesty Mary the Second, Queen of England. London: printed for R. Simpson, 22 pp.
The "Proem" to the essay alludes to Dryden's Virgil, then in progress: predicts that "Dryden . . . will of a certain make Maro speak better than ever Maro thought." Makes several other laudatory references to Dryden in the course of defending modern poetry. Reprinted: 1975.15.

1698

1 ANON. The Fatal Discovery; or, Love in Ruines. A Tragedy. London: printed by J. Orme for R. Wellington, 50 pp.
The preface, over the name of the actor George Powell, responds to Dryden's prologue to Granville's Heroick Love. Makes fun of him for having given away his laurels (in the prologue) for the fourth time. Defends the actors against Dryden's complaint that they made a poor job of a revival of The Conquest of Granada: the problem was that the play is nonsense. Reprinted: 1975.15.

2 COLLIER, JEREMY. A Short View of the Profaneness and Immorality of the English Stage, etc. London.
Attacks modern plays for blasphemy, immorality, abuse of the clergy and of authority, and wrong teaching. Draws examples from several of Dryden's plays: Don Sebastian, Love Triumphant, The Mock Astrolger, King Arthur, and especially Amphitryon. Defends ancient, and older English, playwrights. Attacks, point by point, Dryden's defense of the ending of The Mock Astrologer; attacks Dryden's use of Jonson's The Alchemist as a precedent for an apparent ill-distribution of rewards. Attacks Absalom and Achitophel for the fundamental blasphemy of its scheme. Many times reprinted. Excerpted: 1909.7; 1971.45.

3 MILBOURNE, LUKE. Notes on Dryden's Virgil. In a Letter to a Friend With an Essay on the same Poet. London: printed for R. Cavill, 232 pp.
An abusive attack on Dryden and his translation. Goes through the translation almost line by line, criticizing its accuracy, diction, and decorum. Interjects ad hominem attacks on Dryden. Appends his own translation of Georgics 1 to show how it should be done. Reprinted: 1975.15; excerpted: 1971.45. See 1729.2.

<u>1699</u>

1   GILDON, JOSEPH. <u>Lives and Characters of the English Dramatick</u>
    <u>Poets</u>. London: printed for Thomas Leigh and William Turner,
    182 pp.
        Arranged alphabetically by author. The Dryden section (pp.
    40-47) lists and dates Dryden's plays, and suggests sources for
    many. Asserts that Dryden "has met with Applause often above his
    Merit," and that his plays while often sublime are rarely pathetic:
    "he has not touch'd Compassion above thrice."

2   PITTIS, WILLIAM. <u>An Epistolary Poem to John Dryden, Esq.;</u>
    <u>Occasion'd by the much Lamented Death of the Right Honourable</u>
    <u>James Earl of Abingdon</u>. London: printed for H. Walwyn, 9 pp.
        Urges Dryden to commemorate the Earl's death "lest some rude
    Hand the sacred Work prophane." Sympathizes with Dryden's position
    out of favor: "<u>Great Bard</u>, whose hoary Merits claim/The <u>Laureat's</u>
    Place, without the <u>Laureat's</u> name." Reprinted: 1975.15.

<u>1700</u>

1   ANON. <u>An Epistle to Sr. Richard Blackmore, Occasion'd by The</u>
    <u>New Sessions of the Poets</u>. London: printed for A. Baldwin,
    12 pp.
        Contains a vision of Dryden in Hell, "crown'd with a wreath
    of flaming Sulphur," burning in a fire fueled with his "impious
    Plays." A hind and panther stare him in the face. Nominates Sir
    Samuel Garth as Dryden's successor, as he also is "Malicious,
    Envious, and Uncivil." Reprinted: 1975.15.

2   ANON. <u>To the Memory of Mr. Dryden</u>. London: printed for
    Charles Brome, 11 pp.
        Praises, among many other things, Dryden's ability to angli-
    cize the classics, his continual vigor, and his skill at arousing
    emotion. Reprinted: 1975.15.

3   BROWN, TOM. <u>A Description of Mr. D----n's Funeral</u>. London:
    printed for A. Baldwin, 8 pp.
        Ridicules Dryden; occasionally echoes <u>MacFlecknoe</u>. Reprinted:
    1975.15.

4   BYSSHE, EDWARD. <u>The Art of English Poetry</u>. London: printed
    for R. Knaplock, E. Castle, and B. Tooke, 384 pp.
        Frequently quotes Dryden's poetry to illustrate discussions
    of versification, rhyme, and stanza forms. Includes an anthology
    of "the most natural, agreeable, and noble thoughts . . . in the
    best English poets." Arranged by subject matter: many are from
    Dryden.

5   FARQUHAR, GEORGE. [Letter.]

Comments in a letter on Dryden's funeral: "his burial was the same as his life, variety and not of a piece:--the quality and mob, farce and heroicks; the sublime and ridicule mix'd in a piece; --great Cleopatra in a hackney coach." Excerpted: 1971.45.

6   PLAYFORD, HENRY, and ABEL ROPER, comps. Luctus Britannici: or The Tears of the British Muses; for the Death of John Dryden, Esq. London: printed for Henry Playford and Abel Roper, 79 pp.
    "Written by the most Eminent Hands in the two Famous Universities, and by several Others." Contains twenty-six poems in English, twenty-four in Latin, and two in Greek. The poems are conventional elegies which stress Dryden's literary domination of the age, his having immortalized his subjects (for good or ill), his modernizing of the classics, and his political contributions. He is frequently compared to Homer and Virgil, and to Chaucer and Spenser. Addison, Garth, and especially Congreve are suggested as his heirs. Reprinted: 1975.15.

7   WESLEY, SAMUEL. An Epistle to a Friend Concerning Poetry. London: printed for Charles Harper, 30 pp.
    Praises Dryden's poetry highly, but laments his immorality; calls on him to repent. Reprinted: 1947.17; 1967.63.

1702

1   ANON. A Comparison Between the Two Stages. London, 227 pp.
    In the form of a dialogue, the work not only discusses Dryden's work (see especially pp. 34-37) but frequently echoes his opinions. Emphasizes his dependence upon sources, but one of the speakers ("Ramble") asserts that he has improved everything he has taken. Reprinted: 1942.13.

1704

1   DENNIS, JOHN. Britannia Triumphans. London.
    The preface attacks Dryden's version of Paradise Lost as part of a general attack on rhyme. Reprinted: 1939.9 (1:374-79).

2   SWIFT, JONATHAN. A Tale of a Tub: . . . To which is added, An Account of a Battel Between the . . . Books. London: printed for John Hunt, 330 pp.
    In The Battle of the Books Dryden and Virgil (in armor of rusty iron and gold, respectively) challenge each other, and ex-change armor, but in the end Dryden is afraid to fight.

1706

1 HUGHES, JABEZ. "Verses Occasion'd by Reading Mr. Dryden's Fables." In <u>Miscellanies in Verse and Prose</u>. London: printed by John Watts, 1737.

The poem, written in 1706, praises Dryden for renewing English style, for his versatility, for recovering Chaucer's poetry, and for the power of his St. Cecila odes. Complains that no poet has replaced him. Reprinted: 1971.45.

1708

1 DOWNES, JOHN. <u>Roscius Anglicanus</u>. London: H. Playford, 52 pp.

Gives the original casts of the most popular plays, including several by Dryden, during the period 1660-1706. Comments occasionally on a play's financial success. Is not wholly reliable. Reprinted: 1928.15; 1969.20; 1974.10.

1709

1 FELTON, HENRY. <u>A Dissertation on Reading the Classics and Forming a Just Style</u>. London: printed for Jonah Bowyer, 248 pp.

Briefly evaluates a large number of ancient and modern writers. Claims that while Dryden wrote under the bondage of rhyme, he "could make the Tinkling of his Chains harmonious." Also he improved upon everything he borrowed from earlier writers.

1711

1 ADDISON, JOSEPH. <u>Spectator</u> 40 (16 April).

Illustrates a discussion of "rants" in tragedy with two quotations from the Dryden-Lee <u>Oedipus</u>. Such passages are examples of "blemishes or false beauties" but are popular nevertheless. Reprinted: 1965.1 (1:168-73).

2 _____. <u>Spectator</u> 62 (11 May).

Commends Dryden for avoiding "false wit" (word-play). Asserts that his definition of wit ("a propriety of words and thoughts adapted to the subject") is actually a definition of any kind of good writing. Reprinted: 1965.1 (1:263-70).

3 DENNIS, JOHN. <u>Reflections . . . upon An Essay upon Criticism</u>. London.

Denies (against Pope's prediction) that Dryden can ever fail to be understood, as happened to Chaucer, because unlike Chaucer he has "Justness of Numbers, and some Truth of Harmony and of Versification." Reprinted: 1939.9 (1:396-419); excerpted: 1971.45.

1712

1   ADDISON, JOSEPH. Spectator 279 (19 January).
     Criticizes Dryden for occasionally "misrepresenting" Virgil
in his translation of the Aeneid, by introducing "affected or unnatural" and "mean or vulgar" thoughts. Reprinted: 1965.1
(2:585-90).

2   _____. Spectator 512 (17 October).
     Gives Absalom and Achitophel as an example of a poem which
pleases by exercising the reader's mind. Notes that it is "one of
the most popular poems that [has] ever appeared in English." Reprinted: 1965.1 (4:317-20).

3   BUDGELL, EUSTACE. Spectator 341 (1 April).
     Praises Dryden's epilogue to Tyrannic Love. Claims that "if
[Dryden] was not the best writer of Tragedies in his Time, [he]
was allowed by every one to have the happiest Turn for a Prologue
or an Epilogue." Reprinted: 1965.1 (3:265-69).

1713

1   DENNIS, JOHN. Remarks upon Cato, a Tragedy. London.
     Favorably compares the quarrel and reconcilement of Antony
and Ventidius in All for Love with a similar scene in Addison's
Cato. Reprinted: 1939.9 (2:41-80).

1714

1   LUTTRELL, NARCISSUS. A Brief Historical Relation of State
     Affairs from September 1678 to April 1714.
     Printed in six volumes in 1857 (1857.3). Contains several
mentions of Dryden, including the Rose Alley attack (1:30), the
censorship of Cleomenes (2:413, 422), and Dryden's death and funeral (4:640, 645, 655).

1715

1   DENNIS, JOHN. Letter "To Mr. Jac. Ton. Sen. [Jacob Tonson] on
     the Conspiracy against the Reputation of Mr. Dryden."
     Elevates Dryden above Pope and other contemporary writers
"for the pomp and Solemnity and Majesty of his Style." Predicts
that Pope will be as little regarded as Settle in thirty years.
Reprinted: 1939.9 (2:399-400); 1971.45.

1717

1   CONGREVE, WILLIAM. Dedication to The Dramatick Works of John Dryden, Esq. London: printed for Jacob Tonson.
    Praises, in general terms, Dryden's character, learning, generosity, modesty, versatility, and originality.

1718

1   GILDON, CHARLES. The Complete Art of Poetry. 2 vols. London: printed for Charles Rivington, 830 pp.
    Volume 1 contains five dialogues on poetry; volume 2 contains examples of poetic uses of a series of words, arranged alphabetically. Praises Dryden for bringing English versification "to its last and greatest Perfection." Ranks Dryden with Spenser and Milton. Contrasts Dryden's Nourmahal (in Aureng-Zebe) with Euripides's Phaedra; criticizes Dryden's play for faults in diction. Praises Dryden's versification. Volume 2 contains many quotations from Dryden to illustrate various poetic usages.

2   TRAPP, JOSEPH. The Aeneis of Virgil Translated into Blank Verse. 2 vols. London.
    The preface defends Trapp's decision to follow Dryden in translating the Aeneid. Charges that Dryden was overly free, and that he interposes himself between Virgil and the reader. Claims that Dryden often mistakes even the spirit of Virgil, and so distorts his original. Gives many examples of substantial changes Dryden introduced. Concludes that his own translation, being in blank verse, "may be considered as an Undertaking of another Kind, rather than as an Attempt to excel His."

1719

1   JACOB, GILES. The Poetical Register: or, the Lives and Characters of the English Dramatick Poets. London: printed for E. Curll, 475 pp.
    · The Dryden section (pp. 72-86) defends Dryden from his attackers, especially Gerard Langbaine (1691.1). Quotes extensively from Congreve's encomium (1717.1). Lists and briefly describes the plays, and gives some biographical information.

1720

1   DENNIS, JOHN. Character and Conduct of Sir John Edgar (Third Letter). London.
    Attacks MacFlecknoe as slanderous; places Shadwell above Dryden as a comic writer. Reprinted: 1939.9 (2:200-206); excerpted: 1971.45.

2   JACOB, GILES. An Historical Account of the Lives and Writings
     of Our Most Considerable English Poets. London: printed for
     E. Curll, 369 pp.
         The Dryden section (pp. 261-65) lists and describes his poems
     and translations. Includes John Dennis's ode on Dryden's transla-
     tion of the third book of Virgil's Georgics.

1721

1   [GILDON, CHARLES.] The Laws of Poetry, as laid down by the
     Duke of Buckinghamshire, . . . the Earl of Roscommon, and . . .
     the Lord Landsdowne . . . . London: printed for W. Hinchcliffe
     and J. Walthoe, 362 pp.
         Refers frequently to Dryden. Complains, in the discussion of
     Buckingham, that Alexander's Feast has not been properly set to
     music. Also contrasts, unfavorably, The State of Innocence with
     Paradise Lost. Likewise finds Dryden's tragedies weak beside
     Thomas Otway's. The essay on Roscommon praises Dryden's Ovid and
     Virgil, and defends him against the charge that he behaved badly
     toward Thomas Creech, the translator of Lucretius. The brief dis-
     cussion of Lansdowne includes a defense of Dryden against charges
     of bad judgment, arguing that he was forced to please his audiences.

1724

1   WELSTED, LEONARD. "A Dissertation Concerning the Perfection of
     the English Language, the State of Poetry, etc.," in Epistles,
     Odes, &c., Written on Several Subjects. London: printed for
     J. Walthoe and J. Peele.
         Describes Dryden's prefaces as "a pretty amusing mixture of
     wit and ribaldry, good sense and impropriety, and vanity and modes-
     ty oddly jumbled together." Claims that "there is a liveliness in
     them that never tires one, but they want solidity and justness to
     give full satisfaction." Reprinted in Eighteenth-Century Critical
     Essays, ed. Scott Elledge (Ithaca: Cornell University Press, 1961),
     1:320-48.

1728

1   OLDMIXON, JOHN. The Arts and Logick of Rhetorick. London:
     printed for John Clark et al., 450 pp.
         Uses many illustrations from Dryden; acknowledges that he is
     "the Father of our present Numbers," but mainly attacks him for
     various violations of literary decorum. Reprinted: 1976.44.

2   _____. An Essay on Criticism. London: printed for J.
     Pemberton, 94 pp.
         Contains many brief quotations from and citations of Dryden.

Occasionally comments on his work: praises especially his <u>Aeneid</u>
and <u>Fables</u>. Finds his wordplay often indecorous. Notes his critical inconsistency, but attributes it to the occasional nature of
most of his writing. Reprinted: 1964.38.

3   SPENCE, JOSEPH. <u>Anecdotes, Observations, and Characters of</u>
     <u>Books and Men</u>.
          Covers the period from 1728 to 1744. Contains several very
     brief stories, comments, and reminiscences (of varying degrees of
     authenticity) about Dryden's life and views. Printed: 1820.2.

<u>1729</u>

1   LAMOTTE, CHARLES. <u>An Essay upon Poetry and Painting</u>. London:
     printed for F. Fayram and J. Leake, 202 pp.
          Attacks Dryden and Lee for anachronism in their version of
     <u>Oedipus</u>, because they have Oedipus refer to a theatrical stage.
     Assumes that the error was Lee's, because Dryden kept "all the
     Graces and Beauties to himself" (p. 6). Accuses Dryden of pla-
     giarism from French writers, even as he ridicules them (p. 163).
     Reprinted in facsimile (New York: Garland, 1970).

2   POPE, ALEXANDER. "A Parallel of the Characters of Mr. Dryden
     and Mr. Pope, as drawn by certain of their Cotemporaries" [sic].
     In <u>The Dunciad</u>.
          "Appendix VI" prints, on facing pages, closely parallel ex-
     cerpts from hostile commentaries on the works of the two poets.
     The excerpts on Dryden are drawn from Milbourne's <u>Essay on Dryden's</u>
     <u>Virgil</u> (1698.3), the anonymous <u>Whip for the Fool's Back</u>, Christopher
     Nesse's <u>Key (With the Whip)</u> (1682.3), and Oldmixon's <u>Essay on</u>
     <u>Criticism</u> (1728.2). Many times reprinted. The standard modern
     edition is by James Sutherland in <u>The Twickenham Edition of the</u>
     <u>Poems of Alexander Pope</u>, vol. 5 (New Haven: Yale University Press;
     London: Methuen, 1943.)

<u>1736</u>

1   BIRCH, THOMAS. "John Dryden." In <u>A General Dictionary,</u>
     <u>Historical and Critical</u>, by Pierre Bayle. Rev. and enl. by John
     Peter Barnard, Thomas Birch, John Lackman et al. 7 vols.
     London: printed for G. Strahan et al., 1734-41.
          The Dryden section (4:677-87) contains a survey of his life
     and works, based upon earlier published accounts. The footnotes
     have much information about contemporary responses, especially to
     his political and religious views. See 1940.21.

2   VOLTAIRE. Second épitre dedicatoire to <u>Zaïre</u>.
          Criticizes Dryden, "<u>un très grand génie</u>," for putting lan-
     guage "<u>opposée à la tendresse</u>" into the mouths of his heroes.
     <u>Oeuvres</u> (2:552-53), ed. Moland (Paris: Garnier, 1877-85).

1738

1   ANON. "The Importance of Justice." Gentleman's Magazine 8
     (May):251-52.
          Praises Dryden's even-handedness in allowing "Achitophel"
     some credit for his performance as a judge. Contrasts modern
     writers, who "absolutely deny Common Sense and Common Honesty to
     every Man without the Pale of their Faction."

1740

1   CIBBER, COLLEY. An Apology for the Life of Colley Cibber, with
     an Historical View of the Stage during his own Time. London:
     printed for John Watts.
          Contains several references to Dryden. Describes his reading
     of Amphitryon to his cast ("cold . . . flat . . . unaffecting").
     Describes how Kynaston, Nokes, Mrs. Barry, and Mrs. Monfort played
     roles in Dryden's heroic plays; believes Dryden meant some passion-
     ate speeches to be funny.

1745

1   G., W. "To S.G. on the Foregoing." Gentleman's Magazine 15
     (February):99.
          The author, now eighty-seven, recalls "plain John Dryden (be-
     fore he paid his court with success to the great) in one uniform
     cloathing of Norwich drugget." Describes him as "the mildest crea-
     ture breathing, and the readiest to help the young and deserving."
     Recalls eating tarts with Dryden and Mrs. Reeve (an actress, pos-
     sibly Dryden's mistress). Describes the first production of
     Marriage a-la-Mode: "I solemnly declare that you have seen no
     such acting, not in any degree since."

1747

1   SPENCE, JOSEPH. Polymetis: or, an Enquiry concerning the
     Agreement Between the Works of the Roman Poets, and the Remains
     of the Antient Artists. London: printed for R. Dodsley, 374 pp.
          Attacks Dryden's translation of Virgil for its misunderstand-
     ing and consequent misrepresentation of allegorical figures.
     Charges that Dryden did not recognize the unity in ancient litera-
     ture of natural and allegorical actions. Examines many passages
     in support of his argument (pp. 309-20).

1750

1   [BROUGHTON, THOMAS.] In Biographica Britannica: or, the Lives

of the Most eminent Persons who have flourished in Great Britain and Ireland. Edited by William Oldys. 6 vols. in 7. London: printed for W. Innys et al., 1747-66.
Gives a brief, derivative account of the life and works, with copious notes and citations (3:1749-61).

2   JOHNSON, SAMUEL. Rambler 31 (3 July).
Briefly comments on Dryden's "warmth and fancy" and consequent occasional inaccuracy. The standard modern edition is by W.J. Bate and Albrecht B. Strauss, in The Yale Edition of the Works of Samuel Johnson, vols. 3-5 (New Haven: Yale University Press, 1969), 3:167-73.

1751

1   JOHNSON, SAMUEL. Rambler 125 (28 May).
Uses scenes from Don Sebastian and Aureng-Zebe to show how tragedy can be turned to farce by the introduction of buffoonery or inappropriate and improbable speeches and emotions. The standard modern edition is by W.J. Bate and Albrecht B. Strauss, in The Yale Edition of the Works of Samuel Johnson, vols. 3-5 (New Haven: Yale University Press, 1969), 4:299-305.

1753

1   CIBBER, THEOPHILUS. The Lives of the Poets of Great Britain and Ireland. 5 vols. London: printed for R. Griffiths.
Contains an anecdotal and selective account of Dryden's life and works (3:64-94). Gives much space to a story concerning astrology and Dryden's son Charles, and to an account of Dryden's funeral and Lord Jeffery's supposed interruption. Lists and describes the plays; his accounts are dependent upon Giles Jacob (1720.2).

1756

1   HUME, DAVID. The History of England from the Invasion of Julius Caesar to the Revolution of 1688. Vol. 2. Edinburgh: printed for Hamilton, Balfour, and Neill.
Excoriates Dryden for "indecency and bad taste," but admits that among the bulk of his writings ("the refuse of our language") there are a few fine things: the St. Cecilia's Day odes and Absalom and Achitophel. Abridged: with an introduction by Rodney W. Kilcup (Chicago: University of Chicago Press, 1975), (pp. 382-83).

2   WARTON, JOSEPH. An Essay on the Genius and Writings of Pope. London: printed for R. and J. Dodsley.

Praises Dryden for occasionally introducing common and
familiar words into his poetry. Suggests that he may have had a
greater genius than Pope, even though Pope was the better artist.
Praises Alexander's Feast for passion and variety; praises the
Fables, especially Palamon and Arcite for its rendering of passion and Theodore and Honoria ("incomparable wildness"). Excerpted
in Eighteenth-Century Critical Essays, ed. Scott Elledge (Ithaca:
Cornell University Press, 1961), 2:717-63; 1971.45.

1758

1   [MURPHY, ARTHUR.] [The Spanish Friar.] London Chronicle,
      14-16 November.
          A review of a performance at the Drury Lane Theatre. De-
scribes the piece as a "hermaphrodite," which "partakes of two
species, without being perfect in either." Reprinted: 1963.49.

1759

1   YOUNG, EDWARD. Conjectures on Original Composition. London:
      printed for A. Millar . . . and R. & J. Dodsley.
          Asserts that Dryden "was a stranger to the pathos" and there-
fore failed as a tragic writer. His use of rhyme in serious plays
was particularly abominable. Praises Alexander's Feast. Excerpted:
1971.45.

1760

1   DERRICK, SAMUEL. "The Life of John Dryden, Esq." In The
      Miscellaneous Works of John Dryden, Esq. 4 vols. London:
      printed for J. and R. Tonson.
          The "Life" (1:xiv-xxxiv) gives more details than any previous
biography. Surveys Dryden's life and career, with particular attention to the relationships between the works and their historical contexts. Prints the contract for the Fables between Dryden
and Jacob Tonson. Casts doubt on several traditions originating
in hostile attacks by Tom Brown (1688.2; 1690.1-2; 1700.3), Gerard
Langbaine (1687.5; 1691.1), and others. Defends the sincerity of
Dryden's conversion. Evaluates his work as a whole: "his fancy was
always vigorous, his imagination fertile, his sentiments spirited,
his language . . . elegant, and his versification smooth and grace-
ful; he was copious in invention; in translation [gave] the spirit
of his author." See 1940.21.

1762

1   ANON. [Letter.] St. James Magazine, October, pp. 149-52.

A letter to the magazine. Prints several passages from
Aureng-Zebe which seem to echo Samson Agonistes and, in one case,
Paradise Lost. Accuses Dryden of plagiarism.

1763

1   WARTON, JOSEPH. The Works of Virgil in English Verse. Translated by Christopher Pitt and Joseph Warton. Notes by Joseph
Warton. 4 vols. London: printed for R. and J. Dodsley.
      The "Prefatory Dedication" criticizes Dryden's Virgil for
inaccuracies, with examples (1:xi-xix). Frequently cites Dryden
in the notes to the text.

1764

1   BAKER, DAVID ERSKINE. The Companion to the Playhouse. 2 vols.
London: printed for T. Becket.
      The sections on Dryden (unpaginated) survey his career, often
repeating inaccurate material from such previous surveys as those
of Jacob (1720.2) and Theophilus Cibber (1753.1). Gives details
about the plays' theatrical and publication histories, and sometimes information about sources. Revised: 1812.1. Reprinted:
1966.4.

1769

1   GRANGER, JAMES. A Biographical History of England, from Egbert
the Great to the Revolution. 3 vols. London: printed for T.
Davies.
      Has two brief mentions of Dryden, under the reigns of Charles
II and James II. The first praises his influence on poetry: "The
chains of our English bards were formerly heard to rattle only; in
the age of Waller and Dryden, they became harmonious" (2:331-32).
The second mention (2:546) deals with his conversion: "Dryden, who
had panegyric for all characters, and religion for all changes of
the times, turned Roman-Catholic, upon the accession of James."

2   WEBB, DANIEL. Observations on the Correspondence between Poetry
and Music. London: printed for J. Dodsley, 162 pp.
      Calls Alexander's Feast the most perfect poem (in English) of
the kind that stimulates emotions by describing them in others.
Concludes that in this poem "music unites with poetry in the character of a descriptive art."

1770

1   GENTLEMAN, FRANCIS. The Dramatic Censor; or Critical Companion.

2 vols. London: printed for J. Bell.
      Attacks Dryden for lack of realism and for licentiousness,
but admits that All for Love, the character of Dorax in Don
Sebastian, and Dryden's scenes in Oedipus have merit. Attributes
his overall failure to "servile compliance with false taste"
(2:460-61).

1776

1   BEATTIE, JAMES. Essays. Edinburgh: printed for William
      Creech; London: printed for E. and C. Dilly, 555 pp.
      A lengthy footnote (pp. 16-20) in the essay "On Poetry and
Music, as they affect the Mind" finds Dryden's chief characteristics to be energy and ease. Claims, however, that "his attachment
to the vernacular idiom, as well as the fashion of his age, often
betrays him into a vulgarity, and even meanness of expression."
He is too witty for pathos, too familiar for sublimity. Places
Dryden closer to Horace than to any other ancient or modern author.

1779

1   ANON. "The Works of the English Poets." Gentleman's Magazine
      49 (June):312-13; (July):362-64; (September):453-57; (October):
      505-7.
      A review of Johnson's Lives (1779.2-4). Is critical of the
choice of Dryden's poems in the anthology, and of a general lack
of annotation. Adds an anecdote about Dryden's quarrel with Jacob
Tonson. Concludes that Johnson wrote "this article, if any, con
amore."

2   JOHNSON, SAMUEL. "John Dryden." In The Works of the English
      Poets, With Prefaces, Biographical and Critical, by Samuel
      Johnson. 68 vols. in 58. London: printed by H. Hughes for C.
      Bathurst et al., 1779-81. [Lives of the Poets.]
      Surveys Dryden's life. Quotes copiously to illustrate his
attitudes and style. Praises him as a dramatist, critic, and
theorist, but notes his lack of financial success. Defends him
against the charge of expediency in his conversion. Finds the
translation of Virgil the "most laborious and difficult of all his
works." Credits him with being "the father of English criticism,"
and with establishing the heroic couplet. Assesses and analyzes
his major poems. Concludes that "what was said of Rome, adorned
by Augustus, may be applied . . . to English poetry embellished by
Dryden, . . . he found it brick, and he left it marble." Many
times reprinted. See 1905.2 (1:331-487) for the standard modern
edition.

3   _____ . "Christopher Pitt." In The Works of the English Poets,
      with Prefaces, Biographical and Critical, by Samuel Johnson.

68 vols. in 58. London: printed by H. Hughes for C. Bathurst et al., 1779-81.

Contrasts Dryden's and Pitt's Aeneids. Finds Dryden's more lifelike, Pitt's more accurate. See 1905.2 (3:277-80) for the standard modern edition.

4 _____. "Alexander Pope." In The Works of the English Poets, with Prefaces, Biographical and Critical, by Samuel Johnson. 68 vols. in 58. London: printed by H. Hughes for C. Bathurst et al., 1779-81.

Sees Dryden as a model for Pope. Contrasts them at length: Dryden has more energy, and more unevenness. See 1905.2 (3:82-276) for the standard modern edition.

5 "Scrutator." "Strictures on Dr. Johnson's Prefaces to the English Poets." Gentleman's Magazine 49 (December):593-95.

Proposes some corrections and additions to Johnson's life of Dryden.

1784

1 ANON. Critical Review 58 (July):59.

A review of Thomas Davies's Dramatic Miscellanies (1784.2). States that "Dryden, as a dramatic writer, is now little known; though he possesses great merit, blended perhaps with still greater faults. We know not a better field for a candid and discerning critic."

2 DAVIES, THOMAS. Dramatic Miscellanies. 3 vols. London: printed for the author.

Asserts, in "Dryden" (3:153-75), that no one can read heroic plays without laughter and contempt (mixed with esteem and admiration). Makes fun of Maximin, the villain of Tyrannic Love; praises Aureng-Zebe for its strength of passion and its diction, "familiar and dramatic." Credits All for Love with being the first play after the Restoration to revive the "true dramatic style." But disparages, relative to the Elizabethans, all Restoration comic writers except Etherege. Concludes that "English versification is more indebted to [Dryden] than to half the poets from Chaucer's time to the present." See 1784.1.

1785

*1 OWEN, EDWARD. A Translation of Juvenal and Persius into English Verse. London: Rivington & Sons.

Cited by Howard Weinbrot in 1969.82.

2 X., A. [Original Love-Letter of the Poet Dryden] Gentleman's Magazine 55 (May):337.

A correspondent prints a letter to Honor Dryden, dated 23 May 164[?]. See 1942.12.

<hr>

1786

1 WAKEFIELD, GILBERT. The Poems of Mr. Gray with Notes by Gilbert Wakefield, B.A.
      Objects to Johnson's praise of "TO . . . Anne Killigrew." Calls the poem a "performance infinitely inferiour to any production of Mr. Gray; a model indeed of almost every vice of composition; full fraught with sentiments at once puerile, low, and turgid; and debased by meanness of expression." Quoted by Leopold Damrosch, Jr., in The Uses of Johnson's Criticism (Charlottesville: University Press of Virginia, 1976), p. 188n.

2 Z. [Particulars of Dryden's Funeral.] Gentleman's Magazine 56 (April):291-93.
      Prints the account in Ned Ward's London Spy (1701). Notes that it contradicts the traditional sensational account originally accepted by Samuel Johnson.

<hr>

1787

1 A., J. "Remarks on Dryden's Ode to the Memory of Mrs. Killigrew." Gentleman's Magazine 57 (November):965-67.
      Differs with Johnson's high praise of the poem. Finds it extravagant in its statements and indecorous in its religious implications. Is surprised that Johnson liked it in view of his attitude toward Cowley.

2 "EUGENIO." [Three Dryden Letters.] Gentleman's Magazine 57 (November):943-44.
      Prints three letters to Richard Busby, Headmaster of Westminster School. Two are by Dryden; one is by Elizabeth Dryden. Each involves one or another of their sons. See 1942.12.

3 P., R.O. [Imagination and Judgement.] Gentleman's Magazine 57 (November):969-72.
      Gives several examples in which poets have committed absurdities due to judgment failing to restrain imagination. The allegory in The Hind and the Panther is one.

<hr>

1788

1 WESTON, JOSEPH. "An Essay on the Superiority of Dryden's Versification over that of Pope and of the Moderns." Printed with Philotoxi Ardenae, by John Morfitt. Birmingham: printed for the authors.

Weston's essay (pp. vii-xxvi) defends Dryden against those who charge him with being careless and lacking in passion. Claims that Pope's supposed advantages over Dryden--greater correctness, regularity, polish, dignity--are actually defects. See 1789.1, 3-5; 1790.2, 4-9.

1789

1   M--s. [Defense of Weston and Dryden.] Gentleman's Magazine 59 (August):682-83.
    Criticizes Anna Seward (1789.3) for being too hard on Dryden. Suggests that he intentionally "kept down certain parts of his writings to serve as foils to the rest," and that he would have written more carefully had his finances allowed him more leisure. Claims that Seward's choice of examples is biased, and offers alternatives.

2   [POTTER, ROBERT.] The Art of Criticism; as exemplified in Dr. Johnson's Lives of the Most Eminent English Poets. London: printed for T. Hookham, 250 pp.
    Gives a running commentary on Johnson's life of Dryden (pp. 49-66). Jeers at both authors from a strict common sense position. Is particularly annoyed with the lack of verisimilitude in the heroic plays and satires.

3   SEWARD, ANNA. "Strictures . . . on a Preface by Mr. Weston." Gentleman's Magazine 59 (April):291-92; (May):389-91; (June): 510-12.
    Attacks Weston's praise of Dryden at the expense of Pope (1788.1). Criticizes Dryden for breaches of literary decorum, for allowing the sense to overflow the bounds of the couplet, for overusing Alexandrines. Contrasts his practice in these matters with that of Pope. Attacks Dryden's moral failings, and careless attitude toward revision. Finds him without fixed principles. See 1789.2, 4-5; 1790.2, 4-9.

4   _____. [The Comparative Merits of Dryden and Pope.] Gentleman's Magazine 59 (September):818-21.
    Answers her critics (1788.1; 1789.1). Reiterates her preference for Pope on moral and artistic grounds. Defends her choice of passages illustrating Dryden's weaknesses. Makes further comparison between the two authors, especially as translators.

5   WESTON, JOSEPH. [Vindication from the Strictures of Mrs. Seward.] Gentleman's Magazine 59 (December):1101-6; 60 (January 1790):27-33.
    Quotes extensively from his preface to The Woodmen of Arden (1788.1) to familiarize his readers with it. Responds to Seward's "Strictures" (1789.3). Accuses her of errors of fact and interpretation. Argues that even with more time for revising Dryden's

style would have remained unchanged. Defends Dryden's use of
familiar words. See 1790.4-9.

1790

1   ELDERTON, J. Gentleman's Magazine 60 (July):583.
         Contributes the transcript of a letter from Dryden to one of
Charles II's ministers (March 1673/4), in which he asks for his
half-year's salary. See 1942.12.

2   M--s. [On the Comparative Merits of Pope and Dryden.]
     Gentleman's Magazine 60 (February):120-21.
         Repeats previous arguments preferring Dryden (1789.1), and
explaining his faults. Quotes Gray's and Warton's praise for
Dryden (1756.2).

3   MONBODDO, JAMES BURNETT, Lord. Unpublished MS c. 1790.
         Discussed by Emily L. Cloyd in James Burnett Lord Monboddo
(1972.9). The manuscript would have been the seventh volume of
the Origin and Progress of Language (1773-92). Monboddo analyzes
Alexander's Feast line by line, showing in detail the function of
sound (pp. 150-52).

4   MORFITT, J[OHN]. [On the Merits of Pope and Dryden.]
     Gentleman's Magazine 60 (January):6-7.
         Prefers Dryden to Pope because of his greater variety. Tries
to adjudicate the dispute between Seward and Weston, but essentially sides with the latter. See 1788.1; 1789.1, 3-5; 1790.2, 5-9.

5   SEWARD, ANNA. [Final Sentiments on Pope and Dryden.]
     Gentleman's Magazine 60 (June):523-25.
         Asserts that Weston has never proven his charge that Pope
encouraged his friends to undercut Dryden's fame. Repeats several
of her complaints about Dryden's style. See 1789.5.

6   _____. [On the Merits of Pope and Dryden.] Gentleman's
     Magazine 60 (February):118-20.
         Responds to Weston (1789.5) and Morfitt (1790.4). Accuses
Weston of not supporting his attacks on Pope's character. Criticizes Dryden's metrics, especially "his Alexandrines in the middle
of sentences, his perpetual triplets, his everlasting expletives."

7   W., R., or "BARDUS ORDOVICENSIS." [Pope and Dryden.]
     Gentleman's Magazine 60 (December):1197-98.
         Prefers Dryden to Pope. Finds Pope monotonous and Dryden
careless, but sublime. Pope "may be said to offend by his perfection; Dryden, to please by his imperfection."

8   WESTON, JOSEPH. [Defence of . . . the Preface to The Woodmen
     of Arden.] Gentleman's Magazine 60 (December):1067-68, 1169-72.

Continues his defense of himself and Dryden, and his attack
on Anna Seward, especially her use of quotations. Responds especially to her complaints against Dryden's prosody. See 1788.1;
1789.3-5; 1790.4-6, 9.

9   _____. [On the Comparative Merits of Dryden, &c.] Gentleman's
     Magazine 60 (September):777-80; (November):974-77.
     Argues that Anna Seward misconstrued his charge that Pope
allowed his friends to deprecate Dryden (1789.5; 1790.5). Attacks
other details in her essays on Dryden and Pope. Again accuses her
of bias in her choice of illustrations. See 1788.1; 1789.3-5;
1790.4-6, 8.

1800

1   MALONE, EDMOND, ed. The Critical and Miscellaneous Prose of
     John Dryden. 3 vols. London: printed for T. Cadell and W.
     Davies.
     Volume 1, part 1 consists of "Some Account of the Life and
Writings of John Dryden" (570 pp.). This is the first scholarly
biography, written to correct earlier errors and to publish newly
discovered facts. Discusses his birth and family relationships
and his financial situation. Dates and describes the works chronologically, correcting many previous datings. Puts the prose into
its literary, religious, and political perspectives. Discusses his
controversies with Howard, Buckingham, Rochester, Settle, and
Shadwell. Defends the sincerity of his conversion, and discusses
his loss of the laureateship. Corrects previous sensational accounts of his funeral, using contemporary sources. Gives miscellaneous information about such matters as Dryden's family tie with
Swift, St. Cecilia's Day observances, and Dryden's family after
his death. Prints (as appendixes) Dryden's patent as laureate,
his agreement for producing the Fables, the undertaker's bill for
his funeral, the text of the Dryden monument in Titchmarsh,
Northamptonshire, and a list of "persons in whose cabinets letters
written by Dryden may be found." See 1808.3; 1940.21; 1961.57.

1802

1   GIFFORD, WILLIAM, trans. The Satires of Decimus Junius
     Juvenalis. London: printed for G. and W. Nicol and R. Evans,
     533 pp.
     Contains "An Essay on the Roman Satirists" (pp. xxxvii-lxvi)
which begins by attacking Dryden's "Discourse . . . of Satire."
Finds it wonderfully written but insufficiently learned.

1804

1   GODWIN, WILLIAM. Life of Geoffrey Chaucer. 4 vols. London:

printed for Richard Phillips.
Makes occasional reference to Dryden's translations of
Chaucer, and to his misunderstanding of Chaucer's versification.
Classes Dryden's translation of "The Flower and the Leaf" with "the
most successful productions of human genius." Feels that Dryden's
comparison of "The Knight's Tale" with Homer and Virgil is absurd.

*2   MITFORD, WILLIAM. An Inquiry into the Principles of Harmony in
      Language, and of the Mechanism of Verse, Modern and Antient.
      2d ed. London: T. Cadell & W. Davies, 434 pp.
      Cited by Paul Fussell in Theory of Prosody in Eighteenth-
Century England (1954.7).

1805

1   WORDSWORTH, WILLIAM. Letter to Sir Walter Scott, 7 November.
     Admires Dryden but asserts that "his is not a poetical
Genius." His language has neither imagination nor "the amiable,
the ennobling or intense passions." Concludes that "there is not
a single image from Nature in the whole body of his works; and in
his translation from Vergil whenever Vergil can be fairly said to
have his eye upon his subject, Dryden always spoils the passage."
Printed in The Letters of William and Dorothy Wordsworth, 2d ed.,
ed. E. de Selincourt, rev. Chester Shaver (Oxford: Clarendon
Press, 1957. Reprinted: 1971.45.

1807

1   R., C.L. "Dryden censured." Gentleman's Magazine 77 (May):
     428-29.
     Complains that Dryden is blasphemous in his parody of the
biblical description of John the Baptist in MacFlecknoe.

1808

1   [HALLAM, HENRY.] "Scott's Edition of Dryden." Edinburgh Review
     13 (October):116-35.
     Attacks Scott's life and edition of Dryden (1808.3) as pedan-
tic and meaningless. Disparages the heroic plays, preferring The
Indian Emperour for its moderate style. Concludes that All for
Love and The Spanish Friar are the best plays. Attacks Scott and
Dryden for their Toryism. Gives Dryden credit for having written
so well in spite of his material. Criticizes his prose style as
too informal to be a model for didactic or historical writing.

2   SCHLEGEL, AUGUSTUS WILLIAM von. Lecture delivered in Vienna,
     1808.
     Attacks Dryden's plays, and Dryden himself, for immodesty,

immorality, confusion, inconsistency, improbability, lack of heart,
and bombast. Grants that he possessed an "uncommon facility of
rhyming." Published in Lectures on Dramatic Art, trans. John
Black, 1846. Reprinted: 1971.45.

3   SCOTT, Sir WALTER, ed. The Works of John Dryden. 18 vols.
    London: W. Miller.
        The first (and as yet the only) complete works of Dryden.
Contains extensive commentary. Revised by George Saintsbury,
1882-93 (1882.4). Volume 1 is "The Life of John Dryden," published
separately in 1826, and in 1834 as volume 1 of Scott's Miscellaneous
Prose Works (Edinburgh: Robert Cadell). Reprinted with an introduction and notes by Bernard Kreissman (1963.21). The life is
based on Edmond Malone's research (1800.1), but is the first to
place Dryden fully in his setting, as well as to marshal all the
facts then uncovered (together with much conjecture) in readable
chronological fashion. Also contains extensive critical commentary, especially showing how the historical and literary contexts
of the works (including the works' occasions) can illuminate them.
See 1940.21.

                              1810

1   [GREEN, THOMAS.] Extracts from the Diary of a Lover of
    Literature. Ipswich: to be printed by John Raw, 248 pp.
        Contains several scattered comments on Dryden. Is astonished
at the fulsomeness of his flattery. Asserts that "for disputing
in rhyme, Dryden has certainly no equal: his spirit is inextin-
guishable." Notes that Dryden's definition of wit ("propriety of
words and thoughts") is much more general than the definition current in his (Green's) own time. Remarks on the occasional and
various nature of Dryden's work: "whatever immediately occupied
[his] fervid mind, appears to have assumed a disproportionate importance there." Discussed by Stanley Archer in 1973.4.

                              1811

*1   TODD, H.J., ed. The Poetical Works of John Dryden. Notes by
     Joseph Warton et al. 4 vols. London.
        Cited by Upali Amarasinghe in 1962.2. Amarasinghe uses
Warton's notes, written in the late eighteenth century, as an
example of "transitional uncertainties" about Dryden's worth:
Warton anticipates the feeling of the nineteenth century that
Dryden did not sufficiently appreciate the "pathetic."

                              1812

1   BAKER, DAVID ERSKINE. Biographica Dramatica; or, a Companion

to the Playhouse. 3 vols. London: printed for Longman.
    An updated version, "with very considerable Additions and
Improvements throughout" by Stephen Jones, of 1764.1. Adds in-
formation about Dryden drawn from a contributor to Gentleman's
Magazine (1745.1), and anecdotes about Shadwell's reaction to
MacFlecknoe and Dryden's high opinion of Alexander's Feast. Re-
printed: 1966.4.

2   D'ISRAELI, ISAAC. Calamities of Authors. 2 vols. London:
     Murray; Edinburgh: Blackwood.
    Sympathizes with Dryden for the poor treatment he received
from critics during his lifetime. Quotes an opinion of the time
that the success of a rival's play will "vex huffing Dryden and
Congreve to madness." Comments as follows: "Dryden and Congreve!
The one the first genius, the other the most exquisite wit of our
nation, are to be vexed to madness!--their failures are not to ex-
cite sympathy, but contempt or ridicule!" The standard edition is
by Benjamin D'Israeli (London: Frederick Warne, 1881). Reprinted
in facsimile [Hildesheim (Germany) and New York: Georg Ohms, 1969].

                              1813

1   P. "Notice of Mr. Scott's Edition of Dryden." Analectic
     Magazine 2 (August):139-46.
    Laments that Scott has brought Dryden's immoral plays, writ-
ten only to make money, back to light. Is sickened by the "baneful industry of research." See 1808.3.

                              1817

1   COLERIDGE, SAMUEL TAYLOR. Biographia Litteraria. 2 vols.
     London: Rest Fenner.
    Notes "the vividness of [Dryden's] description" (2:56).
Modern edition ed. J. Shawcross. 2 vols. (Oxford: Clarendon
Press, 1909).

2   [MATURIN, CHARLES ROBERT, and WILLIAM GIFFORD.] "The Tragic
     Drama." Quarterly Review 17 (April):248-60.
    Surveys the history of drama. Contrasts two stages in
English drama: the earlier, original stage and the later stage,
heavily influenced (to its discredit) by French and classical
drama. Portrays Dryden as occasionally breaking through the re-
straints imposed by foreign forms, with his "argumentative and
often sublime poetry."

                              1818

1   HAZLITT, WILLIAM. "On Dryden and Pope." Lecture delivered at

the Surrey Institute.
   Discusses Dryden briefly, mainly in contrast with Pope.
Finds Dryden a better prose writer, and a bolder and more varied
poet. Concludes that The Hind and the Panther is his greatest
work. Printed in Works, ed. A.R. Waller and Arnold Glover (London:
J.M. Dent; New York: McClure, Phillips, 1902), 5:68-85.

1819

1   SHANAHAN, W. "A correspondence on several literary matters."
    Gentleman's Magazine 89, no. 2 (August):119-22.
       Speculates about the locations of hard-to-find copies of
various of Dryden's works. Notes that modern satirists have preferred Dryden's vigorous but unpleasant style to Pope's more difficult but more poetic style.

1820

1   [SOUTHERN, H.]. "The Dramatic Works of John Dryden, Esq."
    Retrospective Review 1, pt. 1:112-61.
       Evaluates Dryden's plays to separate the "flowers" from the
"thorns and brushwood." Finds him generally deficient in pathos,
though occasionally capable of writing affecting scenes. Criticizes his use of homely metaphors. Notes that beautiful passages
are often juxtaposed with absurdities. Concludes that All for Love
and Don Sebastian are the two best plays. Suggests that Dryden
might have written too many plays, that his genius was "dribbled
away" in coarse and indecent comedies.

2   SPENCE, JOSEPH. Anecdotes, Observations, and Characters, of
    Books and Men. Edited by S.W. Singer. London: W.H. Carpenter,
    530 pp.
       Edition of 1728.3. Reprinted, with an introduction by
Bonamy Dobrée (Carbondale: Southern Illinois University Press,
1964).

1821

1   ANON. "Memoirs of the Kit-Kat Club." Gentleman's Magazine 91,
    no. 2 (November):434-37; (December):532-35.
       Quotes at length (pp. 532-34) an account of Dryden's deal-
ings with Jacob Tonson, especially over the translation of the
Aeneid.

2   [BARKER, C.]. "Dryden's Prose Works." Retrospective Review 4,
    pt. 1:55-72.
       Compares the styles of Dryden and Addison, emphasizing
Dryden's vigor and force. Notes however that these qualities
sometimes appear at the expense of grace and propriety.

3   [SOUTHEY, ROBERT, and H.H. MILMAN.] "The Spanish Drama."
    Quarterly Review 25 (April):1-24.
        Complains in passing that no one has traced Dryden's
    Almanzor and the heroes of The Indian Emperour "to their proto-
    types on the Spanish stage."

1823

1   [SOUTHEY, ROBERT.] "Bishop Burnet's History of his Own Time."
    Quarterly Review 29 (April):165-213.
        Defends Dryden's life and plays against Burnet's charges of
    immorality. Mocks Dryden for his attempts to improve upon
    Shakespeare and Milton.

1825

1   [KEBLE, JOHN.] "Sacred Poetry." Quarterly Review 32 (June):
    211-32.
        Discusses the nature and history of religious poetry in
    English. Cites Dryden's paraphrase of the Veni Creator as an
    example of English Catholic poetry at its best.

1828

1   [MACAULAY, THOMAS BABINGTON.] "Dryden." Edinburgh Review 47
    (January):1-36.
        Attacks Dryden for immorality, lack of realism, and political
    and artistic expediency. Opposes Dryden's use of rhyme in drama,
    but credits him with occasional "good description and magnificent
    rhetoric." Praises his "power of reasoning in verse," especially
    in Absalom and Achitophel and The Hind and the Panther.

2   [WILSON, JOHN.] "The Man of Ton. A Satire." Blackwood's
    Magazine 23 (June):835-55.
        Praises Dryden as a satirist, despite his "wavering princi-
    ples." Singles out his ear for music, and clear diction.

1831

1   [WILSON, JOHN.] "An Hour's Talk About Poetry." Blackwood's
    Magazine 30 (September):475-90.
        Attacks contemporary poetry, contrasting it unfavorably with
    that of the past. Concludes that Paradise Lost is the "one Great
    Poem." Briefly discusses Dryden (pp. 486-87), finding him glori-
    ous but "insensible to the pathetic and the sublime."

2   _____ . "Sotheby's Homer." Blackwood's Magazine 29 (April):

668-87; (May):829-66.
Compares Dryden's translation of several passages from Book 1 of the Iliad with those of Chapman, Tickel, Pope, Cowper, and Sotheby. Finds none wholly satisfactory: Dryden "wilfully violates throughout both the style and the spirit of Homer," despite his vigor and "majestic flow." Attacks Dryden's criticisms of Homer; suggests that he was partial to Virgil.

1832

1 COLERIDGE, SAMUEL TAYLOR. Table Talk and Omniana. Edited by H.N. Coleridge. London: J. Murray. 6 August.
Prefers Dryden's to Pope's way of building a character: in his Achitophel and Zimri "every line adds to or modifies the character, which is, as it were, a-building up to the very last verse." Modern edition ed. T. Ashe (London: Bell, 1888).

2 GENEST, JOHN. Some Account of the English Stage from the Restoration in 1660 to 1830. 10 vols. Bath: printed by H.E. Carrington.
Gives accounts, interspersed with commentary, of productions at each theater, arranged year by year. Notes actors and actresses, and dates where available. Volumes 1 (1660-90) and 2 (1691-1719) contain material on plays by Dryden. Brings together several key sources: Malone (1800.1); Joseph Wright; Langbaine (1687.5; 1691.1); Downes (1708.1); Samuel Pepys; and Colley Cibber (1740.1).

1833

1 ANON. "Sharpe's British Peerage." Gentleman's Magazine 103, no. 2 (July):52-54.
Notes that Sharpe discovered the record of Dryden's marriage, which had eluded Malone and Scott.

2 COLERIDGE, SAMUEL TAYLOR. Table Talk and Omniana. 1 November.
"Dryden's genius was of that sort which catches fire by its own motion; his chariot wheels get hot by driving fast." Modern edition ed. T. Ashe (London: Bell, 1888).

1839

1 HALLAM, HENRY. Introduction to the Literature of Europe in the Fifteenth, Sixteenth, and Seventeenth Centuries. 4 vols. London: John Murray, 1837-39.
Volume 4, chapter 6 ("History of Dramatic Literature from 1650 to 1700") discusses and evaluates Dryden's plays, concluding that The Spanish Friar (in its tragic scenes) and All for Love are his best, matched by few or none "in dignity, in animation, in

striking images and figures" (pp. 484-88). Chapter 7 of the same
volume treats the prose: credits him with a style "superior to
any that England had seen," but argues that as a critic he "is
not to be numbered with those who have sounded the depths of the
human mind" (pp. 532-38). Chapter 5 contains general praise of
the poetry (pp. 430-38).

1842

1   ANON. "Life and Times of Dryden." Eclectic Review 75:47-72.
        Supercilious recounting of Dryden's life. Violently attacks
him and his plays for immorality: "[he] indulged . . . in heinous
fornication."

1845

1   [WILSON, JOHN.] "North's Specimens of the British Critics."
        Blackwood's Magazine 57 (February):133-58; (March):369-400;
        (April):503-28; (May):617-46; (June):771-93; 58 (July):114-28;
        (August):229-56; (September):366-88.
        A repetitive and digressive account of aspects of Dryden's
criticism. Emphasizes his relations with other great authors:
his translation of Chaucer, his comments on Shakespeare, his version of Paradise Lost, his influence on Pope, his similarities to
Johnson as a critic. Sees his version of Chaucer as his greatest
achievement, as it made Chaucer readable. Finds his attitude toward Shakespeare puzzlingly inconsistent. Describes The State of
Innocence in detail, mockingly. Quotes at great length from
MacFlecknoe and Absalom and Achitophel; dismisses all satire in
English since Pope. Reprinted: 1979.47.

1848

1   MACAULAY, THOMAS BABINGTON. The History of England from the
        Accession of James II. 6 vols. London: Longmans.
        Harshly criticizes Dryden on moral grounds. Uses the shift
in attitudes towards Anglicans and Dissenters in The Hind and the
Panther as a manifestation of shifts in court policy (2:850-55).
Many times reprinted. The standard edition is by C.H. Firth
(1914.4).

1849

1   KENNEDY, CHARLES RANN. The Works of Virgil. Translated by the
        Rev. Rann Kennedy and Charles Rann Kennedy. 2 vols. London.
        The preface to volume 2 (pp. iii-xxxi) discusses previous
translations of the Aeneid. Asserts that while Dryden's is the
best in English, it is one of his worst performances: it deviates
too far from the original, and the style is insufficiently grave.

1850

1   B., C. "Dryden's 'Absalom and Achitophel.'" N&Q [1st ser.] 2
    (7 December):468.
        A reply to "The Hermit of Holyport" (1850.3), identifying
Thomas Fuller's Profane State (1642) as the source of the passage
about Shaftesbury which "the Hermit" quoted from Absalom and
Achitophel.

2   CUNNINGHAM, PETER. "Dryden's Quarrel with Flecknoe."
    Gentleman's Magazine, n.s. 34 (December):597-99.
        Suggests that the R.F. who attacked Dryden in A Letter from
a gentleman to the Honourable Ed. Howard (1668.1) was Richard
Flecknoe, thus giving Dryden a reason for satirizing him.

3   "The Hermit of Holyport." "Dryden's 'Essay upon Satire.'" N&Q
    [1st ser.] 2 (23 November):422-23.
        Argues, principally from internal evidence, that Dryden, not
the Earl of Mulgrave, wrote the "Discourse . . . of Satire." Cites
a passage describing Shaftesbury which seems to echo a similar passage in Absalom and Achitophel. See 1850.1; 1851.4-5.

4   . "Gray.--Dryden.--Playing Cards." N&Q [1st ser.] 2
    (7 December):462-63.
        Reaffirms statement (in 1850.3) that Dryden was the sole
author of the "Discourse . . . of Satire."

1851

1   BREEN, HENRY H. "On Two Passages in Dryden." N&Q [1st ser.]
    3 (21 June):492.
        Asserts that Dryden blunders in The Spanish Friar in speaking
of the pleasures of madness that "none but madmen know." Dryden
could not know them without being himself mad.

2   CAMPKIN, HENRY. "Suppressed Epilogue by Dryden." N&Q [1st
    ser.] 4 (13 December):472.
        Notes the existence of an unspoken epilogue to The Duke of
Guise, and urges that it be reprinted in toto by its owner J.
Payne Collier.

3   CLOUGH, ARTHUR HUGH. "Dryden and His Times." Two lectures
    given at University College (London) in 1851-52.
        The first lecture deals with his life, emphasizing the long
span of his career and his thorough involvement with public affairs. Defends his conversion. Praises him for renovating the
language. The second lecture deals with the translations. Finds
them weak not because they distort their originals but because of
an inherent difference of character between Dryden and the authors
he was translating. Concludes that he is not a great poet, but is

rewarding and interesting. Praises his "vigour of mere writing, in manliness and force of style." Printed: 1964.8, pp. 85-106.

4   CORNEY, BOLTON. "The Essay on Satire." N&Q [1st ser.] 3 (15 March):162-63.
    Rejects Dryden's authorship of the "Discourse of Satire"; ascribes it to Mulgrave. See 1850.3; 1851.5.

5   CROSSLEY, JAS. "Dryden's Essay Upon Satire." N&Q [1st ser.] 3 (22 February):146.
    A reply to 1850.3 and 1850.4, agreeing that Dryden wrote the "Discourse of Satire." See also 1851.4.

1852

1   B., C., ed. Selections from the Poetry of Dryden. London: John W. Parker.
    The preface (pp. iii-xv) argues for a revaluation of Dryden. Celebrates his capacity for turning "every thing into imagination."

1854

1   ANON. "Glorious John." Fraser's Magazine 50:157-72.
    Reviews Bell's edition of Dryden's poetry (1854.2). Imaginatively reconstructs life in the theaters in Dryden's time. Defends Dryden against charges of immorality; notes Bell's publication of new evidence supporting the sincerity of his conversion. Credits Dryden with having produced, next to Chaucer and Shakespeare, "the most enduring effect upon the poetical literature of England."

2   BELL, ROBERT, ed. Poetical Works. 3 vols. The Annotated Edition of the English Poets. London: John W. Parker.
    Volume 1 contains a "memoir" of Dryden (pp. 9-98) which adds some new information, mostly from letters, to Malone's and Scott's lives. Treats Dryden's life and works chronologically, with comment on the works and their literary, political, and religious backgrounds. Relates his style and changes of opinion to his temperament. Defends his character and conversion, but not the moral tenor of the plays. Affirms his importance in the development of English poetry and criticism. Concludes that he was "of all English poets . . . the most English."

3   CORNEY, BOLTON. "Dryden on Shakespeare." N&Q [1st ser.] 9 (4 February):95-96.
    Conjectures that an anonymous "Prologue to Julius Caesar" (published in the Covent Garden Drolery, 1672) was actually written by Dryden.

4   [MASSON, DAVID.] "The Literature of the Restoration: Dryden."

British Quarterly Review 20:1-44.
Emphasizes the impingement of historical events on the development of Dryden and his contemporaries. Treats his career,
with little comment on individual works. Defends his conversion,
asserting its essential consistency. Ranks him fifth among English
poets, stressing the time span and quantity of his works. Notes
their great variation in quality, attributing it to Dryden's ro-
bust nature. Reprinted in Essays Biographical and Critical
(Cambridge: Macmillan, 1856), pp. 88-139.

1855

1 ANON. "Dryden: His Character and Writings." Eclectic Review
n.s. 9:71-88.
Reviews Bell's edition (1854.2). Sees Dryden as a transitional figure between Elizabethan and modern poetry. Laments the
lack of a good biography. Credits him with being the "first and
greatest" of controversial poets, but attacks The Hind and the
Panther (and his conversion). Ruefully acknowledges the accuracy
of his portrayal in that poem of the awkward compromises of the
Anglican Church.

2 ANON. "Dryden and his Times." Westminster Review 63 (1 April):
336-67.
Reviews Bell's edition (1854.2) and the selections published
by Parker (1852.1). Argues for the continuing value of Dryden's
work. Examines his career, and its close relationship with its
age. Explains the immorality of the plays by reference to the
standards of the time. Sees Dryden as "the first English critic
who applied general laws to particular cases in literature." Includes material on attacks on Dryden. Concludes that he was a
great writer, but sadly unhappy in his time.

3 GILFILLAN, G., ed. Poetical Works. 2 vols. Edinburgh: James
Nichol.
The prefatory matter to volume 1 (pp. i-xxiv) includes a
brief life interspersed with comments on the poetry. Attacks the
immorality of the plays and the conversion. The preface to volume
2 (pp. i-xxiv) repeats the charges, but also praises the poetry
for its easy, various style and its intellect. Finds it deficient
in sublimity, natural imagery, and "true tenderness of feeling."
Wishes Dryden had lived in a novelwriting age; suggests that he
might have rivalled Cervantes and Scott. Includes notes.

4 J., D. "Johnson's 'Life of Dryden.'" N&Q [1st ser.] 12
(4 August):83.
Denies Johnson's assertions (in 1779.2) that the plays were
printed in the order in which they were written, and that Dryden
did not suffer much financially after the loss of his offices.

5   T., W.M. "Dryden, Pope, and Curll's 'Corinna.'" N&Q [1st
     ser.] 12 (13 October):277-79.
         Identifies "Corinna" (mentioned in letters by Dryden) as
     Mrs. Elizabeth Thomas. Suggests that she might have been his
     mistress.

6   WILKINS, J.W. "The Genius of Dryden." Edinburgh Review 102
     (July):1-40.
         Denies significant French influence on Dryden's works.
     Puzzles over the decline of interest in his poetry, after its
     dominance for a century. Decides that modern readers reacted
     against "the degenerate productions of [Dryden's and Pope's] fol-
     lowers." Defends Dryden's conversion; discusses and praises the
     allegory of The Hind and the Panther. Examines the poem in detail,
     emphasizing Dryden's ways of handling problems inherent in his sub-
     ject. Calls the poem "the ablest existing illustration of the
     great religious controversy in the reign of James II."

                              1857

1   GLADSTONE, W.E. "Homeric Characters In and Out of Homer."
     Quarterly Review 102 (July):204-51.
         Briefly contrasts Dryden's treatment of Troilus and Cressida
     with those of Chaucer and Homer.

2   HUSK, WILLIAM HENRY. An Account of the Musical Celebrations on
     St. Cecilia's Day in the Sixteenth, Seventeenth, and Eighteenth
     Centuries. London: Bell & Daldy, 242 pp.
         Describes, among others, the festivals of 1687 and 1697, to
     which Dryden contributed A Song for St. Cecilia's Day and
     Alexander's Feast. Gives information on composers, singers, and
     music; relates anecdotes related with the occasions.

3   LUTTRELL, NARCISSUS. A Brief Historical Relation of State
     Affairs from September 1678 to April 1714. 6 vols. Oxford:
     Oxford University Press.
         Prints 1714.1.

                              1858

1   [HANNEY, JAMES.] "Horace and his Translators." Quarterly
     Review 104 (October):325-61.
         Describes Dryden's theory of the three kinds of translation
     (metaphrase, paraphrase, imitation), and praises Dryden's "para-
     phrase" of Horace's Tyrrhena regum progenies. Asserts that Dryden
     has produced something which is better than a translation, but "is
     not Horace" (pp. 340-41).

1859

1   L.   "Dryden and King William." N&Q [2d ser.] 7 (26 February):
168.
    Points to Dryden's abusive allusions to the Dutch and King
William in his translations from Virgil, especially the Aeneid 6,
line 608 and 6, line 621. This abuse is sometimes obtained by
perverting the sense of the original. See 1860.1.

2   R., R.J. "Dryden." N&Q [2d ser.] 7 (9 April):301.
    States, in response to 1859.3, that the complimentary verses
prefixed to the second edition of Religio Laici were also prefixed
to the first, so cannot be used as evidence against the poem's cold
reception.

3   VINE, GEO[RGE] ROB[ERT]. "Dryden." N&Q [2d ser.] 7 (19 March):
233.
    Argues against Bell's statement (in 1854.2) that Religio
Laici "was the least popular of Dryden's poems." Points to a
second edition within a year of the first, containing three compli-
mentary prefatory poems. See 1859.2.

1860

1   L.   "Allusions to William III and the Dutch in Dryden's
Translation of Virgil." N&Q [2d ser.] 10 (6 October):263.
    Points out hostile allusions in Georgics 3, lines 381-82 and
4, line 137. See 1859.1.

1861

1   [CONINGTON, JOHN.] "The English Translators of Virgil."
Quarterly Review 110 (July):73-114.
    Argues that while no translator has successfully preserved
Virgil's character, Dryden is the only one who "has an individuality of his own of sufficient mark to interest and impress the
reader" (pp. 95-98). Contrasts Wordsworth's translation of a passage from Aeneid 1 with Dryden's, to Dryden's advantage: "he
possessed that rapidity of movement which is absolutely necessary
[to an epic narrative] to a degree greater perhaps than any other
English poet" (pp. 102-3). Reprinted: 1872.3.

2   [HANNEY, JAMES.] "Plutarch." Quarterly Review 110 (October):
459-84.
    Discusses and evaluates Dryden's Plutarch, criticizing the
translations (done by many hands) and praising the preface and
biography, the latter for its "real insight into Plutarch's character," and its "acute remarks on biography" (pp. 466-68).

3   "PARATHINA." "Dryden's Prefaces." <u>N&Q</u> [2d ser.] 11 (16
    February):125.
        Calls for a collection of the prefaces in one volume; quotes
Johnson's praise of Dryden's criticism in support.

4   W., H. "John Dryden's Parents." <u>N&Q</u> [2d ser.] 12 (14
    September):207.
        Notes the discovery, in Pilton, Northamptonshire, of the
marriage license of Dryden's parents. The date (21 October 1630)
proves that Dryden (born 9 August 1631) was their eldest child.

1862

1   ANON. "Corneille and Dryden. Principles of the Drama."
    <u>Fraser's Magazine</u> 66:383-98.
        Finds Dryden a great reasoner, and the rhyme he defends in
drama "a development of reason in verse." Calls his style "quite
French," unlike that of other English writers of his time.

2   CUNNINGHAM, PETER. "Inedited Lines by Dryden." <u>N&Q</u> [3d ser.]
    2 (13 September):205.
        Asserts that Dryden's "Epistle to Sir Godfrey Kneller" was
not "thrown off at heart," but consciously worked over. Compares
the poem's final form with earlier versions.

3   HERAUD, JOHN A. "John Dryden." <u>Temple Bar</u> 7 (December):77-100.
        Attempts to reconcile Dryden's achievement with the portrait
of him as immoral and inconstant. Argues that his taste and skill
improved as his career went on. Suggests that his conversion followed naturally from the philosophy which can be seen developing
in his work. Praises his public poetry, especially the satires,
but finds him lacking in spirituality. Concludes that his achievement was limited, but perfect within those limits.

4   PALGRAVE, F.T. "English Poetry from Dryden to Cowper."
    <u>Quarterly Review</u> 112 (July):146-79.
        Examines the "change inaugurated by Dryden," and traces the
course of poetry from his time down to the present. Argues that
there never was a "French school" in the Restoration, although the
aim of the new poetry "was to give to poetry greater clearness,
condensation, and straightforwardness of style." Dryden was a
master of this style. Suggests that the "didactic and critical
temper," combined with a "false and shallow classical tone," has
led to the modern lack of interest in Restoration verse.

1863

1   BULWER-LYTTON, EDWARD G. "Caxtonia: A Series of Essays on
    Life, Literature, and Manners. No. xxiv." <u>Blackwood's Magazine</u>

94 (September):267-92.
Discusses (p. 269) the extent of French influence on Dryden.
Concludes that he remained essentially English in spirit if not in
form. Argues that Pope frenchified Dryden's style, effeminizing
it by refining away "the old native freedom of rhythm and cadence."

2   TAINE, HIPPOLYTE ADOLPHE. Histoire de la litterature anglaise.
     Paris: Hachette.
     The Dryden section (3:162-253 in the second edition, revised
and enlarged, 1866) surveys his life and career, especially against
the background of earlier English literature. Discusses the heroic
and tragic plays, especially praising All for Love. Contrasts
Dryden with Otway. Finds Dryden more at home with verse essays,
satires, translations, and imitations than with drama. Praises
his skill at argument.

1864

1   CUNNINGHAM, PETER. "Of Wit." N&Q [3d ser.] 5 (9 January):30.
     Discusses the changing meaning of the word "wit," with sever-
al examples of Dryden's uses of the word.

2   MERRYWEATHER, F. SOMNER. "Dryden." Gentleman's Magazine, 2d
     n.s. 16 (June):682.
     Notes the presence of Dryden and his family among Roman
Catholics in Westminster in September 1689, and also that he is
listed among those who paid a fine rather than swear loyalty to
William and Mary.

1865

1   HOOPER, RICHARD. [Life of Dryden.] In The Poetical Works of
     John Dryden. 5 vols. London: Bell & Daldy.
     The life (1:i-cxxx) is based on those of Malone (1800.1),
Scott (1808.3), and Bell (1854.2). Emphasizes the relationships
between Dryden's major works and political and religious issues.

2   [SKELTON, J.]. "John Dryden. A Vindication." Fraser's
     Magazine 72:160-79.
     Sets out the social background of Dryden's career, especially
the role of the Court. Describes Dryden's personality, emphasizing
his inconsistency. Defends his conversion against Macaulay
(1828.1), noting the obvious sincerity of The Hind and the Panther.
Praises the directness and fertility of his poetry, especially the
satires.

1866

1   BROOKE, W.T. "Dryden and Milbourne." N&Q [3d ser.] 10 (14
    July):27.
        Suggests as a cause for the quarrel between the two the
    failure of Milbourne's translation of Aeneid 1 and his subsequent
    jealousy of Dryden's success with Virgil.

1867

1   [COLLINS, W. LUCAS.] "Conington's Translation of the AEneid."
    Blackwood's Magazine 101 (January):35-53.
        Compares previous translations with Conington and with each
    other. Praises the vigor and beauty of Dryden's version, but ac-
    cuses it of paraphrase and misrepresentation.

2   HUSK, W.H. "Dryden's 'MacFlecknoe.'" N&Q [3d ser.] 12 (19
    October):319.
        Identifies two streets known as Pissing Alley in Dryden's
    time. (In response to a query.)

3   _____. "Dryden's Ode on the Death of Henry Purcell." N&Q
    [3d ser.] 12 (30 November):446.
        Feels that Dryden wrote the ode's last line as it was printed
    in 1696: "And list'ning and silent, and silent and list'ning, and
    list'ning and silent obey." (In response to a query.)

4   K., D.J. "Dryden References." N&Q [3d ser.] 12 (21 December):
    512.
        Identifies the source of two references in Britannia Rediviva
    as Pliny, Nat. Hist. I.iii.c.9. (In response to a query.)

5   SKEAT, WALTER W. "Dryden Queries: 'Neyes.'" N&Q [3d ser.] 12
    (20 July):56.
        "Neyes" probably means "eyes" in the phrase (from Troilus
    and Cressida) "Do the neyes twinkle at him?" (In response to a
    query.)

1868

1   "CHITTELDROOG." "Dryden's 'Negligences.'" N&Q [4th ser.] 1
    (14 March):238.
        Challenges assertions of Johnson (1779.2) and Bell (1854.2)
    that several lines in Alexander's Feast are defective or negligent
    because they do not rhyme. See 1868.4.

2   CHRISTIE, W.D. "Drydeniana." N&Q [4th ser.] 1 (25 April):
    383-84.
        Continues to wonder, despite some response from correspond-
    ents, if Dr. Thomas Hobbs was in attendance at Charles II's last

illness and death, as suggested by the 1701 Tonson folio edition
of Dryden's Threnodia Augustalis. Calls for an authoritative edition of Absalom and Achitophel, and more research into identifying
persons in the poem. See 1868.5.

3   FARRAR, F.W. "Epochs in English Poetry." Gentleman's Magazine
    3d n.s. 5 (January):35-45; (February):188-206.
        Praises Dryden as a stylist but charges that he "desecrated
those high powers" (pp. 197-98).

4   G., J.A. "Dryden's 'Negligences.'" N&Q [4th ser.] 1 (18
    April):378.
        Compares Pope's rhyming habits in odes with Dryden's in
Alexander's Feast; finds Pope's "more imperfect." See 1868.1.

5   H., R. "Hobbes [sic], the Surgeon." N&Q [3d ser.] 12 (2
    November):356-57.
        Identifies (based on annotations in his copy of the 1681
second edition) Issachar with Sir William Courtenay, and "Him of
the Western Dome" with the Bishop of Salisbury, Seth Ward. Suggests that Tonson inserted Hobbs's name in Threnodia Augustalis
after Dryden's death. Feels that Dryden was not in abject circumstances at his death. See 1868.2.

6   LOWELL, JAMES RUSSELL. "Dryden." North American Review 107
    (July):186-248.
        Describes and evaluates Dryden's works, and characterizes
his achievement in general. Calls him the "earliest complete type
of the purely literary man," and criticizes his attempts to please
his audience. Characterizes his critical opinions as inconsistent
but always well argued. Disparages the plays on moral grounds,
but gives examples of "great" passages. Praises Dryden as an unrivalled satirist and pleader, much better (and fairer) than Pope.
Concludes that Dryden was not a great poet but "a strong thinker
who sometimes carried common sense to a height where it catches
the light of a diviner air." Cannot decide whether his influence
has been beneficial. Reprinted: 1890.5.

7   NICK, K.F.J. De Virgili Carminibus a Drydeno Poeta in Linguam
    Britannicam Translatis. Ph.D. dissertation, Jena. Bochum:
    Stumpf, 27 pp.
        Describes Dryden's translations of Virgil, emphasizing his
metrical and other poetic devices, and the relation of these
translations to his theory of metaphrase, paraphrase, and imitation. Finds Dryden's versions relatively loose and generally
praiseworthy.

8   RIEDEL, OTTO. Dryden's Influence on the Dramatical Literature
    of England. Ph.D. dissertation, Rostock. Crossen: Ferd, Riep,
    29 pp.
        Surveys Dryden's career. Concludes that his major

contributions to English drama were his introduction of "French
taste" and, especially, his dramatic criticism (because of its
style and in spite of his inconsistency).

1869

1   ANON. "From the Restoration to the Revolution (According to
    Dryden's Prologues and Epilogues)." Once a Week 21 (20
    November):347-50; (27 November):358-61; (4 December):380-83;
    (11 December):409-12.
        Sketches the theatrical and literary contexts of the pro-
logues and epilogues, and classifies them according to occasion
and subject matter. Uses them to illustrate an account of Dryden's
career, and the social, political, religious, and theatrical issues
of the times.

2   DELIUS, N. "Dryden und Shakespeare." Shakespeare Jahrbuch
    4:6-40.
        Traces Dryden's references to and uses of Shakespeare, with
emphasis on his negative comments, and the way his adaptations
alter Shakespeare. Concludes that Dryden's wasted, forgotten attempts stand as a warning example to others.

1870

1   CHRISTIE, W.D., ed. The Poetical Works of John Dryden. Globe
    Edition. London: Macmillan, 749 pp.
        "Edited with a memoir, revised text, and notes." The memoir
(pp. xv-lxxxvii) contains some information not in Malone (1800.1),
Scott (1808.3), and Bell (1854.2), such as more factual detail
about Dryden's birth and family, as well as false information
which is corrected by later biographers, especially Osborn
(1940.21) and Ward (1961.57). Gives much background information
on the poems, especially Absalom and Achitophel. Takes Macaulay's
side (see 1828.1) on the conversion: "self-respect and a fine
sense of the becoming were not to be expected from one who had
led a life of mendicancy and adulation."

1871

1   AINGER, ALFRED. "Absalom and Achitophel." N&Q [4th ser.] 7
    (24 June):532-33.
        Explicates ll. 196-97, describing Achitophel (Shaftesbury):
"David for him his tuneful harp had strung,/ And Heaven had wanted
one immortal song."

2   CLARKE, CHARLES COWDEN. "English Satirists." Gentleman's
    Magazine, 3d n.s. 229 (November):691-719.

Praises Dryden's invention and style; criticizes his lack
of tenderness and humor. Asserts that his two great mistakes were
to persist in writing plays, and to oscillate in religion, no matter how sincerely.

1872

1   B., O.B. "'Absalom and Achitophel' and 'MacFlecknoe.'" N&Q
    [4th ser.] 10 (3 August):86.
        Points to the fact that Dryden was not the first to apply
the names Absalom and Achitophel to Monmouth and Shaftesbury.

2   CHRISTIE, W.D. "Dryden's Departure from Cambridge University."
    N&Q [4th ser.] 10 (9 November):370.
        Asserts that Dryden left college soon after receiving his
B.A. (1654), and did not continue to reside there until 1657, as
others had suggested. Bases his argument on a newly discovered
letter.

3   CONINGTON, JOHN. "The English Translations of Virgil." In
    Miscellaneous Writings. Vol. 1. Edited by J.A. Symonds.
    London: Longmans, Green, pp. 137-97.
        Reprint of 1861.1.

4   HETTNER, HERMANN. Literaturgeschichte des achtzehnten
    jahrhunderts. 3 vols. 3d ed. Braunschweig: Vieweg & Sohn.
        Chronicles Dryden's career. Emphasizes classical French
influences on his work, especially the influence of Boileau. Asserts that he is more critic than poet (1:84-99).

1874

*1 DICKMANN, J. "Dryden's Virgil Compared with the Latin Original."
    Ph.D. dissertation, Rostock.
        Cited by Helene M. Hooker in 1946.8.

1876

1   BELJAME, A[LEXANDRE]. "Buckingham and Dryden: 'My wound is
    great,' etc." N&Q [5th ser.] 6 (9 September):213.
        Doubts a story that an actress who spoke the above (supposed-
ly suppressed) line (in The Rival Ladies?) was permanently hissed
from the stage. Remarks that although some of Dryden's plays were
unsuccessful, it is not clear that he ever lost a benefit night.
See 1925.16.

2   "EREM." "Dryden." N&Q [5th ser.] 6 (8 July):24.
        Suggests that modern editions have mispunctuated the opening
line of The Flower and the Leaf.

3   VILDHAUT, BERNARD. Dryden's Fable of The Hind and Panther
     Considered with Regard to the Ecclesiastical Policy of James
     the Second. Lüdinghausen: H. Rademann, 29 pp.
          Argues that the poem is essentially a political rather than
     a theological poem. Sees Dryden as primarily interested in justi-
     fying James's attempt to establish toleration of Catholicism.

                              1877

1   ANON. "The Select Dramatic Works of John Dryden." Dublin
     University Magazine 89 (May):658-62.
          Explains the moral and literary failures of Dryden's drama
     by reference to the standards of the audience for which he wrote.
     Summarizes and comments briefly on All for Love and Don Sebastian.

2   [COURTHOPE, W. J.]. "Mr. Elwin's Pope." Quarterly Review 143
     (April):321-61.
          A review of Elwin's edition of Pope (1871-72). Contrasts
     Dryden and Pope as "historical portrait painters," arguing that
     Dryden excelled at presenting public figures in action, Pope "the
     secret springs and motives of human conduct" (p. 346). Contrasts
     the two poets' use of the couplet (pp. 352-55), finding Dryden's
     individual couplets more powerful, while Pope excelled at building
     them into paragraphs.

3   SPENCE, R.M. "Dryden." N&Q [5th ser.] 7 (19 May):338.
          Explicates, in response to a query, 11. 105-108 of Heroic
     Stanzas.

4   TAYLOR, JOHN. "Drydeniana." N&Q [5th ser.] 7 (19 May):386.
          Presents some notes from a MS of Dryden's belonging to a Mr.
     R. Graham that shed some light on his relations with Tonson. The
     MS also mentions Dryden's plans to translate Homer, and contains
     a rough draft of a translation of Ovid's Ars Amatoria.

                              1878

1   [COLLINS, JOHN CHURTON.] "John Dryden." Quarterly Review 146
     (October):289-331.
          Reviews the biographical work of Malone (1800.1), Scott
     (1808.3), the Aldine Edition, and Christie (1870.1). Finds Scott
     the best, though none are adequate. Surveys the course of Dryden's
     reputation. Defends him against moral attacks, stating that he was
     "the noble scapegoat of an ignoble and dissolute generation."

2   KENNEDY, HUGH A. "Dryden's Triplet on Jacob Tonson." N&Q
     [5th ser.] 10 (10 August):104-5.
          Suggests two circumstances under which Dryden might have
     written "Lines on Tonson": as a threat to get Tonson to repay a

debt, and upon the completion of Sir Godfrey Kneller's picture of Tonson.

1 ELZE, K. "Zu Dryden." Anglia 2:174-75.
   Two textual notes on Annus Mirabilis. The first argues that "people" is the correct reading in Stanza 12, despite an apparent grammatical need for "peoples"; the second suggests "breasts" as an emendation for "creasts" in Stanza 66. See 1892.4.

2 HAMILTON, WALTER. The Poets Laureate of England, Being a History of the Office of Poet Laureate. London: Elliot Stock, 333 pp.
   Surveys his career, emphasizing his public poetry. Lists and describes the plays (pp. 81-111). Reprinted: 1970.36.

3 SHÖPKE, O. "Über Dryden's Bearbeitung Chaucer's Gedichte." Anglia 2:314-53; 3 (1880):35-58.
   Classifies Dryden's changes, emphasizing how much he has altered the original, both in style and substance, fitting it to the tastes of his own time.

1880

1 ANON. "Dryden as a Dramatist." Temple Bar 59 (June):163-78.
   Divides the plays into four kinds: heroic plays, blank verse plays, alterations of Shakespeare, and comedies. Surveys his career; pays particular attention to The Conquest of Granada and the excesses of the heroic style. Concludes that Don Sebastian is Dryden's masterpiece. Finds that "notwithstanding the splendid poetry . . . and the noble language" Dryden lacks sublimity.

2 ARNOLD, MATTHEW. "The Study of Poetry." In The English Poets. Vol. 1. Edited by T.H. Ward. London: Macmillan.
   Asks whether Dryden and Pope are "poetical classics." Credits Dryden with establishing a fit English prose, involving "some repression and silencing of poetry." Concludes that Dryden and Pope "are not classics of our poetry, they are classics of our prose." Many times reprinted. See The Complete Prose Works of Matthew Arnold, ed. R.H. Super (Ann Arbor: University of Michigan Press, 1973), 9:161-88.

3 _____. "Thomas Gray." In The English Poets. Vol. 3. Edited by T.H. Ward. Macmillan.
   Laments Gray's indebtedness to Dryden. Disparages the poetry of Dryden and Pope relative to that of the nineteenth century. Claims that their poetry is not genuine because it is not "conceived and composed in the soul." See The Complete Prose Works of

Matthew Arnold, ed. R.H. Super (Ann Arbor: University of Michigan Press, 1973), 9:189-204.

4   SWINBURNE, A.C. "A Relic of Dryden." Gentleman's Magazine 247 (September):416-23.
    Argues that two passages in The Mistaken Husband are by Dryden, because of their grave and high style. Prints lengthy passages. Concludes that "a reader must be very imperfectly imbued with the spirit or skilled in the manner of his work, who imagines that the sole representative and distinctive qualities of his tragic or serious dramatic verse are to be sought or found in the resonant reverberations of amoebaean rant which roll and peal in prolonged and portentous echoes of fulminant epigram through the still dilating dialogue of his yet not undelightful heroic plays." Reprinted in Complete Works, ed. Sir Edmund Gosse and Thomas James Wise (London: Heinemann; New York: Gabriel Wells, 1926), 14:411-21.

5   WARD, A.W. "Dryden's Verse." In The English Poets. Vol. 2, Edited by T.H. Ward. London: Macmillan.
    A general summary and evaluation of Dryden's career and achievement in nondramatic verse. Praises his odes in particular, but finds him "incapable of true sublimity." Reprinted: 1921.9.

1881

1   BELJAME, ALEXANDRE. Le public et les hommes de lettres en Angleterre au dix-huitième siècle. Paris: Hachette.
    Surveys the status of authors, especially in relation to their audiences. Demonstrates the effect upon their work of their need for financial support. Contains two chapters which treat ⌣ Dryden. Traces the improvement in the condition of men of letters as their public increased, but emphasizes their overwhelming dependence, especially in the late seventeenth century, on patronage, particularly that of the Court. Uses many examples from Dryden's life and works. Reprinted: 1897.1 (with index). Translated: 1948.2; translation reprinted: 1971.8.

2   _____. Quae e Gallicis Verbis in Anglicam Linguam Johannes Dryden Introduxerit. Paris: Hachette, 106 pp.
    Discusses Dryden's role in bringing French words into the English vocabulary, in the broad context of French influence on English from the Norman Conquest forward. Notes Dryden's frequent retention, in his poetry, of French accentuation. Concludes that in Dryden's time there was a second wave of French words entering English (for which Dryden had a major responsibility), but that in contrast to the result of the first wave French accentuation was largely retained.

3   BOBERTAG, FELIX. "Drydens Theorie des Dramas." Englische

Studien 4, no. 3:373-404.
Argues that classical and native elements are stronger than
French in Dryden's criticism.

4   HASELL, ELIZABETH J. "A Talk About Odes." Blackwood's Magazine
    129 (June):783-802.
    In dialogue form. Notes the mixture of narration and song
in Alexander's Feast. Comments, on the conclusion of the same
poem, that "while unrivalled at depicting the power of music in
earthly things, Dryden's venal muse could not get far in delineat-
ing its higher uses."

5   J., A. "Dryden?" N&Q [6th ser.] 4 (9 July):24-25.
    Asserts, and attempts to prove, that "To Mr. Creech upon his
translation of Lucretius into English" is by Dryden.

6   SAINTSBURY, GEORGE. Dryden. English Men of Letters. London:
    Macmillan; New York: Harper, 198 pp.
    A critical biography and appreciation. Describes and evalu-
ates the works. Defends Dryden against charges of immorality, inconsistency, and materialism. Notes the great variety in Dryden's
output: finds this variety one of his most distinctive characteristics. Finds fault with many previous accounts of events in
Dryden's career, and of the nature of his achievement; strives to
correct misimpressions and truisms. Praises his satiric and didactic poems; concludes that his drama is inferior to his other
work. Asserts that "there was never . . . so great a writer who
was so thoroughly occasional in the character of his greatness."
Praises the Fables for their originality, and Dryden in general
for being "so far in advance of his time." Calls him "the greatest craftsman in English letters." Reprinted many times: most
recently 1969.66. See 1940.21.

1882

1   D., E.A. "'Cadua': 'Woots': 'Diana's Grove.'" N&Q [6th
    ser.] 6 (12 August):132.
    In response to a query, suggests meanings for these words
or phrases in The Wild Gallant.

2   ROSBUND, MAX. Dryden als Shakespeare-Bearbeiter. Ph.D.
    dissertation, Halle-Wittenberg. Halle: Plotz'sche, 72 pp.
    Deals with verbal parallels, spectacle, style, and metrics.
Notes many differences; comes to no general conclusions.

3   SAINTSBURY, GEORGE, ed. The Works of John Dryden. 18 vols.
    Edinburgh: printed for William Paterson, 1882-93.
    A revision and correction of Scott's edition (1808.3).

4   [SHAIRP, J.C.]. "English Poets and Oxford Critics." Quarterly

Review 153 (April):431-63.
    Surveys the history of English poetry. Discusses Dryden's career in the context of this history (pp. 450-54): his break with styles and attitudes of the past, his unsurpassed achievement as a political satirist, his greatness as a translator and weakness as a lyricist.

1883

*1   OHLSEN, FRIEDRICH. "Dryden as a Dramatist and Critic." Ph.D. dissertation, Altona.
      Cited by C.G. Child in 1904.2.

1884

1   ANON. "Dryden and Drummond as Hymnologists--Dryden." Saturday Review 58:370-72.
    Argues that Dryden translated Catholic hymns, and that these are printed in the Primer of 1706. Uses tradition and chronology as evidence. See 1884.4; 1937.13.

2   B., G.S. A Study of the Prologue and Epilogue in English Literature from Shakespeare to Dryden. London: Kegan Paul, Trench, 198 pp.
    Traces the history of the form, and describes major examples. Distinguishes among various types, primarily by subject matter. Calls Dryden the best and most voluminous writer of prologues and epilogues.

3   GOTCH, J. ALFRED. "Round Dryden's Birthplace." Building News, 22 February.
    Describes Aldwinckle All Saints, Titchmarsh, and Oundle, and identifies many locations associated with Dryden. Reprinted: 1888.2.

4   SHIPLEY, ORBY. "Dryden as a Hymnodist." Dublin Review, 3d ser. 12 (October):245-69.
    Argues that it is "not improbable" that Dryden translated Catholic hymns which appeared anonymously in 1706. Bases the argument on similarities of style and wording between the hymns and Dryden's poetry, and on the belief that there was no other person at the time with qualifications for doing the work. See 1884.1; 1937.13.

1885

1   ANON. "Hymns Attributed to Dryden." Saturday Review 59:284-85.
    Argues for Dryden's authorship of hymns in the 1706 Primer

on the basis of stylistic similarities to his poetry.   See 1884.1,
4; 1937.13.

2   COURTHOPE, W.J.   "The Liberal Movement in England, pt. 6."
    National Review 5:770-86.
        Cites Dryden several times as an exemplar of conservatism in
    literature. Charges that modern poets have lost touch with liter-
    ary language and with reality; admires those poets who, like
    Dryden, have "the power of reproducing the idea of external
    Nature."

3   GILLOW, JOSEPH. Bibliographical Dictionary of the English
    Catholics. 5 vols. London: Burns & Oates; New York: Catholic
    Publication Society.
        The Dryden entry (2:112-31) surveys his life and works, em-
    phasizing his religious development and conversion. Lists his
    works chronologically, with very brief commentary.

4   GOSSE, EDMUND. From Shakespeare to Pope: An Inquiry Into the
    Causes and Phenomena of the Rise of Classical Poetry in England.
    Cambridge: Cambridge University Press, 308 pp.
        Denies Dryden a place among the pioneers of the classical
    movement in England: he is less sublime and less austere "than
    such as Waller and Cowley" (pp. 226-28). Reprinted: 1968.28.

5   HARTMANN, KARL. Einfluss Molières auf Dryden's romischdrama-
    tische Dichtungen. Ph.D. dissertation, Leipzig: Joachim und
    Jüstel, 40 pp.
        Examines each of Molière's plays and Dryden's comedies,
    noting similarities, mostly verbal. Suggests that Molière was a
    major influence on Dryden.

6   OTT, PHILIPP. Über das Verhältnis des Lustspiel-Dichters Dryden
    zur gleichzeitigen französischen Komödie, ins besondere zu
    Molière. Ph.D. dissertation, München. Landshut: Jos.
    Thomann'schen, 35 pp.
        Examines Sir Martin Mar-All and An Evening's Love, noting
    their verbal and structural similarities to plays by Molière (and,
    in the case of Sir Martin Mar-All, Quinault). Finds Sir Martin
    below its original in artistic merit; An Evening's Love above.

7   TÜCHERT, ALOYS. John Dryden als Dramatiker in seinen
    Beziehungen zu Madeleine de Scudérys Romandichtung. Ph.D.
    dissertation, Zweibrücken: A. Kranzbühler, 44 pp.
        Discusses the significance of French romances as sources
    and influences in early Restoration drama. Emphasizes de Scudéry
    and Dryden. Deals with Secret Love, The Conquest of Granada, and
    Marriage a-la-Mode.

1886

1   SKEAT, WALTER W. "Dryden's Use of Instinct." N&Q [7th ser.]
    1 (17 April):306-7.
        Condemns Bell's note (in 1854.2) to Absalom and Achitophel,
    1. 219. (Bell had found the line prosaic, and suggested an emenda-
    tion.) Shows how, if one accents "instinct" on the second sylla-
    ble, the line scans.

1887

1   DÖHLER, E. "Der Angriff George Villiers auf die heroischen
    Dramen und Dichter Englands im 17. Jahrhundert." Anglia 10:
    38-75.
        Speculates upon the particular targets Buckingham had in
    mind at various stages in writing The Rehearsal; includes various
    scenes and plays by Dryden, and critical statements made by him.

2   HOPKINS, GERARD MANLEY. Letter to Robert Bridges, 6 November.
        Calls Dryden "the most masculine of our poets," whose "style
    and rhythms lay the strongest stress of all our literature on the
    naked thew and sinew of the English language." Printed in The
    Letters of Gerard Manley Hopkins to Robert Bridges, ed. Claude
    Collier Abbott (London: Oxford University Press, 1935).

3   PANZNER, MAX. John Dryden als Übersetzer altklassischer
    Dichtungen. Pt. 1, "Vergils Aeneis." Ph.D. dissertation,
    Breslau: Breslauer Genossenschafts-Buchdruckerei, 47 pp.
        Reviews previous scholarship on Dryden as translator. Demon-
    strates Dryden's loose practice in translation. Emphasizes his ex-
    pansion of the Latin, especially at moments of emotion and vivid
    action. Notes his use of devices, such as parallelism, which are
    typical of the heroic couplet.

1888

1   FIRTH, C.H. "Dryden's Stanzas on Oliver Cromwell." N&Q [7th
    ser.] 5 (26 May):404.
        Suggests that lines in the thirty-fifth stanza of Heroic
    Stanzas refer to the capture of a whale in the Thames (a bad omen,
    in this case portending Cromwell's death).

2   GOTCH, J. ALFRED. "Round Dryden's Birthplace." Northamptonshire
    Notes and Queries 2:173-81.
        Reprint of 1884.3.

3   LOWE, ROBERT W. A Bibliographical Account of English Theatrical
    Literature from the Earliest Times to the Present Day. New
    York: J.W. Bouton; London: J.C. Nimmo, 396 pp.

Gives bibliographical information about published plays and books about the theater. Reprinted: 1966.34. Revised and updated: 1970.4.

4   LYNN, W.T. "Dryden's Funeral and Lord Jeffreys." N&Q [7th ser.] 6 (29 December):507.
      Suggests that the story of Jeffrey's scandalous interruption of the funeral was a fabrication by Elizabeth Thomas.

5   S[TEPHEN], L[ESLIE]. "John Dryden." In The Dictionary of National Biography. Vol. 16. Edited by Leslie Stephen. London: Smith, Elder, pp. 64-75.
      Surveys Dryden's life and works, making use of what biographers and editors had discovered or surmised about Dryden to date. Concludes that he is "the least unworldly of great poets," and therefore his work reflects his time for good and ill. Lists his works, and editions after his death. Reprinted: The Dictionary of National Biography (London: Oxford University Press, 1921-22), 6:64-75.

1889

1   HOLZHAUSEN, P. "Dryden's heroisches Drama." Englische Studien 13, no. 3:414-45; 15, no. 1 (1891):13-52; 16, no. 2 (1892): 201-29.
      Defines the form and describes its evolution in England. Analyzes the plays, emphasizing characterization. Discusses themes, especially that of moral choice. Examines the prologues and epilogues. Looks at the metrics. Concludes that Dryden's heroic drama is a comprehensive failure.

1890

1   BLACK, WILLIAM GEORGE. "Log-Rolling." N&Q [7th ser.] 9 (8 February):106.
      Cites Dryden's "To Mr. Lee on his Alexander," in which Dryden questions the propriety of one author noticing favorably the work of a friend.

2   EVANS, JOHN AMPHLETT. "Dryden." Temple Bar 88 (March):380-91.
      An appreciation of Dryden, moral aspects aside. Speculates about Dryden's influence on Tennyson. Takes issue with Macaulay's attack on the heroic plays (1828.1); examines The Conquest of Granada, linking it to the epic and historical romance. Praises its political realism. Concludes that Dryden is "the greatest craftsman in English literature."

3   _____. "Dryden and Scott." Temple Bar 90 (September):84-94.
      Draws parallels between the two writers. Argues for the

influence of Dryden on Scott. Notes similarities in their political outlooks and in their personalities, except that Dryden lacks
"consistent elevation of moral or religious tone." Defends Dryden
against Wordsworth's charge that he makes no use of natural imagery
(1805.1).

4   _____. "Dryden's Prose Works." Temple Bar 89 (August):549-58.
         Credits Dryden with being the "pivot, on which turns the
whole history of English literature" (for his role in improving
English prose style). Compares a passage by Macaulay with the
opening of Dryden's Essay of Dramatic Poesy, upon which it is based.
Quotes a passage from Marriage a-la-Mode to demonstrate Dryden's
skill as a comic writer.

5   LOWELL, JAMES RUSSELL. "Dryden." In The Complete Writings of
         James Russell Lowell. Vol. 3. London: Macmillan, pp. 95-191.
         Reprint of 1868.6.

                              1892

1   BENNETT, H. LEIGH. "John Dryden." In A Dictionary of
         Hymnology. Edited by John Julian. London: John Murray.
         Includes a brief life; discusses the available evidence re-
garding Dryden's authorship of hymns in The Primer, or Office of
the B.V. Mary, in English (1706). Accepts Shipley's argument
(1884.4) that the bulk of them are Dryden's. Reprinted: 1907
(2d ed. rev.); 1957 (New York: Dover). See 1937.13.

2   COLLINS, GEORGE STUART. Dryden's Dramatic Theory and Praxis.
         Ph.D. dissertation, Leipzig: Oswald Schmidt, 69 pp.
         Describes and summarizes, chronologically, Dryden's major
critical statements on drama. Disparages their "personal, sub-
jective, and occasional" nature. Briefly discusses the relation
of each of eighteen of the plays to his critical statements. Concludes that there is little real connection between his dramatic
theory and practice.

3   DEIGHTON, KENNETH, ed. Aureng-Zebe, A Tragedy. Westminster:
         Archibald Constable, 215 pp.
         Briefly relates the life. Discusses (pp. 9-22) the heroic
plays, quoting copiously from the opinions of previous critics.
Concludes that Aureng-Zebe is the best of the heroic plays because
it is the least extreme in characterization and style. With memoir
and notes.

4   KÖLBING, E[UGEN]. "Zu Drydens Annus Mirabilis." Englische
         Studien 16, no. 1:158-59.
         Argues against emending "crests" to "breasts" in l. 264, on
the ground that "crest" is correct when used of a swan. See
1879.1.

5   LOUNSBURY, THOMAS R. Studies in Chaucer: His Life and Writings.
    3 vols. New York: Harper.
        Credits Dryden with having revived Chaucer's reputation.
    Defends his decision to modernize and paraphrase: notes that his
    versions were preferred to the originals throughout the eighteenth
    century. Praises Dryden's understanding of the "spirit" and
    "sense" of Chaucer. Compares passages in the original to Dryden's
    version, arguing Chaucer's superiority (3:99-110, 156-79).

1893

1   ADAMS, F. "Thomas Shadwell and Dryden." N&Q [8th ser.] 4
    (21 October):334.
        Feels there is no ground for supposing that Dryden borrowed
    the line "Great wits are sure to madness near allied" from Shadwell
    (as suggested in 1893.2). Notes that Shadwell's line is a trans-
    lation of a passage in Seneca, describing a theory of Aristotle's.

2   TROLLOPE, HENRY M. "Thomas Shadwell and Dryden." N&Q [8th
    ser.] 4 (23 September):243.
        Notes the similarity between Dryden's line "Great wits are
    sure to madness near allied" (Absalom and Achitophel 1, line 163)
    and Shadwell's "Great wits, you know, have always a mixture of
    madness" (The Sullen Lovers, 1668). See 1893.1.

3   WESELMANN, FRANZ. Dryden als Kritiker. Ph.D. dissertation,
    Gottingen. Mulheim a.d. Ruhr: Marks, 54 pp.
        Quotes excerpts to illustrate Dryden's critical opinions on
    various aspects of literature. Discusses in a brief introduction,
    Dryden's classical, English, and continental sources.

1894

1   KÖLBING, EUGEN. "Zu Dryden." Englische Studien 19, no. 3:465.
        Notes Dryden's use of "reed" in the sense of "marsh" at 1.
    194 of The Wife of Bath's Tale.

*2 LUNDBECK, TORBEN. Dryden som tragediedigter. Copenhagen:
    G.E.C. Gad, 195 pp.
        In Danish. Cited in 1912.3.

3   PUGHE, FRANCIS H. John Drydens Übersetzungen aus Theokrit.
    Ph.D. dissertation, Breslau: Nischkowsky, 49 pp.
        Defends Dryden's versions of Theocritus, arguing that their
    relative looseness better preserves the spirit of the original
    Greek than a stricter rendering. Compares Dryden's versions to
    others, and to Dryden's own translations from Latin.

4   WARD, C.A. "The Funeral and Monument of Dryden." N&Q [8th

ser.] 5 (28 April):322-23; (19 May):382-84; (16 June):463-64.
Rehashes the funeral stories, asserting that the sensational
accounts current through the eighteenth century were false.
Praises Tom Brown's "A Description of Mr. D----n's Funeral"
(1700.3). Laments that Dryden's grave in Westminster Abbey still
remains improperly marked.

5   WYLIE, LAURA JOHNSON. Studies in the Evolution of English
     Criticism. Boston: Ginn, 212 pp.
         Chapter 1 (pp. 1-53) discusses Dryden's criticism, especially
in the context of its distant and immediate sources. Comments in
detail upon the Essay of Dramatic Poesy. Concludes that the key
strengths of Dryden's criticism are his "catholic taste" and "daring and ardor of mind." Reprinted: 1976.63; 1977.52.

1895

1   ANON. "Art of Translation." Quarterly Review 182 (October):
     324-53.
         Surveys and defends the art of translation, especially
theories of translation. Credits Dryden as the first translator
fully to espouse liberal rather than literal rendering.

*2   COLLINS, JOHN CHURTON. "John Dryden." In Essays and Studies.
     London.
         Cited by Margaret P. Sherwood in 1898.3. May be a reprint
of 1878.1.

3   DIERBERGER, JOSEF. John Drydens Reime: Ein Beitrag zur
     Geschichte der englischen Tonvokale. Ph.D. dissertation,
     Freiburg: Lehmann, 115 pp.
         Studies Dryden's rhymes as a means of understanding English
pronunciation in the late seventeenth century. Gives many examples,
classified by vowel sound.

4   GARNETT, RICHARD. The Age of Dryden. London: Bell, 298 pp.
         Has two chapters on Dryden, covering the poetry and drama
(pp. 7-41, 76-100). Outlines the life; describes and evaluates
the poetry, emphasizing its relation with Dryden's life and times.
Surveys the drama, from a generally hostile viewpoint. Reprinted:
1971.35.

5   LYNN, W.T. "Dryden and Greek." N&Q [8th ser.] 7 (18 May):386.
         Suggests that the Greek spelling of "eureka" at Religio
Laici, l. 43, is wrong. See 1895.6, 8-9.

6   _____. "Dryden and Greek." N&Q [8th ser.] 8 (6 July):14.
         Claims that the argument in 1895.8 assumes that Dryden did
no proofreading, an impossibility. See also 1895.5, 9.

7   [PALMER, ARTHUR.] "Horace and his Translators." Quarterly

Review 180 (January):111-37.
        Praises Dryden's paraphrases and translations of Horace
(p. 123). Claims that his version of Tyrrhena regum progenies is
"probably the one poem written in imitation of Horace that is superior to the original."

8   T., D.C. "Dryden and Greek." N&Q [8th ser.] 7 (8 June):451-52.
        Argues, in response to 1895.5, that Dryden's Greek spelling
of "eureka" reflects the pronunciation he learned at Westminster
School. See also 1895.6, 9.

9   _____. "Dryden and Greek." N&Q [8th ser.] 8 (3 August):97-98.
        Dryden's spelling of "eureka" could have been his mistake,
but the point about pronunciation (made in 1895.8) still holds.
See also 1895.5-6.

1896

*1   ANON. "John Dryden." Citizen 1:291-93; 2:17-19.
        Cited in Latt and Monk, 1976.30.

2   C., B.L.R. "Literary Parallel." N&Q [8th ser.] 9 (25 January):
     65.
        Notes a parallel between the opening lines of The Hind and
the Panther and two lines from an elegy in memory of Admiral Deane.

3   PUGHE, F. "Kleine Bemerkungen." Englische Studien 22, no. 3:
     455.
        Agrees with 1892.4 that there is no need to emend "crests"
to "breasts" at Annus Mirabilis, 1. 264.

1897

1   BELJAME, ALEXANDRE. Le public et les hommes de lettres en
     Angleterre au dix-huitième siècle. Paris: Hachette.
        Reprint of 1881.1, adding an index. Translated 1948.2;
translation reprinted 1971.8.

2   HAMELIUS, PAUL. Die Kritik in der englischen Literatur des
     17. und 18. Jahrhunderts. Ph.D. dissertation, Liège. Leipzig:
     Th. Grieben, 206 pp.
        Sees Dryden as a crucial mediating figure between the criti-
cal views of the seventeenth and eighteenth centuries.

3   MEYER, PAUL. Metrische Untersuchung über den Blankvers John
     Dryden's. Ph.D. dissertation, Halle: Wischan und Wettengel,
     84 pp.
        Analyzes Dryden's prosodic practice in eight blank verse
plays, with many examples and tables. Concludes that Dryden's

blank verse is typical of its time, and generally reflects conventional modern pronunciation and accent.

*4   SMITH, HERBERT A. "Classicism and Criticism in English Literature from Dryden to Pope." Ph.D. dissertation, Yale University.
     Cited in Latt and Monk, 1976.30.

5   SPEERSCHNEIDER, OTTO. Metrische Untersuchungen über den heroischen Vers in John Drydens Dramen. Ph.D. dissertation, Halle: Wischan und Wettengel, 88 pp.
     Classifies, with examples but little commentary, Dryden's characteristic diction and metrical practice in the heroic plays.

6   TUPPER, FREDERICK, Jr. "Dryden and Speight's Chaucer." MLN 12 (June):347-53.
     Argues that Dryden's Chaucer was indebted to Speight's edition. Gives several examples of how Dryden's wording seems to derive from Speight's annotations.

1898

*1   NOYES, G[EORGE] R. "Dryden as Critic, with Special Reference to the French Influence." Ph.D. dissertation, Harvard University.
     Cited in Latt and Monk, 1976.30.   .

2   SCHELLING, FELIX E. "Ben Jonson and the Classical School." PMLA 13, no. 2:221-49.
     Asserts that "there is not a trait which came to prevail in the poetry of the new classic school as practiced by Waller and Dryden, and later by Pope, which is not directly traceable to the influence or to the example of Ben Jonson." Reprinted: 1961.45.

3   SHERWOOD, MARGARET P. Dryden's Dramatic Theory and Practice. Boston, New York, and London: Lamson, Wolfee, 110 pp.
     Sees a gulf between Dryden's critical theory and practice. Summarizes his major critical pieces. Treats comedies, heroic plays, and tragedies, finally asserting that "Dryden's dramatic work is imitation, not organic creation. It lacks a vital centre, and it has not endured." Reprinted: 1966.51.

1899

1   DAY, E. MORTON. "Drydeniana." N&Q [9th ser.] 3 (4 March):165.
     Questions Saintsbury's interpretation of a stage direction in The Indian Emperour.

2   ELTON, OLIVER. The Augustan Ages. Periods of European

Literature 8. New York: Scribners; Edinburgh and London: Blackwood, 439 pp.
   A general literary history of the period. Surveys and praises Dryden's criticism, finding him the greatest English critic (besides Gray) before Coleridge. Also praises his prose style.

*3   KUCHENBACKER, KARL. Dryden as a Satirist. Magdeburg: n.p.
   Cited in Latt and Monk, 1976.30.

*4   WITT, OTTO. "'The Tempest or the Enchanted Island.' A Comedy by John Dryden, 1670. 'The Sea Voyage.' A Comedy by Beaumont and Fletcher, 1647. 'The Goblin's Tragi-Comedy' by Sir John Suckling, 1646. In ihren Verhältnis zu Shakespeares 'Tempest' und den übrigen Quellen." Ph.D. dissertation, Rostock.
   Cited in Latt and Monk, 1976.30.

1900

1   GROLIER CLUB. Exhibition of First and Other Editions of the Works of John Dryden (1631-1700). New York: De Vinne Press, 88 pp.
   Contains 146 items, including Drydeniana and portraits. Gives brief bibliographical description and occasional notes.

2   KER, W.P., ed. Essays of John Dryden. Oxford: Clarendon Press.
   A general introduction to Dryden's criticism, followed by brief introductory essays on several of the works in the collection, pointing out what is important about them. Emphasizes his independence and lack of dogmatism, and praises his forthright style. Relates his work to that of his contemporaries in England and the continent (pp. xiii-lxxi). Reprinted: 1925.8; 1970.47.

*3   SCOTT, ANNA M. "Über das Verhältnis von Drydens State of Innocence zu Miltons Paradise Lost." Ph.D. dissertation, Halle.
   Cited in Latt and Monk, 1976.30.

1901

1   GROLIER CLUB. An Exhibition of Selected Works of the Poets Laureate of England. New York: De Vinne Press, 95 pp.
   Contains six Dryden items.

2   HENNEMAN, JOHN B. "Dryden After Two Centuries (1700-1900). SR 9 (January):57-72.
   Celebrates Dryden as a major contributor to the histories of English prose style and poetic form. Claims that the two St. Cecilia poems are his greatest achievements.

3 NEWDIGATE-NEWDEGATE, Lady [ANNE]. <u>Cavalier and Puritan in the Days of the Stuarts</u>. New York: Longmans, Green: London: Smith, Elder, 382 pp.
   Compiled from the papers of Sir Richard Newdigate (1644-1710). Includes reports of Dryden's beating in Rose Alley, and the political delay in the production of <u>The Duke of Guise</u>. Gives 18 November 1682 as the date of one performance.

1902

1 KRÜGER, WILHELM. <u>Das Verhältnis von Colley Cibbers Lustspiel "The Comical Lovers" zu John Drydens "Marriage A La Mode" und "Secret Love, or, the Maiden Queen."</u> Ph.D. dissertation, Halle: Wischan und Wettengel, 56 pp.
   Prints parallel passages, showing Cibber's extensive use of the wording in Dryden's plays. Points out, however, that Cibber has softened Dryden's explicit sexual and religious references.

1903

1 BRIDGES, ROBERT. "Dryden on Milton." <u>Speaker</u>, 24 October.
   Accuses Dryden of inconsistency in his public attitude toward Milton; attacks his translations of Chaucer; quotes several passages to show that his poetry is bad. Reprinted: 1932.2.

2 CHASE, LEWIS N. <u>The English Heroic Play: A Critical Description of the Rhymed Tragedy of the Restoration</u>. Studies in Comparative Literature. New York: Columbia University Press, 262 pp.
   Characterizes English heroic drama with many examples from Dryden. Emphasizes its foreignness to English taste, but asserts that "it was a wholesome antidote" to the indecency of contemporary comedy. Reprinted: 1965.11.

3 COURTHOPE, W.J. <u>A History of English Poetry</u>. 6 vols. London and New York: Macmillan.
   "John Dryden and the Satirists of the Country Party" (3: 482-533) credits Dryden with bringing the language into a new era. "Dryden and the Romantic Drama after the Restoration" (4:397-453) categorizes and describes Dryden's plays, with reference to Dryden's various critical statements on drama. Defends the plays against their attackers: claims that Dryden was an important transitional figure in the history of English drama. Reprinted: 1962.7.

4 HANNMANN, FRIEDRICH. <u>Drydens Tragödie "All for Love or the World well Lost" und ihr Verhältnis zu Shakespeares "Antony and Cleopatra"</u>. Ph.D. dissertation, Rostock: Carl Boldt'sche, 82 pp.
   Summarizes Dryden's theory and practice leading up to <u>All for Love</u>, emphasizing his comments on and adaptations of

Shakespeare. Compares plot, characterization, and style of the
two plays in detail. Concludes that Dryden's play is far inferior
to Shakespeare's.

5   RZESNITZEK, FLORIAN. Das Verhaltnis der Fables von John Dryden
    zu den entsprechenden mittelenglischen Vorlagen. Ratibon:
    Lindner, 178 pp.
        Compares Dryden's translations of Chaucer with the originals.
    Emphasizes differences in the plots and character development.
    Concludes that the translations can serve as models of excellence.

1904

1   BAILEY, JOHN. "Dryden and Shakespeare." TLS, 1 April, p. 97.
        Compares All for Love and Antony and Cleopatra. Praises
    Dryden's craftsmanship as a dramatist. Reprinted: 1911.3;
    1968.39.

2   CHILD, C.G. "The Rise of the English Heroic Play." MLN 19
    (June):166-73.
        Defends the traditional credit given to Davenant as the
    founder of English heroic drama. Traces the development of the
    form up to Dryden's The Indian Emperour.

3   COUPER, RAMSAY W. "John Dryden's First Funeral." Athenaeum
    4005 (30 July):145-46.
        Asserts, on the basis of parish records, that Dryden was
    buried at St. Anne's Soho on Thursday, 2 May 1700, then removed,
    embalmed, and laid in state in the College of Physicians and
    Westminster Abbey. See 1904.4.

4   HARVEY, WILLIAM J. "John Dryden's First Funeral." Athenaeum
    4009 (27 August):271; 4017 (22 October):552.
        Claims priority for the discovery of Dryden's burial at St.
    Anne's Soho (see 1904.3). Prints extracts from contemporary news-
    papers about Dryden's death and funeral, and prints the College of
    Physicians official motion that Dryden be carried to Westminster
    Abbey.

5   LAWRENCE, W.J. "Did Thomas Shadwell Write an Opera on 'The
    Tempest?'" Anglia 27:205-17.
        Attributes the anonymous 1674 opera obviously based on the
    Dryden-Davenant Tempest to Shadwell. See 1906.6, 8; 1925.16;
    1946.21; 1947.6.

*6 MILLER, RAYMOND D. "Secondary Accent in Modern English Verse
    (Chaucer to Dryden)." Ph.D. dissertation, Johns Hopkins.
        Cited in Latt and Monk, 1976.30. Reprinted: 1975.39;
    1976.39.

7   NOYES, GEORGE R. "An Unnoticed Edition of Dryden's Virgil."
    MLN 19 (May):125-27.
        Claims that a collation of two copies shows that a second
    edition appeared in 1697, correcting the first; and that no one
    has noticed the differences between the two. See 1909.5 for a re-
    traction.

8   PARSONS, EDWARD S. "A Note Upon Dryden's Heroic Stanzas on the
    Death of Cromwell." MLN 19 (February):47-49.
        Suggests that the reference to Cromwell's palms thriving al-
    though they were not weighted (1. 57) alludes to the frontispiece
    of Eikon Basilike, where two weighted palms appear in the picture
    of Charles I at prayer.

9   WENDELL, BARRETT. The Temper of the Seventeenth Century in
    English Literature. Clark Lectures for 1902-03. New York:
    Scribners; London: Macmillan.
        Surveys Dryden's life and work as epitomizing developments
    in English life and literature during the later seventeenth century
    (pp. 327-55). Reprinted: 1967.62.

10 WIERUSZOWSKI, KURT E. Untersuchungen über John Drydens
    Boccaccio-Paraphrasen. Ph.D. dissertation, Bonn: Foppen, 75
    pp.
        Contrasts the originals to Dryden's reworkings; argues that
    Dryden has greatly changed them. Describes and classifies the
    changes under such categories as amplification, dramatic and styl-
    istic heightening, use of political allusions, and echoes of pre-
    vious authors other than Boccaccio.

11 ZENKE, HERMANN. Dryden's Troilus and Cressida im Verhältnis zu
    Shakespeare's Drama und die übrigen Bearbeitungen des Stoffes
    in England. Ph.D. dissertation, Rostock: Carl Boldt'sche, 48
    pp.
        Argues that Dryden used the First Folio text. Summarizes
    the plot, with interspersed commentary. Prints a table of cor-
    responding passages. Concludes that Dryden's most important change
    was to streamline Shakespeare's plot.

1905

1   EVERETT, WILLIAM. "Six Cleopatras." Atlantic Monthly 95
    (February):252-63.
        Contrasts six portrayals from Shakespeare to Delphine Gay
    (1847), including Dryden's.

2   JOHNSON, SAMUEL. Lives of the English Poets. Edited by George
    Birkbeck Hill. 3 vols. Oxford: Clarendon Press.
        The standard modern edition. Includes 1779.2 (1:331-487);
    1779.3 (3:277-80); 1779.4 (3:82-276).

3   SCHRODER, EDWIN. Drydens letztes Drama: "Love Triumphant or
    Nature will Prevail." Ph.D. dissertation, Rostock: Adlers
    Erben, 70 pp.
        Describes the characters and plot. Compares the play un-
    favorably with Beaumont and Fletcher's A King and No King. Con-
    cludes that the play has too many absurdities and improbabilities
    to work.

4   TUPPER, JAMES W. "The Relation of the Heroic Play to the
    Romances of Beaumont and Fletcher." PMLA 20, no. 3:584-621.
        Asserts that the heroic play developed out of Jacobean drama
    through Davenant. Uses many examples from Dryden in support, com-
    paring them with examples drawn from Jacobean playwrights, espe-
    cially Beaumont and Fletcher. Emphasizes similarities of plot and
    types of character.

1906

1   ALBRECHT, LOUIS. Drydens "Sir Martin Mar-All" in Bezug auf
    seine Quellen. Ph.D. dissertation, Rostock: Adlers Erben.
        Compares Dryden's play (1667) with Quinault's L'Amant
    Indiscret (1654) and Molière's L'Etourdi (1653). Cites parallel
    passages to argue that Dryden was indebted to the two French plays.
    Concludes that Sir Martin Mar-All is inferior to its source.

2   ANON. "Religio Laici." Spectator 97:673-74.
        An appreciative summary of the poem.

*3 BOHN, WILLIAM E. "The Development of John Dryden's Critical
    Theory." Ph.D. dissertation, University of Michigan.
        Cited in Latt and Monk, 1976.30. See 1907.1.

4   CHARLANNE, LOUIS. L'Influence française en Angleterre au XVIIe
    siècle. Paris: Société Française d'Imprimerie et de Librairie,
    633 pp.
        A comprehensive survey of French influence on English society
    and literature during the period, especially the drama. Refers
    frequently to Dryden: discusses his attitudes toward introducing
    French words into English, his work as Historiographer Royal, and
    especially his use of French materials in his drama and dramatic
    criticism. Reprinted: 1971.15.

5   CHURCHILL, GOERGE B. "The Relation of Dryden's 'State of
    Innocence' to Milton's 'Paradise Lost' and Wycherley's 'Plain
    Dealer': an Inquiry into Dates." MP 4 (October):381-88.
        Asserts that The State of Innocence was published in 1677,
    despite David Masson's suggestion (in his life of Milton) that
    Marvell alluded to it in his prefatory poem to the second edition
    of Paradise Lost (1673). There is no other evidence for an edi-
    tion earlier than 1677.

6   CLARKE, Sir ERNEST. "'The Tempest' as an 'Opera.'" Athenaeum
     4113 (25 August):222-23.
          Suggests that Shadwell turned the Dryden-Davenant Tempest
     into an opera. See 1904.5, 1906.8.

7   KILBOURNE, FREDERICK W. Alterations and Adaptations of
     Shakespeare. Boston: Poet Lore, 190 pp.
          Describes each of Dryden's adaptations of Shakespeare. Is
     scornful of The Tempest; critical of Troilus and Cressida; calls
     All for Love a masterpiece, but asserts that it is really a new
     play.

8   LAWRENCE, W.J. "Did Thomas Shadwell Write an Opera on 'The
     Tempest?'" Anglia 29:539-41.
          Accuses Sir Ernest Clarke (1906.6) of having plagiarized
     his (Lawrence's) earlier article (1904.5).

*9 MYERS, CLARA L. "Opera in England from 1656 to 1728." Western
     Reserve University Bulletin 9, no. 5:129-56.
          Cited in Latt and Monk, 1976.30.

10 "RANGER." "John Dryden." Bookman (London) 31 (November):68-70.
          Praises Dryden's poetry and prose; belittles his drama.
     Surveys the life.

11 SAINTSBURY, GEORGE. A History of English Prosody From the
     Twelfth Century to the Present Day. 2 vols. London and New
     York: Macmillan.
          Describes and analyzes Dryden's prosody. Surveys his poetry
     chronologically, emphasizing his increasing skill in a variety of
     forms. Credits Dryden with establishing the supremacy of the coup-
     let. Places his achievement in the form on a par with Shakespeare's
     and Milton's in blank verse, Spenser's in the stanza, and William
     Morris's in octosyllabics. Reprinted: 1961.43.

                              1907

1   BOHN, WILLIAM E. "The Development of John Dryden's Literary
     Criticism." PMLA 22, no. 1:56-139.
          Attempts to make sense of the seeming contradictions in
     Dryden's criticism; concludes that "Dryden's critical activity
     was an organic part of his life." Finds five stages in his de-
     velopment, roughly corresponding to stages in his personal circum-
     stances. These stages alternate between "romanticism" and "ration-
     alism," with the culminating fifth stage (1690-1700) a combination
     of the two.

*2 KERBY, W. MOSELEY. "Molière and the Restoration Comedy in
     England." Ph.D. dissertation, Rennes.
          Cited in Latt and Monk, 1976.30.

3   MAYNARDIER, HOWARD. <u>The Arthur of the English Poets</u>. Boston
    and New York: Houghton Mifflin, 461 pp.
        Summarizes and briefly interprets <u>King Arthur</u> (pp. 296-98).
    Reprinted: 1969.47.

4   ROOT, ROBERT. "Dryden's Conversion to the Roman Catholic
    Faith." <u>PMLA</u> 22, no. 2:298-308.
        Defends Dryden's conversion as following consistently from
    his conservative political attitudes, which valued order above all
    else.

5   TUCKER, T.G. <u>The Foreign Debt of English Literature</u>. London:
    G. Bell, 264 pp.
        Describes the influence of classical and modern literatures
    upon English literature. Gives several examples of works which
    might have influenced works of Dryden's. Reprinted: 1966.63.

<u>1908</u>

1   FRYE, PROSSER H. "Dryden and the Critical Canons of the
    Eighteenth Century." In <u>Literary Reviews and Criticisms</u>.
    London: Putnam, pp. 130-89.
        An appreciative treatment of Dryden's style, emphasizing how
    it forms the basis for the standards of eighteenth-century poetry.
    Defends the style against modern attack. Reprinted: 1968.24.

2   HINCHMAN, WALTER S., and FRANCIS B. GUMMERE. <u>Lives of Great</u>
    <u>English Writers from Chaucer to Browning</u>. Boston and New York:
    Houghton Mifflin, 575 pp.
        Gives a derivative summary of Dryden's life and career (pp.
    128-39).

3   MUSTARD, W.P. "Virgil's Georgics and the British Poets."
    <u>American Journal of Philology</u> 29:1-32.
        Identifies allusions to the <u>Georgics</u> in <u>The Medal</u> and
    <u>Alexander's Feast</u>.

4   SPURGEON, CAROLINE F. <u>Five Hundred Years of Chaucer Criticism</u>
    <u>and Allusion: 1357-1900</u>. Chaucer Society Second Series 48-50,
    52-56. London: Chaucer Society, 1908-17.
        Identifies, dates, quotes, and occasionally annotates allu-
    sions to Chaucer. The introduction credits Dryden with "the first
    detailed and careful criticism of Chaucer," and emphasizes his in-
    fluence upon eighteenth-century attitudes toward Chaucer. Re-
    printed: 1925.15; 1960.24.

5   THORNDIKE, ASHLEY H. <u>Tragedy</u>. The Types of English Literature.
    Boston and New York: Houghton Mifflin, 396 pp.
        Surveys English tragedy down to the middle of the nineteenth
    century. Uses Dryden's career as an illustration of the rise and

fall of heroic drama. Credits him with an important impact on
dramatic theory; concludes with moderate praise for his over-all
achievement (pp. 259-63).

1909

1   HOWARD, WILLIAM GUILD. "Ut Pictura Poesis." PMLA 24, no. 1:
     40-123.
         Discusses Dryden's "Parallel between Painting and Poetry"
     together with his translation of Du Fresnoy's De arte graphica
     and its annotations by De Peles. Asserts that these works provide
     the handiest introduction to the ut pictura poesis theory. Sum-
     marizes De arte graphica at length, dwelling on its similarity to
     Vida's Ars Poetica.

2   JOHNSON, CHARLES F. Shakespeare and His Critics. Boston and
     New York: Houghton Mifflin, 397 pp.
         Summarizes Dryden's attitudes toward Shakespeare, in a gen-
     eral chapter on the Restoration period (pp. 58-65).

3   MUNRO, JOHN, ed. The Shakespeare Allusion-Book: A Collection
     of Allusions to Shakespeare from 1591 to 1700. 2 vols. New
     York: Duffield; London: Chatto & Windus.
         Dates, identifies, and prints allusions, with occasional
     annotation. Dryden's allusions are in volume 2.

4   NOYES, GEORGE R., ed. The Poetical Works of Dryden. Cambridge
     Edition. Boston: Houghton Mifflin.
         Includes all of Dryden's nondramatic poetry, based on "a
     careful collation of the entire text with the original editions."
     The notes reprint "a considerable portion of . . . Scott's com-
     mentary." Includes a biographical sketch. Second edition revised
     and enlarged: 1950.18.

5   NOYES, GEORGE R. [Retraction of "An Unnoticed Edition of
     Dryden's Virgil."] MLN 24 (January):31.
         Retracts 1904.7. The copy on which his argument was based
     proves to be of the real second edition with a title page taken
     from the first edition. Accepts Malone's date of 1698 for the
     second edition.

*6   RICHARDSON, CHARLES F. A Study of English Rhyme. Hanover,
     N.H.: University Press.
         Cited in Latt and Monk, 1976.30, which notes the relevant
     chapter as "Formal Rhyme" (pp. 146-57).

7   SPINGARN, JOEL E., ed. Critical Essays of the Seventeenth
     Century. Vol. 3. Oxford: Clarendon Press.
         Contains excerpts from Gerard Langbaine (1691.1) and Jeremy
     Collier (1698.2). The introduction (1:ix-cvi) traces the sources

and development of English criticism during the seventeenth century, emphasizing questions of influence. Sees Dryden (whose
criticism is not included in the anthology, as being readily
available) as the culmination of this development. Notes that
Essay on Dramatic Poesy first introduces French criticism fully
into England, and applies its criteria to English works. Calls
Dryden "the first great modern critic." Reprinted: 1957.34;
1963.53.

8   WHEATLEY, HENRY B. "Dryden's Publishers." Transactions of the
    Bibliographical Society 11:17-38.
        Traces the history of Dryden's relations with his publishers,
especially Henry Herringman and Jacob Tonson. Pays particular attention to the arrangements for the subscription of Virgil's
Aeneid.

1910

1   BALLEIN, JOHANNES. Jeremy Collier's Angriff auf die englische
    Bühne. Ph.D. dissertation, Marburg: N.G. Elwert'sche, 261 pp.
        Discusses (pp. 153-66) Dryden's explicit and implicit re-
sponses to Collier's Short View (1698.2).

2   BENTZIEN, WERNER. Studien zu Drydens "Oedipus". Ph.D. disser-
    tation, Rostock: Carl Boldt'sche, 100 pp.
        Puts the play in the context of contemporary English drama;
studies its relation to previous versions by Sophocles, Seneca,
and Corneille; summarizes its plot; remarks on its style. Concludes that the sensationalism of Dryden and Lee diminished the
tragic effect of the story.

3   BROWN, FRANK C. Elkanah Settle: His Life and Works. Chicago:
    University of Chicago Press, 180 pp.
        Deals briefly with Settle's rivalry with Dryden, quoting
extensively from the relevant materials (pp. 51-60).

4   HILL, HERBERT WYNFORD. "La Calprenède's Romances and the
    Restoration Drama." University of Nevada Studies 2, no. 3:1-56;
    3, no. 2 (1911):57-158.
        Notes and documents the similarity of the plots of La
Calprenède's Cassandra and Cleopatra to The Indian Queen, The
Indian Emperour, and The Conquest of Granada; suggests that they
were among the influences on Dryden's early heroic plays. Reprinted: 1911.5.

5   MACPHERSON, CHARLES. Über die Vergil-Übersetzung des John
    Dryden. Ph.D. dissertation, Berlin: Mayer und Müller, 102 pp.
        Analyzes Dryden's translation of Virgil, emphasizing verbal
and syntactical detail. Places it in its literary contexts, and
discusses its significance in publishing history as a subscription

venture. Compares it with other translations: concludes that it
is the most readable.

6   MILES, DUDLEY H. The Influence of Molière on Restoration
     Comedy. New York: Columbia University Press, 283 pp.
          Traces the influence of Molière on Dryden, among others.
     Asserts that Dryden drew mainly on Molière for characterization,
     rather than plot. Examines especially Marriage a-la-Mode and
     Amphitryon, emphasizing Dryden's use of "metaphysical" language
     in the latter. Has an alphabetical "list of borrowings" in an
     appendix.

7   MONROE, B.S. "An English Academy." MP 8 (July):107-22.
          Traces the development of interest in an English Academy.
     Alludes to Dryden's activities with the Royal Society, and quotes
     several passages from his prose.

8   MOORE, JOHN L. "Tudor-Stuart Views of the Growth, Status, and
     Destiny of the English Language." Studien zur englischen
     Philologie 41:1-173.
          Briefly treats Dryden's statements on the language, particu-
     larly his attitudes toward anglicizing foreign words. Reprinted:
     1970.56.

9   PREVITÉ-ORTON, C.W. Political Satire in English Poetry.
     Cambridge: Cambridge University Press, 244 pp.
          Discusses Absalom and Achitophel and The Hind and the Panther
     (pp. 96-105). Finds Dryden to be the greatest satirist of his
     time, but a hireling: he "praised or blamed as the court-wind
     blew."

10   RISTINE, FRANK HUMPHREY. English Tragicomedy: Its Origin and
     History. Columbia University Studies in English. New York:
     Columbia University Press, 262 pp.
          Discusses Dryden's early defense of tragicomedy, and his
     later condemnation of it. Compares the plots of Dryden's tragi-
     comedies with each other (pp. 168-75). Reprinted: 1963.44.

11   SARGEAUNT, JOHN, ed. Poems of John Dryden. London: Oxford
     University Press, 629 pp.
          The introduction (pp. ix-xxiii) deals with the inadequacies
     of previous editions. The notes are strictly concerned with textu-
     al matters. Reprinted: 1929.8.

                                  1911

1   ALDEN, RAYMOND M. "The Doctrine of Verisimilitude in French
     and English Criticism of the Seventeenth Century." In the
     Matzke Memorial Volume. Stanford: Stanford University, pp.
     38-48.

Briefly contrasts Dryden and Rymer: asserts that Dryden's good taste led him into inconsistencies which avoided the other's hidebound devotion to the "rules."

2   BAAS, DAVID. Drydens heroische Tragödie: Eine ästhetische Untersuchung. Ph.D. dissertation, Freiburg: Wagner, 78 pp.
    Discusses the antecedents of Dryden's heroic plays, especially in Shakespeare and Corneille. Links his plain style to an effort to combine the two. Emphasizes relationships between Dryden's artistic personality and the psychology of the tragedies. Praises his power of invention, but finds him unable to rise above his time.

3   BAILEY, JOHN. "Dryden and Shakespeare." In Poets and Poetry. Oxford: Clarendon Press, pp. 72-79.
    Reprint of 1904.1. Reprinted: 1968.39.

4   FRIEDLAND, LOUIS S. "The Dramatic Unities in England." JEGP 10, no. 1:56-89; no. 2:280-99; no. 3:453-67.
    Following Bohn's division of Dryden's career as a critic into five periods (1907.1), chronologically summarizes his views on the unities. Emphasizes his inconsistencies and departures from authority, but defends these as pragmatic choices. Asserts that his dramatic tenets combine "classic" and "romantic" attitudes.

5   HILL, HERBERT WYNFORD. La Calprenède's Romances and the Restoration Drama. Chicago: University of Chicago Press.
    Reprint of 1910.4.

6   MERRILL, ELIZABETH. The Dialogue in English Literature. New Haven: Yale University Press, 135 pp.
    Briefly summarizes Essay of Dramatic Poesy. Comments on the appropriateness of the dialogue form. Reprinted: 1969.48.

7   SAINTSBURY, GEORGE. "Dryden and his Contemporaries." In A History of English Criticism. Edinburgh and London: Blackwood, pp. 105-46.
    Gives a full account of Dryden's prose pieces, with examples and commentary. Compares Dryden with Boileau, to the credit of Dryden. Claims that Dryden "is the first critic to ask, not whether he ought to like such and such a thing, but whether he does like it, and why he likes it."

*8 SCENNA, DESIDERATO. Spigolature critichi: Minuzie carducciane. Dryden e Boccaccio. Chieti.
    Cited in Latt and Monk, 1976.30.

9   WILLIAMS W.H. "'Loves Extreamest Line.'" MLR 6 (July):386.
    Glosses this phrase (Palamon and Arcite 1, line 404), correcting Saintsbury (1882.3) and Noyes (1909.4).

1912

1 DIEDE, OTTO. Der Streit der Alten und Modernen in der englischen Literaturgeschichte des XVI. und XVII. Jahrhunderts. Ph.D. dissertation, Greifswald: Adler, 139 pp.
Deals with Dryden's relation to "the battle of the books" (pp. 78-95). Examines his major critical prose, concluding that while he tends to favor the moderns, his views are balanced by reverence for the ancients.

2 GRÜBNER, WILLY. Der Einfluss des Reims auf den Satzbau der englischen "Heroic Plays." Ph.D. dissertation, Königsberg: Karg und Manneck, 68 pp.
Deals in general with the disruption to normal word order caused by the demands of rhyming. Includes a treatment of Dryden (pp. 11-21).

3 HEIGL, FRANZ. Die dramatischen Einheiten bei Dryden. Ph.D. dissertation, Munich: Hueber, 95 pp.
Traces the history of concern about the unities up to Dryden's time. Summarizes his critical comments on the unities and describes his actual practice. Asserts that Dryden is more consistent in his use of the unities of time and place than of the unity of action. Concludes that Dryden's attempt to adapt the unities to the English tradition was useful in the long run.

4 LAWRENCE, W.J. "Did Thomas Shadwell Write an Opera on 'The Tempest?'" In The Elizabethan Playhouse and Other Studies. Stratford-upon-Avon: Shakespeare Head Press, pp. 193-206.
Combines 1904.5 and 1906.8.

5 REED, EDWARD BLISS. English Lyric Poetry from Its Origins to the Present Time. New Haven: Yale University Press, 616 pp.
Contains generally disparaging comment on Restoration lyrics, though it praises "To . . . Anne Killigrew." Quotes examples from Dryden's songs to demonstrate their inferiority to those of the Elizabethans. Reprinted: 1967.48.

6 SAINTSBURY, GEORGE. A History of English Prose Rhythm. London: Macmillan, 503 pp.
Remarks that Dryden's great contribution was to develop a conversational style well suited to argument. His prose, for the most part, cannot be arranged in quantitative rhythm. Concludes that he "set a model for all time." Reprinted: 1965.49; 1978.48.

7 STEEVES, HARRISON ROSS. "'The Athenian Virtuosi' and the 'Athenian Society.'" MLR 7 (July):358-71.
Distinguishes between the two. The former name was assumed by a group who attacked Dryden under its cover (see 1673.5); the second name denoted an actual club, which carried on respectable literary activities.

8   WARD, A.W., and A.R. WALLER, eds. The Cambridge History of
    English Literature. Vol. 8, The Age of Dryden. New York:
    G.P. Putnam; Cambridge: Cambridge University Press.
        "Dryden," by A.W. Ward (pp. 1-64), reviews his life, sum-
    marizing and commenting upon his plays and other major works,
    chronologically. Emphasizes his influence upon his own time and
    the period immediately after him. "The Prosody of the Seventeenth
    Century," by George Saintsbury (pp. 253-73), traces Dryden's cru-
    cial role in the development of the heroic couplet as the period's
    dominant form. "The Essay and the Beginning of Modern English
    Prose," by A.A. Tilley (pp. 421-46), discusses Dryden's style among
    that of many others. Emphasizes his influence over his contempo-
    raries as well as eighteenth-century prose writers. Revised and
    condensed: 1941.13.

1913

1   BESING, MAX. Molières Einfluss auf das englische Lustspiel bis
    1700. Ph.D. dissertation, Munster. Leipzig: Noske, 112 pp.
        Discusses each of Molière's plays, attempting to establish
    which English plays derive from it. Finds parallels between many
    Molière and Dryden plays, strongly suggestive of influence.

*2 GILLET, J.C. "Molière en Angleterre, 1660-1670." Memoires de
    l'académie royale de Belgique, 2d ser. 9.
        Cited in Latt and Monk, 1976.30.

3   HEARNSHAW, F.J.C. English History in Contemporary Poetry:
    Court and Parliament 1588-1688. London: G. Bell for the
    Historical Association.
        Describes major political poems during the period. Quotes
    Dryden frequently.

4   MILLER, G.M. The Historical Point of View in English Literary
    Criticism from 1570-1770. Anglistische Forschungen 35.
    Heidelberg: C. Winter, 164 pp.
        Reviews Dryden's major criticism, emphasizing his incon-
    sistency and lack of originality. Sees Dryden as less important
    than others in the field of historical criticism (pp. 94-100).
    Reprinted: 1968.44.

*5 REUSS, ADAM. "Das persönliche Geschlecht und unpersönlicher
    Substantive bei John Milton und John Dryden." Ph.D. disserta-
    tion, Kiel.
        Cited in Latt and Monk, 1976.30.

6   RHYS, ERNEST. Lyric Poetry. Channels of English Literature.
    London and Toronto: J.M. Dent; New York: E.P. Dutton.
        An appreciative description of Dryden's lyrics, with exam-
    ples (pp. 241-46).

7   ROUTH, JAMES. "The Classical Rule of Law in Criticism of the
     Sixteenth and Seventeenth Centuries." JEGP 12, no. 4:612-30.
        Sees three central factors in English classical criticism:
adherence to authority, the growth of polite conversation, and the
aristocratic "court temper." The key concept is decorum. Claims
that Dryden's work is "the supreme manifestation of English classicism," but that in its servility it begins to decay. Documents
Dryden's fallacies and inconsistencies, and his misreading of
Aristotle. Finds romanticism and realism to be virtually nonexistent during Dryden's period.

                                 1914

1   GRAY, W. FORBES. The Poets Laureate of England: Their History
     and Their Odes. London: Sir Isaac Pitman & Sons, 326 pp.
        Surveys Dryden's laureateship. Asserts that "the most vivid
impression we gain is that of a man of rare poetical gifts allay-
ing [sic] himself with fluid conviction and cupidity."

2   HOUSTON, PERCY H. "The Inconsistency of John Dryden." SR 22
     (October):469-82.
        Argues that Dryden's inconsistency was consistent given the
times, which made making a living very hard for an author. Illustrates the scope of Dryden's changes of mind.

*3   LEO, Brother, C.S.C. "Dryden as a Prose Writer." Catholic
     University Bulletin 20:211-23.
        Cited in Latt and Monk, 1976.30.

4   MACAULAY, THOMAS BABINGTON. "Dryden." In The History of
     England. Vol. 2. Edited by C.H. Firth. London: Macmillan,
     pp. 850-55.
        Reprint of 1848.1.

5   ROUTH, JAMES. "The Purpose of Art as Conceived in English
     Literary Criticism of the Sixteenth and Seventeenth Centuries."
     Englische Studien 48 (July):124-44.
        Surveys attitudes toward the ends of art during the period.
Mentions Dryden among many others who take a Horatian position.
Finds Dryden's views on the importance of art's moral purpose in-
teresting, "considering some of his own questionable acts."

6   STRACHAN, L.R.M. "Dryden's 'Character of Polybius.'" N&Q
     [11th ser.] 9 (7 February):103-5.
        Points out errors in the Scott-Saintsbury edition of the
piece (1882.3), and annotates several passages.

7   SUMMERS, MONTAGUE, ed. The Rehearsal, by George Villiers, Duke
     of Buckingham. Stratford-upon-Avon: Shakespeare Head Press.
        The introduction treats the character of John Bayes at

length, asserting that Dryden, though the major satiric object in the characterization, is not the only one. Notes Dryden's mild reaction to the play, and gives a stage history as well as extensive commentary upon the work itself.

8   VERRALL, A.W. Lectures on Dryden. Edited by Margaret de G. Verrall. Cambridge: Cambridge University Press, 278 pp.
      A wide-ranging study of Dryden's work which also contains close readings of several pieces. Pays particular attention to Absalom and Achitophel and to the criticism. Shows how the biblical fiction of Absalom and Achitophel perfectly suits Dryden's needs, and categorizes it as an "epyllion," emphasizing its uniqueness. Analyzes the poem's metrics. Surveys the controversy over the unities, placing Dryden in the tradition as it developed from Aristotle. Analyzes the odes, crediting Dryden with great influence on the later development of the English ode. Compares All for Love with Antony and Cleopatra. Reprinted: 1963.59.

9   WILLIAMS, W.H. "'Palamon and Arcite' and 'The Knight's Tale.'" MLR 9 (April):161-72; (July):309-23.
      Compares Dryden's "paraphrase" with its original to demonstrate Dryden's greater polish and artificiality.

1915

1   MUNDY, PERCY DRYDEN. "Dryden and Swift." N&Q [11th ser.] 11 (27 March):257-58.
      Argues that Swift's grandmother was probably the daughter of Nicholas Dryden, the poet's great-uncle. See 1924.9.

2   PETSCH, ROBERT. "Dryden und Rymer." Germanisch-romanische Monatschrift 7 (March):137-48.
      Discusses the controversy between the two over dramatic theory.

3   ROUTH, JAMES. The Rise of Classical English Criticism: A History of the Canons of English Literary Taste and Rhetorical Doctrine, from the Beginning of English Criticism to the Death of Dryden. New Orleans: Tulane University Press, 101 pp.
      Attempts to discover "what canons of art men held during the period." Makes heavy use of Dryden, especially Essay of Dramatic Poesy. Calls Dryden a "rationalist" who blends the "classic" and "romantic" strains in criticism. Reprinted: 1978.47.

1916

*1 BUTTERWORTH, RICHARD. "Dryden and the Methodist Hymn-Book." Proceedings of the Wesley Historical Society 10:159-62.
      Cited in Latt and Monk, 1976.30.

2   DUTTON, GEORGE B. "Theory and Practice in English Tragedy,
    1650-1700." Englische Studien 49 (January):190-219.
        Discusses, among the works of others, Dryden's heroic plays
    and tragedies, showing that he repeatedly strained and broke the
    neoclassic "rules." In general he conformed more and more as his
    career developed, but was always liable to depart from tradition
    for pragmatic or artistic purposes.

3   WRIGHT, ROSE A. The Political Play of the Restoration.
    Montesano, Wash.: A.E. Veatch, 197 pp.
        Classifies the plays by political position; mentions several
    plays by Dryden as examples of "anti-Whig" drama. States that
    Dryden's works provide "possibly an exception" to the conclusion
    that "scarcely a single Restoration political play . . . possesses
    qualities that make for permanency of literary interest."

                              1917

1   GAW, ALLISON. "Tuke's Adventures of Five Hours in Relation to
    the 'Spanish Plot' and to John Dryden." In Studies in English
    Drama. Edited by Allison Gaw. Publications of the University
    of Pennsylvania Series in Philology and Literature 14. New
    York: Appleton for the University of Pennsylvania, pp. 1-61.
        Deals with the nature and significance of the play. Traces
    "the reciprocal relations . . . between it and the early criticism
    of John Dryden." Dryden was antagonistic to the play from the
    start, but The Rival Ladies shows the influence of the "Spanish
    plot" Tuke had popularized. The 1671 revision of the Adventures
    suggests that Tuke was trying to disarm further criticism from
    Dryden.

2   LEO, Brother, C.S.C. "How Dryden Became a Catholic." Catholic
    World 105 (July):483-94.
        Investigates Dryden's "religious mutations" to show that his
    conversion was sincere, consistent, and inevitable.

*3 PAUL, FRANCIS. "John Dryden." American Catholic Quarterly
    Review 42:454-62.
        Cited in Latt and Monk, 1976.30.

4   ROSENBERG, ALFRED. Longinus in England bis zum Ende des 18.
    Jahrhunderts. Berlin: Mayer und Müller, 159 pp.
        Notes (pp. 19-29) Dryden's various direct references to
    Longinus. Finds Dryden to be a "Longinian" critic, even in his
    early works, before he had apparently read Longinus.

                              1918

1   BABINGTON, PERCY L. "Dryden Not the Author of 'MacFlecknoe.'"

MLR 13 (January):25-34.
Asserts that John Oldham wrote the poem, on the grounds that a manuscript of the poem exists among Oldham's papers, dated 1678, and that the poem is more in Oldham's satirical vein than Dryden's. See 1918.2, 5.

2   BELDEN, H.M. "The Authorship of MacFlecknoe." MLN 33 (December):449-56.
Defends Dryden's authorship against Babington's suggestion (1918.1) that Oldham wrote it. See 1918.5.

3   DOBELL, PERCY JOHN. The Literature of the Restoration: Being a Collection of the Poetical and Dramatic Literature Produced Between the Years 1660 and 1700, with Particular Reference to the Writings of John Dryden. London: P.J. and A.E. Dobell, 108 pp.
A bibliography, with some annotation: "a fuller and better list of the names of the writers and titles of their productions than can be obtained elsewhere."

4   PERRY, HENRY TEN EYCK. The First Duchess of Newcastle and Her Husband as Figures in Literary History. Harvard Studies in English 4. Boston and London: Ginn, 335 pp.
Contains scattered references to Dryden's contacts with the Duke and Duchess; deals in some detail with the relative contributions of Dryden and the Duke to Sir Martin Mar-All. Reprinted: 1968.49.

5   THORN-DRURY, GEORGE. "Dryden's MacFlecknoe, A Vindication." MLR 13 (July):276-81.
Replies to 1918.1. States that John Oldham was poetically incapable of writing the poem. Points out that the manuscript in question is only a transcript of parts of the poem, containing obvious errors which also appeared in the poem's first edition. Cites several contemporary attributions of the poem to Dryden. Reprinted: 1966.57.

6   WALLACE, LEONARD DeLONG. "A New Date for The Conquest of Granada." MP 16 (September):271-72.
On the basis of a contemporary letter, asserts that part 1 was first performed between 10 December 1670 and the close of the year, and part 2 on or before 9 January 1671.

7   WANN, LOUIS. "The Oriental in Restoration Drama." University of Wisconsin Studies in Language and Literature 2:163-86.
Lists and classifies plays "whose dramatis personae contains at least one Oriental." Concludes that while they fall short of the Elizabethans in the accurate portrayal of character, Restoration playwrights portray customs more realistically. Praises several of Dryden's plays and characters as being above the level of most contemporary examples.

1919

1 HAVENS, RAYMOND D. "Mr. Dryden Meets Mr. Milton." <u>Review</u>
(New York) 1 (14 June):110.
   Notes an account of Dryden's visit to Milton, given in 1713,
that adds a few details to Aubrey's. See 1925.6, 16.

2 NITCHIE, ELIZABETH. <u>Vergil and the English Poets</u>. New York:
Columbia University Press, 259 pp.
   Describes Dryden's translation; criticizes it for its de-
partures from Virgil (pp. 152-58).

1920

1 AMOS, FLORA ROSS. <u>Early Theories of Translation</u>. Studies in
English and Comparative Literature. New York: Columbia
University Press, 198 pp.
   Fully treats Dryden's theory of translation, and looks at
his practice. Asserts that he takes a middle course between imita-
tion and literal translation (pp. 153-62).

2 CLOUGH, BEN. C. "Notes on the Metaphysical Poets." <u>MLN</u> 35
(February):115-17.
   Notes several parallels between lines by Dryden and lines
by Donne, Carew, and Herbert.

3 HUXLEY, ALDOUS. "Forgotten Satirists." <u>London Mercury</u> 1
(March):565-73.
   Describes, with much quotation, the political poetry aroused
by the Popish Plot and its aftermath. Emphasizes poems written in
response to <u>Absalom and Achitophel</u>.

4 JACK, ADOLPHUS ALFRED. <u>A Commentary on the Poetry of Chaucer
and Spenser</u>. Glasgow: Maclehose, Jackson, 378 pp.
   Briefly discusses and evaluates Dryden's versions of Chaucer:
finds them praiseworthy. Attributes their success to "a similar
flow, a similar moral easiness, a similar good sensible knowledge
of the world" (pp. 127-31).

5 JONES, RICHARD FOSTER. "The Background of <u>The Battle of the
Books</u>." <u>Washington University Studies</u>, 2d humanistic ser. 7
(April):99-162.
   Briefly mentions Dryden as one who typified the chaos that
resulted when English critics tried to reconcile their tastes and
imported French standards. Reprinted in condensed form: 1951.18.

6 L., G.G. "Dryden's 'Alexander's Feast.'" <u>N&Q</u> [12th ser.] 7
(31 July):87-88.
   Suggests that Dryden got his subject from a reference to the
story of Timotheus and Alexander in Jeremy Collier's <u>Moral Essays</u>
(1697).

7   NICOLL, ALLARDYCE. "The Origin and Types of the Heroic
     Tragedy." Anglia 44:325-26.
          Categorizes the types and sources of the form, and distin-
     guishes the channels through which influence came. Emphasizes
     Davenant, Howard, Dryden, and Orrery. Denies that the form totally
     died with the seventeenth century.

8   ODELL, GEORGE C.D. Shakespeare from Betterton to Irving. 2
     vols. New York: Scribners; London: Constable.
          Contains accounts, mainly disparaging, of Dryden's adapta-
     tions of Shakespeare. Reprinted: 1963.37.

9   PARKER, KARL THEODORE. Oliver Cromwell in der schönen Literatur
     Englands: Eine literarische Studie. Ph.D. dissertation,
     Freiburg: Speyer und Kaerner, 112 pp.
          Discusses Heroic Stanzas (pp. 41-47) in the context of
     Cromwell's history and the various pieces written to or about him.

10   VAN DOREN, MARK. The Poetry of John Dryden. New York:
     Harcourt, Brace, 367 pp.
          Describes and evaluates Dryden as a poet. Puzzles over his
     unevenness: concludes that "fancy" occasionally overcame "judg-
     ment," leading to breaches of poetic decorum. Finds his poetry
     at its best the "poetry of statement." Praises his handling of
     the couplet, and devices of rhythm and repetition. Suggests that
     writing for the theaters had a beneficial effect on his nondramatic
     poetry. Attributes the success of his occasional poetry to his
     skill at "grouping and shaping"; finds the prologues and epilogues
     the "best and richest" of his occasional verse. Classifies them
     nine different ways. Celebrates the "abounding metrical energy"
     of his lyric poetry, and his skill at using couplets in narrative
     poetry, especially in the Fables. An appendix supports the case
     for Dryden as the author of MacFlecknoe (see 1918.1, 5). Reprinted:
     1931.38 (rev.); 1946.19; 1960.26. Chapter 6, "The Lryic Poet," is
     reprinted in 1962.21 and 1971.42.

                                1921

1   BROADUS, E.K. The Laureateship: A Study of the Office of Poet
     Laureate in England with Some Account of the Poets. Oxford:
     Clarendon Press, 245 pp.
          Discusses the dates at which Dryden became laureate (1668)
     and historiographer royal (1670), and the accompanying pensions.
     Concludes that the posts had no formal duties, but that Dryden's
     "powers of argument and satire" would be expected to be at the
     service of the King (pp. 59-74).

2   CRAIG, HARDIN. "Dryden's Lucian." Classical Philology 16
     (April):141-63.
          Surveys translations of Lucian previous to the edition for

which Dryden wrote the life. Discusses translators of the edition,
and the circumstances of its delayed publication in 1711.

3   ELIOT, T.S. "John Dryden." TLS, 9 June, pp. 361-62.
      Praises Dryden; claims that he is "one of the tests of a
catholic appreciation of poetry." Defends him against the attacks
of the nineteenth century. Closely analyzes several passages from
Dryden's work. Suggests that "in the next revolution of taste
. . . poets may turn to the study of Dryden," whose standards "it
is desperate to ignore." Reprinted: 1927.3; 1950.7; 1963.46.

4   EMERSON, OLIVER FARRAR. "John Dryden and a British Academy."
      Proceedings of the British Academy 10:45-58.
      Credits Dryden as the source for four suggestions for a
British Academy (1664, 1667, 1679, 1683), the second and third of
which had been attributed to Thomas Sprat and the Earl of Roscommon
respectively. Briefly reviews Dryden's pronouncements on the
English language. Reprinted: 1966.57; 1974.13. See 1924.2.

5   NETTLETON, GEORGE H. English Drama of the Restoration and
      Eighteenth Century (1642-1780). New York: Macmillan Co.,
      381 pp.
      Surveys Dryden's career as a dramatist, summarizing and
evaluating the plays, and relating them to their backgrounds and
to contemporary trends.

6   NICOLL, ALLARDYCE. "Dryden, Howard, and Rochester." TLS,
      13 January, p. 27.
      Describes a single scene in British Museum Add. MS. 28,692
possibly from the nonextant The Conquest of China by the Tartars,
by Sir Robert Howard. Suggests that the scene may be by Rochester
(the other material in the manuscript is Rochester's) or by Dryden,
who is known to have intended to help Howard with the play.

7   _____. "Political Plays of the Restoration." MLR 16 (July-
      October):224-42.
      Surveys and categorizes these plays, many of which were never
acted. Finds three chief subjects among them: the restoration of
monarchy, the political-religious struggles of 1679-85, and the
events surrounding the Revolution of 1688. Contains several references to works by Dryden.

8   SQUIRE, WILLIAM BARCLAY. "The Music of Shadwell's 'Tempest.'"
      Musical Quarterly 7 (October):565-78.
      Identifies as far as possible the music to Shadwell's oper-
atic version of the Dryden-Davenant Tempest; gives one song in
full.

9   WARD, A.W. "Dryden's Verse." In Collected Papers. Vol. 4.
      Cambridge: Cambridge University Press, pp. 64-79.
            Reprint of 1880.5.

1922

1 BOASE, T.S.R. "The Danger of Unity." New Statesman, 11
   February, p. 531.
      Reviews an Oxford production of All for Love. Finds the
   play's weakness in Dryden's observance of the unities, which re-
   stricts the full development of Cleopatra's character.

2 BRADLEY, J.F., and J.Q. ADAMS. The Jonson Allusion-Book: A
   Collection of Allusions to Ben Jonson from 1597 to 1700. New
   Haven: Yale University Press, 472 pp.
      Prints allusions, with occasional annotation. Contains many
   allusions by Dryden, and also some to him in connection with
   Jonson. See 1941.1.

3 DOBELL, PERCY JOHN. John Dryden: Bibliographical Memoranda.
   London: P.J. and A.E. Dobell, 32 pp.
      An annotated and descriptive bibliography of several of
   Dryden's works. Does not claim to be complete. See 1939.12.

4 HAVENS, RAYMOND D. The Influence of Milton on English Poetry.
   Cambridge, Mass.: Harvard University Press, 734 pp.
      Discusses Dryden's comments on Milton; examines The State of
   Innocence (pp. 118-20). Finds it "feeble and absurd." Notes that
   Dryden has subordinated the action and verse to spectacular the-
   atrical effects. Reprinted: 1961.18.

5 JONES, VIRGIL L. "Methods of Satire in the Political Drama of
   the Restoration." JEGP 21, no. 4:662-69.
      Categorizes methods of political satire in Restoration drama.
   Asserts that "there was little that was new" about them. Contains
   several references to Dryden's works.

6 NETHERCOT, ARTHUR H. "The Term 'Metaphysical Poets' before
   Johnson." MLN 37 (January):11-17.
      Cites many examples of the term; suggests that Johnson did
   not necessarily take it from Dryden's "Discourse . . . of Satire."

7 NICOLL, ALLARDYCE. Dryden as an Adapter of Shakespeare.
   Shakespeare Association Papers 8. London: Shakespeare
   Association, 35 pp.
      Treats Restoration adaptations of Shakespeare; classifies
   and illustrates the kinds of changes made. Analyzes The Tempest,
   All for Love ("more suggested than adapted"), and Troilus and
   Cressida, contrasting them with their originals. Contains "a
   brief bibliography of Shakespeare adaptations 1660-1700." Re-
   printed: 1975.43; 1977.30.

8 STRACHAN, L.R.M. "Reputed Song by Dryden." N&Q [12th ser.]
   11 (28 October):341-42.
      Questions the attribution (in A Golden Treasury of Song,
   1906?) of "What shall I do to show how much I love her" to Dryden.

9   THALER, ALWIN. <u>Shakespeare to Sheridan: A Book about the</u>
     <u>Theatre of Yesterday and To-Day</u>. Cambridge, Mass.: Harvard
     University Press, 357 pp.
        Contains material on the working conditions and financial
     arrangements of playwrights: several references to Dryden.

1923

1   AURNER, ROBERT RAY. "The History of Certain Aspects of the
     Structure of the English Sentence." <u>PQ</u> 2 (July):187-208.
        Analyzes changes in sentence structure from Caxton to
     Macaulay. Credits Dryden with ending the "period of isolation
     and individualism, in which there was no reasonably clear, service-
     able, and straightforward sentence medium available for everyday
     use."

2   JAMESON, R.D. "Notes on Dryden's Lost Prosodia." <u>MP</u> 20
     (February):241-53.
        Abstracts Dryden's theory of prosody from his scattered
     statements. Contrasts his positions with those of Edward Bysshe
     (1700.4).

3   NICOLL, ALLARDYCE. <u>Dryden and His Poetry</u>. Poetry and Life
     Series 32. London: Harrap, 149 pp.
        Surveys, chronologically, Dryden's life and work. Emphasizes
     the pioneering nature of his poetry, while noting also how much of
     the Elizabethan spirit he preserved. Discusses how Dryden's poetry
     connects with his personal, literary, and historical circumstances.
     Concludes that as a "poet of the intellect . . . he should have had
     nothing to do with the workings of the human heart." Reprinted:
     1976.42; 1977.29.

4   _____. <u>A History of Restoration Drama, 1660-1700</u>. Cambridge:
     Cambridge University Press.
        Discusses "The Theatre," "Tragedy," and "Comedy." Treats
     the drama chronologically within these categories. Emphasizes
     questions of influence. Briefly describes and evaluates Dryden's
     plays individually. Appendixes deal with "The History of the
     Playhouses" and "The History of the Stage." There is a "Handlist
     of Restoration Plays." Revised: 1928.10; 1940.20; 1952.23 (as
     vol. 1 of <u>A History of English Drama 1660-1900</u>); 1965.45.

5   NOYES, GEORGE R. "'Crites' in Dryden's <u>Essay of Dramatic</u>
     <u>Poesy</u>." <u>MLN</u> 38 (June):333-37.
        Argues that Sir Robert Howard, not the Earl of Roscommon
     (as Edmond Malone thought, in 1800.1) is the original for Crites,
     on the ground that Crites's arguments echo those in Howard's
     printed works.

6   PENDLEBURY, B.J. <u>Dryden's Heroic Plays: A Study of the Origins</u>.

London: Selwyn & Blount, 138 pp.
    Discusses Dryden's relationships with the heroic tradition
in continental and English literature, especially in drama. Summarizes Dryden's dramatic theories, and defends his heroic plays:
praises especially his creation of character and manipulation of
plot.

7   RALEIGH, Sir WALTER. "John Dryden and Political Satire." The
     Henry Sidgwick Memorial Lecture, delivered at Newnham College,
     Cambridge, November 1913. In Some Authors. Oxford: Clarendon
     Press, pp. 156-73.
        Praises, with frequent quotation, Dryden's satires as models
of the poetic treatment of public affairs.

*8   SENCOURT, ROBERT [R.E.G. George]. India in English Literature.
     London: Simpkin, Marshall, Hamilton, Kent.
        Cited in Latt and Monk, 1976.30.

9   WOLLSTEIN, ROSE HEYLBUT. English Opinions of French Poetry
     1660-1750. Studies in Romance Philology and Literature. New
     York: Columbia University Press, 113 pp.
        Uses Dryden as the representative example of English atti-
tudes toward French drama during the Restoration. Takes many examples from his criticism to show that the attitude was favorable
(with reservations).

10   WYLD, HENRY C. Studies in English Rhymes from Surrey to Pope.
     London: Murray, 153 pp.
        Uses many examples from Dryden in a study of rhyming prac-
tices and their relationship to pronunciation. Reprinted:
1965.65.

1924

1   DOBRÉE, BONAMY. Restoration Comedy 1660-1720. Oxford:
     Clarendon Press.
        Contains an extended and highly appreciative treatment of
Marriage a-la-Mode; calls it "the epitome of Dryden's comedy at
its best." Praises his "great critical intelligence," which makes
up for his lack of "great creative capacity." Reprinted: 1964.10.

2   FREEMAN, EDMUND. "A Proposal for an English Academy in 1660."
     MLR 19 (July):291-300.
        Argues against Emerson's conclusion that Dryden should be
given credit for suggesting a British Academy (1921.4). Gives
evidence to show that the idea was not new when Dryden first pro-
posed it, having been raised in several works published in 1660
and the years shortly before.

3   HOLLAND, BERNARD. "John Dryden." Dublin Review 175 (July,

August, September):29-47.
A summary and description of Dryden's life and works.

4   KAYE, F.B. "La Rochefoucauld and the Character of Zimri." <u>MLN</u>
    39 (April):251.
        Notes parallels between Zimri in <u>Absalom and Achitophel</u> and
    La Rochefoucauld's <u>Portrait du Cardinal de Retz</u>.

5   KRUTCH, JOSEPH WOOD. <u>Comedy and Conscience after the Restora-</u>
    <u>tion</u>. Studies in English and Comparative Literature. New York:
    Columbia University Press, 280 pp.
        Primarily concerned with the backgrounds and aftermath of
    Jeremy Collier's attack on the stage (1698.2). Credits Dryden
    with being a pioneer in Restoration comedy; calls <u>The Wild Gallant</u>
    the first typical example of the form. Sees social cynicism as a
    main characteristic of early Restoration comedy. Reprinted:
    1949.8; 1967.33.

6   LEGOUIS, PIERRE, and LOUIS CAZAMIAN. <u>Histoire de la litterature</u>
    <u>anglaise</u>. 2 vols. Paris: Hachette.
        Surveys, in their chronological places, Dryden's lyrics,
    satires, dramas, and prose. Translated by Helen Douglas Irvine
    and W.D. MacInnes (London: J.M. Dent; New York: Macmillan Co.,
    1926, 1927). Many times reprinted in French and in translation.

7   McCUTCHEON, R.P. "Dryden's Prologue to the <u>Prophetess</u>." <u>MLN</u>
    39 (February):123-24.
        Suggests that Shadwell caused the prologue not to be spoken.
    Cites an account printed with the prologue in the <u>Muses Mercury</u>
    for January 1707.

8   MARK, JEFFREY. "Dryden and the Beginnings of Opera in England."
    <u>Music and Letters</u> 5 (July):247-52.
        Notes that in spite of his "obvious contempt for [opera],"
    as expressed in several prologues and epilogues, Dryden succumbed
    to the demands of his audience and reluctantly collaborated with
    composers.

9   MUNDY, PERCY DRYDEN. "Dryden and Swift: Their Relationship."
    <u>N&Q</u> 147 (4 October):243-44; (18 October):279-80; (8 November):
    334.
        Argues that Swift's mother was the daughter of Dryden's
    great-uncle Nicholas Dryden, so that the two poets were second
    cousins once removed. See 1915.1.

10   NETHERCOT, ARTHUR H. "The Reputation of the 'Metaphysical
     Poets' during the Seventeenth Century." <u>JEGP</u> 23, no. 2:173-98.
         Uses Dryden as the chief example in a survey of seventeenth-
     century attitudes toward the "metaphysical" school. Sees in his
     distinction between a "great poet" and a "great writer" (applied
     to Cowley) the emerging neoclassical attitude toward literature.

11 QUAYLE, THOMAS. <u>Poetic Diction, A Study of Eighteenth Century</u>
<u>Verse</u>. London: Methuen, 219 pp.
Analyzes the diction of eighteenth-century poetry: finds
it restrictive and artificial. Sees Dryden as the founder of this
diction. Reprinted: 1977.37.

12 WESTERFRÖLKE, HERMANN. <u>Englische Kaffeehauser als Sammelpunkte</u>
<u>der literarischen Welt im Zeitalter von Dryden und Addison</u>.
Jenaer germanistische Forschungen 5. Jena: Biedermann, 100 pp.
"Dryden und sein Kreis bei <u>Will's</u>" (pp. 27-50) recounts anec-
dotes about Dryden and others who were associated with Will's
Coffeehouse during Dryden's life. Summarizes his literary posi-
tions and others' views of him and them.

1925

1 [DOANE, GILBERT H.]. "First Collation of an Interesting Dryden
Item." <u>Bookman's Journal</u> 12:163-64.
Collates "Miscellaneous Essays" by St. Evremond (1692), con-
taining a character written in part by Dryden.

2 BONDURANT, ALEXANDER. "The <u>Amphitruo</u> of Plautus, Moliere's
<u>Amphitryon</u>, and the <u>Amphitryon</u> of Dryden." <u>SR</u> 33 (October):
455-68.
Contrasts the plots of the plays, concluding that each mir-
rors its age. Dryden's play is "immoral."

3 CLARK, A.F.B. <u>Boileau and the French Classical Critics in</u>
<u>England (1660-1830)</u>. Paris: Champion, 550 pp.
Deals extensively with the influence of Boileau and others
(Le Bossu, Bouhours, Rapin, Dacier) upon Dryden. Emphasizes the
<u>Art Poetique</u> and <u>Le Lutrin</u>, which is seen as a major source of
<u>MacFlecknoe</u>, and therefore of the mock-heroic form in English.
Examines the French elements in Dryden's dramatic criticism; argues that Corneille's and Boileau's practice in verse had a significant effect on the development of the English heroic couplet
(pp. 127-33, 150-58). Reprinted: 1965.13.

4 ELLIS, AMANDA M. "Horace's Influence on Dryden." <u>PQ</u> 4
(January):39-60.
Analyzes Dryden's Horatian quotations and allusions, and
his use of Horatian materials drawn through other writers. Concludes that Dryden was a crucial transmitter of Horace's influence
to English literature.

5 EMERSON, OLIVER FARRAR. "Dryden and the English Academy."
<u>MLR</u> 20 (April):189-90.
Restates his position that Dryden's proposal for an English
Academy antedated the Royal Society committee to consider such an
Academy. See 1921.4; 1924.2.

6   HAVENS, RAYMOND D. "Dryden's Visit to Milton." RES 1 (July):
     348-49.
          Points out that he published in 1919 the passage used by
     Thorn-Drury (in 1925.16) to show that Dryden did visit Milton.
     Argues further that the visit is adequately documented without
     reference to the passage. See 1919.1.

7   JAEGER, HERMAN. Dryden og hans tid. Oslo: J.W. Cappelens,
     150 pp.
          In Norwegian. A generally chronological survey of Dryden's
     career, emphasizing its literary and historical backgrounds.

8   KER, W.P. "The Style of Dryden's Prose." In Collected Essays.
     London: Oxford University Press.
          Reprint of 1900.2. Reprinted: 1970.47.

9   LOW, D.M. "An Error in Dryden." TLS, 30 April, p. 300.
          Argues for an emendation in Theodore and Honoria.

10   LUBBOCK, ALAN. The Character of John Dryden. Hogarth Essays
     9. London: Hogarth Press, 31 pp.
          Emphasizes Dryden's intellectual integrity and consistency,
     and his natural and open style. Asserts that he combined "lack
     of originality" and "brilliant individual taste." Claims that
     "his permanent object was to refine the English language." Re-
     printed: 1977.26; 1978.32.

11   LYNCH, KATHLEEN M. "D'Urfé's L'Astrée and the 'Proviso' Scenes
     in Dryden's Comedy." PQ 4 (October):302-8.
          Argues that Dryden's later "proviso" scenes (especially in
     Secret Love and Amphitryon) derive from Honoré D'Urfé's pastoral
     romance L'Astrée. Gives evidence that the work was very well
     known in England, and cites parallel passages between it and plays
     by Dryden.

12   NICOLL, ALLARDYCE. British Drama: A Historical Survey from
     the Beginnings to the Present Time. London: Harrap; New York:
     Crowell, 515 pp.
          "Restoration Drama" (pp. 215-58) provides a general intro-
     duction to the theatrical conditions and literature of the period.
     Finds Dryden's rhymed heroic tragedies disappointing, but superior
     to his blank verse tragedies. Sees his comedy as a link between
     Jonsonian comedy and comedy of manners. Updated 1927, 1932, 1947,
     1962, and 1978 (by J.C. Trewin).

13   PAYNE, F.W. "The Question of Precedence between Dryden and the
     Earl of Orrery with Regard to the English Heroic Play." RES 1
     (April):173-81.
          Argues on circumstantial evidence that Orrery's The Black
     Prince was written before the end of 1661 and first performed in
     1663. Points out that Johnson and Dryden himself seemed to believe
     that Orrery was the first to write heroic plays in English.

14 SMITH, JOHN HARRINGTON. "Dryden's Critical Temper." Washington University Studies, humanistic ser. 12 (April): 201-20.
　　Deals with Dryden's apparent critical inconsistency by arguing that his literary appreciations are the only relevant and worthy parts of his essays.

15 SPURGEON, CAROLINE F. Five Hundred Years of Chaucer Criticism and Allusion: 1357-1900. 3 vols. Cambridge: Cambridge University Press.
　　Reprint of 1908.4. Reprinted: 1960.24.

16 THORN-DRURY, GEORGE. "Some Notes on Dryden." RES 1 (January): 79-83; (April):187-97; (July):324-30.
　　1. "Dryden and Daniel." Cites parallels between speeches in Daniel's Cleopatra and All for Love.
　　2. "Dryden and Milton." Quotes a passage from The Monster (1713) telling a version of Aubrey's story about Dryden getting permission to "tag" Paradise Lost. See 1925.6.
　　3. "Dryden and the Duke of Buckingham." Throws doubt on a story about Buckingham's impromptu capping (at a performance) of a line by Dryden. See 1876.1.
　　4. "Poetical Reflections On A Late Poem Entituled, A. & A. By A Person of Honour, fol. 1682." Argues that it was not written by Buckingham. Suggests Edward Howard as a possible author. See 1681.3.
　　5. "Dryden's Pecuniary Circumstances." Cites an entry in Thomas Howard's book of expenses about a payment "in Charitye" to Lady Elizabeth Dryden.
　　6. "Dryden and Shadwell." (a) Argues that MacFlecknoe had circulated in manuscript for several years before its publication. (b) Doubts that Shadwell wrote The Medal of John Bayes (1682.6).
　　7. "Mr. Dryden's Poem to King William." Prints the title and "discourse" prefixed to the poem.
　　8. "Dryden, Creech, and Tonson." Prints an extract from a letter from Jacob Tonson to his nephew stating that he (Jacob Tonson) wrote the puff verses for Creech's translation of Lucretius. The verses had been ascribed to Dryden.
　　9. "The Medal." Prints a letter (15 March 1682) anticipating the imminent publication of the poem.
　　10. "Dryden's Prologues and Epilogues in Sir W. Howard's MS." Cites manuscript versions of prologues and epilogues which contain unrecorded variants.
　　11. "Absalom and Achitophel." Cites earlier examples of applications of the biblical story to contemporary political events.
　　12. "Dryden and the opera on The Tempest." Doubts, with evidence, that Shadwell had anything to do with it. See 1904.5; 1906.6, 8.

17 WALKER, HUGH. English Satire and Satirists. Channels of

English Literature. London and Toronto: J.M. Dent; New York:
E.P. Dutton, 332 pp.
    Calls Dryden the first master of modern satire. Demonstrates
his qualities through analyses of Absalom and Achitophel and
MacFlecknoe. Finds his "instinct for the apt word" the cause of
his success. Looks briefly at satirical elements in Religio Laici
and The Hind and the Panther (pp. 150-65). Reprinted: 1972.94.

1926

*1   CORVESOR, D. "Shakespeare Adaptations from Dryden to Garrick."
      Ph.D. dissertation, London (Birkbeck College).
          Cited in Latt and Monk, 1976.30.

*2   DIFFENBAUGH, GUY L. The Rise and Development of the Mock Heroic
      Poem in England from 1660 to 1714. Urbana: University of
      Illinois Press.
          Cited in Latt and Monk, 1976.30.

 3   LEGOUIS, EMILE, and LOUIS CAZAMIAN. A History of English
      Literature. Translated by Helen Douglas Irvine and W.D.
      MacInnes. 2 vols. London: J.M. Dent; New York: Macmillan
      Co.
          A translation from the French original (1924.6). Reprinted
      many times.

 4   LYNCH, KATHLEEN M. The Social Mode of Restoration Comedy.
      University of Michigan Publications in Language and Literature
      2. New York: Macmillan Co., 253 pp.
          Attempts to define and account for Restoration comedy of
      manners. Briefly treats several of Dryden's early plays in con-
      nection with the tradition. Reprinted: 1965.37.

 5   WALMSLEY, D.M. "Shadwell and the Operatic Tempest." RES 2
      (October):463-66.
          Argues on circumstantial evidence that Shadwell had a hand
      in the work. See 1904.5; 1906.6, 8; 1925.16; 1927.15-16.

1927

*1   ASHBY, STANLEY R. "The Treatment of the Themes of Classic
      Tragedy in English Tragedy between 1660-1738." Ph.D. disserta-
      tion, Harvard University.
          Cited in Latt and Monk, 1976.30. Abstracted in Harvard
      University Summaries of Theses 3:141-43.

 2   CLARK, WILLIAM S. "Dryden's Relations with Howard and Orrery."
      MLN 42 (January):16-20.
          Notes that Dryden was living with Sir Robert Howard in

London in the summer of 1663, and through him had connections with the Earl of Orrery. These relationships were crucial in the development of the heroic play in England.

3   ELIOT, T.S. "John Dryden." In Homage to John Dryden: Three Essays on the Poetry of the Seventeenth Century. Hogarth Essays 1, no. 4. London: Leonard and Virginia Woolf.
    Reprint of 1921.3. Reprinted: 1950.7.

4   HAM, ROSWELL G. "Shadwell and 'The Tory Poets.'" N&Q 152 (1 January):6-8.
    Attributes the poem to Shadwell on internal evidence. Describes and briefly annotates it. See 1682.2.

5   HARDER, FRANZ. "Eine deutsche Anregung zu Dryden's 'Alexander's Feast?'" Englische Studien 61 (May):177-82.
    Suggests that a heroic poem by Jakob Vogel (1626) might have introduced Dryden to the story of Timotheus and Alexander.

6   HARRISON, T.P., Jr. "Othello as a Model for Dryden in All for Love." Studies in English (University of Texas) 7:136-43.
    Cites parallels to suggest the character of Alexas is "to some extent" inspired by that of Iago.

7   HUGHES, MERRITT Y. "Dryden as a Statist." PQ 6 (October): 334-50.
    Asserts that Dryden's political positions were fundamentally consistent, rooted in reaction against "mobocracy," and in belief in idealized monarchy. Suggests that his public's disillusion with the heroic play showed that the latter idea had little vitality left. Argues that Dryden's affinity for and familiarity with "Hobbism" can be seen in The Conquest of Granada and Absalom and Achitophel. Concludes that Dryden felt that "the correct position on every question is an independent and realistic attitude, guided by respect for the law."

8   LOVEJOY, ARTHUR O. "'Nature' as Aesthetic Norm." MLN 42 (November):444-50.
    Classifies meanings given to "nature" when used as an aesthetic standard. Draws several examples from Dryden.

9   MAGNUS, LAURIE. English Literature in its Foreign Relations 1300 to 1800. London: Kegan Paul, Trench, Trubner; New York: E.P. Dutton, 302 pp.
    Contains an appreciation of Dryden, with some emphasis on his role in internationalizing English literature. Surveys, generally, his allusions to and use of French literature, especially in his criticism (pp. 143-70).

10 NOLDE, JOHANNA. "Die Bühnenanweisungen in John Drydens Dramen." Ph.D. dissertation, Westfälischen Wilhelms-Universität, Münster. 52 pp.

A study of stage directions in Dryden's plays, and of
theatrical facilities generally during his period.

11   PRINZ, JOHANNES. John Wilmot Earl of Rochester, His Life and
     Writings. Palaestra 154. Leipzig: Mayer und Müller, 468 pp.
        Deals briefly with Rochester's patronage of and quarrel with
     Dryden. Blames Rochester for the Rose Alley beating of Dryden
     (pp. 192-99).

12   SEEGAR, OSKAR. Die Auseinandersetzung zwischen Antike und
     Moderne in England bis zum Tode Dr. Samuel Johnsons. Leipzig:
     Mayer und Müller, 117 pp.
        Describes controversies over drama, epic, and satire asso-
     ciated with Dryden and writers of his period (pp. 49-55). Empha-
     sizes Dryden's role as a spokesman for modern literature.

13   SPENCER, HAZELTON. Shakespeare Improved: The Restoration
     Versions in Quarto and on the Stage. Cambridge, Mass.: Harvard
     University Press, 418 pp.
        Includes a detailed annotated summary of Dryden's Shake-
     spearean plays. Includes stage and publication histories. Re-
     printed: 1963.52.

14   SUMMERS, MONTAGUE, ed. The Complete Works of Thomas Shadwell.
     5 vols. London: Fortune Press.
        The general introduction treats the personal and artistic
     relationships between Dryden and Shadwell at length. Reprinted:
     1968.57.

15   THORN-DRURY, GEORGE. "Shadwell and the Operatic Tempest." RES
     3 (April):204-8.
        Attacks D.M. Walmsley's argument that Shadwell was involved
     in the operatic version of the Dryden-Davenant Tempest. See
     1925.16; 1926.5; 1927.16.

16   WALMSLEY, D.M. "Shadwell and the Operatic Tempest." RES 3
     (October):451-53.
        Defends and further explains his contention that Shadwell
     had a hand in the operatic Tempest. See 1925.16; 1926.5; 1927.15.

                                  1928

 1   BREDVOLD, LOUIS I. "Dryden, Hobbes, and the Royal Society."
     MP 25 (May):417-38.
        Criticizes the neglect of the importance of Dryden's member-
     ship in the Royal Society. Examines the extent to which he pos-
     sessed ideas or attitudes characteristic of the Society. Distin-
     guishes Hobbes's materialism and Descartes' idealism as typical
     seventeenth-century philosophies. Finds elements of both in
     Dryden, but emphasizes his essential skepticism. Cites several

passages to show his appreciation of the new science. Links his "ingenuous changeableness in literary opinions" to his intellectual experiences. Reprinted: 1966.57. See 1930.8; 1931.2, 21, 29, 32.

2   CLARK, WILLIAM S. "The Sources of the Restoration Heroic Play." RES 4 (January):49-63.
    Argues against emphasis on native sources. Shows evidence to suggest that Dryden's heroic plays derive primarily from French romances both in plots and style. Claims that Dryden's theory, as expressed in his essay "Of Heroic Plays," is mainly a defense of what he had done in The Conquest of Granada and is heavily dependent on Davenant's "Preface to Gondibert." See 1929.7; 1930.1-2, 9.

3   DENT, EDWARD J. Foundations of English Opera: A Study of Musical Drama in England During the Seventeenth Century. Cambridge: Cambridge University Press, 253 pp.
    Discusses and evaluates The Tempest (pp. 136-44), Albion and Albianus (pp. 160-70), and King Arthur (pp. 20-15). Summarizes the plots, music, and staging. Praises King Arthur, suggesting that it is successful in part because it was written from the outset as an opera. Reprinted: 1965.16.

4   DOBRÉE, BONAMY. "Cleopatra and 'That Criticall War.'" TLS, 11 October, pp. 717-18.
    Compares the versions of Shakespeare, Samuel Daniel, and Dryden. Concludes that each has a different way of telling the tale: while there is no main theme in Shakespeare, Daniel emphasizes the character of Cleopatra and Dryden that of Antony. Concludes that All for Love is "more decorously a tragedy" than Antony and Cleopatra, but that Shakespeare's play is greater because of his "poetic genius in the use of metaphor." Reprinted: 1929.4; 1968.39.

5   FLASDIECK, HERMANN M. Der Gedanke einer englischen Sprach-akademie in Vergangenheit und Gegenwart. Jenaer germanistische Forschungen 11. Jena: Frommannschen, 254 pp.
    Notes Dryden's recurring advocacy of a project to refine and stabilize the language.

6   HAM, ROSWELL G. "Dryden Versus Settle." MP 25 (May):409-16.
    Traces the course of the conflict, trying to account for the vituperativeness of Dryden's attack in Absalom and Achitophel, part 2. Suggests that Settle was the author of Azaria and Hushai (1682.4), The Medal Revers'd, and much of Absalom Senior (1682.5).

7   ____. "Uncollected Verse by John Dryden." TLS, 27 December, p. 1025.
    Argues for Dryden's authorship of a broadside prologue and epilogue to Nathaniel Lee's Mithridates (1681).

8   HOTSON, LESLIE. The Commonwealth and Restoration Stage.

Cambridge, Mass.: Harvard University Press, 433 pp.
Briefly discusses, with documentary details, Dryden's artistic and financial connections with the King's Company. Reprinted:
1962.17.

9   LEGOUIS, PIERRE. André Marvell: poète, puritain, patriote
     1621-1678. Paris: Didier; London: Oxford University Press,
     525 pp.
          Contains many references to Dryden's poetry (primarily as a
     point of contrast to Marvell), especially in the area of political
     satire. Briefly contrasts Absalom and Achitophel and Marvell's
     satires, to Dryden's advantage. Suggests that Dryden's relative
     moderation in the poem (a cause of its success) may be a result of
     a less passionate commitment. Touches briefly on the personal re-
     lations of the two poets. Reprinted (in English): 1965.34.

10   NICOLL, ALLARDYCE. A History of Restoration Drama 1660-1700.
     2d. ed. Cambridge: Cambridge University Press, 416 pp.
          An updated and revised version of 1923.4. Further editions:
     1940.20; 1952.23 (as vol. 1 of A History of English Drama 1660-
     1900); 1965.45.

*11 PRAZ, MARIO. "Poets and Wits of the Restoration." ES 10
     (April):41-53.
          Cited in Latt and Monk, 1976.30.

12   ROSENFELD, SYBIL, ed. The Letterbook of Sir George Etherege.
     London: Oxford University Press, 450 pp.
          Contains a letter from Dryden (16 February 1687) and
     Etherege's letter in answer to it. Also contains a letter by
     Etherege commenting on The Hind and the Panther and MacFlecknoe
     (23 June/3 July 1687).

13   SMITH, DAVID NICHOL. Shakespeare in the Eighteenth Century.
     Oxford: Clarendon Press, 91 pp.
          Summarizes Dryden's views on Shakespeare, with quotations;
     briefly treats All for Love as a fine example of adapting
     Shakespeare (pp 5-11, 16-19).

14   STARNES, D.T. "More about Dryden as an Adapter of Shakespeare."
     Studies in English (University of Texas) 8:100-106.
          Cites parallels between All for Love and As You Like It,
     Julius Caesar, Hamlet, and Macbeth.

15   SUMMERS, MONTAGUE, ed. Roscius Anglicanus by John Downes.
     London: Fortune Press, 299 pp.
          An edition of 1708.1. Reprinted: 1968.58.

16   WALMSLEY, D.M. "The Influence of Foreign Opera on English
     Operatic Plays of the Restoration Period." Anglia 52, no. 1:
     37-50.

Gives many instances of English works so influenced. In general sees Dryden as less affected than his contemporaries by these influences (which are mostly French).

17   WILD, B. JOSEF. Dryden und die römische Kirche. Ph.D. dissertation, Freiburg. Leipzig: Robert Noske, 99 pp.
Surveys Dryden's life and works chronologically, emphasizing his attitudes toward Roman Catholicism. Argues that his conversion was sincere and consistent with his development as a writer and thinker.

18   WOOD, PAUL SPENCER. "The Opposition to Neo-Classicism in England Between 1600 and 1700." PMLA 43 (March):182-97.
Examines the period's attempt to reconcile its appreciation of Elizabethan literature with neoclassical principles. Claims that in this reconciliation, "modern English literary criticism had its beginnings." Uses Dryden as an important example. Reprinted: 1961.45.

19   YOUNG, Sir GEORGE. An English Prosody on Inductive Lines. Cambridge: Cambridge University Press, 310 pp.
Discusses Dryden's heroic couplets and blank verse (pp. 244-47). Briefly analyzes his characteristic habits. Emphasizes his innovations; relates him to the history of English prosody.

1929

1   ANON. Prefatory remarks to All for Love. San Francisco: -printed for William Andrews Clark, Jr., 126 pp.
A reprint with "Bibliographical Note and Prefatory Remarks." The remarks discuss the play's relation with Antony and Cleopatra. Shakespeare's play is superior, but All for Love is a "significant milestone" in the development of English drama. Contains thirteen plates from a mural illustrating All for Love in Clark's library.

2   ANON. "Stage Speech." TLS, 19 December, pp. 1065-66.
Describes the quarrel between Dryden and Sir Robert Howard over rhyme on the stage. Argues that the real issue is the relation of art to life. See 1668.1-2, Essay of Dramatic Poesy, and "A Defence of an Essay of Dramatic Poesy."

3   [DOBRÉE, BONAMY.] "Dryden and Artificial Tragedy." TLS, 15 August, pp. 629-30.
Asserts that Dryden's tragedy is based on ideas rather than passions; that his major accomplishment was in his forms, his "grace of structure." Reprinted as part of a chapter in 1929.4.

4   DOBRÉE, BONAMY. Restoration Tragedy 1660-1720. Oxford: Clarendon Press, 189 pp.
Uses many examples from Dryden to illustrate various aspects

of Restoration tragedy. One chapter contrasts Dryden's treatment of the story of Antony and Cleopatra with Shakespeare's and Samuel Daniel's, arguing that Dryden's form gives his play superior coherence (see 1928.4). Another chapter (part of which appeared as 1929.3) deals with the central characteristics of Dryden's tragedies. Emphasizes his success at keeping decorum and giving pleasure. Reprinted: 1950.5.

5   GHOSH, J.C. "Prologue and Epilogue to Lee's 'Constantine the Great.'" TLS, 14 March, p. 207.
        Questions the attribution of the prologue to Otway and the epilogue to Dryden.

6   GRIERSON, H.J.C. Cross-Currents in English Literature of the Seventeenth Century. London: Chatto & Windus, 361 pp.
        Praises Dryden's vigor and variety, but finds in him a "want of spiritual content." Claims that he is too rhetorical, and too bound up with the circumstances of his time. Finds Alexander's Feast to be the "finest piece of noise" before Vachel Lindsay (but Lindsay has more "true poetry"). Reprinted: 1958.15.

7   LYNCH, KATHLEEN M. "Conventions of Platonic Drama in the Heroic Plays of Orrery and Dryden." PMLA 44 (June):456-71.
        Argues (against W.S. Clark in 1928.2) for the influence of native Platonic drama, which provided a dramatic structure for the stories derived from French romance. Closely examines several of Dryden's early plays in this light. See 1930.1-2, 9.

8   SERGEAUNT, JOHN, ed. Poems of John Dryden. London: Oxford University Press.
        Reprint of 1910.11.

9   WHITE, H.O. "Dryden and Descartes." TLS, 19 December, p. 1081.
        Sees the influence of Descartes on a speech of Adam's in The State of Innocence.

10   WOLFE, HUMBERT. Notes on English Verse Satire. Hogarth Lectures on Literature 10. London: Hogarth Press, 158 pp.
        Calls Dryden the greatest English satirist, and his age "the golden age of English satire." Credits Dryden with establishing the proper use of the heroic couplet (pp. 75-95). Reprinted: 1978.62.

                                1930

1   CLARK, WILLIAM S. "The Platonic Element in the Restoration Heroic Play." PMLA 45 (June):623-24.
        Accuses Kathleen M. Lynch (1929.7) of distorting his argument (1928.2) and her evidence. See 1930.2, 9.

2   CRANE, R.S. [Review-abstract of Kathleen M. Lynch's "Conventions of Platonic Drama in the Heroic Plays of Orrery and Dryden" (1929.7).] PQ 9 (April):178.
      Argues that if the debate over the nature of the English heroic play is to be continued, there should be an investigation of the meaning and nature of the heroic form in all genres. See 1928.2; 1929.7; 1930.1, 9.

3   ELLIS, AMANDA. John Dryden and Prose Fiction. Colorado College Publication, General Series 168, Studies Series 4. Colorado Springs: Colorado College, 10 pp.
      Lists, in chart form, Dryden's references to works of prose fiction. Finds them widely scattered, but suggests they make up a consistent attitude toward the form: they should be exemplary and true to life. Concludes, however, that "the time for prose fiction to assume its rightful place was not yet ripe."

4   FAIRCLOUGH, H.R. "The Influence of Virgil Upon the Forms of English Verse." Classical Journal 26 (October):74-94.
      Credits Dryden with being the most successful translator of Virgil in English; notes (quoting Dryden's own statement) that he was much influenced by Virgil, and that he transmitted this influence to later English literature.

5   HAM, ROSWELL G. "Some Uncollected Verse of John Dryden." London Mercury 21 (September):421-26.
      Discusses the Oxford prologues and epilogues. Prints the prologue and epilogue to Aphra Behn's History of Bacon in Virginia from a rare copy in the Bodleian. Suggests that Dryden was interested in a post at Oxford. See 1931.1A; 1934.9; 1937.3.

6   HERRICK, MARVIN T. The Poetics of Aristotle in England. Cornell Studies in English 17. New Haven: Yale University Press; London: Oxford University Press, 205 pp.
      Considers Dryden's use of Aristotle: finds him "not a faithful servant." Notes his critical inconsistency with regard to the unities and plot in general (pp. 62-75).

7   LAMAR, MARY. Dramatic Criticism by English Dramatists to 1750. Dallas: Lamar Press, 76 pp.
      Chapter 3, "Restoration Criticism (1660-1698)," pp. 26-47, describes and summarizes Dryden's major critical essays in chronological order.

8   LLOYD, CLAUDE. "John Dryden and the Royal Society." PMLA 45 (December):967-76.
      Questions Dryden's continuing interest in the science of the day. Dryden was in arrears and was then dropped by the Society. He was never satirized as a "virtuoso" and there is little in his poetry to suggest an understanding of modern science. Therefore there is no need to try to reconcile his "scientific" beliefs with those of real scientists. See 1928.1; 1931.2, 21, 29, 32.

9   LYNCH, KATHLEEN M.   "The Platonic Element in the Restoration
     Heroic Play."   PMLA 45 (June):625-26.
         Defends her method; argues that W.S. Clark (in 1928.2) under-
     estimates the popularity of Platonic drama in the Restoration.   See
     1929.7; 1930.1-2.

10   NEWDIGATE, B.H.   "An Overlooked Ode by Dryden."   London Mercury
     22 (September):438-42.
         Prints the "Ode on the Marriage of . . . Mrs. Anastasia
     Stafford."   It was first published in 1813.

11   OLIVERO, F.   "Virgil in Seventeenth and Eighteenth Century
     English Literature."   Poetry Review 21:171-92.
         Lists echos of Virgil's poetry in Dryden.

12   STAUFFER, DONALD A.   English Biography before 1700.   Cambridge,
     Mass.: Harvard University Press, 402 pp.
         Praises Dryden's life of Plutarch as a model: calls it the
     best literary biography of its time.   Also discusses Dryden's com-
     ments on biography (pp. 231-32, 249-50).   Reprinted: 1964.46.

13   TANNER, LAWRENCE E.   "Dryden's Monument in Westminster Abbey."
     N&Q 158 (15 March):191.
         Gives the history of its changes.

14   T[HORN]-D[RURY], G[EORGE].   "Dryden's Verses 'To the Lady
     Castlemaine, upon Her Incouraging His First Play'."   RES 6
     (April):193-94.
         Collates the version in Examen Poeticum (1693) with that in
     "A New Collection of Poems and Songs" (1674).

15   VINES, SHERARD.   The Course of English Classicism From the Tudor
     to the Victorian Age.   Hogarth Lectures on Literature 12.
     London: Hogarth Press, 160 pp.
         Relates Dryden to Baroque styles in visual arts and music.
     Deals exclusively with his drama and dramatic criticism (pp.
     67-75).

16   WHITING, GEORGE W.   "Political Satire in London Stage Plays,
     1680-83."   MP 28 (August):29-43.
         Deals briefly with The Spanish Friar and The Duke of Guise,
     among many other plays by other playwrights.

17   WILLIAMSON, GEORGE.   The Donne Tradition: A Study in English
     Poetry from Donne to the Death of Cowley.   Cambridge, Mass.:
     Harvard University Press, 274 pp.
         Suggests that Dryden's comment on Donne in the "Discourse
     . . . on Satire" (1693) ("were he translated into numbers, and
     English, he would yet be wanting in the dignity of expression")
     "begins the alienation of Donne from the main tradition of English
     poetry."   Notes also Dryden's comments in the "Preface to the

Fables" (1700) which accuse the metaphysicals of want of judgment. Points out, however, Donne's significant influence on Dryden, especially when Dryden argues in verse. Reprinted: 1958.34; 1980.31.

18   _____. "Dryden as Critic." <u>University of California Chronicle</u> 32 (January):71-76.
A general evaluation of Dryden's criticism, mentioning his inconsistencies and "coarse" taste, but crediting him with establishing the dictum that the best critics of poetry are themselves poets.

19   WISE, THOMAS J. <u>A Dryden Library. A Catalogue of Printed Books, Manuscripts, and Autograph Letters by John Dryden</u>. London: printed for private circulation only.
Has an introduction by C.H. Wilkinson. A bibliographical description, with annotation, of books by and related to Dryden owned by T.J. Wise.

<u>1931</u>

1   BOSWELL, ELEANORE. "Chaucer, Dryden and the Laureateship: A Seventeenth-Century Tradition." <u>RES</u> 7 (July):337-39.
Quotes Dryden's patent as laureate to suggest that the offices of poet laureate and historiographer royal had traditional pedigrees.

1A   BREDVOLD, LOUIS I. "Dryden and the University of Oxford." <u>MLN</u> 46 (April):218-24.
Argues against the suggestion by Roswell G. Ham (in 1930.5) that an Oxford prologue and two epilogues indicate that Dryden angled for an Oxford appointment. See 1934.9; 1937.3.

2   _____. "John Dryden and the Royal Society." <u>PMLA</u> 46 (September):954-57.
Points out, against Claude Lloyd (1930.8), that Dryden's praise of the Society in <u>Annus Mirabilis</u> was written while he was in arrears. Argues that Dryden's scientific views were no more confused than those of others at the time. See 1931.21, 29, 32.

3   BRUNNER, FRIEDA. <u>John Dryden's Hymnen</u>. Ph.D. dissertation, Freiburg: Karl Henn, 134 pp.
Analyzes versions of Latin hymns, attributed to Dryden, published in 1706. Summarizes the history of English Catholic hymnody. Pays close attention to verbal and rhythmic details; praises their artistry. See 1937.13.

4   D., S.N. "Dryden's Ode on St. Lucy's Day." <u>Month</u> 158:540-44.
Reprints and annotates the ode "On the Marriage of . . . Mrs. Anastasia Stafford," emphasizing its reference to the Popish Plot crisis and its Catholic martyrs.

5   DEANE, CECIL V. <u>Dramatic Theory and the Rhymed Heroic Play</u>.
     London: Oxford University Press, 241 pp.
          Deals with the shifting relationships between Restoration
     heroic plays and the neoclassic "rules." Argues that the plays
     moved from a relatively strict conformity to them, then moved back
     to a moderate conformity. Sees Dryden as a major example and in-
     fluence in these changes. Emphasizes his concern with the develop-
     ment of a native English drama. Looks at <u>The Indian Queen</u>, <u>The</u>
     <u>Rival Ladies</u>, and <u>Tyrannic Love</u> in detail. Reprinted: 1976.13;
     1977.9.

6   [DOBRÉE, BONAMY.] "John Dryden." <u>TLS</u>, 6 August, pp. 601-2.
          An appreciation commemorating his three-hundredth anniversary.
     Notes his emphasis on giving delight; calls him "the supreme English
     man of letters." Credits him with having consciously undertaken to
     create a language "fit for civilized Englishmen to use." Reprinted:
     1932.8; 1967.16.

7   EDDY, WILLIAM ALFRED. "Dryden Quotes Ben Jonson." <u>MLN</u> 46
     (January):40-41.
          Notes that 1. 54 in <u>Song for St. Cecilia's Day</u> ("Mistaking
     earth for heav'n") is identical to a line in Jonson's "The Musical
     Strife."

8   ELIOT, T.S. "John Dryden: The Poet, the Dramatist, the Critic."
     <u>Listener</u> 5:621-22, 681-82, 724-25.
          Credits Dryden with having "for all time, established a
     <u>normal</u> English speech, a speech valid for both verse and prose."
     Surveys his development as a poet, and notes his great influence.
     Evaluates Dryden's drama, emphasizing its poetry. Contrasts it
     with Shakespeare's, arguing that Dryden although not so great a
     poet had a better influence. Praises Dryden's heroic couplets;
     predicts that Dryden's example will benefit future writers of
     English poetic drama. Claims that Dryden was "positively the
     first master of English criticism." Calls him "the <u>normal</u> critic"
     who is "concerned neither with appreciation nor with aesthetics."
     Reprinted: 1932.9.

9   FLETCHER, EDWARD G. "The Date of Dryden's Birth." <u>TLS</u>,
     21 November, p. 894.
          Points out that John Aubrey gives both 9 August and 19 August
     1631, at different times, as the date of Dryden's birth. See
     1931.12-13, 23-24.

10   GLAZIER, GEORGE E. <u>John Dryden's Associations with</u>
     <u>Northamptonshire: A Tercentenary Recapitulation</u>. Northampton:
     n.p., 12 pp.
          Sets out Dryden's local activities and connections, and the
     background of his family. "Contains no new discoveries and no new
     theories." Reprinted from the <u>Journal of the Northamptonshire</u>
     <u>Natural History Society</u> 26, no. 205 (July).

11   GRANVILLE-BARKER, HARLEY. On Dramatic Method. London:
        Sidgwick & Jackson, 192 pp.
           Disparages heroic drama, and the use of the heroic couplet
     in drama; closely examines the plot of Aureng-Zebe, but finds it
     mechanical (pp. 113-55).

12   HAM, ROSWELL G. "The Date of Dryden's Birth." TLS, 20 August,
        p. 633.
           Asserts that Dryden was born on 19 August 1631, on the evi-
     dence of a horoscope for Dryden in a manuscript in the Bodleian
     Library. See 1931.9, 13, 23-24.

13   _____. "The Date of Dryden's Birth." TLS, 17 September, p.
        706.
           Argues against Duncan MacNaughton (1931.23) that 19 August
     cannot be an error for 9 August, because the horoscope clearly
     states that the date is New Style. See 1931.9, 12, 24.

14   _____. Otway and Lee: Biography from a Baroque Age. New
        Haven: Yale University Press; London: Oxford University Press,
        257 pp.
           Has extensive material on Dryden's collaboration with Lee,
     especially with regard to The Duke of Guise and its political as-
     pects. Contains other scattered references to Dryden's connections
     with both Otway and Lee (pp. 156-73).

*15 HASWELL, RICHARD E. "The Heroic Couplet Before Dryden (1550-
        1675)." Ph.D. dissertation, University of Illinois.
           Cited in Latt and Monk, 1976.30.

16   HISCOCK, W.G. "A Dryden Epilogue." TLS, 5 March, p. 178.
           Announces the discovery, in Christ Church Library, Oxford,
     of a broadside of the epilogue "Spoken to the King . . . at Oxford
     on . . . March the Nineteenth 1681." See 1932.13.

17   JONES, RICHARD FOSTER. "The Originality of Absalom and
        Achitophel." MLN 46 (April):211-18.
           Gives many instances of seventeenth-century uses of the bib-
     lical Achitophel as a type of the traitorous politician. Also
     gives many examples of the association of David with the reigning
     English monarch. Reprinted: 1966.6, 57; 1976.7.

18   JORDAN, ARNOLD. "The Conversion of John Dryden." Month 158:
        18-25.
           Defends Dryden's moral character from attack; sees in his
     works "on the whole a progress from error to truth." Calls for a
     vindication of the conversion.

19   LAWRENCE, W.J. "Dryden's Abortive Opera." TLS, 6 August, p.
        606.
           Argues, on internal evidence, that The State of Innocence

was "written for representation at Court," for a celebration of
the marriage of the Duke of York and Mary of Modena (1673), but
was deemed unsuitable. See 1931.34, 39, 41.

20   LEGOUIS, PIERRE. "Quinault et Dryden: Une source de The
      Spanish Fryar." RLC 11, no. 2:398-415.
          Examines the verbal and structural similarities between
      Dryden's play and Quinault's L'Astrate. Concludes that although
      Dryden improved upon Quinault, and changed the nature of the play
      from tragedy to tragicomedy, his debt is substantial.

21   LLOYD, CLAUDE. "John Dryden and the Royal Society." PMLA 46
      (September):961-62.
          Replies to 1931.2, 29, and 32. Accepts correction of some
      points of detail, but repeats his earlier attack on the reliability
      of John Evelyn's reference to Dryden's attendance at committee
      meetings. See 1930.8.

*22   MacDONALD, W.L. "John Dryden: 1631-1931." Bookman (New York)
      72:481-88.
          Cited in Latt and Monk, 1976.30.

23   MacNAUGHTON, DUNCAN. "The Date of Dryden's Birth." TLS,
      3 September, p. 664.
          Asserts, against Roswell G. Ham (1931.12), that 19 August
      is either an error for 9 August, or that 19 August is New Style
      rather than Old Style. See 1931.9, 13, 24.

24   _____. "The Date of Dryden's Birth." TLS, 24 September, p.
      730.
          Asserts that Dryden was born on either 9 August or 19 August.
      All we need to know is which calendar we are using. Charges that
      Roswell G. Ham (1931.12-13) was unfair in saying that Pope was in
      error about the date, because Pope was using the Old Style calen-
      dar. See also 1931.9, 23.

25   MEISSNER, PAUL. "Die rationalistische Grundlage der englischen
      Kultur des 17. Jahrhunderts." Anglia 55 (October):321-67.
          Deals briefly with Dryden's Shakespearean and heroic plays
      as examples of a rationalistic approach to behavior and motivation.

26   No entry.

*27   NICHOLLS, NORAH. "Some Early Editions of John Dryden."
      Bookman (London) 80:266-67.
          Cited in Latt and Monk, 1976.30.

28   PFITZNER, KÄTHE. Die Ausländertypen im englischen Drama der
      Restorationzeit. Ph.D. dissertation, Breslau: Lebenslauf,
      99 pp.
          Classifies foreign characters in Restoration drama by

nationality, and notes their typical natures. Draws many examples
from Dryden. Finds that these characters are consistently seen as
inferior.

29   RISKE, ELLA THEODORA. "John Dryden and the Royal Society."
      PLMA 46 (September):951-54.
         Points out that John Evelyn mentions Dryden as active on a
      committee to investigate an English Academy. See 1930.8; 1931.2,
      21, 32.

30   SOTHEBY and Co. Catalogue of the Very Extensive and Well-Known
      Library of English Poetry, Drama and Other Literature, Princi-
      pally of the XVII and Early XVIII Centuries, Formed by the Late
      George Thorn-Drury, Esq., K.C., and Sold by Order of his Execu-
      tors. London: printed by J. Davy, 362 pp.
         Contains many Dryden items (see especially pp. 301-17).

31   STRAHAN, SPEER. "A Wreath for John Dryden." Commonweal 14
      (26 August):400-401.
         An appreciation of Dryden's life and works, with a Catholic
      emphasis.

32   STROUP, THOMAS B. "John Dryden and the Royal Society." PMLA
      46 (September):957-61.
         Notes Dryden's praise for scientific method in "To . . . Dr.
      Charleton." Cites many other examples in Dryden's work which sug-
      gest his interest in science. See 1930.8; 1931.2, 21, 29.

33   SUMMERS, MONTAGUE, ed. The Dramatic Works of John Dryden. 6
      vols. London: Nonesuch Press.
         Each volume contains explanatory notes for the plays in that
      volume. The introduction (1:xvii-cxxix) digressively surveys
      Dryden's life and times, pausing to describe and evaluate each of
      the plays. Concludes that only Chaucer and Shakespeare match
      Dryden's greatness.

34   SUMMERS, MONTAGUE. "Dryden's Abortive Opera." TLS, 13 August,
      p. 621.
         Agrees with W.J. Lawrence (1931.19) that The State of
      Innocence was designed for representation at Court. Adds two manu-
      scripts of the work to the one Lawrence mentions.

35   TAYLOR, DANIEL CRANE. William Congreve. London: Oxford
      University Press, 262 pp.
         Deals at some length with the Collier controversy (see
      1698.2) and Dryden's role in it. Also has material on Dryden's
      relationship with Congreve. Reprinted: 1963.57.

36   THOMAS, P.G. Aspects of Literary Theory and Practice, 1550-
      1870. London: Heath Cranton, 210 pp.
         Contains a general summary of Dryden's career (pp. 64-77).
      Reprinted: 1971.70.

37   TREADWAY, THOMAS J.   "The Religious Sincerity of John Dryden."
     Ecclesiastical Review 85:277-90.
          Asserts that Dryden's conversion to Catholicism was sincere,
     consistent, and inevitable.

38   VAN DOREN, MARK.   The Poetry of John Dryden.   Rev. ed., with
     an introduction by Bonamy Dobrée.   Cambridge: Minority Press,
     307 pp.
          Reprint of 1920.10.   Dobrée's introduction calls for a rise
     in the relative valuation of Dryden.   Reprinted: 1946.19; 1960.26.

39   WAGNER, BERNARD M.   "Dryden's Abortive Opera."   TLS, 1 October,
     p. 754.
          Mentions a further manuscript of The State of Innocence to
     those mentioned by W.J. Lawrence (1931.19) and Montague Summers
     (1931.34).   See also 1931.41.

*40 WHITE, ARTHUR F.   "The Office of Revels and Dramatic Censorship
     during the Restoration Period."   Western Reserve University
     Bulletin, Studies in English Literature 34:5-45.
          Cited in Latt and Monk, 1976.30.

41   WHITING, GEORGE W.   "Dryden's Abortive Opera."   TLS, 24 December,
     p. 1041.
          Mentions two more manuscripts of The State of Innocence.   See
     1931.19, 34, 39.

*42 W[ILLIAMSON], H.R.   "Portrait of a Man of Letters: The Career
     of Mr. John Dryden."   Bookman (London) 80:239-42.
          Cited in Latt and Monk, 1976.30.

                                    1932

1   BREDVOLD, LOUIS I.   "Political Aspects of Dryden's Amboyna and
     The Spanish Fryar."   University of Michigan Publications,
     Language and Literature 8:119-32.
          Attacks the attitude that these plays betray Dryden's lack
     of principle.   Argues that the factual circumstances of the produc-
     tion of Amboyna, and the tone of the dedication, do not suggest
     political pamphleteering.   Shows that Dryden was being paid his
     pension regularly, and was not out of favor at Court when he wrote
     The Spanish Friar, and therefore did not write it out of anger or
     spite.   Furthermore, the play is loyalist in spirit.   Reprinted:
     1966.57.

2   BRIDGES, ROBERT.   "Dryden on Milton."   In Collected Essays,
     Papers, &c.   Vol. 10.   London: Oxford University Press, pp.
     271-82.
          Reprint of 1903.1.

3   BRINKLEY, ROBERTA FLORENCE. Arthurian Legend in the Seventeenth
    Century. Johns Hopkins Monographs in Literary History 3.
    Baltimore: Johns Hopkins University Press, 237 pp.
        Examines Dryden's Arthurian projects and completed works,
    emphasizing their relation to contemporary politics. Summarizes
    and contrasts Albion and Albianus and King Arthur (pp. 142-46).
    Deals with Dryden's influence upon later Arthurian works, especial-
    ly Sir Richard Blackmore's (pp. 174-76).

4   CASSON, T.E. "John Dryden." Poetry Review 23:47-51.
        Defends Dryden's work against post-Romantic prejudice; empha-
    sizes his celebration of the reigning Stuarts.

5   CLARK, WILLIAM S. "The Definition of the 'Heroic Play' in the
    Restoration Period." RES 8 (October):437-44.
        Reviews contemporary occurrences of the term. Concludes
    that in the mind of its audience it was "a wholly serious play,
    composed in rimed verse, with a tone befitting heroic poetry, and
    concerned with the lofty sentiments of persons in high stations."

6   DAY, CYRUS LAWRENCE, ed. The Songs of John Dryden. Cambridge,
    Mass.: Harvard University Press, 215 pp.
        Prints the songs, with textual annotation and commentary.
    Gives several in facsimile, with music. The introduction (pp.
    xi-xvi) claims that Dryden's lyrics are "his most enduring tri-
    umph." Notes however that many of the songs are "marred by a re-
    current note of cynicism and sensuality."

7   de BEER, E.S. "Mr. Montague Summers and Dryden's Essay of
    Dramatic Poesy." RES 8 (October):453-56.
        Attacks Summers for expropriating the substance of notes
    (in 1931.33) from previous editors he had depreciated. See
    1933.3, 12.

8   DOBRÉE, BONAMY. "John Dryden." In Variety of Ways: Discussions
    on Six Authors. Oxford: Clarendon Press, pp. 1-16.
        Reprint of 1931.6. Reprinted: 1967.16; 1976.15; 1977.11.

9   ELIOT, T.S. John Dryden: The Poet, the Dramatist, the Critic.
    New York: Holliday, 68 pp.
        Reprint of 1931.8, with inconsequential expansion.

10 FORNELLI, GUIDO. La Restaurazione inglese nell'opera di John
    Dryden. Florence: La Nuova Italia, 55 pp.
        Stresses Dryden's immersion in the events of his time down
    to the Revolution of 1688; sees him withdrawing into himself after
    that point. Traces the course of his career, emphasizing the po-
    litical events which shaped his work. Concludes that Dryden is a
    crucial transitional figure in the development of modern literature.

11 HARVEY-JELLIE, WALLACE R. Le théâtre classique en Angleterre,
    dans l'âge de John Dryden. Montréal: Librairie Beauchemin,

109 pp.
    Surveys Restoration drama, emphasizing the French influence. Finds classicism dominant during this period, in which Dryden "seul merité le nom de génie."

*12 HECHT, J. Der heroische Frauentyp in Restaurationsdrama. Leipzig.
    Cited in Latt and Monk, 1976.30.

13 HISCOCK, W.G. "Oxford History." TLS, 13 October, p. 734.
    Identifies the occasion of Dryden's epilogue "As from a darkn'd Roome some Optick glass." See 1931.16.

14 HOLLAND, A.K. Henry Purcell: The English Musical Tradition. London: G. Bell, 248 pp.
    Deals briefly with Dryden's attitude toward music, and praises his ability to write for composers. Analyzes King Arthur at length, concentrating upon Purcell's music (pp. 211–16). Claims that Dryden is the only respectable librettist in English opera.

15 JUNEMANN, WOLFGANG. Drydens Fabeln und ihre Quellen. Britannica 5. Hamburg: de Gruyter, 103 pp.
    Discusses the Chaucerian imitations and Sigismonda and Guiscardo. Describes each piece from beginning to end, noting Dryden's modifications of his sources.

16 LEGOUIS, PIERRE. "La religion dans l'oeuvre de Dryden avant 1682." Révue Anglo-Americaine 9:383–92, 525–36.
    Traces Dryden's religious references and allusions prior to Religio Laici. Finds that religion occupied a prominent place in his thought. Concludes that in line with his general skepticism, his major attitudes are antifanatic and anticlerical. Reprinted: 1973.41.

17 LIESER, PAUL. Die englische Ode im Zeitalter Klassizismus. Ph.D. dissertation, Bonn: Plasnick, 102 pp.
    Deals briefly with Dryden's odes. Credits him with having taken Cowley's irregular Pindaric ode and made it into powerful art (pp. 29–37).

18 McKEITHEN, D[ANIEL] M[ORELY]. "The Authorship of 'The Medal of John Bayes.'" Studies in English (University of Texas) 12: 92–97.
    Reaffirms the attribution to Shadwell, because "[it] echoes Shadwell's earlier works, and Shadwell's later works echo [it]." See 1682.6.

19 McKEITHEN, DANIEL MORELY. "The Occasion of MacFlecknoe." PMLA 47 (September):766–71.
    Argues that the occasion was Shadwell's insult of Dryden in the dedication of The History of Timon of Athens, the Man-Hater (1678). Surveys in detail the quarrel between Shadwell and Dryden.

20   MANN, WOLFGANG. <u>Drydens heroische Tragödien als Ausdruck</u>
      <u>höfischer Barockkultur in England</u>. Ph.D. dissertation, Tübingen.
      Württemberg: Gatzer und Hahn, 72 pp.
          Discusses the heroic plays; asserts that they are prime ex-
      amples of English "courtly baroque." Sees in them a consonance
      with the values of the court of Charles II. Emphasizes the pas-
      sion and individualism of Dryden's heroes; praises their psycho-
      logical validity.

21   RALLI, AUGUSTUS. <u>A History of Shakespearean Criticism</u>. 2 vols.
      London: Oxford University Press.
          Briefly summarizes and evaluates Dryden's contributions
      (1:4-6). Reprinted: 1959.36.

*22   STEVENSON, SAMUEL W. "Romantic Tendencies in the Works of
      Dryden, Addison, Pope." Ph.D. dissertation, Johns Hopkins
      University.
          Cited in Latt and Monk, 1976.30.

23   WARD, CHARLES E. "A Biographical Note on John Dryden." <u>MLR</u>
      27 (April):206-10.
          Surveys what is known about Dryden's finances. Asserts
      that Dryden was not in financial distress until after the Revolution
      of 1688.

24   _____. "Was John Dryden Collector of Customs?" <u>MLN</u> 47 (April):
      246-49.
          Asserts that there is no evidence that Dryden was ever
      Collector of Customs: in fact such evidence as does exist points
      the other way.

25   WHITING, G[EORGE] W. "The Ellesmere MS of 'The State of
      Innocence.'" <u>TLS</u>, 14 January, p. 28.
          Describes the texts of two manuscripts in the Huntington
      Library. Suggests that their existence confirms Dryden's state-
      ment that copies of the opera were widely dispersed before print-
      ing.

26   WOLF, J.Q. "A Note on Dryden's Zimri." <u>MLN</u> 47 (February):
      97-99.
          Notes two biblical Zimris, an adulterer and a traitor, who
      could both be behind Dryden's choice of a name for his portrait
      of Buckingham in <u>Absalom and Achitophel</u>.

                              <u>1933</u>

1   BREDVOLD, LOUIS I. "Notes on John Dryden's Pension." <u>MP</u> 30
      (February):267-74.
          Gives the facts about Dryden's pension from 1670 to 1688,
      based upon the <u>Calendar of Treasury Books</u>. Attacks those who

accuse Dryden of converting to Roman Catholicism for reasons of
expedience: there is little or no evidence to support them.

*2   BURROWS, DOROTHY. "The Relation of Dryden's Serious Plays and
      Dramatic Criticism to Contemporary French Literature." Ph.D.
      dissertation, University of Illinois.
           Cited in Latt and Monk. 1976.30.

3   de BEER, E.S. "Mr. Montague Summers and Dryden's Essay of
      Dramatic Poesy." RES 9 (April):203.
           Responds to Summers's defence of his notes in 1931.33 by
      leaving it to the readers to decide. See 1932.7; 1933.12.

4   ELIOT, T.S. "The Age of Dryden." In The Use of Criticism:
      Studies in the Relation of Criticism to Poetry in England.
      The Charles Eliot Norton Lectures 1932-33. Cambridge, Mass.:
      Harvard University Press; London: Faber & Faber, pp. 53-65.
           Interprets Dryden's statement on the three happinesses of
      the poet's imagination (in the preface to Annus Mirabilis). Dis-
      tinguishes among Dryden, Addison, and Johnson and their ages. Re-
      printed: 1948.5.

5   ELLEHAUGE, MARTIN. English Restoration Drama: Its Relation
      to Past English and Past and Contemporary French Drama.
      Copenhagen: Levin & Munksgaard, 322 pp.
           Examines its subject in the light of the broader development
      of European drama. Refers often to Dryden's plays and criticism.
      Concludes that Restoration drama completes "the transference of
      the scene of action from the regions of heroism and idealism to
      the world of reality." Reprinted: 1970.27.

6   ELTON, OLIVER. The English Muse: A Sketch. London: G. Bell,
      478 pp.
           Surveys Dryden's poetry, praising his mastery of technique,
      especially in Absalom and Achitophel (pp. 259-71).

7   HOLLIS, CHRISTOPHER. Dryden. London: Duckworth, 224 pp.
           A life, derived from secondary materials. Contains scattered
      comment on the works, occasional notes, and a brief bibliography.
      Reprinted: 1974.23; 1977.17.

8   HOUSMAN, A.E. "The Name and Nature of Poetry." The Leslie
      Stephen Lecture for 1933.
           Disparages the poetry of the eighteenth century for its use
      of unnatural poetic diction and lack of sublimity. Uses Dryden's
      translations of Chaucer as major examples, but admits that when
      Dryden uses the vernacular he is a great poet. Printed in 1961.21.

9   MUNDY, PERCY DRYDEN. "Portraits of Dryden." N&Q 164 (17 June):
      423-24; 165 (16 September):194.
           Lists known portraits of Dryden, and asks for information
      about the locations of those which are missing.

10   PRAZ, MARIO. "Restoration Drama." ES 15 (February):1-14.
        Disparages Montague Summers's edition of Dryden's plays
   (1931.33). Examines characteristic plots and language in Restoration drama, with an emphasis on its use of figures of speech. Relates the drama to contemporary continental literature.

*11   SHEWRING, W.H. "The Office Hymns of John Dryden." Ampleforth
        Journal 39:18-27.
           Cited in Latt and Monk, 1976.30.

12   SUMMERS, MONTAGUE. "Mr. Montague Summers and Dryden's Essay of
        Dramatic Poesy." RES 9 (April):202-3.
           Defends himself against E.S. de Beer's charge (1932.7) that
   he had used the notes of others in his edition of Dryden's plays
   (1931.33). Argues that much of the substance of his and others'
   notes is common property. See 1933.3.

13   THORP, WILLARD. "A New Manuscript Version of Dryden's Epilogue
        to Sir Fopling Flutter." RES 9 (April):198-99.
           Gives variants from Sloane MS. 1458 at the British Museum;
   urges that this version is nearer to Dryden's intention than those
   printed previously.

14   WILLIAMSON, GEORGE. "The Restoration Revolt Against Enthusiasm."
        SP 30 (October):571-603.
           Attributes the development of plainer style to a reaction
   against rhetoric, already present in Bacon and bolstered by painful
   memories of zealous pulpit excesses during the Interregnum. Relates Dryden to Hobbes in his laying out of the proper relationship
   between imagination and judgment. Sees Dryden as the epitome,
   especially in poetry, of the movement to a new style. Reprinted:
   1960.28; 1969.85.

*15   WOOLF, LEONARD. "Dryden." Nation (London) 33:575.
           Cited in Latt and Monk, 1976.30.

1934

1   ANON. "Dryden a Hymnodist?" TLS, 12 April, p. 258.
        Discusses Dryden's possible authorship of translations of
   hymns for the Benedictine Vesperal; concludes that no convincing
   evidence exists either way.

2   BECKINGHAM, C.F. "Selvaggi and Dryden." N&Q 167 (8 September):
        169.
           Suggests that Dryden's lines on Milton derive from Selvaggi's
   couplet printed in the 1645 edition of Milton's poems.

3   BREDVOLD, LOUIS I. The Intellectual Milieu of John Dryden:
        Studies in Some Aspects of Seventeenth Century Thought.

University of Michigan Publications in Language and Literature
12. Ann Arbor: University of Michigan Press, 189 pp.
Deals generally with "Dryden's characteristic thought and
its background in the seventeenth century." Defends Dryden against
charges that his work lacks intellectual content: finds in him a
"skeptical temper and thought." Traces the development of philosophic skepticism from the Greeks, especially Pyrrho, down to
Dryden's own time. Ties Dryden to such contemporary scientists as
Joseph Glanvill and Robert Boyle. Asserts that "Pyrrhonism . . .
is patent for all to see" in Religio Laici and The Hind and the
Panther; links this to fideistic, antirationalistic attitudes
among English Catholics. Argues that Dryden's reading of the
translation of Father Simon's Critical History of the Old Testament
was the "most critical event in his intellectual life." Sees
Dryden's Toryism as a natural consequence of his skepticism. Concludes that Dryden's work is "one of the classic expressions of
the conservative temperament." Reprinted: 1957.7. The introduction and conclusion are reprinted in 1963.46.

4   BRENNECKE, ERNEST, Jr. "Dryden's Odes and Draghi's Music."
     PMLA 49 (March):1-36.
        Examines the poetry, music, and occasions of St. Cecilia's
Day observances in London previous to Dryden's first participation
in 1687. Claims that Dryden was the first poet to be asked to take
part who had the skill to write properly for the occasion. Analyzes Draghi's music for Song for St. Cecilia's Day, indicating
the competence with which Dryden's words are set. Argues that
Dryden learned from the difficulties posed by his libretto, and
that the differences between Alexander's Feast (1697) and the 1687
Song reflect his greater awareness of the problems inherent in
writing for music. Reprinted: 1966.57.

5   CHESTER, ALLAN GRIFFITH. "Dryden and Thomas May." TLS, 19
     July, p. 511.
        Argues that Dryden's translation of the Georgics is indebted
to that of Thomas May. Prints parallel passages in illustration.

6   CLARK, Sir GEORGE. The Later Stuarts 1660-1714. Oxford History
     of England. Oxford: Clarendon Press, 502 pp.
        The brief treatment of Dryden (pp. 366-68) emphasizes his
supremacy as a political satirist. Many times reprinted. Second
edition: 1955.

7   DOWLIN, CORNELL MARCH. Sir William Davenant's "Gondibert," Its
     Preface, and Hobbes's Answer: A Study in English Neo-Classicism.
     Philadelphia: University of Pennsylvania, 127 pp.
        Argues for Davenant as the major influence on Dryden's heroic
plays (pp. 85-105).

8   GREEN, CLARENCE C. The Neo-Classical Theory of Tragedy in
     England During the Eighteenth Century. Harvard Studies in

English 11. Cambridge, Mass.: Harvard University Press.
Cites Dryden frequently as exemplary of the "liberal" critical view regarding the "rules" in the late seventeenth century. This view held that they should not be slavishly followed. Reprinted: 1966.21.

9 HAM, ROSWELL G. "Dryden and the Colleges." MLN 49 (May): 324-32.
Brings forward more evidence to argue, against Louis Bredvold (1931.1), that Dryden was seriously interested in obtaining a post at Oxford. See 1930.5; 1937.3.

10 MAYO, THOMAS. Epicurus in England (1650-1725). Dallas: Southwest Press, 265 pp.
Deals with Dryden's translations of Lucretius, and with his relationships with other translators. Discusses Epicurean elements in Dryden's work.

11 PAUL, HENRY N. "Players' Quartos and Duodecimos of Hamlet." MLN 49 (June):369-75.
Suggests that Dryden did the editorial work on the 1683 quarto of Hamlet.

12 RICHTER, WALTER. Der Hiatus im englischen Klassizismus (Milton, Dryden, Pope). Ph.D. dissertation, Freiburg. Schramberg: Gatzer und Hahn, 139 pp.
Lists and classifies instances in which final and initial vowels fall together. Draws examples from Annus Mirabilis, Absalom and Achitophel, and The Hind and the Panther. Compares frequency of "hiatus" with selected examples from Milton and Pope.

*13 ROSE MARIE, Sister. "Dryden's Prose." Catholic World 139: 432-38.
Cited in Latt and Monk, 1976.30.

*14 _____. "John Dryden--Poet or Not?" Catholic World 139:283-89.
Cited in Latt and Monk. 1976.30.

15 SHARP, ROBERT L. "The Pejorative Use of Metaphysical." MLN 49 (December):503-5.
This use existed well before Dryden's statement that Donne "affects the metaphysics" (1693).

16 SUMMERS, MONTAGUE. A Bibliography of the Restoration Drama. London: Fortune Press, 143 pp.
"As far as possible" lists, chronologically for each author, all the plays (including those unacted or unprinted) between 1660 and 1700. Includes eight pages on Dryden (pp. 55-62).

17 _____. The Restoration Theatre. London: Routledge & Kegan Paul, 373 pp.

A study of theatrical conditions: publicity, prices, the
audience, stagecraft, stage conventions, scenery, costumes. Draws
many examples from Dryden's plays and criticism. Reprinted:
1964.48.

18   TILLYARD, E.M.W. <u>Poetry Direct and Oblique</u>. London: Chatto
     & Windus, 294 pp.
        Questions the belief that Dryden is "so preeminently the
     poet of statement." Gives three examples of important "obliqui-
     ties" in his work, from <u>All for Love</u>, <u>Religio Laici</u>, and <u>Threnodia
     Augustalis</u>. But concludes that Dryden was so occupied "in re-
     creating the poetry of statement" that he could not take full ad-
     vantage of his great gifts for obliquity (pp. 81-91). Reprinted
     (revised): 1959.42; 1977.43.

*19 WARD, CHARLES E. "Dryden's Drama 1662-1677: A Study in the
     Native Tradition." Ph.D. dissertation, Duke University.
        Cited in Latt and Monk, 1976.30.

                                1935

1   ALLEN, NED BLISS. <u>The Sources of John Dryden's Comedies</u>.
     University of Michigan Publications in Language and Literature
     16. Ann Arbor: University of Michigan Press, 313 pp.
        Argues that Dryden's comedies are heavily dependent upon
     borrowing from other works, native and foreign. Asserts that his
     "rule was to sacrifice everything to please the public," and there-
     fore he was eclectic and self-contradictory in his use of forms of
     comedy. Classifies the comedies into various types, depending
     upon their ancestry, and deals with each comedy, indicating its
     likely source or sources. Argues that critics have not paid enough
     attention to Langbaine's treatment of Dryden's borrowing (1691.1).
     Based on a Ph.D. dissertation, University of Michigan. Reprinted:
     1976.1.

*2   BODDY, MARGARET P. "The Translations of Virgil into English
     Verse from Douglas through Dryden: A Study in the Development
     of Poetic Expression." Ph.D. dissertation, University of
     Minnesota.
        Cited in Latt and Monk, 1976.30.

3   BROOKS, HAROLD. "Some Notes on Dryden, Cowley, and Shadwell."
     <u>N&Q</u> 168 (9 February):94-95.
        Quotes passages from two contemporary volumes, owned present-
     ly by Sir Charles Firth, containing various remarks on three poets.

4   _____. "When Did Dryden Write <u>MacFlecknoe</u>--Some Additional
     Notes." <u>RES</u> 11 (January):74-78.
        Brings forward seven further arguments in favor of Thorn-
     Drury's dating of 1678 (1925.16). Reprinted: 1966.57.

5   CASE, ARTHUR E. A Bibliography of English Poetic Miscellanies
     1521-1750. Oxford: Oxford University Press, 401 pp.
         Includes collation and annotation of miscellanies in which
     Dryden's work appears.

6   DEANE, C[ECIL] V. Aspects of Eighteenth Century Nature Poetry.
     Oxford: Blackwell, 145 pp.
         Disparages Dryden's translation of Virgil as negligent of
     the original and overreliant on stock phraseology (pp. 33-50).

7   HAM, ROSWELL G. "Dryden as Historiographer-Royal: The
     Authorship of His Majesties Declaration Defended, 1681." RES
     11 (July):284-98.
         Suggests works Dryden may have written as a consequence of
     his post as historiographer royal; argues on both external and
     internal evidence that Dryden wrote His Majesties Declaration
     Defended. Reprinted: 1966.57. See 1978.50.

8   _____. "Dryden's Dedication for The Music of the Prophetesse,
     1691." PMLA 50 (December):1065-75.
         Discusses the manuscript dedication, attributed to Dryden,
     though signed (in Dryden's hand) with Purcell's name. Examines
     changes in the manuscript, suggesting what they show us about
     Dryden's composing technique.

9   HARBAGE, ALFRED. "Elizabethan and Seventeenth-Century Play
     Manuscripts." PMLA 50 (September):687-99.
         Identifies and locates manuscripts. Arranged by author:
     includes three by Dryden (The State of Innocence, The Indian
     Emperour, and The Indian Queen).

10   _____. Sir William Davenant Poet Venturer 1606-1668.
     Philadelphia: University of Pennsylvania Press, 319 pp.
         Deals at length with Davenant's contacts with Dryden. Dis-
     cusses Dryden's critical remarks on Davenant's work, and analyzes
     (pp. 260-63) their collaboration on The Tempest.

11   HAVENS, P.S. "Dryden's 'Tagged' Version of 'Paradise Lost.'"
     In Essays in Dramatic Literature: The Parrott Presentation
     Volume. Edited by Hardin Craig. Princeton: Princeton
     University Press, pp. 383-97.
         Argues that Dryden wrote The State of Innocence to test his
     convictions about the propriety of Milton's use of the epic form
     in Paradise Lost. Asserts that Dryden believed that the dramatic
     form is better suited to tragedy than the epic. Also suggests
     that Dryden was trying to grasp the essentials of writing an epic,
     in order to prepare for his own. Reprinted: 1967.24.

12   HOOKER, EDWARD N. "Dryden's Allusion to the Poet of Excessive
     Wit." N&Q 168 (15 June):421.
         Supports John Dennis's identification of Wycherley as the
     poet thus alluded to in the "Parallel of Poetry and Painting."

13   LANGE, VICTOR. Die Lyrik und ihr Publikum im England des 18.
     Jahrhunderts. Eine geschmacksgeschichtliche Untersuchung über
     die englischen Anthologien von 1670-1780. Literatur und Leben
     2. Weimar: H. Böhlaus, 125 pp.
          Examines poetic miscellanies, including the Dryden-Tonson
     collection, one of the earliest of the period. Concentrates on
     publishing arrangements and public reception. Concludes that the
     practice of the period established the pattern for anthologies
     that has persisted to the present.

14   LEAVIS, F.R. "English Poetry in the Seventeenth Century."
     Scrutiny 4 (December):236-56.
          Briefly disparages Dryden in contrast to Pope and Jonson:
     he is too much a part of his particular time and community, and
     his "effects are all for the public ear." Reprinted: 1936.14
     (slightly revised); 1962.21.

15   MACAULAY, T.C. "French and English Drama in the Seventeenth
     Century." Essays and Studies 20:45-74.
          A broad comparison, emphasizing distinctions and differing
     trends. Contains a brief treatment of The Conquest of Granada.

*16 MAURER, DAVID W. "The Spanish Intrigue Play on the Restoration
     Stage." Ph.D. dissertation, Ohio State University.
          Cited in Latt and Monk, 1976.30.

17   NETTLETON, GEORGE H. "Author's Changes in Dryden's Conquest of
     Granada, Part I." MLN 50 (June):360-64.
          Examines four changes between the first quarto (1672) and
     the second quarto (1673), arguing that they represent the author's
     changes or, if not, "the sanction of authority above that of the
     compositor."

18   PARSONS, COLEMAN O. "Dryden's Letter of Attorney." MLN 50
     (June):364-65.
          Prints a letter (14 December 1680) by which Dryden gave
     George Ward power of attorney to collect his (Dryden's) pension.

19   PINTO, V. de SOLA. Rochester: Portrait of a Restoration Poet.
     London: Bodley Head, 316 pp.
          Discusses Dryden's relations with Rochester; gives particular
     attention to the quarrel between them. Speculates on Dryden's role
     in An Essay on Satyr, and on its relationship to the Rose Alley
     beating, which is blamed on the Duchess of Portsmouth (pp. 199-
     205).

20   ROSENFELD, SYBIL. "The Restoration Stage in Newspapers and
     Journals, 1660-1700." MLR 30 (October):445-59.
          Prints, with annotations, "items of theatrical and dramatic
     interest" from newspapers in the Burney Collection (British
     Museum) and elsewhere. Refers occasionally to Dryden or to his
     works.

21 SUMMERS, MONTAGUE. The Playhouse of Pepys. New York:
Macmillan Co.; London: Kegan Paul, Trench, Trubner, 500 pp.
   Contains many scattered references to Dryden, especially in
relation to the two acting companies. Reprinted: 1964.47.

22 TURNELL, G.M. "Dryden and the Religious Elements in the
Classical Tradition." Englische Studien 70 (August):244-61.
   Argues that Dryden's Catholicism derived from his view that
Man, in a state of sin, needed authority. His poetry likewise was
classic rather than romantic in that it represented what he saw
and not what he felt. Both faith and poetry were based on logic
and discipline, not spiritual experience.

23 WARD, CHARLES E. "Massinger and Dryden." ELH 2 (November):
263-66.
   Argues for Dryden's indebtedness to Massinger's The Virgin
Martyr in Tyrannic Love.

24 WILLIAMSON, GEORGE. "The Rhetorical Pattern of Neo-Classic
Wit." MP 33 (August):55-81.
   Argues that the neoclassical couplet developed in a straight
line from Jonson to Dryden, and was ultimately derived from certain
sententious figures in Latin rhetoric which Puttenham and others
advocated. Demonstrates how reliance on these figures strongly influenced prosody, especially sentence structure. Reprinted:
1960.28; 1969.85.

1936

*1 BROWER, REUBEN. "John Dryden's Use and Criticism of Virgil."
Ph.D. dissertation, Harvard University.
   Cited in Latt and Monk, 1976.30. Abstracted in Harvard
University Summaries of Theses 12:310-12.

2 COLBY, ELBRIDGE. English Catholic Poets: Chaucer to Dryden.
Milwaukee: Bruce, 227 pp.
   Contains an impressionistic survey of Dryden's life and
works (pp. 176-90).

3 de BEER, E.S. [A Poem Attributed to Dryden.] TLS, 16 May,
p. 420.
   Argues against W.G. Hiscock's attribution of "The Triumph of
Levy" to Dryden (1936.8), on the grounds of lack of positive evidence, and the poem's poor quality. See also 1936.4, 9-11.

4 _____. [A Poem Attributed to Dryden.] TLS, 30 May, p. 460.
   Replies (to Hiscock in 1936.10) that four volumes of miscellanies containing poems by Dryden did appear during his life,
and these must have contained most of his original minor poems.
See also 1936.3, 8-9, 11.

5   DOBRÉE, BONAMY. "Milton and Dryden: A Comparison in Poetic
     Ideas and Poetic Method." ELH 3 (March):83-100.
          Compares their early development, finding many parallels.
     Contrasts their mature styles, finding Milton the more original,
     while Dryden "used and developed the tradition of English poetry."
     Concludes that "to discuss which of them is the greater poet is
     invidious." Reprinted: 1970.25.

6   EIDSON, JOHN ODIN. "Dryden's Criticism of Shakespeare." SP
     33 (April):273-80.
          Brings together and paraphrases Dryden's various statements
     about Shakespeare.

7   HARBAGE, ALFRED. Cavalier Drama: An Historical and Critical
     Supplement of the Study of the Elizabethan and Restoration
     Stage. New York: Modern Language Association; London: Oxford
     University Press, 311 pp.
          An exhaustive survey of English drama from 1626 to 1669.
     Contains many scattered references to Dryden. Lists, chronologi-
     cally, plays written during the period. Reprinted: 1964.17.

8   HISCOCK, W.G. "A Poem Attributed to Dryden." TLS, 18 April,
     p. 340.
          Prints "The Triumph of Levy" from Christ Church Library,
     Oxford, and attributes it either to Dryden or to a plagiarist of
     Dryden, primarily on internal evidence. See 1936.3-4, 9-11.

9   _____. [A Poem Attributed to Dryden.] TLS, 25 April, p. 360.
          Adds circumstantial evidence to 1936.8, linking the poem to
     Dryden. See 1936.3-4, 10-11.

10   _____. [A Poem Attributed to Dryden.] TLS, 23 May, p. 440.
          Repeats his attribution to Dryden, arguing that the poem
     ("The Triumph of Levy") is equal in quality to many of Dryden's
     prologues and epilogues. Points out that no edition of Dryden's
     poems appeared during his lifetime. See 1936.3-4, 8-9, 11.

11   _____. [A Poem Attributed to Dryden.] TLS, 10 October, p. 815.
          Lists additional resemblances between "The Triumph of Levy"
     and lines by Dryden. See 1936.3-4, 8-10.

12   KELLY, BLANCHE M. The Well of English. New York and London:
     Harper, 420 pp.
          Surveys and appreciates Dryden's career (pp. 125-33). De-
     plores the plays on moral grounds. Emphasizes his religious views.
     The book as a whole deals with the Roman Catholic strain in English
     literature.

13   LEAVIS, F.R. "'Antony and Cleopatra' and 'All for Love': A
     Critical Exercise." Scrutiny 5 (September):158-69.
          Contrasts the two plays, primarily using close readings of

parallel passages to argue that Shakespeare's play has "life," while Dryden's has only "eloquence." Emphasizes imagery and metaphor, in which Shakespeare is seen to be complex, Dryden simple. Reprinted: 1975.32.

14 _____. "The Line of Wit." In Revaluation: Tradition and Development in English Poetry. London: Chatto & Windus; New York: Goerge W. Stewart, pp. 10-36.
     Reprint of 1935.14 (slightly revised). Reprinted: 1962.21.

15 MACDONALD, HUGH. "'A Journal from Parnassus': An Unpublished Satire on Dryden." TLS, 17 October, p. 844.
     Describes and discusses the manuscript poem, recently acquired by the Bodleian. Reprinted: 1937.11.

16 _____. "The Attacks on Dryden." Essays and Studies 21:41-74.
     States the "meagre" list of known facts about Dryden's life; notes the confusing effect of the mass of attacks upon him; states that "the curious collection may be worth assembling once more." Thoroughly reviews the attacks on him from 1668 up to and beyond his death. Concludes that "it is not easy to find any parallel in English literature to so much violence and ridicule directed against one man of letters in his life-time unless Pope is a competitor." Suggests that something in Dryden's character, perhaps "some shade of ineffectiveness," caused such extraordinary resentment. Reprinted: 1966.57.

17 MUNDY, PERCY DRYDEN. "Portraits of Dryden." N&Q 170 (2 May): 318-19.
     Describes a copy of a portrait of Dryden (by G.P. Harding) which he has just acquired.

*18 MURPHY, DENNIS. "Metaphor and Simile in Dryden's Non-Dramatic Poetry." Ph.D. dissertation, University of Iowa.
     Cited in Latt and Monk, 1976.30.

*19 PULVER, JEFFREY. "Purcell and Dryden." Musical Opinion and Musical Trade Review 59:589-90.
     Cited in Latt and Monk. 1976.30.

20 ROSENFELD, SYBIL. "Dramatic Advertisements in the Burney Newspapers 1660-1700." PMLA 51 (September):123-52.
     Prints and annotates the advertisements, several of which are for plays by Dryden.

21 SWAYNE, MATTIE. "The Progress Piece in the Seventeenth Century." Studies in English (University of Texas) 16:84-92.
     Discusses, among the works of others, Dryden's "Discourse . . . of Satire." States that the work is "much too complicated" to be a typical progress piece.

22   TEETER, LOUIS. "The Dramatic Use of Hobbes's Political Ideas."
     ELH 3 (June):140-69.
          Argues that typical Hobbesian political doctrines never ap-
     peared in a favorable light in Restoration drama. Emphasizes
     Hobbes's belief that obedience was owed to authority, whatever it
     was: this belief "could never be admitted by a Stuart or a Tory."
     Dryden may have used Hobbes's ethical or psychological ideas, but
     "no king who is not a tyrant ever . . . demands obedience in the
     terms of the Leviathan." Discusses relevant parts of several of
     Dryden's plays, including especially The Conquest of Granada, The
     Duke of Guise, and Tyrannic Love. Reprinted: 1966.57.

23   WALCOTT, FRED G. "John Dryden's Answer to Thomas Rymer's The
     Tragedies of the Last Age." PQ 15 (April):194-214.
          Argues that Dryden had read Rymer's work before completing
     his preface to All for Love, where he suggests that he is coming
     forth with an answer. Asserts that there is an "identity" between
     Dryden's "Heads of an Answer to Rymer" and the preface to Troilus
     and Cressida ("The Grounds of Criticism in Tragedy"). Analyzes
     this piece to suggest that it contains the principles upon which
     Dryden would base a detailed response to Rymer's argument.

*24 WANNING, ANDREWS. "Some Changes in the Prose Style of the
     Seventeenth Century." Ph.D. dissertation, Cambridge University.
          Cited in Latt and Monk, 1976.30.

25   WARD, CHARLES E. "The Dates of Two Dryden Plays." PMLA 51
     (September):786-92.
          Dates Marriage a-la-Mode in 1671 (rather than 1672), and
     Amboyna near the beginning of the Third Dutch War in 1672 (rather
     than 1673).

26   ZEUTHEN, RALPH M. John Dryden: Poet and Dramatist.
     Minneapolis: n.p., 8 pp.
          Sees two periods in Dryden's career: the "attempts at the
     popular, indecent drama . . . and the turn to critical poetry."
     Describes each period generally; concludes that while he was not
     a poetic genius "his surpassing wealth of language and excellent
     versification have already taken their rightful places among the
     highest ranks of literature."

                                   1937

1   ANON. "Dryden's Conversion: The Struggle for Faith." TLS,
     17 April, pp. 281-82.
          Defends Dryden's sincerity and consistency; appreciates The
     Hind and the Panther.

2   ANTHONY, Sister ROSE. The Jeremy Collier Stage Controversy,
     1698-1726. Milwaukee: Marquette University Press, 343 pp.

Treats the controversy by summarizing and commenting briefly on Collier's Short View of the Immorality . . . of the English Stage (1698.2), and, chronologically, a large number of the replies to it, including four by Dryden. Notes Dryden's apparent reluctance to answer Collier directly: suggests that in part he recognized the justice of his allegations.

3   BENNETT, J.A.W. "Dryden and All Souls." MLN 52 (February): 115–16.
Prints a letter from a fellow of All Souls (Oxford), 19 January 1686, explicitly referring to Dryden as a (losing) candidate for the wardenship of the college.

4   CLARK, WILLIAM S. "Corpses, Concealments, and Curtains on the Restoration Stage." RES 13 (October):438–48.
Describes and discusses the use of the traverse. Takes a major example from The Duke of Guise.

5   _____, ed. The Dramatic Works of Roger Boyle, Earl of Orrery. 2 vols. Cambridge, Mass.: Harvard University Press.
Discusses, in the introduction (1:3–97), Orrery's literary relations with Dryden, especially the question of his possible influence on The Rival Ladies.

*6   GALLAWAY, WILLIAM FRANCIS. "English Adaptations of Roman Satire, 1660–1800." Ph.D. dissertation, University of Michigan. Cited in Latt and Monk, 1976.30.

7   HAM, ROSWELL G. "Dryden's Epilogue to The Rival Ladies, 1664." RES 13 (January):76–80.
Argues that a manuscript poem in the Bodleian Library, on the same sheet as manuscript copy of the prologue, is the missing epilogue.

8   HARTSOCK, MILDRED E. "Dryden's Plays: A Study in Ideas." In Seventeenth Century Studies. Second Series. Edited by Robert Shafer. Princeton: Princeton University Press for the University of Cincinnati, pp. 69–176.
Relates Dryden's ideas to those of Hobbes and Montaigne. Finds Dryden's characters, in their self-interest and determinism, and their passion-driven natures, to reflect Hobbes's view of Man. Sees a similarity between Dryden's Pyrrhonist skepticism in religion and Montaigne's religious views. Relates Dryden's antipathy to the clergy to both Hobbes and Montaigne. Suggests that both skepticism and materialism ("and their offspring disillusion") may finally have brought Dryden into the Church.

9   KNIGHTS, L.C. "Restoration Comedy: The Reality and the Myth." Scrutiny 6 (September):122–43.
Charges that Restoration comedies are "trivial, gross, and dull." Finds their language commonplace, their characters cold,

their plots remote from life. Emphasizes the comedies' reliance
upon empty conventions. Argues that the "dominating mood" is
cynicism, but without "the tragic strength of disillusion." Uses
Marriage a-la-Mode as a major example. Reprinted: 1946.10;
1966.31.

10   LEGOUIS, PIERRE. "Dryden and Eton." MLN 52 (February):111-15.
       Discusses Settle's implied charge that Dryden coveted, and
was refused, the appointment as Provost of Eton in 1680/1; discusses, in relation to this issue, the question of whether Dryden
was thinking of taking orders.

11   MACDONALD, HUGH. Introduction to A Journal from Parnassus Now
       Printed from A Manuscript circa 1688. London: P.J. Dobell.
       Gives the background of the "seminar of the poets" mode,
and suggests 1687 or 1688 as the journal's date. Prints the text.
See 1936.15; 1938.7.

12   MUNDY, PERCY DRYDEN. "The Baptism of John Dryden." N&Q 173
       (25 September):225.
       Argues that Dryden was almost certainly baptized, despite
charges to the contrary (repeated most recently by Christopher
Hollis, 1933.7). Notes that nine of his brothers and sisters were
baptized at Titchmarsh, and that the parish registers for the period of his birth are missing.

13   NOYES, GEORGE RAPALL, and GEORGE REUBEN POTTER, eds. Hymns
       Attributed to John Dryden. University of California Publica-
       tions in English 6. Berkeley: University of California Press,
       231 pp.
       Reprints the Primer of 1706, a collection of English trans-
lations of Roman Catholic hymns. Argues that "there is no valid
reason why a single one of the hymns other than Veni, Creator
Spiritus should be ascribed to Dryden." Demolishes at great length
the arguments of those who have claimed that Dryden made some or
all of the translations. See 1884.1, 4; 1885.1; 1892.1; 1931.3.

14   STROUP, THOMAS B. "Scenery for The Indian Queen." MLN 52
       (June):408-9.
       Argues that a stage direction referring to "an Indian cave"
in Tyrannic Love proves that the scenery from The Indian Queen was
still in use at Drury Lane.

15   _____. "Supernatural Beings in Restoration Drama." Anglia 61
       (April):186-92.
       Argues that Restoration dramatists distinguished between
spirits from unearthly regions and ghosts of departed mortals, and
that only the second type was used functionally. Draws several
examples from Dryden.

16   VALLESE, TARQUINIO. Politics and Poetry: Political Influences

on English Poetry. Milan: Società Anonima Editrice Dante Alighieri, 111 pp.

Briefly describes and evaluates Dryden's political poetry. Finds Dryden's satires successful "because they are the outburst of personal virulence . . . what is natural in man's heart." Reprinted: 1976.58; 1978.57.

17 WARD, CHARLES E. "Some Notes on Dryden." RES 13 (July): 297–306.

Contains eight biographical notes:

1. "Dryden's loan to Charles II." Prints and annotates the relevant document from the Public Record Office.

2. "'Mr. Dreiden's Serge Bed.'" The Dreiden alluded to in a letter to Sir Robert Howard (quoted by W.S. Clark in 1927.2) is not the poet. See 1938.2.

3. "Honoria in The Rival Ladies." If the character is named after anyone it is Sir Robert Howard's wife Honoria, not Dryden's cousin Honor Dryden. See 1944.5.

4. "The Milk-White Hind." The estate of Lord Clifford, where Dryden visited after 1686, contained several white deer.

5. "The Agreement for the Virgil." Summarizes the contract between Dryden and Jacob Tonson.

6. "Two 'New' Songs of Dryden." Prints songs from The Husband his own Cuckold, by Dryden's son John, arguing that they are the senior Dryden's, as his contract with Tonson specifically allowed him to do this work.

7. "An Advertisement for the Virgil." Transcribes it, from a manuscript in Dryden's hand, and suggests a date for it.

8. "Dryden, Higden, and Tonson." Gives details of a suit between Higden and Tonson, suggesting that Dryden's knowledge of this suit (1686) prompted him to secure a written agreement with Tonson.

1938

*1 CAMERON, LESTER W. "A Study of Dryden's Prose Style." Ph.D. dissertation, University of Wisconsin.

Cited in Latt and Monk, 1976.30. Abstracted in Summaries of Doctoral Dissertations, University of Wisconsin 2:292–94.

2 CLARK, W[ILLIAM] S. "Some Notes on Dryden." RES 14 (July): 330–32.

Rebuts C.E. Ward's argument that the "Dreidon" referred to in Hanley's letter about the "serge bed" is not the poet. See 1927.2; 1937.17.

*3 HARMAN, ROLAND N. "Sir Walter Scott as Editor of John Dryden." Ph.D. dissertation, Yale University.

Cited in Latt and Monk, 1976.30.

*4   KNIPP, GEORGE W.   "The Stage History of John Dryden's Plays."
      Ph.D. dissertation, Johns Hopkins University.
            Cited in Latt and Monk, 1976.30.

*5   LADRIERE, JAMES C.   "Sarmoni Propivs: A Study of the Horatian
      Theory of the Epistle and of Dryden's Allusion to it in the
      Preface of Religio Laici."   Ph.D. dissertation, University of
      Michigan.
            Cited in Latt and Monk, 1976.30.

 6   LEGOUIS, PIERRE.   "Corneille and Dryden as Dramatic Critics."
      In Seventeenth Century Studies Presented to Sir Herbert Grierson.
      Oxford: Clarendon Press, pp. 269-91.
            Contrasts the two, concluding that "Dryden is as much more
      living a dramatic critic than Corneille, as he is a less living
      dramatic poet."   Credits Corneille with more independence and
      originality in his criticism than history has allowed him.   Sug-
      gests that Dryden's superiority as a critic is largely a matter
      of style.   Reprinted: 1973.41.

 7   _____.   "A Journal from Parnassus."   EA 2, no. 2:151-55.
            Describes the piece, and adds annotations and comments to
      those of Hugh Macdonald in 1937.11.

 8   MUNDY, PERCY DRYDEN.   "Dryden's Hermitage."   N&Q 174 (5
      February):102.
            Asks for information about an undated French article con-
      cerning an incident involving Dryden, Dryden's niece, Sir Charles
      Blount, George Earl of Lindsay, and a "Woolwich brewer's hovel"
      which becomes an "elegant mansion."

 9   NETHERCOT, ARTHUR H.   Sir William D'Avenant: Poet Laureate and
      Playwright-Manager.   Chicago: University of Chicago Press, 494
      pp.
            Discusses Dryden's relationship with Davenant; emphasizes
      his great liking and admiration for him.   Summarizes, analyzes,
      and evaluates The Tempest, finding it "not quite an abortion"
      (pp. 398-403).

10   NOYES, ROBERT GALE.   "Contemporary Musical Settings of the
      Songs in Restoration Dramatic Operas."   Harvard Studies and
      Notes in Philology and Literature 20:99-121.
            Lists, annotates, and gives locations if known.   Includes
      many settings of songs by Dryden.

11   _____.   "Conventions of Song in Restoration Tragedy."   PMLA 53
      (March):162-88.
            Surveys types of songs, and their dramatic contexts, with
      many examples, several drawn from Dryden.   Concludes that tragic
      dramatists "consciously endeavored to place their lyrics in natur-
      al relationship to the context of the play."

12   PARSONS, A.E.   "The English Heroic Play."   MLR 33 (January):
     1-14.
          Argues that the form developed from the heroic poem and the
     heroic prose romance.   Asserts that Davenant thoroughly understood
     the form's background, and that the Howard-Dryden Indian Queen fol-
     lows the form, but that Dryden soon abandoned it in favor of other
     models.

13   PINTO, V. de SOLA.   Introduction to English Literature.   Edited
     by Bonamy Dobrée.   Vol. 2, The English Renaissance 1510-1688.
     London: Cresset, 381 pp.
          Contains a general description of Dryden's characteristics,
     primarily in poetry, and a brief survey of his career (pp. 115-18).

*14 ROSECKE, INGO.   "Drydens Prologe und Epiloge."   Ph.D. disserta-
     tion, Hamburg.
          Cited in Latt and Monk, 1976.30.

*15 S., E.   "Dryden's Conversion to Catholicism."   More Books 13:
     437.
          Cited in Latt and Monk, 1976.30.

16   SHEWRING, WALTER.   "Dryden and the Primer of 1706."   Downside
     Review 56:303-10.
          Recants his former statement (see 1933.11) that Dryden is
     the author of some or all of the hymns in the Primer.

17   [SUMMERS, MONTAGUE.]   "John Dryden."   In Great Catholics.
     Edited by Fr. Claude Williamson, O.S.C.   London: Nicholson &
     Watson, pp. 264-76.
          Summarizes Dryden's life and work, emphasizing and celebrat-
     ing his religious beliefs from a Roman Catholic viewpoint.

18   SWEDENBERG, H.T., Jr.   "Fable, Action, Unity, and Supernatural
     Machinery in English Epic Theory, 1650-1800."   Englische Studien
     73 (November):39-48.
          Attempts to synthesize Restoration and eighteenth-century
     epic theory on these four "phases" of the form.   Refers frequently
     to Dryden, concluding that the theory derives primarily from
     "Aristotle, Horace, and the French critics of the seventeenth
     century."

19   _____.   "Rules and English Critics of the Epic, 1650-1800."
     SP 35 (October):566-87.
          Sees increasing respect for the "rules" and authority in the
     epic theory of the late seventeenth century.   Cites passages from
     Dryden (among other writers) as representative.   Reprinted:
     1961.45; 1966.6; 1976.7.

20   TRAUB, WALTHER.   Auffassung und Gestaltung der Cleopatra in der
     englischen Literatur.   Wurzburg: Triltsch, 108 pp.

One subchapter (pp. 48-61) deals with All for Love. Asserts that it is the only treatment of the character of Cleopatra worthy of comparing to Shakespeare's, but concludes that the conception of Cleopatra has been domesticated and narrowed.

21 WARD, CHARLES E. "The Publication and Profits of Dryden's Virgil." PMLA 53 (September):807-12.
    Analyzes the contract between Dryden and Jacob Tonson to show that Dryden's official profits (setting aside gifts) from his translation of Virgil were £590, 8/8, much less than Malone (1800.1) and Saintsbury (1881.5) had estimated.

22 _____. "An Unpublished Dryden Letter." TLS, 29 October, p. 700.
    Prints and comments on a letter to Viscount Latimer, son of the Earl of Danby, in 1677. Relates details in the letter to the writing of Mr. Limberham, and to Dryden's financial circumstances.

23 WILCOX, JOHN. The Relation of Molière to Restoration Comedy. New York: Columbia University Press, 249 pp.
    Contains many scattered references to Dryden, and surveys his career as a comic dramatist. Discusses Dryden's acknowledged and unacknowledged borrowings from Molière, and Langbaine's charges of plagiarism (in 1691.1). Concludes that Dryden did not make much direct use of Molière (pp. 105-17). Reprinted: 1964.54.

1939

1 BALL, ALICE DULANY. "An Emendation of Dryden's Conquest of Granada, Part One." ELH 6 (September):217-18.
    Argues that 11. 151-52 should be given to Selin rather than to Zulema.

*2 BARRON, M. "Dryden the Catholic." Dominicana 24:111-15.
    Cited in Latt and Monk, 1976.30.

3 BOYCE, BENJAMIN. Tom Brown of Facetious Memory: Grub Street in the Age of Dryden. Harvard Studies in English 21. Cambridge, Mass.: Harvard University Press, 224 pp.
    Describes and examines Brown's The Reasons of Mr. Bays Changing His Religion (1688.2) (pp. 19-31); discusses the contributions of both Brown and Dryden to the translation of Lucian; gives the evidence for and against Brown's authorship of A Description of Mr. D----n's Funeral (1700.3).

4 BRONOWSKI, JACOB. The Poet's Defence. Cambridge: Cambridge University Press, 258 pp.
    A chapter on Dryden (pp. 89-125) treats him as the last poet dramatist who could hold together a view of both "Ideal Nature" and human society. Studies All for Love, seeing Antony as

representative of "Heroic Nature," finally defeated by the world. Concludes that "the Augustan Age had begun."

5   BROOKS, CLEANTH. "A Note on the Death of Elizabethan Tragedy." In Modern Poetry and the Tradition. Chapel Hill: University of North Carolina Press; London: Poetry London, pp. 203-18.
        Suggests that "the tendency toward order and simplification" in scientific and poetic thought at the end of the seventeenth century destroyed Elizabethan tragedy by overrefining it. Invokes Dryden's theory and practice as typical of this development. Reprinted: 1965.7.

6   BROWER, REUBEN. "Dryden's Poetic Diction and Virgil." PQ 18 (April):211-17.
        Traces the influence of Virgil on Dryden's diction, especially in the translation and the Fables. Although much of Dryden's "Latinized circumlocutions" could have come from Milton or "the combined force of the Roman poetical tradition," there is a clear and direct relationship to Virgil which carried over into the Fables. Concludes that "the poetic diction which Dryden and his contemporaries innocently bequeathed to the eighteenth century may thus be traced in part to the 'best of poets.'"

7   HAMMETT, E.A. "A Note for the NED." MLN 54 (June):449.
        Lists, following Beljame (1881.1), several words derived from French which Dryden used before the earliest citation in the Oxford English Dictionary.

*8 HARASZTI, ZOLTAN. "Dryden's Adaptations and Operas (with a facsimile)." More Books 8:89-99.
        Cited in Latt and Monk, 1976.30.

9   HOOKER, EDWARD N., ed. The Critical Works of John Dennis. 2 vols. Baltimore: Johns Hopkins University Press, 1939, 1943.
        Contains many references to Dryden. See 1693.2; 1704.1; 1711.3; 1713.1; 1715.1; 1720.1.

10 HUNTLEY, FRANK L. "Dryden, Rochester, and the Eighth Satire of Juvenal." PQ 18 (July):269-84.
        Analyzes the preface to All for Love in the light of Dryden's quarrel with Rochester. Argues that Juvenal's eighth satire provides the framework for the essay, which "is more significant as rhetoric than as criticism." Reprinted: 1966.57.

11 LEWIS, C.S. "Shelley, Dryden, and Mr. Eliot." In Rehabilitations and Other Essays. London: Oxford University Press, pp. 3-34.
        Rebuts Eliot's disparagement of Shelley relative to Dryden (1921.3). Finds Dryden, although at times brilliant, incapable of sustaining decorum, especially in his heroic poetry and plays. Reprinted: 1960.13; 1976.32; 1977.25.

12   MACDONALD, HUGH. John Dryden: A Bibliography of Early
      Editions and of Drydeniana. Oxford: Oxford University Press,
      368 pp.
          Collates and annotates, with bibliographical description,
      "every edition of Dryden's writings published during his lifetime,
      and every contemporary book or pamphlet I have been able to trace
      in which he is praised, attacked, or alluded to." Arranged by
      categories of works; chronologically within each category. Re-
      printed: 1966.35. See 1941.11; 1942.5; 1965.45A.

13   SCHWEITZER, JEROME W. "Dryden's Use of Scudéry's Almahide."
      MLN 54 (March):190-92.
          Points out errors in annotation in Montague Summers's edition
      of The Conquest of Granada (1931.33), and clarifies the relation-
      ship between the play, the Scudéry novel, and its English transla-
      tions.

14   SMITH, BYRON P. Islam in English Literature. Beirut: American
      Press, 267 pp.
          Notes Dryden's various uses of Islamic settings and charac-
      ters; describes the plays involved. Evaluates Dryden's knowledge
      of Islamic history and traditions. Emphasizes Don Sebastian (pp.
      19-54).

15   WILSON, JOHN HAROLD. "Rochester, Dryden, and the Rose-Street
      Affair." RES 15:294-301.
          Criticizes the inferences drawn from the evidence that had
      been used to blame the Rose Alley cudgelling on Rochester. Sug-
      gests other innocuous implications of the documents involved.

                                1940

1   BREDVOLD, LOUIS I., and HUGH MACDONALD. "John Dryden." In
      The Cambridge Bibliography of English Literature. Vol. 2.
      Edited by F.W. Bateson. Cambridge: Cambridge University
      Press, pp. 262-75.
          Lists publication dates of Dryden's works, with occasional
      annotation. Lists selected books and essays on Dryden. Revised:
      1971.7.

2   BROWER, REUBEN. "Dryden's Epic Manner and Virgil." PMLA 55
      (March):119-38.
          Argues the heavy indebtedness of Dryden to Virgil. Gives
      examples of echoes of Virgil, drawn from the plays as well as the
      nondramatic poetry. Concludes that Dryden tended to use Virgilian
      allusions when his purpose was to "convey the impression of epic
      rather than the reality." Reprinted: 1966.57; 1975.1.

*3   CUNNINGHAM, HUGH T. "The Political and Literary Backgrounds
      of Dryden's Absalom and Achitophel." Ph.D. dissertation, Yale

University.
      Cited in Latt and Monk, 1976.30.

4   DAY, CYRUS L., and ELEANORE BOSWELL MURRIE. English Song-
      Books, 1651-1702: A Bibliography with a First-Line Index of
      Songs. Oxford: Oxford University Press for the Bibliographical
      Society, 460 pp.
           The index includes many songs by Dryden: these are cross-
      referenced to the list of song books, which contains annotation
      and bibliographical description.

5   de BEER, E.S. "Dryden: Date of a Prologue, 'Gallants, a
      Bashful Poet.'" N&Q 179 (21 December):440-41.
           Dates it between 1689 and 1693, because of a topical allu-
      sion to the prologue.

6   ____. "Dryden: 'The Kind Keeper': The 'Poet of Scandalous
      Memory.'" N&Q 179 (24 August):128-29.
           Argues that Marvell, rather than Flecknoe, is the poet
      Dryden alludes to in the dedication to Mr. Limberham, or The Kind
      Keeper. The argument is based on Marvell's greater stature as a
      poet.

7   ____. "Dryden's Anti-Clericalism." N&Q 179 (12 October):
      254-57.
           Suggests that the increase in anticlerical passages begin-
      ning around 1677 followed some disappointment involving the Church.
      Suggests that he might have been refused ordination, which would
      have made him ineligible for a sinecure.

*8   DOBELL, PERCY JOHN, and A.E. DOBELL. A Catalogue of the Works
      of John Dryden and Drydeniana. London: P.J. and A.E. Dobell.
           Cited in Latt and Monk, 1976.30.

9   EVANS, B. IFOR. Tradition and Romanticism: Studies in English
      Poetry from Chaucer to W.B. Yeats. London: Methuen.
           Contains a general summary and evaluation of Dryden's poetry
      (pp. 61-75). Asserts that Dryden "invented English satire," and
      made possible "a poetry widely read and fully intelligible." Re-
      printed: 1964.11.

10   GALLAWAY, FRANCIS. Reason, Rule, and Revolt in English
      Classicism. New York: Scribners, 383 pp.
           Uses many examples from Dryden in the course of an examina-
      tion of the "artistic outlook of English classicism." Argues
      that this classicism "nourished the seeds of its own destruction."
      Reprinted: 1965.19.

*11 GIOVANNINI, G. "The Theory of Tragedy as History in Renaissance
      and Neo-classical Criticism." Ph.D. dissertation, University of
      Michigan.
           Cited in Latt and Monk, 1976.30.

12   HARBAGE, ALFRED. Annals of English Drama 975-1700: An
      Analytical Record of All Plays, Extant or Lost, Chronologically
      Arranged and Indexed by Authors, Titles, Dramatic Companies,
      etc. Philadelphia: University of Pennsylvania.
            Includes Dryden entries. Second revised edition: 1964.18.

13   _____. "Elizabethan-Restoration Palimpsest." MLR 35 (July):
      287-319.
            Includes an argument that The Mistaken Husband and The Wild
      Gallant are rewritings of plays by Richard Brome. Reprinted:
      1972.29.

14   HARRIS, BRICE. Charles Sackville Sixth Earl of Dorset: Patron
      and Poet of the Restoration. Illinois Studies in Language and
      Literature 26, no. 3-4. Urbana: University of Illinois Press,
      269 pp.
            Treats Dorset's patronage of Dryden (pp. 195-200).

15   HUGHES, LEO. "Attitudes of Some Restoration Dramatists Toward
      Farce." PQ 19 (July):268-87.
            Discusses, in part, Dryden's dislike of farce, using his
      direct statements and his practice in drama as evidence.

16   JEFFERSON, D.W. "The Significance of Dryden's Heroic Plays."
      PLPLS-LHS 5, no. 3:125-39.
            Argues that the wittiness of Dryden's heroic plays has never
      been appreciated. Uses examples drawn from The Conquest of Granada
      and Aureng-Zebe to show that "Dryden deliberately used heroic melo-
      drama as a playground for his powers of wit and rhetoric." Seen
      in this way, the heroic plays are a natural prelude to his major
      satirical poems. Also emphasizes Dryden's use of imagery in the
      plays, which is likened to techniques in metaphysical poetry. Re-
      printed: 1966.31, 43.

17   JONES, RICHARD FOSTER. "Science and Criticism in the Neo-
      Classical Age of English Literature." Journal of the History
      of Ideas 1 (October):381-412.
            Sees Dryden's literary criticism as exemplary of the skepti-
      cism which was crucial to the development of science. Sees also
      in Dryden's criticism the inductive method of reasoning, "when not
      in his neo-classic moods." Suggests that Dryden's belief in poetic
      progress is a parallel to the spirit of the Royal Society. Re-
      printed: 1951.18; 1961.45.

*18   MARTIN, MILDRED. "Influences on Dryden's Prose Style." Ph.D.
      dissertation, University of Illinois.
            Cited in Latt and Monk, 1976.30.

19   MUIR, KENNETH. "The Imagery of All for Love." PLPLS-LHS 5,
      no. 3:140-47.
            Examines and evaluates the imagery, concluding that it is
      much inferior to Shakespeare's in Antony and Cleopatra. Shows how

much of it is indebted to Shakespeare, and also to Samuel Daniel's
Cleopatra. Asserts that Shakespeare's play is more deeply unified,
because its unity is "based on the poetic conception and expressed
in a style which . . . is never led into bathos or bombast." Reprinted: 1968.39.

20 NICOLL, ALLARDYCE. A History of Restoration Drama 1660-1700.
3d ed. Cambridge: Cambridge University Press.
A revised and updated version of 1923.4 and 1928.10. Reprinted: 1952.23 (as vol. 1 of A History of English Drama 1660-
1900); 1965.45.

21 OSBORN, JAMES M. John Dryden: Some Biographical Facts and
Problems. New York: Columbia University Press, 309 pp.
Contains two parts: the first describes and evaluates previous biographies, and the second presents miscellaneous "collater-
al investigations" of biographical problems. The first part traces
the growth of knowledge about Dryden from his own time to the
twentieth century. Examines in detail the work of Burch (1736.1),
Derrick (1760.1), Johnson (1779.2), Malone (1800.1), Scott (1808.3),
and Saintsbury (1881.5). The second part consists of the following
sections:
1. "The Medal of John Bayes." Argues, against Thorn-Drury
(1925.16), that Shadwell was the author. Reprinted: 1963.46.
2. "Was Dryden in Herringman's Employ?" Discusses the evidence but is unable to answer the question.
3. "Dryden and the King's Playhouse in 1678." Discusses
the implications of the company's petition against Dryden; examines its cancelled passages.
4. "Dryden's London Residences." Lists those which are
known.
5. "Dryden's Absences from London." Lists and discusses
trips Dryden is known to have made or is thought to have made.
6. "Dryden and William Walsh." Discusses their relationship; prints several passages from letters between them.
7. "Dryden and Langbaine." Suggests the cause of Langbaine's
grievance against Dryden; argues that his attack on Dryden has dis-
torted literary history.
8. "Books from Dryden's Library." Comments on several books
known to have belonged to Dryden.
9. "Dryden Family Traditions in 1799." Prints and annotates
letters to Malone on the subject.
10. "Shorter Studies." These very short notes have the following titles: "Dryden's Verses to Koningsmark," "Dryden and
Thomas Sprat," "Dryden and His 'Cosen Salwey,'" "William Oldys on
Dryden," "The Dryden Letters at Knole," "John Dryden, jr. and the
Duke of Shrewsbury," "Dryden's 'Heads of an Answer to Rymer,'" and
"Dryden's Baptism." Reprinted (revised):1965.45A.

22 PINTO, V. de SOLA. "Rochester, Dryden, and the Duchess of
Portsmouth." RES 16 (April):177-78.

Argues, on the evidence of Narcissus Luttrell and Anthony à
Wood, for her responsibility in the Rose Alley cudgelling.

23   SHARP, ROBERT L.   From Donne to Dryden: The Revolt Against
     Metaphysical Poetry.   Chapel Hill: University of North Carolina
     Press, 234 pp.
          Sees Dryden as the figure most responsible for the death of
     the metaphysical style.   Traces his movement away from the style
     of Cowley and Waller, who influenced him early.   Contrasts Donne
     and Dryden as representative of the metaphysical and antimetaphysi-
     cal styles at their best.   Examines Dryden's direct and implicit
     judgments of metaphysical poetry.   Reprinted: 1965.51.

24   SHUSTER, GEORGE N.   The English Ode from Milton to Keats.
     Columbia University Studies in English and Comparative Litera-
        ture 150.   New York: Columbia University Press, 320 pp.
          Credits Dryden with having kept the tradition of the ode
     alive during an inhospitable period.   Surveys the types of ode
     written during the Restoration, emphasizing the satiric.   Examines
     Dryden's odes, stressing their loyalty to tradition.   Concludes
     that "Dryden established the irregular ode as a valuable and in-
     teresting genre" (pp. 123-45).

25   THORPE, CLARENCE DeWITT.   The Aesthetic Theory of Thomas Hobbes.
     University of Michigan Publications in Language and Literature
        18.   Ann Arbor: University of Michigan Press, 346 pp.
          Devotes a chapter to "The Psychological Approach in Dryden"
     (pp. 189-220), which argues for Dryden's position "in the Hobbian
     tradition of the psychological approach to aesthetic problems."
     Cites Dryden's use of Hobbes's terminology ("fancy," "judgment,"
     "memory") and outlines his theory of invention.   Argues that his
     brief for the importance of fancy under the restriction of judgment
     exemplifies Hobbes's theory of fancy.   Concludes that Dryden is
     directly in the line from Hobbes to the Romantics in his belief
     that excitement is itself pleasure, and in his continuing appeal
     to the criterion of taste.   Reprinted: 1964.50.

*26 TREADWAY, THOMAS J.   "The Critical Opinions of John Dryden."
     Ph.D. dissertation, St. Louis University.
          Cited in Latt and Monk, 1976.30.   Abstracted in DA 2, no.
     2:49-50.

27   WILEY, AUTREY NELL, ed.   Rare Prologues and Epilogues 1642-1700.
     London: George Allen & Unwin, 403 pp.
          Prints and annotates, with bibliographic information, many
     of Dryden's prologues.   Includes a historical and critical intro-
     duction.

28   WORCESTER, DAVID.   The Art of Satire.   Cambridge, Mass.:
     Harvard University Press, 198 pp.
          Briefly treats Dryden in the context of the development of

English satire. Credits him with diverting English satire "into the channel of high burlesque" (pp. 157-59). Reprinted: 1960.30.

1941

1   BENTLEY, G.E. "Seventeenth-Century Allusions to Ben Jonson." HLQ 5 (October):65-113.
      Adds allusions to those collected by Bradley and Adams (1922.2). Includes twenty-six by Dryden.

*2   BROADUS, E.K. "The Date of Dryden's Appointment as Poet-Laureate." Nation (London) 98:751-52.
      Cited in Latt and Monk, 1976.30.

3   de BEER, E.S. "Absalom and Achitophel: Literary and Historical Notes." RES 17 (July):298-309.
      Suggests various general ways in which Dryden's background had fitted him for writing the poem. Discusses the identities of various characters. Suggests that Amnon (murdered by Absalom) might have been William Fanshawe (not murdered by Monmouth but by Monmouth's brother-in-law). Also suggests the following identifications: Balaam = Lord Grey, Caleb = Essex, Agag = Sir William Scroggs. See 1955.16; 1956.10, 19.

*4   FOSTER, GEORGE H. "British History on the London Stage, 1660-1700." Ph.D. dissertation, University of North Carolina.
      Cited in Latt and Monk, 1976.30.

5   HODGES, JOHN C. William Congreve the Man: A Biography from New Sources. The Modern Language Association General Series 9. New York: Modern Language Association; London: Oxford University Press, 168 pp.
      Makes many scattered references to Dryden's personal and literary associations with Congreve.

6   HOLLIS, CHRISTOPHER. "Dryden's Conversion." Tablet 177:470-71.
      Defends and explains Dryden's Catholicism, particularly in its relation to the politics of his time. Discusses Macaulay's antagonism to Dryden.

7   HOOKER, HELENE MAXWELL. "Charles Montagu's Reply to The Hind and the Panther." ELH 8 (March):51-73.
      Prints an edited text of Montagu's manuscript poem in reply to The Hind and the Panther. Analyzes the poem, and discusses the history of its form (the dialogue). Asserts that the poem identifies "the essential weakness of Dryden's paradoxical position": that he failed to draw a line between the provinces of reason and faith. Montagu's firm insistence that "a solid faith could be built only upon reason" (identifying reason with beliefs that men commonly hold) was traditional in contemporary Anglican apologetics.

*8   LITTLE, EVELYN S. "Homer and Theocritus in English Translation:
      A Critical Bibliography Designed as a Guide for Librarians in
      the Choice of Editions for the General Reader." Ph.D. disser-
      tation, University of Michigan.
          Cited in Latt and Monk, 1976.30. Abstracted in DA, 3, no.
      2:60-61.

 9   LONG, RALPH BERNARD. "Dryden's Importance as Spokesman of the
      Tories." Studies in English (University of Texas) 21:79-99.
          Deprecates Dryden's contribution to Tory propaganda. Sur-
      veys the bulk of topical political literature during the period,
      and sets Dryden's against it. Argues that poetry, in which Dryden
      excelled, never had the appeal and influence of prose, in which
      his work was mediocre. Credits Roger L'Estrange with being the
      most effective Tory writer, although Dryden's verse has "remained
      in Tory memories." Notes that even down to the present, Dryden's
      chief admirers have been, for the most part, "staunchly Tory."

*10   O'BRIEN, ROBERT DAVID. "What About Dryden?" America 66:101-2.
      Cited in Latt and Monk, 1976.30.

11   OSBORN, JAMES M. "Macdonald's Bibliography of Dryden: An
      Annotated Check List of Selected American Libraries." MP 39
      (August):69-98; (November):197-212.
          Indicates, with occasional annotation, where copies of items
      listed by Macdonald in 1939.12 are to be found in America.

12   POTTLE, FREDERICK A. The Idiom of Poetry. Ithaca: Cornell
      University Press.
          In a chapter entitled "The Critic's Responsibility" (pp.
      43-57), cites Dryden as a model of the responsible critic whose
      chief function "is to recognize and define the emergent idiom."
      Reprinted (revised):1946.14; second edition (rev. and enl.):
      1963.41.

13   SAMPSON, GEORGE, ed. The Concise Cambridge History of English
      Literature. Cambridge: Cambridge University Press; New York:
      Macmillan Co., 1108 pp.
          The section on Dryden (pp. 401-9) surveys his career and
      accomplishment. A condensation of 1912.8.

14   SMITH, R. JACK. "Drydeniana." TLS, 27 December, p. 655.
          Adds an anonymous translation of St. Evremond (1687) to
      Macdonald's "Drydeniana" (in 1939.12).

15   WELLEK, RENÉ. The Rise of English Literary History. Chapel
      Hill: University of North Carolina Press, 282 pp.
          Briefly discusses Dryden's criticism (pp. 28-31) in the
      course of a treatment of the growth of the concepts of "individu-
      ality" and "development" in seventeenth-century literary history.

*16 WILLIAMS, WELDON M. "The Early Political Satire of the Restoration." Ph.D. dissertation, University of Washington. Cited in Latt and Monk, 1976.30. Abstracted in University of Washington, Abstracts of Theses 5:297-303.

17 WILSON, JOHN HAROLD, ed. The Rochester-Savile Letters: 1671-1680. Graduate School Studies: Contributions in Languages and Literature 8. Columbus: Ohio State University Press, 136 pp.
Several of the letters refer to Dryden: the editor's notes explain the references.

1942

1 ALLEMAN, GILLERT SPENCER. Matrimonial Law and the Materials of Restoration Comedy. Wallingford, Pa.: n.p., 162 pp.
Examines the plays in the light of contemporary matrimonial law. Refers to several plays by Dryden, especially The Wild Gallant and Sir Martin Mar-All.

2 DUNNE, JOSEPH W. "John Dryden: Catholic Apologist." Clergy Review 21:15-22.
An appreciation of Dryden, especially The Hind and the Panther. Defends Dryden against non-Catholic critics still under the sway of Macaulay (1828.1).

3 EVANS, G. BLAKEMORE. "Dryden's 'State of Innocence.'" TLS, 21 March, p. 144.
Analyzes the Harvard manuscript, which has corrections in Dryden's hand. Argues that "these readings preserve Dryden's original text, instead of the type-setter's interpretation of it." Also notes an echo of Paradise Lost in Tyrannic Love (1669), which would be Dryden's earliest notice of the poem.

4 GREENE, GRAHAM. British Dramatists. London: Collins, 48 pp.
Briefly discusses Dryden's career (pp. 26-30), emphasizing his influence on his own and modern theater. Concludes that he "was . . . the great organizer."

5 OSBORN, JAMES M. "Macdonald's Bibliography of Dryden." MP 39 (February):313-19.
Criticizes the "bibliographical shortcomings" of 1939.12. Reprinted: 1966.57.

6 RANDOLPH, MARY CLAIRE. "The Structural Design of the Formal Verse Satire." PQ 21 (October):368-84.
Summarizes the "Discourse on Satire," stressing its insistence upon formal unity in satire. Suggests that the formula proved unworkable in practice. Reprinted: 1961.45.

7 RICHARDS, I.A. "The Interactions of Words." In The Language

of Poetry. Edited by Allen Tate. Princeton: Princeton
University Press, pp. 65-87.
    Compares Donne's First Anniversary with "To the Memory of
Anne Killigrew." Examines the wording of Dryden's poem, arguing
that close study of it is not repaid by any discovery of greater
meaning (as contrasted with Donne's poem). Reprinted: 1960.20.

8   SMITH, R. JACK. "The Date of MacFlecknoe." RES 18 (July):
     322-23.
    Cites an allusion to the poem in The Tory-Poets (1682.2),
which was printed 4 September, a month before MacFlecknoe. This
provides further proof that the poem was available before publication.

*9   _____. "Dryden and Shadwell: A Study in Literary Controversy."
      Ph.D. dissertation, Cornell University.
    Cited in Latt and Monk, 1976.30. Abstracted in Cornell
University, Abstracts of Theses (1942):54-56.

10   TILLOTSON, GEOFFREY. "Absalom and Achitophel." Listener 27:
     51-52.
    An appreciation of the poem, emphasizing Dryden's skill in
characterization and his moderation. Compares the poem with the
General Prologue to The Canterbury Tales.

11   _____. "Eighteenth-Century Poetic Diction (I)." In Essays in
      Criticism and Research. Cambridge: University of Cambridge,
      pp. 53-62.
    Discusses Dryden (among other poets): is mainly concerned
with the effect of the heroic couplet on the way poets saw nature.
Reprinted: 1961.55; 1967.58.

12   WARD, CHARLES E., coll. and ed. The Letters of John Dryden
     With Letters Addressed to Him. Durham, N.C.: Duke University
     Press, 213 pp.
    Prints seventy-seven letters, including fifteen addressed to
Dryden. The notes (pp. 143-89) give the current location of each
letter, and explain allusions and details. The preface (pp. vii-
xiv) discusses the significance of the letters, most of which are
from Dryden's last years. Notes their casual, nonliterary nature,
but argues that they "form almost the only real source for a study
of the man." Traces the course of their discovery and publication
from Edmond Malone's edition of most of them (1800.1) onwards.
Reprinted: 1965.58. See 1965.45A.

13   WELLS, STARING B., ed. A Comparison Between the Two Stages:
     A Late Restoration Book of the Theatre. Princeton Studies in
     English 26. Princeton: Princeton University Press, 227 pp.
    An edition of 1702.1.

1943

1 BOTTKOL, JOSEPH McG. "Dryden's Latin Scholarship." MP 40
    (February):241-54.
    Defends Dryden's ability as a Latinist by reference to the
seventeenth-century editions he actually used. Argues that "his
departures from the original are due to aesthetic or stylistic
reasons." Identifies the editions Dryden used, and notes how not
only their texts but their commentaries influenced him. Reconsti-
tutes his working method. Calls for a re-edition of the translations. Reprinted: 1966.57.

2 CRANE, R.S. "English Neoclassical Criticism: An Outline
    Sketch." In The Dictionary of World Literature. Edited by
    Joseph T. Shipley. New York: Philosophical Library, pp. 116-
    27.
    Finds the "basic historical affinities" of criticism within
the period to be "Roman and rhetorical" rather than "Greek and
philosophical." Notes three lines of development: the rules of
art are found in the mind rather than in the works of great writers; works are seen as appealing to particular audiences instead
of universally; and the artist is increasingly thought of as creating through imagination and invention, rather than judgment. Refers frequently to Dryden. Reprinted: 1952.8.

3 DeARMOND, ANNA J. "Some Aspects of Character-Writing in the
    Period of the Restoration." Delaware Notes, 16th ser.:55-89.
    Surveys character writing in its various formal manifesta-
tions. Sees Dryden as "incomparably" the greatest writer of characters in poetry during the period.

4 HATHAWAY, BAXTER. "John Dryden and the Function of Tragedy."
    PMLA 58 (September):665-73.
    Sees Dryden as an intermediate figure between two theories
of the function of tragedy: that it "demonstrates the dangers
resulting from action based upon passion," and that it "does and
should increase compassion." Despite the primacy in his time of
the first theory, Dryden leaned toward the second, and therefore
"moved in the direction of the new age."

5 HOOKER, HELENE M. "Dryden's and Shadwell's Tempest." HLQ 6
    (February):224-28.
    Argues for Shadwell's authorship of the operatic version of
The Tempest, based on a variant last line of a Huntington Library
manuscript of Dryden's "Prologue Spoken at the Opening of the
Theatre Royal, March 26, 1674."

*6 HUNTLEY, FRANK L. "The Unity of John Dryden's Dramatic Criti-
    cism, 1664-1681." Ph.D. dissertation, University of Chicago.
    Cited in Latt and Monk, 1976.30. One chapter is reprinted
as 1944.3.

7   LOANE, GEORGE W.   "Notes on the Globe 'Dryden.'"   N&Q 185
     (6 November):272-81.
          Gives many notes and references the Globe Dryden (1870.1)
     lacks. Most are literary allusions and echoes.

8   McMANAWAY, JAMES G.   "Notes on 'A Key . . . to . . . Absalom
     and Achitophel.'"   N&Q 184 (19 June):365-66.
          Gives bibliographical information about the work (1682.3)
     which may help elucidate the contemporary response to Absalom and
     Achitophel.

9   MONTGOMERY, GUY.   "Dryden and the Battle of the Books."
     University of California Publications in English 14:57-72.
          Finds Dryden impossible to classify as either an Ancient or
     a Modern. Notes that he was a Modern in that he judged a work ac-
     cording to its truth to its subject, but that he "was an Ancient
     so far as he turned to the past for support when he needed author-
     ity for what was just in taste, universal in humanity."

10   MUNDY, PERCY DRYDEN.   "The Baptism of John Dryden."   N&Q 184
     (8 May):286; (5 June):352.
          Notes J.M. Osborn's discovery of a transcript of the parish
     register giving Dryden's baptismal record (1940.21).

11   SPENCER, THEODORE.   "Antaeus, or Poetic Language and the Actual
     World."   ELH 10 (September):173-92.
          Uses Dryden as one of two examples of poets who had to find
     their proper language through a process of "poetic self-analysis
     and discipline" (Yeats is the other). Contrasts "Upon the Death
     of the Lord Hastings" and "The Secular Masque" to demonstrate how
     Dryden achieved, over the years, a simplicity closer to the reality
     of actual speech.

*12   STALLMAN, ROBERT W.   "Dryden in Modern Poetry and Criticism."
      Ph.D. dissertation, University of Wisconsin.
           Cited in Latt and Monk, 1976.30. Abstracted in Summaries of
      Doctoral Dissertations, University of Wisconsin 7:302-4.

13   TROWBRIDGE, HOYT.   "Dryden's Essay on the Dramatic Poetry of
     the Last Age."   PQ 22 (July):240-50.
          Reads the work in relation to Essay of Dramatic Poesy. Sug-
     gests through an analysis of its structure that it is best under-
     stood not as a revision of the Essay of Dramatic Poesy but as "a
     supplement, footnote, or appendix." Reprinted: 1977.44.

14   WALLERSTEIN, RUTH.   "Dryden and the Analysis of Shakespeare's
     Techniques."   RES 19 (April):165-85.
          Analyzes All for Love, and suggests its relevance for under-
     standing Dryden's conception of poetry. Asserts that Dryden was
     trying to "realize [passion] in its direct flow, rather than ana-
     lyze it as in Aureng-Zebe." Gives a close reading of Antony's

behavior in the early scenes to suggest Dryden's difficulty in
presenting an emotion (melancholy) which was not conventional in
his time. Discusses Dryden's use of figures, noting and evaluating the effectiveness with which he imitates Shakespeare. Contrasts the characters of Cleopatra, suggesting that Dryden adapted
his Cleopatra to what he could do best ("analytical drama" and
"reflection and logical statement"). Concludes that his attempt
to join what was great in Shakespeare to what was great in the Age
of Reason "doomed the play to essential failure and disunity."
Reprinted: 1966.57.

15 _____. "To Madness Near Allied: Shaftesbury and His Place in
the Design and Thought of Absalom and Achitophel." HLQ 6
(August):445-71.
    Investigates the philosophical and psychological backgrounds
of Dryden's portrait of Achitophel. Finds the English tradition
of the literary character to be primarily concerned with presenting ethical attitudes, especially having to do with the definition
and defense of reason. Traces the development of the idea of the
kinship of great wit and madness through the period, and relates
it to Dryden's political and religious attitudes. Sees the psychological contrast of Achitophel and David as the unifying center of
the poem.

16 WILLIAMS, WELDON M. "The Genesis of John Oldham's Satyrs Upon
the Jesuits." PMLA 58 (December):958-70.
    Notes some close parallels (the use of the name "Corah" and
of a clearly topical biblical parallel) between Absalom and
Achitophel and an aborted draft satire (1678) of Oldham's poem.

1944

*1 CUBBAGE, VIRGINIA C. "The Reputation of John Dryden, 1700-
1779." Ph.D. dissertation, Northwestern University.
    Cited in Latt and Monk, 1976.30. Abstracted in Summaries of
Doctoral Dissertations, Northwestern University 12:10-15.

2 GRIERSON, H.J.C., and J.C. SMITH. A Critical History of English
Poetry. London: Chatto & Windus, 535 pp.
    Surveys Dryden's poetic career, emphasizing his relation to
the development of English poetry. Sees him as a poet, like
Spenser, who "[took up], completed, and combined" the "tentatives"
of his precursors, and whose influence was immediate and continuing
(pp. 172-90). Revised 1947.2.

3 HUNTLEY, FRANK L. The Unity of John Dryden's Dramatic Criticism:
The Preface to Troilus and Cressida (1679). Chicago: University
of Chicago.
    Chapter 10 (pp. 179-212) of the author's doctoral disserta-
tion (1943.6). Reviews the contradictory critical opinion of the

preface. Closely analyzes the piece to show its fundamental originality and unity. Emphasizes Dryden's attempt to find "a criterion
of excellence that . . . accounts for [his] pleasure in reading
Shakespeare and Fletcher," despite the authority of Rymer's neo-
classical criteria. Concludes that Dryden grounds his standards
in the older English poets' treatment of passion.

4   PELTZ, CATHERINE WALSH. "The Neo-Classic Lyric 1660-1725."
     ELH 11 (June):92-116.
          Treats some of Dryden's dramatic lyrics in a study of short
     stanzaic poems. Emphasizes conventional themes and verse forms.
     Concludes that the achievement of the neoclassic lyric is its
     "perfect expression of a restricted, thoroughly familiar subject
     matter in familiar language and verse forms."

5   SCOTT, FLORENCE R. "Lady Honoria Howard." RES 20 (April):
     158-59.
          Brings forward facts which make C.E. Ward's identification
     of her with Honoria in The Rival Ladies unlikely. See 1937.16.

*6   SHERWOOD, JOHN C. "The Source of John Dryden's Critical
     Essays." Ph.D. dissertation, Yale University.
          Cited in Latt and Monk, 1976.30.

7   SMITH, R. JACK. "Shadwell's Impact on John Dryden." RES 20
     (January):29-44.
          Argues that Shadwell, of all Dryden's enemies, influenced
     him most. Discusses Dryden's various replies to, and attacks on,
     Shadwell: shows how often they brought forth significant critical
     statements. Suggests that Dryden's opinion of Jonson declined as
     a result of Shadwell's advocacy, and that his theory of translation
     likewise developed in opposition to Shadwell's opinions.

8   SWEDENBERG, H.T., Jr. The Theory of the Epic in England, 1650-
     1800. University of California Publications in English 15.
     Berkeley and Los Angeles: University of California Press, 407
     pp.
          Examines Dryden's attitudes toward classical theory of the
     epic, particularly his simultaneous respect for the "rules" and
     for the importance of the poet's own reason. Uses many examples
     from Dryden to illustrate attitudes toward major characteristics
     of the epic: fable and action, the moral, unity, the probable and
     marvelous, machines, character, language, and versification. Re-
     printed: 1972.82.

                              1945

1   AVERY, EMMETT L. "A Tentative Calendar of Daily Theatrical
     Performances, 1660-1700." Research Studies (Washington State
     University) 13:225-83.

Lists, with occasional annotation, the date and theater of known performances during the period.

2 BROWN, WALLACE C. "Dramatic Tension in Neoclassic Satire." CE 6 (February):263-69.
Analyzes Absalom and Achitophel (among three other neoclassic examples) to argue that disapproval of neoclassic satire on the ground that it has no dramatic tension is unjustified.

*3 _____. "The 'Heresy' of the Didactic." University of Kansas City Review 11:178-84.
Cited in Latt and Monk, 1976.30.

4 BULLITT, JOHN, and WALTER JACKSON BATE. "Distinctions between Fancy and Imagination in Eighteenth-Century English Criticism." MLN 60 (January):8-15.
Deals briefly with Dryden's treatment of the terms in the preface to Annus Mirabilis; sees this passage as manifesting "a distinct transition from the traditional to the subsequent interpretation of the terms."

*5 BURKE, MARGARET J. "Dryden and Eliot: A Study in Literary Criticism." Ph.D. dissertation, Niagara University.
Cited in Latt and Monk, 1976.30.

*6 CASEY, LUCIAN T. "The Biographies and Biographers of John Dryden." Ph.D. dissertation, Niagara University.
Cited in Latt and Monk, 1976.30.

7 EVANS, G. BLAKEMORE. "A Seventeenth-Century Reader of Shakespeare." RES 21 (July):271-79.
Prints some manuscript notes by an anonymous person writing 1687-c.1689. Contains comments on Religio Laici, Sir Martin Mar-All, Oedipus, and Secret Love.

8 WOODWARD, GERTRUDE L., and JAMES G. McMANAWAY. A Check List of English Plays 1641-1700. Chicago: Newberry Library, 162 pp.
Lists and locates (in fifteen U.S. libraries) editions of individual or collected plays for the period. Contains a section on Dryden (pp. 42-54). See 1949.4 (a "supplement" by Fredson Bowers).

9 WRIGHT, HERBERT G. "Some Sidelights on the Reputation and Influence of Dryden's 'Fables.'" RES 21 (January):23-37.
Surveys eighteenth- and nineteenth-century response to the Fables, emphasizing cases of possible influence.

1946

1 BATE, WALTER JACKSON. From Classic to Romantic: Premises in

Eighteenth-Century England. Cambridge, Mass.: Harvard University Press, 205 pp.
A discussion of decorum as a central neoclassic principle is illustrated by several passages from Dryden's criticism. Reprinted: 1961.2.

2   CARVER, GEORGE. Alms for Oblivion: Books, Men and Biography. Milwaukee: Bruce, 335 pp.
Chapter 9, "Dryden and Plutarch" (pp. 105-11), credits Dryden's introduction to Plutarch's Lives (1683-86) with being "one of the earliest examples of critical biography," and with including the first distinguished discussion of biography as a form.

3   DAVIES, GODFREY. "The Conclusion of Dryden's Absalom and Achitophel." HLQ 10 (November):69-82.
Argues that King Charles suggested both the "object" and the "framework" of the poem, and that he did so after he decided to try Shaftesbury, perhaps in July 1681. Suggests further that he asked to Dryden to "incorporate in his satire the substance of the official defense of the dissolutions of Parliament." Discusses this piece, showing its closeness to the poem. Reprinted: 1966.57.

4   DICKSON, ARTHUR. "Dryden's Absalom and Achitophel, 192-197." Expl 5 (October): note 2.
Suggests, in response to a query, that the lines mean that Heaven would have wanted a song (one of the Psalms) because David would have written it in praise of Achitophel, not God. See 1947.4, 9, 18.

5   FROST, WILLIAM. "Dryden and the Art of Translation." Ph.D. dissertation, Yale University.
Cited in Latt and Monk. 1976.30. See 1955.11.

6   HOEFLING, Sister MARY CHRYSANTHA. A Study of the Structure of Meaning in the Sentences of the Satiric Verse "Characters" of John Dryden. Washington, D.C.: Catholic University of America, 142 pp.
Analyzes and classifies the characteristics of Dryden's sentences in the satiric character portraits, and the relation of these characteristics to the rhetoric of the passages. Concludes that Dryden found a "free and loose" style more useful in narration than the "'closed' style of fully elaborated rhetorical periods."

7   HOOKER, EDWARD N. "The Purpose of Dryden's Annus Mirabilis." HLQ 10 (November):49-67.
Discusses the poem in the context of works earlier in the decade--some of which share its title--which predict or interpret prodigies as judgments upon England. Asserts that Dryden's purpose was "to show that the disasters were merely trials" which "had

served to draw the King and his people together in the bonds of mutual suffering and affection." Analyzes the poem in support of this assertion. Concludes that "Dryden's poem was a piece of inspired journalism." Reprinted: 1966.6, 57; 1976.7.

8 HOOKER, HELENE MAXWELL. "Dryden's Georgics and English Predecessors." HLQ 9 (May):273-310.
   Demonstrates the extent of Dryden's borrowings from other English translators. Categorizes types of borrowing; traces the descent of borrowing from translator to translator, where possible. Points out that "by far the greatest part of his borrowings are confined to rhyme words and phrases," suggesting that he "was glad to dispense with the drudgery of rhyming, preferring to spend his talents on the creation of poetry."

9 HUSTVEDT, SIGURD B. William Andrews Clark Memorial Library: Report of the First Decade, 1934-1944. Berkeley and Los Angeles: Clark Memorial Library, University of California, 85 pp.
   "The Age of Dryden" (pp. 34-42) describes the library's holdings in the 1641-1700 period.

10 KNIGHTS, L.C. "Restoration Comedy: The Reality and the Myth." In Explorations: Essays in Criticism. London: Chatto & Windus, pp. 131-49.
   Reprint of 1937.9. Reprinted: 1966.31.

11 LEGOUIS, PIERRE, ed. and trans. Dryden: Poèmes choisis. Paris: Aubier, 442 pp.
   The introduction (pp. 5-64) summarizes Dryden's career for the general French reader and discusses the poetry, emphasizing its historical contexts and links to French literature. Discusses the problems of translating Dryden into French because of his "dense and elliptic" style, and his vocabulary, which seems similar to that of the modern day, but in fact is not. See 1965.45A.

12 MACDONALD, HUGH. "Banter in English Controversial Prose after the Restoration." Essays and Studies 32:21-39.
   Traces the shift in the tone of controversial prose from abuse to banter. Mentions Dryden's dispute with Sir Robert Howard, and several pamphlets attacking and defending Dryden's heroic plays.

13 MANDACH, ANDRÉ. Molière et la comedie de moeurs en Angleterre (1660-68): Essai de littérature comparée. Neuchâtel: Baconnière, 128 pp.
   Discusses the question of the authorship of Sir Martin Mar-All. Attributes it to the Duke of Newcastle rather than Dryden on internal evidence (pp. 63-80).

14 POTTLE, FREDERICK A. "The Critic's Responsibility." In The Idiom of Poetry. Rev. ed. Ithaca: Cornell University Press, pp. 43-57.
   Reprint of 1941.12. Reprinted: 1963.41.

15   RIBNER, IRVING. "Dryden's Shakespearean Criticism and the Neo-
     Classical Paradox." Shakespeare Association Bulletin 21
     (October):168-71.
          Asserts that Dryden's application of the "rules" to
     Shakespeare, in violation of his own taste, laid the groundwork
     for the collapse of neoclassic criticism.

16   RUSSELL, TRUSTEN W. Voltaire, Dryden, and Heroic Tragedy.
     New York: Columbia University Press, 186 pp.
          Surveys Dryden's works as background to a study of Voltaire's
     debt to him. Emphasizes Dryden's heroic plays and typical atti-
     tudes of his characters. Reprinted: 1966.48.

17   RUST, ISABEL B. "Theory of the Ode Applied to the English Ode
     Before 1700." Ph.D. dissertation, University of Michigan.
          Cited in Latt and Monk, 1976.30. Abstracted in DA 7, no. 1:
     83-85.

18   TROWBRIDGE, HOYT. "The Place of the Rules in Dryden's Criti-
     cism." MP 44 (November):84-96.
          Attempts to "recover [Dryden's] theory of criticism and to
     define its nature, as he himself conceived it." Concludes that
     Dryden's principles were that taste was an improper standard of
     judgment, that objective standards did exist, and that the "rules"
     were not dogmatic or unchangeable. Asserts that the philosophic
     basis of this position exists not in Pyrrhonic or Academic skepti-
     cism, but in the Aristotelean distinction between demonstrative
     and probable proof. "He agreed with Cicero that certainty can
     never be attained in criticism but that probability is a sufficient
     basis for the arts; the rules . . . are tentative or hypothetical
     and are to be accepted with a 'doubtful academical assent.'" Re-
     printed: 1966.57; 1977.44.

19   VAN DOREN, MARK. The Poetry of John Dryden. New York:
     Rinehart.
          Reprint of 1931.38; originally printed 1920.10. Reprinted:
     1960.26.

20   WARD, CHARLES E. "Religio Laici and Father Simon's History."
     MLN 61 (June):407-12.
          Gives new information about Henry Dickinson, the translator
     of the History; suggests that Dryden "was well aware of the
     Critical History before the end of 1681," at least a full year
     before the appearance of Religio Laici. Reprinted: 1966.57.

21   _____. "The Tempest: A Restoration Opera Problem." ELH 13
     (June):119-30.
          Argues against the attribution of the operatic version to
     Shadwell (see 1904.5). Uses several pieces of external evidence;
     argues tentatively that Thomas Betterton was responsible. See
     1947.6.

22 WILLIAMSON, GEORGE. "The Occasion of An Essay of Dramatic Poesy." MP 44 (August):1-9.
Suggests that Sorbière's Voyage to England (1664) provided the occasion. Shows how Sorbière, and Thomas Sprat in his answer to him, raised issues which are central to Dryden's essay. Places the statement of the essay's speakers in relation to points made by Sorbière, Sprat, and Sir Robert Howard. Reprinted: 1960.28; 1966.57; 1969.85.

1947

*1 ALBRAUGH, RALPH M. "Dryden's Liberary Relationships, 1689-1700." Ph.D. dissertation, Ohio State University.
Cited in Latt and Monk, 1976.30.

2 GRIERSON, H.J.C., and J.C. SMITH. A Critical History of English Poetry. Rev. ed. London: Chatto & Windus.
Reprint of 1944.2, with minor correction and updating.

3 GRIFFITH, R.H. "Dryden's Absalom and Achitophel, 192-97." Expl 6 (December): note 17.
Suggests Psalm 109 as the one David wouldn't have written. See 1946.5; 1947.9, 18.

4 HUNTLEY, FRANK L. "Dryden's Discovery of Boileau." MP 45 (November):112-17.
Asserts that Dryden had just come upon, and was now making use of, Boileau's Art poetique in the writing of "The Author's Apology for Heroic Poetry and Poetic Licence" (1677). Examines the similarities between the two pieces: concludes that they hold "the common point of view of universal bon sens against the private bias of the few, a preoccupation with genres, and, in the genre of the epic, an emphasis upon words and thoughts, figures and machines."

5 MIGNON, ELISABETH. Crabbed Age and Youth: The Old Men and Women in the Restoration Comedy of Manners. Durham, N.C.: Duke University Press, 201 pp.
Discusses the old characters in The Wild Gallant and The Assignation (pp. 61-72).

6 MILTON, WILLIAM M. "Tempest in a Teapot." ELH 14 (March): 207-18.
Discusses the controversy over the authorship of the operatic version. Defends W.J. Lawrence's theory that Shadwell wrote the opera (1904.5). Concludes that although it is seriously flawed, Lawrence's theory is "the most believable supposition which has yet appeared." Attacks the argument of C.E. Ward in 1946.21.

7   MONK, SAMUEL HOLT. "Dryden Studies: A Survey, 1920-1945."
    ELH 14 (March):46-63.
        Surveys and evaluates work during the period. Concludes
that "almost everything" remains to be done. Notes especially the
need for a definitive edition of the complete works, further studies of the heroic plays, a treatment of Dryden's influence, a study
of the criticism, and a concordance. Reprinted: 1966.57.

8   MYERS, ROBERT MANSON. "Neo-Classical Criticism of the Ode for
    Music." PMLA 62 (June):399-421.
        Examines the age's standards for evaluating the musical ode.
Cites several examples from Dryden's criticism, and from others'
praise of Dryden's skill at writing words for music. Concludes
that there are "ten distinct qualities required of any perfect ode
for musical setting." Notes that Dryden's two musical odes were
the most popular of all his poems during the neoclassical period.

9   PETTIT, HENRY. "Dryden's Absalom and Achitophel 192-197."
    Expl 5 (June): note 61.
        Suggests 2 Samuel 22 as the song that would have been un-
written. See 1946.5; 1947.4, 18.

10 PINTO, V. de SOLA. "Dryden and Thomas Shipman." N&Q 192:389.
        Notes a resemblance between a figure of speech in Dryden's
dedication of the Fables (1700) and Shipman's "The Virgin" (1677).

11 PRIOR, MOODY E. "Tragedy and the Heroic Play." In The Language
    of Tragedy. New York: Columbia University Press, pp. 154-212.
        Attempts to determine the essential character of heroic
drama. Analyzes Aureng-Zebe and All for Love in detail as characteristic examples of the form at its best. Emphasizes plot, language, and imagery. Notes the propriety of the rhymed couplet for
the typical situations of heroic drama, but praises Dryden's success with blank verse in All for Love. Reprinted: 1950.20 (rev.);
1963.46; 1966.46.

*12 RUNDLE, JAMES U. "The Influence of the Spanish Comedia on
    Restoration Comedy: A First Essay." Ph.D. dissertation,
    University of Cincinnati.
        Cited in Latt and Monk, 1976.30.

13 _____. "The Source of Dryden's 'Comic Plot' in The Assignation."
    MP 45 (November):104-11.
        Identifies Calderón's Con quien vengo vengo as the play's
source. Argues that Scarron's Roman Comique, sometimes linked
with Dryden's play, in fact derives from Calderón. Summarizes
Con quien vengo vengo and shows Dryden's apparent use of it, including several direct verbal borrowings.

14 SCHWEITZER, JEROME W. "Another Note on Dryden's Use of Georges
    de Scudéry's Almahide." MLN 62 (April):262-63.

Argues against Summers's inference (in 1931.33) that Dryden used the episode of Osman and Alibech (in de Scudéry's Ibrahim) in The Conquest of Granada.

15 SNUGGS, HENRY L. "The Comic Humours: A New Interpretation." PMLA 62 (March):114-22.
Asserts that "Jonson, Shadwell, Dryden, and Congreve are on the whole consistent with their expressed purpose" in their presentation of comic humors, and are generally consistent with each other.

16 WALLERSTEIN, RUTH. "On the Death of Mrs. Killigrew: The Perfecting of a Genre." SP 44 (July):519-28.
Contrasts the Hastings elegy and the Killigrew ode to show "Dryden's evolution out of the dying metaphysical age into full neo-classicism." Notes Dryden's ability, even at an early age, to draw together disparate materials into a unified poem, even though the result is "callow." Sees in the later poem a union of "the tradition of the Greek and Latin elegy with the tradition of Donne." Finds the poem "at once illustrative of the grandeur of Dryden's analysis and reconstitution of the great formal genres of literature, and of the thin spiritual air he often had to breathe in his perennial struggle between the fading mediaeval world and the rising world of science and social enlightenment." Reprinted: 1950.26; 1962.21; 1966.57; 1971.42.

17 WESLEY, SAMUEL. Epistle to a Friend concerning Poetry and Essay on Heroic Poetry. Introduction by Edward N. Hooker. Series Two: Essays on Poetry 2. Ann Arbor: Augustan Reprint Society.
The first item is a reprint of 1700.7. Reprinted: 1967.63.

18 ZIMANSKY, CURT A. "Dryden's Absalom and Achitophel 192-197." Expl 5 (March):note 34.
Suggests 2 Samuel 18:33 as the unwritten song. See 1946.5; 1947.4, 9.

1948

1 AVERY, EMMETT L., and A.H. SCOUTEN. "A Tentative Calendar of Daily Theatrical Performances in London, 1700-1701 to 1704-1705." PMLA 63 (March):114-80.
Lists performances by day and theater, with some annotation. Refers to several productions of plays by Dryden.

2 BELJAME, ALEXANDRE. Men of Letters and the English Public in the Eighteenth Century, 1660-1744: Dryden, Addison, Pope. Edited by Bonamy Dobrée. Translated by E.O. Lorimer. London: Kegan Paul, 516 pp.
Translation of 1881.1. Reprinted: 1971.8.

3   BROWN, WALLACE CABLE. <u>The Triumph of Form: A Study of the
     Later Masters of the Heroic Couplet</u>. Chapel Hill: University
     of North Carolina Press, 220 pp.
         Deals with Dryden as the first master of the heroic couplet.
     Stresses the point that he uses the form in a wide variety of kinds
     of poem. Analyzes several poems and passages to suggest the char-
     acteristics of Dryden's mature couplets (pp. 14-31).

*4   CABLE, CHESTER. "Methods of Non-Dramatic Verse Satire, 1640-
     1700." Ph.D. dissertation, University of Chicago.
         Cited in Latt and Monk, 1976.30.

5   ELIOT, T.S. "The Age of Dryden." In <u>The Use of Poetry and
     the Use of Criticism</u>. London: Faber & Faber, pp. 53-65.
         Reprint of 1933.4.

*6   EICH, LOUIS M. "Alterations of Shakespeare 1660-1710: And an
     Investigation of the Critical and Dramatic Principles and
     Theatrical Conventions which Prompted These Revisions." Ph.D.
     dissertation, University of Michigan.
         Cited in Latt and Monk, 1976.30. Abstracted in <u>DA</u> 8, no.
     1:90-91.

7   ELLEDGE, SCOTT. "Cowley's Ode <u>Of Wit</u> and Longinus on the
     Sublime: A Study of One Definition of the Word <u>Wit</u>." <u>MLQ</u> 9
     (June):185-98.
         Briefly links Cowley's ode to Dryden's various definitions
     of wit. Notes that, like Dryden, Cowley first identified wit with
     the sublime, but later came to equate it with decorum. Finds in
     Cowley's association of wit and decorum, as transmitted through
     Dryden, the origin of Pope's view of wit in his <u>Essay on Criticism</u>.

8   FREEMAN, PHYLLIS. "William Walsh and Dryden: Recently Recov-
     ered Letters." <u>RES</u> 24 (July):195-202.
         Discusses the background of two unpublished letters from
     Walsh to Dryden; relates them to two of Walsh's involvements with
     women, and sets them in the context of his friendship with Dryden.

9   GARDNER, WILLIAM B[RADFORD]. "Dryden and the Authorship of the
     Epilogue to Crowne's <u>Calisto</u>." <u>Studies in English</u> (University
     of Texas) 27:234-38.
         Argues that both the text printed by Crowne and that attrib-
     uted to Dryden by his early editors are by Crowne. Suggests that
     the differences between the two texts reflect political censorship.

*10 GOHN, ERNEST S. "Seventeenth-Century Theories of the Passions
     and the Plays of John Dryden." Ph.D. dissertation, Johns
     Hopkins University.
         Cited in Latt and Monk, 1976.30.

11   HERRICK, MARVIN T. "The Place of Rhetoric in Poetic Theory."

Quarterly Journal of Speech 34 (February):1-22.
Cites Dryden as a modern example of a critic who uses rhetorical categories in literary criticism.

12   HUNTLEY, FRANK L. "On the Persons in Dryden's Essay of Dramatic
Poesy." MLN 63 (February):88-95.
Argues that the characters are probably not portraits of real
people but "embodiments of attitude." Shows how each of the tradi-
tional identifications, including Neander=Dryden, is inappropriate.
Reprinted: 1966.57.

*13   LEGOUIS, PIERRE. "A propos de Dryden." Les Langues Modernes
42:A40-A41.
Cited in Latt and Monk, 1976.30.

*14   MERRIN, JAMES T., Jr. "The Theory of Comedy in the Restoration."
Ph.D. dissertation, University of Chicago.
Cited in Latt and Monk, 1976.30.

15   MILES, JOSEPHINE. The Primary Language of Poetry in the 1640's.
University of California Publications in English 19, no. 1.
Berkeley and Los Angeles: University of California Press, 160
pp.
Quantitative analysis of verbal usage of representative major
and minor poets. Devotes several pages to examples from Dryden
(pp. 82-85, 92-94, 116-19). Places Dryden in a group (with Milton,
Waller, and others) which is characterized by a relatively high use
of substantives and epithets. Contrasts this group with another
including Donne, Jonson, and others.

16   MUNDY, PERCY DRYDEN. "The Dryden-Swift Relationship." N&Q
193 (30 October):470-74.
Gives a pedigree of the line of Nicholas Dryden (the poet's
great-uncle) through whom Dryden and Swift were related.

17   NOYES, GEORGE R., and HERMAN RALPH MEAD, eds. An Essay Upon
Satyr (1680), in University of California Publications in
English 7, no. 3. Berkeley and Los Angeles: University of
California Press, pp. 139-55.
Discusses the strange publishing history of a pamphlet, an-
nounced in 1680 and recently found in two American libraries, supposed to be by Mulgrave and Dryden. Shows that it was in fact
written by a "poor but dishonest poet" who published it in 1648
over Cowley's name.

18   OPPENHEIMER, MAX, Jr. "Supplementary Data on the French and
English Adaptations of Calderón's El astrólogo fingido." RLC
22, no. 3:547-60.
Describes Dryden's An Evening's Love, or The Mock Astrologer.
Discusses Dryden's various sources, finding eleven. Argues that
Dryden did not use Calderón's work directly, but relied on French
versions of it.

19   SHERBURN, GEORGE. "The Restoration and Eighteenth Century
      (1660-1789)." In A Literary History of England. Edited by
      Albert C. Baugh. New York: Appleton-Century-Crofts, pp. 699-
      1108.
          Deals with Dryden's criticism (pp. 716-18), his poetry (pp.
      722-32), and his serious plays (pp. 752-56). Argues against sim-
      plistic views of Dryden; stresses his originality and independence.
      Praises his "directness and pungency of expression." Surveys his
      poetic career: notes that the poetry is predominantly occasional.
      Praises the brilliance and eloquence of the style. Summarizes his
      work as a dramatist, dealing almost exclusively with the serious
      plays. Concludes that "his tragedies suffer from the fact that
      they remind us of better things." Second edition: 1967.53.

20   SMITH, JOHN HARRINGTON. The Gay Couple in Restoration Comedy.
      Cambridge, Mass.: Harvard University Press, 263 pp.
          Discusses Secret Love (pp. 55-61), An Evening's Love (pp.
      66-68), Marriage a-la-Mode (pp. 69-71), and Mr. Limberham (pp.
      95-96). Sees these as examples of early "gay comedies." Credits
      Dryden with breaking new ground with the witty couple in Secret
      Love. States that Marriage a-la-Mode "anatomizes the code of the
      period more deeply than . . . any other of his comedies." Re-
      printed: 1971.68.

21   SUTHERLAND, JAMES R. A Preface to Eighteenth Century Poetry.
      Oxford: Clarendon Press, 181 pp.
          Frequently cites Dryden as a pioneer in the concepts of
      poetry which came to dominate the century. Emphasizes his influ-
      ence on poetic diction and questions of decorum.

22   SWEDENBERG, H.T., Jr., and ELIZABETH SWEDENBERG, eds. George
      Stepney's Translation of the Eighth Satire of Juvenal. Berkeley:
      University of California Press for the Clark Memorial Library,
      68 pp.
          The introduction (pp. 1-15) discusses the possibility that
      Dryden had a hand in revising the translation before publication.

23   THOMSON, J.A.K. The Classical Background of English Literature.
      London: George Allen & Unwin, 272 pp.
          Discusses Dryden as an influential interpreter of the clas-
      sics. Concentrates on his use of Latin models, especially Juvenal,
      in satire; on his theory of translation; and on his prose style,
      which has "the classical virtues of definition and lucidity"
      (pp. 201-4, 211-14).

24   TILLYARD, E.M.W. "Dryden: Ode on Anne Killigrew, 1686." In
      Five Poems 1470-1870: An Elementary Essay on the Background
      of English Literature. London: Chatto & Windus, pp. 49-65.
          Briefly analyzes the poem's form. Discusses the poem's
      relevance in five areas: the theological world picture it em-
      bodies, its decorum, what it reflects about Dryden's classicism,

its assurance about the value of the arts, and its use of the heroic convention. Finds in it an affirmation of "faith in the value of good manners and of an ordered way of life." Reprinted: 1955.27; 1963.46.

*25   WIKELUND, PHILIP R. "The Fettered Muse: Aspects of the Theory of Verse Translation in Augustan England, 1640-1750." Ph.D. dissertation, University of California at Los Angeles.
      Cited in Latt and Monk, 1976.30.

26   WILSON, JOHN HAROLD. The Court Wits of the Restoration. Princeton: Princeton University Press, 270 pp.
      Deals primarily with Buckingham, Mulgrave, Rochester, Buckhurst, Sedley, Etherege, and their circles. Refers frequently to their personal and literary relations with Dryden. Gives extended treatment to Dryden's quarrels with Rochester. Reprinted: 1967.64.

*27   WINTERBOTTOM, JOHN A. "Patterns of Piety: Studies in the Intellectual Background of Dryden's Tragedies." Ph.D. dissertation, Yale University.
      Cited in Latt and Monk, 1976.30.

1949

1   ADAMS, HENRY HITCH. "A Note on the Date of a Dryden Letter." MLN 64 (December):528-31.
      Argues that a letter in C.E. Ward's edition of Dryden's letters (1942.12) is wrongly dated. Dryden's letter to William Walsh (17 August 1693) should be dated 20 July 1693.

2   ARTHOS, JOHN. The Language of Natural Description in Eighteenth-Century Poetry. University of Michigan Publications in Language and Literature 24. Ann Arbor: University of Michigan Press, 477 pp.
      Makes copious use of Dryden to illustrate the standardized vocabulary of neoclassic poetry; argues that this vocabulary, when it is used to describe nature, is related "to the language of earlier poetry and scientific literature." Prints an "alphabetical list of certain words found frequently in the English poetry of the eighteenth century," with many examples drawn from Dryden.

3   BEALL, CHANDLER B. "A Quaint Conceit From Guarini to Dryden." MLN 64 (November):461-68.
      Traces the influence of a song of Guarini's, containing the euphemistic sexual sense of "die", down to Dryden's song "Whil'st Alexis lay prest" in Marriage a-la-Mode.

4   BOWERS, FREDSON. Supplement to A Check List of English Plays 1641-1700. Charlottesville: Bibliographical Society of the

University of Virginia, 22 pp.
   The Dryden section deletes two "ghosts" from 1945.8, makes
several corrections, and adds holdings from some American libraries.

5   _____. "Variants in Early Editions of Dryden's Plays." HLB
       3 (Spring):278-88.
   Describes several important variants, and comments on their
significance. Notes some unrecorded minor variants. See 1949.7.

6   BROOKS, HAROLD F. "The 'Imitation' in English Poetry, Especial-
       ly in Formal Satire, Before the Age of Pope." RES 25 (April):
       124-40.
   Discusses the development of the concept of "imitation" in
England before the eighteenth century. Emphasizes, and distin-
guishes among, the theoretical and practical contributions of
Cowley, Denham, Dryden, Rochester, and Oldham. Relates English
to continental imitations, especially those of Boileau.

7   DUNKIN, PAUL S. "The Dryden Troilus and Cressida Imprint:
       Another Theory." SB 2:185-89.
   Suggests a hypothesis about the printing sequence which resulted in five imprints of the 1679 Troilus and Cressida. See
1949.5.

8   KRUTCH, JOSEPH WOOD. Comedy and Conscience after the Restora-
       tion. New York: Columbia University Press.
       Reprint of 1924.5. Reprinted: 1967.33.

9   _____. "Pope and our Contemporaries." In Pope and His
       Contemporaries: Essays Presented to George Sherburn. Edited
       by James L. Clifford and Louis A. Landa. New York: Oxford
       University Press, pp. 251-59.
   Contrasts Dryden with Pope in terms of their relative popularity with twentieth-century students. Concludes that Dryden is
more popular because he is more nearly "metaphysical." Reprinted:
1977.23.

10   PERKINSON, RICHARD H. "A Note on Dryden's Religio Laici." PQ
       28 (October):517-18.
   Cites Gilbert Burnet's identification of the anonymous writer
of a commendatory poem as John Vaughan. Identifies a tract to
which Dryden refers in the Preface.

11   STECK, JAMES S. "Dryden's Indian Emperour: The Early Editions
       and their Relation to the Text." SB 2:139-52.
   Gives the textual history of the play, discussing significant
changes, especially their implications for the genealogy of the
editions.

12   TURNER, W. ARTHUR. "Milton, Marvell, and 'Dradon' at Cromwell's

Funeral." PQ 28 (April):320-23.
Cites a list of those assigned to assemble at Somerset House
for the funeral procession. Thinks it probable that "Dradon" is
the poet.

1950

1 BOWERS, FREDSON. "Current Theories of Copy-Text, with an
Illustration from Dryden." MP 48 (August):12-20.
Discusses various methods of choosing a copy-text and dealing with variants. Concludes that authors usually "concentrated
on substantive revision and [were] content . . . to accept the ac-
cidents [changes in punctuation, spelling, etc.] which normal
printing practice imposed on [their] work." Analyzes the problems
involving different editions of The Indian Emperour to support his
conclusion that the first edition of a work, set from an authoritative manuscript, is the best copy-text. Reprinted: 1969.5.

2 _____. "The First Edition of Dryden's Wild Gallant, 1669."
Library, 5th ser. 5 (June):51-54.
Demonstrates on internal evidence that Macdonald's 72b, not
72a, is the first edition (see 1939.12).

3 BUSH, DOUGLAS. Science and English Poetry: A Historical
Sketch, 1590-1950. The Patten Lectures, Indiana University,
1949. New York: Oxford University Press, 174 pp.
Briefly discusses Dryden (pp. 48-50). Traces the course by
which Dryden's skepticism led to his conversion to Roman Catholicism.

4 BUTT, JOHN. The Augustan Age. Hutchinson's University Library.
New York and London: Hutchinson, 160 pp.
Gives a general treatment of Dryden's poetry, emphasizing
his pioneering work in developing the heroic couplet, the Pindaric
ode, and the philosophic poem (pp. 9-27). States that "above all
he is interested in experiment, in exploring the frontier regions
. . . where satire is near to tragedy." Reprinted: 1966.7.

5 DOBRÉE, BONAMY. Restoration Tragedy. Oxford: Clarendon
Press.
Reprint of 1929.4.

*6 EIDMANS, KATHLEEN M.D. "Dryden's 'Medal,' a Text and a Study."
Ph.D. dissertation, London University (Birkbeck).
Cited in Latt and Monk, 1976.30.

7 ELIOT, T.S. "John Dryden." In Selected Essays. Rev. ed.
New York: Harcourt, Brace, pp. 264-74.
Reprint of 1921.3; 1927.3.

8   GARDNER, WILLIAM BRADFORD. "John Dryden's Interest in Judicial
     Astrology." SP 47 (July):506-21.
         Classifies Dryden's allusions to astrology. Finds that he
     uses astrology four ways: seriously, satirically, humorously, and
     merely for embellishment. Notes that "Dryden's belief in astrology
     has caused him to be severely criticized."

*9   GEIS, WALTER. "Die Anschauungen von den religiösen und
     politischen Ordnungen in der Dichtung John Drydens, dargestellt
     vornehmlich auf Grund der Interpretation der Lehrgedichte in
     Zusammenhang des Gesamtwerkes." Ph.D. dissertation, Frankfurt
     am Main.
         Cited in Latt and Monk, 1976.30.

10   HORSMAN, E.A. "Dryden's French Borrowings." RES, n.s. 1
     (October):346-51.
         Lists French words which Dryden was apparently the first to
     use in English. Analyzes his Gallicisms: concludes that for the
     most part he used words and phrases which had already entered con-
     versation.

11   KAPLAN, CHARLES. "Dryden's An Essay of Dramatic Poesy." Expl
     8 (March): note 36.
         Notes the parallel between the English victory in the Naval
     battle and that in the critical discussion.

*12 KING, ANNE R. "Translation from the Classics during the
     Restoration with Special Reference to Dryden's Aeneis." Ph.D.
     dissertation, Cornell University.
         Cited in Latt and Monk, 1976.30.

*13 KINSLEY, JAMES. "Diction and Style in the Poetry of John
     Dryden." Ph.D. dissertation, Edinburgh University.
         Cited in Latt and Monk, 1976.30.

14   KOSSMAN, H. "A Note on Dryden's 'All for Love,' V.165ff."
     ES 31 (August):99-100.
         Interprets the passage by reference to the scholastic view
     of the soul: finds Dryden guilty of anachronism.

15   LEECH, CLIFFORD. "Restoration Tragedy: A Reconsideration."
     DUJ 42:106-15.
         Assesses the stature of Restoration tragedy, emphasizing
     its morality. Argues that its insistence upon poetic justice
     makes real tragedy impossible, although Dryden comes closest to
     achieving it. Gives examples of the harmful effects of the au-
     thors' straining after extraordinary theatrical and emotional im-
     pact: several of these are from Dryden. Concludes that Restora-
     tion tragedy is no longer viable on the stage. Reprinted:
     1966.31.

16 MacMILLAN, DOUGALD. "The Sources of Dryden's The Indian
Emperour." HLQ 13 (August):355-70.
 Argues that Davenant's "entertainment" The Cruelty of the
Spaniards in Peru (1658) and Purchas His Pilgrimage (1625) are
specific sources. Shows how Dryden's adaptation of historical ac-
counts helped him solve dramaturgical problems.

17 MONK, SAMUEL HOLT. John Dryden: A List of Critical Studies
Published from 1895 to 1948. Minneapolis: University of
Minnesota Press; London: Oxford University Press, 57 pp.
 Lists, as completely as possible, works about, or significant
for, Dryden. Arranged alphabetically by subject. Stars items of
special importance. Revised and enlarged: 1976.30. See 1951.20.

18 NOYES, GEORGE R., ed. The Poetical Works of John Dryden. The
Cambridge Edition. 2d ed. rev. and enl. Boston: Houghton
Mifflin.
 A new edition of 1909.4. Takes recent scholarship into account: the biographical sketch has been revised and expanded,
some poems now thought to be Dryden's have been added, and the
notes have been extensively corrected. The "biographical sketch"
(pp. xvii-lxxii) is in fact an essay on Dryden's literary career,
with many references to the products of twentieth-century scholarship and criticism. Emphasizes the skill of Dryden's technique in
each form he tried. See 1965.45A.

19 PRIOR, MOODY E. "Poetic Drama: An Analysis and a Suggestion."
In English Institute Essays (1949). Edited by Alan S. Downer.
New York: Columbia University Press, pp. 3-32.
 Cites Dryden's critical method as typical of a new spirit
which had a "great and prolonged effect on European drama," for
Dryden judged not only by taste but by reference to critical principles. Uses the debate over rhyme in the Essay of Dramatic Poesy
to illustrate the argument over verisimilitude, in which Dryden
was ultimately on the losing side. Concludes that the desire for
verisimilitude is a major factor in the modern decline of poetic
drama. Reprinted: 1950.20; 1966.46.

20 _____. "Tragedy and the Heroic Play." In The Language of
Tragedy. Rev. ed. New York: Columbia University Press, pp.
154-212.
 Reprint of 1947.11. Reprinted: 1963.46; 1966.46.

21 PURPUS, EUGENE R. "The 'Plain, Easy, and Familiar Way': The
Dialogue in English Literature, 1660-1725." ELH 17 (March):
47-58.
 Attempts to define what was meant by "dialogue" during the
period. Uses Dryden's comment on the impartiality of the form (in
Essay of Dramatic Poesy) as a major example.

22 _____. "Some Notes on a Deistical Essay Attributed to Dryden."

PQ 29 (July):347-49.
  Attributes "Of Natural Religion" (1695) to "A.W." rather
than to Dryden or to Charles Blount.

23 SHERWOOD, JOHN C. "Dryden and the Rules: the Preface of
   Troilus and Cressida." CL 2 (Winter):73-83.
   Argues that the essay is heavily dependent upon French critics, especially LeBossu and Rapin. Asserts that Dryden by this
time (1679) had reconciled his respect for the "rules" and his
love for Shakespeare. Finds the essay sounder and more satisfying
than the Essay of Dramatic Poesy.

24 SMITH, DAVID NICHOL. John Dryden. Clark Lectures on English
   Literature, 1948-49. Cambridge: Cambridge University Press,
   93 pp.
   Consists of four lectures: "Early Verse and Criticism,"
"Plays," "Satires and Religious Poems," and "Translations, Odes,
Fables." "Early Verse and Criticism" emphasizes Dryden's stature
as a pioneer in English criticism. "Plays" deals only with the
heroic plays and tragedies, and includes a comparison of All for
Love and Antony and Cleopatra. "Satires and Religious Poems" again
emphasizes Dryden's innovations, especially in satire. It also relates Religio Laici and The Hind and the Panther to the religious
issues they deal with. "Translations, Odes, Fables" is primarily
appreciative and descriptive. It praises Dryden's openings;
credits the Fables with making Chaucer better known. Reprinted:
1966.52; 1976.55; 1977.41. "Plays" is reprinted in 1968.39.

25 SWEDENBERG, H.T., Jr. "On Editing Dryden's Early Poems." In
   Essays Critical and Historical Dedicated to Lily B. Campbell.
   University of California Publications in English Studies 1.
   Berkeley and Los Angeles: University of California Press, pp.
   73-84.
   Discusses an editor's problems in assessing variants, mostly
in punctuation, among editions during Dryden's lifetime. Notes
that while he expressed irritation at errors introduced during
printing, it is impossible to infer what his own punctuation
standards were. Concludes that the safe procedure is to use the
best state of the first edition as the copy-text.

26 WALLERSTEIN, RUTH. Studies in Seventeenth-Century Poetic.
   Madison and Milwaukee: University of Wisconsin Press, 431 pp.
   Includes an expansion (pp. 115-42) of 1947.16. Treats more
deeply than formerly the structure of the Hastings ode; includes
a brief look at Dryden's late elegiac poems Eleonora and "For a
Fair Maiden Lady." Finds in Dryden, among elegists of the century,
"the most purely formal embodiment of the type of society's lament
for its lost members."

27 WEDGWOOD, C.V. Seventeenth-Century English Literature. London
   and New York: Oxford University Press, 186 pp.

"A short general history." Deals briefly with Dryden; emphasizes how rooted his work is in his time. Claims that he is
closer in spirit to Milton and the metaphysicals than to Pope.
Credits him with having shown "by his example that written English
could <u>appear</u> as spontaneous as spoken." Reprinted: 1961.59;
1977.47.

<u>1951</u>

1   ADAMS, HENRY HITCH. "A Prompt Copy of Dryden's <u>Tyrannic Love</u>."
     <u>SB</u> 4:170-74.
          Describes a copy in the Folger Library; suggests that it is
     a King's Company prompt copy. Discusses its annotations and their
     possible significance for the production.

*2   ADEN, JOHN. "The Question of Influence in Dryden's Use of the
     Major French Critics." Ph.D. dissertation, University of North
     Carolina.
          Cited in Latt and Monk, 1976.30.

3   ANON. "John Dryden, Poet." <u>TLS</u>, 16 February, pp. 93-95.
          A review-article on George Noyes's new edition of the poems
     (1950.18). Emphasizes Dryden's kinship with the poets of the
     Renaissance, especially in the importance he placed on the prin-
     ciple of decorum. Discusses several of the poems in this light.
     Concludes that "his poems form a dogged and brilliant attempt to
     work out the Renaissance conception in a manner which would suit
     the temper of the new age."

*4   ARNOLDT, JOHANNES. "Das Charakterbild des Earl of Shaftesbury
     in der politischen Satire der Restaurationzeit unter Beruck-
     sichtigung des historischen Hintergrundes." Ph.D. dissertation,
     Marburg.
          Cited in Latt and Monk, 1976.30.

5   ATKINS, J.W.H. <u>English Literary Criticism: 17th and 18th
     Centuries</u>. London: Methuen; New York: Barnes & Noble, 394 pp.
          Summarizes Dryden's critical works before 1674, and puts them
     in the context of "the transitional stage" between the Renaissance
     and neoclassicism (pp. 52-69). The main chapter on Dryden ("The
     Father of English Criticism") deals with the remainder of his work
     and evaluates his total contribution. Emphasizes the broadening
     of his critical interests beyond drama; summarizes his statements
     on various literary forms. Concludes that he brought to English
     criticism a "larger and more generous conception" of the critic's
     role: not to find fault but to find excellence.

6   BORINSKI, LUDWIG. <u>Englischer Geist in der Geschichte seiner
     Prosa</u>. Freiburg: Herder, 253 pp.
          Makes frequent use of examples from Dryden in characterizing

classic prose. Contrasts a passage from the preface to <u>Absalom and Achitophel</u> with one from <u>Gulliver's Travels</u>, noting Dryden's directness and Swift's Latinate abstraction.

7   BOWERS, FREDSON. "The 1665 Manuscript of Dryden's <u>Indian Emperour</u>." <u>SP</u> 48 (October):738-60.
      Argues that the manuscript is the most authoritative text extant. Describes its history. Interprets Dryden's revisions in the printed text of 1667. Suggests that a revised publisher's transcript was the printer's copy, and probably also the copy for the 1665 manuscript.

8   BROWER, REUBEN. <u>The Fields of Light: An Experiment in Critical Reading</u>. New York: Oxford University Press, 230 pp.
      In the course of a discussion of the nature of irony, analyzes Dryden's portrait of Corah (Titus Oates) in <u>Absalom and Achitophel</u> (pp. 51-57). Uses the passage to exemplify different types and levels of irony. Notes how much of the impact depends upon a continuity of beliefs between author and audience.

*9   CARTER, ALBERT HOWARD. "The Conception of Character in Dryden and Corneille." <u>SCN</u> 9:58.
      Cited in Latt and Monk, 1976.30.

10   COOKE, ARTHUR L. "Did Dryden Hear the Guns?" <u>N&Q</u> 196 (12 May):204-5.
      Asserts that Dryden, Pepys, and others who commented on hearing, in London, the noise of the Battle of Lowestoft (see the opening of the <u>Essay of Dramatic Poesy</u>) were actually hearing thunder.

*11   DOBBINS, AUSTIN C. "The Employment of Chaucer by Dryden and Pope." Ph.D. dissertation, University of North Carolina.
      Cited in Latt and Monk, 1976.30.

12   FROST, WILLIAM. "Dryden's Prologue and Epilogue to <u>All for Love</u>." <u>Expl</u> 10 (October): note 1.
      Suggests that the "plenteous autumn" now past is the period of Elizabethan and early Jacobean drama, and that the "last age" of the epilogue refers to the same period.

13   HARTNOLL, PHYLLIS, ed. <u>The Oxford Companion to the Theatre</u>. Oxford: Oxford University Press.
      Surveys Dryden's dramatic career. Gives a few details of the stage histories of a few plays. Reprinted: 1957.18; 1967.25.

*14   HOFFMAN, ARTHUR W. "Some Aspects of Dryden's Imagery." Ph.D. dissertation, Yale University.
      Cited in Latt and Monk, 1976.30.

15   HOOKER, EDWARD N. "Pope on Wit: The <u>Essay on Criticism</u>." In

The Seventeenth Century: Studies in the History of English
Thought and Literature from Bacon to Pope, by Richard Foster
Jones et al. Edited by Francis R. Johnson et al. Stanford:
Stanford University Press, pp. 225-46.
Briefly discusses Dryden's definition of wit as "propriety."
Asserts that it implies a "threefold relationship, between thoughts,
words, and subject, effected in such a way that the three elements
appear to belong to one another" (pp. 244-45).

16   HUNTLEY, FRANK L. On Dryden's "Essay of Dramatic Poesy."
     University of Michigan Contributions in Modern Philology 16.
     Ann Arbor: University of Michigan Press, 78 pp.
     Deals with the background, structure, and significance of
the work. Analyzes the argument, in the form of a running commentary, and fits Dryden's arguments on rhyme here and in his
"Defence" of the Essay (1668) to the points of Sir Robert Howard
they were intended to refute. Notes the argumentative nature of
the work, and stresses the importance of the terms "just" and
"lively," used in his definition of a good play, to all his dramatic criticism.

17   JOHNSON, MAURICE. "Dryden's Note on Depilation." N&Q 196
     (27 November):471-72.
     Prints one of Dryden's notes to his translation of Persius's
fourth satire, suppressed by Dryden's editors.

18   JONES, RICHARD FOSTER, et al. The Seventeenth Century: Studies
     in the History of English Thought and Literature from Bacon to
     Pope. Edited by Francis R. Johnson, Majorie H. Nicolson, George
     B. Parks, George Sherburn, and Virgil K. Whitaker. Stanford:
     Stanford University Press, 378 pp.
     Includes Jones's abridgment of 1920.5; reprint of 1940.17.
Also includes 1951.15, 33.

19   JUMP, J.D. "Thomas Philipott and John Dryden. And John Keats!"
     N&Q 196 (8 December):535-36.
     Suggests that Dryden took the phrase "tenement of clay"
(applied to Achitophel) from Philipott's several uses of it. Notes
in passing a possible anticipation by Philipott of some lines by
Keats.

20   KEAST, W.R. "Dryden Studies, 1895-1948." MP 48 (February):
     205-10.
     Adds titles missed by Samuel H. Monk in 1950.17.

21   KNIGHT, DOUGLAS. Pope and the Heroic Tradition: A Critical
     Study of His "Iliad." Yale Studies in English 117. New Haven:
     Yale University Press, 131 pp.
     Treats in several places the extent of Pope's indebtedness
to Dryden. Emphasizes the general value for Pope of Dryden's example in translating a classical epic; notes also specific examples
of borrowing.

22   KORN, A.L. "MacFlecknoe and Cowley's Davideis." HLQ 14
      (February):99-127.
            Argues that there is a close relationship between the poems.
      Analyzes specific examples in which Dryden seems to be explicitly
      or implicitly parodying Cowley. Examines similarities of theme,
      and in the use of biblical overtones. Analyzes several examples
      of biblical allusion in MacFlecknoe in the light of similar pas-
      sages in Davideis. Asserts that MacFlecknoe is Dryden's "genial
      criticism of the neo-classic epic of [his] own period," and that
      it also contains an element of self-satire. Reprinted: 1966.57.

23   LEGOUIS, PIERRE. "Dryden's Letter to 'Ormond.'" MLN 66
      (February):88-92.
            Argues that this letter (dated "The first day of Winter,
      1698") is genuine, and that it is addressed to the Duchess of
      Ormond, not the Duke (as modern annotators have assumed).

24   LEISHMAN, J.B. The Monarch of Wit. London: Hutchinson,
      285 pp.
            Makes several brief references to Dryden. Asserts that in
      his satiric poetry Dryden was really a follower of Donne's: com-
      pares passages from The Hind and the Panther and Donne's Satire II
      to illustrate the point. Five further editions (1955, 1957, 1959,
      1962, 1965) did not alter the Dryden material.

25   LENGEFELD, WILHELM FREIHERR KLEINSCHMIT von. "Ist Shakespeares
      Stil barock? Bemerkungen zur Sprache Shakespeares und Drydens."
      In Shakespeare-Studien: Festschrift für Heinrich Mutschmann.
      Edited by Walter Fischer and Karl Wentersdorf. Marburg:
      Elwert, pp. 88-106.
            Compares the language of Antony and Cleopatra and All for
      Love. Takes Dryden to be the "greatest virtuoso of the baroque
      style," but associates Shakespeare with mannerism. Finds
      Shakespeare a poet of directness and Dryden a poet of reflection
      and sentiment.

26   MARTIN, R.H. "A Note on Dryden's Aeneid." PQ 30 (January):
      89-91.
            Notes how much Dryden has omitted from, and added to, Aeneid
      1. 459-63.

*27   RUSSELL, DORIS A. "Dryden's Relation with His Critics." Ph.D.
      dissertation, Columbia University.
            Cited in Latt and Monk, 1976.30. Abstracted in DA 11:117-18.

28   SALERNO, LUIGI. "Seventeenth-Century English Literature on
      Painting." JWCI 14 (July-December):234-58.
            Briefly discusses Dryden's "Parallel Of Poetry and Painting."
      Links Dryden's association of painting and the theater to Aristotle
      and French theorists of drama (p. 251).

*29 SCHILLING, BERNARD N. "The Man of Letters as Conservative:
     John Dryden." SCN 9:1.
          Cited in Latt and Monk, 1976.30.

*30 SIMPSON, FRIENCH, Jr. "The Relationship between Character and
     Action in Neo-classical Tragedy, with Special Reference to Some
     Tragedies by John Dryden." Ph.D. dissertation, Stanford
     University.
          Cited in Latt and Monk, 1976.30.

31   SÖDERLIND, JOHANNES. Verb Syntax in Dryden's Prose, Part I.
     Essays and Studies on English Language and Literature 10.
     Uppsala: Lundeqvistska Bokhandeln; Copenhagen: Ejnar
     Monksgaard; Cambridge, Mass.: Harvard University Press, 283 pp.
          A "descriptive-analytic" study of Dryden's characteristic
     syntax, with many examples and frequent comparisons with English
     writers before, during, and after his time. Examines how, "by
     means of morphemes and word-order, verb concepts are brought into
     relation with one another and with other concepts, and what the
     nature of these relations is." Concludes that "the main outlines
     of Elizabethan syntax still obtain in Dryden's prose." Suggests
     that Dryden's seeming modernity is a function of his style, not
     his syntax. Part 1 deals with predicate verbs in clauses; part 2
     (1958.30) with "non-finite forms."

32   THOMSON, J.A.K. Classical Influences on English Poetry.
     London: George Allen & Unwin, 271 pp.
          Touches upon the Roman sources of Dryden's poetry, especially
     in satire (pp. 225-29). Finds the influence of Juvenal particular-
     ly apparent. Credits Dryden with an original contribution to sa-
     tire in his character-drawing. Discusses, very briefly, Dryden's
     odes (pp. 142-45) and elegies (pp. 170-71).

33   TILLYARD, E.M.W. "A Note on Dryden's Criticism." In The
     Seventeenth Century: Studies in the History of English Thought
     and Literature from Bacon to Pope, by Richard Foster Jones et
     al. Edited by Francis R. Johnson et al. Stanford: Stanford
     University Press, pp. 330-38.
          Attempts to account for Dryden's greatness as a critic.
     Finds his "paramount critical achievement" in his ability to look
     freshly and objectively at ancient as well as modern literature,
     and in the energetic application of his skill. Reprinted: 1962.46.

34   WHITE, ERIC WALTER. The Rise of English Opera. London:
     Lehman, 335 pp.
          Briefly discusses the contributions of Dryden and others to
     Restoration opera (pp. 37-46). An appendix gives the dates and
     places of the first performances of selected English operas and
     semi-operas, including Albion and Albianus and King Arthur. Also
     gives the same information for "The Secular Masque."

*35   WILCOX, ANGELINE T. "The 'True Critic' in England in the
       Eighteenth Century." Ph.D. dissertation, Northwestern
       University.
            Cited in Latt and Monk, 1976.30.

 36   WILLIAMSON, GEORGE. The Senecan Amble: A Study in Prose From
       Bacon to Collier. Chicago: University of Chicago Press;
       London: Faber & Faber, 377 pp.
            Discusses Dryden's theories and practice in prose. Uses
       selections from his work as major examples of developments in the
       later seventeenth century. Relates his style to the Royal Society's
       approach to language. Examines his treatment of other writers,
       especially Ben Jonson. Traces and analyzes his development of
       relatively conversational, idiomatic style.

 37   WOODHOUSE, A.S.P. "Romanticism and the History of Ideas." In
       English Studies Today: Papers Read at the International Confer-
       ence of University Professors of English held in Magdalen Col-
       lege, Oxford, August 1950. Edited by C.L. Wrenn and Geoffrey
       Bullough. London: Oxford University Press, pp. 120-40.
            Traces the early development of romanticism. Cites Dryden
       as an early proponent of the freedom and power of the imagination
       (pp. 131-32).

                                 1952

*1   ANON. "All for Love." Catholic World 175:393.
            Cited in Latt and Monk. 1976.30.

 2   BOWERS, FREDSON. "The Pirated Quarto of Dryden's State of
       Innocence." SB 5:166-69.
            Argues that the pirate quarto (1695 or later) took its text
       from the most recent printing for the sake of convenience while,
       for purposes of disguise, imitating in certain peculiarities the
       out-of-date fourth quarto (1684). See 1952.14.

 3   BOYS, RICHARD C., ed. Studies in the Literature of the Augustan
       Age: Essays Collected in Honor of Arthur Ellicott Case. Ann
       Arbor: George Wahr for the Augustan Reprint Society.
            Includes 1931.17; 1938.19; 1946.7. Reprinted: 1966.6;
       1976.7.

 4   BROWER, REUBEN. "An Allusion to Europe: Dryden and Tradition."
       ELH 19 (March):38-48.
            Argues that Dryden's work "marks the reaffirmation of 'Europe'
       in English poetry and culture." Demonstrates how Dryden draws on
       classical, Christian, and native traditions for his distinctive
       style. Through an analysis of the portrait of Corah (Titus Oates)
       in Absalom and Achitophel, shows how by using opposing styles and
       levels of diction Dryden is able to appeal to different audiences.

Concludes that "thanks to Dryden the tone of Augustan poetry is less parochial than it might have been: it is resonant with echoes of other literary worlds, or larger manners and events." Reprinted: 1959.6; 1962.21; 1963.46; 1971.42.

5   BUSH, DOUGLAS. English Poetry: The Main Currents from Chaucer to the Present. New York: Oxford University Press, 231 pp.
Treats Dryden as lyricist, as satirist, and as discursive poet in the course of a chapter on "The Age of Reason and Sensibility." Finds his satire his great achievement: Dryden keeps his temper, . . . and his emotional and artistic control intensifies the effect."

6   CALDER-MARSHALL, ARTHUR. "Dryden and the Rise of Modern Publishing." History Today 2 (September):641-45.
Sees Dryden's relationship with Jacob Tonson as the prototype of the modern relationship of author and publisher; surveys Dryden's career as a professional writer.

7   CAZAMIAN, LOUIS. The Development of English Humor. Durham, N.C.: Duke University Press, 421 pp.
Briefly discusses Dryden's use of the word "humour." Notes that his use of "humour" in the modern sense antedates the first OED citation (pp. 396-97). Reprinted: 1965.10.

8   CRANE, RONALD S. "English Neoclassical Criticism: An Outline Sketch." In Critics and Criticism: Ancient and Modern. Edited by R.S. Crane. Chicago and London: University of Chicago Press, pp. 372-88.
Reprint of 1943.2.

9   DAVIE, DONALD. "Dramatic Poetry: Dryden's Conversation-Piece." Cambridge Journal 5 (June):553-61.
Argues that the relaxation of Essay of Dramatic Poesy damages it as criticism. Finds the arguments unfocused and the various intentions of the work in conflict with one another. Suggests that to maintain his realistic fiction Dryden had to make the arguments vague enough not to give offense. Analyzes several arguments in the piece, pointing out their inadequacy.

*10   FEDER, LILLIAN. "John Dryden's Interpretation and Use of Latin Poetry." Ph.D. dissertation, University of Minnesota.
Cited in Latt and Monk, 1976.30.

11   FUJIMURA, THOMAS H. The Restoration Comedy of Wit. Princeton: Princeton University Press, 239 pp.
Cites Dryden frequently, especially his criticism. Uses several of his critical statements and definitions to help establish the theoretical basis of the work. Reprinted: 1968.25; 1978.13.

12   GREENE, DONALD. "'Logical Structure' in Eighteenth-Century
      Poetry." PQ 31 (July):315-36.
           Attacks the commonplace that the period was one in which
      poetry with "logical structure" was paramount. Discusses Absalom
      and Achitophel, The Hind and the Panther, and Religio Laici, argu-
      ing that in fact "the characteristic quality of Dryden's didactic
      poetry . . . is not excellence of logical arrangement but a pleas-
      ing sort of informal, almost anti-logical impressionism."

*13   HAMILTON, MARION H. "Dryden's The State of Innocence: An Old-
      Spelling Edition with a Critical Study of the early Printed
      Texts and Manuscripts." Ph.D. dissertation, University of
      Virginia.
           Cited in Latt and Monk, 1976.30.

14   _____. "The Early Editions of Dryden's State of Innocence."
      SB 5:163-66.
           Establishes the proper order of the first nine editions;
      argues that the ninth (falsely dated 1684) is a piracy. See
      1952.2.

15   JACK, IAN. Augustan Satire: Intention and Idiom in English
      Poetry 1660-1750. Oxford: Clarendon Press, 173 pp.
           Contains chapters on MacFlecknoe (pp. 43-52) and Absalom and
      Achitophel (pp. 53-76). Asserts that MacFlecknoe is a mock-heroic
      poem; defines that term through an analysis of passages in the
      poem. Argues that Absalom and Achitophel is basically a heroic
      poem, with "occasional base details" in the portraits. Analyzes
      the poem in support of this thesis, but points out that the struc-
      ture is not typical of the heroic poem, because it lacks narrative.
      Concludes that the poem's characteristic tone is the result of a
      blend of a "strong element of wit" with a "heroic basis." The
      chapter on MacFlecknoe is reprinted in 1962.21 and 1971.42.

16   JOHNSON, MAURICE. "A Literary Chestnut: Dryden's 'Cousin
      Swift?'" PMLA 67 (December):1024-34.
           Notes the wide currency and significance given over the
      years to Dryden's supposed comment about Swift's future as a writ-
      er ("Cousin Swift, you will never be a poet"). Argues that there
      is no evidence that Dryden ever spoke to Swift; that no persistent
      malevolence toward Dryden can be found in Swift's works or letters;
      that the phrase as it has come down to us was probably formulated
      by Samuel Johnson.

17   JOOST, NICHOLAS. "Poetry and Belief: Fideism from Dryden to
      Eliot." Dublin Review 226, no. 455 (1st Quarter):35-53.
           Defends Dryden's religious belief against the modern charge
      that his appeal to authority in religion inevitably leads to au-
      thoritarianism in politics and literature. Emphasizes Dryden's
      belief in intellectual and artistic freedom.

18   KINSLEY, JAMES. "Dryden's 'Character of a Good Parson' and
      Bishop Ken." RES, n.s. 3 (April):155-58.
           Brings forth several pieces of evidence which suggest that
      Ken was Dryden's original; also suggests that Dryden was given the
      idea by Pepys.

19   KLIGER, SAMUEL. The Goths in England; A Study in Seventeenth
      and Eighteenth Century Thought. Cambridge, Mass.: Harvard
      University Press, 304 pp.
           Briefly treats King Arthur, asserting that the conflict be-
      tween Arthur and his Saxon enemy Oswald reflects the conflict be-
      tween royalism and Saxon democracy (pp. 192-94).

20   KRONENBERGER, LOUIS. "Dryden: The Spanish Friar, Marriage a
      la Mode." In The Thread of Laughter: Chapters on English Stage
      Comedy from Jonson to Maugham. New York: Knopf, pp. 81-92.
           Describes and evaluates the two plays. Praises the serious
      plot of The Spanish Friar and the comic plot of Marriage a-la-Mode,
      while disparaging their other plots. Concludes that Dryden was not
      quite a top class playwright.

*21   MACE, DEAN TOLLE. "English Musical Thought in the Seventeenth
      Century: A Study of an Art in Decline." Ph.D. dissertation,
      Columbia University.
           Cited in Latt and Monk, 1976.30. Abstracted in DA 12:620.

22   MacLEAN, NORMAN. "From Action to Image: Theories of the Lyric
      in the Eighteenth Century." In Critics and Criticism: Ancient
      and Modern. Edited by R.S. Crane. Chicago and London:
      University of Chicago Press, pp. 408-60.
           Analyzes Alexander's Feast as a typical example of "the early
      sublime ode." Shows its similarity to epideictic rhetoric: it
      achieves its purpose of glorifying the power of music by the in-
      direct method of showing its powerful effects (pp. 434-36). As a
      whole the essay sees the neoclassic ode as transitional between
      two concepts of lyric: that the lyric should move men to good,
      and that it should express the poet's soul.

23   NICOLL, ALLARDYCE. A History of English Drama 1660-1900. Vol.
      1, Restoration Drama. Cambridge: Cambridge University Press.
           A revised and expanded version of 1923.4, 1928.10, and
      1940.20. Follows each chapter with a short new chapter, which in-
      corporates new material. Takes note at several points at the up-
      surge in studies of Dryden and the Restoration period, and of the
      positive revaluation of his work, especially in comedy. Two of
      the appendixes, "History of the Playhouses: 1660-1700" and "Hand-
      list of Restoration Plays," have been completely rewritten in the
      light of modern scholarship. Further updated: 1965.45.

*24   PURSER, K.L. "The Exclusion Bill Controversy in Imaginative
      Literature, 1678-1682." Ph.D. dissertation, London University

(King's College).
Cited in Latt and Monk, 1976.30.

*25   RUSHTON, URBAN JOSEPH PETERS. "The Development of Historical
      Criticism in England 1532-1700." Ph.D. dissertation, Princeton
      University.
      Cited in Latt and Monk, 1976.30. Abstracted in DA 12:308.

*26   SINGH, SARUP. "A Study of the Critical Theory of the Restora-
      tion Drama as Expressed in Dedications, Prefaces, Prologues,
      Epilogues and Other Dramatic Criticism of the Period." Ph.D.
      dissertation, London University (University College).
      Cited in Latt and Monk, 1976.30.

27   SMITH, HAROLD WENDELL. "Nature, Correctness, and Decorum."
      Scrutiny 18 (June):287-314.
           Presents Dryden as the major case in the collapse of litera-
      ture after the Elizabethan period. Argues that his career as "the
      first openly professional writer" was governed by a drive for
      bourgeois success in which financial gain and respectability were
      most important. Finds in his critical statements on style symptoms
      of a "seismic" split between "the abstract form" and "the living
      concrete expression of society itself."

28   SOUTHERN, RICHARD. Changeable Scenery: Its Origin and
      Development in the British Theatre. London: Faber & Faber,
      411 pp.
           Alludes briefly to stage directions in The Wild Gallant,
      Albion and Albianus, and The Tempest. Discusses the evidence
      these directions provide about scenery, especially moveable scen-
      ery, in Dryden's time.

29   SPECTOR, ROBERT D. "Dryden's Palamon and Arcite." Expl 11
      (November): note 7.
           Asserts that by reducing Chaucer's four books to three
      Dryden has given the work greater unity.

30   SUCKLING, NORMAN. "Dryden in Egypt: Reflexions on All for
      Love." DUJ 45:2-7.
           Asserts that the play is worthy of comparison with Corneille
      and Racine; that it is a true classical tragedy; that it is a
      tragedy of love such as neither Shakespeare nor Corneille nor
      Racine created, in which we are presented with a love for which
      the world is well lost. Abridged: 1968.39.

                              1953

1   ADEN, JOHN. "Dryden and Boileau: The Question of Critical
      Influence." SP 50 (July):491-509.
           Deals with Dryden's direct contacts with Boileau's work,

his use of Boileau's Longinus, and Boileau's general influence.
Treats the contacts chronologically, but finds in none of them
"acceptable evidence" of Boileau's influence. Examines Dryden's
use of Longinus, concluding that Boileau acted only as a transmitter: the ideas which affected Dryden are all Longinian. Discusses
Boileau's central critical concepts without finding any which seem
to have influenced Dryden, except the idea of adapting classical
satires to contemporary conditions. Concludes that Dryden "ignored
or rejected" much that was characteristic of Boileau.

*2   ANDERSON, AUGUSTUS E. "Theory of Fancy and Imagination in
      English Thought from Hobbes to Coleridge." Ph.D. dissertation,
      Vanderbilt University.
            Cited in Latt and Monk, 1976.30. Abstracted in DA 13:226.

*3   BEVAN, ALLAN R. "Dryden as a Dramatic Artist." Ph.D. disser-
      tation, University of Toronto.
            Cited in Latt and Monk, 1976.30.

4   BOWERS, FREDSON. "Dryden As Laureate: The Cancel Leaf in
      'King Arthur.'" TLS, 10 April, p. 244.
            Records a reference by Dryden to his removal as laureate,
      preserved in one copy in the Bodleian Library (all the others hav-
      ing the reference cancelled). Gives the bibliographic circum-
      stances of the problem and speculates on their causes. Suggests
      that the reference may indicate that the government presented some
      terms for accepting the post which Dryden found unacceptable. See
      1953.26.

5   BRODERSEN, G.L. "Seventeenth Century Translations of Juvenal."
      Phoenix 7 (Summer):57-76.
            Discusses seventeenth-century theories of translation; uses
      Dryden's classification (metaphrase, paraphrase, imitation) as a
      model. Surveys translations of Satires 1, 2, and 10. Finds
      Dryden's translation inadequate, but claims that his alone can
      "stand as an original work."

6   CAMERON, W.J. "An Overlooked Dryden Printing." N&Q 198
      (August):334.
            Claims that a 1697 text of Dryden's verses to Etherege has
      been overlooked, and asks for the matter to be cleared up.

7   EVANS, G. BLAKEMORE. "The Text of Dryden's MacFlecknoe." HLB
      7 (Winter):32-54.
            Studies the relationship between the 1682 and 1684 texts in
      the light of seven manuscripts containing all or part of the poem.
      Collates the 1682 text and the manuscripts with the 1684 text, and
      gives a statistical analysis of variants. Concludes that the 1682
      text has no more (or less) authority than any of the manuscripts,
      and that no temporal relationship among them can be determined.
      Argues that insufficient attention has been paid to the value of

manuscript evidence in determining seventeenth-century texts.
See 1955.8.

8   FOLKIERSKI, WLADYSLAW. "Ut Pictura Poesis: ou l'étrange
     fortune du De Arte Graphica de Du Fresnoy en Angleterre." RLC
     27, no. 3:385-402.
         Summarizes Dryden's preface to his translation of De Arte
     Graphica, finding it an extreme statement of the ut pictura poesis
     position.

9   KINSLEY, JAMES. "Dryden and the Art of Praise." ES 34 (May):
     57-64.
         Studies Dryden's panegyrics, arguing that too much has been
     made of their use of flattery. Asserts that they are better seen
     as occasional poems and exercises of wit. Relates the panegyrics
     to the satires: they provide the heroic ideal against which the
     reality is measured. Reprinted: 1966.57.

10   _____. "Dryden and the Encomium Musicae." RES, n.s. 4
     (July):263-67.
         Links Alexander's Feast to the tradition of encomium musicae.
     Shows how Dryden uses the story of Alexander and Timotheus selec-
     tively to make the illustration of music's effects more complicated
     than was traditional.

11   _____. "Dryden's Bestiary." RES, n.s. 4 (October):331-36.
         Deals with the reliance of The Hind and the Panther on tra-
     ditional beast fable. Shows that each of his animals is not arbi-
     trarily chosen but has antecedents in the tradition.

*12 MOORE, FRANK HARPER. "Dryden's Theory and Practice of Comedy."
     Ph.D. dissertation, University of North Carolina.
         Cited in Latt and Monk, 1976.30. See 1963.31.

13   MORGAN, EDWIN. "Dryden's Drudging." Cambridge Journal 6
     (April):414-29.
         Evaluates Dryden's poetry; examines his strengths and weak-
     nesses in the light of his age's concept of the poet's function.
     Finds in him the characteristic limitation of his period: over-
     emphasis on correctness and refinement. Asserts that he is at
     his best--in All for Love, the satires, and the translations of
     satires--when he is most free of the strictures of literary en-
     vironment. Concludes that Dryden's work demonstrates "the varie-
     ties of effect possible within a narrow and unpromising critical
     view of the poet's function." Reprinted: 1963.46.

*14 MORTON, R.E. "The Prologue and Epilogue in Restoration
     Literature." Ph.D. dissertation, Oxford University.
         Cited in Latt and Monk, 1976.30.

*15 ROMMEL, GEORGE W. "The Concept of France in England in the

Restoration Period." Ph.D. dissertation, Northwestern University.
Cited in Latt and Monk, 1976.30. Abstracted in <u>DA</u> 13:1198-99.

*16 SCHMIDT, KARLERNST. <u>Vorstudien zu einen Geschichte des Komischen Epos</u>. Halle: Niemeyer.
Cited in Latt and Monk, 1976.30.

17 SHERWOOD, JOHN C. "Dryden and the Rules: The Preface to the Fables." <u>JEGP</u> 52 (January):13-26.
Argues that Dryden is not only internally consistent but generally faithful to the neoclassical rules. Analyzes the preface to support his thesis. Shows that most of Dryden's statements on Homer, Virgil, and even Chaucer are not original but firmly based on neoclassical precepts. Maintians that his achievement is in style rather than originality: he applies the rules masterfully, even to unpromising material (as with his treatment of Chaucer).

*18 SINCLAIR, GILES M. "The Aesthetic Function of Rime in Dryden's Work." Ph.D. dissertation, University of Michigan.
Cited in Latt and Monk, 1976.30. Abstracted in <u>DA</u> 13:801-2.

19 SMITH, DANE FARNSWORTH. <u>The Critics in the Audience of the London Theatres from Buckingham to Sheridan: A Study of Neoclassicism in the Playhouse 1671-1779</u>. University of New Mexico Publications in Language and Literature 12. Albuquerque: University of New Mexico Press, 192 pp.
Frequently quotes Dryden on critics in the audience, and on what a critic should be. Discusses <u>The Rehearsal</u> (pp. 38-39); notes a previously unnoticed attack on Dryden in the anonymous "On Mr. Higden's Comedy." Reprinted: 1974.62; 1978.53.

20 SMITH, JOHN HARRINGTON. "Dryden's Prologue and Epilogue to <u>Mithridates</u>, Revived." <u>PMLA</u> 68 (March):251-67.
Presents an annotated text, based on a 1681 printing emended in the margin by Narcissus Luttrell. Argues that Luttrell's changes improve the text, and are likely to be closer to what Dryden intended. Asserts that the study demonstrates how the new [California] edition of Dryden will "add substantially to the findings of its predecessors."

21 SUTHERLAND, JAMES. <u>The English Critic</u>. London: H.K. Lewis for University College, London, 19 pp.
Discusses Dryden (pp. 5-9) as one of four representative English critics. Credits Dryden with having "started a tradition of unpedantic literary discussion" which has persisted in England but is unknown in America.

22 SWEDENBERG, H.T., Jr. "England's Joy: <u>Astraea Redux</u> in Its Setting." <u>SP</u> 50 (January):30-44.

Considers the poem in the light of others on the same occasion, and of the "ideas and sentiments of the day." In its emphasis on joy at the present rather than recrimination for the past
its tone is typical. Also its praise for General Monk, and its
expectation that Charles has benefited from exile, appear in many
other poems. The title "suggests not merely the return of justice
. . . but the return of law and of kingly power."

23 TRICKETT, RACHEL. "The Augustan Pantheon: Mythology and
    Personification in Eighteenth-Century Poetry." Essays and
    Studies 6:71-86.
       Discusses "the way in which mythological characters gave
place to personified abstractions" in the Augustan Age: notes the
strength of the ut pictura poesis concept in the eighteenth century. Quotes Dryden's "Parallel of Poetry and Painting" several
times in support of her thesis. Notes especially how his comments
suggest "the point at which heroic action and pictorial representation can meet" in the figure of a hero, caught just at the moment
of action.

*24 WATSON, GEORGE. "Contributions to a Dictionary of Critical
    Terms: Imagination and Fancy." EIC 3:201-14.
       Cited by George Hammerbacher, 1978.19.

25 WINTERBOTTOM, JOHN A. "The Development of the Hero in Dryden's
    Tragedies." JEGP 52 (April):161-73.
       Compares the heroes of Dryden's tragedies (except All for
Love) to argue that from play to play they progress from social
iconoclasts to embodiments of the social ideal. Before Almanzor
(in The Conquest of Granada) they are iconoclasts; Almanzor develops from one type to the other; Aureng-Zebe confirms the completed development. In his early plays Dryden condemns the anti-
social hero, but recognizes in The Conquest of Granada the
possibility that through education in virtue a hero may change
enough to fit into civilized society.

26 YOUNG, KENNETH. "Dryden as Laureate." TLS, 8 May, p. 301.
       Suggests that the unacceptable "terms" Dryden refers to in
the cancelled statement in the first edition of King Arthur (see
1953.4) may have been political as well as religious.

                              1954

1 ADEN, JOHN. "Dryden and St. Evremond." CL 6 (Summer):232-39.
      Argues that St. Evremond was not a major influence on Dryden.
Notes many specific points on which the two took different views.
Points out that Dryden published his criticism before St. Evremond,
and that his few direct references to him came too late in his
career to be meaningful.

2   COOKE, ARTHUR L.   "Two Parallels between Dryden's Wild Gallant and Congreve's Love for Love." N&Q, n.s. 1:27-28.
    Points out that two key episodes in Congreve's play (1695) closely parallel two incidents in Dryden's (1663).

3   FEDER, LILLIAN. "John Dryden's Use of Classical Rhetoric." PMLA 69 (December):1258-78.
    Discusses the rhetorical theories of Cicero and Quintilian and argues for their influence on the structure and content of Dryden's critical essays. Traces the development of Dryden's characteristic rhetorical stances, arguing that they move from declamatio to oratio. Reprinted: 1966.57.

*4 FINK, JACK E. "St. Evremond in the French and English Critical Traditions." Ph.D. dissertation, Stanford University.
    Cited in Latt and Monk, 1976.30. Abstracted in DA 14:971-72.

*5 FREEDMAN, MORRIS. "Milton and Dryden." Ph.D. dissertation, Columbia University.
    Cited in Latt and Monk, 1976.30. Abstracted in DA 14:109.

6   _____. "A Note on Milton and Dryden as Satirists." N&Q, n.s. 1:26-27.
    Suggests that 1. 200 of MacFlecknoe ("Thy inoffensive satires never bite") refers to Milton's gibe at Bishop Hall in Apology for Smectymnuus ("toothless satires"). Points to "neglected resemblances" between Milton and Dryden as satirists.

7   FUSSELL, PAUL, Jr. Theory of Prosody in Eighteenth-Century England. Connecticut College Monograph 5. New London: Connecticut College, 180 pp.
    Makes several brief references to Dryden. Makes the point that Dryden was typical of his time in believing that the proper English verse had ten syllables, divided into disyllabic feet.

8   GAGEN, JEAN ELIZABETH. The New Woman: Her Emergence in English Drama, 1600-1730. New York: Twayne, 193 pp.
    Uses brief examples from several of Dryden's plays in an examination of learned, witty, and independent female characters.

*9 GAINES, ERVIN J. "Merchant and Poet: A Study of Seventeenth-Century Influences." Ph.D. dissertation, Columbia University.
    Cited in Latt and Monk, 1976.30. Abstracted in DA 14:110.

10 GOODMAN, PAUL. The Structure of Literature. Chicago: University of Chicago Press, 289 pp.
    Analyzes MacFlecknoe (pp. 117-26) in the course of a discussion of comic plots. Emphasizes the role of the narrator, whose "systematic interference" is necessary in poems in which the comic and the serious are mixed. Shows how the narrator puts his point of view through "a series of deflating epigrams." Discusses the

temporal unity of the poem; shows that it has a beginning, middle, and end.

11   HAMILTON, MARION H. "The Manuscripts of Dryden's The State of Innocence and the Relation of the Harvard MS to the First Quarto." SB 6:237–46.
     Analyzes the variants in the five extant manuscripts to establish an ancestral tree. Argues on internal evidence that the Harvard manuscript contains emendations by Dryden, but that the first quarto derives from a missing manuscript which like the Harvard manuscript descends directly from the archetype. Concludes that the first quarto is "clearly the text of highest substantive authority."

12   HAMMOND, H. "'One Immortal Song.'" RES, n.s. 5 (January):60–62.
     Interprets 11. 196–97 of Absalom and Achitophel as referring to Psalm 109, which was believed by many scriptural commentators in Dryden's time to be a violent attack by David upon Achitophel.

*13 HAUN, EUGENE. "The Libretti of the Restoration Opera in English: A Study in Theatrical Genres." Ph.D. dissertation, University of Pennsylvania.
     Cited in Latt and Monk, 1976.30. Abstracted in DA 14:1395.

*14 HOWLING, ROBERT T. "Moral Aspects of Restoration Comedy." Ph.D. dissertation, Pennsylvania State University.
     Cited in Latt and Monk, 1976.30.

15   HUGHES, R.E. "Dryden and Juvenal's Grandmother." N&Q, n.s. 1:521.
     Argues that Dryden's seeming mistranslation of 1. 112 of Juvenal's third satire is a result not of prudery but because he was using a variant text.

16   JEFFERSON, D.W. "Aspects of Dryden's Imagery." EIC 4 (January):20–41.
     Discusses the "mature" imagery of the rhymed heroic plays and the satires, arguing that it is more "metaphysical" than has been admitted. Produces many examples of successful images and groups of images. Traces recurring motifs in the imagery; relates his characteristic imagery to his ideas and those of his time. Also looks briefly at The Hind and the Panther and some of the translations. Reprinted: 1969.40.

17   KINSLEY, JAMES. "A Dryden Play at Edinburgh." Scottish Historical Review 33:129–32.
     Argues that lines in one of the Oxford prologues suggest that The Indian Emperour was produced in Edinburgh during James Duke of York's residence there in 1682.

*18 LILL, JAMES VERNON. "Dryden's Adaptations from Milton,

Shakespeare, and Chaucer." Ph.D. dissertation, University of Minnesota.
Cited in Latt and Monk, 1976.30. Abstracted in <u>DA</u> 14:1214.

*19 MACE, AGNES K. "The Public Verse Epistle from Dryden to Burns." Ph.D. dissertation, Catholic University of America.
Cited in Latt and Monk, 1976.30.

20 MOORE, FRANK HARPER. "Dr. Pelling, Dr. Pell, and Dryden's Lord Nonsuch." MLR 49 (July):349-51.
Argues that Dr. John Pell, not Dr. Edward Pelling, was the person (alluded to in a note by George Steevens to <u>The Rape of the Lock</u>) who believed himself with child, and who therefore may have been the model for Lord Nonsuch in <u>The Wild Gallant</u>.

21 _____. "Heroic Comedy: A New Interpretation of Dryden's <u>Assignation</u>." <u>SP</u> 51 (October):585-98.
Argues that Dryden's purpose was to combine high comedy with "still higher, or heroic comedy." Describes the play's two plots, showing that Dryden raises the level of the comedy above the potential coarseness of his sources. Concludes that the play occupies a middle level between high comedy and the heroic plays, and that Corneille's discussion of "comédie heroïque" may have provided his theoretical basis.

22 RØSTVIG, MAREN-SOFIE. <u>The Happy Man: Studies in the Metamorphoses of a Classical Ideal 1600-1700</u>. Oslo Studies in English 2. Oslo: Akademisk Forlag; Oxford: Basil Blackwell, 496 pp.
Discusses Dryden's translation of Horace's <u>beatus ille qui procul negotiis</u>, noting how its freedom as a paraphrase enables it to reflect Dryden's view of Horace's Epicureanism. Asserts that his translations generally reflect his "Epicurean leanings." Looks at translations from Virgil and Lucretius as well as those from Horace: uses Dryden's translation of 11. 485-86 from <u>Georgics</u> 2 as a "striking" example of how a translation can betray the ideas of its own time.

23 SMITH, JOHN HARRINGTON. "Dryden and Buckingham: The Beginnings of the Feud." <u>MLN</u> 69 (April):242-45.
Argues that the feud began in 1667, with Buckingham's epilogue to his adaptation of John Fletcher's <u>The Chances</u>: the epilogue is an implicit attack on Dryden throughout. Dryden responded in the prologue to a revival of Tomkin's <u>Albumazar</u>, in which he seems to hint that Buckingham is a plagiarist.

24 _____. "Dryden and Flecknoe: A Conjecture." <u>PQ</u> 33 (July): 338-41.
Suggests that Richard Flecknoe angered Dryden by alluding, in the prologue to his <u>Emilia</u> (1672), to excesses in heroic drama.

25   _____. "The Dryden-Howard Collaboration." SP 51 (January):
      54-74.
           Attempts to distinguish Dryden's from Howard's scenes in
      The Indian Queen. Suggests that a study of Howard's The Vestal
      Virgin (1664 or 5) illuminates the problem. Notes possible paral-
      lels between Howard's play and scenes in The Indian Queen. Con-
      cludes that Howard planned the play and assigned about half of it
      to Dryden.

26   TILLYARD, E.M.W. The English Epic and Its Background. Oxford:
      Oxford University Press, 558 pp.
           Discusses Dryden's attitudes toward the epic, and speculates
      about what Dryden's epic, had he written one, would have been like.
      Suggests that the age was unpropitious for the epic because of
      political disillusion and the prevailing philosophical skepticism.
      Asserts that had Dryden written an epic a "profoundly critical
      estimate of human nature and [a] profound belief in honest work
      and achieved culture" would have been at its core. Suggests that
      he decided that he lacked the materials for an epic--a proper sub-
      ject and a proper verse form. Praises his translation of the
      Aeneid. Reprinted: 1966.61.

*27   WEISS, SAMUEL ABBA. "Hobbism and Restoration Comedy." Ph.D.
      dissertation, Columbia University.
           Cited in Latt and Monk, 1976.30. Abstracted in DA 14:114.

*28   WIKELUND, PHILIP. "Restoration Literature: An Annotated
      Bibliography." Folio 19, no. 2:135-55.
           Cited in Latt and Monk, 1976.30.

29   WORTSHORNE, SIMON T. Venetian Opera in the Seventeenth Century.
      Oxford: Clarendon Press, 201 pp.
           Touches briefly on Dryden as typical of the "trend of
      [aesthetic] thought" in the later seventeenth century. Mentions
      as particularly relevant to opera his comment that poetry and
      painting "are not only true imitations of nature, but of the best
      nature, of that which is wrought up to a nobler pitch" ("A Parallel
      of Poetry and Painting").

30   YOUNG, KENNETH. John Dryden: A Critical Biography. London:
      Sylvan Press, 256 pp.
           Relates Dryden's life chronologically, using secondary ma-
      terials. Summarizes many of the more important works as a basis
      for biographical speculation. Reprinted: 1969.86.

                              1955

1   ADEN, JOHN. "Dryden and Swift." N&Q, n.s. 2 (June):239-40.
           Points out possible sources in Dryden for two passages in
      Swift: the clothes allegory in Tale of a Tub (from The Hind and

the Panther), and Swift's attack on Dryden in The Battle of the Books (from the preface to Troilus and Cressida).

2 _____. "Dryden, Corneille, and the Essay of Dramatic Poesy." RES, n.s. 6 (April):147-56.
Attempts to distinguish true from apparent influence. Admits that Dryden is "clearly and rather extensively" indebted to Corneille, but claims that Corneille's influence on Neander's views, when they are distinct from those of the other speakers, is essentially nonexistent.

3 _____. "Shakespeare in Dryden's First Published Poem?" N&Q, n.s. 2 (January):22-23.
Finds an echo of Hamlet in 11. 9-12 of "Upon the Death of the Lord Hastings." Suggests a "reconsideration of the influences at work, however faintly, in Dryden's apprenticeship to poetry."

4 BALDINI, GABRIELE. Teatro inglese della restaurazione e del settecento: Dryden, Otway, Congreve, Farquhar, Gay, Lillo, Goldsmith, Sheridan. Florence: Sansoni.
Translates All for Love (Tutto per Amore), pp. 3-94. The introduction to the anthology (pp. xix-cxx) frequently cites Dryden as example and authority.

5 BERKELEY, DAVID S. "Some Notes on Probability in Restoration Drama." N&Q, n.s. 2 (June):237-39; (August):342-44; (October): 432.
Inquires into "Restoration methods of improbable characterization." Finds these mainly done through the verse medium and the remoteness of action in time and space. Cites Dryden's characterization of the Saxons in King Arthur.

*6 BERNARD, Sister ROSE. "The Character of Dryden in the Twentieth Century." Catholic Educator 25:423-25.
Cited in Latt and Monk, 1976.30.

7 BRINKLEY, ROBERTA FLORENCE, ed. Coleridge on the Seventeenth Century. Durham, N.C.: Duke University Press.
The section on Dryden (pp. 630-33) reprints various published and unpublished comments. Coleridge consistently praises Dryden's craftsmanship. See 1817.1; 1832.1; 1833.2.

8 DEARING, VINTON A. "Dryden's MacFlecknoe: The Case for Authorial Revision." SB 7:85-102.
Uses evidence given by G.B. Evans (in 1953.7) to suggest a sequence of seven early manuscripts and the 1682 and 1684 printed texts. Discusses the theory of authorial revision. Argues that his suggested order may shed light on Dryden's methods of revising.

9 EMERSON, EVERETT H.; HAROLD E. DAVIS; and IRA JOHNSON. "Intention and Achievement in All for Love." CE 17 (November):

84-87.
Argues that the play is at odds with its stated intention
(to show the consequences of unlawful love). Concludes that the
result is not unsuccessful, but full of confusions. Reprinted:
1968.39.

10   FREEDMAN, MORRIS. "Dryden's 'Memorable Visit' to Milton."
      HLQ 18 (February):99-108.
      Suggests that John Aubrey's story about Dryden's visit to
Milton may have come from Dryden himself. Notes that each of the
"prefaces" to Paradise Lost deal with its lack of rhyme, and argues
that Dryden may have written The State of Innocence to show what
could be done on the same topic in rhyme.

11   FROST, WILLIAM. Dryden and the Art of Translation. Yale
      Studies in English 128. New Haven: Yale University Press,
      100 pp.
      Studies and evaluates Dryden's translations, especially from
Virgil and Chaucer. Argues that the theory of translation has
been hampered by false expectations; that a good translator must
not be literalistic but must strive to discover the "pillar sym-
bols" of the original and preserve them. Examines Dryden's treatments of words, lines, couplets, and verse paragraphs, showing how
Dryden is generally able to recreate what is significant in the
original (if not always literally). Discusses the translations
in relation to the heroic and mock-heroic modes of the Augustan
Age; notes the degree to which contemporary poetic, political,
and personal concerns affect the translations. Suggests that
Virgil's themes were closer than Homer's to Dryden's interests.
Concludes that the "official" and "play" modes of Augustan verse
were interdependent: there could not have been The Rape of the
Lock without Dryden's Aeneid. Reprinted: 1969.22.

*12   HADLEY, PAUL E. "Principles of English Literary Translation."
       Ph.D. dissertation, University of Southern California.
       Cited in Latt and Monk, 1976.30.

13   HERRICK, MARVIN T. Tragicomedy: Its Origin and Development
      in Italy, France, and England. Urbana: University of Illinois
      Press, 338 pp.
      Briefly examines "the historical-tragical-comical heroic
play," such as The Conquest of Granada, The Spanish Friar, and Don
Sebastian. Finds this type the final episode in the history of
tragicomedy, carrying on from William Davenant a mixture of French
and native English strains.

*14   HUGHES, R.E. "The Sense of the Ridiculous: Ridicule as a
       Rhetorical Device in the Poetry of Dryden and Pope." Ph.D.
       dissertation, University of Wisconsin.
       Cited in Latt and Monk, 1976.30. Abstracted in Summaries
of Doctoral Dissertations, University of Wisconsin 15:613-15.

15 KER, W.P. "John Dryden." In On Modern Literature: Lectures and Addresses. Edited by Terence Spencer and James Sutherland. Oxford: Clarendon Press, pp. 19-29.

Taken from a written account of classroom lectures at University College, London. Points out that in fact "the classical strain" is not easy to find in Dryden, especially in the plays. Emphasizes Dryden's role as literary innovator, and his variety and flexibility. Tries to account for The Hind and the Panther ("the most extraordinary contradiction of everything one is told about the classical spirit"). Concludes that the beast fable itself is not central to the poem and can be ignored.

16 KINSLEY, JAMES. "Absalom and Achitophel: Literary and Historical Notes." RES, n.s. 6 (July):291-97.

Argues against identifications of characters made by E.S. de Beer in 1941.2. Points out that the biblical parallel is not meant to be complete. Suggests the following identifications: Amnon= Sir John Coventry, Balaam=Theophilus Hastings, Agag=Lord Stafford, Issachar=Thomas Thynne. Can make no positive identification of Caleb. See 1956.10, 19.

17 LAWLOR, JOHN. "Radical Satire and the Realistic Novel." Essays and Studies 8:58-75.

Uses Dryden's identification of the satiric with the heroic as the starting point for a meditation on what happens when it is realized that satire may have no corrective force. Emphasizes Gulliver's Travels.

18 MARKS, EMERSON R. Relativist and Absolutist: The Early Neoclassical Debate in England. New Brunswick, N.J.: Rutgers University Press, 182 pp.

Briefly discusses Dryden as a critic. Finds him to be an absolutist, but one whose absolutism derives from a view of literature itself rather than from authority. Notes also that Dryden was frequently a "relativist of means."

*19 MAURER, A.E. WALLACE. "Dryden's View of History." Ph.D. dissertation, University of Wisconsin.

Cited in Latt and Monk, 1976.30. Abstracted in Summaries of Doctoral Dissertations, University of Wisconsin 15:617-18.

20 MERZBACH, MARGARET KOBER. "The Third Source of Dryden's Amphitryon." Anglia 73, no. 2:213-14.

Claims on internal evidence that Thomas Heywood's The Silver Age is a source (as well as the obvious Plautus and Molière).

21 MILES, JOSEPHINE. "Eras in English Poetry." PMLA 70 (September):853-75.

Uses ten lines from Absalom and Achitophel as part of the evidence for her argument that eras can be distinguished on the basis of sentence structure. Reprinted: 1957.28.

22   MONK, SAMUEL HOLT. "Dryden's 'Eminent French Critic' in a
     Parallel of Poetry and Painting." N&Q, n.s. 2 (October):433.
          Identifies the "eminent French critic" whom Dryden quotes
     in the "Parallel" as André Dacier.

23   PETTIT, HENRY. "'The Pleasing Paths of Sense': The Subject
     Matter of Augustan Literature." In Literature and Science.
     International Federation for Modern Languages and Literatures:
     Proceedings of the Sixth Triennial Congress, Oxford, 1954.
     Oxford: Blackwell, pp. 169-74.
          Examines Alexander's Feast as "a simple lyric exposition of
     the role of sensation in controlling the association of ideas,
     moods, and actions."

*24 PROUDFOOT, L. "Dryden's Aeneis and Its Seventeenth Century
     English Sources." Ph.D. dissertation, Manchester University.
          Cited in Latt and Monk, 1976.30. See 1960.19.

25   RAMSEY, PAUL, Jr. "Dryden's Essay of Dramatic Poesy." Expl
     13 (May): note 46.
          Analyzes the setting of the opening of the work, showing
     how it invokes "a range of relations between the great and the
     small, the permanent and the transient."

26   SYPHER, WYLIE. Four Stages of Renaissance Style: Transforma-
     tions in Art and Literature 1400-1700. Garden City, N.Y.:
     Doubleday, 312 pp.
          The final chapter, "Late Baroque," deals in part with
     Dryden's heroic plays as "a transitional phase in the transforming
     of baroque into late-baroque art," during which the older form re-
     tains its "grandiose proportions and gestures," but moves "into a
     more formal and metrical space or 'scene.'"

27   TILLYARD, E.M.W. "Dryden: Ode on Anne Killigrew, 1686." In
     Poetry and Its Background: Illustrated by Five Poems. London:
     Chatto & Windus.
          Reprint of (retitled) 1948.24. Reprinted: 1963.46.

28   WALTON, GEOFFREY. Metaphysical to Augustan: Studies In Tone
     and Sensibility in the Seventeenth Century. London: Bowes &
     Bowes, 171 pp.
          Treats changes in the nature and definition of wit during
     the century: uses statements by Dryden as major examples. Briefly
     discusses Dryden's possible indebtedness to Cowley in Song for St.
     Cecilia's Day.

29   WHITLOCK, BAIRD W. "Elijah and Elisha in Dryden's MacFlecknoe."
     MLN 70 (January):19-20.
          Annotates the last four lines of the poem, arguing that the
     scriptural context, involving the close relationship of Elisha to
     Elijah, is crucial to their meaning.

1956

*1   BEAUCHAMP, VIRGINIA W. "Dramatic Treatment of Antony and
      Cleopatra in the Sixteenth and Seventeenth Centuries: Varia-
      tions in Dramatic Form upon a Single Theme." Ph.D. disserta-
      tion, University of Chicago.
          Cited in Latt and Monk, 1976.30.

2   BIGGINS, D. "Source Notes for Dryden, Wycherley, and Otway."
     N&Q, n.s. 3:298-301.
          Suggests that a masque in John Fletcher and William Rowley's
     The Maid in the Mill is a source for a similar masque in The Rival
     Ladies.

3   BROSSMAN, S.W. "Dryden's Cassandra and Congreve's Zara." N&Q,
     n.s. 3:102-3.
          Asserts that Cassandra (in Cleomenes) is the prototype for
     Zara (in The Mourning Bride).

4   CAMERON, L.W. "The Cold Prose Fits of John Dryden." RLC 30,
     no. 3:371-79.
          Compares The History of the League and The Life of St.
     Francis Xavier with their originals and with Dryden's original
     prose. Notes that The History of the League is written in a style
     very different from Dryden's, while The Life of St. Francis Xavier
     is written in a similar style. Credits Dryden the translator with
     preserving the style of his original, even when it differs from
     his own.

5   COPE, JACKSON I. "Science, Christ, and Cromwell in Dryden's
     Heroic Stanzas." MLN 71 (November):483-85.
          Notes that Dryden uses a scientific simile to associate
     Cromwell with divinity at a crucial moment in the poem.

*6   CORNELIUS, DAVID K. "The Caustic Muse: A Study in Seventeenth-
      Century Verse Satire." Ph.D. dissertation, Columbia University.
          Cited in Latt and Monk, 1976.30. Abstracted in DA 16:747.

7   CROSS, GUSTAV. "Ovid Metamorphosed: Marston, Webster, and
     Nathaniel Lee." N&Q, n.s. 3:244-45, 508-9.
          Sees an Ovidian influence (through Arthur Golding's transla-
     tion) at one point in Act 5 of Dryden and Nathaniel Lee's Oedipus.

8   DAICHES, DAVID. Critical Approaches to Literature. Englewood
     Cliffs, N.J.: Prentice-Hall, 415 pp.
          Contains a summary and discussion of Dryden's basic critical
     positions (pp. 183-231). Emphasizes the Essay of Dramatic Poesy,
     and also deals with Dryden on Chaucer. Admires the "free play be-
     tween theory and practice" in Dryden's work. Relates his handling
     of various critical problems to other critics and other approaches.

9   DEARING, BRUCE. "Some Views of a Beast." MLN 71 (May):326-29.
        Notes the ambiguity of Dryden's metaphor "Thy chase had a
    beast in view" (in the address to Diana, or King James, in "The
    Secular Masque"). Claims that the metaphor has been increasingly
    misunderstood.

10 de BEER, E.S. "Absalom and Achitophel: Literary and Historical
        Notes." RES, n.s. 7 (October):410-14.
        Replies to James Kinsley (1955.16). Finds his arguments and
    identifications unsatisfactory. See 1941.2; 1956.19.

11 DEMMERY, MORTON. "The Hybrid Critic." Music and Letters 37
        (April):128-40.
        Uses Song for St. Cecilia's Day as his major example in a
    consideration of how criticism can deal jointly with words and
    music. Shows how Handel's music enhances the rhythms of Dryden's
    poetry, although in most circumstances, where lesser talents are
    involved, musical rhythms tend to obscure verbal rhythms.

12 DOBBINS, AUSTIN C. "Dryden's 'Character of a Good Parson':
        Background and Interpretation." SP 53 (January):51-59.
        Notes parallels between the political contexts of Chaucer's
    and Dryden's works. Sees both writers as attacking clergy who
    called for the overthrow of rightful monarchs (Richard II and
    James II). Concludes that in Dryden's view of Chaucer the Good
    Parson "was the clergyman who cherished the established doctrines
    and devoted his attention primarily to the affairs of the spirit."

13 DOBRÉE, BONAMY. John Dryden. Writers and Their Work. London
        and New York: Longmans, 48 pp.
        Surveys Dryden's life and works, with a "select bibliogra-
    phy." Revised: 1961.11.

*14 ELKIN, P.K. "In Defence of Hippocentaurs." Journal of the
        Australasian Universities Language and Literature Association
        5:18-25.
        Cited in Latt and Monk, 1976.30.

15 FREEDMAN, MORRIS. "All for Love and Samson Agonistes." N&Q,
        n.s. 3:514-17.
        Argues that Dryden was greatly influenced by Milton's drama-
    tic poem in writing his play, and that Antony and Cleopatra are
    much closer to Milton's Samson and Dalila than to Shakespeare's
    characters. Suggests that Dryden was following Milton's neoclassic
    guidelines for drama, as laid down in the preface to Samson
    Agonistes.

16 HOOKER, EDWARD N., and H.T. SWEDENBERG, Jr., eds. The Works of
        John Dryden. Volume I: Poems 1649-1680. Vinton A. Dearing,
        textual editor. Berkeley and Los Angeles: University of
        California Press, 430 pp.

The definitive edition. The commentary (pp. 171-369) discusses the nature, circumstances, and significance of each poem, treats its verse (if significant), and gives explanatory and interpretive notes for various words, verses, and passages. Refers frequently to secondary criticism (especially from the twentieth century). Includes extensive textual notes. Further volumes in the "California Dryden" to date: 1962.42 (8); 1966.32 (9); 1969.52 (3); 1970.59 (10); 1971.58 (17); 1972.83 (2); 1974.7 (4); 1974.54 (18); 1976.41 (15); 1978.29 (11); 1979.30 (19). See 1965.45A.

17   HUGHES, LEO. A Century of English Farce. Princeton: Princeton University Press, 313 pp.
      Credits Dryden with being the first critic to treat farce as a form. Also makes several brief references to plays by Dryden. Reprinted: 1979.16.

18   JONES, CLAUDE E. "'The Critical Review' and Some Major Poets." N&Q, n.s. 3:114-15.
      Reviews thirty years of critical opinion in the Critical Review (1756-85). States that during the period critics "did not have a very high opinion of Dryden, apparently on linguistic rather than poetic grounds."

19   KINSLEY, JAMES. "Absalom and Achitophel: Literary and Historical Notes." RES, n.s. 7 (October):414-15.
      Reaffirms his argument against E.S. de Beer. See 1941.2; 1955.16; 1956.10.

20   _____. "The 'Three Glorious Victories' in Annus Mirabilis." RES, n.s. 7 (January):30-37.
      Points out that these victories (in the Second Dutch War) were not victories at all. Shows how Dryden has shaped history to the ends of heroic poetry.

21   LEYBURN, ELLEN DOUGLAS. Satiric Allegory: Mirror of Man. Yale Studies in English, 130. New Haven: Yale University Press, 149 pp.
      Analyzes Absalom and Achitophel (pp. 15-22) and MacFlecknoe (pp. 34-37) as examples of satiric allegory. Notes how Dryden creates a "doubleness of perception" which allows us to understand the application of the satiric allegory independently.

*22 McCOLLUM, JOHN I., Jr. "Dryden's 'Adaptations': The Tragedies." Ph.D. dissertation, Duke University.
      Cited in Latt and Monk, 1976.30.

23   MANIFOLD, JOHN STREETER. The Music in English Drama from Shakespeare to Purcell. London: Rockliff, 217 pp.
      Notes Dryden's heavy use of trumpets in the stage directions to The Conquest of Granada; quotes his defense of drums and trumpets as useful to "raise the imagination of the audience" at a

heroic play. Mentions several instances in which Dryden calls for
or suggests various musical effects in his plays. Argues that
properly contemporary music should be used in modern productions;
suggests that Amphitryon be staged with Purcell's original music.

24   MANLEY, FRANCIS. "Ambivalent Allusions in Dryden's Fable of
     the Swallows." MLN 71 (November):485-87.
          Argues that the complexity of the episode (in The Hind and
     the Panther) reflects the ambivalence of the Catholic attitude
     toward repeal of the Test Act. Concentrates on the Raven's warn-
     ing (3, lines 465 ff.).

*25 MANUEL, M. "The Seventeenth-Century Critics and Biographers of
     Milton." Ph.D. dissertation, Ohio State University.
          Cited in Latt and Monk, 1976.30.

*26 MARSH, ROBERT H. "Major Conceptions of Criticism and Taste in
     England from Dryden to Hume." Ph.D. dissertation, Johns
     Hopkins University.
          Cited in Latt and Monk, 1976.30.

27   MINER, EARL. "Dryden's MacFlecknoe." N&Q, n.s. 3:335-37.
          Suggests possible sources and analogues for lines in
     MacFlecknoe in poems by Abraham Cowley, Edmund Waller, and Elkanah
     Settle.

28   MYERS, ROBERT MANSON. Handel, Dryden, and Milton. London:
     Bowes & Bowes, 158 pp.
          A chapter on "Handel and Dryden" (pp. 17-44) deals primarily
     with Handel. Gives evidence showing how Handel's setting of
     Alexander's Feast enhanced the poem's great popularity during the
     eighteenth century. Appendixes contain the texts of Song for St.
     Cecilia's Day and Alexander's Feast that were used by composers
     Jeremiah Clarke, Thomas Clayton, Handel, and Giovanni Baptista
     Draghi.

29   PADGETT, LAWRENCE E. "Dryden's Edition of Corneille." MLN
     71 (March):173-74.
          Argues that Dryden used the 1660 edition of Trois Discours
     in writing Essay of Dramatic Poesy.

*30 RAMSAY, PAUL, Jr. "The Image of Nature in John Dryden." Ph.D.
     dissertation, University of Minnesota.
          Cited in Latt and Monk, 1976.30. Abstracted in DA 16:2461.
     See 1969.64.

31   SERONSY, CECIL C. "Chapman and Dryden." N&Q, n.s. 3:64.
          Suggests the influence of Chapman's continuation of Hero and
     Leander on the third stanza of Song for St. Cecilia's Day.

32   SPECTOR, ROBERT D. "Dryden's Translation of Chaucer: A Problem

in Neo-Classical Diction." N&Q, n.s. 3:23-26.
Argues that in order to show Chaucer's poetry in its best light (as a superior poet to Boccaccio and Ovid), Dryden chose those tales for translation in which the diction is strongest. Argues against the position that he avoided the fabliaux on moral grounds.

33 STAMM, RUDOLF. "Englischer Literaturbarock?" In Die Kunstformen des Barockzeitalters. Edited by Rudolf Stamm. Berne: Francke, pp. 383-412.
Briefly discusses Dryden as a dramatist, emphasizing his mixing of forms (as in Marriage a-la-Mode) and his reworking of Shakespearean material.

*34 STROUP, THOMAS B. "Type Characters in the Serious Drama of the Restoration with Special Attention to the Plays of Davenant, Dryden, Lee, and Otway." Kentucky Microcards, Series A, 5. Lexington: University of Kentucky.
Cited by John Zamonski in 1975.59.

35 SUTHERLAND, JAMES. "Restoration Prose." In Restoration and Augustan Prose: Papers delivered . . . at the Third Clark Library Seminar, 14 July 1956. Los Angeles: Clark Memorial Library, University of California, pp. 1-18.
Notes, in an overview of the period, how Dryden seems almost always conscious of a friendly reader, often of a specific reader.

36 SUTHERLAND, W.O.S., Jr. "Dryden's Use of Popular Imagery in The Medal." University of Texas Studies in English 35:123-24.
Identifies many images which seem to be drawn from a wide range of contemporary pamphlets and periodicals. Suggests how Dryden adapted these to his purposes by playing upon stock partisan reactions. Notes also the original and reworked materials which elevate The Medal above the level of mediocre party poetry.

37 VAN der WEELE, STEVEN J. "The Critical Reputation of Restoration Comedy in Modern Times." Ph.D. dissertation, University of Wisconsin.
Cited in Latt and Monk, 1976.30. Abstracted in DA 16:344-45.

38 WASSERMAN, EARL R. "Dryden's Epistle to Charleton." JEGP 55 (April):201-12.
Argues that the poem's primary content is political: that the scientific material is presented in political terms and then becomes the vehicle for the political thesis, which is that an elective monarchy (on the Danish model) is a desirable alternative for England. Reprinted: 1959.43; 1963.46; 1979.44.

39 WHEATLEY, KATHERINE E. Racine and English Classicism. Austin: University of Texas Press, 356 pp.

Discusses French influences on Dryden's theory of tragedy (pp. 240-43). Defends Racine against Dryden's complaints about verisimiltude in Phèdre. Suggests Racine's Bérénice as a model for All for Love.

40 ZIMANSKY, CURT A., ed. The Critical Works of Thomas Rymer. New Haven: Yale University Press, 350 pp.
The introduction discusses Dryden's relationship with Rymer, including brief analyses of "Heads of an Answer to Rymer" and "The Grounds of Criticism in Tragedy" (pp. xxxiii-xxxix). The notes and commentary refer frequently to Dryden.

1957

1 ALLEN, JOHN. Masters of British Drama. London: Dobson, 192 pp.
Gives a basic introductory account of the plays. Finds that unlike those of the Elizabethans, the plays of the Restoration do not have the "conscience" of the age "embedded" in them.

2 ALLEN, NED B. "The Sources of Dryden's The Mock Astrologer." PQ 36 (October):453-64.
Argues, with detailed evidence, that Madeleine de Scudéry's Ibrahim is a major, unacknowledged, source.

3 ARBER, AGNES. "Dryden and Cowley." TLS, 7 June, p. 349.
Responds to 1957.8. Suggests that both Dryden and Cowley, in their associations of stars with jelly or slime, were drawing on a folk belief. See also 1957.32.

4 BARBER, C.L. The Idea of Honour in the English Drama, 1591-1700. Goethenburg Studies in English 6. Göteborg: Elanders Boktryckeri Aktiebolag, 364 pp.
Studies the word "honour" in 235 plays, "to give a kind of map of usage during the century." Suggests that the changes represent changes in social values. Draws examples and statistics from many of Dryden's plays.

*5 BLEULER, WERNER. Das heroische Drama John Drydens als Experiment dekorativer Formkunst. Berne: Francke, 118 pp.
Cited by John Zamonski in 1975.59.

6 BOWERS, R.H. "Dryden's Influence on Cuthbert Constable." N&Q, n.s. 4 (January):13-14.
Shows that most of the definitions of literary terms in Cuthbert's unpublished dictionary are taken from Dryden without acknowledgment, thus testifying to Dryden's influence in the early eighteenth century.

7 BREDVOLD, LOUIS I. The Intellectual Milieu of John Dryden.

London: Oxford University Press.
Reprint of 1934.3.

8   BROOKS, HAROLD F. "Dryden and Cowley." <u>TLS</u>, 19 April, p. 245.
Argues for echoes of Cowley, missed by the editors of the
California Edition (1956.16), in several passages in Dryden's
poems. On the passages relating stars to jelly and slime (in
<u>Annus Mirabilis</u>), see also 1957.3, 32.

9   BROSSMAN, SIDNEY W. "Dryden's <u>Cleomenes</u> and Fletcher's <u>Bonduca</u>."
<u>N&Q</u>, n.s. 4 (February):66–68.
Notes the resemblance of Dryden's Cleonidas and Fletcher's
Hengo. Concludes that Dryden probably relied on Fletcher's play
for situations and characterization.

10   CAMERON, WILLIAM J. "John Dryden and Henry Heveningham."
<u>N&Q</u>, n.s. 4 (May):199–203.
Argues that Heveningham, not Dryden, wrote "The Fair
Stranger" (published in 1701).

11   CAZAMIAN, LOUIS, and EMILE LEGOUIS. <u>A History of English
Literature</u>. Translated by Helen Douglas Irvine and W.D.
MacInnes. Rev. ed. London: J.M. Dent.
Revised edition of 1926.3. First edition (in French) 1924.6.

12   COSHOW, BETTY GAY. "Dryden's 'Zambra Dance.'" <u>Expl</u> 16
(December): note 16.
Notes that the song (from <u>The Conquest of Granada</u>) "uses
most of the conventions of love poetry [and] unites them in ritual." See 1959.22.

13   CRINÒ, ANNA MARIA. <u>John Dryden</u>. Biblioteca dell'"Archivum
Romanicum." Serie I: Storia-Lettaratura-Paleografia 50.
Florence: Olschki, 404 pp.
Introduces Dryden's work to Italian readers. Surveys his
life, discusses the influences on him and his chief characteristics
as a writer, and analyzes his major works, genre by genre. Celebrates Dryden as a synthesizer of "the spirit of a society shaped
in an epoch of great historical change." Surveys the course of
Dryden's reputation in Italy (pp. 348–50).

*14 EMSLIE, McDONALD. "The Relationship Between Words and Music
in the English Secular Song, 1622-1700." Ph.D. dissertation,
Cambridge University.
Cited in Latt and Monk, 1976.30.

*15 EVANS, BETTY D. "Dryden's Imagery in His Nondramatic Poetry."
Ph.D. dissertation, University of Oklahoma.
Cited in Latt and Monk, 1976.30. Abstracted in <u>DA</u> 17:1749.

16   FALLE, GEORGE G. "Dryden: Professional Man of Letters." <u>UTQ</u>

26 (July):443-55.
    Celebrates Dryden's great service to professional letters: he upheld the "integrity of literary activity within the social framework." Characterizes his intellectual outlook as one which could assimilate a range of ideas. Suggests that the contradictions in his thought derive from conflicts between his individual responses and his sense of his responsibility to instruct and delight his audience.

*17   GRIFFITH, RICHARD R. "Science and Pseudo-Science in the Imagery of John Dryden." Ph.D. dissertation, Ohio State University.
    Cited in Latt and Monk, 1976.30. Abstracted in DA 17:1072-73.

18   HARTNOLL, PHYLLIS, ed. The Oxford Companion to the Theatre. 2d ed. Oxford: Oxford University Press.
    First edition: 1951.13. Second edition reprinted: 1967.25.

*19   HAUSER, DAVID R. "The Neo-Classical Ovid: Ovid in English Literature, 1660-1750." Ph.D. dissertation, Johns Hopkins University.
    Cited in Latt and Monk, 1976.30.

20   HEMPHILL, GOERGE. "Dryden's Heroic Line." PMLA 72 (December): 863-79.
    Discusses Dryden's "purely metrical variations from the norm of the heroic line, rhymed and unrhymed." Classifies clear variations into twelve types, and examines each, with examples. Makes heavy use of Dryden's own discussions of prosody, and of the practices of poets before Dryden. Concludes that Dryden was careful to match the type and frequency of variations to the elevation of the poem. Reprinted: 1966.57.

21   HOOKER, EDWARD N. "Dryden and the Atoms of Epicurus." ELH 24 (June):177-90.
    Asserts that Religio Laici's ends are essentially political and philosophical. Sees it as a document in a controversy beginning with Martin Clifford's A Treatise of Human Power (1674), which argued the right of every man to decide truth for himself. Analyzes Dryden's critique of rational systems, arguing that he has in mind the atomism of Epicurus and its modern effects, as he saw them in the politics of Shaftesbury and Buckingham. Reprinted: 1963.46; 1966.57.

22   KERMODE, FRANK. "The Poet and His Public: Dryden, A Poet's Poet." Listener 57:877-78.
    Speaks of Dryden's two audiences: the paying public and the "more ghostly audience" of other poets. Concludes that his heroic-comic mode, as in Annus Mirabilis or MacFlecknoe, is really addressed to this second audience.

*23 KORNBLUTH, MARTIN L. "Friendship in Fashion: The Dramatic Treatment of Friendship in the Restoration and Eighteenth Century." Ph.D. dissertation, Pennsylvania State University.
Cited in Latt and Monk, 1976.30. Abstracted in DA 17:361-62.

*24 LAKAS, ROBERT RAYMOND, S.J. "The Hind and the Panther: Dryden's Use of the Three Styles." Ph.D. dissertation, Yale University.
Cited in Latt and Monk, 1976.30.

25 LEES, F.N. "John Dryden." In The Pelican Guide to English Literature. Vol. 4. Edited by Boris Ford. Harmondsworth, U.K.: Penguin, pp. 97-113.
A general survey of Dryden's work. Gives a nonchronological, discursive description of the major works, emphasizing style. Many times reprinted.

*26 MARTZ, WILLIAM J. "Dryden's Religious Thought: A Study of The Hind and the Panther and Its Background." Ph.D. dissertation, Yale University.
Cited in Latt and Monk, 1976.30.

27 MAURER, A.E. WALLACE. "Dryden and Pyrrhonism." N&Q, n.s. 4 (June):251-52.
Cites a passage in Dryden's life of Plutarch which suggests that Dryden might in fact have rejected Pyrrhonism, contrary to the assertions of Louis Bredvold in 1934.3.

28 MILES, JOSEPHINE. Eras and Modes in English Poetry. Berkeley and Los Angeles: University of California Press, 244 pp.
The introduction appeared in an earlier form as 1955.21. "Dryden and the Classical Mode" (pp. 33-47) examines Dryden's most frequent "referential words," "metrical structures," and "sentence structures" to establish a norm for "classic" English style in poetry. Notes that this style has the same traits as the Roman Augustan style. Reprinted: 1976.38.

29 MONTGOMERY, GUY, and LESTER A. HUBBARD, eds. Concordance to the Poetical Works of John Dryden. Los Angeles and Berkeley: University of California Press, 722 pp.
Based on Noyes's edition (1950.18). Lists appearances of words by work and line; does not quote the line. The preface briefly compares Dryden's word frequencies with those of other writers. Notes that his characteristic vocabulary seems to empha- size the heroic and the deliberative. Reprinted: 1967.42.

30 NATHANSON, LEONARD. "The Context of Dryden's Criticism of Donne's and Cowley's Love Poetry." N&Q, n.s. 4 (February): 56-59; (May):197-98.
Discusses the attitude of Dryden and his friend William Walsh toward love poetry as a genre. Both Dryden and Walsh attack Donne and Cowley for their "failure to observe decorum in their

amorous verse" by bringing learning into it. Cites an analogue
to their censure in René Rapin's Réflexions sur la Poétique.

31 PERKINS, MERLE L. "Dryden's The Indian Emperour and Voltaire's
       Alzire." CL 9 (Summer):229-37.
            Argues the significance of Dryden's influence on Voltaire's
    work. Concludes that the structure of Dryden's play allowed
    Voltaire "to adapt the heroic genre to his serious philosophic
    purpose--the discussion of a religious problem within an authentic
    historical context."

32 SCUDAMORE, W.K. "Dryden and Cowley." TLS, 14 June, p. 365.
            Supports 1957.3 in associating "star-slime" (Annus Mirabilis)
    with folk beliefs. Cites Charles Lamb. See 1957.8.

33 SMITH, JOHN HARRINGTON. "Some Sources of Dryden's Toryism,
       1682-1684." HLQ 20 (May):233-43.
            Discusses Dryden's use of his sources for the postscript to
    The History of the League and the first scene of The Duke of Guise.
    Notes a wide range of borrowings, some of them exact (and "un-
    scrupulous by modern standards"). Concludes that Dryden was "far
    more a literary man than a scholar or student of political theory."

34 SPINGARN, JOEL E., ed. Critical Essays of the Seventeenth
       Century. 3 vols. Bloomington: Indiana University Press.
            Reprint of 1909.7. Reprinted: 1963.53.

35 SUTHERLAND, JAMES. On English Prose. Alexander Lectures.
       Toronto: University of Toronto Press, 131 pp.
            Emphasizes the conversational quality of Dryden's prose.
    Argues that the change in prose style associated with Dryden's
    period was not related to the wishes of the Royal Society but to
    the imitation, by writers like Dryden and Halifax, of the conver-
    sation of aristocratic gentlemen.

36 WIMSATT, WILLIAM K., Jr., and CLEANTH BROOKS. Literary Criti-
       cism: A Short History. New York: Knopf, 773 pp.
            Includes "English Neo-Classicism: Jonson and Dryden" (pp.
    174-95) and "Dryden and Some Later Seventeenth-Century Themes"
    (pp. 196-220). Describes and summarizes Essay of Dramatic Poesy:
    praises Dryden's ability, here and elsewhere, "to retain . . . an
    openness to contrary argument almost approaching skepticism."
    Calls his basic belief "probabilist": he admits that total pre-
    cision is not possible in many fields of knowledge. Relates
    Dryden's interest in wit to the shift from comedy of humors to
    comedy of manners. Notes his distinction between comedy and trag-
    edy in terms of tragedy's greater moral responsibility. Remarks
    on his introduction of the term "poetic justice" and (for this
    time) his relative lack of concern for it. Uses Dryden's theory
    of types of translation to introduce the "aesthetic of imitation"
    in the earlier eighteenth century. Many times reprinted.

37   WRIGHT, HERBERT G.   <u>Boccaccio in England from Chaucer to</u>
      <u>Tennyson</u>. London: Athlone Press, 504 pp.
            Describes Dryden's three translations from the <u>Decameron</u>.
      Notes and interprets Dryden's additions and other changes.   Praises
      the quality of his work (pp. 264-77).

                                    1958

1   ALDEN, JOHN.   <u>The Muses Mourn: A Checklist of Verses Occasioned</u>
      <u>by the Death of Charles II</u>.   Charlottesville: University of
      Virginia Press, 78 pp.
            Gives bibliographic description and location of commemorative
      poems.   Includes Dryden's <u>Threnodia Augustalis</u> (in eight different
      editions).

*2   ARNOLD, CLAUDE.   "Reflections of Political Issues in the Plays,
      Prologues, and Epilogues of John Dryden."   Ph.D. dissertation,
      Case Western Reserve University.
            Cited in Latt and Monk, 1976.30.

3   BAWCUTT, N.W.   "More Echoes in Pope's Poetry."   <u>N&Q</u>, n.s. 5
      (May):220-21.
            Points out two parallels between Pope and Dryden:
      <u>MacFlecknoe</u> 1. 84 and <u>Dunciad</u> 5, line 359, and "To . . . the
      Duchess of Ormond," 1. <u>245</u> and <u>Dunciad</u> 5, 67.

4   BIRRELL, T.A.   "Dryden's Library."   <u>N&Q</u>, n.s. 5 (September):409.
            Calls for information concerning books owned by Dryden.

*5   BOLGAR, R.R.   <u>The Classical Heritage and Its Benefactors</u>.
      Cambridge: Cambridge University Press.
            Cited in Latt and Monk, 1976.30.

6   BROWNE, RAY B.   "Dryden and Milton in Nineteenth-Century
      'Popular' Songbooks."   <u>Bulletin of Bibliography</u> 22 (May-August):
      143-44.
            Lists twelve songs by Dryden, and indicates the nineteenth-
      century songbooks in which they appeared.

*7   BUHTZ, GEORG.   "Dryden's moralische Gedankenwelt."   Ph.D.
      dissertation, Hamburg.
            Cited in Latt and Monk, 1976.30.

8   BURTON, K.M.P.   <u>Restoration Literature</u>. London: Hutchinson
      University Library, 240 pp.
            A literary history of the period.   Deals with Dryden through-
      out, discussing his work in different genres.   Claims that "no
      other English writer was consistently successful in so many
      fields."

9   CABLE, WILLIAM G. "Absalom and Achitophel as Epic Satire."
     In Studies in Honor of John Wilcox. Edited by A. Dayle Wallace
     and Woodburn A. Ross. Detroit: Wayne University Press, pp.
     51-60.
         Asserts that Dryden adapted epic devices for use in persua-
     sive satire. Points out epic qualities in the poems. Concludes
     that Dryden established a model for satirists of the Augustan per-
     iod.

10   COPE, JACKSON I. "Dryden vs. Hobbes: An Adaptation from the
     Platonists." JEGP 57 (July):444-48.
         Asserts that Dryden employed arguments used by More and
     Glanvill in his opposition to Hobbes's denial of the existence of
     spirits in nature. Concludes that while Dryden "could experiment
     with Hobbes's central ideas . . . he saw that the aesthetic natur-
     alism was the unpalatable fruit of the philosophic materialism."

11   CRINÒ, ANNA MARIA. Dryden: Poeta satirico. Biblioteca dell'
     "Archivum Romanicum." Serie I: Storia-Litteratura-Paleografica
     55. Florence: Olschki, 137 pp.
         Examines Absalom and Achitophel, The Medal, MacFlecknoe, The
     Hind and the Panther, and the prologues and epilogues. Places
     Dryden in the context of English satire, emphasizing his links to
     Spenser and to the "wits" of his own time. Describes each of the
     works, noting especially its historical background. Concludes that
     satire was the form best suited for what Dryden wanted to express.

12   FREEDMAN, MORRIS. "Dryden's Miniature Epic." JEGP 57 (April):
     211-19.
         Generally examines Dryden's debt, in Absalom and Achitophel,
     to Paradise Lost and Paradise Regained. Suggests that Achitophel's
     temptation of Absalom resembles the comparable scene in Paradise
     Regained more than the one in Paradise Lost. Concludes that
     Dryden's poem meets E.M.W. Tillyard's specifications for a Restora-
     tion epic (as expressed in The Miltonic Setting, Cambridge, 1938).

13   _____. "Dryden's Reported Reaction to Paradise Lost." N&Q,
     n.s. 5 (January):14-16.
         Argues that Dryden's praise of Paradise Lost was neither a
     spurning of rhyme nor a confirmation of blank verse.

*14 GRACE, JOHN WILLIAM. "Theory and Practice in the Comedy of
     John Dryden." Ph.D. dissertation, University of Michigan.
         Cited in Latt and Monk, 1976.30. Abstracted in DA 18:2141.

15   GRIERSON, H.J.C. Cross-Currents in English Literature of the
     Seventeenth Century. New York: Harper, 361 pp.
         Reprint of 1929.6.

16   HAGSTRUM, JEAN. The Sister Arts: The Tradition of Literary
     Pictorialism and English Poetry from Dryden to Gray. Chicago:

University of Chicago Press, 359 pp.
"John Dryden" (pp. 173-209) discusses the significance of painting to Dryden's poetry, concentrating on his practice rather than his critical statements. Examines Absalom and Achitophel as a display of personages dramatically arranged. Sees All for Love as the culmination in Dryden of the classically pictorial: draws a parallel between historical painting and the "pictorially static" characters of the play. Relates Dryden's conception of Antony to paintings on the theme of "The Choice of Hercules." Looks at the "baroque" odes, finding in them the "splendour" and "excesses" of continental art. Part of the discussion of All for Love (pp. 184-197) is reprinted in 1968.39.

17   HOWARTH, R.G. "Dryden's Letters." English Studies in Africa 1 (September):184-94.
Comments on the letters in general, noting that though few and brief, they are "full of interest to the student of the man and his work."

18   KIMMEY, JOHN L. "John Cleveland and the Satiric Couplet in the Restoration." PQ 37 (October):410-23.
Argues for the crucial influence of Cleveland upon Dryden and other Restoration satirists. Uses parallel examples to suggest that Dryden learned how to adapt the couplet to satire from Cleveland.

19   KINSLEY, JAMES, ed. The Poems of John Dryden. Oxford English Poets. 4 vols. Oxford: Clarendon Press.
Provides the first "complete text of Dryden's original poems and verse translations based on a critical review of all the early printings." Includes textual variants with the poems; the commentary is in volume 4. The commentary puts the poems in context, identifies allusions, and elucidates verbal difficulties. See 1965.45A.

20   Le COMTE, EDWARD S. "Samson Agonistes and Aureng-Zebe." EA 11 (January-March):18-22.
Gives several examples of verbal parallels; argues that they are direct borrowings. Concentrates on the Dalila episode in Samson Agonistes.

21   LINDBERGER, ÖRJAN. The Transformations of Amphitryon. Stockholm Studies in the History of Literature 1. Stockholm: Almqvist & Wiksell, 232 pp.
Examines Dryden's Amphitryon to see what he has adapted from other versions, mainly Molière's, and what he has added on his own. Generally finds that he has diminished the story by adding more comic material, some of it in poor taste (pp. 90-102).

*22   McCALL, JOHN JOSEPH. "Gerard Langbaine's An Account of the English Dramatic Poets (1691): Edited with an Introduction and

Notes." Ph.D. dissertation, Florida State University.
Cited in Latt and Monk, 1976.30. Abstracted in DA 18:
1788-89.

23   MAURER, A.E. WALLACE. "Dryden's Bad Memory and A Narrow
Escape." N&Q, n.s. 5 (May):212-13.
Argues that Dryden made an obvious error in his controversy
with Stillingfleet by misrepresenting Lord Herbert of Cherbury on
Henry VIII. Suggests that he escaped a charge of falsification
because Stillingfleet did not notice the error. See 1967.39.

24   _____. "From Renaissance to Neo-Classic." N&Q, n.s. 5 (July):
287.
Compares Ulysses' speeches on degree in Shakespeare's and
Dryden's versions of Troilus and Cressida. Finds in Shakespeare
"the fresh expanding infinitude of the Renaissance" and in Dryden
"the incipient consolidation and definition of Neo-classicism."

25   _____. "The Immortalizing of Dryden's 'One Immortal Song.'"
N&Q, n.s. 5 (August):341-43.
Argues that David's song of thanksgiving in 2 Samuel 22 is
the one meant in Absalom and Achitophel ll. 192-97.

26   MOORE, JOHN ROBERT. "Alexander's Feast: A Possible Chronology
of Development." PQ 37 (October):495-98.
Suggests that Dryden was inspired to use the story of
Timotheus and Alexander by reading Jeremy Collier's "Of Musick"
(1697). Fits this possibility into the traditional chronology of
the poem's composition.

27   _____. "Political Allusions in Dryden's Later Plays." PMLA 73
(March):36-42.
Emphasizes Don Sebastian; identifies political allusions and
relates them to contemporary events. Notes the heavy censorship
his plays underwent from 1689 on. Comments on the political implications of Dryden's relationships with his patrons during this period.

28   MORTON, RICHARD. "'By No Strong Passion Swayed': A Note on
John Dryden's Aureng-Zebe." English Studies in Africa 1
(March):59-68.
Argues that while he is otherwise heroic, Aureng-Zebe is "in
his love less than ideal," since he is swayed by his passion to a
potentially tragic extent. Indicates how the passion/reason theme
is reinforced by the play's imagery.

29   OSBORN, SCOTT C. "Heroical Love in Dryden's Heroic Drama."
PMLA 73 (December):480-90.
Argues that this love is not Platonic, as has been believed,
but is a disease created by an imbalance of humors. Uses Robert
Burton's treatment of "heroical love" in Anatomy of Melancholy to

interpret Dryden's view of it. Shows how in Dryden's plays love
leads to violent and tragic action. Concludes that "the true
basic conflict in Dryden's heroic drama is between passion . . .
and reason."

30   SÖDERLIND, JOHANNES. Verb Syntax in Dryden's Prose, Part 2.
      Essays and Studies on English Language and Literature 19.
      Copenhagen: Ejnar Monksgaard; Cambridge, Mass.: Harvard
      University Press, 259 pp.
          Completes 1951.31. Part 2 deals with "nonfinite" verb forms.

*31   SUTHERLAND, JAMES. English Satire. Clark Lectures. Cambridge:
      Cambridge University Press.
          Cited in Latt and Monk, 1976.30.

32   WASSERMAN, EARL R. "The Meaning of 'Poland' in The Medal."
      MLN 73 (March):165-67.
          Asserts that Dryden identifies the Whigs with the Poles be-
      cause their monarchy was elective. Cites references to the Polish
      system by both Whig and Tory controversialists.

33   WHITE, ERIC WALTER. "Early Theatrical Performances of Purcell's
      Operas: with a Calendar of Recorded Performances, 1690-1710."
      TN 13 (Winter):43-65.
          Includes plays and libretti by Dryden.

34   WILLIAMSON, GEORGE. The Donne Tradition: A Study of English
      Poetry from Donne to the Death of Cowley. New York: Noonday.
          Reprint of 1930.17.

35   WILSON, JOHN HAROLD. All the King's Ladies: Actresses of the
      Restoration. Chicago: University of Chicago Press, 215 pp.
          Credits Dryden with having "perfected the gay couple"; refers
      occasionally to Dryden's contacts with actresses and actors.

36   WINTERBOTTOM, JOHN A. "The Place of Hobbesian Ideas in Dryden's
      Tragedies." JEGP 57 (October):665-83.
          Argues that Dryden's tragedies do not have a Hobbesian basis.
      Examines The Indian Emperour, The Conquest of Granada, Aureng-Zebe,
      and Don Sebastian. Claims that Dryden's heroes express his belief
      that something "akin to Reason as it was traditionally conceived"
      can control the passions. Reprinted: 1966.57.

                              1959

1   ADEN, JOHN. "Dryden and the Imagination: The First Phase."
      PMLA 74 (March):28-40.
          Discusses the development of Dryden's theory of the imagina-
      tion down to 1672. Notes his shifting definitions of such terms
      as "fancy," "imagination," and "wit." Associates the increased

importance given to imagination with the rise of Dryden's career
as an author of heroic plays. Finds the "Essay of Heroic Plays"
(1672) to be the climax of Dryden's increasing belief in the importance of imagination to the creative process.

*2   ALSSID, MICHAEL. "Dryden's Rhymed Heroic Tragedies: A Critical
      Study of the Plays and Their Place in Dryden's Poetry." Ph.D.
      dissertation, Syracuse University.
           Cited in Latt and Monk, 1976.30. Abstracted in DA 20:3281.
      See 1974.1.

3   ALVAREZ, A. "Public Poet." New Statesman 57 (3 January):18-19.
           Discusses the "decline" of Dryden's reputation; suggests that
      the modern age has no taste for "the public voice of poetry," of
      which Dryden was the creator and master. Calls him "the most com-
      petent poet in the language" and "the most unflinchingly sensible."

*4   BEVAN, ALLAN R. "Poetry and Politics in Restoration England."
      Dalhousie Review 39:314-35.
           Cited in Latt and Monk, 1976.30.

5   BORINSKI, LUDWIG. "Ideale der Restaurationszeit." In
      Festschrift für Walther Fischer. Heidelberg: Winter, pp.
      49-64.
           Claims that the heroic ideal is the most characteristic of
      the literature of the period. Discusses Dryden's Don Sebastian
      as well as his early heroic plays.

6   BROWER, REUBEN. Alexander Pope: The Poetry of Allusion.
      Oxford: Clarendon Press, 378 pp.
           Reprint of 1952.4 as one of its chapters. The essay is re-
      printed in 1963.46.

*7   BULLOUGH, GEOFFREY. "The Grand Style in English Poetry." Cairo
      Studies in English 3:9-25.
           Cited in Latt and Monk, 1976.30.

8   CHAMBERS, A.B. "Absalom and Achitophel: Christ and Satan."
      MLN 74 (November):592-96.
           Suggests that Dryden's identification of Achitophel with
      Satan "provides an ironic Christhood for Absalom as well." Notes
      Miltonic passages, especially from Christ's speeches in Paradise
      Regained, which Dryden seems to echo.

*9   CORDER, JIMMIE WAYNE. "The Restoration Way of the World: A
      Study of Restoration Comedy." Ph.D. dissertation, University
      of Oklahoma.
           Cited in Latt and Monk, 1976.30. Abstracted in DA 19:1739.

10   DEARING, VINTON A. A Manual of Textual Analysis. Berkeley and
      Los Angeles: University of California Press, 119 pp.

Uses Dryden's epilogue to Etherege's The Man of Mode as a
sample problem to illustrate a method of textual analysis (pp.
69–72). Also uses the question of authorial revision in MacFlecknoe
(see 1955.8) as an example (pp. 79–86).

11 DOBRÉE, BONAMY. "Dryden's Poems." SR 67 (Summer):519–26.
    An appreciative overview of the poetry, emphasizing Dryden's
craftsmanship.

*12 EBBS, JOHN D. "The Principle of Poetic Justice Illustrated in
     Restoration Tragedy." Ph.D. dissertation, University of North
     Carolina.
         Cited in Latt and Monk, 1976.30. Abstracted in DA 19:2087–
88.

*13 GRIFFIN, ERNEST G. "The Dramatic Chorus in English Literary
     Theory and Practice." Ph.D. dissertation, Columbia University.
         Cited in Latt and Monk, 1976.30. Abstracted in DA 20:3726–
27.

*14 HEATH-STUBBS, JOHN. "Baroque Ceremony: A Study of Dryden's
     'Ode to the Memory of Mistress Anne Killigrew' (1686)." Cairo
     Studies in English 3:76–84.
         Cited in Latt and Monk, 1976.30.

15 HOFFMAN, ARTHUR W. "Note on a Dryden Ode." TLS, 19 June, p.
    369.
        Suggests that by referring to Epictetus's lamp in l. 82 of
the poem Dryden implies that Anne Killigrew has passed a "stern
moral test." See 1959.24.

16 HOLLAND, NORMAN N. The First Modern Comedies: The Significance
    of Etherege, Wycherley, and Congreve. Cambridge, Mass.:
    Harvard University Press, 274 pp.
        Deals with the Davenant–Dryden Tempest (pp. 217–21). Argues
that it "tells us more than all the other [adaptations of Elizabethan plays] about Restoration social comedy, because it is based
upon a view of sex as the source of rivalry and deception that only
learning how to deal with the facts of an imperfect world can reme-
dy."

*17 HOPE-WALLACE, PHILIP. "The Enchanted Island." Time and Tide
     40:708.
         Cited in Latt and Monk, 1976.30.

*18 HOWELL, ELMO H. "The Role of the Critic in the Restoration
     and Early Eighteenth Century." Ph.D. dissertation, University
     of Florida.
         Cited in Latt and Monk, 1976.30. Abstracted in DA 20:1363–
64.

*19   JOOST, NICHOLAS. "Dryden's <u>Medall</u> and the Baroque in Politics and the Arts." <u>Modern Age</u> 3:148–55.
Cited in Latt and Monk, 1976.30.

*20   KANE, Sister MARY FRANZITA. "John Dryden's Doctrine of <u>Wit</u> as <u>Propriety</u>: A Study of the Terms and Relations Involved in the Definition of 1677." Ph.D. dissertation, University of Notre Dame.
Cited in Latt and Monk, 1976.30. Abstracted in <u>DA</u> 19:1741.

*21   KING, BRUCE. "Dryden's Treatment of Ideas and Themes in His Dramatic Works, with Some Reference to the Intellectual Movement of His Time." Ph.D. dissertation, Leeds University.
Cited in Latt and Monk, 1976.30.

22   _____. "Dryden's Zambra Dance." <u>Expl</u> 18 (December): note 18.
Argues that the song's source is in Hobbes's <u>Leviathan</u>.
See 1957.12.

23   KOLB, GWIN J. "Johnson Echoes Dryden." <u>MLN</u> 74 (March):212–13.
Suggests that 11. 295-98 of "The Vanity of Human Wishes" echo two lines in <u>The State of Innocence</u>.

24   LEGOUIS, PIERRE. "Note on a Dryden Ode." <u>TLS</u>, 3 July, p. 399.
Complains that he has priority on the point made by Arthur Hoffman in 1959.15. Suggests that American and British scholars should consult foreign-language criticism more frequently.

25   LOWENS, IRVING. "St. Evremond, Dryden, and the Theory of Opera." <u>Criticism</u> 1 (Summer):226–48.
Discusses St. Evremond's letter to Buckingham on opera (1677), and Dryden's various statements on opera as well as his practice in <u>Albion and Albianus</u>. Praises St. Evremond, and disparages Dryden for shoddiness and inconsistency. Argues that Dryden's views on opera were not influenced by St. Evremond.

26   McARTHUR, HERBERT. "Romeo's Loquacious Friend." <u>SQ</u> 10 (Winter):35–44.
Discusses Dryden's comments on Mercutio (in "Defence of the Epilogue"), and subsequent critics' quotation and misquotation of it, as a prelude to a general treatment of the character.

*27   MAGOON, J. "Dryden and the Language of Poetry." Ph.D. dissertation, Swansea University.
Cited in Latt and Monk, 1976.30.

28   MAURER, A.E. WALLACE. "Dryden's <u>Absalom and Achitophel</u>, 745–746." <u>Expl</u> 17 (May): note 56.
Argues that "specious" in 1. 746 must carry "the positive meaning of resplendent winsomeness," despite the <u>OED</u> use of this line as an example of the modern negative sense. See 1961.32.

29 _____. "Dryden's Balaam Well Hung?" <u>RES</u>, n.s. 10 (November): 398-401.
   Suggests that Balaam (<u>Absalom and Achitophel</u>, 1. 574) is Sir Francis Winnington.

30 _____. "Dryden's Knowledge of Historians, Ancient and Modern." <u>N&Q</u>, n.s. 6 (July-August):264-66.
   Credits Dryden with a wide knowledge of historians. Suggests that he used ancient historians in support of conservative judgments, and modern historians "in the lively contentiousness of contemporary political and religious polemic."

*31 MUIR, KENNETH. "Three Shakespeare Adaptations." <u>PLPLS-LHS</u> 8:233-40.
   Cited in Latt and Monk, 1976.30.

32 NÄNNY, MAX. <u>John Drydens rhetorische Poetik: Versuch eines Aufbaus aus seinem kritischen Schaffen</u>. Schweizer Anglistische Arbeiten 49. Berne: Franke, 118 pp.
   Attempts to establish Dryden's basic critical principles. Finds these to be related to classical rhetoric; classifies the critical works and stances on the basis of the three divisions of rhetoric (demonstrative, deliberative, judicial).

33 O'REGAN, M.J. "Two Notes on French Reminiscences in Restoration Comedy." <u>Hermathena</u> 93 (May):63-70.
   Notes that Dryden's character Damon in <u>An Evening's Love</u> is very similar to Molière's Alceste in <u>Le Misanthrope</u>.

*34 PARK, HUGH W. "Revenge in Restoration Tragedy." Ph.D. dissertation, University of Utah.
   Cited in Latt and Monk, 1976.30. Abstracted in <u>DA</u> 20:1097-98.

*35 POLLARD, ARTHUR. "Five Poets on Religion: 1. Dryden, Pope, and Young." <u>Church Quarterly Review</u> 160:352-62.
   Cited in Latt and Monk, 1976.30.

36 RALLI, AUGUSTUS. <u>A History of Shakespeare Criticism</u>. New York: Humanities Press.
   Reprint of 1932.21.

*37 ROMAGOSA, Sister EDWARD, O. Carm. "A Compendium of the Opinions of John Dryden." Ph.D. dissertation, Tulane University.
   Cited in Latt and Monk, 1976.30. Abstracted in <u>DA</u> 19:3296.

*38 SELLERS, WILLIAM H. "Literary Controversies Among Restoration Dramatists, 1660-1685." Ph.D. dissertation, Ohio State University.
   Cited in Latt and Monk, 1976.30. Abstracted in <u>DA</u> 20:3306-08.

*39   SIMON, IRENE. "'Pride of Reason' in the Restoration and
Earlier Eighteenth Century." RLV 25:375-96, 453-73.
      Cited in Latt and Monk, 1976.30.

*40   SPINGARN, EDWARD. "The Restoration Heroic Play." Ph.D. dis-
sertation, Columbia University.
      Cited in Latt and Monk, 1976.30. Abstracted in DA 20:3732-
33.

41   STRANG, BARBARA M.H. "Dryden's Innovations in Critical Vocabulary." DUJ, n.s. 20 (June):114-23.
      Looks at critical terms thought by the OED to have been in-
troduced by Dryden. Notes also terms wrongly attributed to him,
and terms used by him before the OED's first citation.

42   TILLYARD, E.M.W. Poetry Direct and Oblique. New York: Barnes
& Noble.
      Reprint of 1934.18.

43   WASSERMAN, EARL. The Subtler Language. Baltimore: Johns
Hopkins University Press.
      Includes 1956.38, which is also later reprinted in 1963.46.
The book is reprinted (1979.44).

1960

1   AVERY, EMMETT L., ed. The London Stage 1660-1800. Part 2:
1700-1729. 2 vols. Carbondale: Southern Illinois University
Press.
      Includes dates and places of productions of plays by Dryden
during the period, with available information about the cast. For
other parts see 1961.47 (Part 3); 1962.44 (Part 4); 1965.56 (Part
1); 1968.37 (Part 5).

*2   BAIZER, ASHER. "The Theory of Imitation in English Neoclassical
Criticism." Ph.D. dissertation, New York University.
      Cited in Latt and Monk, 1976.30. Abstracted in DA 20:194.

*3   BENSON, DONALD R. "John Dryden and the Church of England: The
Conversion and the Problem of Authority in the Seventeenth Century." Ph.D. dissertation, University of Kansas.
      Cited in Latt and Monk, 1976.30. Abstracted in DA 20:4106-7.

4   CAMERON, W.J. John Dryden in New Zealand: An Account of Early
Editions . . . Found in Various Libraries Throughout New Zealand.
Library School Bulletin 1. Wellington: Wellington Library
School, 32 pp.
      Gives a bibliographical description of, and locates, volumes
published in the seventeenth and eighteenth centuries.

*5 CULIOLI, ANTOINE. "Dryden, traducteur et adaptateur de Chaucer et de Bocace." Ph.D. dissertation, Sorbonne.
     Cited in Latt and Monk, 1976.30.

6 DAICHES, DAVID. A Critical History of English Literature. 2 vols. New York: Ronald Press, 1177 pp.
     "The Restoration" (pp. 537-89) deals with Dryden throughout. Emphasizes the poetry: summarizes and comments on the major (and some minor) poems chronologically.

7 EMSLIE, McDONALD. "Dryden's Couplets: Imagery Vowed to Poverty." Critical Quarterly 2 (Spring):51-57.
     Asserts that Dryden's emphasis in "poetry of statement" is on argument rather than suggestiveness: the imagery is "clear and explicit," and does not rely on subtlety for its effect. Looks at the portraits of Og and Doeg in Absalom and Achitophel (Part 2) as unusual examples, using rich and suggestive imagery. Looks also at several passages in Part 1 of the poem which share this uncharacteristic feature. But concludes that overall Dryden's metaphors "[build up] the attitude he wishes to communicate" (without Shakespearean ambiguity).

8 FUJIMURA, THOMAS H. "The Appeal of Dryden's Heroic Plays." PMLA 75 (March):37-45.
     Tries to account for their popularity with contemporary audiences. Argues that they display an essentially naturalistic and primitive view toward sex (love) and glory (honor), a "romantic revolt against Christian humanism" which Restoration audiences would have found appealing.

9 HINMAN, ROBERT. Abraham Cowley's World of Order. Cambridge, Mass.: Harvard University Press, 381 pp.
     Argues (pp. 9-11) that Cowley was not the poet Dryden had in mind when in the preface to the Fables he wrote of "one of our late great poets . . . sunk in his reputation, because he could never forgive any conceit which came in his way; but swept like a dragnet great and small." Suggests that John Cleveland or Edward Benlowes may have been meant.

10 HOFFMAN, ARTHUR W. "Dryden's To Mr. Congreve." MLN 75 (November):553-56.
     Suggests that 1. 14 ("The second temple was not like the first") refers not to the Temple in Jerusalem but to Christopher Wren's St. Paul's, which replaced the medieval cathedral destroyed in the Great Fire.

*11 HUGHES, R.E. "Dryden's All for Love: The Sensual Dilemma." Drama Critique 3, no. 2:68-72.
     Cited in Latt and Monk, 1976.30.

*12 JACK, IAN. "'The True Raillery.'" Cairo Studies in English

4:9-23.
Cited in Latt and Monk, 1976.30.

13   LEWIS, C.S. "Shelley, Dryden, and Mr. Eliot." In English
      Romantic Poets. Edited by M.H. Abrams. New York: Oxford
      University Press, pp. 247-67.
          Reprint of 1939.11.

14   MILES, JOSEPHINE. Renaissance, Eighteenth-Century, and Modern
      Language in English Poetry: A Tabular View. Berkeley and Los
      Angeles: University of California Press, 76 pp.
          Contains five tables which indicate various forms of verbal
      repetition in poets. Includes statistics for Dryden drawn from
      Absalom and Achitophel.

15   MINER, EARL. "Dryden's Messianic Eclogue." RES, n.s. 11
      (August):299-302.
          Suggests on internal evidence (and some circumstantial ex-
      ternal evidence) that Dryden's translation of Virgil's Fourth
      Eclogue was originally intended to celebrate the birth of the
      first child of Princess (later Queen) Anne in 1684.

16   MONK, SAMUEL HOLT. "Shadwell's 'Flail of Sense.'" N&Q, n.s.
      7 (February):67-68.
          Argues that the description of MacFlecknoe as a "flail of
      sense" (1. 89) may refer to Shadwell's "extreme anti-Catholicism
      at the time of the Popish Plot." The reference is to the "Pro-
      testant flail," a weapon alluded to by anti-Papist controversial-
      ists.

17   PRINCE, F.T. "Dryden Redivivus." Review of English Literature
      (Leeds University) 1, no. 1 (January):71-79.
          A review-article on Kinsley's edition of the poems (1958.19).
      Surveys modern attitudes toward Dryden's poetry; hopes that in any
      new revival the religious poems are given their due.

18   _____. "Dryden's Political Satires." Listener 64 (28 February):
      148-49.
          A talk on the BBC Third Programme, as part of the series "The
      Birth of Modern England." Relates the poems to their political
      backgrounds; emphasizes Absalom and Achitophel.

19   PROUDFOOT, L. Dryden's "Aeneid" and Its Seventeenth Century
      Predecessors. Manchester: Manchester University Press, 286 pp.
          Prints passages from Book 4, together with Dryden's transla-
      tion and those of earlier English translators, suggesting Dryden's
      various sources. Concludes that Lauderdale is the unacknowledged
      "mediator" between Dryden and earlier versions. Finds Dryden's
      translation strong in political and moral passages, but lacking
      Virgil's pathos and frequently losing his subtle verbal effects
      through overelaboration and overemphasis. Claims that Dryden's

commentary on Virgil is superficial. Suggests that he was derivative because he sought a "definitive" version of the poem which
would embody a whole tradition of translation. Reprinted:
1978.45.

20   RICHARDS, I.A. "The Interactions of Words." In The Language
      of Poetry. Edited by Allen Tate. New York: Russell & Russell,
      pp. 65-87.
          Reprint of 1942.7.

*21   RIPPY, FRANCIS MAYHEW. "Imagery, John Dryden, and 'The Poetry
      of Statement.'" Ball State Teachers College Forum 1, no. 2:
      13-20.
          Cited in Latt and Monk, 1976.30.

22   SCHULTE, EDVIGE. Profilo storico della metrica inglese.
      Naples: Instituto Universitario Orientale, 265 pp.
          Deals briefly with Dryden (pp. 121-27). Notes that his
      metrical effects have great variety even though his forms are very
      regular.

*23   SOULE, GEORGE ALAN, Jr. "Dryden and the Poetry of Public
      Action." Ph.D. dissertation, Yale University.
          Cited in Latt and Monk, 1976.30.

24   SPURGEON, CAROLINE. Five Hundred Years of Chaucer Criticism
      and Allusion, 1357-1900. New York: Russell & Russell.
          Reprint of 1908.4; 1925.15.

25   STEADMAN, JOHN M. "Timotheus in Dryden, E.K., and Gafori."
      TLS, 16 December, p. 819.
          Suggests that Franchino Gafori's De Harmonia Musicorum
      Instrumentorum (1518) may have contributed to Alexander's Feast.

26   VAN DOREN, MARK. John Dryden: A Study of His Poetry.
      Bloomington: Indiana University Press.
          Reprint of 1920.10; 1931.38 (rev.); 1946.19.

27   WEDGWOOD, C.V. Poetry and Politics Under the Stuarts. Clark
      Lectures, 1958. Cambridge: Cambridge University Press, 227 pp.
          Discusses several of Dryden's political poems in terms of
      their historical contexts. Emphasizes Absalom and Achitophel (pp.
      162-68) as an example of Tory reaction against the Puritans.

28   WILLIAMSON, GEORGE. Seventeenth Century Contexts. London:
      Faber & Faber, 291 pp.
          Includes 1933.14; 1935.24; 1946.22 (which is also reprinted
      in 1966.57). Reprinted: 1969.85.

29   WILSON, F.P. Seventeenth Century Prose. Five Lectures.
      Berkeley and Los Angeles: University of California Press,

129 pp.
     Praises Dryden's prose style in general terms. Reprinted:
1976.62.

30   WORCESTER, DAVID. The Art of Satire. New York: Russell &
     Russell.
          Reprint of 1940.28.

*31 YOUNG, DONALD L. "The Reputation of John Dryden, 1895-1956."
     Ph.D. dissertation, Boston University.
          Cited in Latt and Monk, 1976.30. Abstracted in DA 21:908-9.

1961

1   BALL, ALBERT. "Charles II: Dryden's Christian Hero." MP
     59 (August):25-35.
          Argues that in Absalom and Achitophel Dryden models Charles
     on the pattern of a Christian epic hero. Surveys Dryden's interest
     in the epic, and his statements about epic heroes. Notes that
     Charles's movement from inaction to assertiveness is typical of
     heroes in Christian epic.

2   BATE, WALTER JACKSON. From Classic to Romantic: Premises in
     Eighteenth-Century England. New York: Harper & Row.
          Reprint of 1946.1.

3   BIRRELL, T.A. "John Dryden's Purchases at Two Book Auctions,
     1680 and 1682." ES 42 (August):193-217.
          Lists and classifies the purchases noted as having been made
     by Dryden in two auctioneers' catalogues.

4   BROWN, DAVID D. "Dryden's 'Religio Laici' and the 'Judicious
     and Learned Friend.'" MLR 56 (January):66-69.
          Suggests that he is John Tillotson, and that his complaint,
     which Dryden alludes to in the poem's preface, had to do with
     Dryden's presentation of Athanasius as intolerant towards Arius
     (11. 220-23).

5   _____. "John Tillotson's Revisions and Dryden's 'Talent for
     English Prose.'" RES, n.s. 12 (February):24-39.
          Examines Tillotson's methods of revision to try to shed some
     light on his possible influence on Dryden. Finds nothing about
     their many stylistic similarities which would point inevitably to
     influence. Suggests that Dryden may have discussed methods of re-
     vision with Tillotson at various times, and seen some of his ser-
     mons in manuscript.

*6   CARROLL, J.T. "Dryden and the Great Chain of Being." Ph.D.
     dissertation, National University of Ireland.
          Cited in Latt and Monk, 1976.30.

7   CHIASSON, ELIAS J.   "Dryden's Apparent Skepticism in <u>Religio</u>
     <u>Laici</u>." <u>Harvard Theological Review</u> 54 (July):207-21.
          Argues that Dryden belongs to the "tradition of Christian
     humanism . . . common to patristic, medieval, and Renaissance
     Christendom"; opposes Bredvold's view (in 1934.3) that Dryden was
     a philosophic skeptic. Discusses seventeenth-century Anglican
     attitudes toward reason. Sees in the opening image of <u>Religio</u>
     <u>Laici</u> a view of reason that conforms to these attitudes. Analyzes
     the poem to argue Dryden's kinship with the Anglican Christian-
     humanist position. Reprinted: 1966.57; 1969.40.

8   CONGLETON, JAMES E.   "The Effect of the Restoration on Poetry."
     <u>Tennessee Studies in Literature</u> 6:93-101.
          Briefly surveys Dryden's poetry, emphasizing its difference
     from pre-Restoration poetry.

9   COOK, RICHARD I.   "Dryden's <u>Absalom and Achitophel</u> and Swift's
     Political Tracts, 1710-1714." <u>HLQ</u> 24 (August):345-48.
          Notes a "kinship . . . of theme and structure" between
     Dryden's poem and Swift's <u>History of the Four Last Years of the</u>
     <u>Queen</u>.

*10   DAVIS, IRA B.   "Religious Controversy: John Dryden's 'The
     Hind and the Panther.'" <u>College Language Association Journal</u>
     4:207-14.
          Cited in Latt and Monk, 1976.30.

11   DOBRÉE, BONAMY.   <u>John Dryden</u>. Writers and Their Work. Rev.
     ed. London and New York: Longmans.
          Revised edition of 1956.13 (updates bibliography).

*12   ELLIS, HARRY JAMES.   "A Critical Analysis of John Dryden's
     <u>The Hind and the Panther</u>." Ph.D. dissertation, University of
     Pennsylvania.
          Cited in Latt and Monk, 1976.30. Abstracted in <u>DA</u> 22:563-64.

13   EMSLIE, McD[ONALD].   "Dryden's Couplets: Wit and Conversation."
     <u>EIC</u> 11 (July):264-73.
          Finds the basis for Dryden's diction in satire to be the
     colloquial conversation of gentlemen. Relates this thesis to
     Dryden's statements about wit, and to his practice.

14   EVANS, G. BLAKEMORE.   "Dryden's <u>MacFlecknoe</u> and Dekker's
     <u>Satiromastix</u>." <u>MLN</u> 76 (November):598-600.
          Argues that 11. 87-89 refer to two "prophecies" in
     <u>Satiromastix</u> (2. 2. 55-62 and 5. 2. 338-39).

15   FREEDMAN, MORRIS.   "Milton and Dryden on Rhyme." <u>HLQ</u> 24
     (August):337-44.
          Argues that Milton's remarks on rhyme, prefatory to <u>Paradise</u>
     <u>Lost</u>, use and respond to arguments made in the Dryden-Howard con-
     troversy. Notes several parallels in thought and wording,

concluding that in Milton's paragraph "almost every phrase is the
distillation of lengthy matter in Dryden and Howard."

16   FUJIMURA, THOMAS H. "Dryden's Religio Laici: An Anglican
      Poem." PMLA 76 (June):205-17.
          Argues against Bredvold (1934.3) that the poem is in the
      mainstream of Anglican apologetics. Notes that the procedure of
      the work is rational, that its attitude toward authority is ortho-
      dox, and that its reasonableness is in the Anglican spirit. Sees
      Dryden as compatible with the Latitudinarian wing of the Church.

17   HANZO, THOMAS A. Latitude and Restoration Criticism.
      Anglistica 12. Copenhagen: Rosenkilde & Bagger, 153 pp.
          "John Dryden and the Failure of Latitude" (pp. 84-117) ex-
      amines Dryden's criticism, especially Essay of Dramatic Poesy.
      Claims that while it is a primary document of "latitudinarian"
      criticism, it is self-contradictory in its appeal both to universal
      laws and to historical developments. Traces this split through the
      rest of Dryden's criticism, arguing that Dryden recognized it and
      was therefore consistently uncertain.

18   HAVENS, RAYMOND D. The Influence of Milton on English Poetry.
      New York: Russell & Russell.
          Reprint of 1922.4.

*19   HENIGAN, ROBERT H. "English Dramma per Musica: A Study of
      Musical Drama in England from The Siege of Rhodes to the Opening
      of the Haymarket Theatre." Ph.D. dissertation, University of
      Missouri.
          Cited in Latt and Monk, 1976.30.

20   HOLLANDER, JOHN. The Untuning of the Sky: Ideas of Music in
      English Poetry 1500-1700. Princeton: Princeton University
      Press, 479 pp.
          Argues that Song for St. Cecilia's Day and Alexander's Feast
      both transcend their occasions and "represent with unqualified suc-
      cess the attitudes toward music of the community that commissioned
      and praised them." Notes that although the Song alludes to both
      the music of the spheres and the last trump it basically praises
      worldly music. Analyzes Alexander's Feast to show how it both
      demonstrates and celebrates the affective power of music: con-
      cludes that it is "the goddess Persuasion" who is finally commended.
      Sees both works as the culmination of "the untuning of the sky,"
      the process by which the old notion of heavenly music has been re-
      placed by a celebration of music as it is actually made on earth
      (pp. 394-422). This section is reprinted in 1963.46.

21   HOUSMAN, A.E. "The Name and Nature of Poetry." In Selected
      Prose. Edited by John Carter. Cambridge: Cambridge University
      Press, pp. 168-95.
          Reprint of 1933.8.

22 HOY, CYRUS. "The Effect of the Restoration on Drama."
    Tennessee Studies in Literature 6:85-91.
        Argues, with several examples from Dryden and others, that
    Restoration drama was at its best in naturalistic satiric comedy,
    and at its worst in serious drama. Sees both forms as "the final
    working out of tendencies present in English drama for at least
    half a century prior to 1660."

23 HUGHES, R.E. "John Dryden's Greatest Compromise." TSLL 2
    (Winter):458-63.
        Relates Dryden's satires to Aristotelian rhetoric, arguing
    that he uses its devices to organize his arguments.

24 HYMAN, STANLEY EDGAR. Poetry and Criticism: Four Revolutions
    in Taste. New York: Atheneum, 178 pp.
        "English Neo-Classicism" (pp. 40-84) takes Antony and
    Cleopatra and All for Love as examples to illustrate the book's
    argument that works which establish a standard for a period tend
    to create, in time, their antithesis (and its theoretical defense)
    which in turn establishes a new standard.

*25 JOHNSON, JAMES WILLIAM. "Dryden's 'Epistle to Robert Howard.'"
    Ball State Teachers College Forum 2, no. 1:20-24.
        Cited in Latt and Monk, 1976.30.

26 JONES, HAROLD WHITMORE, ed. Anti-Achitophel (1682): Three
    Verse Replies to "Absalom and Achitophel" by John Dryden.
    Gainesville, Fla.: Scholars' Facsimiles & Reprints, 112 pp.
        Includes Absalom Senior by Elkanah Settle (1682.6), Poetical
    Reflections (anonymous, 1681.3), and Azaria and Hushai by Samuel
    Pordage (1682.4). The introduction (pp. iii-vii) sets out what is
    known about the circumstances of the three pieces, and provides a
    "table of allusions" and some notes.

*27 KIRSCH, ARTHUR C. "Dryden's Theory and Practice of the Rhymed
    Heroic Play." Ph.D. dissertation, Princeton University.
        Cited in Latt and Monk, 1976.30. Abstracted in DA 22:1979.
    See 1965.33.

*28 KNIGHT, L.H. "Stage Adaptations of Shakespeare, 1660-1900."
    Ph.D. dissertation, University of Wales (Swansea).
        Cited in Latt and Monk, 1976.30.

29 KNOX, NORMAN. The Word "Irony" and Its Context, 1500-1755.
    Durham, N.C.: Duke University Press, 272 pp.
        Draws evidence from Dryden's criticism about his period's
    definitions of and attitudes toward irony and its types.

*30 LEEMAN, RICHARD K. "Corneille and Dryden: Their Theories of
    Dramatic Poetry." Ph.D. dissertation, University of Wisconsin.
        Cited in Latt and Monk, 1976.30. Abstracted in DA 22:1158-
    59.

31   McFADDEN, GEORGE. "Dryden's 'Most Barren Period'--and Milton."
      HLQ 24 (August):283-96.
          Suggests that 1672-74 was "a period of intense study and ex-
      periment in versification." Speculates that during this time
      Dryden was studying Paradise Lost to improve his own poetry; that
      he particularly learned from Milton (and Virgil) techniques for
      "interweaving and internal reinforcement of sound." Argues that
      Aureng-Zebe shows the result of his work during this period.
      Claims that revisions made between the manuscript and the 1677
      printed versions of The State of Innocence also support his case.

32   MAURER, A.E. WALLACE. "Dryden's Absalom and Achitophel, 745-
      746." Expl 20 (September): note 6.
          Qualifies the point made in his former note on this passage
      (see 1959.28). Now feels that the connotations of "specious" and
      other key words are pejorative as well as positive.

33   _____. "Who Prompted Dryden to Write Absalom and Achitophel?"
      PQ 40 (January):130-38.
          Suggests that Edward Seymour ("Amiel" in the poem, and
      Speaker of the House of Commons) may have done so.

34   MAVROCORDATO, ALEXANDRE. "La critique classique anglaise et la
      fonction de la tragédie (1660-1720)." EA 14 (January-March):
      10-24.
          Discusses, and discriminates among, the critics' positions
      on poetic justice and catharsis. Concludes that they failed to
      establish coherent positions because of their inadequate under-
      standing of psychology.

*35   MELL, DONALD CHARLES, Jr. "Variations on Elegiac Themes:
      Dryden, Pope, Prior, Gray, Johnson." Ph.D. dissertation,
      University of Pennsylvania.
          Cited in Latt and Monk, 1976.30. Abstracted in DA 22:1159-
      60.

*36   MERZBACH, MARGARET KOBER. "Kleist and Dryden." South Central
      Bulletin 21, no. 4:11-16.
          Cited in Latt and Monk, 1976.30.

37   MINER, EARL. "Dryden and the Issue of Human Progress." PQ 40
      (January):120-29.
          Examines Dryden's poetry in order to illuminate his views on
      the idea of progress, and the use he makes of it. Notes that
      Dryden's attitudes do not fall into conventional categories. As-
      serts that Dryden's contemplation of the idea of progress gave him
      a source of metaphor, and a useful (and unusual) awareness of the
      relation of the past to the present.

38   MOORE, ROBERT ETHERIDGE. Henry Purcell and the Restoration
      Theatre. London, Melbourne, and Toronto: Heinemann; Cambridge,

Mass.: Harvard University Press, 238 pp.
Discusses the Dryden-Purcell King Arthur and The Indian Queen at length. Finds the active collaboration of the two in the former work a tribute by Dryden to the much younger Purcell, especially since Dryden clearly felt uncomfortable with the constraints of writing for music. Claims, however, that the opera is very successful. Gives The Indian Queen high praise as well, especially noting Purcell's skill at setting Dryden's words. Discusses the opera's similarities to Aïda. Reprinted: 1974.45.

39   PINTO, V. de SOLA. "Rochester and Dryden." Renaissance and Modern Studies 5:29-48.
Finds in Dryden and Rochester an example of the "semi-antagonistic literary partnership" between the industrious professional and the brilliant amateur which has recurred in English poetry. Traces the course of their personal relationship. Argues that the flowering of Dryden's career in the 1670s is due to Rochester's influence.

*40   PORTE, MICHAEL S. "The Servant in Restoration Comedy." Ph.D. dissertation, Northwestern University.
Cited in Latt and Monk, 1976.30. Abstracted in DA 21:3093.

41   RICKS, CHRISTOPHER. "Dryden's Absalom." EIC 11 (July):273-89.
Asserts that "Absalom is culpably vulnerable" and that an accurate reading of the poem requires his condemnation. Sketches the political situation involving Monmouth. Analyzes the diction and context of relevant passages to show that Dryden's praise of Absalom is ironic.

*42   ROPER, ALAN H. "Dryden and the Stuart Succession." Ph.D. dissertation, Johns Hopkins University.
Cited in Latt and Monk, 1976.30.

43   SAINTSBURY, GEORGE. A History of English Prosody from the Twelfth Century to the Present Day. 2 vols. New York: Russell & Russell.
Reprint of 1906.11.

44   SCHILLING, BERNARD N. Dryden and the Conservative Myth: A Reading of "Absalom and Achitophel." New Haven and London: Yale University Press, 337 pp.
Reads the poem as an expression of the "conservative myth," whose manifestations derive from a belief that order should control energy. Sees the work as Dryden's substitute for an epic, in which his skills and what the age wanted came together. Looks at the various ways the myth is expressed: artistically, by the "rules" and the restraining force of the heroic couplet; intellectually and emotionally by the alliance of "great wit" and "madness" and the sense of danger this and other attributes of the rebels engender. Sees the satiric mode as an essential form in which the

conservative poet (like Dryden) expresses his fear of the mob.
Finds Dryden's personal temper compatible with the myth: "his
conservatism is freely chosen, the natural unforced result of what
he was." Gives a passage-by-passage reading, illustrating how the
conservative myth supports the poem's style, structure, rhetoric,
ideas, and dramatic situations. Concludes that it is a poem of
argument, skillfully controlled, in which the mythic dimension is
crucial.

45   ., ed. Essential Articles for the Study of English
     Augustan Backgrounds. Hamden, Conn.: Archon Books, 426 pp.
         Includes 1898.2; 1928.18; 1938.19; 1940.17; 1942.6.

46   SCHLESS, HOWARD H. "Dryden's Absalom and Achitophel and A
     Dialogue Between Nathan and Absolome. PQ 40 (January):139-43.
         Describes and summarizes the Dialogue and briefly compares
     it with Dryden's poem.

47   SCOUTEN, ARTHUR H., ed. The London Stage, 1660-1800. Part 3:
     1729-1747. 2 vols. Carbondale: Southern Illinois University
     Press.
         Lists performances of Dryden's plays during this period,
     with dates, theaters, and cast list (if available). For other
     parts in the series, see 1960.1 (Part 2); 1962.44 (Part 4);
     1965.56 (Part 1); 1968.37 (Part 5).

*48   SHARMA, R.C. "Conventions of Speech in the Restoration Comedy
     of Manners." Indian Journal of English Studies 2:23-38.
         Cited in Latt and Monk, 1976.30.

*49   SINGH, SARUP. "Dryden and the Unities." Indian Journal of
     English Studies 2:78-90.
         Cited in Latt and Monk, 1976.30.

50   STEINER, GEORGE. The Death of Tragedy. New York: Knopf, 375
     pp.
         Credits Dryden with being the "first of the critic-
     playwrights." Emphasizes his attempts to reconcile classic and
     native ideals, his theory and his taste. Evaluates his plays,
     finding the comedies excellent, the tragedies (because of that
     inner conflict) less good. Claims that All for Love is weakened
     by the consciousness of the imitation.

51   TANNER, J.E. "The Messianic Image in MacFlecknoe." MLN 76
     (March):220-23.
         Sees a pervasive identification of Shadwell with the Messiah
     as one of the poem's unifying devices.

*52   TAYLOR, MYRON W. "Two Analogies for Poetry in the Seventeenth
     Century." Ph.D. dissertation, Washington University (St. Louis).
         Cited in Latt and Monk, 1976.30. Abstracted in DA 21:3772.

*53 THALE, MARY. "John Dryden's Use of the Classics in his Literary Criticism." Ph.D. dissertation, Northwestern University.
Cited in Latt and Monk, 1976.30. Abstracted in DA 22:574.

54 TIEMANN, HERMANN. "Die Bedeutung der 'Spanish Plots' fur das englischen Drama der Fruhrestuaration." Romantisches Jahrbuch 12:278-311.
Discusses several of Dryden's early comedies in terms of their use of the "Spanish Plot"; relates them to contemporary works by other authors.

55 TILLOTSON, GEOFFREY. Augustan Studies. London: Athlone Press, 266 pp.
Reprints (in slightly revised form) 1942.11 (pp. 13-22). Also includes "More About Poetic Diction" (pp. 46-110), which discusses the various meanings currently given to "poetic diction," and attempts to describe it from the perspective of the eighteenth and nineteenth centuries. Notes that Dryden avoided the word "diction" as insufficiently English: his term was "expression." Argues that modern disparagement of heightened or circumlocutory diction mistakes its intent: suggests that when Dryden used a phrase such as "watery ranks" for "waves" he was not being shoddy but demonstrating his interest in science and natural phenomena. Includes as an appendix "English and Latin" (pp. 98-108), which cites Dryden as one of several critics who deplored the overuse of Latin-based words in English, and who clearly felt that English was not inferior to Latin as a language for poetry.

56 VAN LENNEP, WILLIAM. "Plays on the English Stage 1669-1672." TN 16 (Autumn):12-20.
Contains new information about the date of the first performance of Sir Martin Mar-All.

57 WARD, CHARLES E. The Life of John Dryden. Chapel Hill: University of North Carolina Press, 388 pp.
The standard biography. Assembles all available material about Dryden's life. Excludes, "in general, critical pronouncement upon Dryden's work." Includes five appendixes and extensive notes.

58 WASSERMAN, EARL. "Pope's 'Ode for Musick.'" ELH 28 (June): 163-86.
Analyzes the opening stanza of Song for St. Cecilia's Day. Shows how the form of the stanza, drawing upon the tradition of musical symbolism, embodies the poem's theme of order brought out of chaos.

59 WEDGWOOD, C.V. Seventeenth-Century English Literature. London and New York: Oxford University Press.
Reprint of 1950.27.

60　WILLIAMSON, GEORGE. The Proper Wit of Poetry. Chicago:
　　　University of Chicago Press; London:　Faber & Faber, 136 pp.
　　　　　Uses many examples from Dryden.　Discusses his definitions
　　of wit, and his views about wit in other writers.　Looks at his
　　practice, especially in mock-heroic.　Reprinted:　1980.32.

61　WILSON, JOHN HAROLD.　"Theatre Notes from the Newdigate News-
　　　letters."　TN 15 (Spring):79-84.
　　　　　Contains two contemporary notes on The Duke of Guise.

<u>1962</u>

1　ALSSID, MICHAEL W.　"The Perfect Conquest:　A Study of Theme,
　　　Structure and Characters in Dryden's The Indian Emperour."　SP
　　　59 (July):539-59.
　　　　　Discusses rhymed heroic drama generally:　sees the play as
　　typical of the form in its use of a central moral design, a trou-
　　bled monarchy, and a conflict involving love.　Gives a close read-
　　ing of the play:　emphasizes conquest as a basic theme.　Finds
　　three stages in the plot.　In the first (Spain invades Mexico),
　　civilization makes a heroic and tragic impact on a primitive so-
　　ciety.　In the second (military conflict), Cortez is revealed as
　　a complex but unnatural figure.　In the third (Spain's victory),
　　the play moves toward a celebration of male vigor, as the aging
　　Montezuma and his nation are defeated.　Links Cortez to both
　　Almanzor and Aureng-Zebe as a figure who is "an instrument of
　　destiny" but is also "driven by strong sexual and military pas-
　　sions" and must therefore learn control.

2　AMARASINGHE, UPALI.　Dryden and Pope in the Early Nineteenth
　　　Century:　A Study of Changing Literary Tastes, 1800-1830.
　　　Cambridge:　Cambridge University Press, 255 pp.
　　　　　Describes and analyzes editions of the period, especially
　　Scott's (1808.3).　Notes the light their critical standards throw
　　on contemporary attitudes toward Dryden.　Surveys the periodical
　　literature, and the views of poets and critics.　Concludes that
　　while Dryden (and the Augustans generally) suffered a decline in
　　esteem during the period, their work was much more influential on
　　nineteenth-century poetry than is commonly thought.

3　ANON.　"A Poet Hidden."　TLS, 14 September, p. 688.
　　　　　A review-article on Ward's Life (1961.57) and Schilling's
　　Dryden and the Conservative Myth (1961.44).　Laments that so lit-
　　tle is known about Dryden as a person.

4　BAUMGARTNER, A.M.　"Dryden's Caleb and Agag."　RES, n.s. 13
　　　(November):394-97.
　　　　　Argues on internal evidence that Caleb (in Absalom and
　　Achitophel) is Arthur Capel, Earl of Essex, and (agreeing with
　　Kinsley against de Beer) that Agag is Lord Stafford.　See 1941.2;
　　1955.16; 1956.10, 19.

*5   BLONDEL, JACQUES. "The Englishness of Dryden's Satire in
        <u>Absalom and Achitophel</u>." Travaux du Centre d'Études Anglaises
        et Américaines, vol. 1. Aix-en-Provence: Faculté des Lettres
        et Sciences Humaines.
           Cited in Latt and Monk, 1976.30.

*6   BRETT, RICHARD D. "Ironic Harmony: Poetic Structure in Donne,
        Marvell, and Dryden." Ph.D. dissertation, Cornell University.
           Cited in Latt and Monk, 1976.30. Abstracted in <u>DA</u> 22:2783-
  84.

7   COURTHOPE, W.J. <u>A History of English Poetry</u>. 6 vols. New
        York: Russell & Russell.
           Reprint of 1903.3.

*8   CRINÒ, ANNA MARIA. "Ritorno al Dryden." <u>Cultura e Scuola</u> 1,
        no. 4:65-71.
           Cited in Latt and Monk, 1976.30.

9   DEARING, VINTON A. <u>Methods of Textual Editing</u>. Los Angeles:
        Clark Memorial Library, University of California, 35 pp.
           Describes some of the methods used by the textual editors
    of the California Dryden (1956.16, etc.). Reprinted: 1969.18.

10   FORKER, CHARLES R. "Romeo and Juliet and the 'Cydnus' Speech
        in Dryden's <u>All for Love</u>." <u>N&Q</u> n.s. 9:382-83.
           Sees an echo of <u>Romeo and Juliet</u> 2. 2. 23 in <u>All for Love</u>
    3, lines 169-72. Suggests also that Dryden patterned his Cleopatra
    on Shakespeare's Juliet the better to fit his "'heroic conception
    of tragedy."

11   FORREST, JAMES E. "Dryden, Hobbes, Thomas Goodwin and the
        Nimble Spaniel." <u>N&Q</u>, n.s. 9:381-82.
           Maintains that Dryden's comparison of wit to a "nimble
    spaniel" (in his "Account" of <u>Annus Mirabilis</u>) originated in
    Goodwin's <u>The Vanity of Thoughts Discovered</u> (1650), and was trans-
    mitted to Dryden through Hobbes's <u>Leviathan</u> (1651). See 1963.8,
    64.

12   GAGEN, JEAN. "Love and Honor in Dryden's Heroic Plays." <u>PMLA</u>
        77 (June):208-20.
           Surveys and defines the concept of honor in the Renaissance;
    finds it inseparably linked with virtue. Analyzes Dryden's prac-
    tice: concludes that while heroes' and heroines' views of love
    and honor are essentially ethical, villians treat the concepts
    naturalistically.

13   GOLDEN, SAMUEL A. "A Numismatic View of Dryden's <u>The Medal</u>."
        <u>N&Q</u>, n.s. 9:383-84.
           Points out the differences between the actual medal cast to
    commemorate Shaftesbury's acquittal and Dryden's description of it
    in his poem.

14   GROOM, BERNARD. The Diction of Poetry from Spenser to Bridges.
      Toronto: University of Toronto Press, 292 pp.
         "Dryden" (pp. 95-111) looks at Dryden's career chronological-
      ly, with emphasis on his characteristic vocabulary; places his dic-
      tion in both the "neoclassical" and "Spenserian" traditions. Com-
      pares (pp. 119-22) "Homeric diction" in Dryden and Pope.

15   HARDING, DAVIS P. The Club of Hercules: Studies in the
      Classical Background of "Paradise Lost." Illinois Studies in
      Language and Literature 50. Urbana: University of Illinois
      Press, 145 pp.
         Uses Dryden's discussion of the difficulties of translating
      Virgil to suggest why Milton used blank verse in his epic. Looks
      at Aeneid 1, lines 305-13 and Dryden's translation of it to illus-
      trate Dryden's complaints about the inadequacy of English. Attrib-
      utes Dryden's failure to use Virgil's verse-paragraph rhythm to his
      decision to preserve Virgil's "smoothness and grace" in heroic
      couplets without caesuras (pp. 116-23).

16   HOFFMAN, ARTHUR W. John Dryden's Imagery. Gainesville:
      University of Florida Press, 183 pp.
         Treats "imagery characteristically used by Dryden," and the
      range of his methods of employing imagery in poetry. Also deals
      with his stylistic development as a poet. Emphasizes not only
      Dryden's characteristic images, but the ways in which images func-
      tion as part of his arguments. Notes that his analogic uses of
      imagery distinguish him from the classical tradition of which he
      is a part. The first chapter is reprinted in 1969.40, the sixth
      in 1963.46.

17   HOTSON, LESLIE. The Commonwealth and Restoration Stage. New
      York: Russell & Russell.
         Reprint of 1928.8.

*18   HUGHES, R.E. "'Wit': The Genealogy of a Theory." College
      Language Association Journal 5:142-44.
         Cited in Latt and Monk, 1976.30.

*19   IRIE, KEITARO. "The Auxiliary Do in John Dryden's Plays."
      Anglica 5:1-19.
         Cited in Latt and Monk, 1976.30.

20   KAUFMANN, R.J. "On the Poetics of Terminal Tragedy: Dryden's
      All for Love." In All for Love. Edited by R.J. Kaufmann. San
      Francisco: Chandler, 78 pp.
         Suggests that during the period between Annus Mirabilis and
      Absalom and Achitophel Dryden perfected his craft in the series of
      plays culminating in All for Love. Sees the heroic plays as an
      "organic cycle," climaxing in All for Love. Also sees this cycle
      as "the death agony of the tragic drama in England." Emphasizes
      "divided vision" in All for Love: the play combines "political

realism" and "romantic nostalgia." Calls the result "terminal tragedy," which involves as its central situation the end of an empire. While each of the heroic plays contains elements of this form, All for Love is its perfect embodiment. Reprinted: 1963.46.

21 KEAST, WILLIAM R., ed. Seventeenth-Century English Poetry: Modern Essays in Criticism. New York: Oxford University Press.
  Includes 1920.10 (chapter 6); 1936.14; 1947.16; 1952.4, 15. Revised: 1971.42.

22 KING, BRUCE. "Don Sebastian: Dryden's Moral Fable." SR 70 (Autumn):651-70.
  Claims that this is Dryden's best play, for it alone has a sufficient organizing structure (as a moral fable of "guilt and original sin").

23 ___. "Dryden's Absalom and Achitophel, 150-166." Expl 21 (December): note 28.
  Argues against A. Verrall (1914.8) and others that Dryden had Hobbes's theory of madness, not Aristotle's theory of soul and body, in mind in his portrait of Achitophel.

24 KIRSCH, ARTHUR C. "Dryden, Corneille, and the Heroic Play." MP 59 (May):248-64.
  Argues that Dryden derived his concept of the heroic play largely from Corneille. Surveys previous theories about the origins of heroic drama. Describes Corneille's typical plots and characters; links these to Dryden's practice. Concludes that Dryden accommodated Corneille's "heroic elevation and magnificence" to the English stage.

25 ___. "The Significance of Dryden's Aureng-Zebe." ELH 29 (June):160-74.
  Sees the play as a turning point in Dryden's career as a dramatist, in that his interests were changing from the heroic play of passion to the play of sentiment and domesticity. Argues that the change from rhymed couplets to blank verse is a symptom of this shift in the purpose of serious drama. Reprinted: 1966.31, 43.

26 KNIGHT, G. WILSON. The Golden Labyrinth: A Study of British Drama. New York: Norton, 416 pp.
  Comments briefly on some of the comedies and heroic plays. Concludes that Dryden's "thinking is too rational for drama," although "he alone among his contemporaries . . . ambitiously and uncompromisingly, if overconfidently, wills the romantic, the superhuman, guest."

*27 LAVINE, ANNE R. "This Bow of Ulysses: Shakespeare's Troilus and Cressida and Its Imitation by Dryden." Ph.D. dissertation, Bryn Mawr College.

Cited in Latt and Monk, 1976.30. Abstracted in <u>DA</u> 22:3186-88.

28   LEVINE, JAY ARNOLD. "The Status of the Verse Epistle Before
      Pope." <u>SP</u> 59 (October):658-84.
         Briefly discusses Dryden's poems to Congreve, Sir Godfrey
      Kneller, and John Driden of Chesterton. Argues that only the lat-
      ter is a "fully rhetorical epistle."

29   MACE, DEAN T. "Dryden's Dialogue on Drama." <u>JWCI</u> 25 (January-
      June):87-112.
         Sees <u>Essay of Dramatic Poesy</u> as the first treatment of an
      opposition which would come to dominate criticism: the debate be-
      tween historical truth and psychological truth as foundations of
      poetry. Argues that the essay is a serious attempt to consider
      alternatives, and does not come down on one side or the other.
      Lisideius presents the standard view of French dramatic theory,
      that a play is "unlimited by the necessity of conforming to any-
      thing but an inward and hidden psychological truth." Neander, on
      the other hand, believes that "the stage must be carefully control-
      led and limited by external fact." This is why he defends English
      tragicomedy, as it more closely conforms to the reality of experi-
      ence.

30   McGANN, JEROME J. "The Argument of Dryden's <u>Religio Laici</u>."
      <u>Thoth</u> 3 (Spring):78-89.
         Analyzes the argument of the poem to demonstrate that it
      proceeds on nonrational lines. Suggests, on verbal and circum-
      stantial grounds, that it has a close connection with Donne's
      <u>Biathanatos</u>.

31   MARKS, EMERSON R. "Pragmatic Poetics: Dryden to Valéry."
      <u>Bucknell Review</u> 10 (March):213-23.
         Discusses various poets' self-serving critical manifestos
      which attempt to bring about changes in public attitudes toward
      their own poetry. Cites <u>Essay of Dramatic Poesy</u> as a case in point.

32   MAXWELL, J.C. "Dryden's Epilogue to <u>Oedipus</u>, 11. 5-6." <u>N&Q</u>,
      n.s. 9:384-85.
         Points out that the lines echo Horace's <u>Ars Poetica</u>, 11.
      38-40.

33   MILLER, CLARENCE H. "The Styles of <u>The Hind and the Panther</u>."
      <u>JEGP</u> 61 (July):511-27.
         Argues that although the poem is written in a middle style,
      it has distinct gradations within that style. Supports his argu-
      ment with a detailed examination of the poem's imagery, diction,
      allusions, and versification.

34   MINER, EARL. "Some Characteristics of Dryden's Use of Metaphor."
      <u>SEL</u> 2 (Summer):309-20.

Discusses Dryden's use of metaphor as a key to his strength as a poet. Analyzes the opening lines of Absalom and Achitophel, showing the complexity of their uses of metaphor: they "make up a tissue of temporal states likened to each other (and therefore metaphors) in a complex development." The passage also introduces us to the complex tone and allegory of the poem. Suggests "controlling metaphor" as an appropriate term for this characteristic procedure of Dryden's. Examines MacFlecknoe as another example, showing that religion, art, and the figure of the monarch become controlling metaphors there. Reprinted: 1963.46.

35 RAMSAY, PAUL. The Lively and the Just: An Argument for Propriety. University of Alabama Studies 15. Montgomery: University of Alabama Press, 153 pp.

Discusses "To . . . Anne Killigrew" as an ode which is good because it "display[s] propriety to genre, to subject, and to intent" (pp. 65-70). Finds the poem "the most Christian, social, and impersonal" of the three odes under discussion (the others are by Wordsworth and Allen Tate).

36 REICHERT, JOHN. "A Note on Buckingham and Dryden." N&Q, n.s. 9:220-21.

Notes the swipes at Marriage a-la-Mode in Buckingham's The Rehearsal. Cites particularly Buckingham's use of an improbability that also appears in Dryden's play: a letter written by someone after death.

37 ROPER, ALAN H. "Dryden's Medal and the Divine Analogy." ELH 29 (December):396-417.

Argues that the poem has a thematic unity, established in the imagery of the opening lines, in which Shaftesbury is identified with a false monarchy (and with Satan). Analyzes the poem to show how its various aspects are assisted and integrated by its basic imagery. Reprinted with slight changes in 1965.48.

38 _____. "Dryden's 'Secular Masque.'" MLQ 23 (March):29-40.

Asserts that the poem is more complex than has been granted. Relates it to the sequence of metallic ages, associating the iron age with the reign of William III. Notes that the poem's commentator is Momus, the god of laughter: concludes that the poem's attitude to folly is Democritean laughter rather than Heraclitean tears.

39 ROTHSTEIN, ERIC. "English Tragic Theory in the Late Seventeenth Century." ELH 29 (September):306-23.

Sees two strains: "fabulist" (in which the value of the play is in the moral) and "affective" (in which the value is in the exercise of the emotions for moral effect). Argues that the "affective" line of thought proved the stronger, which made the shift from the heroic play to the sentimental play inevitable. Makes heavy use of Dryden's "Heads of an Answer to Rymer" and "The Grounds of Criticism in Tragedy." Forms the basic thesis for 1967.51.

*40   _____. "Unrhymed Tragedy, 1660-1702." Ph.D. dissertation,
      Princeton University.
            Cited in Latt and Monk, 1976.30. Abstracted in DA 23:1689.

*41   SÁNCHEZ ESCRIBANO, FEDERICO. "Lope de Vega según una alusión
      de John Dryden." Hispanó 16:101-2.
            Cited in Latt and Monk, 1976.30.

42   SMITH, JOHN HARRINGTON, and DOUGALD MacMILLAN, eds. The Works
      of John Dryden. Volume VIII: Plays. The Wild Gallant, The
      Rival Ladies, The Indian Queen. Vinton A. Dearing, textual
      editor. Berkeley and Los Angeles: University of California
      Press, 385 pp.
            The commentary (pp. 235-304) gives each play a headnote
      which places it in its context and briefly touches on its major
      themes, strengths, and weaknesses. The headnote is followed by
      notes which explain individual words, phrases, or passages. Essays
      on "Staging" (pp. 307-16) and "The Actors" (pp. 319-21) deal with
      the theatrical circumstances of the first productions, as far as
      they are known or can be suggested. Includes the texts of the
      songs added to the operatic Indian Queen (1695). Textual notes to
      the three plays follow. Other volumes in the series to date:
      1956.16 (1); 1966.32 (9); 1969.52 (3); 1970.59 (10); 1971.58 (17);
      1972.83 (2); 1974.7 (4); 1974.54 (18); 1976.41 (15); 1978.29 (11);
      1979.30 (19).

43   SORELIUS, GUNNAR. "The Unities Again: Dr. Johnson and Delu-
      sion." N&Q, n.s. 9:466-67.
            Notes that Johnson's assertion that the spectators at a play
      always know it is a fiction (in the "Preface to Shakespeare") is
      anticipated by Dryden in his "Epistle Dedicatory" to Love Triumphant
      (1694).

44   STONE, GEORGE WINCHESTER, Jr., ed. The London Stage, 1660-1800.
      Part IV: 1747-1776. 3 vols. Carbondale: Southern Illinois
      University Press.
            Includes information about date, place, and cast of per-
      formances of Dryden's plays during the period. For other parts
      see 1960.1 (Part 2); 1961.47 (Part 3); 1965.56 (Part 1); 1968.37
      (Part 5).

*45   SWAIN, VICTOR C. "On the Meaning of 'Wit' in Seventeenth-
      Century England." Ph.D. dissertation, Columbia University.
            Cited in Latt and Monk, 1976.30. Abstracted in DA 22:3189-
      90.

46   TILLYARD, E.M.W. "A Note on Dryden's Criticism." In Essays
      Literary and Educational. London: Chatto & Windus, pp. 80-88.
            Reprint of 1951.33.

47   van der WELLE, J.A. Dryden and Holland. Groningen: Wolters,
      153 pp.

Investigates what Dryden "as a spokesman of the Restoration government" felt toward Holland and the Dutch. Also tries to determine the extent of Dutch influence on his work. Notes and summarizes Dryden's mentions of Holland and the Dutch. Concentrates on Annus Mirabilis and Amboyna; asserts that the latter may be seen as propaganda in the context of the Third Dutch War. Notes allusions to Dryden in Dutch literature, but concludes that he was not well known in Holland. Argues that in spite of his aversion to Holland and the Dutch Dryden studied and respected many Dutch writers.

48   WAITH, EUGENE M. The Herculean Hero in Marlowe, Chapman,
       Shakespeare and Dryden. New York: Columbia University Press;
       London: Chatto & Windus, 224 pp.
       Defines the "Herculean hero" as "a warrior of great stature who is guilty of striking departures from the morality of the society in which he lives." The chapter on Dryden (pp. 152-201) discusses The Conquest of Granada, Aureng-Zebe, and All for Love. Sees Dryden's major innovation in the tradition as the introduction of love, which "sometimes leads to the resolution of a major paradox in the situation of the Herculean hero, the opposition between his freedom and the demands of society." Concentrates on the moral development of Almanzor (in Conquest); suggests that in Aureng-Zebe the hero acquires the self-discipline of Almanzor, while the antagonist Morat has his irregularity. Sees Antony in All for Love as a Herculean hero, but concludes that the play's moral concerns "the tragic limitations imposed by human existence on the infinite aspirations of heroic passion." The discussion of All for Love is reprinted in 1966.43 and 1968.39.

49   WATSON, GEORGE. The Literary Critics: A Study of English
       Descriptive Criticism. Baltimore: Penguin, 222 pp.
       "John Dryden" (pp. 32-57) surveys his career as a critic, emphasizing the originality of his achievement. Describes, and comments on, the major essays. Concludes that despite his inconsistency he provided "the inestimable example of showing that literary analysis is possible at all." Revised: 1964.53. Second edition: 1973.90.

50   WILSON, JOHN HAROLD. "The Duke's Theatre in March, 1680."
       N&Q, n.s. 9:385-86.
       Considers the generally assigned date of the first production of The Spanish Friar (March 1680) doubtful.

51   _____ . "Six Restoration Play-Dates." N&Q, n.s. 9:221-23.
       Conjecturally dates the plays on available evidence. Includes The Mistaken Husband (early March 1674) and Oedipus (early September 1678).

52   WINTERBOTTOM, JOHN A. "Stoicism in Dryden's Tragedies."
       JEGP 61 (October):868-83.

Attempts to establish Dryden's attitude toward ancient and
modern stoics. Notes that Dryden dedicated two tragedies to well-
known stoics. Finds many examples of stoic behavior in the characters of Dryden's tragedies, especially restraint in the powerful
and resignation in the weak.

53   YOUNGREN, WILLIAM H. "Generality in Augustan Satire." In In
     Defense of Reading. Edited by Reuben A. Brower and Richard
     Poirier. New York: E.P. Dutton, pp. 206-34.
         Analyzes the portrait of Achitophel, along with passages
     from Pope's Epistle to a Lady and Johnson's The Vanity of Human
     Wishes, to argue that Augustan satire characteristically makes use
     of the non-narrative, "clear satiric portrait."

1963

*1   ADAM, DONALD G. "John Dryden: A Study of His Prose Achieve-
     ment." Ph.D. dissertation, University of Rochester.
         Cited in Latt and Monk, 1976.30. Abstracted in DA 24:2025-
     26.

2   ADEN, JOHN. The Critical Opinions of John Dryden: A Dictionary.
     Nashville: Vanderbilt University Press, 318 pp.
         Prints brief excerpts from Dryden's criticism to illustrate
     his opinions, including changed opinions, on various subjects.
     Arranged alphabetically by subject, and chronologically within
     subjects. Cross referenced. A "selective index" lists "familiar
     phrases, quotations, titles, topics, and allusions with the subject-
     entries under which they occur."

*3   ANTHONY, GERALDINE M. "Divine Imagery in Dryden's Lyric
     Poetry." Ph.D. dissertation, St. John's University.
         Cited in Latt and Monk, 1976.30.

4   BARNARD, JOHN. "The Dates of Six Dryden Letters." PQ 42
     (July):396-403.
         Argues against some of Margaret Boddy's contentions (in
     1963.6); suggests dates on external evidence for six letters
     written during the period in question (1694-96).

5   _____. "Dryden, Tonson, and Subscriptions for the 1697 Virgil."
     PBSA 57 (2d Quarter):129-51.
         Reviews attempts to ascertain Dryden's profit from the trans-
     lation, and how it was divided. Agrees with Ward (1961.57) that
     it was £1400, but argues that only a third (rather than more than
     half) came from patrons: the venture therefore was largely com-
     mercial. Examines the conflict between Dryden and Jacob Tonson
     over the contract. Relates the venture to the development of
     publication by subscription.

6 BODDY, MARGARET. "Dryden-Lauderdale Relationships. Some Bibliographical Notes and a Suggestion." PQ 42 (April):267-72.
   Discusses various matters having to do with Dryden's and Lauderdale's translations of Virgil. Suggests that Dryden might have sent Lauderdale "various parts of his translation as he finished them." See 1963.4.

7 BROWER, REUBEN A. "Dryden and the 'Invention' of Pope." In Restoration and Eighteenth Century: Essays in Honor of Alan Dugald McKillop. Edited by Carroll Camden. Chicago and London: University of Chicago Press for William Marsh Rice University, pp. 211-33.
   Examines the "late Horatian" style of Dryden, from 1685 to the end of his life. Finds an increasing celebration of rural retirement, in ways that anticipate Pope.

8 DAVIES, H. NEVILLE. "Dryden, Hobbes, and the Nimble Spaniel." N&Q, n.s. 10 (September):349-50.
   Suggests that Hobbes's Leviathan is the source of Dryden's comparison of wit to a "nimble spaniel." See 1962.11; 1963.64.

*9 DOYLE, ANNE. "The Empress of Morocco: A Critical Edition of the Play and the Controversy Surrounding It." Ph.D. dissertation, University of Illinois.
   Cited in Latt and Monk, 1976.30. Abstracted in DA 24:296.

10 FITZGERALD, ROBERT. "Dryden's Aeneid." Arion 2, no. 3 (Autumn):17-31.
   Praises Dryden's translation, but claims that a better one could have been made during the English Renaissance or the nineteenth century. Suggests that Dryden's haste led to some of his problems, but overall "no one else . . . has yet achieved a version as variously interesting and as true to the best style of a later age."

11 FRENCH, DAVID P. "Dryden's MacFlecknoe, 48." Expl 21 (January): note 39.
   Speculates about the meaning of the reference to "Aston Hall"; suggests several possibilities.

*12 GIBB, CARSON. "Figurative Structure in Restoration Comedy." Ph.D. dissertation, University of Pennsylvania.
   Cited in Latt and Monk, 1976.30. Abstracted in DA 23:4683-84.

*13 GOUSSEFF, JAMES W. "The Staging of Prologues in Tudor and Stuart Plays." Ph.D. dissertation, Northwestern University.
   Cited in Latt and Monk, 1976.30. Abstracted in DA 23:3548.

*14 HALE, PAUL V. "'Enthusiasm' Rejected and Espoused in English Poetry and Criticism, 1660-1740." Ph.D. dissertation, New York

University.
Cited in Latt and Monk, 1976.30.   Abstracted in <u>DA</u> 24:727.

15   HAMILTON, K.G.   <u>The Two Harmonies: Poetry and Prose in the</u>
     <u>Seventeenth Century</u>.   Oxford: Clarendon Press, 224 pp.
          Quotes Dryden frequently in illustration. Discusses his
     attitudes toward proper styles in poetry and prose, and how
     these attitudes differ from each other. Asserts that Dryden felt
     rhymed verse to be more persuasive (and less objective) than blank
     verse. Relates Dryden's view of poetry to his view of discourse.
     Concludes that there was no radical distinction between attitudes
     toward prose and poetry in the seventeenth century. Reprinted:
     1978.18.

16   HOPE, A.D.   "Anne Killigrew, or the Art of Modulating."
     <u>Southern Review</u> (Adelaide, Australia) 1:4-14.
          Sees Dryden as handling the problem of the disparity between
     the truth of Anne Killigrew's limited accomplishment and the needs
     of his elegy by "modulating" his tone between "the most elevated
     fervour" and "familiar and ironic tenderness." Asserts that Dryden
     praises her not because of what she had written but because she
     shared in "the great world of arts and letters." Concludes that
     the "triviality of the subject" is a crucial part of the poem's
     overall success. Reprinted: 1965.24; 1969.40.

17   ILLO, JOHN.   "Dryden, Sylvester, and the Correspondence of
     Melancholy Winter and Cold Age." <u>ELN</u> 1 (December):101-4.
          Suggests that Dryden's attack upon Sylvester's comparison of
     old age to winter (in the dedication of <u>The Spanish Friar</u>) reflects
     the loss of the belief in the correspondence between man and nature.

18   KING, BRUCE.   "<u>Absalom and Achitophel</u>: Machiavelli and the
     False Messiah." <u>EA</u> 16 (July-September):251-54.
          Suggests that Absalom's rise may echo that of the false
     Messiah James Naylor, and that 11. 230-61 contain ironic echoes of
     passages in <u>The Prince</u>.

19   _____.   "Dryden's Intent in <u>All for Love</u>." <u>CE</u> 24 (January):
     267-71.
          Argues that Dryden's statement of moral intent should be
     ignored, because of the three-year lapse between the play and the
     preface in which it appears. Argues that "the raising of emotional
     sympathy" for Antony and Cleopatra is his true intention, and that
     the preface shows Dryden coming under the moralizing influence of
     Le Bossu.

20   KLIMA, S.   "Some Unrecorded Borrowings from Shakespeare in
     Dryden's <u>All for Love</u>." <u>N&Q</u>, n.s. 10 (November):415-18.
          Points to several hitherto unnoticed borrowings from plays
     other than <u>Antony and Cleopatra</u>.

21 KREISSMAN, BERNARD, ed. The Life of John Dryden, by Sir Walter
Scott. Lincoln: University of Nebraska Press, 490 pp.
Reprint of vol. 1 of 1808.3. The introduction (pp. vii-xiii)
places the work in the history of biography. Claims that "the
clear perspective of time--the faithful representation of a past
period and the vivid description of an older social setting super-
imposed on the life of a figure of the past--was first achieved in
this volume." The notes explain (and sometimes correct) details
in the biography.

*22 KURAK, ALEX. "Imitation, Burlesque Poetry, and Parody: A
Study of Some Augustan Critical Distinctions." Ph.D. dissertation, University of Minnesota.
Cited in Latt and Monk, 1976.30. Abstracted in DA 24:2014-
15.

*23 LARSON, RICHARD L. "Studies in Dryden's Dramatic Technique:
The Use of Scenes Depicting Persuasion and Accusation." Ph.D.
dissertation, Harvard University.
Cited in Latt and Monk, 1976.30. See 1975.31.

24 LAWRENCE, W.J. The Elizabethan Playhouse and Other Studies.
New York: Russell & Russell.
Reprint of 1912.4, which includes 1904.5.

25 LeCOMTE, EDWARD S. "'Amnon's Murther.'" N&Q, n.s. 10
(November):418.
Suggests that the allusion (Absalom and Achitophel, 1. 39)
refers to Monmouth's murder of a watchman, not to his mutilation
of Sir John Coventry.

26 LOFTIS, JOHN. The Politics of Drama in Augustan England.
Oxford: Clarendon Press, 173 pp.
"Political Themes of Restoration Drama" (pp. 7-34) discusses
political elements in Dryden's plays. Notes his Toryism and neo-
classicism: asserts that "he shows for kings the devotion which
Addison a few years later shows for liberty."

27 LØSNES, ARVID. "Dryden's Aeneis and the Delphin Virgil." In
The Hidden Sense and Other Essays. Edited by Kristian Schmid.
Norwegian Studies in English 9. Oslo: Universitats-forlaget;
New York: Humanities Press, pp. 113-57.
Investigates the relationship between Dryden's translation
and the second edition of the 1682 Delphin text. Argues that
Dryden used this text. Calls for further close study of Dryden's
translations.

*28 MALTBY, JOSEPH. "The Effect of Irony on Tone and Structure in
Some Poems of Dryden." Ph.D. dissertation, University of
Wisconsin.
Cited in Latt and Monk, 1976.30. Abstracted in DA 24:2463-
64.

*29   MERRIMAN, JAMES DOUGLAS. "The Flower of Kings: A Study of the
      Arthurian Legend in England Between 1485 and 1835." Ph.D. dis-
      sertation, Columbia University.
           Cited in Latt and Monk, 1976.30.   Abstracted in DA 23:3354-
      55.

 30   MINER, EARL. "The Wolf's Progress in The Hind and the Panther."
      Bulletin of the New York Public Library 67 (October):512-16.
           Interprets the account of the Wolf as "proferring alternative
      origins" of a heresy which should not be limited to modern Presby-
      terianism. Discusses the relevant scriptural and historical mater-
      ial, in which pre-Reformation types of the "heresies" of voluntarism
      and antipathy to kingship appear.

 31   MOORE, FRANK HARPER. The Nobler Pleasure: Dryden's Comedy in
      Theory and Practice. Chapel Hill: University of North Carolina
      Press, 264 pp.
           Based partly on 1953.12. Discusses the comic plays chrono-
      logically, with full summary, commentary, and evaluation. Reads
      the plays in the light of the criticism, and vice-versa. Finds no
      single theory of comedy, but infers a general trend toward refine-
      ment, and an increasing interest in moral questions. Emphasizes
      Dryden's craftsmanship as a playwright and a critic, but admits
      he is not a "comic genius." Credits him with a positive influence
      upon the development and refinement of Restoration comedy.

*32   MURAKAMI, SHIKŌ. "Reverence for Human Nature: The Poetry of
      Dryden and Pope." The Journal of the Faculty of Letters, Osaka
      University 10, nos. 1-6:1-84.
           Cited in Latt and Monk, 1976.30.

 33   NAZARETH, PETER. "All for Love: Dryden's Hybrid Play."
      English Studies in Africa 6 (September):154-63.
           Asserts that Dryden is influenced by French neoclassical
      dramatists as well as by Shakespeare, and that the combination is
      harmful.

 34   NEVO, RUTH. The Dial of Virtue: A Study of Poems on Affairs
      of State in the Seventeenth Century. Princeton: Princeton
      University Press, 293 pp.
           Contains scattered comments on several of Dryden's public
      poems; analyzes Absalom and Achitophel at length (pp. 244-65).
      Notes how Dryden makes use of dramatic characters, as opposed to
      the static "character" typical of much satire in the period. Com-
      pares the poem with The Medal and The Hind and the Panther to "make
      clear the great gain in ironic deflation which the scriptural mech-
      anism allows." Shows also the classical, especially Virgilian,
      standards against which the satirized characters are judged. Con-
      cludes by noting that those on the wrong side were real contenders
      for real power; that the poem is the last great poem on affairs of
      state.

*35   NICHOLS, JAMES WILLIAM. "Satiric Insinuation: A Study of the Tactics of English Indirect Satire." Ph.D. dissertation, University of Washington.
        Cited in Latt and Monk, 1976.30. Abstracted in DA 24:302.

*36   NORRELL, LEMUEL N. "The Cuckold in Restoration Comedy." Ph.D. dissertation, Florida State University.
        Cited in Latt and Monk, 1976.30. Abstracted in DA 23:3889.

37   ODELL, GEORGE D.C. Shakespeare from Betterton to Irving. 2 vols. New York: Blom.
        Reprint of 1920.8.

38   OLIVER, H.J. Sir Robert Howard (1626–1698): A Critical Biography. Durham, N.C.: Duke University Press, 358 pp.
        Treats Howard's personal and literary relations with Dryden. Recounts the events of Dryden's collaboration with Howard (pp. 61–87) and his controversy with him over the use of rhyme in drama (pp. 88–120).

39   No entry

*40   PARSONS, P.E. "The Siege of Rhodes and Restoration Tragedy: An Interpretation of Some Formal Developments in the Serious Drama of the Restoration." Ph.D. dissertation, Cambridge University.
        Cited in Latt and Monk, 1976.30.

41   POTTLE, FREDERICK A. "The Critic's Responsibility." In The Idiom of Poetry. 2d ed., rev. and enl. Bloomington: Indiana University Press, pp. 43–57.
        Reprint of 1941.12; 1946.14.

42   REINERT, OTTO. "Passion and Pity in All for Love: A Reconsideration." In The Hidden Sense and Other Essays. Edited by Kristian Schmid. Norwegian Studies in English 9. Oslo: Universitats-forlaget; New York: Humanities Press, pp. 159–95.
        Asserts that they play is unified thematically. Summarizes critical attitudes toward the play. Analyzes its symbolism and imagery; finds its central theme in the "paradoxical triumph" of passion over reason. Reprinted (abridged): 1968.39.

43   RINGLER, RICHARD N. "Two Sources for Dryden's The Indian Emperour." PQ 42 (July):423–29.
        Suggests Donne's First Anniversarie and two scenes from The Fairie Queene (1. 7 and 2. 6).

44   RISTINE, FRANK HUMPHREY. English Tragicomedy: Its Origin and History. New York: Russell & Russell.
        Reprint of 1910.10.

45   RUDD, NIALL. "Dryden on Horace and Juvenal." UTQ 32
     (January):155-69.
         Attacks Dryden's treatment of Horace and Juvenal in "Discourse
     . . . of Satire." Emphasizes Dryden's "misunderstanding" of style
     and intention, and also his inconsistencies and historical inaccu-
     racies. Reprinted: 1966.47.

46   SCHILLING, BERNARD N., ed. Dryden: A Collection of Critical
     Essays. Twentieth Century Views. Englewood Cliffs, N.J.:
     Prentice-Hall.
         Contains 1921.3; 1934.3 (two chapters); 1940.21 (one chapter);
     1947.11; 1948.24; 1952.4; 1953.13; 1956.38; 1957.21; 1961.20;
     1962.16 (one chapter); 1962.20; 1962.34.

*47 SCHLUETER, ANNE R. "John Drydens All for Love: Eine Interpre-
     tation." Ph.D. dissertation, Göttingen.
         Cited in Latt and Monk, 1976.30.

*48 SELLIN, PAUL R. "The Poetic Theory of Daniel Heinsius and
     English Criticism of the Seventeenth Century: Jonson, Milton,
     and Dryden." Ph.D. dissertation, University of Chicago.
         Cited in Latt and Monk, 1976.30.

49   SHERBO, ARTHUR, ed. New Essays, by Arthur Murphy. East Lansing:
     Michigan State University Press.
         Reprint of 1758.1, with an introduction.

50   SIMON, IRÈNE. "Dryden's Revision of the Essay of Dramatic
     Poesy." RES, n.s. 14 (May):132-41.
         Analyzes the revision: finds the 1684 version less collo-
     quial and lively, more controlled and easier to read. Concludes
     that the revision is "nearer to the models Dryden was presumably
     trying to emulate."

51   SINGH, SARUP. The Theory of Drama in the Restoration Period.
     Foreword by James R. Sutherland. New Delhi: Orient Longmans;
     London: Longmans, Green, 311 pp.
         Makes heavy use of Dryden's criticism, claiming that "no one
     perhaps reflects so accurately as Dryden the changes in the spiri-
     tual climate of the age." Traces Dryden's shift from seeing moral
     to seeing sentimental ends in serious drama; discusses his views
     on poetic justice, rhyme in tragedy, opera, tragicomedy, comedy of
     manners, and farce. Stresses Dryden's relative independence from
     the French neoclassic reliance on the unities; argues that Johnson's
     rejection of the unities as irrelevant to verisimilitude is heavily
     indebted to Dryden's criticism.

52   SPENCER, HAZELTON. Shakespeare Improved: The Restoration
     Versions in Quarto and on the Stage. New York: Ungar.
         Reprint of 1927.13.

53 SPINGARN, JOEL E., ed. Critical Essays of the Seventeenth
   Century. 3 vols. Bloomington: Indiana University Press.
       Reprint of 1909.7; 1957.34.

54 STRATMAN, CARL J., C.V.S. "John Dryden's All for Love: Unrecorded Editions." PBSA 57 (1st Quarter):77-79.
       Gives publication details for twelve editions between 1710
   and 1792.

55 SUTHERLAND, JAMES R. "The Impact of Charles II on Restoration
   Literature." In Restoration and Eighteenth Century: Essays in
   Honor of Alan Dugald McKillop. Edited by Carroll Camden.
   Chicago: University of Chicago Press for William Marsh Rice
   University, pp. 251-63.
       Is briefly concerned with Dryden's relationship with (and
   attitudes toward) Charles.

56 _____. John Dryden: The Poet as Orator. The Twentieth W.P.
   Ker Memorial Lecture delivered in the University of Glasgow,
   21 February 1962. Glasgow: Jackson, 29 pp.
       Discusses Dryden's public poetry. Calls him "a Public Orator
   of genius"; likens his sincerity in encomia to that of a university
   public orator. Praises him for his ability to overcome his material with his art.

57 TAYLOR, DANIEL CRANE. William Congreve. New York: Russell &
   Russell.
       Reprint of 1931.35.

58 TOWERS, TOM H. "The Lineage of Shadwell: An Approach to
   MacFlecknoe." SEL 3 (Summer):323-24.
       Argues that Shadwell is connected with Dekker, Heywood, and
   Shirley because all were associated with Christopher Beeston's
   theaters, which emphasized lavish elaboration and vulgarity, and
   were the forerunners of Dryden's rival theater (the Duke's).
   Shadwell and Flecknoe are therefore commercial rivals to Dryden
   as well as epitomes of dullness.

59 VERRALL, A.W. Lectures on Dryden. Edited by Margaret deG.
   Verrall. New York: Russell & Russell.
       Reprint of 1914.8.

60 VIETH, DAVID. Attribution in Restoration Poetry: A Study of
   Rochester's Poems of 1680. New Haven and London: Yale
   University Press, 557 pp.
       Contains many scattered references to Dryden, mainly having
   to do with his relations with Rochester. Criticizes his attack on
   Rochester in the preface to All for Love as too one-sided to be
   effective or acceptable. Contrasts it with Rochester's "An Allusion to Horace" (1680.2), which admits Dryden's poetic ability
   while savaging him in other ways.

61   WAITH, EUGENE M. "The Voice of Mr. Bayes." SEL 3 (Summer):
      335-43.
          Discusses different "voices" Dryden uses in addressing his
      patrons, his reading audience, and his theater audience. Suggests
      that he has in mind, and with his rhetoric tries to create, an
      ideal audience for whom the heroic play could be truly heroic.

*62   WATSON, GEORGE. "Dryden and the Scientific Image." Notes and
      Records of the Royal Society of London 18:25-35.
          Cited in Latt and Monk, 1976.30.

63   _____. "Dryden's First Answer to Rymer." RES, n.s. 14
      (February):17-23.
          Argues for the superiority of Jacob Tonson's text of "Heads
      of an Answer to Rymer" over Johnson's. Credits the work with being
      the only piece of English criticism between the Restoration and
      Johnson to attack Aristotle's Poetics frontally. Denies that the
      "Heads" are essentially a first draft of "The Grounds of Criticism
      in Tragedy," for the latter is much less outspoken and innovative.

64   _____. "Dryden, Hobbes, and the Nimble Spaniel." N&Q, n.s.
      10 (June):230-31.
          Asserts, in response to 1962.11, that the spaniel metaphor
      is not necessarily Puritan. See also 1963.8.

*65   ZEBOUNI, SELMA ASSIR. "The Hero in Dryden's Heroic Tragedy:
      A Revaluation." Ph.D. dissertation, Pennsylvania State
      University.
          Cited in Latt and Monk, 1976.30. Abstracted in DA 24:2467.
      See 1965.66.

                                    1964

*1   AUSPRICH, HARRY. "A Rhetorical Analysis of the Restoration
      Prologue and Epilogue." Ph.D. dissertation, Michigan State
      University.
          Cited in Latt and Monk, 1976.30. Abstracted in DA 25:1400.

2   BATELY, JANET M. "Dryden's Revisions in the Essay of Dramatic
      Poesy: The Preposition at the End of the Sentence and the
      Expression of the Relative." RES, n.s. 15 (August):268-82.
          Analyzes and classifies some of Dryden's grammatical prac-
      tices not only in the revised Essay but generally. Emphasizes his
      decreasing use of prepositions at the ends of sentences, and his
      increasing distinction between the relative pronouns "which" (for
      nonpersons) and "who" (for persons).

3   BENSON, DONALD R. "Halifax and the Trimmers." HLQ 27
      (February):115-34.
          Notes the seeming inconsistency of Dryden's praise of Halifax

(in Absalom and Achitophel and elsewhere) and his enthusiastic
participation in the Trimmer controversy on the Tory side. Surveys the controversy; concludes that Halifax was not viewed as a
"Trimmer" at the time (1682-85).

4 _____. "Theology and Politics in Dryden's Conversion." SEL 4
   (Summer):393-412.
   Argues that the major factor in Dryden's conversion was not
philosophical skepticism but political conservatism. Examines
Religio Laici, The Hind and the Panther, and the intervening prose
for evidence that Dryden was increasingly convinced that the
Established Church did not have the will to enforce its doctrines,
which he always believed reasonable, against Presbyterians and
other dissenters. Notes Dryden's consistent belief that Dissent
led inevitably to political chaos; concludes that he became a
Catholic in large part because he felt that only enforced uniform-
ity could create the "common quiet" that was always his goal in
politics or religion.

*5 BRADHAM, JO ALLEN. "English Lucilian Satire: The Augustan
   Mode." Ph.D. dissertation, Vanderbilt University.
      Cited in Latt and Monk, 1976.30. Abstracted in DA 25:450-51.

6 BRETT, R.L. "Thomas Hobbes." In The English Mind: Studies in
   the English Moralists Presented to Basil Willey. Edited by
   Hugh Sykes Davies and George Watson. Cambridge: Cambridge
   University Press, 30-54.
      Discusses Dryden's debt to Hobbes, especially in the reli-
gious poems and Absalom and Achitophel. Suggests that Dryden's
way of bringing poetry and rhetoric together probably owes something to Hobbes (pp. 49-53).

7 CARACCIOLO, PETER. "Some Unrecorded Variants in the First
   Edition of Dryden's All for Love, 1678." Book Collector 13
   (Winter):498-500.
      Adds variants to those noted by Fredson Bowers (in 1949.5),
and discusses their significance. Calls for further study of the
printing of All for Love.

8 CLOUGH, ARTHUR HUGH. "Dryden and His Times." In Selected
   Prose Works. Edited by Buckner B. Trawick. University, Ala.:
   University of Alabama Press, pp. 85-106.
      Reprint of 1851.3.

*9 DAVIES, H. NEVILLE. "Dryden's Libretti in the Light of
   Seventeenth-Century Ideas About Words and Music." Ph.D. dissertation, Liverpool University.
      Cited in Latt and Monk, 1976.30.

10 DOBRÉE, BONAMY. Restoration Comedy 1660-1720. London and New
   York: Oxford University Press.
      Reprint of 1924.1.

11   EVANS, B. IFOR. <u>Tradition and Romanticism</u>. London: Archon
     Books.
          Reprint of 1940.9.

12   FISCH, HAROLD. <u>Jerusalem and Albion: The Hebraic Factor in
     Seventeenth Century Literature</u>. London: Routledge & Kegan
     Paul; New York: Schocken, 310 pp.
          Briefly discusses Dryden as typical, in style and subject
     matter, of the positivistic, antispiritual attitudes of the Resto-
     ration (pp. 257-59).

13   FLEISCHMANN, WOLFGANG BERNARD. <u>Lucretius and English Literature
     1680-1740</u>. Paris: Nizet, 285 pp.
          Emphasizes the influence of Dryden's translations upon the
     English understanding of Lucretius. Argues that the passages he
     chose to translate, and his view of Lucretius as a poet and natur-
     alist (not simply a philosopher), formed the dominant English atti-
     tude for the eighteenth century.

14   GALLAGHER, MARY. "Dryden's Translation of Lucretius." <u>HLQ</u> 28
     (November):19-29.
          Analyzes Dryden's translation to show how he changed the
     original to make a pleasing English poem. Relates the work to
     Dryden's other compositions of the period, noting their compati-
     bility.

*15 GOGGIN, L.P. "This Bow of Ulysses." <u>Essays and Studies in
     Language and Literature</u> (Duquesne University) 5:49-86.
          Cited in Latt and Monk, 1976.30.

16   GREANY, HELEN T. "On the Opening Lines of <u>Absalom and
     Achitophel</u>." <u>Satire Newsletter</u> 2 (Fall):29-31.
          Analyzes the first forty-two lines, pointing out verbal de-
     vices which assist the satire.

17   HARBAGE, ALFRED. <u>Cavalier Drama: An Historical and Critical
     Supplement to the Study of the Elizabethan and Restoration
     Stage</u>. New York: Russell & Russell.
          Reprint of 1936.7.

18   _____, and S. SCHOENBAUM. <u>Annals of English Drama 975-1700:
     An Analytical Record of All Plays, Extent or Lost, Chronologi-
     cally Arranged and Indexed by Authors, Titles, Dramatic Compan-
     ies, etc</u>. 2d rev. ed. Philadelphia: University of Pennsylvania.
          Update of 1940.12.

*19 HART, JEFFREY. "John Dryden: The Politics of Style." <u>Modern
     Age</u> 8:399-408.
          Cited in Latt and Monk, 1976.30.

20   KING, BRUCE. "The Significance of Dryden's <u>State of Innocence</u>."
     <u>SEL</u> 4 (Summer):371-91.

Argues that the work is more important than has been realized. Claims that "its imagery and themes dominate his most important works." Discusses its intellectual background, emphasizing its relation to Descartes and Hobbes. Analyzes the plot, showing how carefully and thoroughly it is constructed.

21 KINSLEY, JAMES. "The Music of the Heart." Renaissance and Modern Studies 8:5-52.
 Discusses eighteenth-century attitudes toward the union of poetry and music in a single work. Quotes Dryden several times on his frustrating experiences with libretto-writing.

22 KIRSCH, ARTHUR C. "'An Essay on Dramatick Poetry' (1681)." HLQ 28 (November):89-91.
 Reprints and discusses the essay (1681.1). Notes that it is the most extravagant of the comparatively rare works which praise Dryden during the period.

*23 KRAMER, L.J. "Formal Satire and Censorship in the Seventeenth Century." In Proceedings of the 8th Congress of the Australasian Universities' Languages and Literature Association. Canberra: Australian National University, pp. 44-45.
 Cited in Latt and Monk, 1976.30.

24 LEVINE, JAY ARNOLD. "John Dryden's Epistle to John Driden." JEGP 63 (July):450-74.
 Analyzes the poem in detail. Relates it to its political context, suggesting that it is really a deliberative address not only to Driden or to Parliament but to the English people, arguing for moderation in many different ways. Relates the poem to the celebrations of rural retirement in Horace and others; discusses its main metaphors and their implications. Concludes by examining the poem's rhetorical strategy, noting that John Driden plays a dual role as audience and as subject, and that John Dryden himself also identifies with Driden. Reprinted: 1969.40.

25 LEWALSKI, BARBARA KIEFER. "David's Troubles Remembered: An Analogue to Absalom and Achitophel." N&Q, n.s. 11 (September): 340-43.
 Notes several strong similarities between Dryden's poem and Robert Aylett's David's Troubles Remembered; suggests possible influence on Dryden.

*26 LOFTIS, JOHN. "The Hispanic Element in Dryden." Emory University Quarterly 20:90-100.
 Cited in Latt and Monk, 1976.30.

27 MACE, DEAN T. "Musical Humanism, the Doctrine of Rhythmus, and the Saint Cecilia Odes of Dryden." JWCI 27:251-92.
 Argues that Dryden followed modern developments of the tradition of musical humanism in writing his St. Cecilia odes.

Suggests that he was using the theory of rhythmus propounded by
Isaac Vossius in De poematum cantu (1673), which held that classical feet (in poetry and song) could communicate specific emotions.
Analyzes the forms of the two odes, emphasizing their lack of
regularity in rhyme, stanza, rhythm, or line length. (Musical
humanists saw "harmony"--regular repetition in music--as the cause
of modern music's failure to communicate specific passions and
ideas as ancient music presumably had done.) Notes that modern
composers had difficulty setting Dryden's texts because of their
rhythmic complexity. Traces the theory of rhythmus through the
seventeenth century, emphasizing its increasing emphasis on the
affective power of rhythmic proportion. See 1966.10, 36.

*28 McFADDEN, GEORGE. "Dryden and the Numbers of His Native
     Tongue." Duquesne Studies, Philological Series 5:87-109.
          Cited in Latt and Monk, 1976.30.

29   _____. "Elkanah Settle and the Genesis of MacFlecknoe." PQ
     43 (January):55-72.
          Argues that the poem is the long-matured product of Dryden's
     conception of the true poet, and of his experiences with Settle
     and Shadwell. Traces in detail Dryden's and Settle's mutual an-
     tagonism, concentrating on Notes and Observations on "The Empress
     of Morocco." Sees there in the concept of a kind of antipoet the
     germ of MacFlecknoe. Suggests that Dryden finally turned on
     Shadwell rather than Settle because of what appear to be attacks
     on Dryden in Shadwell's version of Timon of Athens.

30   MARY ELEANOR, Mother, S.H.C.J. "Anne Killigrew and MacFlecknoe."
     PQ 43 (January):47-54.
          Reads the poems as mirror images of each other. Notes their
     many ironic similarities; suggests that together they present the
     fall and restoration of poetry.

*31 MASSON, DAVID I. "Dryden's Phonetic Rhetoric: Some Passages
     from His Original Poems." PLPLS-LHS 11:1-5.
          Cited in Latt and Monk, 1976.30.

32   MAVROCORDATO, ALEXANDRE. La critique classique en Angleterre
     de la restauration à la mort de Joseph Addison. Paris: Didier,
     736 pp.
          Divides the development of "classic" English criticism into
     three stages: 1660-74, 1674-94, and 1694-1719. Sees Essay of
     Dramatic Poesy as a major document of the first period ("incuba-
     tion"). Asserts that in the second period ("expansion") Dryden
     as a critic was subordinate to Thomas Rymer. Admires Dryden's
     criticism during the third period ("stabilization") but finds him
     out of the mainstream.

33   MINER, EARL. "Dryden and 'The Magnified Piece of Duncomb.'"
     HLQ 28 (November):93-98.

Suggests that the phrase (in the preface to The Hind and the
Panther) is specific rather than proverbial. Suggests that it refers to the Rev. Eleazar Duncon.

34 _____ . "Dryden as Prose Controversialist: His Role in A
    Defence of the Royal Papers." PQ 43 (July):412-19.
        Argues (against Charles Ward in 1961.57) that Dryden wrote
only the defense of the Duchess of York, and not those of the King.
Examines the evidence on both sides: concludes that differences in
style between the first two tracts and the third strengthen his
position.

35 MONK, SAMUEL HOLT. "Dryden and the Beginnings of Shakespeare
    Criticism in the Augustan Age." In The Persistence of
    Shakespeare Idolatry: Essays in Honor of Robert W. Babcock.
    Edited by Herbert M. Schueller. Detroit: Wayne State
    University Press, pp. 47-75.
        Relates Dryden's response to Shakespeare to his own pragmatic
needs as a playwright. Traces the influence of Restoration critical debates upon eighteenth-century criticism. Concludes that
Dryden's view of Shakespeare is consistent, and of enormous and
beneficial impact upon the development of Shakespeare criticism.

36 MORTON, RICHARD. "'Silver at the Bottom of the Melting Pot':
    Dryden's Troilus and Shadwell's Timon." In Stratford Papers on
    Shakespeare, 1963. Edited by B.W. Jackson. Toronto: W.J. Gage
    for McMaster University, pp. 126-50.
        Describes Dryden's version; attempts to account for its
changes. Concludes that Dryden was trying to interpret and clarify
an obscure and difficult play; argues that Dryden interpreted it as
dealing with "concepts of power and duty in the state of war."

*37 NEWMAN, ROBERT STANLEY. "The Tragedy of Wit: The Development
    of the Heroic Drama from Dryden to Addison." Ph.D. disserta-
    tion, University of California at Los Angeles.
        Cited in Latt and Monk, 1976.30. Abstracted in DA 25:5262.

38 OLDMIXON, JOHN. An Essay on Criticism. The Augustan Reprint
    Society 107-108. Los Angeles: Clark Memorial Library,
    University of California at Los Angeles.
        A facsimile reprint of 1728.2.

*39 PETERSON, RICHARD G. "The Roman Image in English Literature
    from 1660 to 1700." Ph.D. dissertation, University of Minnesota.
        Cited in Latt and Monk, 1976.30. Abstracted in DA 25:2518.

40 PRICE, MARTIN. To the Palace of Wisdom: Studies in Order and
    Energy from Dryden to Blake. Garden City, N.Y.: Doubleday,
    479 pp.
        "Dryden and Dialectic" (pp. 28-78) deals in detail with
Dryden's original poetry, including the serious plays. Asserts

that "the crucial theme in the dialectic of Dryden's poetry is the
struggle for the mind by both flesh and spirit." Traces this theme
(also seen in terms of the opposition of order and energy) throughout the poetry. Finds in the heroic plays the dialectic unresolved
but powerful: "the vigor of the heroic characters' deep feelings
and proud demands is a necessary part of the order Dryden creates,
an order that risks anarchy and division so that it may include
energy and greatness." Sees the satires as involving a dialectic
between natural and divine order (through which David moves in
Absalom and Achitophel). Emphasizes the satiric aspect of the
poems: sees it as especially crucial in The Hind and the Panther.
In a separate discussion of All for Love (pp. 237-42), asserts that
the play "embodies Dryden's characteristic tragic situation--the
assertion of integrity in a world of conflicting claims or of sheer
fortuitousness." Also notes the play's dialectical structure.
Overall the book concludes that in English literature between
Dryden and Blake there is a shift from the primacy of order to
that of energy (although both are always present).

41   PRINCE, F.T. "The Study of Form and the Renewal of Poetry."
     Proceedings of the British Academy 50:45-61.
         Sees a basic "incongruity" in Absalom and Achitophel:
Dryden's apparent perception that "if the Heroic poem is to be
modern, it can only be as a kind of burlesque." But concludes
that his search for the heroic in poetry enabled him to make this
discovery.

42   RINGLER, RICHARD N. "Two Dryden Notes." ELN 1 (June):256-61.
         Sees allusions to Archimedes' sphere in "Upon the Death of
the Lord Hastings" (1649) and "Prologue to the University of
Oxford, 1674." Suggests that Dryden was influenced by reading the
discussion of Archimedes' sphere in John Wilkins's Mathematicall
Magick (1648).

43   ROSENBERG, BRUCE A. "Annus Mirabilis Distilled." PMLA 79
     (June):254-58.
         Argues that the poem is unified by alchemical and astrologi-
cal metaphors. Sees the Great Fire as the alchemist's purifying
fire that will produce Philosopher's Gold, "the new golden London,
reborn from its own ashes of a baser mold."

44   RUSS, JON R. [Note on The Hind and the Panther.] RES, n.s. 15
     (August):303-4.
         Suggests that Edward Topsell's Historie of Four-Footed
Beastes (1607) is the source of Dryden's "milk-white hind."

45   STARNES, D.T. "Imitation of Shakespeare in Dryden's All for
     Love." TSLL 6 (Spring):39-46.
         Claims that in addition to Antony and Cleopatra and other
Shakespeare plays which have been noted (see 1927.6; 1928.14;
1963.20), Dryden used passages from The Merchant of Venice, Julius
Caesar, As You Like It, Othello, Macbeth, and Coriolanus.

46   STAUFFER, DONALD A. English Biography before 1700. New York:
     Russell & Russell.
          Reprint of 1930.12.

47   SUMMERS, MONTAGUE. The Playhouse of Pepys. New York:
     Humanities Press.
          Reprint of 1935.21.

48   _____. The Restoration Theatre. New York: Humanities Press.
          Reprint of 1934.17.

49   SUTHERLAND, JAMES. "Prologues, Epilogues and Audience in the
     Restoration Theatre." In Of Books and Humankind: Essays and
     Poems Presented to Bonamy Dobrée. Edited by John Butt. London:
     Routledge & Kegan Paul, pp. 37-54.
          Traces the development of the form. Discusses Dryden's
     typical practice, emphasizing his craftsmanship. Praises his
     "ability to develop a theme," and his pertinent and lively use of
     allusion and metaphor.

50   THORPE, CLARENCE DeWITT. The Aesthetic Theory of Thomas Hobbes.
     New York: Russell & Russell.
          Reprint of 1940.25.

51   TRICKETT, RACHEL. "The Idiom of Augustan Poetry." In
     Discussions of Poetry: Form and Structure. Edited by Francis
     Murphy. Boston: Heath, pp. 111-26.
          Asserts that the Augustans "deal consistently with the forms
     of things known, with the world as it is, and in place of the myths
     of an earlier age they elevate the past, history, the ancients and
     the record of actual human experience." Emphasizes the influence
     of the epic upon the period's poetry, especially in the Augustans'
     use of the simile. Uses the opening lines of Religio Laici as an
     example. Concludes that the "prevailing idiom" of Augustan poetry
     is "discoursive."

52   WASSERMAN, GEORGE R. John Dryden. Twayne English Authors
     Series. New York: Twayne, 174 pp.
          Attempts "to convey to the reader unfamiliar with Dryden the
     new enthusiasm for the poet" which characterizes modern scholarship.
     Contains a chronology, a survey of Dryden's life and times, brief
     commentary and summary, and a selective annotated bibliography of
     secondary material.

53   WATSON, GEORGE. The Literary Critics. Rev. ed. New York:
     Barnes & Noble, 222 pp.
          Revised edition of 1962.49: contains "additions, corrections,
     and revisions, both to the text and to the bibliography." Re-
     printed: 1973.90.

54   WILCOX, JOHN. The Relation of Molière to Restoration Comedy.

New York: Blom.
     Reprint of 1938.23.

55   WILSON, JOHN HAROLD. Mr. Goodman the Player. Pittsburgh:
     University of Pittsburgh Press, 161 pp.
          Deals occasionally with productions of plays by Dryden per-
     formed by the King's or Duke's Companies, especially those of the
     King's in which Cardell Goodman had a part.

                              1965

1   ADDISON, JOSEPH, and RICHARD STEELE, et al. The Spectator.
     Edited by Donald F. Bond. 5 vols. Oxford: Clarendon Press.
          The standard modern edition. Includes 1711.1-2; 1712.1-3.

2   ALSSID, MICHAEL W. "The Design of Dryden's Aureng-Zebe." JEGP
     64 (July):452-69.
          Argues that both the literal and figurative actions in the
     play suggest "that Dryden's basic structural design . . . is con-
     ceived in terms of the sun analogy." Describes the moral ideas
     incarnated in each of the major characters; relates these to the
     sun analogy.

*3   ARCHER, STANLEY. "John Dryden and the Earl of Dorset." Ph.D.
     dissertation, University of Mississippi.
          Cited in Latt and Monk, 1976.30. Abstracted in DA 26:1018-
     19.

4   BATELY, JANET M. "Dryden and Branded Words." N&Q, n.s. 12
     (April):134-39.
          Discusses vocabulary changes in the second edition of Essay
     of Dramatic Poesy. Concludes that the changes move away from col-
     loquialism, and in the direction of modern usage.

*5   BLAIR, JOEL. "Dryden and Fanciful Poetry." Ph.D. dissertation,
     Harvard University.
          Cited in Latt and Monk, 1976.30.

6   BRADBROOK, M.C. English Dramatic Form: A History of Its
     Development. London: Chatto & Windus, 214 pp.
          In a brief discussion of The Conquest of Granada (pp. 115-
     18), links Almanzor's rhetorical extremity to the frustration of
     the Cavaliers after the Restoration, who "felt a need to believe
     in the heroic together with an incapacity to do so."

7   BROOKS, CLEANTH. Modern Poetry and the Tradition. New York:
     Oxford University Press.
          Reprint of 1939.5.

8   BROWN, F. ANDREW. "Shakespeare in Germany: Dryden, Langbaine,

and the <u>Acta Eruditorum</u>." <u>Germanic Review</u> 40 (March):87–95.
Argues that the favorable comment on Dryden appearing in
the journal <u>Acta Eruditorum</u> (Leipzig) in 1700 is a response to
Langbaine's attack (1691.1). Cites a summary of <u>Essay of Dramatic
Poesy</u> in the same journal; concludes that German discussions of
Shakespeare in the early eighteenth century took their cue from
these treatments of Dryden's criticism.

9   BROWN, JOHN RUSSELL, and BERNARD HARRIS, eds. <u>Restoration
     Theatre</u>. Stratford-on-Avon Studies 6. London: Edward Arnold.
     Includes, among others not on Dryden, original essays by
Bernard Harris (1965.21), D.W. Jefferson (1965.26), W. Moelwyn
Merchant (1965.41), Anne Righter (1965.47), and Roger Sharrock
(1965.52).

10   CAZAMIAN, LOUIS. <u>The Development of English Humor</u>. New York:
     AMS Press.
         Reprint of 1952.7.

11   CHASE, LEWIS N. <u>The English Heroic Play: A Critical Descrip-
     tion of the Rhymed Tragedy of the Restoration</u>. New York:
     Russell & Russell.
         Reprint of 1903.2.

12   CHERNAIK, WARREN L. "The Heroic Occasional Poem: Panegyric
     and Satire in the Restoration." <u>MLQ</u> 26 (December):523–35.
         Looks at examples of the form, especially in Edmund Waller
and Andrew Marvell; relates them to Dryden's association of satire
with epic.

13   CLARK, A.F.B. <u>Boileau and the French Classical Critics in
     England (1660–1830)</u>. New York: Russell & Russell.
         Reprint of 1925.3.

14   CRIDER, J.R. "Dryden's 'Absalom and Achitophel,' 169–172."
     <u>Expl</u> 23 (April): note 63.
         Suggests that the lines do more than insult Shaftesbury's
son: they support the attack on Shaftesbury because of the current
belief that physical and mental qualities were passed from parent
to child.

15   DAVIES, H. NEVILLE. "Dryden's <u>All for Love</u> and Thomas May's
     <u>The Tragedie of Cleopatra Queen of AEgypt</u>." <u>N&Q</u>, n.s. 12
     (April):139–44.
         Suggests that May's play, not Shakespeare's, is the major
source of <u>All for Love</u>.

16   DENT, EDWARD J. <u>Foundations of English Opera: A Study of
     Musical Drama in England During the Seventeenth Century</u>. New
     York: Da Capo.
         Reprint of 1928.3.

*17   FOSTER, EDWARD E. "Dryden and the Poetry of Conversion: A
       Reading of The Hind and The Panther." Ph.D. dissertation,
       University of Rochester.
            Cited in Latt and Monk, 1976.30. Abstracted in DA 26:3301-2.

*18   FRIED, GISELA. "Das Charakterbild Shakespeares im 17. und 18.
       Jahrhundert." In Jahrbuch der Deutschen Shakespeare-
       Gesellschaft West. Edited by Hermann Hever. Heidelberg:
       Quelle & Mayer, pp. 161-83.
            Cited in Latt and Monk, 1976.30.

 19   GALLAWAY, FRANCIS. Reason, Rule, and Revolt in English Classic-
       ism. New York: Octagon Books.
            Reprint of 1940.10.

 20   HAMM, VICTOR M. "Dryden's Religio Laici and Roman Catholic
       Apologetics." PMLA 80 (June):190-98.
            Suggests that Dryden made use of such writers as Hugh de
       Cressy, William Rushworth, Thomas White, John Canes, John Sargeant,
       Edward Worsley, and Abraham Woodhead. Cites verbal parallels and
       echoes of ideas. Suggests that the reading Dryden did while writ-
       ing Religio Laici may have caused him to question Anglicanism.

 21   HARRIS, BERNARD. "The Dialect of those Fanatic Times." In
       Restoration Theatre. Edited by John Russell Brown and Bernard
       Harris. Stratford-on-Avon Studies 6. London: Edward Arnold,
       pp. 11-40.
            Printed in 1965.9. Compares dramatic and nondramatic prose.
       Finds, in opposition to L.C. Knights (in 1937.9), dramatic prose
       to be vigorous and lifelike. Asserts that prose should not be
       considered except in its contexts, whether broadly social or spe-
       cifically circumstantial. Claims that the use of low language made
       "more possible in the drama the fuller presentation of experience."

*22   HAYMAN, JOHN GRIFFITHS. "Raillery during the Restoration Period
       and Early Eighteenth Century." Ph.D. dissertation, Northwestern
       University.
            Cited in Latt and Monk, 1976.30. Abstracted in DA 25:4146-
   47.

 23   HOPE, A.D. "All for Love, or Comedy as Tragedy." In The Cave
       and the Spring. Adelaide: Rigby, pp. 144-63.
            Asserts that the play is actually a comedy. It lacks the
       conflict of values that Antony and Cleopatra has, substituting for
       it a conflict for possessions. Notes a "middle-class commercial"
       language and tone. Concludes that Dryden's lovers "mistake in-
       fatuation for passion and delirium for imaginative vision." Re-
       printed: 1970.38.

 24   _____. "Anne Killigrew, or the Art of Modulating." In The
       Cave and the Spring. Adelaide: Rigby, pp. 129-43.
            Reprint of 1963.16. Reprinted: 1969.40; 1970.38.

25 JACKSON, WALLACE. "Dryden's Emperor and Lillo's Merchant: The Relevant Bases of Action." MLQ 26 (December):536-44.
     Argues that The London Merchant is in "the line of descent" from All for Love. Both plays see excessive passion as the central evil. Concludes that it is more useful to think of the plays as "theatre of a closed society" than as "domestic tragedy."

26 JEFFERSON, D.W. "'All, all of a piece throughout': Thoughts on Dryden's Dramatic Poetry." In Restoration Theatre. Edited by John Russell Brown and Bernard Harris. Stratford-on-Avon Studies 6. London: Edward Arnold, pp. 159-76.
     Printed in 1965.9. Argues for the essential unity of Dryden's drama in such matters as mood, imagery, and theme. Uses Don Sebastian as a major example, showing how themes, characters, and sentiments echo those in others of Dryden's plays from all periods of his career.

27 KERNAN, ALVIN B. The Plot of Satire. New Haven: Yale University Press, 233 pp.
     Cites "Discourse of Satire" as the culmination of Renaissance attempts to sum up the form. Emphasizes Dryden's articulation of morality and wit as touchstones of satire (pp. 6-9). Examines Dryden's portrait of Zimri; asserts that here "art and morality . . . are locked together in an intricate and continuing conflict which generates the plot of satire."

28 KIEHL, JAMES M. "Dryden's Zimri and Chaucer's Pardoner: A Comparative Study of Verse Portraiture." Thoth 6, no. 1 (Winter):3-12.
     Compares the two portraits: emphasizes how each reflects its author's purpose. Analyzes the two poets' couplets, showing that Dryden's are much more formal and rhetorical.

29 KING, BRUCE. "Absalom and Dryden's Earlier Praise of Monmouth." ES 46 (August):332-33.
     Notes two allusions in Absalom and Achitophel to Dryden's dedication of Tyrannic Love to Monmouth (1670). Points out the irony in Dryden's earlier praise of Monmouth's naturalism: in Absalom and Achitophel he portrays him as artificial.

30 _____. "Anti-Whig Satires in The Duke of Guise." ELN 2 (March):190-93.
     Suggests three possible sources for Whig ideas satirized in the play: the anonymous A Letter from a Person of Quality to his Friend Concerning His Majesties late Declaration, Shadwell's Epistle to the Tories, and the anonymous Letter to a Friend in the Country.

31 _____. "Dryden, Tillotson, and Tyrannic Love." RES, n.s. 16 (November):364-77.
     Notes parallels between some of St. Catherine's speeches in

the play and passages in Tillotson's early sermons. Suggests that
Dryden may have been asked, possibly by someone at the Court, for
a religious play, and turned naturally for ideas to Tillotson.
Concludes that Dryden was probably a Latitudinarian, like Tillotson,
at the time of writing the play (1669).

*32   _____. "Dryden's Marriage a la Mode." Drama Survey 4:28-37.
            Cited in Latt and Monk, 1976.30.

33   KIRSCH, ARTHUR. Dryden's Heroic Drama. Princeton: Princeton
          University Press, 157 pp.
              Studies the relation of Dryden's heroic plays to his theory:
      argues that he "subordinated theoretical commitments to his prac-
      tice." Questions the view that Dryden based his concept of heroic
      drama on the epic; finds native and continental drama much more
      potent influences. Emphasizes two aspects of Dryden's heroes:
      their libertinism and their "resemblance to the protagonists of
      Cornélian drama." Discusses his development from The Rival Ladies
      to The Conquest of Granada. Finds the geometric complexity of the
      plot of The Rival Ladies typical of his earliest serious plays.
      Sees the key theme of the conflict between public and private vir-
      tue beginning to develop in The Indian Emperour and becoming cru-
      cial in The Conquest of Granada. Finds in Aureng-Zebe the emergence
      of a new kind of hero who wins the audience's sympathy rather than
      admiration; ties this change to Dryden's shift from heroic couplets
      to the more realistic blank verse. Analyzes All for Love, empha-
      sizing its sentimental and domestic aspects. Suggests that in
      moving in this direction Dryden was responding to the success of
      plays by Nathaniel Lee and Thomas Otway. Concludes that Dryden
      was "at once the last of the Elizabethans and the first of the
      Moderns." Reprinted: 1972.40. The section of All for Love is
      reprinted in 1968.39.

34   LEGOUIS, PIERRE. Andrew Marvell: Poet, Puritan, Patriot.
          Oxford: Clarendon Press, 261 pp.
              The author's translation from the French of 1928.9.

35   LEVINE, JAY ARNOLD. "Dryden's Song for St. Cecilia's Day,
          1687." PQ 44 (January):38-50.
              Defends the poem against Johnson's criticism of it (in
      1779.2); analyzes the opening stanza to show its symmetry of meter,
      and argues that "diapason," far from being an unduly technical
      term, is a key to the poem's use of the tradition of cosmic harmony.
      Reads the rest of the poem in this light. Notes that it departs
      from the standard of Cecilian tributes, being more "complex and
      serious."

36   LEWALSKI, BARBARA KIEFER. "The Scope and Function of Biblical
          Allusion in Absalom and Achitophel." ELN 3 (September):29-35.
              Argues that "biblical allusions are much more extensive and
      even more important to the poem than has heretofore been realized."
      Shows how widely these allusions range throughout the Bible.

37   LYNCH, KATHLEEN M.   The Social Mode of Restoration Comedy.
     New York: Octagon Books.
        Reprint of 1926.4.

*38   McNAMARA, PETER LANCE.   "John Dryden's Contribution to the
      English Comic Tradition of Witty Love-Play." Ph.D. disserta-
      tion, Tulane University.
         Cited in Latt and Monk, 1976.30. Abstracted in DA 25:5910-
      11.

39   MAYHEAD, ROBIN.   Understanding Literature.   Cambridge:
     Cambridge University Press, 189 pp.
        Discusses "To the Memory of Mr. Oldham" (pp. 154-58). De-
     fends the poem against the charge that it is too "neat" to express
     real grief. Praises its technical excellence.

40   MELLERS, WILFRID. Harmonious Meeting: A Study of the Rela-
     tionship between English Music, Poetry and Theatre, c. 1600-
     1900. London: Dobson, 317 pp.
        Discusses Purcell's music to Shadwell's The Tempest, which
     is based in turn on the Davenant-Dryden version of Shakespeare's
     play. Finds the opera a total failure except for the music (pp.
     220-24).

41   MERCHANT, W. MOELWYN.   "Shakespeare 'Made Fit.'" In Restoration
     Theatre.   Edited by John Russell Brown and Bernard Harris.
     Stratford-on-Avon Studies 6. London: Edward Arnold, pp.
     195-219.
        Printed in 1965.9. Presents a sympathetic treatment of
     Dryden's Shakespearean adaptations. Finds in them clear examples
     of the differences between Restoration and Elizabethan dramatic
     intentions: Dryden's versions are unambiguous in their moral
     sentiments; poetic justice is clearly distributed; the plays are
     more regular in structure than Shakespeare's.

42   MINER, EARL.   "The Significance of Plot in The Hind and the
     Panther." Bulletin of the New York Public Library 69
     (September):446-58.
        Links the absence of conventional plot in the poem to
     Dryden's other great poems of the eighties. Examines ll. 639-63,
     in which the progress of the plot seems to be particularly diffi-
     cult to grasp. Suggests that the dialogue between the Hind and
     the Panther reflects a dialogue within Dryden himself, which may
     account in part for the poem's difficulty and complexity. Proposes
     that the allusion to the Battle of Sedgemoor (1685) in these lines
     may indicate the approximate date of Dryden's conversion.

43   MIRÓ, CÉSAR.   "México y Perú en la tragedia clásical occidental."
     Cuadernos del Congreso por la libertad de la cultura 100:66-70.
        Cited in Latt and Monk, 1976.30.

44   MURPHREE, A.A.   "Wit and Dryden."   In <u>All These to Teach:</u>
     <u>Essays in Honor of C. A. Robertson</u>.   Edited by Robert A. Bryan,
     Alton C. Morris, A.A. Murphree, and Aubrey L. Williams.
     Gainsville: University of Florida Press, pp. 159-70.
          Enumerates, categorizes, and gives references for seventeen
     different uses of "wit" in Dryden's work.

45   NICOLL, ALLARDYCE.   <u>A History of English Drama, 1660-1900</u>.   6
     vols.   Cambridge: Cambridge University Press.
          Volume 1 ("Restoration Drama") is an updated edition of
     1923.4; 1928.10; 1940.20; 1952.23.

45A OSBORN, JAMES M.   <u>John Dryden: Some Biographical Facts and</u>
     <u>Problems</u>.   Rev. ed.   Gainesville: University of Florida Press,
     332 pp.
          A revised edition of 1940.21.   Adds "Postscript: Another
     Quarter Century" (pp. 114-29), which reviews scholarship since
     the first edition.   Discusses the strengths and weaknesses of Hugh
     Macdonald's bibliography (1939.12), and Charles E. Ward's edition
     of Dryden's letters (1942.12) and his life of Dryden (1961.57), and
     editions by Pierre Legouis (1946.11), George Noyes (1950.18), James
     Kinsley (1958.19), as well as the beginning of the California
     Edition (1956.16, etc.).

*46 PALMER, RODERICK.   "Treatments of Antony and Cleopatra."   <u>CEA</u>
     <u>Critic</u> 27, no. 4:8-9.
          Cited in Latt and Monk, 1976.30.

47   RIGHTER, ANNE.   "Heroic Tragedy."   In <u>Restoration Theatre</u>.
     Edited by John Russell Brown and Bernard Harris.   Stratford-
     on-Avon Studies 6.   London: Edward Arnold, pp. 135-57.
          Printed in 1965.9.   Argues the essential emptiness of
     Restoration tragedy.   Contends that in the period comedy and trag-
     edy were "implacably opposed forms" which could not coexist in the
     same play.   Condemns Restoration drama for excesses of plot, lan-
     guage, and character.   Claims that the tragedies present "a world
     of absolutes, of black and white without any mitigating shades of
     grey."   Concludes that in the last quarter of the century tragedy
     and comedy began moving together, toward sentimentality and pathos
     ("a senile marriage of opposites").   Draws several examples from
     Dryden's plays, especially <u>Tyrannic Love</u>.

48   ROPER, ALAN H.   <u>Dryden's Poetic Kingdoms</u>.   London: Routledge
     & Kegan Paul, 220 pp.
          Explicates Dryden's public poetry, emphasizing his use of
     figurative language.   Argues that his successes and failures have
     to do (in part) with the degree of imagination and resonance in
     his figures; suggests that his relative weakness in drama is tied
     to this question.   Notes his ability to tie sound to sense.   Looks
     at "poems in which the subject is an event or person exemplifying
     the government of England" (<u>Heroic Stanzas</u>, <u>Astraea Redux</u>, <u>Annus</u>

Mirabilis, The Medal): analyzes the structural patterns of analogy and imagery which unify each. Discusses the relationship between Dryden's political and literary views, especially as expressed in his use of analogy. Briefly applies his method to Absalom and Achitophel; concludes that "without Dryden our literature would be deficient in a poetry that successfully celebrates the public values of peace, security, authority, and political order."

49   SAINTSBURY, GEORGE. A History of English Prose Rhythm. Bloomington: Indiana University Press.
         Reprint of 1912.6.

*50   SAMPSON, HERBERT GRANT. "The Anglican Tradition in Eighteenth-Century Verse." Ph.D. dissertation, Michigan State University.
         Cited in Latt and Monk, 1976.30. Abstracted in DA 25:6602.

51   SHARP, ROBERT L. From Donne to Dryden: The Revolt Against Metaphysical Poetry. Hamden, Conn.: Archon Books.
         Reprint of 1940.23.

52   SHARROCK, ROGER. "Modes of Satire." In Restoration Theatre. Edited by John Russell Brown and Bernard Harris. Stratford-on-Avon Studies 6. London: Edward Arnold, pp. 109-32.
         Printed in 1965.9. Claims that in Restoration satire "the assertion of an attitude and a style of life was often as important, if not more important" than railing at chronic vices. Compares pre- and post-Restoration satire to show how the later writers better understood the nature of Latin satire, and had also, in their political circumstances, a greater amount of material. Compares John Oldham's Satires upon the Jesuits and Absalom and Achitophel to show how, as in Dryden's poem, "political good sense becomes a necessary constituent of poetic merit."

53   SIMON, IRÈNE. "Dryden's Prose Style." RLV 31:506-30.
         Cited in Latt and Monk, 1976.30.

54   SUTHERLAND, W.O.S. Jr. The Art of the Satirist: Essays on the Satire of Augustan England. Austin: University of Texas Press, 134 pp.
         Comments passage-by-passage on Absalom and Achitophel (pp. 38-53). Discusses various characters and what they represent; emphasizes the poem's moral complexity and maturity. Notes several organizing motifs: religious imagery and symbolism, animal imagery, antithesis and contrast.

*55   TAYLOR, CHARLENE M. "Aspects of Social Criticism in Restoration Comedy." Ph.D. dissertation, University of Illinois.
         Cited in Latt and Monk, 1976.30. Abstracted in DA 26:7301-2.

56   VAN LENNEP, WILLIAM, ed. The London Stage 1660-1800. Part 1: 1660-1700. With a critical introduction by Emmett L. Avery and

Arthur H. Scouten. Carbondale: Southern Illinois University
Press, 824 pp.
Lists plays performed during the period, with information
about the productions (date, theater, actors and actresses) and
some contemporary comment. Arranged chronologically. For other
parts see 1960.1 (Part 2); 1961.47 (Part 3); 1962.44 (Part 4);
1968.37 (Part 5).

57   VIETH, DAVID. "Irony in Dryden's Ode to Anne Killigrew." SP
      62 (January):91-100.
Suggests that Dryden's portrayal is in part ironic: he views
her simultaneously as a "potentially divine figure of atonement"
and as an "average, even if charming, mortal." Concludes that the
double-edged result is fundamental to the poem's success.

58   WARD, CHARLES E., coll. and ed. The Letters of John Dryden With
      Letters Addressed to Him. New York: AMS Press.
            Reprint of 1942.12.

59   WASSERMAN, GEORGE R. "The Domestic Metaphor in Astraea Redux."
      ELN 3 (December):106-11.
Argues that the similarities between Dryden's use of this
metaphor and the "imagery of Hebraic covenant lore" suggests that
he saw an Old Testament parallel to contemporary events not unlike
that in Absalom and Achitophel.

*60   WEIDHORN, MANFRED. "Dreams in Seventeenth-Century English
      Literature." Ph.D. dissertation, Columbia University.
            Cited in Latt and Monk, 1976.30. Abstracted in DA 26:1638.

*61   WEST, MICHAEL D. "Dryden's Attitude Toward the Hero." Ph.D.
      dissertation, Harvard University.
            Cited in Latt and Monk, 1976.30.

62   WILLIAMSON, GEORGE. "Dryden's View of Milton." In Milton and
      Others. London: Faber & Faber; Chicago: University of Chicago
      Press, pp. 103-21.
Examines The State of Innocence in the light of Dryden's various comments on Paradise Lost and related issues such as blank
verse, heroic poetry, and epic poetry. Concludes that in general
Dryden's work does not reflect Dryden's later criticism of Milton's
poem, bound as it is by its original.

63   WILSON, JOHN HAROLD. A Preface to Restoration Drama. Riverside
      Studies in Literature. Boston: Houghton Mifflin, 215 pp.
Makes frequent reference to Dryden's work, especially the
criticism, to illustrate various aspects of the overall subject.
Summarizes the plots of The Conquest of Granada and All for Love.
Evaluates them as examples of the heroic play and the "high tragedy." Finds the former not a tragedy and the latter "perhaps a little too coldly classical."

64 WOODHOUSE, A.S.P. "Religion and Poetry, 1660-1780." In The
Poet and His Faith: Religion and Poetry in England from Spenser
to Eliot and Auden. Chicago and London: University of Chicago
Press, pp. 123-59.
    Briefly treats Religio Laici and The Hind and the Panther.
Credits Dryden with initiating a rational and lucid mode in poetry
which had its effect on religious verse during the period.

65 WYLD, HENRY C. Studies in English Rhyme from Surrey to Pope.
New York: Russell & Russell.
    Reprint of 1923.10.

66 ZEBOUNI, SELMA ASSIR. Dryden: A Study in Heroic Characterization. Louisiana State University Studies, Humanities Series 16.
Baton Rouge: Louisiana State University Press, 118 pp.
    Argues that Dryden's heroic plays, properly understood, are
"a true reflection of the period and of the author and an important
link in the evolution of English drama." Asserts that modern critics have failed to understand the psychology of Dryden's heroes.
Argues that the basic trait of the hero is his "dominion, or even-
tual dominion, over his passion or passions." Looks at heroes in
Dryden's other serious plays: finds that they share the same basic
psychology. Argues that Dryden's concept of the hero is essentially identical to that of Corneille; contrasts Racine's heroes, who
seem to act in response to inner rather than outer drives.

67 ZIMBARDO, ROSE A. Wycherley's Drama: A Link in the Development
of English Satire. Yale Studies in English 156. New Haven and
London: Yale University Press, 182 pp.
    Discusses Dryden's "Discourse of Satire" (pp. 116-24). Ar-
gues that it "provides clear evidence" of a new perception of satire, that like other literary kinds it must have a "generically
determined form."

1966

1 ANSELMENT, RAYMOND A. "Martin Marprelate: A New Source for
Dryden's Fable of the Martin and the Swallows." RES, n.s. 17
(August):256-67.
    Notes that Martin Marprelate was conventially regarded as
a dangerous fool; suggests that Dryden's characterization of the
Martin in The Hind and the Panther comes not from beast fable but
from the anti-Martinist literature which was current during the
Elizabethan period and after.

2 ARCHER, STANLEY. "Benaiah in Absalom and Achitophel II." ELN
3 (March):183-85.
    Argues that the proper identification is the Colonel Edward
Sackville who commanded the garrison at Tangier, not the Edward
Sackville who denounced Titus Oates (as Sir Walter Scott had
thought).

3   _____. "The Persons in An Essay of Dramatic Poesy." PLL 2
         (Fall):305-14.
            Defends Edmond Malone's identifications (in 1800.1) of
      Eugenius (Lord Buckhurst), Lisideius (Sir Charles Sedley), Crites
      (Sir Robert Howard), and Neander (Dryden).

4   BAKER, DAVID ERSKINE. Biographica Dramatica: or, a Companion
         to the Playhouse. New York: AMS Press.
            Reprint of 1912.1, which is a revised version (by Stephen
      Jones) of 1764.1.

5   BENSON, DONALD R. "Who 'Bred' Religio Laici?" JEGP 65
         (April):238-51.
            Asserts that Dryden had probably not read Father Simon's
      Critical History of the Old Testament when he wrote the poem, de-
      spite what he says in his dedication. Argues that his points
      against the Deists in the first half of the poem are based on the
      writings of Richard Baxter and Edward Stillingfleet, and that the
      second part of the poem contains a refutation (probably unwitting)
      of Simon's most important points.

6   BOYS, RICHARD C., ed. Studies in the Literature of the Augustan
         Age: Essays Collected in Honor of Arthur Ellicott Case. New
         York: Gordian Press.
            Reprint of 1952.3, which includes 1931.17; 1938.19; 1946.7.
      Reprinted: 1976.7.

7   BUTT, JOHN. The Augustan Age. New York: Norton.
            Reprint of 1950.4.

8   CRINÒ, ANNA MARIA. "Dryden MS." TLS, 22 September, p. 879.
            Announces that she has found an early manuscript of Heroic
      Stanzas.

9   CUNNINGHAM, JOHN E. Restoration Drama. Literature in Perspec-
         tive. London: Evans, 160 pp.
            "John Dryden" (pp. 59-76) provides a general introduction,
      thematically arranged, to Dryden's life and career as a dramatist.
      Emphasizes his professionalism in contrast to the other writers--
      Etherege, Wycherley, Otway, Congreve--the book deals with.

10   DAVIES, H. NEVILLE. "Dryden and Vossius: A Reconsideration."
         JWCI 29:282-95.
            Argues, against Dean T. Mace (1964.27), that Dryden was not
      indebted to Vossius's theory of rhythmus. Explains his allusion
      to rhythmus in the preface to Albion and Albanus as a reference
      to the prosody, based on Virgil's practice, that he had prepared
      for his own use. Suggests that Dryden's views about the difficulty
      of singing in English may have come from William Holder's Elements
      of Speech (1669). Criticizes Mace's interpretation of several con-
      temporary theories about the inadequacy of modern music. See
      1966.36.

11   DOYLE, ANNE. "Dryden's Authorship of <u>Notes and Observations on</u>
     <u>The Empress of Morocco</u> (1674)." <u>SEL</u> 6 (Summer):421-45.
          Argues on internal evidence (largely parallels with ideas
     and wording Dryden used elsewhere) that Dryden wrote the preface,
     the postscript, most of the second act, and "The Errata's in the
     Epistle." Finds it impossible to attribute authorship for the
     rest of the work.

12   EHRMAN, MADELINE. <u>The Meanings of the Modals in Present-Day</u>
     <u>English</u>. The Hague: Mouton, 106 pp.
          Compares, in "Appendix B" (pp. 98-103), Dryden's use of
     modal auxiliaries with Shakespeare's and with present-day English.
     Takes examples from <u>Essay of Dramatic Poesy</u> and <u>All for Love</u>; con-
     cludes that the essay is much closer to present-day English than
     the play.

*13 ELKIN, P.K. "The Defence of Satire from Dryden to Johnson."
     Ph.D. dissertation, Oxford University.
          Cited in Latt and Monk, 1976.30. See 1973.24.

14   ELLOWAY, D.R., ed. <u>Dryden's Satire</u>. London: Macmillan; New
     York: St. Martin's, 238 pp.
          The introduction places Dryden in his literary context, and
     describes and evaluates the selections in the anthology. Asserts
     that "almost all his verse that is chiefly valued today" is satir-
     ic. Provides a "historical introduction" to <u>Absalom and Achitophel</u>
     and <u>The Medal</u>.

*15 EMERY, JOHN P. "Restoration Dualism of the Court Writers."
     <u>RLV</u> 32:238-65.
          Cited in Latt and Monk, 1976.30.

16   GATTO, LOUIS C. "An Annotated Bibliography of Critical Thought
     Concerning Dryden's <u>Essay of Dramatic Poesy</u>." <u>RECTR</u> 5, no. 1
     (May):18-29.
          Briefly describes the contents of each entry; "makes no ef-
     fort to catalogue . . . anthologies which contain the <u>Essay</u>, nor
     does it attempt any citation of the more general literary histor-
     ies."

17   GEREVINI, SILVANO. <u>Dryden e Teocrito: Barocco e neoclassicismo</u>
     <u>nella Restaurazione inglese</u>. Milan: Mursia, 157 pp.
          Notes the critical neglect of Dryden's work as a translator.
     Discusses his version of four idylls of Theocritus: compares them
     with those of his predecessors and contemporaries, especially
     Thomas Creech. Suggests that Dryden used Creech's translations
     as a basis for his own, despite his contention to the contrary.
     Analyzes each translation, almost line by line.

18   GOLDEN, SAMUEL A. "Dryden's <u>Cleomenes</u> and Theophilus Parsons."
     <u>N&Q</u>, n.s. 13 (October):380.

Proposes that Parsons, whose prefatory poem was published
with the play in 1693, was first cousin to Nahum Tate. Suggests
that Dryden's publication of the poem shows his continued interest
in helping young writers.

19   _____. "Dryden's Praise of Dr. Charleton." Hermathena 103
      (Autumn):59-65.
      Argues that the poem should not be separated from the context
of Dryden's other panegyrics. Notes that unlike the others, which
are highly ornamental, the poem "is stripped clean of all decora-
tive devices." Suggests that this form is a tribute to Charleton
as a member of the Royal Society.

20   _____. "Dryden's 'To My Honored Friend, Dr. Charleton,' 37-44."
      Expl 24 (February): note 53.
      Argues that Dryden embedded a reference to Charleton's
Spiritus Gorgonicus (which has to do with stony growths in the
human body) in ll. 43-44.

21   GREEN, CLARENCE C. The Neo-Classical Theory of Tragedy in
      England During the Eighteenth Century. New York: Blom.
            Reprint of 1934.8.

22   KALLICH, MARTIN. "Oedipus: From Man to Archetype." Comparative
      Literature Studies 3, no. 1:33-46.
            Discusses the Dryden-Lee Oedipus as one version of the myth.
Suggests that its innovation, the "tragic love" theme, is a reflection of the fashion of the time.

23   KING, BRUCE. Dryden's Major Plays. Edinburgh and London:
      Oliver & Boyd, 225 pp.
            Asserts that the conflict of passion and resignation is at
the heart of Dryden's drama. Argues that the heroic plays are
basically satiric, and reflect Dryden's dislike of Hobbesian materialism: he uses characters like Maximin in Tyrannic Love and
Almanzor in The Conquest of Granada to illustrate "man in his
natural state." Also discusses The Rival Ladies, The Indian Queen,
and The Indian Emperour. Sees Marriage a-la-Mode as reflecting
Dryden's anti-Hobbesianism. Finds in The State of Innocence a reflection of the controversy between Hobbes and Bishop Bramhall
over necessity and liberty. Adam and Eve fall because they accept
Hobbesian arguments: for Dryden Milton's "paradise within . . .
has come to represent those virtues of temperament and self-
regulation that Dryden felt were necessary if man was to avoid
life's unrest." Calls Aureng-Zebe, whose main theme is "the dis-
quieting effects of the imagination," the best of the heroic plays,
even though the form was no longer adequate for what Dryden wanted
to do. Finds All for Love disappointing, due to the insufficiency
of its aims, although it does succeed in raising sympathy for its
major figures. Relates The Spanish Friar to political questions
of the time, especially in its support of monarchy and divine

right. Asserts that <u>Don Sebastian</u> is Dryden's best play, because
it has "a mature critical theory" behind it, and a plot directly
related to its moral. Sees in the play a conflict between Christian
and Stoic views of death. The tragic ending "illustrates Dryden's
view that human passion will break through all social laws unless
resignation is forced on man by his fear of an unknown after-life."
Finds finally in <u>Love Triumphant</u> an illustration of "the contrast
between the life of passion and the life of fortitude, which is
the essential subject of Dryden's plays." Concludes that "Dryden
was the first of the great Augustan critics of the modern world
and of its intellectual justifications."

24 _____. "'Lycidas' and 'Oldham.'" <u>EA</u> 19 (January–March):60–63.
Cites verbal parallels between the two poems; suggests that
the relationship between them illustrates Dryden's interest in
"Milton's achievement at imitating classical poetics in English."

*25 KINNEAVY, GERALD B. "Judgment in Extremes: A Study of Dryden's
<u>Absalom and Achitophel</u>." <u>University of Dayton Review</u> 3, no. 1:
15–30.
Cited in Latt and Monk, 1976.30.

*26 KLAVER, PETER ROBERTS. "The Meaning of the Term <u>Wit</u> in English
Literary Criticism, 1680–1712." Ph.D. dissertation, University
of Michigan.
Cited in Latt and Monk, 1976.30. Abstracted in <u>DA</u> 27:478A–
79A.

27 LANGHANS, EDWARD A. "Restoration Manuscript Notes in Seventeenth
Century Plays." <u>RECTR</u> 5, no. 1 (May):30–39; no. 2 (November):
2–17.
Lists and describes these: nine (out of fifty-two) entries
relate to Dryden.

28 LEED, JACOB. "A Difficult Passage in <u>Astraea Redux</u>." <u>ES</u> 47
(April):127–30.
Argues that the meaning of 11. 159–68 is that while success
is easy in imagination, it is hard in action; that General Monk's
task in bringing about the King's return was particularly hard despite strong support for it.

29 LEGOUIS, PIERRE. "Dryden's Scipio and Hannibal." <u>TLS</u>, 15 July,
p. 602.
Quarrels with Alan Roper's readings of <u>The Medal</u> and "To
. . . Mr. Congreve" (in 1965.48).

30 LOFTIS, JOHN. "Exploration and Enlightenment: Dryden's <u>The
Indian Emperour</u> and Its Background." <u>PQ</u> 45 (January):71–84.
Discusses and evaluates the play. Asserts that despite its
inconsistencies (especially in the portrayal of Montezuma) it has
"intellectual vigor." Suggests several possible sources for the

historical material: The Tempest, the operas of Davenant, and the
histories of Purchas and especially Lopez de Gómara (where the
theme of Spanish cruelty and destructiveness can be found).

31   _____, ed. Restoration Drama: Modern Essays in Criticism.
      New York: Oxford University Press, 382 pp.
          Includes 1937.9; 1940.16; 1950.15; 1962.25.

32   _____, ed. The Works of John Dryden. Volume IX: Plays. The
      Indian Emperour, Secret Love, Sir Martin Mar-All. Vinton A.
      Dearing, textual editor. Berkeley and Los Angeles: University
      of California Press, 451 pp.
          The commentary (pp. 291-375) and other editorial material
      follow the format of 1962.42 (vol. 8). Other volumes in the series
      to date: 1956.16 (1); 1969.52 (3); 1970.59 (10); 1971.58 (17);
      1972.83 (2); 1974.7 (4); 1974.54 (18); 1976.41 (15); 1978.29 (11);
      1979.30 (19).

33   LOVE, H.H.R. "The Authorship of the Postscript of Notes and
      Observations on The Empress of Morocco." N&Q, n.s. 13
      (January):27-28.
          Argues on the internal evidence that Shadwell, not Dryden,
      wrote the piece.

34   LOWE, ROBERT W. A Bibliographical Account of English Theatrical
      Literature from the Earliest Times to the Present Day. Detroit:
      Gale Research.
          Reprint of 1888.3. Revised and updated: 1970.4.

35   MACDONALD, HUGH. John Dryden: A Bibliography of Early Editions
      and of Drydeniana. London: Dawsons of Pall Mall.
          Reprint of 1939.12.

36   MACE, DEAN T. "A Reply to Mr. H. Neville Davies's 'Dryden and
      Vossius: A Reconsideration.'" JWCI 29:296-310.
          Replies to 1966.10. Defends his interpretation of musical
      theories of Dryden's period. Quotes extensively from John Wallis's
      The Strange Effects Reported of Musick in Former Times, Examined
      (1732). Also defends his interpretation of Dryden's reference to
      Vossius in his preface to Albion and Albianus. See 1964.27.

*37   McFADDEN, GEORGE. "Dryden, Boileau, and Longinian Imitation."
      In Proceedings of the IVth Congress of the International Com-
      parative Literature Association. Vol. 2. Edited by Francois
      Jost. The Hague: Mouton, pp. 751-55.
          Cited in Latt and Monk, 1976.30.

*38   MARTIN-CLARKE, M.F. "Studies in Dryden's Criticism, with
      Particular Reference to His Critical Terminology and to Certain
      Aspects of His Dramatic Theory and Practice." Ph.D. disserta-
      tion, Oxford University.
          Cited in Latt and Monk, 1976.30.

39   MAURER, A.E. WALLACE. "The Design of Dryden's The Medall."
      PLL 2 (Fall):293-304.
        Argues that Dryden "struck his own medal" in the poem, rely-
ing on his audience's familiarity with conventional medallic design:
he presents the obverse of the coin in 11. 22-144 and the reverse
in 11. 145-324. Concludes that his convention derives from emblematic poetry and advice-to-the-painter poems, but that the result
here is original. Points out that Samuel Pordage's parody The
Medal Revers'd (1682.5) gives a clear indication that Dryden's pattern was perceptible.

40   _____. "The Structure of Dryden's Astraea Redux." PLL 2
      (Winter):13-20.
        Analyzes the poem to show that it is organized like a clas-
sical oration, in which Dryden uses each of the three types: demonstrative, deliberate, judicial. Concludes that when viewed this
way the poem is not disorganized, as many critics have suggested.

41   MILBURN, D. JUDSON. The Age of Wit 1650-1750. New York:
      Macmillan Co.; London: Collier-Macmillan, 348 pp.
        Refers frequently to Dryden's various discussions of wit.
Uses "Upon the Death of Lord Hastings" and MacFlecknoe to show how
conventional attitudes toward wit changed during the century (pp.
69-75). Narrates Dryden's argument with Shadwell over the relative importance of wit and judgment (pp. 120-24).

42   MINER, EARL. "Dryden's Annus Mirabilis, 653-656." Expl 24
      (May): note 75.
        Argues that the image of the ocean leaning on the sky is not
an absurdity but a "very fair and exciting representation of English
experience of exploration in his day and for a century preceding."

43   _____, ed. Restoration Dramatists: A Collection of Critical
      Essays. Twentieth Century Views. Englewood Cliffs, N.J.:
      Prentice-Hall.
        Includes 1940.16; 1962.25, 48.

44   NOVAK, MAXIMILLIAN E. "The Demonology of Dryden's Tyrannick
      Love and 'Anti-Scot.'" ELN 4 (December):95-98.
        Asserts that A Discourse Concerning the Nature and Substance
of Devils and Spirits (1665), by "Anti-Scot," is an important
source of the incantation scene in the play.

43   NOVARR, DAVID. "Swift's Relation with Dryden, and Gulliver's
      Annus Mirabilis." ES 47 (October):341-54.
        Discusses Swift's "ambivalent attitude toward Dryden." Cites
negative references, implicit as well as overt, in Swift's works
and letters, but argues that Swift also had a "grudging admiration"
for Dryden's work, especially in the heroic mode. Suggests that
Annus Mirabilis served as one model for Swift's presentation of
Gulliver's heroic actions in Book 1, chapter 5.

46   PRIOR, MOODY. The Language of Tragedy. Bloomington: Indiana
      University Press.
           Reprint of 1950.20 (the revised edition of 1947.11).

47   RUDD, NIALL. The Satires of Horace. Cambridge: Cambridge
      University Press.
           Includes 1963.45.

48   RUSSELL, TRUSTEN W. Voltaire, Dryden, and Heroic Tragedy. New
      York: AMS Press.
           Reprint of 1946.16.

49   SHERGOLD, N.D., and PETER URE. "Dryden and Calderón: A New
      Spanish Source for The Indian Emperour." MLR 61 (July):369-83.
           Asserts that "a substantial part of Dryden's plot is directly
      adapted" from Calderón's El príncipe constante (1628 to 1629).
      Cites many structural and verbal parallels, as well as similarities
      in characterization. See 1970.52.

50   SHERWOOD, JOHN C. "Dryden and the Critical Theories of Tasso."
      CL 18 (Fall):351-59.
           Argues that Tasso was an important influence on Dryden.
      Cites parallels between them; suggests that they shared "the prob-
      lem of reconciling the native and classical traditions." Notes
      that their ideas are particularly close when they deal with the
      relation of heroic poetry to heroic drama.

51   SHERWOOD, MARGARET P. Dryden's Dramatic Theory and Practice.
      New York: Haskell House.
           Reprint of 1898.3.

52   SMITH, DAVID NICHOL. John Dryden. Clark Lectures on English
      Literature, 1948-49. Hamden, Conn.: Archon Books.
           Reprint of 1950.24.

*53   SMITH, J.L. "Some Aspects of the Verse-Epistle in English
      Literature before Pope." Ph.D. dissertation, Oxford University.
           Cited in Latt and Monk, 1976.30.

54   SORELIUS, GUNNAR. "The Giant Race Before the Flood": Pre-
      Restoration Drama on the Stage and in the Criticism of the
      Restoration. Studia Anglistica Upsaliensia 4. Uppsala:
      Almqvist & Wiksell, 227 pp.
           Refers frequently to Dryden's plays and criticism. Argues
      that there was a general trend toward sentimentalism in both seri-
      ous and comic drama which Dryden at first resisted and then suc-
      cumbed to. Finds Dryden typical of the playwrights of the period
      who "both loved and hated the dramatic heritage."

55   STRATMAN, CARL J., C.S.V., ed. Bibliography of English Printed
      Tragedy 1565-1900. Carbondale: Southern Illinois University

Press; London and Amsterdam: Feffer & Simons.
Lists (chronologically) editions containing Dryden's heroic or tragic plays. Gives publisher, date, other relevant information when available, and occasional bibliographical commentary. Indicates where copies may be found (pp. 165-85).

*56 STUCKEY, JOHANNA HEATHER. "The Reputation and Influence of C. Petronius Arbiter Among English Men of Letters from 1600-1700." Ph.D. dissertation, Yale University.
Cited in Latt and Monk, 1976.30. Abstracted in DA 27:188A-89A.

57 SWEDENBERG, H.T., Jr., ed. Essential Articles for the Study of John Dryden. Hamden, Conn.: Archon Books, 602 pp.
Contains the following essays: 1918.5; 1921.4; 1931.17; 1932.1; 1934.4; 1935.4, 7; 1936.16, 22; 1939.10; 1940.2; 1942.5; 1943.1, 14; 1946.3, 7, 18, 20, 22; 1947.7, 16; 1948.12; 1951.22; 1953.9; 1954.3; 1957.20, 21; 1958.36; 1961.7.

*58 SWEDENBERG, H.T., Jr. "Literature: 1640-1750. In Report of the Third Decade 1956-1966. Los Angeles: Clark Memorial Library, University of California.
Cited in Latt and Monk, 1976.30.

59 THALE, MARY. "Dryden's Critical Vocabulary: The Imitation of Nature." PLL 2 (Fall):315-26.
Examines the phrase "imitation of nature," which Dryden seems to have been the first to use. Finds both "nature" and "imitation" used in several different senses; concludes that it is an "inclusive phrase intended to synthesize apparently opposite features of ancient and modern drama." Notes that the phrase appears most frequently at the beginning of Dryden's career, when he was looking for a vocabulary to use in his defense of English drama.

60 _____. "Dryden's Dramatic Criticism: Polestar of the Ancients." CL 18 (Winter):36-54.
Shows how Dryden uses the ancients to justify modern drama. He supplements and reinterprets their theories, he appeals to classical nondramatic sources to expand the number and nature of his standards and, most importantly, he elevates "to primacy a concept of the imitation of nature." This last practice enables him to show the superiority of the English drama over the French. Concludes that Dryden is a great critic because he makes the classics relevant to his modern literary situation.

61 TILLYARD, E.M.W. The English Epic and Its Background. New York: Barnes & Noble.
Reprint of 1954.26.

62 TRAUGOTT, JOHN. "The Rake's Progress from Court to Comedy: A Study in Comic Form." SEL 6 (Summer):381-407.

Considers what seems to be a contradictory value system inherent in Restoration drama. Notes Dryden's oscillation between posturing about and ridiculing love and honor; finds this "paradoxical and absurb sentiment . . . the very quality of the age." Cites Tyrannic Love (with its epilogue) and Absalom and Achitophel as examples of an uneasy coexistence of the two attitudes; sees Marriage a-la-Mode as a "deliberate counterpointing" of the two.

63 TUCKER, T.G. The Foreign Debt of English Literature. New York: Haskell House.
       Reprint of 1907.5.

64 WASSERMAN, GEORGE. "Dryden's The Hind and the Panther, III, 1-21." Expl 24 (April): note 71.
       Argues that these lines "wittily anticipate two reactions . . . to the first two parts of the poem": Protestant anger, and Catholic fear of their new freedoms under James II.

65 _____. "A Note on Dryden's Panther." N&Q, n.s. 13 (October): 380-82.
       Looks at 3. 639-43: sees there evidence of a change in Dryden's characterization of the Panther from that of the first two parts of the poem. Suggests that the change is a response to James II's Declaration of Indulgence.

66 WEIMANN, ROBERT. "Shakespeares Publikum and Platformbühne im Spiegel Klassizistischer Kritik (bei Rymer, Dryden u. a.)." Shakespeare Jahrbuch 102:60-96.
       Discusses neoclassic attitudes toward the old Elizabethan-style open stage and the acting style it fostered. Notes Dryden's marked preference for the indoor stage with scenery: relates this attitude to his belief that his own age surpassed that of the Elizabethans in wit. Suggests that neoclassic critics may have also been influenced by seeing plays at the open-air Red Bull Theatre.

67 WELLINGTON, JAMES E. "Conflicting Concepts of Man in Dryden's Absalom and Achitophel." Satire Newsletter 4 (Fall):2-11.
       Argues that the poem contains a "fundamental conflict," unresolved, between two concepts of human nature. The poem takes both the orthodox Christian view (that man is depraved and needs restraints) and the libertine naturalistic view (that he is free to do as he pleases). This conflict primarily resides in the characterization of King Charles.

1967

1 ADAMS, PERCY G. "'Harmony of Numbers': Dryden's Alliteration, Consonance, Assonance." TSLL 9 (Autumn):333-43.
       Demonstrates Dryden's heavy use of each of these devices. Argues that his use of them was frequently onomatopoetic.

2   ALSSID, MICHAEL W. "Shadwell's <u>MacFlecknoe</u>." <u>SEL</u> 7 (Summer):
      387–402.
          Asserts that "Dryden subverted Shadwell's critical ideas
      and dramatic practice to create <u>MacFlecknoe</u> and . . . that the
      poem reveals Dryden's awareness of the enemy's incipient Whiggism
      and its implications." Suggests possible sources in Shadwell's
      plays and criticism for several of the poem's allusions. Proposes
      that Dryden turns Shadwell into a "humor" character in retaliation
      for Shadwell's characterization of "Drybob" in <u>The Humorists</u>. Ar-
      gues that Dryden singled out Shadwell's <u>Psyche</u> for special attack
      because of its association with Monmouth's rise to fame.

3   _____. <u>Thomas Shadwell</u>. Twayne English Authors Series. New
      York: Twayne, 191 pp.
          Deals with the points at which Shadwell's and Dryden's ca-
      reers intertwined.

3A   ANGEL, MARC D. "Five Translations of the <u>Aeneid</u>." <u>Classical</u>
      <u>Journal</u> 62 (April):295–300.
          Compares versions of 4.700–705 (those of Dryden, Rolfe
      Humphries, C. Day Lewis, J.W. Mackail, and Kevin Guinagh).
      Praises Dryden for capturing the spirit of the original, but
      faults his literal accuracy. Suggests that he was more interested
      in interpreting than translating the original. Finds Lewis's the
      best of the five.

4   ARCHER, STANLEY. "Dryden's 'MacFlecknoe,' 47–48." <u>Expl</u> 26
      (December): note 37.
          Suggests that "Aston Hall" be emended to "Santon Hall,"
      Shadwell's birthplace near Norwich.

5   AVERY, EMMETT L. "Rhetorical Patterns in Restoration Prologues
      and Epilogues." In <u>Essays in American and English Literature</u>
      <u>Presented to Bruce Robert McElderry, Jr</u>. Edited by Max F.
      Schultz with William D. Templeton and Charles R. Metzger.
      Athens: Ohio University Press, pp. 221–37.
          Discusses the strategies various authors used to deal with
      problems of being continually original within the form of the
      prologue and epilogue. Emphasizes their use of comparison in their
      attempt to secure a sympathetic response from their audience. Uses
      several examples from Dryden.

5A   BARNES, T.R. <u>English Verse: Voice and Movement from Wyatt to</u>
      <u>Yeats</u>. Cambridge: Cambridge University Press, 334 pp.
          The book "is intended to encourage the student and . . .
      general reader to listen to poetry." The overall emphasis is on
      sound and tone. Looks at several passages drawn from Dryden, show-
      ing his clarity and technical craft. Notes the public nature of
      his work, as contrasted with such poets as John Donne (pp. 106–16).

6   BEAURLINE, L.A., and FREDSON BOWERS, eds. <u>Four Comedies</u>.

Curtain Playwrights. Chicago and London: University of Chicago Press.

Old-spelling texts of Secret Love, An Evening's Love, Sir Martin Mar-All, and Marriage a-la-Mode. The general introduction (pp. 1-22) notes Dryden's low opinion of his comic writing: suggests that it derives from his low estimate of comedy's audience. Points out his use of the Jonsonian humor tradition and his own introduction of wit and repartee to comedy. Concludes by praising Dryden's skill at blending farce with regular comedy. Also contains brief individual introductions to each play.

7 _____, and _____, eds. Four Tragedies. Curtain Playwrights. Chicago and London: University of Chicago Press.

Old-spelling texts of The Indian Emperour, Aureng-Zebe, All for Love, and Don Sebastian. The introduction (pp. 1-25) praises Dryden's ability to sharpen dramatic conflict, but finds fault with his lack of variety. Notes the importance of Dryden's attitude that "the purpose of drama was to produce certain emotional and moral effects in the audience." This required, in serious plays, a kind of hero remote from ordinary life, like a figure in an epic. Notes that Dryden tried to produce pity rather than admiration in his later serious plays, which required a more realistic central figure. Also contains brief introductions to each of the four plays.

8 BELLER, MANFRED. Philemon und Baucis in der europaischen Literatur. Heidelberg: Winter, 164 pp.

Describes Dryden's version (in the Fables). Credits him with having avoided sentimentality in the climactic parting scene by concentrating on the representation of the metamorphosis (pp. 74-77).

*9 BIDDLE, EVELYN Q. "A Critical Study of the Influence of the Classical and Christian Traditions upon the Character of the Hero as Revealed Through the Concepts of 'Love' and 'Honor' in Three Restoration Tragedies." Ph.D. dissertation, University of Southern California.

Cited in Latt and Monk, 1976.30. Abstracted in DA 27:3969A-70A.

10 BROICH, ULRICH. "Litertin und heroischer Held: Das Drama der englischen Restuarationszeit und seine Leitbilder." Anglia 85, no. 1:34-57.

Finds links between comedies of manners and heroic plays. Sees in both a central pair of lovers (enduring similar conflicts), idealistic heroes, military language and imagery, and an emphasis on wit and honor as proper heroic qualities. Concludes that both forms were developing in the direction of sentimental drama. Discusses The Conquest of Granada, Aureng-Zebe, The Man of Mode (by Sir George Etherege), The Country Wife (by William Wycherley), and The Way of the World (by William Congreve).

*11   BUDICK, SANFORD. "Dryden's <u>Religio Laici</u>: A Study in Context
      and Meaning." Ph.D. dissertation, Yale University.
              Cited in Latt and Monk, 1976.30. Abstracted in <u>DA</u> 27:4216A.
      See 1970.17.

 12   COHEN, RALPH. "The Augustan Mode in English Poetry." <u>ECS</u> 1
      (September):3-32.
              Attempts to define the mode "so that it provides for relia-
      ble generalizations of poetic habits of thought and expression in
      the poetry from 1660 to 1750." Analyzes the opening eleven lines
      of <u>Religio Laici</u> and ll. 187-192 of <u>MacFlecknoe</u>, among many other
      passages by other poets, to discover the mode's characteristics.
      Finds nine "habits" characteristic of the period. Claims that
      while all do not appear in every poem, all poems of the period use
      one or more of them.

 13   CORDER, JIM W. "Rhetoric and Meaning in <u>Religio Laici</u>." <u>PMLA</u>
      82:245-49.
              Argues that the poem is an exercise in judicial oratory.
      Shows how the poem follows the conventional model of a classical
      oration, with its <u>exordium</u> (ll. 1-24), <u>narratio</u> (ll. 25-41),
      <u>confirmatio-confutatio</u> (ll. 42-426), and <u>peroratio</u> (ll. 427-end).
      Suggests that the poem is a debate in which Dryden upholds a golden
      mean against the extremes of deism, traditionalism, and enthusiasm.

 14   DANIELSSON, BROR, and DAVID M. VIETH, eds. <u>The Gyldenstolpe</u>
      <u>Manuscript Miscellany of Poems by John Wilmot, Earl of Rochester,</u>
      <u>and other Restoration Authors</u>. Stockholm Studies in English 17.
      Stockholm: Almqvist & Wiksell, 392 pp.
              Argues for 1676 as the date of <u>MacFlecknoe</u>, primarily because
      while it refers to many "events up to and including the publication
      of <u>The Virtuoso</u>" (1676), it is silent about events after it. Finds
      the date also plausible because it falls between <u>Aureng-Zebe</u> and
      <u>All for Love</u>, when Dryden was pessimistic about drama and inter-
      ested in the epic (pp. 343-47).

 15   DAVIES, H. NEVILLE. "Dryden's <u>All for Love</u> and Sedley's <u>Antony</u>
      <u>and Cleopatra</u>." <u>N&Q</u>, n.s. 14 (June):221-27.
              Argues that Dryden was indebted to Sedley's play for the
      selection of action to be dramatized, and for the central incident
      of the plot (Antony's loss of faith in Cleopatra).

 16   DOBRÉE, BONAMY. "John Dryden." In <u>Varieties of Ways: Discus-</u>
      <u>sions of Six Authors</u>. Essay Index Reprint Series. Freeport,
      N.Y.: Books for Libraries, pp. 1-16.
              Reprint of 1931.6; 1932.8.

 17   EADE, CHRISTOPHER. "Some English Iliads: Chapman to Dryden."
      <u>Arion</u> 6 (Autumn):336-45.
              Prints several passages as translated by Chapman, Dryden,
      and Hobbes.

18   ERSKINE-HILL, HOWARD. "Augustans on Augustanism: England,
      1655-1759." Renaissance and Modern Studies 11:53-83.
          Cites Dryden among others as a writer who used versions of
      the term "Augustan" and saw his own age in Augustan terms. Shows
      in general the complexity of what was meant by the concept.

19   FOWLER, ALISTAIR, and DOUGLAS BROOKS. "The Structure of
      Dryden's Song for St. Cecilia's Day, 1687." EIC 17 (October):
      434-47.
          Argues that the poem's structural pattern "is built according
      to a coherent system of number symbolism." The system derives from
      numerical ratios associated with musical harmony. Reprinted:
      1970.34.

20   GRANT, DOUGLAS. "Samuel Johnson: Satire and Satirists." New
      Rambler, ser. C 3:5-17.
          Deals with Johnson's and Dryden's attitudes toward the use
      of personal attack in satire. Cites their distinctions between
      satire and lampoon. Notes Dryden's two justifications for lampoon
      (revenge and promotion of the public good). Claims that sometimes
      (as in Absalom and Achitophel or The Vanity of Human Wishes) the
      poets are able through the epic manner to "merge the particular in
      the general."

*21   HAGESTAD, WILLIAM THOMSON. "Restoration Patronage." Ph.D.
      dissertation, University of Wisconsin.
          Cited in Latt and Monk, 1976.30. Abstracted in DA 28:1050A.

22   HALEWOOD, WILLIAM H. "'The Reach of Art' in Augustan Poetic
      Theory." In Studies in Criticism and Aesthetics, 1660-1800:
      Essays in Honor of Samuel Holt Monk. Edited by Howard Anderson
      and John S. Shea. Minneapolis: University of Minnesota Press,
      pp. 193-212.
          Argues that the familiar analogy between poetry and painting
      helped poetry "in resisting its danger from a too narrowly under-
      stood mimetic purpose." Suggests that Dryden's frequent advocacy
      of license (as in the case of Shakespeare) "suggests understanding
      of the freedoms (theoretically) allowed the painter."

23   HAMILTON, K.G. John Dryden and the Poetry of Statement. St.
      Lucia, Brisbane: University of Queensland Press, 203 pp.
          Discusses the term "poetry of statement," applied by Mark
      Van Doren to Dryden's poetry in 1920.10. Asserts that it must be
      "successful both as poetry and as statement, and not as either
      statement or poetry alone." Uses the opening lines of Absalom and
      Achitophel to illustrate "poetry of statement." Claims that Religio
      Laici is "poetry of statement in the purest form it can achieve."
      Contrasts it with The Hind and the Panther, but shows that even
      when a poem does not make a direct argument "poetry of statement"
      can give its subject "an appearance of reality." Discusses the
      portrait of Zimri (Buckingham) in Absalom and Achitophel, arguing

that the passage's meaning is in part conveyed by its style: "a
direct meaning is expressed by the discursive statement, and it is
given life and vitality . . . by being cast into a form where
metre, texture, alliteration, rhyme, set up a pattern in sound
and movement that gives a richer significance to the statement."
Remarks on Dryden's "relatively slight use of imagery": links
this to his success in the public forms of poetry. Relates his
use of ornamentation to the rhetorical device of amplification.
Concludes that Dryden's poetry "shows that poetry need not necessarily be a thing of emotion." Reprinted: 1969.27.

24   HAVENS, P.S. "Dryden's 'Tagged' Version of 'Paradise Lost.'"
     In Essays in Dramatic Literature: The Parrott Presentation
     Volume. Edited by Hardin Craig. New York: Russell & Russell,
     pp. 383-97.
          Reprint of 1935.11.

25   HARTNOLL, PHYLLIS, ed. The Oxford Companion to the Theatre.
     3d ed. Oxford: Oxford University Press.
          First edition 1951.13; second edition 1957.18.

26   HOGAN, FLORIANA T. "Notes on Thirty-One English Plays and
     Their Spanish Sources." RECTR 6, no. 1 (May):56-59.
          Asserts that An Evening's Love and The Assignation contain
     direct borrowings; that The Wild Gallant has been erroneously at-
     tributed to a Spanish source; that it is questionable whether The
     Rival Ladies, The Indian Emperour, and The Conquest of Granada
     have Spanish sources.

27   HÖLTGEN, KARL J. "John Dryden's 'nimble spaniel': Zur
     Schnelligkeit der 'inventio' und 'imaginatio.'" In Lebende
     Antike: Symposium für Rudolf Sühnel. Edited by Horst Meller
     and Hans-Joachim Zimmermann. Berlin: Schmidt, pp. 233-49.
          Traces the common metaphor (used by Dryden in the dedication
     to Annus Mirabilis) for the speed of the imagination as it deals
     with material backward from Dryden through earlier rhetorical and
     poetic theory.

*28 JENSEN, H. JAMES. "A Glossary of John Dryden's Critical
     Terms." Ph.D. dissertation, Cornell University.
          Cited in Latt and Monk, 1976.30. Abstracted in DA 28:231A.
     See 1969.36.

29   JOHNSON, JAMES WILLIAM. The Formation of English Neo-Classical
     Thought. Princeton: Princeton University Press, 380 pp.
          Deals with the extent of the Augustan Age's knowledge of the
     ancients, and the effect of that knowledge. Contains many brief
     references to Dryden. Reprinted: 1978.24.

30   JOHNSON, SAMUEL. Lives of the English Poets. Edited by G.B.
     Hill. 2 vols. New York: Octagon Books.
          Reprint of 1905.2 (edition of 1779.2).

31   KING, BRUCE. "Dryden's Ark: The Influence of Filmer." SEL 7
     (Summer):403-14.
           Asserts that the political theories of Sir Robert Filmer on
     the divine right of kings were a major element in Dryden's "con-
     servative myth." Places the source of Dryden's analogy of the
     Restoration to Noah's Ark in Filmer, and gives several more exam-
     ples in which Dryden seems to echo Filmer.

*32 KRUPP, KATHLEEN M. "John Dryden on the Functions of Drama."
     Ph.D. dissertation, Florida State University.
           Cited in Latt and Monk, 1976.30. Abstracted in DA 27:2502A.

33   KRUTCH, JOSEPH WOOD. Comedy and Conscience after the Restora-
     tion. New York: Russell & Russell.
           Reprint of 1924.5; 1949.8.

*34 LEE, RONALD JAMES. "The Satires of John Oldham: A Study of
     Rhetorical Modes in Restoration Verse Satire." Ph.D. disserta-
     tion, Stanford University.
           Cited in Latt and Monk, 1976.30. Abstracted in DA 28:1080A.

35   LEGOUIS, PIERRE. "Dryden plus Miltonien que Milton?" EA 20
     (October-December):370-77.
           Argues that The State of Innocence is a worthy work, and that
     Dryden shows more audacity even than Milton in arguing for free
     will.

*36 LOVE, HAROLD. "The Myth of the Restoration Audience." Komos
     1:49-56.
           Cited in Latt and Monk, 1976.30.

*37 MARTIN, LESLIE H., Jr. "Conventions of the French Romances in
     the Drama of John Dryden." Ph.D. dissertation, Stanford
     University.
           Cited in Latt and Monk, 1976.30. Abstracted in DA 28:1053A-
     54A.

38   MAURER, A.E. WALLACE. "Dryden's Memory Vindicated: Proceed
     with Bibliographical Caution." N&Q, n.s. 14 (September):345-46.
           A retraction of 1958.23. Admits that his charge that Dryden
     had misrepresented a passage in Lord Herbert of Cherbury's history
     of Henry VIII was wrong.

39   MINER, EARL. "Chaucer in Dryden's Fables." In Studies in
     Criticism and Aesthetics, 1660-1800: Essays in Honor of Samuel
     Holt Monk. Edited by Howard Anderson and John S. Shea.
     Minneapolis: University of Minnesota Press, pp. 58-72.
           Examines and classifies the changes Dryden made, arguing
     that they can be "defined in terms of the historia, fabula, and
     argumentum of classical narrative." The first type of change em-
     phasizes or adds to the historical material, the second increases

and clarifies the fabulous element, and the third adds or interprets philosophy.

40   . "Dryden's Ode on Mrs. Anastasia Stafford." <u>HLQ</u> 30
        (February):103-11.
        Gives what is known about the family and historical back-
ground. Suggests that the poem was composed for a wedding in
December 1687. Discusses the poem itself, stressing its similarity
to <u>Britannia Rediviva</u>. Speculates that the missing part of the
poem would, like other similar Dryden poems, shift into prophecy.

41   . <u>Dryden's Poetry</u>. Bloomington: Indiana University
        Press, 374 pp.
        "Discusses the assumptions, ideas, and techniques of Dryden's
major poetry, including not only his nondramatic work but also his
plays, as represented by <u>All for Love</u>, and his translations, as
represented by <u>Fables</u>." Begins by discussing <u>Annus Mirabilis</u>,
emphasizing Dryden's discovery of effective ways of dealing with
historical subject matter in poetry. Finds the world of <u>All for
Love</u> distinguished from that in <u>Annus Mirabilis</u> by "the scope given
to private desires." Finds the essential link between Dryden's
nondramatic and dramatic poetry in his continuing exploration of
"the limits of his forms." Notes Dryden's use of "controlling
metaphors" in <u>MacFlecknoe</u> and <u>Absalom and Achitophel</u> (applies the
term to Dryden's characteristic interchanging of tenor and vehicle). Finds these metaphors to be art, monarchy, and religion in
<u>MacFlecknoe</u> and, in <u>Absalom and Achitophel</u>, the basic biblical
parallel. Praises the effectiveness of the latter poem's dramatic
structure. Asserts that <u>The Hind and the Panther</u> is Dryden's most
difficult poem. Asks how the poem can be "seen whole." Also asks
what we are to make of the "basic absurdity" of the beast fable.
Notes the poem's wittiness. Asserts that Dryden "has created not
only a new but also a most flexible metaphorical convention." Argues that Dryden's political and religious views were consistently
conservative and monarchical, but stresses that <u>Religio Laici</u> and
<u>The Hind and the Panther</u> are very different poems, especially be-
cause of the latter poem's use of fable and imagery. Discusses
its structure: sees a general temporal organization, in which the
first part deals with the present (by affirming Catholic orthodoxy)
and the third with the future (possible effects of resolving political and religious questions). Notes Dryden's debt to John
Donne in <u>Eleonora</u>, but emphasizes his rejection of Donne's cynicism.
Concludes that "what little passion there is in <u>Eleonora</u> is not for
its object, the Countess of Abingdon, but is that of an old man re-
viewing his youth and his art." Discusses the lyrics: emphasizes
their variety and complexity. Finds in "To . . . Anne Killigrew"
"Dryden's own illustration of the faith he has affirmed in human
capacity." Discusses the structure of <u>Fables</u>, arguing that it is
an orderly whole. Suggests the <u>Metamorphoses</u> as a model, both in
structure and theme. Sees the passage on government in "To . . .
John Driden" as "the clearest, surest statement of his lifetime."

Concludes that Dryden's "achievement is a highly varied and digni-
fied late expression of Christian humanism." Reprinted: 1971.57.

42   MONTGOMERY, GUY, and LESTER A. HUBBARD, eds. Concordance to
      the Poetical Works of John Dryden. New York: Russell &
      Russell.
            Reprint of 1957.29.

43   MOORE, FRANK HARPER. "The Composition of Sir Martin Mar-All."
      In Essays in English Literature of the Classical Period Pre-
      sented to Dougald MacMillan. Edited by Daniel W. Patterson and
      Albrecht B. Strauss. Studies in Philology Extra Series 4.
      Chapel Hill: University of North Carolina Press, pp. 27-38.
            Argues that "certain interesting peculiarities" of the first
      edition may be the result of "an imperfectly coordinated collabora-
      tion" between Dryden and the Duke of Newcastle. There are in-
      congruities in the time schemes of the two plots, a large number
      of bibliographic anomalies, and inconsistencies in character.
      Concludes that Newcastle's contribution was limited to a first
      draft of Acts 1-3.

44   NETHERCOT, ARTHUR H. Sir William D'Avenant: Poet Laureate and
      Playwright-Manager. Enl. ed. New York: Russell & Russell.
            An enlarged edition of 1938.9.

45   PAULSON, RONALD. The Fictions of Satire. Baltimore: Johns
      Hopkins University Press, 236 pp.
            Deals with Absalom and Achitophel and MacFlecknoe. Notes
      Dryden's use of a "satiric fiction" in Absalom and Achitophel which
      includes the elements of civil war, a tempter and his dupe, a fic-
      kle mob and a plot to excite it, and the loyal few and their king.
      Sees this "fiction" as dominant in Tory satire during the Restora-
      tion. Finds in MacFlecknoe a different situation: an absurd uni-
      verse in which the mob has become the main element and the villain
      is now king.

46   PETERSON, R.G. "Larger Manners and Events: Sallust and Virgil
      in Absalom and Achitophel." PMLA 82:236-44.
            Argues that more attention should be paid to the classical
      element in the poem, especially to the allusions to Sallust and
      Virgil. The classical references relate the poem to the period of
      chaos and civil war before the ascendancy of Augustus. Demon-
      strates the strong kinship between Dryden's Achitophel and Sallust's
      Catiline. Shows the density of Virgilian allusion in the latter
      parts of the poem, especially in the portrait of Barzillai's son
      (who resembles Marcellus in Aeneid 6) and David, who is modeled in
      part on Virgil's portrayal of Augustus.

*47   RASCO, KAY FRANCES DILWORTH. "Supernaturalism in the Heroic
      Play." Ph.D. dissertation, Northwestern University.
            Cited in Latt and Monk, 1976.30. Abstracted in DA 27:3433A-
      34A.

48 REED, EDWARD BLISS. English Lyric Poetry from Its Origins to the Present Time. New York: Haskell House.
Reprint of 1912.5.

*49 RESTAINO, KATHERINE M. "The Troubled Stream of Translation: A Study of Translation in the Eighteenth Century." Ph.D. dissertation, Fordham University.
Cited in Latt and Monk, 1976.30. Abstracted in DA 27:2507A-8A.

50 ROSCIONI, GIAN CARLO. "Sir Robert Howard's 'Skeptical Curiosity.'" MP 65 (August):53-59.
Suggests that Howard's interests in philosophy and science had a significant effect on Dryden, in particular on Annus Mirabilis.

51 ROTHSTEIN, ERIC. Restoration Tragedy: Eorm and the Process of Change. Madison, Milwaukee, and London: University of Wisconsin Press, 201 pp.
Sees two major theories of the ends of tragedy: the "fabulist," deriving from Horace's point about the instructive value of poetry, and the "affective," ultimately deriving from Aristotle's comment about catharsis. The latter, which emphasized the evocation of emotion in the audience, came to dominate Restoration tragedy. Deals with the change during the period away from heroic drama toward a naturalistic drama which emphasized psychology and emotion. Notes how the continued existence of unrhymed earlier English tragedies in repertory provided playwrights with an alternative to rhymed heroic tragedy when that tradition wore itself out. Concludes that the "affective" nature of Restoration tragedy is the key to its diminished reputation: "a work of art that depends on the creative emotion of the audience . . . grows dated." Contains frequent references to Dryden's work, especially Don Sebastian, which is taken as an example of late Restoration tragedy at its best. Reprinted: 1978.46.

*52 RUSSELL, ROBERT E. "Dryden's Juvenal and Persius." Ph.D. dissertation, University of California at Davis.
Cited in Latt and Monk, 1976.30. Abstracted in DA 28:209A.

53 SHERBURN, GEORGE, and DONALD F. BOND. "The Restoration and Eighteenth Century (1660-1789)." In A Literary History of England. Edited by Albert C. Baugh. 2d ed. New York: Appleton-Century-Crofts, pp. 699-1108.
A corrected reprint of 1948.19 with a "bibliographical supplement."

54 SWEDENBERG, H.T., Jr. "Challenges to Dryden's Editor." In John Dryden: Papers Read at a Clark Library Seminar, February 25, 1967. Introduction by John Loftis. Los Angeles: Clark Memorial Library, University of California, pp. 23-40.

Discusses the problem faced by the editors of the California
Dryden. There are no holographs of any of his significant works.
There are many passages which resist glossing, and many which re-
quire difficult choices about how much should be glossed. Reprinted: 1972.81.

55 _____. "Dryden's Obsessive Concern with the Heroic." In Essays
in English Literature of the Classical Period Presented to
Dougald MacMillan. Edited by Daniel W. Patterson and Albrecht
B. Strauss. Studies in Philology Extra Series 4. Chapel Hill:
University of North Carolina Press, pp. 12-26.
Asserts that "the heroic was the métier toward which his
genius naturally leaned." Surveys Dryden's career, giving examples
of the presence of the heroic throughout.

56 TAYLOR, ALINE M. "Dryden's 'Enchanted Isle' and Shadwell's
'Dominion.'" In Essays in English Literature of the Classical
Period Presented to Dougald MacMillan. Edited by Daniel W.
Patterson and Albrecht B. Strauss. Studies in Philology Extra
Series 4. Chapel Hill: University of North Carolina Press,
pp. 39-53.
Explains the mention of Barbados in MacFlecknoe (one boundary
of Shadwell's dominion) by referring to Dryden and Davenant's The
Tempest, in which they clearly envisioned Shakespeare's isle as
Barbados. The allusion in MacFlecknoe was therefore Dryden's re-
venge for the insult of Shadwell's operatic adaptation of The
Tempest.

*57 THORPE, PETER. "Some Fallacies in the Study of Augustan Poetry."
Criticism 9 (Fall):326-36.
Cited in Latt and Monk, 1976.30.

58 TILLOTSON, GEOFFREY. "Eighteenth-Century Poetic Diction." In
Essays in Criticism and Research. Hamden, Conn.: Archon Books,
pp. 53-85.
Reprint of 1942.11.

59 TRICKETT, RACHEL. The Honest Muse: A Study in Augustan Verse.
Oxford: Clarendon Press, 317 pp.
"Dryden" (pp. 27-84) deals with the nature of his work and
its significance for eighteenth-century poetry. Emphasizes the
public forms of panegyric and satire; sees in both an outlet for
Dryden's strong interest in the heroic and epic. Points out
Dryden's unusual enjoyment in writing panegyrics, and his way of
using them for "general reflection." Suggests that satire gave
him a chance both to use heroic style and, in the right circumstances, mock-heroic style. Sees a turning inward in his later
poetry: suggests that in The Hind and the Panther he may be re-
nouncing his poetic reputation (though not his pride in poetry).
Concludes that Dryden became a model for the Augustans by imposing
the standard of truth to nature and to the art of poetry.

60   WARD, CHARLES E. "Challenges to Dryden's Biographer." In
     John Dryden: Papers Read at a Clark Library Seminar, February
     25, 1967. Introduction by John Loftis. Los Angeles: Clark
     Memorial Library, University of California, pp. 1-21.
          Surveys the types of problems facing the biography, with
     several specific examples. Emphasizes the difficulty of interpret-
     ing and evaluating documentary material. Reprinted: 1972.95.

61   WEINBROT, HOWARD D. "Alexas in All for Love: His Genealogy
     and Function." SP 64 (July):625-39.
          Stresses the importance of Alexas as an "instigating villain."
     Notes that the character of the eunuch who drives the action occurs
     not in Shakespeare but in other plays which must be considered im-
     portant sources: plays by Sedley, Daniel, Corneille, the Countess
     of Pembroke, and Fletcher and Massinger. Asserts that readers of
     the play should be free of the necessity of comparing it to
     Shakespeare.

62   WENDELL, BARRETT. The Temper of the Seventeenth Century in
     English Literature. Essay Index Reprint Series. Freeport,
     N.Y.: Books for Libraries.
          Reprint of 1904.9.

63   WESLEY, SAMUEL. Epistle to a Friend concerning Poetry and the
     Essay on Heroic Poetry. Introduction by Edward N. Hooker. New
     York: Kraus.
          Reprint of 1947.17 (reprint of 1700.7).

64   WILSON, JOHN HAROLD. The Court Wits of the Restoration. New
     York: Octagon Books.
          Reprint of 1948.26.

65   ZIMMERMAN, FRANKLIN B. Henry Purcell, 1659-1695: His Life and
     Times. London: Macmillan; New York: St. Martin's, 446 pp.
          Treats several points at which Dryden's and Purcell's careers
     touched one another, especially the collaboration on King Arthur.
     Notes Dryden's admitted difficulty in writing for a composer, but
     notes also his high praise for Purcell's work (pp. 197-200).

                              1968

1   ADOLPH, ROBERT. The Rise of Modern Prose Style. Cambridge,
     Mass.: M.I.T. Press, 382 pp.
          Discusses Dryden's definition of wit (in the preface to
     Annus Mirabilis). Asserts that despite the classical nature of
     his definition, Dryden's view of language "as a means of persuasion
     easily accessible to all" is "utilitarian." Notes that Dryden seems
     to distinguish the classical plain style from "Senecanism": in the
     plain style "words equal the things of the mind." Concludes that
     Dryden is typical of the Restoration in understanding "prose as a

vehicle for communicating intelligibly rather than revealing the
mind of the author or speaker or showing off his command of literary devices."

*2   ADRIAN, DARYL B.   "Changing Attitudes Toward the English
      Puritans, 1660–1740: A Study of Major Non-Dramatic Works."
      Ph.D. dissertation, University of Missouri.
            Cited in Latt and Monk, 1976.30. Abstracted in DA 28:4113A.

3   ALLEN, JOHN D. Quantitative Studies in Prosody. Johnson City,
      Tenn.: East Tennessee State University Press, 257 pp.
            A statistical study of the relative frequency among major
      poets of alliteration, assonance, and consonance. Includes Dryden,
      but draws no specific conclusions about his practice.

*4   AMIS, GEORGE T.   "Style and Sense in Three Augustan Satires:
      MacFlecknoe, Book I of The Dunciad Variorum, The Vanity of
      Human Wishes." Ph.D. dissertation, Yale University.
            Cited in Latt and Monk, 1976.30. Abstracted in DA 29:558A.

5   ARCHER, STANLEY.   "On Dryden's History of the League (1684)."
      PLL 4 (Spring):103-6.
            Examines the changes Dryden made while translating Maimbourg's
      original. Concludes that while he is generally faithful to the
      text, his changes reflect the extreme Tory position which he held
      at the time.

*6   ATWATER, N.B.   "Dryden's Translation of Chaucer." Ph.D. dis-
      sertation, Exeter University.
            Cited in Latt and Monk, 1976.30.

7   AUSTIN, NORMAN.   "Translation as Baptism: Dryden's Lucretius."
      Arion 7 (Winter):576-602.
            Asserts that in the process of adapting Lucretius to his
      audience Dryden "misrepresented [him] in important ways." Suggests
      that this in part is a result of Dryden's heavy use of Thomas
      Creech's earlier translation. Both translators seem to have been
      trying to put the pagan aspects of the work in a bad light. In
      Dryden's version "Lucretius has surrendered his role as scientist
      and heretic and has been assigned that of the uncompromising moral
      satirist."

*8   BANKS, LANDRUM.   "The Imagery of Dryden's Rhymed Heroic Drama."
      Ph.D. dissertation, University of Tennessee.
            Cited in Latt and Monk, 1976.30. Abstracted in DA 29:224A-
      25A.

*9   BARBEAU, ANNE T.   "John Dryden's Scheme of Values: A Study of
      His Heroic Plays and Early Narrative Poems." Ph.D. dissertation,
      City University of New York.
            Cited in Latt and Monk, 1976.30. Abstracted in DA 29:559A.
      See 1970.10.

*10   BLACKWELL, HERBERT. "Some Formulary Characteristics of John
        Dryden's Comedies." Ph.D. dissertation, University of Virginia.
            Cited in Latt and Monk, 1976.30. Abstracted in DA 28:2642A.

 11   BOYD, JOHN D., S.J. The Function of Mimesis and Its Decline.
        Cambridge, Mass.: Harvard University Press, 331 pp.
            Deals at several points with Dryden as a literary theorist,
        especially with his views on imitation and on the ends of poetry.
        Finds him contradictory and unstable, but characteristic of his
        time. Concludes that "Dryden's fideism and skepticism . . . served
        to limit [his poetry's] potential," and that the poetry "has not
        the mimetic depths of Sophocles, Dante, and Shakespeare."

*12   BROICH, ULRICH. "Drydens MacFlecknoe und seine fruhen
        Nachahmungen." In Studien zum Komischen Epos. Tubingen:
        Niemeyer, pp. 239-42.
            Cited in Latt and Monk, 1976.30.

 13   BROWER, REUBEN. "Form and Defect of Form in Eighteenth-Century
        Poetry: A Memorandum." CE 29 (April):535-41.
            Claims that at times Dryden (and Pope) fell into a kind of
        lifeless automatic style, especially in translation and imitation.

 14   BURNETT, A.D. "An Early Verse Reply to Dryden's The Hind and
        the Panther." N&Q, n.s. 15 (October):378-80.
            Cites a pamphlet entitled The lay-mans answer to The Tay-mans
        opinion: in a Letter to a Friend, published shortly after Dryden's
        poem, which includes a verse fable answering Dryden "on his own
        terms."

*15   BURTON, THOMAS R. "The Animal Lore and Fable Tradition in John
        Dryden's The Hind and the Panther." Ph.D. dissertation,
        University of Washington.
            Cited in Latt and Monk, 1976.30. Abstracted in DA 29:225A-
        26A.

 16   CAMERON, ALLEN BARRY. "Donne and Dryden: Their Achievement in
        the Verse Epistle." Discourse 11 (Spring):252-56.
            Looks at Donne's "To Sir Henry Wotton" and Dryden's "To My
        Honour'd Friend, Dr. Charleton." Finds that Dryden's poem is
        more public, less personal: asserts that this is typical. That
        Dryden published his, while Donne did not, underlines the differ-
        ence.

*17   DANCHIN, PIERRE. "Le public des théatres londoniens a l'époque
        de la Restauration d'après les prologues et les epilogues." In
        Dramaturgie et société: Rapports entre l'oeuvre théatrale.
        Edited by Jean Jacquot. Colloques internationaux du centre
        national de la recherche scientifique: Sciences humaines. 2
        vols. Paris: Editions du centre national de la recherche
        scientifique, 2:847-88.
            Cited in Latt and Monk, 1976.30.

18   DAVIES, H. NEVILLE. "Shakespeare's Sonnet LXVI Echoed in <u>All</u>
      <u>for Love</u>." <u>N&Q</u>, n.s. 15 (July):262-63.
           Suggests that 1. 385 in the play echoes a phrase from the
      sonnet.

19   DAVISON, DENNIS. <u>Dryden</u>. Literature in Perspective. London:
      Evans Brothers, 151 pp.
           Introduces Dryden's poetry to "the ordinary man who reads
      for pleasure." Deals first with the "perspective"--political,
      religious, cultural, and literary backgrounds--and then with the
      poems, grouped by type. Describes, summarizes, and evaluates al-
      most all of the poems, with much quotation.

20   FERRY, ANNE DAVIDSON. <u>Milton and the Miltonic Dryden</u>.
      Cambridge, Mass.: Harvard University Press, 238 pp.
           Decries as artificial the conventional separation of Milton
      and Dryden. Asserts that Dryden was indebted to <u>Paradise Lost</u> in
      <u>Absalom and Achitophel</u>, and to <u>Samson Agonistes</u> in <u>All for Love</u>.
      Sees a relationship between <u>Paradise Lost</u> and <u>Absalom and Achitophel</u>
      in that both works involve "human weakness opportunely exploited by
      the Devil." Sees also an extended allusion to Milton's Satan in
      the portrait of Achitophel. Notes that the degenerate speech of
      the enemy party in Dryden's poem resembles the speech of Adam and
      Eve after the Fall; sees a similar resemblance between Eve's speech
      of reconciliation in Book 10 and David's speech at the end of
      <u>Absalom and Achitophel</u>. Argues that the effect of <u>Samson Agonistes</u>
      on <u>All for Love</u>, though powerful, was probably unconscious. Notes
      many similarities of detail, particularly in the characterization
      of the central figures. Finds the conclusions of the plays similar,
      in that in both the heroes pass into a state of silence, of "un-
      consciousness where even unmixed feelings cannot reach them." But
      finds the end of Dryden's play confused, because it seems to assert
      values which the play has renounced. Concludes that the lack of
      consistency in both poets is a "defining characteristic of poetry
      in this phase of literary history."

21   FOSBERY, M.W. "The Case of John Dryden." <u>Oxford Review</u> 8
      (Trinity Term):65-72; 9 (Michaelmas Term):75-81.
           Disparages Dryden's poetry and ideas; concentrates on <u>Absalom</u>
      <u>and Achitophel</u>.

22   FREEHAFER, JOHN. "Dryden's <u>Indian Emperour</u>." <u>Expl</u> 27: note 24.
           Notes two borrowings of lines from Virgil's <u>Georgics</u> 2 in the
      play, at 5. 1. 115-16 and 1. 1. 5-10.

23   FRENCH, A.L. "Dryden, Marvell, and Political Poetry." <u>SEL</u> 8
      (Summer):397-413.
           Looks at <u>Absalom and Achitophel</u> and Marvell's <u>Horatian Ode</u>.
      Asserts that Dryden's poem has no "unity of impression"; Marvell's,
      on the other hand, though highly complicated is unified. One prob-
      lem is that Dryden's use of classical and biblical material plays

a much less organic role in the poem than Marvell's. Concludes
that while Dryden may have been "the voice of the age," "it was a
thoroughly inferior age."

24 FRYE, PROSSER H. "Dryden and the Critical Canons of the
Eighteenth Century." In Literary Reviews and Criticism. New
York: Gordian, pp. 130-89.
Reprint of 1908.1.

25 FUJIMURA, THOMAS H. The Restoration Comedy of Wit. New York:
Barnes & Noble.
Reprint of 1952.11.

26 GAMBLE, GILES Y. "Dryden's MacFlecknoe, 25-28 and 38-42."
Expl 26 (January): note 45.
Suggests an additional meaning for "supinely" ("leaning back-
ward") at 1. 28, and notes that blanket tossing (1. 42) was an old
method of inducing labor, which is appropriate in the context.

*27 GOLLADAY, GERTRUDE L. "The Rhetorical Poetic Tradition in
Dryden's Two Verse Essays." Ph.D. dissertation, Texas Christian
University.
Cited in Latt and Monk, 1976.30.

28 GOSSE, EDMUND. From Shakespeare to Pope. New York: Burt
Franklin.
Reprint of 1885.4.

*29 GUZZETTI, ALFRED F. "Dryden's Two Worlds: Restoration Society
and the Literary Past." Ph.D. dissertation, Harvard University.
Cited in Latt and Monk, 1976.30.

30 HAMM, VICTOR M. "Dryden's 'The Hind and the Panther' and
Restoration Apologetics." PMLA 83 (May):400-15.
Asserts that Dryden knew several of the leading Roman Catholic
apologetics of his period well, and used them in writing the poem.
Notes echoes of ideas and wording. Concludes that Dryden's conversion came after much reading and thought, not as a mere submission
to authority.

31 HARRIS, BERNARD. "'That Soft Seducer, Love': Dryden's The
State of Innocence and Fall of Man." In Approaches to "Paradise
Lost": The York Tercentenary Lectures. Edited by C.A. Patrides.
Toronto: University of Toronto Press, pp. 119-36.
Asks what the moral of the work is, and Dryden's justification for writing it. Argues that he has changed the emphasis and
hence the moral of Paradise Lost, and that he is interested in "the
desired and achievable state of experience." He emphasizes the
love of Adam and Eve after the Fall, the "heroically human" aspect
of the poem. Notes also how Dryden uses the dramatic form to control and make more accessible "Milton's larger world."

*32   HARRIS, KATHRYN M. "John Dryden: Augustan Satirist." Ph.D.
          dissertation, Emory University.
                 Cited in Latt and Monk, 1976.30. Abstracted in DA 29:1539A-
       40A.

 33   HARTH, PHILLIP. Contexts of Dryden's Thought. Chicago and
          London: University of Chicago Press, 313 pp.
                 Treats Dryden's religious thought, especially in Religio
       Laici and The Hind and the Panther. Shows how the thought relates
       to the poetry, and to historical circumstances. Argues against
       Louis Bredvold's thesis that Dryden was a "Pyrrhonic" skeptic (see
       1934.3): suggests that what looks like skepticism in Dryden is the
       antidogmatic approach favored by the Royal Society. Emphasizes the
       rhetorical qualities of the religious poems: sees Religio Laici as
       a poem in the tradition of the Horatian epistle. Asserts that
       Dryden's arguments against deism in the poem were drawn (for con-
       venience' sake) from Sir Charles Wolseley's The Reasonableness of
       Scripture-Belief (1672). Relates Dryden's position to controver-
       sies within the Anglican Church: associates him with the Lati-
       tudinarian position. Notes Dryden's "pyrotechnic desplay of rhe-
       torical strategies." Denies that Dryden's arguments in Religio
       Laici would lead one to expect his conversion to Roman Catholicism;
       suggests that he may have become bothered by Anglicanism's lack of
       innate authority. Looks at The Hind and the Panther as a poem in
       the mainstream of English Catholic apologetics; notes again his
       rhetorical skill at manipulating arguments. An appendix lays out
       the evidence for Dryden's heavy use of Wolseley.

 34   HAYMAN, JOHN. "Raillery in Restoration Satire." HLQ 31
          (February):107-22.
                 Argues that Dryden's observations on raillery in "Discourse
       . . . of Satire" are related to accepted social modes of raillery.
       Discusses his different uses of it in Absalom and Achitophel, from
       the "inoffensive" mockery of Charles to the portrait of Buckingham
       (Zimri), which is in the social mode. Concludes in general that
       by turning wit in conversation into an artistic device the Restora-
       tion made a valuable contribution to literature.

 35   HINNANT, CHARLES H. "The Background of the Early Version of
          Dryden's The Duke of Guise." ELN 6 (December):102-6.
                 Supports with circumstantial evidence Dryden's claim that he
       composed the play in 1660, even though it was not performed until
       1682. Suggests that it was written in response to dissenters' agi-
       tation at the time of the Restoration: notes that the parallel
       between this agitation and the historical events involving the Duke
       of Guise and the Holy League was drawn at the time. Concludes that
       the evidence gives an exceptionally early sign of how Dryden's po-
       litical attitudes were to develop. See 1973.8, 30.

 36   _____. "Dryden's Gallic Rooster." SP 65 (July):647-56.
                 Notes Dryden's changes in the portrayal of the cock in his

translation of Chaucer's "Nun's Priest's Tale." Suggests that in line with contemporary caricature Dryden meant the cock to represent Louis XIV. Although the poem is not a political allegory, this device provided a way for Dryden to modernize his original.

37   HOGAN, CHARLES BEECHER, ed. The London Stage 1660-1800. Part 5: 1776-1800. 3 vols. Carbondale: Southern Illinois University Press.
    Includes information about performances of Dryden's plays during the period. For other parts of the series, see 1960.1 (Part 2); 1961.47 (Part 3); 1962.44 (Part 4); 1965.56 (Part 1).

38   HUME, ROBERT D. "Dryden's 'Heads of an Answer to Rymer': Notes Toward a Hypothetical Revolution." RES, n.s. 19 (November): 373-86.
    Places the "Heads" in the context of Dryden's thought. Argues that they are speculative questions which Dryden is trying out, and should not be taken as an attempt at refutation. During the 1670s Dryden's and Rymer's views were not far apart: Rymer was more flexible and less prescriptive than he has been given credit for; Dryden always accepted the authority of the classics. Argues that "The Grounds of Criticism in Tragedy" is not inconsistent with the "Heads." Concludes that Dryden's "abiding concern . . . is the reconciliation of the English dramatic tradition with classically derived 'rules.'"

38A   JAUSLIN, CHRISTIAN. "John Dryden's Essay of Dramatic Poesy, 1668." Schweizer Monatshefte 48:215-21.
    Cited by John Zamonski in 1975.59.

39   KING, BRUCE, ed. Twentieth Century Interpretations of "All for Love": A Collection of Critical Essays. Englewood Cliffs, N.J.: Prentice-Hall.
    Includes 1904.1; 1928.4; 1940.19; 1950.24; 1952.30 (abridged); 1955.9; 1958.16; 1962.48; 1963.42 (abridged); 1965.33.

40   LEVINE, GEORGE R. "Dryden's 'Inarticulate Poesy': Music and the Davidic Kings in Absalom and Achitophel." ECS 1 (Summer): 291-312.
    Argues that the poem contains an interaction between a figural use of David in his role as King and harpist, and "a symbolic use of music as an abstract harmonizing principle." Shows the strength of the Davidic concept of kingship in the seventeenth century. Sees in the opening ten lines a structure analogous to "contrapuntal development characteristic of . . . the canzonet, the madrigal, and particularly the fantasia." Also notes frequent use of harmony and cacaphony.

*41   LOTT, JAMES DAVID. "Restoration Comedy: The Critical View, 1913-1965." Ph.D. dissertation, University of Wisconsin.
    Cited in Latt and Monk, 1976.30. Abstracted in DA 28:2688A.

42   MARKS, EMERSON R. The Poetics of Reason: English Neoclassical
      Criticism. New York: Random House, 191 pp.
          "John Dryden" (pp. 60-77) surveys Dryden's criticism chrono-
      logically. Asserts that despite his inconsistencies he is the
      greatest critic of the age. Concludes that his "critical penetra-
      tion is never more evident than in the frequency with which he per-
      ceived and defined the limitations of the very aesthetic of which
      he remains the first great spokesman."

43   MIDDLETON, ANNE. "The Modern Art of Fortifying: Palamon and
      Arcite as Epicurean Epic." Chaucer Review 3:124-43.
          Argues that Dryden tried to make "Palamon and Arcite" ex-
      emplify his concept of heroic poetry. Proposes reasons "why the
      change from romance to epic did not fully succeed." Examines
      Dryden's changes in his original; suggests that he found Chaucer's
      lapse of decorum (in using an ironic narrator) insufficiently moral.
      Concludes that Dryden's "sacrifice of the heroic trappings to the
      truth of the story and to his own profoundest late concerns affirms
      triumphantly the durability of Chaucer's art and the integrity of
      his own."

44   MILLER, G.M. The Historical Point of View in English Literary
      Criticism from 1570-1770. Research Source Works Series 197.
      New York: Burt Franklin.
          Reprint of 1913.4.

*45   MULLIN, JOSEPH E. "The Occasion, Form, Structure, and Design
      of John Dryden's MacFlecknoe: A Varronian Satire." Ph.D. dis-
      sertation, Ohio State University.
          Cited in Latt and Monk, 1976.30. Abstracted in DA 28:3645A.

46   NOVAK, MAXIMILLIAN E. "Dryden's 'Ape of the French Eloquence'
      and Richard Flecknoe." Bulletin of the New York Public Library
      72 (October):499-506.
          Suggests that Dryden is alluding to Flecknoe when he refers
      to an "Ape of French Eloquence" in the preface to The Tempest.
      Shows how Flecknoe fits this description. Argues that Dryden's
      attack on Flecknoe is probably in retaliation for Flecknoe's satire
      Sir William D'Avenant's Voyage to the Other World (1668).

47   PARKER, WILLIAM RILEY. Milton: A Biography. 2 vols. Oxford:
      Clarendon Press, 1509 pp.
          Describes Dryden's meeting with Milton about "tagging"
      Paradise Lost. Suggests that Milton's publisher would not allow
      Dryden to publish The State of Innocence until after the second
      edition of Paradise Lost appeared (1674). Contains several other
      brief references to Dryden.

*48   PATI, P.K. "Dryden's Heroic Plays: A Study of Their Theory
      and Practice." Indian Journal of English Studies 9:87-95.
          Cited in Latt and Monk, 1976.30.

49 PERRY, HENRY TEN EYCK. The First Duchess of Newcastle and Her Husband as Figures in English Literature. New York and London: Johnson Reprints.
Reprint of 1918.4.

50 RINGLER, RICHARD N. "Dryden at the House of Busirane." ES 49 (June):224-29.
Identifies a strong verbal echo of The Fairie Queene 3. 12. 3 in the first scene of All for Love. Suggests that Dryden wanted to invoke "the troubled world of portents" and so went to the poet whom he had praised for his use of "gods and spirits." Notes that the same Spenserian passage comes up in Dryden's translations of Ovid, Virgil, and Chaucer. Concludes that "Spenser . . . would have appreciated the humor of this literary feedback."

51 ROSTON, MURRAY. Biblical Drama in England: From the Middle Ages to the Present Day. Evanston: Northwestern University Press; London: Faber & Faber, 335 pp.
Suggests that in Absalom and Achitophel "Dryden was merely using the biblical text as a novel alternative to classical mythology." Charges that The State of Innocence is "little more than a literary husk."

*52 SCHAFER, WILLIAM J. "The Sources of Augustan Satire: Polemic and Poetry." Ph.D. dissertation, University of Minnesota.
Cited in Latt and Monk, 1976.30. Abstracted in DA 28:5027A-28A.

53 SELLIN, PAUL R. Daniel Heinsius and Stuart England: With a Short-Title Checklist of the Works of Daniel Heinsius. Leiden: At the University Press; London: Oxford University Press, 277 pp.
Considers the question of Heinsius's influence on Dryden. Finds their theories to be "fundamentally quite different": Heinsius follows Aristotle; Dryden follows Horace. Concludes that if Dryden did read Heinsius, he either rejected his ideas, or changed them beyond recognition.

*54 SHEA, JOHN STEPHEN. "Studies in the Verse Fable from La Fontaine to Gay." Ph.D. dissertation, University of Minnesota.
Cited in Latt and Monk, 1976.30. Abstracted in DA 28:5029A.

*55 SLOMAN, JUDITH. "The Structure of Dryden's Fables." Ph.D. dissertation, University of Minnesota.
Cited in Latt and Monk, 1976.30. Abstracted in DA 29:1906A.

*56 STAVES, SARAH SUSAN. "Studies in the Comedy of John Dryden." Ph.D. dissertation, University of Virginia.
Cited in Latt and Monk, 1976.30. Abstracted in DA 28:2658A.

57 SUMMERS, MONTAGUE, ed. The Complete Works of Thomas Shadwell.

5 vols. New York: Blom.
Reprint of 1927.14.

58 _____, ed. Roscius Anglicanus by John Downes. With an
Introduction. New York: Blom.
Reprint of 1928.15.

*59 SWENEY, JOHN R. "Political Attacks on Dryden, 1681-1683."
Ph.D. dissertation, University of Wisconsin.
Cited in Latt and Monk, 1976.30. Abstracted in DA 29:915A.

*60 TRITT, CARLETON S. "Wit and Paradox in Dryden's Serious Plays."
Ph.D. dissertation, University of Washington.
Cited in Latt and Monk, 1976.30. Abstracted in DA 29:882A-
83A.

*61 VISSER, COLIN W. "Dryden's Plays: A Critical Assessment."
Ph.D. dissertation, University of Rochester.
Cited in Latt and Monk, 1976.30. Abstracted in DA 29:1520A-
21A.

62 WELCHER, JEANNE K. "The Opening of Religio Laici and its
Virgilian Associations." SEL 8 (Summer):391-96.
Argues that the opening image echoes the Aeneid 6. 268-72,
both in wording and in its mood of uncertainty and obscurity.
Notes that Dryden's translation of this Virgilian passage echoes
the lines in Religio Laici.

*63 YOUNGREN, MARY ANN. "The Marks of Sovereignty: Authority and
Force in Dryden's Heroic Dramas." Ph.D. dissertation, Harvard
University.
Cited in Latt and Monk, 1976.30.

64 _____. "Generality, Science, and Poetic Language in the
Restoration." ELH 35 (June):158-87.
Attempts to understand what the period meant by "generality"
as a good in poetry. Argues that modern readers have misunderstood
"the central impulse" of Restoration criticism by paying too much
attention to the growth of science and its language during the
period. Poets such as Dryden actually saw poetry as very different
from prose. Insists on the "essential continuity of English criticism from Ascham and Sidney through Dryden and Dennis." Dryden was
in fact highly in favor of figurative language, used judiciously.
Concludes that "general" meant something like "clear in implication."

65 ZWICKER, STEVEN N. "Dryden's Borrowing from Ben Jonson's
'Panegyre.'" N&Q, n.s. 15 (March):105-6.
Points to Dryden's borrowing of the last line of Jonson's
"Panegyre on the Happy Entrance of James" as the last line of his
prologue to John Banks's The Unhappy Favourite.

1969

*1 BACHE, WILLIAM B. "Dryden and Oldham: Hail and Farewell."
    College Language Association Journal 12:237-43.
         Cited in Latt and Monk, 1976.30.

*2 BERNARD, M.L. "Dryden's Aeneid: The Theory and the Poem."
    Ph.D. dissertation, Cambridge University.
         Cited in Latt and Monk, 1976.30.

 3 BERNHARDT, W.W. "Shakespeare's Troilus and Cressida and Dryden's
    Truth Found Too Late." SQ 20 (Spring):129-41.
         Reads Dryden's play as an aid to understanding Shakespeare's.
    Summarizes Dryden's preface ("The Grounds of Criticism in Tragedy").
    Discusses Dryden's changes in the light of his preface: most of
    them attempt to deal with the original's disunity and puzzling
    characterization. Defends Shakespeare, but concludes that Dryden's
    "mistakes" can lead to a discovery of the worth of Troilus and
    Cressida.

 4 BLAIR, JOEL. "Dryden's Ceremonial Hero." SEL 9 (Summer):379-
    93.
         Argues that Dryden's earliest panegyrics essentially have a
    single poetic character as hero: the "ceremonial hero" who repre-
    sents "spiritual processes acting in the world." In Annus Mirabilis,
    Absalom and Achitophel, and especially the late Threnodia Augustalis
    and Britannia Rediviva, however, this hero does not appear, because
    Dryden no longer "believe[s] that the hero should act except as a
    part of the social and political system."

 5 BOWERS, FREDSON. "Current Theories of Copy-Text, with an
    Illustration from Dryden." In Bibliography and Textual Criti-
    cism: English and American Literature, 1700 to the Present.
    Edited by O.M. Brack, Jr. and Warner Barnes. Chicago and
    London: University of Chicago Press, pp. 59-72.
         Reprint of 1950.1.

*6 BREWER, GWENDOLYN W. "The Course of Mirth and Satiric Imagery
    in Selected Comedies of John Dryden." Ph.D. dissertation,
    Claremont Graduate School and University Center.
         Cited in Latt and Monk, 1976.30. Abstracted in DA 29:2206A-
    07A.

 7 BRODWIN, LEONORA LEET. "Miltonic Allusion in Absalom and
    Achitophel: Its Function in the Political Satire." JEGP 68
    (January):24-44.
         Argues that the poem is firmly a satire and not an epic.
    Gives evidence for a close parallel between its sections and the
    sections of Book 1 of Paradise Lost. Concludes that Dryden uses
    Miltonic echoes and allusions not only to elevate his style but to
    turn the memory of Milton against his (Milton's) political follow-
    ers.

8　　BROOKS, HAROLD F.　"Dryden's Juvenal and the Harveys."　PQ 48
　　　(January):12-19.
　　　　　　Identifies the J.H. who translated Juvenal's Tenth Satire
　　as John Harvey (1650-1715).　(He mentions in his preface that
　　Dryden is working on a translation of the same piece.)　Gives
　　biographical information about Harvey and his cousin Stephen
　　Harvey, who translated the Ninth Satire in Dryden's collection.

9　　BUDICK, SANFORD.　"Dryden's 'Mysterious Writ' Deciphered."
　　　TLS, 3 April, p. 371.
　　　　　　Argues that the legend of St. Chad is behind the beast fable
　　in The Hind and the Panther.　See 1969.10, 49-50.

10　　＿＿＿.　"Dryden's 'Mysterious Writ' Deciphered."　TLS, 22 May,
　　　p. 559.
　　　　　　Responds to Earl Miner (1969.49):　charges him with misunder-
　　standing the argument in 1969.9.　See also 1969.50.

11　　＿＿＿.　"New Light on Dryden's Religio Laici."　N&Q, n.s. 16
　　　(October):375-79.
　　　　　　Argues that Dryden's use of Sir Charles Wolseley's The
　　Reasonableness of Scripture-Belief has been exaggerated (see
　　1968.33); suggests instead Hamon L'Estrange's Considerations upon
　　Dr. Bayly's Parenthetical Interlocution (1651) as a source.　As-
　　serts that the primary source was probably Richard Burthogge's
　　Causa Dei (1675).　Suggests also that the "weary, wandring travel-
　　lers" of the opening lines echo The Faerie Queene 7. 6. 9.

12　　CARACCIOLO, PETER.　"Dryden and the Antony and Cleopatra of Sir
　　　Charles Sedley."　ES (Anglo-American Supplement) 50:1-lv.
　　　　　　Notes several apparent borrowings; suggests that All for Love
　　was a response to Sedley's work, which though a bad play was a suc-
　　cess.

13　　CHALKER, JOHN.　The English Georgic:　A Study in the Development
　　　of a Form.　Ideas and Forms in English Literature.　Baltimore:
　　　Johns Hopkins University Press; London:　Routledge & Kegan Paul,
　　　229 pp.
　　　　　　Argues in general that the Georgics were popular in the
　　eighteenth century because the attitudes they expressed "had a
　　particular potency for the period."　Examines Dryden's translation
　　(pp. 21-33):　notes how he brings out the complexity of the origin-
　　al, especially its "oscillation between the heroic and mundane."

*14　　COMPTON, GAIL H.　"The Metaphor of Conquest in Dryden's The
　　　Conquest of Granada."　Ph.D. dissertation, University of
　　　Florida.
　　　　　　Cited in Latt and Monk, 1976.30.　Abstracted in DAI 30:274A.

*15　　CONLON, MICHAEL J.　"Politics and Providence:　John Dryden's
　　　Absalom and Achitophel."　Ph.D. dissertation, University of

Florida.
Cited in Latt and Monk, 1976.30.

16   COPE, JACKSON I.   "Paradise Regained: Inner Ritual."   Milton
Studies 1:51-65.
Asserts that "Milton's defense of blank verse was directed
in part at Dryden's rejection of it," and that "Dryden was influenced by the argument in his later drama."   Suggests that Dryden's
conception of Almanzor was affected by Milton's Satan, although as
Almanzor's character develops, he learns patience.

*17   DARBY, J.E.   "An Examination of Some Restoration Versions of
Shakespeare's Plays."   Ph.D. dissertation, Manchester University.
Cited in Latt and Monk, 1976.30.

18   DEARING, VINTON A.   "Methods of Textual Editing."   In Bibliography and Textual Criticism: English and American Literature,
1700 to the Present.   Edited by O.M. Brack, Jr. and Warner
Barnes.   Chicago and London: University of Chicago Press, pp.
73-101.
Reprint of 1962.9.

19   DOBRÉE, BONAMY.   "Dryden's Prose."   In Dryden's Mind and Art.
Edited by Bruce King.   Edinburgh: Oliver & Boyd, pp. 171-88.
An appreciation, with copious quotation.   Printed in 1969.40.

20   DOWNES, JOHN.   Roscius Anglicanus (1708).   Introduction by John
Loftis; index of performers and plays by David S. Rodes.
Augustan Reprint Society 134.   Los Angeles: Clark Memorial
Library, University of California.
A facsimile reprint of 1708.1.

*21   EBERWEIN, ROBERT T.   "The Imagination and Didactic Theory in
Eighteenth-Century English Criticism."   Ph.D. dissertation,
Wayne State University.
Cited in Latt and Monk, 1976.30.   Abstracted in DAI 30:
1132A-33A.

22   FROST, WILLIAM.   Dryden and the Art of Translation.   Hamden,
Conn.:   Archon Books.
Reprint of 1955.11.

23   _____.   "Dryden's Theory and Practice of Satire."   In Dryden's
Mind and Art.   Edited by Bruce King.   Edinburgh: Oliver & Boyd,
pp. 189-205.
Discusses the "Discourse . . . of Satire," emphasizing
"Dryden's view of satire in relation to society and his view of
satire as a thing in itself."   Notes Dryden's interest in satire
as a device for promoting virtue, "especially good sense."   Summarizes Dryden's consideration of satire as a genre, emphasizing
his insistence on the need for a clear, positive point of view.

Points out that when Dryden wrote, satire (in England) was "still more or less a theoretical possibility." Pope and Johnson perfected it along the lines laid down by Dryden, and no one has equalled them since. Printed in 1969.40.

24   GEDULD, HARRY. <u>Prince of Publishers: A Study of the Work and Career of Jacob Tonson</u>. Indiana University Humanities Series 66. Bloomington and London: Indiana University Press, 245 pp.
         "Dryden's Publisher" (pp. 51-83) surveys Dryden's relations with his publishers, especially Tonson. Deals at length with the production of the translation of Virgil; defends Tonson's conduct. "Miscellany Poems" (pp. 87-109) deals in part with Dryden's role in their publication: concludes that it was basically advisory.

25   GOTTESMAN, LILLIAN. "The Arthurian Romance in English Opera and Pantomime, 1660-1800." <u>RECTR</u> 8, no. 2 (November):47-53.
         Describes <u>King Arthur</u>, its stage history, and its influence in the eighteenth century. Notes Henry Gifford's <u>Merlin</u> (1735), an adaptation of <u>King Arthur</u>, and David Garrick's <u>King Arthur</u> (1770), which derives from either or both of the works by Dryden and Gifford.

26   GUILHAMET, LEON M. "Dryden's Debasement of Scripture in <u>Absalom and Achitophel</u>." <u>SEL</u> 9 (Summer):395-413.
         Argues that Dryden intentionally debased both the scriptural story and seventeenth-century commentary on it in order to make David the most significant figure, an equal to God. Concludes that the poem is "the beginning of a new tradition of literature free of ecclesiastical and medieval restraint."

27   HAMILTON, K.G. <u>John Dryden and the Poetry of Statement</u>. East Lansing: Michigan State University Press.
         Reprint of 1967.23.

28   HARRISON, T.W. "Dryden's <u>Aeneid</u>." In <u>Dryden's Mind and Art</u>. Edited by Bruce King. Edinburgh: Oliver & Boyd, pp. 143-67.
         Sees Dryden's version as a distortion of the original, but also as a "surrogate epic for the seventeenth century." The distortions are the result of Dryden's didacticism, which necessitates that Aeneas be a perfect example of piety. Gives many examples of Dryden's alterations, usually in the direction of greater moral simplicity. Printed in 1969.40.

29   HEATH-STUBBS, JOHN. "Dryden and the Heroic Ideal." In <u>Dryden's Mind and Art</u>. Edited by Bruce King. Edinburgh: Oliver & Boyd, pp. 3-23.
         Asks why Dryden never wrote an epic poem. Concludes that the age was too skeptical, that in fact the mock-heroic mode was truer to the spirit of the time. Sees Dryden's heroic drama as an outlet for "epic aspirations" which finally found their object in <u>Absalom and Achitophel</u> and <u>MacFlecknoe</u>. Printed in 1969.40.

30 _____. <u>The Ode</u>. London: Oxford University Press, 116 pp.
Briefly describes, with quotations, "To . . . Anne Killigrew,"
<u>Song for St. Cecilia's Day</u>, and <u>Alexander's Feast</u> (pp. 42-48).

31 HORN, ANDRÁS. "Gedanken über Rationalität und Illusion.
Apropos John Dryden." In <u>Festscrift Rudolf Stamm</u>. Edited by
Eduard Kolb and Jörg Hasler. Bern and Munich: Franke, pp.
189-201.
Deals generally with verisimilitude in drama: emphasizes
the audience's "willing suspension of disbelief." Uses Dryden's
discussion of these matters (primarily in "Defence of an Essay of
Dramatic Poesy") as a starting point.

*32 HUME, ROBERT D. "Dryden's Criticism." Ph.D. dissertation,
University of Pennsylvania.
Cited in Latt and Monk, 1976.30. Abstracted in <u>DAI</u> 30:
2485A. See 1970.42.

*33 HUNEYCUTT, MELICENT. "The Changing Conceit of the Ideal
Statesman as Reflected in English Verse Drama During the Reign
of Charles II: 1660-1685." Ph.D. dissertation, University of
North Carolina.
Cited in Latt and Monk, 1976.30. Abstracted in <u>DAI</u> 30:
685A-86A.

34 JACKSON, ALLAN S. "Bibliography of 17th and 18th Century Play
Editions in the Rare Book Room of the Ohio State University
Library." <u>RECTR</u> 8, no. 1 (May):30-58.
Cites twenty-four Dryden editions. Gives author, short
title, and date. Indicates what prefatory material is present.

*35 JENKINS, RALPH E. "Some Sources of Samuel Johnson's Literary
Criticism." Ph.D. dissertation, University of Texas.
Cited in Latt and Monk, 1976.30. Abstracted in <u>DAI</u> 30:
1528A.

36 JENSEN, H. JAMES. <u>A Glossary of John Dryden's Critical Terms</u>.
Minneapolis: University of Minnesota Press, 135 pp.
Arranged alphabetically by word or phrase. Gives Dryden's
usage (or usages) for each, with citations. The introduction (pp.
3-11) makes the point that Dryden's critical vocabulary avoids
technical terms and jargon: "his terms are those in common, culti-
vated use, or critical words which came from the French."

37 KELSALL, M.M. "What God, What Mortal? The <u>Aeneid</u> and English
Mock-Heroic." <u>Arion</u> 8 (Autumn):359-79.
Asserts that in a time when the <u>Aeneid</u> was frequently used
for comedy or ridicule, Dryden's translation stands as "the age's
major manifestation of the Virgilian heroic mode." Other writers
of the time had to go to Dryden to find a frame for understanding
the work in its true form. But notes that even Dryden had

difficulty accepting Virgil's use of the marvelous in a non-Christian universe. Therefore he introduced wit into the Aeneid and gave Pope a precedent for the Dunciad.

38   KING, BRUCE. "Absalom and Achitophel: A Revaluation." In
      Dryden's Mind and Art. Edited by Bruce King. Edinburgh:
      Oliver & Boyd, pp. 65-83.
            Reads the poem as self-sufficient, without regard to its
      historical context. Sees as its theme "the dangers of the imagina-
      tion." Argues that Dryden's use of several layers of time enables
      him to suggest the simultaneity of history. Emphasizes the poem's
      links to the Bible as a whole, especially the story of the Fall
      (and other parts of Genesis). Sees Absalom as a parody-Messiah.
      Notes finally how the seeming objectivity of the narrator embodies
      the values of order and reason the poem expresses and supports.
      Printed in 1969.40.

39   _____. "The Conclusion of MacFlecknoe and Cowley." American
      Notes and Queries 7:86-87.
            Links the Elisha-Elijah image at the end of the poem to ll.
      65-72 of Cowley's "On the Death of Mr. Crashaw," which contains a
      similar image. Suggests that the echo is intentional and further
      degrades Flecknoe and Shadwell.

40   _____, ed. Dryden's Mind and Art. Essays Old and New 5.
      Edinburgh: Oliver & Boyd.
            Contains 1954.16; 1961.7; 1962.16 (Chapter 1); 1963.16;
      1964.24; 1969.19, 23, 28-29, 38. American printing: 1970.48.

*41   KING, BRUCE. "Wordplay in Absalom and Achitophel: An Aspect
      of Style." Lang&S 2:330-38.
            Cited in Latt and Monk, 1976.30.

42   McALEER, JOHN J. "John Dryden--Father of Shakespearean Criti-
      cism." Shakespeare Newsletter 19 (February):3.
            Summarizes Dryden's various comments on Shakespeare, and his
      use of Shakespeare in his plays.

*43   MACCUBIN, ROBERT P. "A Critical Study of Odes for St. Cecilia's
      Day, 1683-1697." Ph.D. dissertation, University of Illinois.
            Cited in Latt and Monk, 1976.30. Abstracted in DAI 30:
      1142A-43A.

44   MASON, H.A. "Introducing the Iliad (II): Pope and Dryden as
      Mediators." CQ 4 (Spring):150-68.
            Argues that through the translations of Dryden and Pope we
      can recover the complexity of the original poem. Takes as an ex-
      ample Dryden's version of the description of Hephaestus in Book 1:
      finds it both reverent and irreverent. Concludes that "what places
      Dryden in a class by himself is his command of the 'middle style.'"

*45   MATTEO, GINO JOHN. "Shakespeare's <u>Othello</u>: The Study and the
       Stage, 1604-1904." Ph.D. dissertation, University of Toronto.
           Cited in Latt and Monk, 1976.30. Abstracted in <u>DAI</u> 30:
       689A-90A.

*46   MAVROCORDATO, ALEXANDRE. "Positions de la critique dramatique
       chez Dryden." In <u>Société des anglicistes de l'enseignement</u>
       <u>supérieur: Acts du congrès de Caen</u>, 1966-67. Paris: Didier,
       pp. 103-12.
           Cited in Latt and Monk, 1976.30.

 47   MAYNARDIER, HOWARD. <u>The Arthur of the English Poets</u>. New York
       and London: Johnson Reprints.
           Reprint of 1907.3.

 48   MERRILL, ELIZABETH. <u>The Dialogue in English Literature</u>.
       Hamden, Conn.: Archon Books.
           Reprint of 1911.6.

 49   MINER, EARL. "Dryden's 'Mysterious Writ' Deciphered." <u>TLS</u>,
       1 May, p. 466.
           Argues, against Sanford Budick in 1969.9, that there are
       many sources of the beast fable in <u>The Hind and the Panther</u>, but
       that they do not include the legend of St. Chad. See also 1969.10,
       50.

 50   _____. "Dryden's 'Mysterious Writ' Deciphered." <u>TLS</u>, 3 July,
       p. 730.
           Apologizes for the intemperance of 1969.49. See 1969.9-10.

 51   _____. "From Narrative to 'Description' and 'Sense' in
       Eighteenth-Century Poetry." <u>SEL</u> 9 (Summer):471-87.
           Deals in general with "the disappearance of poetic narrative"
       as a central form. Sees Dryden as a pivotal figure who wished to
       write an epic but lacked the leisure and financial resources to do
       so. After Dryden "heroic virtue" became less and less a subject
       for poetry.

 52   _____, ed. <u>The Works of John Dryden</u>. Volume III: Poems 1685-
       <u>1692</u>. Vinton A. Dearing, textual editor. Berkeley and Los
       Angeles: University of California Press, 595 pp.
           The commentary (pp. 267-513) and other editorial material
       follows the format of volume 1 (1956.16). Other volumes (to date)
       in this definitive edition: 1962.42 (8); 1966.32 (9); 1970.59
       (10); 1971.58 (17); 1972.83 (2); 1974.7 (4); 1974.54 (18); 1976.41
       (15); 1978.29 (11); 1979.30 (19).

*53   MURAKAMI, SHIKŌ. "Kokkakyo ka Kyrkyo ka--<u>Religio Laici</u> no baai"
       [Anglican or Catholic?--the question of <u>Religio Laici</u>]. <u>Eigo</u>
       <u>Seinen</u> 115:10-12.
           In Japanese. Cited in Latt and Monk, 1976.30.

54 MYERS, WILLIAM. "Politics in The Hind and the Panther." EIC
19 (January):19-34.
    Asserts that the poem is not essentially a theological debate
but a political satire, and that therefore many charges laid a-
gainst it (of ridiculousness or indecorum) are baseless. Ties
several passages in the poem to contemporary politics; argues that
when read in this way the poem is unified.

*55 O'CONNOR, GERALD WILLIAM. "Four Approaches to Satire: The
Archtypical, the Historical, the Rhetorical, and the Anthro-
pological." Ph.D. dissertation, Boston University.
    Cited in Latt and Monk, 1976.30. Abstracted in DAI 29:
2222A-23A.

*56 OKERLUND, ARLENE N. "Literature and Its Audience: The Reader
in Action in Selected Works of Spenser, Dryden, Thackeray, and
T.S. Eliot." Ph.D. dissertation, University of California at
San Diego.
    Cited in Latt and Monk, 1976.30. Abstracted in DAI 30:1991A.

57 OSENBURG, F.C. "The Prologue to Dryden's Wild Gallant Reexam-
ined." ELN 7 (September):35-39.
    Argues that the annotation to the prologue in the California
Edition (1962.42) is astrologically uninformed; gives alternative
interpretations.

58 PARKIN, REBECCA PRICE. "Some Rhetorical Aspects of Dryden's
Biblical Allusion." ECS 2 (Summer):341-69.
    Demonstrates ways in which Dryden's use of biblical allusion
reflects his rhetorical situation. While in the secular poems the
allusions are honorific and often incredible, any disparity works
to Dryden's advantage in satire. Shows examples of this in Absalom
and Achitophel. Argues that in the religious poems Dryden had the
problem of making theology concrete and interesting: asserts that
he does this through the use of metaphor.

59 PARRA, ANTON RANIERI. "Considerazioni sulla fortuna di John
Dryden nell'Italia del settecento." Rivista di Letterature
Moderne e Comparate 22 (March):17-46.
    Deals with Dryden's reputation and translators in eighteenth-
century Italy.

*60 PECHTER, EDWARD. "John Dryden's Theory of Literature." Ph.D.
dissertation, University of California at Berkeley.
    Cited in Latt and Monk, 1976.30. Abstracted in DAI 30:33A-
34A. See 1975.46.

61 PETERSON, R.G. "The Unavailing Gift: Dryden's Roman Farewell
to Mr. Oldham." MP 66 (February):232-36.
    Relates the poem to the "conclamatio . . . which was tradi-
tionally spoken to the dead at a Roman funeral." Catullus 101,

which uses the "hail and farewell" formula, may have been a conscious or unconscious influence on Dryden. Concludes that the
form fits the small scope and judicious tone of Dryden's poem better than the elegy.

62   PINKUS, PHILIP. "The New Satire of Augustan England." UTQ 38
      (January):136-58.
          Argues that "satire as we know it"--which makes its point by
      juxtaposing the pretense and the reality--begins in the Augustan
      period. Uses MacFlecknoe as a major example.

63   PIPER, WILLIAM BOWMAN. The Heroic Couplet. Cleveland and
      London: Case Western Reserve University Press, 465 pp.
          "The Heroic Couplet in Dryden" (pp. 99-118) surveys his
      career, emphasizing his contributions to the development of the
      couplet form. Argues that at his best he uses a "dynamic supra-
      couplet movement and organization" in which while the "integrity"
      of individual couplets is maintained, they are interconnected.

64   RAMSAY, PAUL, Jr. The Art of John Dryden. Lexington:
      University of Kentucky Press, 214 pp.
          An analysis and evaluation of the poetry (including All for
      Love). Emphasizes metrical effects and versification. Praises
      Dryden for the fidelity of his imitation of nature, and for his
      poetic decorum. Analyzes the metrics to show how they affect and
      support meaning; provides a "key to scansion." Argues that the
      heroic couplet provides a "firm metrical and rhetorical norm" which
      yet allows great flexibility and variety.

*65   RUTHVEN, K.K. "The Decline of the Conceit." In The Conceit.
      The Critical Idiom. London: Methuen; New York: Barnes &
      Noble, pp. 52-60.
          Cited in Latt and Monk, 1976.30.

66   SAINTSBURY, GEORGE. Dryden. New York: AMS Press.
          Reprint of 1881.6.

*67   SEYMOUR-SMITH, MARTIN. Poets Through Their Letters. London:
      Constable; New York: Harper & Row.
          Cited in Latt and Monk, 1976.30.

*68   SHAWCROSS, JOHN. "Some Literary Uses of Numerology." Hartford
      Studies in Literature 1, no. 1:50-62.
          Cited in Latt and Monk, 1976.30.

69   SHERBO, ARTHUR. "'Characters of Manners': Notes Toward the
      History of a Critical Term." Criticism 11 (Fall):343-57.
          Begins by considering Johnson's distinction between "charac-
      ters of nature" and "characters of manners" (quoted by Boswell).
      Shows how fundamental a distinction this is. Quotes and summarizes
      early uses of "manners" in the literary sense: several of these
      are Dryden's.

*70   . A Computer Concordance of John Dryden's Translation of Virgil's Poetry. 2 vols. East Lansing: Michigan State University Press.
    Cited in Latt and Monk, 1976.30.

71   SHERWOOD, JOHN C. "Precept and Practice in Dryden's Criticism." JEGP 68 (July):432-40.
    Gives many examples in which Dryden manipulates the "rules" to fit particular cases in which he needed to justify his taste. Emphasizes the point that Dryden very rarely "violates" a "rule."

72   SMITH, DENZELL S. "Dryden's Purpose in Adapting Shakespeare's Troilus and Cressida." Ball State University Forum 10, no. 3 (Summer):49-52.
    Attributes the changes Dryden made in his original to his desire to show a world of order rather than disorder.

73   SPÄTH, EBERHARD. Dryden als Poeta Laureatus: Literatur im Dienste der Monarchie. Erlanger Beiträge zur Sprach- und Kunstwissenschaft 36. Nürnberg: Hans Carl, 222 pp.
    Ties Dryden's work to its "sociological and cultural background," emphasizing his official post as laureate from 1668 to 1689. Concludes that during this period "Dryden's literary work was motivated throughout by his will to serve monarchy in whichever way he regarded as appropriate or necessary." Contains an English summary, pp. 207-10.

74   SUTHERLAND, JAMES R. English Literature of the Late Seventeenth Century. Oxford History of English Literature. Oxford: Clarendon Press, 596 pp.
    Surveys Dryden's work by genre. Places it in the literature of the period (1660-1700). Describes and evaluates the major works. Asserts that Dryden "transcended his . . . contemporaries [in poetry] in almost every kind that he attempted." Finds him "by far" the most important critic of the period. Adds a bibliography (by Hugh Macdonald) of important editions and secondary works.

75   THALE, MARY. "Dryden's Unwritten Epic." PLL 5 (Fall):423-33.
    Suggests that Dryden failed to write an epic, or to write perceptively on the epic form, because he was intimidated by the example of Virgil.

*76 THOMAS, RAYMOND L. "Neo-Classical, Romantic, and Twentieth-Century Interpretations of Milton's Satan, 1695-1967." Ph.D. dissertation, Pennsylvania State University.
    Cited in Latt and Monk, 1976.30. Abstracted in DAI 30: 1185A-86A.

77   THOMAS, W.K. "Dryden's Absalom and Achitophel, 581." Expl 27: note 66.
    Finds a parallel to Dryden's use of the name Jonas for Sir William Jones in an anonymous Tory tract of 1681.

78   ____. "The Structure of Absalom and Achitophel." Revue de
       l'Université d'Ottawa/University of Ottawa Quarterly 39 (April-
       June):288-97.
            Asserts that the poem is a unified whole when it is seen as
       a Varronian satire (which allows a witty style and varied subject
       matter) organized like a classical oration, both forensic and de-
       liberative.

79   THORPE, PETER. "The Nonstructure of Augustan Verse." PLL 5
       (Summer):235-51.
            Argues that much Augustan poetry in fact succeeds "without
       unity, structure, coherence, pattern, or . . . design." Uses
       Absalom and Achitophel as one of several examples: despite its
       "disunity" it is a successful work of art, "and everyone knows it."

*80   TISCH, J.H. "Late Baroque Drama--A European Phenomenon?" In
       Proceedings of the Vth Congress of the International Comparative
       Literature Association (Belgrade, 1967). Amsterdam: Swets &
       Zeitlinger, pp. 125-36.
            Cited in Latt and Monk, 1976.30.

81   WALLACE, JOHN M. "Dryden and History: A Problem in Allegorical
       Reading." ELH 36 (March):265-90.
            Argues that seventeenth-century poems with historical content
       should be read as exemplary rather than as allegorical: the role
       of historical poetry was to give precepts and examples through the
       use of parallels and analogies. Discusses "To . . . Dr. Charleton,"
       "To . . . Anne Killigrew," Absalom and Achitophel, and the heroic
       plays as illustrations.

82   WEINBROT, HOWARD D. The Formal Strain: Studies in Augustan
       Imitation and Satire. Chicago and London: University of
       Chicago Press, 245 pp.
            Summarizes "Discourse . . . of Satire" and demonstrates the
       breadth of its influence in the eighteenth century (pp. 65-75).

83   WILDING, MICHAEL. "Allusion and Imitation in MacFlecknoe."
       EIC 19 (October):355-70.
            Argues that the obscene innuendo is as important to the poem
       as the epic allusion; that the "unlikeness of the two sets of
       references [creates] the surprise and tension of wit." Analyzes
       specific examples of allusion and innuendo. Concludes that through
       these complementary devices Dryden avoids direct statement, and
       hence avoids "the rigid or schematic."

84   WILLIAMS, R.D. "Changing Attitudes Toward Virgil." In Virgil.
       Edited by D.R. Dudley. Studies in Latin Literature and its
       Influence. London: Routledge & Kegan Paul, pp. 119-38.
            Discusses the attitudes toward Virgil of English writers from
       Dryden to Tennyson. Sees Dryden as typical of Augustan veneration
       of the original Virgil, freed of medieval allegorizing. Notes that

Dryden praised him for his "artistic control" and "moral and political significance." Asserts that Dryden "does not see the tension in the poet between [Aeneas'] virtues and their disastrous consequences." Goes on to discuss the romantic rejection of Virgil, and the Victorians' appreciation of his pathos.

85   WILLIAMSON, GEORGE. Seventeenth Century Contexts. Rev. ed. Chicago: University of Chicago Press.
Revised edition of 1960.28. No significant changes in the Dryden material.

86   YOUNG, KENNETH. John Dryden: A Critical Biography. New York: Russell & Russell.
Reprint of 1954.30.

1970

1   ADEN, JOHN. "'Nisi Artifex': Dryden and the Poet as Critic." South Atlantic Bulletin 35, no. 4 (November):3-10.
Discusses the "theoretical foundation" of Dryden's habit of being a critic of his own work. Concludes that Dryden's premise, frequently expressed and implied, is that poets are the best judges of poetry.

2   ALDERSON, WILLIAM L., and ARNOLD C. HENDERSON. "Dryden's Fables." In Chaucer and Augustan Scholarship. English Studies 35. Berkeley and Los Angeles: University of California Press, pp. 53-68.
Discusses the text of Chaucer printed with the 1700 folio of the Fables. Notes that it was the first text of Chaucer to use modern typography. Argues that Dryden consulted more than one edition in establishing his basic text; discusses his emendations and modernizations.

3   ARCHER, STANLEY. "Some Early References to Dryden." N&Q, n.s. 17 (November):417-18.
Points out several hitherto unnoticed contemporary references to Dryden as dramatist and critic. Points out that while earlier references during the period are to specific works, later ones are more general.

4   ARNOTT, JAMES FULLARTON, and JOHN WILLIAM ROBINSON. English Theatrical Literature 1559-1900: A Bibliography. London: Society for Theatrical Research, 508 pp.
Revises and updates 1888.3 (reprinted 1966.34). Gives title, place, date, and publisher of printed plays and books about the theater.

*5   ATKINS, GEORGE D. "Dryden and the Clergy." Ph.D. dissertation, University of Virginia.
Cited in Latt and Monk, 1976.30. Abstracted in DAI 30:4396A.

*6 AYCOCK, WENDELL M. "The Irrepressible Characters of Shakespeare's The Tempest: Sequels and Re-Creations." Ph.D. dissertation, University of South Carolina.
Cited in Latt and Monk, 1976.30. Abstracted in DAI 31:351A.

7 BAIER, LEE. "An Early Instance of 'Daydreams.'" N&Q, n.s. 17 (November):409.
Notes that although the OED credits Dryden with the first use of the term (in 1685), Davenant used it about thirty-five years earlier in Gondibert.

*8 BALESTRI, CHARLES A. "English Neoclassicism and Shakespeare: A Study of Conflicting Ideas of Dramatic Form." Ph.D. dissertation, Yale University.
Cited in Latt and Monk, 1976.30. Abstracted in DAI 31:6537A.

9 BANKS, LANDRUM. "Dryden's Baroque Drama." In Essays in Honor of Esmond Linworth Marilla. Edited by Thomas Austin Kirby and William John Olive. Baton Rouge: Louisiana State University Press, pp. 188-200.
Asserts that Dryden's heroic drama is "characteristically baroque," the culmination (along with Paradise Lost) of a process going back as far as Shakespeare. Sees a "simultaneous commitment to more than one viewpoint" as "the essence of baroque." Emphasizes the large scale of action and character in the heroic plays, and the heavy demands the form makes upon the audience's judgment.

10 BARBEAU, ANNE T. The Intellectual Design of John Dryden's Heroic Plays. New Haven and London: Yale University Press, 221 pp.
Asserts that "the heroic plays are essentially plays of ideas, and the early narrative poems, statements about the nature of the historical process." Insists that political ideas are integral parts of the plays, and that the plays are therefore set apart from their literary antecedents. Argues that critics have overemphasized the love vs. honor theme; sees the basic conflict in the plays as political, between "overreachers" and "normative" figures who are aware of their limitations. Relates this conflict to Dryden's conservative view of authority, and to the thought of Thomas Hobbes and Sir Robert Filmer. Analyzes the heroic plays to illuminate their intellectual and moral framework: finds "a gradual deepening of thought" between The Indian Emperour and Aureng-Zebe, in that the latter play deals with private as well as public morality. Discusses Dryden's dramatic techniques; relates them to the intellectual and moral values of order and moderation. Asserts that "the architectural merit of a play . . . is more important to Dryden than the novelty of its content or the language in which it is executed." Looks at the narrative poems; finds the same pattern as in heroic drama: a "state of lawlessness" is gradually replaced by "right government."

11   BATE, WALTER JACKSON. The Burden of the Past and the English
      Poet. Cambridge, Mass.: Harvard University Press, 152 pp.
         Credits Dryden with being "the first great European (not
      merely English) example" of a writer who is strongly aware that
      the existence of a literary past requires him to adopt some kind
      of stance toward it.

*12   BERNET, JOHN W. "Toward the Restoration Heroic Play: The
      Evolution of Davenant's Serious Drama." Ph.D. dissertation,
      Stanford University.
         Cited in Latt and Monk, 1976.30. Abstracted in DAI 30:
      3423A-24A.

*13   BIRD, ROGER A. "Dryden's Medieval Translations." Ph.D. disser-
      tation, University of Minnesota.
         Cited in Latt and Monk, 1976.30. Abstracted in DAI 30:4396A.

14   BLAIR, JOEL. "Dryden on the Writing of Fanciful Poetry."
      Criticism 12 (Spring):89-104.
         Argues against the view that Dryden's criticism is hostile
      to the sublime. Suggests that Dryden saw his task as reconciling
      ancient rules and modern achievements, and that this led him to a
      kind of theory about fanciful poetry. In this theory art should
      "picture a heightened reality . . . a nature more exalted than
      everyday life."

15   BOND, DONALD F. The Age of Dryden. Goldentree Bibliographies
      in Language and Literature. New York: Appleton-Century-Crofts.
         Lists significant editions and secondary works dealing with
      the period from 1660 to 1700.

16   BUDICK, SANFORD. "The Demythological Mode in Augustan Verse."
      ELH 37 (September):389-414.
         Tries to understand the position of the public poet during
      the period. Associates him with the keryx or ancient herald whose
      role is to proclaim matters of great significance, speaking with
      authority derived from a higher power. Sees the "kerygmatic" role
      of the poet in such poems as The Medal and Absalom and Achitophel
      to be that of destroying one myth to replace it with another.

17   _____ . Dryden and the Abyss of Light. Yale Studies in English
      174. New Haven and London: Yale University Press, 285 pp.
         Deals with Religio Laici and The Hind and the Panther. Sur-
      veys Dryden's early theological opinions, emphasizing his rational-
      ism. Asserts that the "doctrine of man's innate capacity for sav-
      ing truths" is the central element of Religio Laici; links this
      idea to the Cambridge Platonists. Notes the doctrine's dominant
      metaphor, in the poem and elsewhere, of the candle for innate
      truth. Reads the poem closely; concludes that its meaning "emerges
      from the poet's attempt to indicate the spiritual role of reason."
      Contrasts it with The Hind and the Panther, suggesting that the

latter poem's differences of meaning and connotation may be related
to Dryden's conversion. Relates the fable to the legend of St.
Chad, noting circumstantial similarities. Claims that the poem
is Dryden's planned Christian epic; concludes that unlike Religio
Laici it "makes a program of the mysterious." Sees Dryden as having recognized "that one of the things poetry and religion have in
common is a sense of intellectual infinitude." Three appendixes
deal with Dryden's possible authorship of a deistical essay, with
similarities between the arguments of Religio Laici and Hamon
L'Estrange's Prerogatives for the Veracity of Scripture, and with
other writers' use of the figure of the "abyss of light."

*18   BURROWS, L.R. "Juvenal in Translation." In Australasian
       Universities Language and Literature Association: Proceedings
       and Papers of the Twelfth Congress Held at the University of
       Western Australia, 5-11 February 1969. Edited by A.P. Treweek.
       Sydney: Australasian Universities Language and Literature
       Association, pp. 193-201.
          Cited in Latt and Monk, 1976.30.

 19   BUTLER, IAN CHRISTOPHER. Number Symbolism. London: Routledge
       & Kegan Paul; New York: Barnes & Noble, 198 pp.
          Summarizes Brooks and Fowler's numerological analysis of
       Song for St. Cecilia's Day (1967.19; 1970.34).

*20   CLARK, JOHN R. "'To the Memory of Mr. Oldham': Dryden's Dis-
       quieting Lines." Concerning Poetry 3, no. 1:43-49.
          Cited in Latt and Monk, 1976.30.

*21   CRIDER, J.R. "The Anti-Poet in MacFlecknoe." Brno Studies in
       English 9:11-18.
          Cited in Latt and Monk, 1976.30.

*22   DAVENPORT, WARREN W. "Private and Social Order in the Drama of
       John Dryden." Ph.D. dissertation, University of Florida.
          Cited in Latt and Monk, 1976.30.

*23   DICKS, GEORGE W. "Dryden's Use of Scripture in His Nondramatic
       Poetry." Ph.D. dissertation, Vanderbilt University.
          Cited in Latt and Monk, 1976.30. Abstracted in DAI 30:4405A.

*24   DILLON, GEORGE L. "The Art How to Know Men: A Study of
       Rationalist Psychology and Neo-Classical Dramatic Theory."
       Ph.D. dissertation, University of California at Berkeley.
          Cited in Latt and Monk, 1976.30. Abstracted in DAI 31:727A.

 25   DOBRÉE, BONAMY. "Milton and Dryden: A Comparison in Poetic
       Ideas and Poetic Method." In Milton to Ouida: A Collection of
       Essays. London: Frank Cass, pp. 1-21.
          Reprint of 1936.5.

*26   ELKIN, P.K. "Dryden's Translation of Juvenal's Sixth Satire."
      In Australasian Universities Language and Literature Association:
      Proceedings and Papers of the Twelfth Congress Held at the
      University of Western Australia, 5-11 February 1969. Edited by
      A.P. Treweek. Sydney: Australasian Universities Language and
      Literature Association, pp. 202-10.
            Cited in Latt and Monk, 1976.30.

 27   ELLEHAUGE, MARTIN. English Restoration Drama: Its Relation
      to Past English and Past and Contemporary French Drama.
      Folcroft, Pa.: Folcroft Press.
            Reprint of 1933.5.

 28   EMPSON, WILLIAM. "Dryden's Apparent Skepticism." EIC 20
      (April):172-81.
            Argues on the basis of a few passages in Religio Laici that
      Dryden was actually a deist. Suggests that his conversion was a
      pragmatic matter. See 1970.37, 41; 1971.26, 55.

 29   FAAS, K.E. "Some Notes on Dryden's All for Love." Anglia 88
      (September):341-46.
            Adds further evidence that Shakespeare's influence on the
      play has been overstated. Notes several verbal parallels with
      passages from plays on the same subject by Samuel Daniel and espe-
      cially Sir Charles Sedley.

 30   FIELD, P.J.C. "Authoritative Echo in Dryden." DUJ 62 (June):
      137-51.
            Discusses biblical echoes, as distinct from direct allusions.
      Argues that unlike most writers of his period Dryden makes echoes
      organic and functional. Emphasizes the satiric contexts of much
      of his echoes, in which "unnatural action" in this world is ironi-
      cally juxtaposed with "supernatural action." Argues that in pane-
      gyric, on the other hand, his standard technique was to use bibli-
      cal typology. Draws the bulk of his examples from MacFlecknoe and
      Absalom and Achitophel.

 31   _____. "Dryden and Rochester." N&Q, n.s. 17 (July):259-60.
            Suggests that the first eleven lines of Religio Laici may
      derive from the opening of Rochester's Satire Against Reason and
      Mankind (and may indeed be a response to it).

*32   FISHER, ALAN S. "The Form, History, and Significance of the
      Augustan Literary Portrait." Ph.D. dissertation, University of
      California at Berkeley.
            Cited in Latt and Monk, 1976.30. Abstracted in DAI 31:386A.

 33   FOWLER, ALISTAIR. Triumphal Forms: Structural Patterns in
      Elizabethan Poetry. Cambridge: Cambridge University Press,
      247 pp.
            Discusses Dryden among many other poets. Asserts that

Dryden's "symmetries generally have pronounced central accents" (numerically significant central lines, central stanzas, etc.).

34   _____, and DOUGLAS BROOKS. "The Structure of Dryden's Song for St. Cecilia's Day, 1687." In Silent Poetry: Essays in Numerological Analysis. Edited by Alistair Fowler. London: Routledge & Kegan Paul, pp. 185-200.
     Reprint of 1967.19.

*35   GRACE, JOAN C. "Tragic Theory in the Critical Works of Thomas Rymer, John Dennis, and John Dryden." Ph.D. dissertation, Columbia University.
     Cited in Latt and Monk, 1976.30. Abstracted in DAI 30: 4410A-11A.

36   HAMILTON, WALTER. The Poets Laureate of England, Being a History of the Office of Poet Laureate. New York: Burt Franklin.
     Reprint of 1879.2.

37   HARTH, PHILLIP. "Empson's Interpretation of Religio Laici." EIC 20 (October):446-50.
     Asserts that Empson (in 1970.28) has misread the passages in question. See also 1970.41; 1971.26, 55.

38   HOPE, A.D. The Cave and the Spring. Chicago: University of Chicago Press.
     Reprint of 1965.24, which contains 1963.16 and 1965.23.

39   HUGHES, DEREK W. "The Significance of All for Love." ELH 37 (December):540-63.
     Interprets the play through an examination of its use of imagery based upon the four elements. Suggests that the play's dependence upon imagery drawn from the natural world helps to dramatize the action's "impasse of conflicting, incompatible, and subjective ideals."

40   HUME, ROBERT D. "Dryden on Creation: 'Imagination' in the Later Criticism." RES, n.s. 21 (August):295-314.
     Explores "Dryden's concept of the nature of the creative process." Although Dryden's critical comments up to 1672 suggest a movement toward a greater reliance on the free imagination, in the later course of his career he moved back toward "judgement," "justness," and "propriety." Concludes that Dryden never really moved far from traditional critical values, and that his experiment in "free creativity" led to a "dead end [the heroic plays] from which he had to retreat."

41   _____. "Dryden's Apparent Skepticism." EIC 20 (October): 492-95.
     Finds Empson's essay (1970.28) "stimulating" but wrong, especially about Dryden's motives for converting to Roman Catholicism. See also 1970.37; 1971.26, 55.

42   _____. Dryden's Criticism. Ithaca and London: Cornell
        University Press, 252 pp.
             Notes the variety of Dryden's purposes in criticism, and the
        problems it raises. Sketches the characteristics of Dryden's criti-
        cal endeavor: it is occasional, unsystematic, pragmatic, undogmat-
        ic, exploratory. It deals with the problem of how the English
        should be writing plays. Suggests that there are three categories
        of Dryden's criticism: speculative, prescriptive, and explanatory.
        Feels that his prescriptive criticism is less good than his specu-
        lative (but the vast majority of his critical work is explanatory).
        Notes that over his career Dryden became less interested in discuss-
        ing forms and more interested in individual poets. Concludes that
        despite his "rhetorical heritage," Dryden moves toward "the sort of
        descriptive and analytic criticism that we practice today." Claims
        that his apparently casual approach is a rhetorical device, useful
        in creating an informal style. Points ou. that his style actually
        varies from work to work, depending upon his purpose. Discusses
        his view of literary history, concluding that he had no real sense
        of literary chronology. Analyzes "Heads of an Answer to Rymer" and
        "The Grounds of Criticism in Tragedy" to show that he is not basi-
        cally opposed to Thomas Rymer's views: he is trying to reconcile
        modern and classical literature. Asks whether Dryden is in fact a
        "neoclassic." Criticizes the term itself; concludes that Dryden
        is trying to build on the classics, but that he is actually less
        "classical" than Milton. Defends his criticism against the charge
        of inconsistency. Suggests that his informal style has misled crit-
        ics into ignoring the fundamental unity of his theory, despite its
        frequent fluctuations. Asserts that his fundamental belief is that
        "literature is the product of imitation heightened for effective-
        ness."

*43   JACKSON, WALLACE. "Satire: An Augustan Idea of Disorder." In
        Proceedings of the MLA Neoclassicism Conferences 1967-1968.
        Edited by Paul J. Korshin. New York: AMS Press, pp. 13-26.
             Cited in Latt and Monk, 1976.30.

44   JAMES, E. NELSON. "Drums and Trumpets." RECTR 9, no. 2
        (November):46-55; 10, no. 1 (May 1971):54-57.
             Discusses battle scenes in heroic plays, including Dryden's.
        Concludes that there are two types, the "classical" (action off
        stage) and the "Elizabethan" (action on stage). See 1971.41.

*45   JOHNSON, JAMES WILLIAM. "John Dryden, His Times, and All for
        Love." In Essays in Honor of Richebourg Gaillard McWilliams.
        Edited by Howard Creed. Birmingham-Southern College Bulletin
        63, no. 2. Birmingham, Ala.: Birmingham-Southern College, pp.
        21-28.
             Cited in Latt and Monk, 1976.30.

*46   JUDKINS, DAVID. "Studies in Seventeenth Century Political
        Poetry of the English Civil War." Ph.D. dissertation, Michigan

State University.
    Cited in Latt and Monk, 1976.30. Abstracted in <u>DAI</u> 31:
2387A.

47   KER, W.P. "The Style of Dryden's Prose." In <u>Literary English</u>
      <u>Since Shakespeare</u>. Edited by George Watson. London: Oxford
      University Press, pp. 231-35.
         Reprint of 1900.2; 1925.8.

48   KING, BRUCE, ed. <u>Dryden's Mind and Art</u>. New York: Barnes &
      Noble.
         Reprint of 1969.40. Includes 1954.16; 1961.7; 1962.16
   (Chapter 1); 1963.16; 1964.26; 1969.19, 23, 28-29, 38.

*49   KUPERSMITH, WILLIAM R., Jr. "Neoclassical English Satire."
      Ph.D. dissertation, University of Texas.
         Cited in Latt and Monk, 1976.30. Abstracted in <u>DAI</u> 30:3012A.

50   LeCLERQ, RICHARD V. "Corneille and <u>An Essay of Dramatic Poesy</u>."
      <u>CL</u> 22 (Fall):319-27.
         Argues that Corneille is not a source of ideas in the essay,
      but a tool which Dryden uses to make his points. Notes that each
      speaker makes use of Corneille in the debate, but Crites and
      Lisideus distort him and Eugenius and Neander transcend him.

51   LOFTIS, JOHN. "Dryden's Criticism of Spanish Drama." In <u>The</u>
      <u>Augustan Milieu: Essays Presented to Louis A. Landa</u>. Edited
      by Henry Knight Miller, Eric Rothstein, and G.S. Rousseau.
      Oxford: Clarendon Press, pp. 18-31.
         Argues that although Dryden frequently used Spanish themes
      (and some Spanish sources) in his earlier plays, he seems to have
      "failed to perceive the magnificence of the Spanish artistic achieve-
      ment." Points out, however, that he did like Spanish criticism; he
      was apparently familiar with Lope de Vega's. Dryden's references
      to Spanish plots suggest that he saw the difference between their
      "busy and complex" nature and that of French drama as analogous to
      the difference he saw between English plays of the previous age
      and those of his own time.

52   _____. "El Príncipe Constante and <u>The Indian Emperour</u>: A
      Reconsideration." <u>MLR</u> 65 (October):761-67.
         Argues, against Shergold and Ure (1966.49), that Calderón's
      play is not a major source of <u>The Indian Emperour</u>. Claims that
      similar passages can be accounted for by their similar points of
      view and subjects. Points out that such positive evidence as we
      do have suggests that Dryden did not know Calderón's work well,
      and did not think highly of it.

53   MARESCA, THOMAS E. "Language and Body in Augustan Poetic."
      <u>ELH</u> 37 (September):374-88.
         Considers the period's "satiric uses of bodies as debasing

devices." Deals especially with MacFlecknoe: sees Shadwell as a travesty of Christ, his "creating word" blocked up in flesh. Finds Shadwell's lack of speech a sign of his total sterility.

54   MEANS, JAMES A. "May's Lucan and The Hind and the Panther." N&Q, n.s. 17 (November):416-17.
        Argues that 2. 161 is indebted not only to Lucan's Bellum Civile 1. 6-7 but to Thomas May's translation of it.

*55   MILOSEVICH, VINCENT M. "Propriety as an Esthetic Principle in Dryden, Shakespeare, and Wagner." Humanities Association Review 21, no. 1:3-13.
        Cited in Latt and Monk, 1976.30.

56   MOORE, JOHN L. "Tudor-Stuart Views of the Growth, Status, and Destiny of the English Language." Studien zur englischen Philologie 2:1-173. College Park, Md.: McGrath.
        Reprint of 1910.8.

*57   MUIR, KENNETH. The Comedy of Manners. London: Hutchinson University Library.
        Cited in Latt and Monk, 1976.30.

58   NEWMAN, ROBERT S. "Irony and the Problem of Tone in Dryden's Aureng-Zebe." SEL 10 (Summer):439-58.
        Asserts that the play has ironic and satiric elements which have been neglected. Classifies and discusses the evidence. Concludes that Dryden "hold[s] up for admiration the continued possibilities of heroic selflessness even as he adjusts these possibilities to a skeptical view of human reality."

59   NOVAK, MAXIMILLIAN E., ed. The Works of John Dryden. Volume X: Plays. The Tempest, Tyrannick Love, An Evening's Love. George Robert Guffey, textual editor. Berkeley, Los Angeles, and London: University of California Press, 563 pp.
        The commentary (pp. 315-481) and other editorial material follows the format of 1962.42 (Vol. 8). Includes a note on staging (pp. 485-88). Further volumes in the "California Dryden" (to date): 1956.16 (1); 1966.32 (9); 1969.52 (3); 1971.58 (17); 1972.83 (2); 1974.7 (4); 1974.54 (18); 1976.41 (15); 1978.29 (11); 1979.30 (19).

60   OGILVIE, R.M. "Two Notes on Absalom and Achitophel." N&Q, n.s. 17 (November):415-16.
        Suggests that ll. 447-54 allude to Lucan's Bellum Civile 1. 205-12 (Caesar decides to cross the Rubicon), and that ll. 270-72 allude to Aeneid 4. 397-98 and 401-404.

*61   PARKIN, REBECCA PRICE. "The Journey Down the Great Scale Reflected in Two Neoclassical Elegies." Enlightenment Essays 1: 197-204.
        Cited in Latt and Monk, 1976.30.

*62   PARSONS, P.E. "Restoration Melodrama and Its Actors." <u>Komos</u>
      2:81–88.
         Cited in Latt and Monk, 1976.30.

 63   POLLARD, ARTHUR. <u>Satire</u>. The Critical Idiom 7. London:
      Methuen, 93 pp.
         A general introduction to the form and its types. Contains
      several brief references to Dryden, and describes <u>Absalom and
      Achitophel</u> and <u>MacFlecknoe</u>.

*64   POLLIN, BURTON R. "'The World Is Too Much With Us': Two More
      Sources--Dryden and Godwin." <u>Wordsworth Circle</u> 1:50–52.
         Cited in Latt and Monk, 1976.30.

*65   POYET, ALBERT. "A Humorous Pun in Dryden's <u>Epistle to the Whigs</u>
      (1682)." <u>Caliban</u> 7:23–24.
         Cited in Latt and Monk, 1976.30.

 66   PROFFITT, BESSIE. "Political Satire in Dryden's <u>Alexander's
      Feast</u>." <u>TSLL</u> 11 (Winter):1307–16.
         Asserts that the poem is "a well-hidden attack upon William
      III." Notes ironies and ambiguities which suggest an undercurrent
      of "illegitimacy and illegality" relating to Alexander and by analo-
      gy to William.

*66A RICE, JULIAN C. "The Allegorical Dollabella." <u>College Language
      Association Journal</u> 13:402–7.
         Cited by John Zamonski in 1975.59.

*67   RIVERS, ISABEL. "The Poetry of Conservatism, 1600–1745: Jonson,
      Dryden, and Pope." Ph.D. dissertation, Columbia University.
         Cited in Latt and Monk, 1976.30. Abstracted in <u>DAI</u> 30:4424A.

*68   RUBIN, BARBARA L. "The Dream of Self-Fulfillment in Restoration
      Comedy: A Study in Two Parts: The Heroic Pattern in Aristophan-
      ic and Roman Comedy and Its Design and Decadence in English
      Comedy from 1660 to 1700." Ph.D. dissertation, University of
      Rochester.
         Cited in Latt and Monk, 1976.30. Abstracted in <u>DAI</u> 30:
      5419A–20A.

*69   SCHARF, GERHARD. <u>Charaktergestaltung und psychologischer Gehalt
      in Drydens Shakespeare-Bearbeitungen</u>. Hamburger Philologie
      Studien. Ph.D. dissertation, Hamburg: H. Buske, 147 pp.
         Cited by John Zamonski in 1975.59.

*70   SCHWARZ, JANET L. "A Labyrinth of Design: A Study of Dryden's
      Dramatic Comedy." Ph.D. dissertation, University of California
      at Berkeley.
         Cited in Latt and Monk, 1976.30. Abstracted in <u>DAI</u> 30:
      4426A.

71 SHAFER, YVONNE BONSALL. "The Proviso Scene in Restoration Comedy of Manners." RECTR 9, no. 1 (May):1-10.
   Classifies various types of the scene. Discusses, among other plays not by Dryden, The Wild Gallant, Secret Love, Marriage a-la-Mode, and Amphitryon.

*72 STALLING, DONALD L. "From Dryden to Lillo: The Course of English Tragedy 1660-1731." Ph.D. dissertation, University of Texas.
   Cited in Latt and Monk, 1976.30. Abstracted in DAI 30:2981A.

73 SWENEY, JOHN R. "The Dedication of Thomas Southerne's The Wives Excuse 1692." Library, 5th ser. 25 (June):154-55.
   Announces that he has discovered a copy of the 1692 quarto containing the dedication, which includes the information that Dryden asked Southerne to write part of Cleomenes. The copy is in the Beinecke Library at Yale University.

74 THOMAS, W.K. "The Matrix of Absalom and Achitophel." PQ 49 (January):92-99.
   Argues that the various elements Dryden chose to put into the poem came out of the vast pamphlet literature of the period which dealt with the Exclusion Crisis, the Popish Plot, and related matters. Finds a particularly close parallel in Thomas D'Urfey's poem The Progress of Honesty.

75 VIETH, DAVID M. "Concept as Metaphor: Dryden's Attempted Stylistic Revolution." Lang&S 3 (Summer):197-204.
   Sets out several different ways in which Dryden makes "abstract principles or concepts perform the traditional functions of metaphor." Draws examples from the heroic plays, All for Love, Absalom and Achitophel, Alexander's Feast, Eleonora, The Medal, "To . . . Dr. Charleton," and Religio Laici.

*76 WEINBROT, HOWARD D. "On the Discrimination of Augustan Satires." In Proceedings of the MLA Neoclassicism Conference 1967-1968. Edited by Paul J. Korshin. New York: AMS Press, pp. 5-12.
   Cited in Latt and Monk, 1976.30.

77 WILLSON, ROBERT F., Jr. "The Fecal Version in MacFlecknoe." Satire Newsletter 8 (Fall):1-4.
   Finds defecation to be the "central satiric metaphor" of the poem. Concludes that by using this metaphor "Dryden has sardonically shown his audience a sharp separation between art and nature, genius and dullness, the spirit and the flesh, immortality and decay."

78 WILSON, GAYLE EDWARD. "Genre and Rhetoric in Dryden's 'Upon the Death of the Lord Hastings.'" Southern Speech Journal 35 (Spring):256-66.
   Asserts that the poem has the structure of an epideictic oration, and defends it as "a model of decorum."

1971

*1 ADAMS, BETTY S. "Dryden's Translation of Vergil and Its Eighteenth-Century Successors." Ph.D. dissertation, Michigan State University.
Cited in Latt and Monk, 1976.30. Abstracted in DAI 32:417A.

*2 ANALA, PHILLIP Z. "John Dryden's Place in the Development of Seventeenth-Century Prose." Ph.D. dissertation, St. Louis University.
Cited in Latt and Monk, 1976.30.

3 ARCHER, STANLEY L. "The Epistle Dedicatory in Restoration Drama." RECTR 10, no. 1 (May):8-13.
Based on a study of 258 dedications; describes the typical pattern of the form. Suggests that publishers were particularly interested in encouraging dedications in their books. Concludes that "the rewards of patronage . . . seem to have been substantial." Makes several references to Dryden.

4 ____. "A Performance of Dryden's Cleomenes." N&Q, n.s. 18 (November):460-61.
Argues that the prologue, written by Matthew Prior, was spoken on the occasion of the play's production at Westminster in 1695 by Lionel Sackville, Lord Buckhurst, the son of Dryden's patron the Earl of Dorset.

5 ATKINS, G. DOUGLAS. "The Function and Significance of the Priest in Dryden's Troilus and Cressida." TSLL 13 (Spring): 29-37.
Discusses the prominence of the priest Calchas; shows that he is responsible for the tragedy. Connects Dryden's characterization of him to his long-standing hatred of clergy, especially those who meddle in politics.

*6 BAKER, VAN R. "Dryden's Military Imagery." Ph.D. dissertation, Columbia University.
Cited in Latt and Monk, 1976.30. Abstracted in DAI 32:3290A.

7 BARNARD, JOHN. "John Dryden." In The New Cambridge Bibliography of English Literature. Vol. 2. Edited by George Watson. Cambridge: Cambridge University Press, pp. 439-63.
Lists major primary and secondary works. Arranged chronologically.

8 BELJAME, ALEXANDRE. Men of Letters and the English Public in the Eighteenth Century, 1660-1714: Dryden, Addison, Pope. Edited by Bonamy Dobrée. Translated from the French by E.O. Lorimer. St. Clair Shores, Mich.: Scholarly Press.
Reprint of 1948.2, which is a translation of 1881.1.

9   BENSON, DONALD R. "The Artistic Image and Dryden's Conception
     of Reason." SEL 11 (Summer):427-35.
         Argues that despite other changes in his beliefs, Dryden was
     never skeptical about the validity of artistic images, or about
     the intuitive reasoning which created them from experience. Con-
     cludes that this is "direct evidence of his intellectual orthodoxy."

10   _____. "Platonism and Neoclassic Metaphor: Dryden's Eleonora
     and Donne's Anniversaries." SP 68 (July):340-56.
         Argues that despite Dryden's avowed imitation of Donne, the
     two poems conceive their subjects quite differently. Donne's "She"
     is a "positive and unitary" image; Dryden's Eleonora is a "synthe-
     tic" pattern of the charitable woman. Relates this difference to
     changing notions of metaphor.

*11 BOATNER, JANET W. "Criseyde's Character in the Major Writers
     from Benoit Through Dryden: The Changes and Their Significance."
     Ph.D. dissertation, University of Wisconsin.
         Cited in Latt and Monk, 1976.30. Abstracted in DAI 31:4705A.

12   BODDY, MARGARET. "Two Notes on Dryden's 'Absalom and
     Achitophel.'" N&Q, n.s. 18 (November):463-64.
         Points out that two passages in Lauderdale's translation of
     the Aeneid echo lines from Dryden's poem.

*13 BODE, ROBERT F. "A Study of the Development of the Theme of
     Love and Duty in English Comedy from Charles I to George I."
     Ph.D. dissertation, University of South Carolina.
         Cited in Latt and Monk, 1976.30. Abstracted in DAI 31:5351A.

*14 CASTROP, HELMUT. "Die Satire in Drydens Prologen und Epilogen."
     Archiv 208:267-85.
         Cited in Latt and Monk, 1976.30.

15   CHARLANNE, LOUIS. L'Influence française en Angleterre au XVIIe
     siècle. Geneve: Slatkine Reprints.
         Reprint of 1906.4.

16   CLARK, JOHN R. "Dryden's 'MacFlecknoe,' 48." Expl 29 (March):
     note 56.
         Suggests that "Aston Hall" is not an actual place but a
     scatological pun.

*17 COLE, ELMER J., Jr. "The Consistency of John Dryden's Literary
     Criticism in Theory and Practice." Ph.D. dissertation,
     University of New Mexico.
         Cited in Latt and Monk, 1976.30. Abstracted in DAI 31:5356A.

*18 CRAWFORD, JOHN W. "Absalom and Achitophel and Milton's Paradise
     Lost." University of Dayton Review 7, no. 2:29-37.
         Cited in Latt and Monk, 1976.30.

19 CRINÒ, ANNA MARIA. *L'opera letteraria di John Dryden*. Verona: Fiorini, 405 pp.

An introductory survey of Dryden's entire canon, beginning with a short biography. Describes the works individually, with extensive quotation, and provides occasional background information. Concludes with a summary of the course of Dryden's critical reputation, including mentions of several early notices in Italy.

20 DILLON, GEORGE L. "The Seventeenth-Century Shift in the Theory and Language of Passion." *Lang&S* 4 (Spring):131-43.

Argues that Restoration playwrights wanted to make the language of passion more accurate than that which the Elizabethans had used, and so introduced several characteristic changes: "the restriction of mind-body metaphors, the limitation on the autonomy of passion . . . and the heightening of the aspect of report, rather than manifestation of passion." Draws most of the Restoration examples from Dryden's adaptations of Shakespeare.

*21 DOEDERLEIN, SUE W. "A Compendium of Wit: The Psychological Vocabulary of John Dryden's Literary Criticism." Ph.D. dissertation, Northwestern University.

Cited in Latt and Monk, 1976.30. Abstracted in *DAI* 31:3542A.

22 DONNELLY, JEROME. "Movement and Meaning in Dryden's *MacFlecknoe*." *TSLL* 12 (Winter):569-82.

Argues that the poem's structural design involves two kinds of movement (horizontal and vertical). But claims that only downward movement is ever completed; the others fail, the vertical becoming horizontal and the horizontal failing to reach a destination.

*23 DYSON, A.E., and JULIAN LOVELOCK. "Beyond the Polemics: A Dialogue on the Opening of *Absalom and Achitophel*." *Critical Survey* 5:133-45.

Cited in Latt and Monk, 1976.30. See 1976.16.

24 EDWARDS, THOMAS R. *Imagination and Power: A Study of Poetry on Public Themes*. New York: Oxford University Press, 232 pp.

Deals at length with *The Medal* (pp. 86-102). Discusses the portrait of Shaftesbury: finds its keynote to be "purposeless activity." As a whole the poem is "a great polemic against popular government" and sees little hope that people will change in the future. Suggests that Dryden sees Shaftesbury's activity as "a special case of a larger restlessness that may inhere in human nature." Links the poem's cynicism and weariness to that of "The Secular Masque," but still concludes that it "is one of our clearest poetic images of a healthy political life."

25 ELKIN, P.K. "Dryden as Intellectual, Playwright, and Critic." *Journal of the Australasian Universities Language and Literature Association* 36:210-16.

Matches the range of recent books on Dryden to Dryden's great range as a writer.

26   EMPSON, WILLIAM. "Dryden's Apparent Skepticism." <u>EIC</u> 21
      (January):111-15.
            Defends his essay on <u>Religio Laici</u> (1970.28). Accuses
      Phillip Harth of misreading the poem (in 1970.37). Finds in
      Dryden's conversion a "sad moral collapse, after the noble and
      generous religious beliefs he had held when he was a Deist and
      wrote <u>Religio Laici</u>." See also 1970.41; 1971.55.

*27   ERSKINE-HILL, HOWARD. "John Dryden." In <u>Dryden to Johnson</u>.
      Edited by Roger Lonsdale. Sphere History of Literature in the
      English Language 4. London: Sphere.
            Cited in Latt and Monk, 1976.30.

28   FAULKNER, THOMAS C. "Dryden and <u>Great and Weighty Considera-
      tions</u>: An Incorrect Attribution." <u>SEL</u> 11 (Summer):417-25.
            Argues that Ward's attribution of this 1679 tract to Dryden
      (in 1961.57) is incorrect because of a lack of convincing positive
      evidence as well as its stylistic dissimilarity to Dryden's other
      work. Concludes that it was written "by an Anglican high Churchman
      serving in a post within the gift of the Crown or as chaplain to a
      prominent Royalist."

*29   FETROW, FRED M. "Dryden's Dramatic Heroes: Conception and
      Mode." Ph.D. dissertation, University of Nebraska.
            Cited in Latt and Monk, 1976.30. Abstracted in <u>DAI</u> 31:4117A.

*30   FORRESTER, KENT A. "Supernaturalism in Restoration Drama."
      Ph.D. dissertation, University of Utah.
            Cited in Latt and Monk, 1976.30. Abstracted in <u>DAI</u> 32:1469A.

31   FREEDMAN, MORRIS. "Milton and Dryden on Tragedy." In <u>English
      Writers of the Eighteenth Century</u>. Edited by John H. Middendorf.
      New York and London: Columbia University Press, pp. 158-71.
            Asserts that Milton and Dryden were carrying on a dialogue
      in their comments on tragedy. Contrasts their views; notes their
      very great differences. Suggests that Dryden was strongly influ-
      enced by <u>Samson Agonistes</u> (and Milton's comments on tragedy in its
      preface) when he wrote <u>All for Love</u>. Points in particular to
      Dryden's rejection of rhyme and the play's greatly compressed plot.

32   _____. "The 'Tagging' of <u>Paradise Lost</u>: Rhyme in Dryden's <u>The
      State of Innocence</u>." <u>Milton Quarterly</u> 5 (March):18-22.
            Makes suggestions about Dryden's motives: he might have
      wanted to write an epic in rhyme, or to make Milton's work more
      accessible. Looks at several parallel passages, showing Dryden's
      general failure. Suggests that if he discovered, while adapting
      Milton, that rhymed couplets were inferior to blank verse the ex-
      perience may have led to his adoption of blank verse for <u>All for
      Love</u>.

33   FROST, WILLIAM. "Dryden and 'Satire.'" <u>SEL</u> 11 (Summer):401-16.

Credits Dryden with clarifying, in "Discourse . . . of
Satire," the nature of the form. Dryden asserts that satire is
nondramatic, that the word derives from the Latin <u>satura</u> (medley)
and not the Greek <u>saturos</u> (satyr), that the satirist's character
is urbane rather than vicious, and that the style should not be
"rough."

*34   GALVIN, Brother RONAN. "<u>The Hind and the Panther</u>: A Varronian
      Satire." Ph.D. dissertation, Fordham University.
         Cited in Latt and Monk, 1976.30. Abstracted in <u>DAI</u> 32:
      2054A-55A.

 35   GARNETT, RICHARD. <u>The Age of Dryden</u>. Essay Index Reprint
      Series. Freeport, N.Y.: Books for Libraries.
         Reprint of 1895.4.

*36   GUIBBORY, ACHSAH. "Attitudes Toward Classical Mythology in
      Seventeenth-Century English Literature." Ph.D. dissertation,
      University of California at Los Angeles.
         Cited in Latt and Monk, 1976.30. Abstracted in <u>DAI</u> 31:4161A.

 37   GUITE, HAROLD. "An Eighteenth-Century View of Roman Satire."
      In <u>The Varied Pattern: Studies in the Eighteenth Century</u>.
      Edited by Peter Hughes and David Williams. Publications of the
      McMaster University Association for 18th-Century Studies 1.
      Toronto: Hakkert, pp. 113-20.
         Attacks the distinction between comic and tragic satire made
      by John Dennis in 1721; claims that the false distinction derives
      from Dryden's "Discourse . . . of Satire." Asserts that Dryden's
      idea is based on an inaccurate understanding of historical fact,
      and on his mistranslation of Roman satires.

*38   HAUN, EUGENE. <u>But Hark! More Harmony: The Libretti of
      Restoration Opera in English</u>. Ypsilanti: Eastern Michigan
      University Press.
         Cited in Latt and Monk, 1976.30.

*39   HENNINGS, THOMAS P. "The Glorious and Loving Hero: Intellectual
      and Dramatic Backgrounds of Dryden's <u>All for Love</u>." Ph.D. dis-
      sertation, University of Wisconsin.
         Cited in Latt and Monk, 1976.30. Abstracted in <u>DAI</u> 32:966A.

 40   HUGHES, LEO. <u>The Drama's Patrons: A Study of the Eighteenth-
      Century London Audience</u>. Austin: University of Texas Press,
      217 pp.
         Deals in general with the audience's self-awareness, with
      its behavior, and with trends "in taste, in manners, and in moral
      attitudes." Notes Dryden's often inconsistent comments on his
      audience. Concludes that "he commonly rests his case on the culti-
      vated taste of the few," but that by the end of his career he seems
      to have given up hope of finding an appreciative audience in the
      theater.

41   JAMES, E. NELSON. "Drums and Trumpets." RECTR 10, no. 1
     (May):54-57.
          Completes essay begun in RECTR 9, no. 2 (November 1970).
     See 1970.44.

42   KEAST, WILLIAM R., ed. Seventeenth-Century English Poetry:
     Modern Essays in Criticism. Rev. ed. New York: Oxford
     University Press.
          A revision of 1962.21. Drops ten essays from the first edi-
     tion and adds twelve. Among those dropped is F.R. Leavis, "The
     Line of Wit" (1936.14).

*43 KELLY, EDWARD H. "Petronius Arbiter and Neoclassic English
     Literature." Ph.D. dissertation, University of Rochester.
          Cited in Latt and Monk, 1976.30. Abstracted in DAI 31:3508A.

44   KINSLEY, JAMES. "John Dryden." In English Poetry: Select
     Bibliographical Guides. Edited by A.E. Dyson. London and New
     York: Oxford University Press, pp. 111-27.
          Gives a brief guide to editions and significant scholarship,
     emphasizing modern work.

45   _____, and HELEN KINSLEY, eds. Dryden: The Critical Heritage.
     The Critical Heritage Series. London: Routledge & Kegan Paul;
     New York: Barnes & Noble, 424 pp.
          Reprints works (often excerpted) of critics and commentators
     on Dryden from the beginning down to the early nineteenth century.
     Many of the pieces are biographical, or contain personal attack or
     defense. The introduction (pp. 1-27) surveys the subject, making
     the point that Dryden was his own best critic (many of the pieces
     in the anthology are by Dryden). Has special praise for Scott's
     edition and life (1808.3).

*46 KISHI, TETSUO. "Dryden and Shakespeare." Shakespeare Studies
     10:39-51.
          Cited in Latt and Monk, 1976.30.

47   KNIGHTS, L.C. Public Voices: Literature and Politics With
     Special Reference to the Seventeenth Century. Clark Lectures
     for 1970-71. London: Chatto & Windus, pp. 94-113.
          Asserts that Dryden's public poetry has only a limited value
     for modern readers because of its "complete absence" of "resonance
     and perspective." His positions are one-sided and lack a sense of
     the potential tragedy in conflict (pp. 94-101). Reprinted:
     1972.41.

*48 KOOMJOHN, CHARLOTTE A. "MacFlecknoe: Dryden's Satire in Theory
     and Practice." Ph.D. dissertation, University of Rochester.
          Cited in Latt and Monk, 1976.30. Abstracted in DAI 32:1478A.

49   LANGBAINE, GERARD. Momus Triumphans: or, the Plagaries of the

English Stage (1688 [1687]). Introduction by David S. Rodes. Augustan Reprint Society 150. Los Angeles: Clark Memorial Library, University of California.
A facsimile reprint of 1687.5.

50 LEGOUIS, PIERRE. "Some Remarks on Seventeenth-Century Imagery: Definitions and Caveats." In Seventeenth-Century Imagery: Essays on Uses of Figurative Language From Donne to Farquhar. Edited by Earl Miner. Berkeley and Los Angeles: University of California Press, pp. 187-97.
Complains about the faulty and ambiguous vocabulary of modern critics in dealing with imagery. Draws several examples from Dryden and criticism on Dryden. Reprinted: 1973.41.

51 LEHMANN, ELMAR. "'If the People Have the Power': Zum Motiv des Volksaufstandes im Drama John Drydens." Poetica 4 (October): 437-61.
Deals with insurrection as a theme throughout Dryden's dramatic career; also looks at earlier treatments of the theme in English drama. Argues that in Dryden's last plays he becomes less a criticizer and more an analyzer of rebellious forces.

52 LINK, FREDERICK M., ed. Aureng-Zebe. Regents Restoration Drama Series. Lincoln: University of Nebraska Press, 154 pp.
The introduction (pp. xiii-xxiii) deals with the play's publication and stage history, and with its sources. Notes the distanced, rhetorical nature of the language, even in scenes of passion. Argues that the play's nature ultimately derives from epic.

53 LYNCH, KATHLEEN M. Jacob Tonson: Kit-Cat Publisher. Knoxville: University of Tennessee Press, 253 pp.
Narrates the course of Dryden's personal and professional relations with Tonson. Notes that despite radical political disagreement (Tonson was a Whig) they remained friends. Emphasizes the mutual advantages their arrangements produced. Gives the financial details of the publication of the translation of Virgil and the miscellanies. Claims that Tonson's miscellanies were the best of their kind, and suggests that the idea for them might have been Dryden's (pp. 17-36).

54 MACE, DEAN T. "Ut pictura poesis: Dryden, Poussin and the Parallel of Poetry and Painting in the Seventeenth Century." In Encounters: Essays on Literature and the Visual Arts. Edited by John Dixon Hunt. London: Studio Vista; New York: Norton, pp. 58-81.
Argues that Poussin's two Phocion pictures perfectly fulfill Dryden's theory about the parallels between poetry and painting. In particular they match in painting what Dryden calls the "greatest work of the soul of man," heroic poetry. Summarizes and discusses Dryden's "Parallel of Poetry and Painting" as an excellent statement of the Renaissance idea of the "sisterhood" of the two

arts. Looks at the earlier history of the idea in Italian theory
of painting and French dramatic theory. Points out that "both arts
became equally concerned with developing powers of expression."

55   MINER, EARL. "Dryden's Apparent Skepticism." EIC 21 (October):
     410-11.
          Notes "a certain creative element in Mr. Empson's reading."
     A response to 1970.28. See also 1970.37, 41; 1971.26.

56   MINER, EARL, ed. "Dryden's Eikon Basilike: To Sir Godfrey
     Kneller." In Seventeenth-Century Imagery: Essays on Uses of
     Figurative Language from Donne to Farquhar. Berkeley and Los
     Angeles: University of California Press, pp. 151-67.
          Closely analyzes the poem's structure, building on a con-
     sideration of the special characteristics of the verse epistle.
     Notes how the kinship of art, linking the poet and the painter,
     dominates the poem's imagery. Finds the unifying element in the
     triple treatment of time: in the past development of painting,
     culminating in Kneller, in the present unfavorable period for art,
     and in the future when "Time as restoring artist will mellow the
     imperfections of present-day art."

57   MINER, EARL. Dryden's Poetry. Bloomington and London: Indiana
     University Press.
          Reprint of 1967.41.

58   MONK, SAMUEL HOLT, ed. The Works of John Dryden. Volume XVII.
     Prose: An Essay of Dramatick Poesie and Shorter Works. Vinton
     A. Dearing, textual editor. Berkeley and Los Angeles: University
     of California Press, 535 pp.
          Contains the shorter prose works which are not attached to
     poems or plays. The commentary (pp. 331-484) includes a headnote
     for each work, and notes on individual words, phrases, and passages.
     Textual notes and appendixes ("His Majesties Declaration" [1681]
     and "Copy of a Paper written by the Late Duchess of York" (1686])
     follow. Further volumes in the "California Dryden" to date:
     1956.16 (1); 1962.42 (8); 1966.32 (9); 1969.52 (3); 1970.59 (10);
     1972.83 (2); 1974.7 (4); 1974.54 (18); 1976.41 (15); 1978.29 (11);
     1979.30 (19).

*59 MOORE, CHARLES A. "The Familiar Verse Epistle from Dryden to
     Pope." Ph.D. dissertation, University of Oregon.
          Cited in Latt and Monk, 1976.30. Abstracted in DAI 31:3513A.

*60 MOORE, JUDITH K. "Early Eighteenth-Century Literature and the
     Financial Revolution." Ph.D. dissertation, Cornell University.
          Cited in Latt and Monk, 1976.30. Abstracted in DAI 31:6561A.

*61 O'SULLIVAN, MAURICE J. "Dryden and Juvenal: A Study in
     Interpretation." Ph.D. dissertation, Case Western Reserve
     University.

Cited in Latt and Monk, 1976.30. Abstracted in DAI 31: 3515A–16A.

*62   RAM, TULSI. The Neo-Classical Epic (1650–1720). Delhi: National.
Cited in Latt and Monk, 1976.30.

*63   REEDY, GERARD, S.J. "Noumenal and Phenomenal Evidence in England, 1622–1682." Enlightenment Essays 2:137–48.
Cited in Latt and Monk, 1976.30.

*64   SEIDEL, MICHAEL A. "Satiric Theory and the Degeneration of State: The Tyrant and the Mob in Satiric Literature of the Restoration and Early Eighteenth Century." Ph.D. dissertation, University of California at Los Angeles.
Cited in Latt and Monk, 1976.30. Abstracted in DAI 31:3519A.

65   SELDEN, RAMAN. "Roughness in Satire from Horace to Dryden." MLR 66 (April):264–72.
Traces attitudes toward "roughness." Places Dryden with those who rejected it, although he is sometimes ambivalent. Distinguishes between two kinds of roughness: the Horatian tradition (to which Dryden belongs) "tries to temper roughness rather than displace it entirely." What the tradition does reject is "primitive and unpolished" roughness.

*66   SHERBO, ARTHUR. Frequency Lists of John Dryden's Translations of Virgil's Poetry. East Lansing: Michigan State University, Computer Center.
Cited in Latt and Monk, 1976.30.

67   SLOMAN, JUDITH. "An Interpretation of Dryden's Fables." ECS 4 (Winter):199–211.
Argues that the book has an inner coherence, and that the poems therefore should be read in terms of their relations to each other. Sees an overall plot involving the development of civilization, in which conventional epic virtues are replaced by Christian charity and patience. Suggests that Dryden learned from Chaucer how to develop themes in a series of tales. Notes that the book ends with "Cymon and Iphigenia," however, in which the ideal world must submit to the real world.

68   SMITH, JOHN HARRINGTON. The Gay Couple in Restoration Comedy. New York: Octagon.
Reprint of 1948.20.

*69   SPENCER, JEFFRY B. "Five Poetic Landscapes, 1650–1750: Heroic and Ideal Landscape in English Poetry from Marvell to Thomson." Ph.D. dissertation, Northwestern University.
Cited in Latt and Monk, 1976.30. Abstracted in DAI 32:3271A.

70   THOMAS, P.G. Aspects of Literary Theory and Practice, 1550–
      1870. Port Washington, N.Y. and London: Kennikat.
        Reprint of 1931.36.

71   WAITH, EUGENE. Ideas of Greatness: Heroic Drama in England.
      New York: Barnes & Noble; London: Routledge & Kegan Paul,
      304 pp.
        A general introduction to the topic. Includes two sections
on Dryden: "Dryden's Plays to 1677" (pp. 203–35) and "Dryden's
Later Plays" (pp. 253–64). Gives detailed plot summaries and
brief evaluations. Emphasizes the importance Dryden placed on en-
gaging the passion of his audience.

*72   WHITE, MAURICE D. "John Dryden's Poetry of Praise: The Ques-
      tion of Irony." Ph.D. dissertation, Ohio State University.
        Cited in Latt and Monk, 1976.30. Abstracted in DAI 32:2071A.

*73   WILKINSON, JOHN. "The Style of Dryden's Early Poetry and of
      Absalom and Achitophel." Ph.D. dissertation, State University
      of New York at Buffalo.
        Cited in Latt and Monk, 1976.30. Abstracted in DAI 31:
4740A–41A.

*74   ZAMONSKI, JOHN. "Redemptive Love in the Plays of John Dryden:
      From Wild Gallant to All for Love." Ph.D. dissertation, Ohio
      University.
        Cited in Latt and Monk, 1976.30. Abstracted in DAI 31:
4139A–40A.

75   ZWICKER, STEVEN N. "The King and Christ: Figural Imagery in
      Dryden's Restoration Panegyrics." PQ 50 (October):582–98.
        Argues that political typology as it was used in the seven-
teenth century provides the key to appreciating Astraea Redux and
To His Sacred Majesty. Surveys the tradition and applies it to
the poems. Concludes that "seen within the framework of sacred
history, the present takes justified meaning from the past; like
their correlative type, the Israelites, the English must endure
suffering and tribulation for past sins, but at the same time they
live in the hope of a renewal of the covenant with God."

1972

1   BAKER, VAN R. "Heroic Posturing Satirized: Dryden's Mr.
      Limberham." PLL 8 (Fall):370–79.
        Suggests that Dryden uses military metaphors in the play to
attack the libertinism of Restoration society as typified by the
Court Wits, who frequently used military imagery in their poetry.
Dryden satirizes the characters of the rake Woodall, the impotent
Father Aldo and Limberham, and the cuckold Brainsick, none of whom
has the martial quality his language might suggest. Concludes that

the language of Dryden's heroic plays forms part of the background:
his heroes had earned the right to be rhetorical, unlike the wits,
few of whom had been soldiers and who were not honorable men.

*2   BHALLA, BRIJ M. "Sex Instinct and Restoration Comedy."
     Visvabharati Quarterly 38, no. 4:79-87.
         Cited in Latt and Monk, 1976.30.

3   BRONSON, BERTRAND. "Some Aspects of Music and Literature in
     the Eighteenth Century." In Stuart and Georgian Moments: Clark
     Library Papers on Seventeenth and Eighteenth Century English
     Literature. Edited by Earl Miner. Berkeley, Los Angeles, and
     London: University of California Press, pp. 127-60.
         Sees two significant phenomena in the relationship of music
     and literature in the eighteenth century. The first is the effort
     to "evolve a language that could convey general and abstract truths
     with a high degree of objectivity, by means of the mutually inter-
     pretive support of which words and tones were capable"; the second
     is the role of popular song in the "transition from classicism to
     individualism." A detailed analysis of Handel's music to Song for
     St. Cecilia's Day illustrates the first phenomenon. Printed in
     1972.60.

4   BROOKS, HAROLD F. "Dryden's Aureng-Zebe: Debts to Corneille
     and Racine." RLC 46 (January-March):5-34.
         Asserts that Dryden drew situations in the play from
     Corneille's Rodogune and Nicomède, and from Racine's Mithridate,
     Britannicus, and Bajazet. Suggests that Milton's Samson Agonistes
     is also a source.

5   BROWER, REUBEN A. "Visual and Verbal Translations of Myth:
     Neptune in Virgil, Rubens, Dryden." Daedalus 101, no. 1:155-82.
         Compares Virgil's treatment of Neptune quelling the waves in
     Aeneid 1 with Rubens's sketch of it and Dryden's translation of it.
     Argues that Rubens harmonizes the Virgilian and Homeric versions,
     while Dryden heightens the imperial and political themes of the
     passage, especially as it seems relevant to his contemporary scene.
     Concludes that such visual elements as there are in his version are
     mainly picked up from earlier illustrators and the "Rubens tradi-
     tion." Reprinted: 1975.1.

6   CAMERON, WILLIAM J. "John Dryden's Jacobitism." In Restoration
     Literature: Critical Approaches. Edited by Harold Love.
     London: Methuen; New York: Barnes & Noble, pp. 277-308.
         Probes the "literary manifestations of Dryden's adherence to
     the lost cause of Jacobitism." While he followed the Tory prin-
     ciples of passive obedience and nonresistance, Jacobite innuendos
     are frequent in Dryden's work after 1688. Analyzes Dryden's Aeneid
     to show, however, that his conception of the hero could serve as a
     model to William, and help to make "the Revolution settlement pas-
     sively acceptable to Jacobites." Printed in 1972.51.

7   CARNOCHAN, W.B. "Some Suppressed Verses in Dryden's Translation
    of Juvenal VI." TLS, 21 January, pp. 73-74.
        Describes verses found written in a copy of Dryden's transla-
    tion of Juvenal and Persius. Despite being described as written by
    Dryden, they are omitted in the printed version of the translation.
    Argues that they are by Dryden and that the hand may be Jacob
    Tonson's. Concludes that the verses were suppressed because of
    the more rigorous moral climate of 1690s. See 1972.43, 46, 63.

8   CASTROP, HELMUT. "Dryden and Flecknoe: A Link." RES, n.s. 23
    (November):455-58.
        Suggests that Richard Flecknoe's Sir William D'Avenant's
    Voyage to the Other World: With His Adventures in the Poets
    Elizium (1668), with its attack upon the laureateship (which Dryden
    had just inherited from Davenant), may have provoked MacFlecknoe.

9   CLOYD, EMILY L. James Burnett Lord Monboddo. Oxford: Clarendon
    Press, 208 pp.
        Describes Monboddo's unpublished manuscript on poetry, which
    would have been volume 7 of the Origin and Progress of Language
    (1773-1792). Monboddo analyzes Alexander's Feast line by line to
    show in detail the function of sound (pp. 150-52). See 1790.3.

*10 CONNELLY, WILLIAM J. "Perspectives in Chaucer Criticism: 1400-
    1700." Ph.D. dissertation, Oklahoma University.
        Cited in Latt and Monk, 1976.30. Abstracted in DAI 33:721A.

*11 CURRENT, RANDALL D. "The Curious Art: A Study of Literary
    Criticism in Verse in the Seventeenth Century." Ph.D. disser-
    tation, University of California at Los Angeles.
        Cited in Latt and Monk, 1976.30. Abstracted in DAI 33:304A.

12 DAVIES, PAUL C. "Restoration Liberalism." EIC 22 (July):
    226-38.
        Finds in Restoration writers, especially the wits, "a spon-
    taneous if unformulated liberalism." Dryden with his history of
    associations with authority is an exception.

*13 DAVIS, FLOYD H., Jr. "The Dramaturgical Functions of Song,
    Dance, and Music in the Comedies of John Dryden." Ph.D. dis-
    sertation, Ball State University.
        Cited in Latt and Monk, 1976.30. Abstracted in DAI 33:2888A.

*14 DORMAN, PETER J. "Chaucer's Reputation in the Restoration and
    Eighteenth Century." Ph.D. dissertation, New York University.
        Cited in Latt and Monk, 1976.30. Abstracted in DAI 32:5734A.

*15 DUGGAN, MARGARET M. "Aspects of Dryden's The Hind and the
    Panther." Ph.D. dissertation, Columbia University.
        Cited in Latt and Monk, 1976.30.

16   FOSS, MICHAEL. The Age of Patronage: The Arts in England,
     1660-1750. Ithaca: Cornell University Press, 243 pp.
          Traces the course of public and private patronage during the
     Augustan Age, with particular emphasis on the artist's economic
     situation and its effect on his art. Refers frequently to Dryden,
     and draws many examples from his life and work.

17   FOWLER, JOHN. "Dryden and Literary Good Breeding." In
     Restoration Literature: Critical Approaches. Edited by Harold
     Love. London: Methuen; New York: Barnes & Noble, pp. 225-46.
          Analyzes Dryden's concept of linguistic development, and its
     relation to his view of Latin literature. Sees in Dryden's trans-
     lations from Latin evidence that he was imposing his own theoreti-
     cal standards upon Latin authors. Suggests that his theory also
     dictates his attitude toward earlier English literature. Printed
     in 1972.51.

18   FREEHAFER, JOHN. "Shakespeare, the Ancients, and Hales of Eton."
     SQ 23 (Winter):63-68.
          Suggests that Dryden's anecdote about Hales (in Essay of
     Dramatic Poesy: that Hales felt Shakespeare to be unequalled as
     a poet) is the "only one which probably adds to our factual know-
     ledge of the opinions of Shakespeare's contemporaries." Argues
     that those of Joseph Gildon and Nicholas Rowe conflict with known
     facts.

19   FRIEDMAN, LENEMAJA. "Bibliography of Restoration and Eighteenth
     Century Plays Containing Children's Roles." RECTR 11, no. 1
     (May):19-30.
          Lists author, play, place of publication, publisher, and
     names of children's roles. Notes seven plays by Dryden.

20   FROST, WILLIAM. "Dryden and the Classics: With a Look at His
     Aeneis." In John Dryden. Edited by Earl Miner. Writers and
     their Background. Athens: Ohio University Press; London: G.
     Bell, pp. 267-96.
          Demonstrates Dryden's close connection with the classics.
     Defends his knowledge of Latin and Greek languages and literature,
     and his understanding of them. Contrasts Dryden's translation of
     Virgil with Douglas's, showing Dryden's characteristics as a trans-
     lator. Traces the influence of Dryden's classicism on later writ-
     ers. Printed in 1972.58.

21   _____. "More About Dryden as a Classicist." N&Q, n.s. 19
     (January):23-26.
          Attempts to "rehabilitate" Dryden's reputation as a classic-
     ist; corrects errors he sees in the Noyes edition (1909.4; 1950.18).
     Concentrates on "Discourse . . . of Satire" and its main source,
     Isaac Casaubon's De Satyrica Graecorum Poesi et Romanorum Satira.

22   FUJIMURA, THOMAS H. "The Personal Drama of Dryden's The Hind

and the Panther." PMLA 87 (May):406-16.
     Asserts that the personal drama of faith in the poem makes
it a moving and vital work. Suggests that both the Hind and the
Panther are Dryden: the latter represents the pride that Dryden
tried to suppress. The beast fable enables him to present his
own struggle and at the same time make a more general statement,
both temporal-historical and universal. Concludes that the poem
succeeds as a religious work because it communicates the pattern
of every Christian's struggle to achieve charity and humanity.

*23   GARRISON, JAMES D. "Dryden and Verse Panegyric." Ph.D. dis-
      sertation, University of California at Berkeley.
           Cited in Latt and Monk, 1976.30. Abstracted in DAI 33:752A.
      See 1975.23.

*24   GEIST, EDWARD V., Jr. "Temple, Dryden, and Saint-Evremond: A
      Study in Libertine Aesthetic and Moral Values." Ph.D. disserta-
      tion, University of Virginia.
           Cited in Latt and Monk, 1976.30. Abstracted in DAI 32:4563A.

 25   HAGSTRUM, JEAN H. "Dryden's Grotesque: An Aspect of the Baroque
      in His Art and Criticism." In John Dryden. Edited by Earl
      Miner. Writers and their Background. Athens: Ohio University
      Press; London: G. Bell, pp. 90-119.
           Relates Dryden's work in the 1660s to the "grotesque," a
      crucial aspect of baroque art. Sees three chief kinds of grotesque
in Dryden's characters: "the social grotesque" (fools and hypo-
crites), "the grotesque of superstition" (savages), and "the grotesque of power" (tyrants). Concludes that ultimately Dryden trans-
formed the grotesque, with its diabolic overtones, from the supernatural to the natural. Printed in 1972.58.

 26   _____. "Verbal and Visual Caricature in the Age of Dryden."
      In England in the Restoration and Early Eighteenth Century:
      Essays on Culture and Society. Edited by H.T. Swedenberg, Jr.
      Berkeley, Los Angeles, and London: University of California
      Press, pp. 173-95.
           Suggests that satirical portraits of individuals may be
      called by the visual term "caricature," of which there are two
types. "Emblematic caricatures" are reductive, as in Swift's
"The Description of a Salamander" (1705); "portrait caricatures,"
while satirically distorting, maintain a realistic surface, as in
the "great verbal portraits of Dryden and Pope." Printed in
1972.83.

 27   HAMILTON, K.G. "Dryden and Seventeenth-Century Prose Style."
      In John Dryden. Edited by Earl Miner. Writers and their
      Backgrounds. Athens: Ohio University Press; London: G. Bell,
      pp. 297-324.
           Examines Dryden's prose style in the context of the histori-
cal development of English style. Contrasts the opening of the

preface to the Fables (1700) with a passage from Milton to show
Dryden's lack of periodicity. Contrasts the same passage with the
opening of Essay of Dramatic Poesy (1668) to suggest that Dryden's
development was toward greater simplicity and ease. Asserts that
Dryden's style is "to be defined primarily by negatives," and that
this "anonymous" quality was essential for the full development
of English prose. Printed in 1972.58.

*28   HAMMIL, CARRIE E.   "The Celestial Journey and the Harmony of
the Spheres in English Literature, 1300-1700." Ph.D. dissertation, Texas Christian University.
     Cited in Latt and Monk, 1976.30. Abstracted in DAI 33:2326A.

29   HARBAGE, ALFRED.   "Elizabethan-Restoration Palimpsest." In
Shakespeare Without Tears and Other Essays. Cambridge, Mass.:
Harvard University Press, pp. 170-218.
     Reprint of 1940.13.

30   HARDIN, RICHARD F.   "Ovid in Seventeenth-Century England." CL
24 (Winter):44-62.
     Cites Dryden's criticism of Ovid's excessive verbal wit as
one of several examples that typify the rejection of him in late
seventeenth-century England.

*31   HEISCH, ELIZABETH A.   "The Problem of Prosody in the Early
English Opera 1660-1700: A Study of the Setting of Words to
Music." Ph.D. dissertation, University of California at Los
Angeles.
     Cited in Latt and Monk, 1976.30. Abstracted in DAI 32:6377A.

32   _____.   "A Selected List of Musical Dramas and Dramas with
Music from the Seventeenth and Eighteenth Centuries." RECTR
11, no. 1 (May):33-58; 11, no. 2 (November):37-59.
     Listed by title. Includes a brief description, and notes
author, composer, date of publication, and location of copy or
copies. Contains twenty-one plays by Dryden.

33   HIRT, A.   "A Question of Excess: Neo-Classical Adaptations of
Greek Tragedy." Costerus 3:55-119.
     Describes at length the plot of Dryden and Lee's Oedipus, as
one example of a neoclassical adaptation of a Greek tragedy.

*34   HOBAN, THOMAS M.   "The Contexts and Structure of Dryden's Fables
Ancient and Modern." Ph.D. dissertation, University of Nebraska.
     Cited in Latt and Monk, 1976.30. Abstracted in DAI 32:
3953A-54A.

35   HOFFMAN, ARTHUR W.   "Dryden's Panegyrics and Lyrics." In John
Dryden. Edited by Earl Miner. Writers and their Backgrounds.
Athens: Ohio University Press; London: G. Bell, pp. 120-55.
     Shows how Dryden fulfilled his concept of the poet's social

responsibility through his poems of satire and compliment, and how
as laureate he handled the special obligations of that office.
Analyzes Dryden's public and personal panegyrics; briefly touches
upon his skill as a lyricist. Printed in 1972.58.

36   HUME, ROBERT D. "Diversity and Development in Restoration
      Comedy 1660-1679." ECS 5 (Spring):365-97.
         Argues that the common concept of the nature and development
      of Restoration comedy is too limited, because too few plays have
      been used to establish it. Suggests that "at any time two or three
      strikingly different modes of comedy exist." Mentions several
      plays by Dryden among many other examples.

37   _____. "Dryden, James Howard, and the Date of All Mistaken."
      PQ 51 (April):422-29.
         Notes that there is some inconclusive evidence that James
      Howard's All Mistaken, or the Mad Couple was written by 1665, which
      would make it precede Dryden's Secret Love, its supposed source.

38   JOHNSON, JAMES WILLIAM. "The Classics and John Bull, 1660-
      1714." In England in the Restoration and Early Eighteenth
      Century: Essays on Culture and Society. Edited by H.T.
      Swedenberg, Jr. Berkeley, Los Angeles, and London: University
      of California Press, pp. 1-26.
         Traces English attitudes toward the classics from 1660 to
      1714. Finds that the humanistic ideal of the continuity of clas-
      sical and Christian thought diminished, despite continuing interest
      in the classics. Cites Dryden's tragedies of the 1670s, satiric
      poems of the 1680s, and translations of the 1690s as evidence of
      shifting attitudes. Printed in 1972.83.

39   JORDAN, ROBERT. "The Extravagant Rake in Restoration Comedy."
      In Restoration Literature: Critical Approaches. Edited by
      Harold Love. London: Methuen, pp. 69-90.
         Argues that the "extravagant rake" is an important type in
      Restoration comedy for whom the problematic moral considerations
      attached to the rake-hero are irrelevant. He is a comic figure,
      not unlike a fop, whose behavior is not seen as a threat to soci-
      ety. Cites several of Dryden's rakes, especially Celadon in Secret
      Love, as examples. Printed in 1972.51.

40   KIRSCH, ARTHUR. Dryden's Heroic Drama. New York: Gordian
      Press.
         Reprint of 1965.33.

41   KNIGHTS, L.C. Public Voices: Literature and Politics with
      Special Reference to the Seventeenth Century. Clark Lectures
      for 1970-71. Totowa, N.J.: Rowman & Littlefield, 133 pp.
         Reprint of 1971.47.

42   KORSHIN, PAUL J. "Figural Change and the Survival of Tradition

in the Later Seventeenth Century." In <u>Studies in Change and Revolution: Aspects of English Intellectual History 1640-1800</u>. Edited by Paul J. Korshin. Menston, Yorkshire: Scolar Press, pp. 99-128.

Argues that there was a significant change in the figurative aspect of literature toward the end of the seventeenth century: "a simplifying reaction began to reject the prevalent trend of imagistic erudition and obscurity." Uses many examples from Dryden.

43 _____. "Some Suppressed Verses in Dryden's Translation of Juvenal VI." <u>TLS</u>, 17 March, pp. 307-8.

Claims that publisher Jacob Tonson's censorship, not "the moral climate of the 1690s," led to the suppression of the verses. A response to 1972.7. See also 1972.46, 63.

*44 LATT, DAVID J. "The Progress of Friendship: The <u>Topoi</u> for Society and the Ideal Experience in the Poetry and Prose of Seventeenth-Century England." Ph.D. dissertation, University of California at Los Angeles.

Cited in Latt and Monk, 1976.30. Abstracted in <u>DAI</u> 32:4616A-17A.

45 LeCLERQ, RICHARD V. "The Academic Nature of the Whole Discourse of <u>An Essay of Dramatic Poesy</u>." <u>PLL</u> 8 (Winter):27-38.

Asserts that Neander's dogmatic defense of rhyme notwithstanding, Dryden has drawn upon the doctrine and method of the later Academics, especially Cicero, in the construction of the "sceptical" <u>Essay</u>. Concludes that an examination of the work shows that Dryden has found in the Academic tradition, as illustrated by such a work as Cicero's <u>De Natura Deorum</u> (which may have been his actual example), a precedent for the nondogmatic nature of Neander's argument, the manipulation of the order of speeches to favor Neander's position, the use of setting, and several other structural devices.

46 LEESON, R.A. "Some Suppressed Verses in Dryden's Translation of Juvenal VI." <u>TLS</u>, 24 March, p. 337.

Agrees with 1972.7 that the atmosphere of the 1690s was inhospitable to bawdy verse. See also 1972.43, 63.

*47 LEVISON, WILLIAM S. "Restoration Adaptations of Shakespeare as Baroque Literature." Ph.D. dissertation, University of Illinois.

Cited in Latt and Monk, 1976.30. Abstracted in <u>DAI</u> 34:730A.

48 LINK, FREDERICK M. "A Decade of Dryden Scholarship." <u>PLL</u> 8 (Fall):427-43.

Reviews editions and books on Dryden for the period 1961-1971. Concludes that much work is still to be done, especially with the plays, some of the poetry, and his influence on later writers.

49   LOFTIS, JOHN. "Dryden's Comedies." In <u>John Dryden</u>. Edited by Earl Miner. Writers and their Background. Athens: Ohio University Press; London: G. Bell, pp. 27-57.
     Characterizes and judges Dryden's comic drama, outlines its origins, and describes each comedy. Emphasizes Dryden's learning, wittiness, and variety. Finds his London comedies disappointing; praises <u>Marriage a-la-Mode</u> and <u>Amphitryon</u>. Concludes that if we "can take them for what the best of them are, superb dramatic achievements combining romantic adventures with acutely observed scenes from familiar life," we can value them properly. Printed in 1972.58.

50   LORD, GEORGE deF. "<u>Absalom and Achitophel</u> and Dryden's Political Cosmos." In <u>John Dryden</u>. Edited by Earl Miner. Writers and their Background. Athens: Ohio University Press; London: G. Bell, pp. 156-90.
     Treats Dryden's political poetry in terms of its use of the "restoration myth": he saw in contemporary events "a recurrence of past events or the re-expression of some archetypal pattern." Sees <u>Absalom and Achitophel</u> as the most prominent instance. Emphasizes the conservatism of Dryden's use of the myth: his rejection of innovation, his defense of the Stuart succession, and his support for "imagined stability," even if autocratic. Printed in 1972.58.

51   LOVE, HAROLD, ed. <u>Restoration Literature: Critical Approaches</u>. London: Methuen; New York: Barnes & Noble.
     An anthology of original essays. Includes 1972.6, 17, 39, 67, 70.

*52   McKEON, MICHAEL. "Meanings of Dryden's <u>Annus Mirabilis</u>." Ph.D. dissertation, Columbia University.
     Cited in Latt and Monk, 1976.30. Abstracted in <u>DAI</u> 33: 2942A-43A. See 1975.35.

53   McNAMARA, PETER L. "Clothing Thought: Dryden on Language." <u>TSE</u> 20:57-70.
     Argues that Dryden's response to living language was flexible rather than prescriptive. His philosophy of language was not fixed by rules but guided by a desire for order and stability: Melantha in <u>Marriage a-la-Mode</u> is an illustration of linguistic modishness. Relates his philosophy of language to his practice of paraphrasing or imitating originals rather than strictly translating them, the better to suit the English language.

54   MARTIN, LESLIE H. "Dryden and the Art of Transversion." <u>Comparative Drama</u> 6 (Spring):3-13.
     Studies <u>Secret Love</u> to show that it is not a routine translation but a skillful adaptation of Madeleine de Scudéry's romance <u>Le Grand Cyrus</u>, in which Dryden compensates for its weaknesses. Some scenes are paraphrased, others are based on narration, and some derive from hints or allusions undeveloped in the original.

55 MINER, EARL. "Forms and Motives of Narrative Poetry." In
    John Dryden. Writers and their Background. Athens: Ohio
    University Press; London: G. Bell, pp. 234-66.
        Traces Dryden's development as a writer of narratives, using
    as a basis for discussion Hobbes's broad definition, which includes
    not only epic but pastoral and satire as possible narrative forms.
    Points to the pervasiveness of narrative characteristics in Dryden's
    nondramatic poetry; treats Annus Mirabilis (at length), MacFlecknoe,
    Absalom and Achitophel, The Medal, Religio Laici, The Hind and the
    Panther and Fables. Finds Fables the high point of Dryden's use of
    narrative: "in its harmony of jarring notes the Fables offer a
    last testament to the much jarring integrity of seventeenth-century
    experience." Printed in 1972.58.

56 _____. "Inclusive and Exclusive Decorums in Seventeenth-Century
    Prose." Lang&S (Summer):192-203.
        Uses an example (among others) from Dryden's "Discourse . . .
    of Satire" (1693) to demonstrate "how periodicity may operate as an
    inclusive decorum that overrides a subordinate exclusive decorum
    expressed by negatives and privatives." Concludes that the "mul-
    tiplicity of decorums" used in seventeenth-century prose included
    "inclusive and exclusive procedures involving prose style."

57 _____. "In Satire's Falling City." In The Satirists's Art.
    Edited by H. James Jensen and Malvin R. Zirker, Jr. Bloomington:
    Indiana University Press, pp. 3-27.
        Uses two of Dryden's statements on satire (from "Discourse
    . . . of Satire" and the preface to Annus Mirabilis) to support the
    argument that satire "is a transforming rather than a mimetic pro-
    cess." Concludes that as panegyric is a vision of apotheosis, so
    satire is a vision of degeneration.

58 _____, ed. John Dryden. Writers and their Background. Athens:
    Ohio University Press; London: G. Bell, 389 pp.
        A collection of original essays on aspects of Dryden's work,
    or specific works or kinds of works. One of a series of volumes
    "presenting major authors in their intellectual, social and artis-
    tic contexts." Includes 1972.20, 25, 27, 35, 49-50, 55, 59, 93,
    98.

59 _____. "On Reading Dryden." In John Dryden. Writers and their
    Background. Athens: Ohio University Press; London: G. Bell,
    pp. 1-26.
        Traces the development of Dryden's reputation; introduces
    the general range of characteristics of his work; sets him against
    the literary and historical background of his age. Emphasizes his
    humanity, generosity, and graciousness. Printed in 1972.58.

60 _____, ed. Stuart and Georgian Moments: Clark Library Seminar
    Papers on Seventeenth and Eighteenth Century English Literature.
    Berkeley, Los Angeles, and London: University of California

Press.
    Collects papers presented at Clark Memorial Library seminars, 1953–1969. Includes 1972.3, 71, 82, 95.

61   MINER, EARL. "The Wild Man Through the Looking Glass." In The Wild Man Within: An Image in Western Thought from the Renaissance to Romanticism. Edited by Edward Dudley and Maximillian E. Novak. Pittsburgh: University of Pittsburgh Press, pp. 87–114.
    Sees the "Wild Man" in seventeenth-century literature as representing actual or potential savagery inherent in the individual or state, toward which the author is often ambivalent. Uses examples from Dryden, especially The Tempest and The Conquest of Granada, as major illustrations. Almanzor, for example, is "at once an aid and a threat to any society."

*62   MITCHELL, ELEANOR R. "Pronouns of Address in English, 1580–1780: A Study of Form Changes as Reflected in British Drama." Ph.D. dissertation, Texas A&M University.
    Cited in Latt and Monk, 1976.30. Abstracted in DAI 32:4593A.

63   MONKMAN, KENNETH. "Some Suppressed Verses in Dryden's Translation of Juvenal VI." TLS, 28 January, p. 99.
    Provides a further bawdy meaning (for "Flats"). See 1972.7, 43, 46.

64   MORGAN, P. "Fop Art: Dryden on Comedy." ES 53 (August): 334–39.
    Asserts that the inconsistent and self-contradictory nature of Dryden's theory and practice of comedy is unimportant in the light of his achievement.

65   MOSKOVIT, LEONARD. "An Echo of Gellius in Dryden's 'Oldham.'" N&Q, n.s. 19 (January):26–27.
    Suggests that 11. 11–21 of Dryden's poem echo Aulus Gellius, Noctes Atticae 13. 2. 3–6.

*66   NELSON, RAYMOND S. "Eros Lost." Iowa English Bulletin: Yearbook 22, no. 3:42–47.
    Cited in Latt and Monk, 1976.30.

67   O'CONNOR, MARK. "John Dryden, Gavin Douglas, and Virgil." In Restoration Literature: Critical Approaches. Edited by Harold Love. London: Methuen, pp. 247–75.
    Assesses the quality of Dryden's Aeneid by comparing it with the original and with Gavin Douglas's translation. Argues that although Dryden's lack of visual imagination does not harm the work, it is less lively than Douglas's, and does not do justice to the ambiguities and obliquities of Virgil. Concludes that the demands of writing in heroic couplets may be to blame. Printed in 1972.51.

68   PARKIN, REBECCA PRICE. "Heroic and Anti-Heroic Elements in
      The Hind and the Panther." SEL 12 (Summer):459-66.
           Cites Samuel Johnson's criticism of The Hind and the Panther
      (that Dryden sometimes lapses from the heroic style into satire).
      Argues that nevertheless much of part 1 of the poem is in fact
      heroic. Concludes that its true genre is mixed heroic-satire,
      which represents the actual situation Dryden and his contemporaries
      experienced.

*69   PARSONS, JAMES H. "A Study of the Political Ideas in John
      Dryden's Absalom and Achitophel." Ph.D. dissertation, University
      of Texas.
           Cited in Latt and Monk, 1976.30. Abstracted in DAI 33:322A.

70   PARSONS, PHILIP. "Restoration Tragedy as Total Theatre." In
      Restoration Literature: Critical Approaches. Edited by Harold
      Love. London: Methuen, pp. 27-68.
           Criticizes Dryden's dramaturgy in his serious plays, by con-
      trast with his contemporaries Settle, Lee, and Otway. Argues that
      although his rhetoric and verbal effects can be brilliant, he lacks
      the visual sense necessary for theatrical power. Suggests that
      Dryden's feeling that his plays were better appreciated by readers
      than playgoers betrays his distrust of the theater. Printed in
      1972.51.

71   PHILLIPS, JAMES. "Poetry and Music in the Seventeenth Century."
      In Stuart and Georgian Moments: Clark Library Seminar Papers on
      Seventeenth and Eighteenth Century English Literature. Edited
      by Earl Miner. Berkeley, Los Angeles, and London: University
      of California Press, pp. 1-21.
           Asserts that the humanistic ideal of the union of poetry and
      music died in the later seventeenth century, because of the increas-
      ing complexity of music. Notes that in both of Dryden's St.
      Cecilia poems, it is significant that it is the saint's voice which
      "enlarges the powers of purely instrumental music." Dryden's com-
      plaint in the preface to Albion and Albianus illustrates the fail-
      ure of the ideal: the English language was not suited to music as
      it had become. Printed in 1972.60.

72   REEDY, GERARD, S.J. "Mystical Politics: The Imagery of Charles
      II's Coronation." In Studies in Change and Revolution: Aspects
      of English Intellectual History 1640-1800. Edited by Paul J.
      Korshin. Menston, Yorkshire: Scolar Press, pp. 19-42.
           Analyzes the imagery in literature about the coronation:
      finds that Charles was characteristically associated with spiritual
      and historical analogues, and that the thunderstorm which occurred
      during the ceremony was given only favorable connotations. Uses
      Dryden's To His Sacred Majesty as a major example.

73   REVERAND, CEDRIC D. "Patterns of Imagery and Metaphor in
      Dryden's The Medal." YES 2:103-14.

Analyzes the poem to demonstrate the complexity of Dryden's
use of imagery, metaphor, and allusions, which most critics, following Mark Van Doren (1929.10), have slighted. Finds complex figurative patterns deriving from the epigraph and its context, and from
the medal itself.

74   ROPER, ALAN. "Dryden's The History of the League and the Early
      Editions of Maimbourg's Histoire de la Ligue." PBSA 66 (3d
      Quarter):245-75.
          Sets out what is known or can be surmised about the process
      by which Dryden was commissioned to translate, and translated,
      Maimbourg's work. Notes that "English evidence" suggests October
      1683 to March 1684 as the period in which the work was done, but
      that "French evidence" indicates that it may have been started and
      finished at a later date. Gives detailed bibliographical descrip-
      tions of editions of the Histoire de la Ligue. Concludes that
      Dryden used the 1684 pirated edition, published at The Hague, and
      on the basis of this conclusion reasons that Dryden could not have
      begun before March 1684, and therefore translated this 150,000 word
      work in no more than four months.

*75   SASLOW, EDWARD L. "Dryden and Achitophel: The Social Context,
      Historical Background and Political Perspective of Dryden's
      Writings Pertinent to the Exclusion Crisis." Ph.D. disserta-
      tion, University of California at Berkeley.
          Cited in Latt and Monk, 1976.30.

76   SEARY, PETER. "Language Versus Design in Drama: A Background
      to the Pope-Theobald Controversy." UTQ 42 (Fall):40-63.
          Argues that the controversy between Dryden and Rymer over
      the relative importance of language and design in drama is in the
      background of the Pope-Theobald controversy: Dryden's anti-
      Aristotelianism strongly influenced Theobald; Pope tended to the
      side of Rymer.

77   SEWARD, PATRICIA M. "Was the English Restoration Theatre
      Significantly Influenced by Spanish Drama?" RLC 46 (January-
      March):95-125.
          Argues that only ten Restoration plays can be shown to have
      demonstrable borrowings from Spanish drama, including Dryden's The
      Indian Emperour (Calderón's El príncipe constante) and The Assigna-
      tion (Calderón's Con quien vengo vengo). Concludes that there was
      no extensive Spanish influence on the Restoration as a whole. Only
      the "intrigue comedy" shows Spanish influence, and this was soon
      anglicized.

*78   SHAHEEN, ABDEL-RAHMAN A. "Satiric Characterization in John
      Dryden's Later Works." Ph.D. dissertation, University of
      Houston.
          Cited in Latt and Monk, 1976.30. Abstracted in DAI 33:
      2905A-06A.

79 SLOMAN, JUDITH. "Dryden's Originality in Sigismonda and Guiscardo." SEL 12 (Summer):445-57.
Cites the work as an outstanding example of Dryden's thorough revision of the originals he translated. Sigismunda resembles Dryden's later tragic heroines, like Almeyda, in asserting her individuality regardless of the consequences, but she also resembles earlier villainous women like Lyndaraxa and Nourmahal, by being overwhelmed by sexual passion. Concludes that this ambivalence is unresolved, but notes that a pattern of light imagery leading from half-light to daylight suggests that she has moved from limited physical knowledge to a somewhat fuller spiritual knowledge by the time of her death.

80 STRAUMANN, BRUNO. John Dryden: Order and Chaos. Zurich: Juris, 239 pp.
Defends Dryden's "ultimate unity," and asserts that his response to "the cultural revolution of the seventeenth century" was central to his work. Examines the Essay of Dramatic Poesy, the heroic drama (especially Aureng-Zebe), and Absalom and Achitophel in the light of his attitude toward "the dualism of order and chaos in human creativity." Concludes that Dryden was an authoritarian conservative out of what he saw as necessity rather than by nature. As a critic he remained a skeptic.

81 SWEDENBERG, H.T., Jr. "Challenges to Dryden's Editor." In Stuart and Georgian Moments: Clark Library Seminar Papers on Seventeenth and Eighteenth Century English Literature. Edited by Earl Miner. Berkeley, Los Angeles, and London: University of California Press, pp. 93-108.
Reprint of 1967.54. Printed in 1972.60.

82 _____. The Theory of the Epic in England, 1650-1800. New York: Russell & Russell.
Reprint of 1944.8.

83 SWEDENBERG, H.T., Jr., ed. The Works of John Dryden. Volume II: Poems 1681-1684. Vinton A. Dearing, textual editor. Berkeley, Los Angeles, and London: University of California Press, 497 pp.
The commentary (pp. 205-406) follows the format of volume 1 (1956.16). Textual notes and appendixes (commendatory poems to Absalom and Achitophel, The Medal, and Religio Laici) follow. Further volumes in the "California Dryden" to date: 1962.42 (8); 1966.32 (9); 1969.52 (3); 1970.50 (10); 1971.58 (17); 1974.7 (4); 1974.54 (18); 1976.41 (15); 1978.29 (11); 1979.30 (19).

84 SWENEY, JOHN R. "Dryden's 'Lines to Mrs. Creed.'" PQ 51 (April):489-90.
Notes that a slip with a variant reading of the poem is pasted in Edmond Malone's copy of his biography of Dryden, which he must have obtained after publication.

85 _____. "The Religion of Lady Elizabeth Howard Dryden." N&Q, n.s. 19 (October):365.
Suggests that a letter from Cardinal Philip Howard (30 June 1693) is important evidence that Dryden's wife had by that time long been a Roman Catholic.

86 THALE, MARY. "The Framework of An Essay of Dramatic Poesy." PLL 8 (Fall):362-69.
Argues that the discontinuity between the style of the framework and the body of the Essay suggests that they may have been written at different times: the framework, with its elaborate, metaphorical style, at the time of Annus Mirabilis (Aug.-Oct. 1666) and the body at an earlier time (between the summer of 1665 and that of 1666). Dryden's inclusion of the framework, which clearly suggests a parallel between English military and literary success, was perhaps designed to raise low morale at the time of publication. Concludes that this motive may have been Dryden's reason for publishing the piece at all, in view of his expressed doubts about its quality.

87 THORPE, PETER. "'No Metaphor Swell'd High': The Relative Unimportance of Imagery or Figurative Language in Augustan Poetry." TSLL 13 (Winter):593-612.
Uses several examples from Dryden, among many others, in arguing that Augustan poetry, modern criticism to the contrary, deemphasizes the image.

*88 UNDERHILL, JOHN H. "Celebration in Eighteenth-Century English Criticism." Ph.D. dissertation, University of Michigan.
Cited in Latt and Monk, 1976.30. Abstracted in DAI 32:6459A.

89 VIETH, DAVID M., ed. All for Love. Regents Restoration Drama Series. Lincoln: University of Nebraska Press, 180 pp.
The introduction (pp. xiii-xxxiv) discusses the play's stage history and reviews the criticism, which has largely been concerned with comparing it to Shakespeare's Antony and Cleopatra. Emphasizes the play's nature as an "imitation"--not only of Antony and Cleopatra but of other plays by Shakespeare, other playwrights, and of Dryden's own heroic plays. Sees the play as overly general and abstract for a tragedy, but with compensating strengths--the character of Alexas, the imagery, the focus on domestic patterns.

90 VIETH, DAVID M. "The Art of the Prologue and Epilogue: A New Approach Based on Dryden's Practice." Genre 5:271-92.
Suggests that the prologues and epilogues can be properly approached by New Criticism because in their own time they were thought to have a separate existence. Dryden's practice suggests that they disrupt "one kind of illusion only to create another, more inclusive one." Classifies eight attributes of the prologue and epilogue. Analyzes three of Dryden's prologues (to An Evening's Love, All for Love, and The Assignation) to demonstrate the success of the New Critical approach.

91 _____. "Irony in Dryden's Verses to Sir Robert Howard." <u>EIC</u>
22 (July):239-43.
　　Suggests that an ironic reading of the poem gives depth to
a work which has been ignored. Asserts that the lines which praise
Howard for improving on Virgil and Statius show that Dryden is writing ironically. Concludes that the predominant tone, however, is
"gentlemanly commendation for the works of his brother-in-law."

*92 VROONLAND, JAMES. "The Dryden-Shadwell Controversy: A Preface
to <u>MacFlecknoe</u>." Ph.D. dissertation, Kansas State University.
　　Cited in Latt and Monk, 1976.30. Abstracted in <u>DAI</u> 33:2399A.

93 WAITH, EUGENE M. "Dryden and the Tradition of Serious Drama."
In <u>John Dryden</u>. Edited by Earl Miner. Writers and their Background. Athens: Ohio University Press; London: G. Bell, pp.
58-89.
　　Links Dryden's serious drama to popular heroic romances,
especially in France, and to contemporary panegyric poetry and
ceremony. Summarizes and characterizes each of Dryden's serious
plays, emphasizing their use of typical heroic themes, such as
magnanimity and heroic self-assertion, but also "generosity and
transcendence." Printed in 1972.58.

94 WALKER, HUGH. <u>English Satire and Satirists</u>. New York: Octagon
Books.
　　Reprint of 1925.17.

95 WARD, CHARLES E. "Challenges to Dryden's Biographer." In
<u>Stuart and Georgian Moments: Clark Library Seminar Papers of
Seventeenth and Eighteenth Century English Literature</u>. Edited
by Earl Miner. Berkeley, Los Angeles, and London: University
of California Press, pp. 73-91.
　　Reprint of 1967.60. Printed in 1972.60.

96 WARNKE, FRANK J. <u>Versions of Baroque: European Literature in
the Seventeenth Century</u>. New Haven and London: Yale University
Press, 240 pp.
　　Attempts to discover the distinctive styles and themes of
baroque literature, defined in part as that "dominant . . . from
the last decades of the sixteenth century to the last decades of
the seventeenth." Sees Dryden as a transitional figure, vestigi-
ally baroque but basically neoclassic.

*97 WEYGANT, PETER S. "Oldham's Versification and the Literary
Style of the English Enlightenment." <u>Enlightenment Essays</u> 3:
120-25.
　　Cited in Latt and Monk, 1976.30.

98 WILDING, MICHAEL. "Dryden and Satire: <u>MacFlecknoe, Absalom
and Achitophel, The Medall</u>, and Juvenal." In <u>John Dryden</u>.
Edited by Earl Miner. Writers and their Background. Athens:

Ohio University Press; London: G. Bell, pp. 191-233.
Credits Dryden as a major innovator in the history of satire,
through his use of "wit, humour, obliqueness, double entendre, and
subtlety" instead of direct diatribe as in Persius.

*99   ZWICKER, STEVEN N. "Dryden and the Sacred History of the
       English People: A Study of Typological Imagery in Dryden's
       Political Poetry 1660-1688." Ph.D. dissertation, Brown
       University.
           Cited in Latt and Monk, 1976.30. Abstracted in DAI 33:737A.
       See 1972.100.

100   _____. Dryden's Political Poetry: The Typology of King and
       Nation. Providence: Brown University Press, 167 pp.
           Treats Dryden's political poetry in the light of the tradi-
       tion of the figural interpretation of scripture, applied to history:
       "Dryden displays a continuous impulse to see in the figures and
       events of past ages models with which he might praise, evaluate,
       and parallel his own time." In this tradition sacred history is
       used to explain, justify, and predict the course of contemporary
       events. Asserts that "Dryden's career as a political poet can be
       read as a series of attempts to forge a sacred history for the
       English nation." Shows how scriptural associations in Annus
       Mirabilis are a means of giving the events of the poem "coherence
       and significance." Sees Dryden's use of the figural tradition
       culminating in Absalom and Achitophel, where "the biblical meta-
       phor, the typological associations, and the contemporary political
       applications are all working to transform the Restoration present
       tense and the biblical past tense into a symbolic eternal tense."
       Suggests that Dryden's turning away from scriptural metaphors and
       typology from The Medal onwards is a symptom of his increasing dis-
       illusion with politics.

                              1973

1   ADAMS, ROBERT. Proteus, His Lies, His Truth: Discussions of
      Literary Translation. New York: Norton, 204 pp.
          Discusses Dryden's version of Juvenal's Tenth Satire, com-
      paring it to Johnson's "The Vanity of Human Wishes." Notes Dryden's
      tendency to expand, to play with language, to generalize and to
      simplify (pp. 102-107).

2   ALEXANDER, JOHN M. "'Ut Musica Poesis' in Eighteenth Century
      Aesthetics." English Miscellany 24:129-52.
          Briefly discusses Dryden's "A Parallel of Painting and
      Poetry" in the context of a shift during the period from seeing
      art "as imitative of sensual form" to seeing it "as expressive of
      emotion." Associates Dryden with the former view.

*3   ANDERBERG, GARY T. "Idea and Passion: The Development of

Dryden's Tragic Drama." Ph.D. dissertation, Stanford University. Cited in Latt and Monk, 1976.30. Abstracted in <u>DAI</u> 33:4327A.

4   ARCHER, STANLEY. "A Dryden Critic of the Romantic Period." <u>South Central Bulletin</u> 33 (Winter):192-93.
   Discusses Thomas Green's <u>Extracts from the Diary of a Lover of Literature</u> (1810.1). Suggests that the scope and enthusiasm of Green's comments demonstrate that interest in neoclassic literature persisted in the romantic era.

5   _____. "Two Dryden Anecdotes." <u>N&Q</u>, n.s. 20 (May):177-78.
   Considers the reliability of two anecdotes concerning Dryden's relations with his patron the Earl of Dorset. Both have to do with Dorset's generosity to Dryden. Concludes that both anecdotes are unreliable.

6   ARMISTEAD, J.M. "The Narrator as Rhetorician in Dryden's <u>The Hind and the Panther</u>." <u>Journal of Narrative Technique</u> 3 (September):208-18.
   Distinguishes four narrative voices in the poem: the inspired convert, the Poet Laureate, the artist defending his technique, and the "Roman Catholic poet-rhetorician whose vision unites the historical perspective of the Poet Laureate with the cosmic and eternal concerns of the Catholic believer." Argues that this use of distinct voices is part of a rhetorical strategy to involve readers in "his newly acquired vision of religious truth."

*7   _____. "A Study of Structure and Poetics in Dryden's <u>The Hind and the Panther</u>." Ph.D. dissertation, Duke University.
   Cited in Latt and Monk, 1976.30. Abstracted in <u>DAI</u> 34:718A.

8   BACHORIK, LAURENCE L. "<u>The Duke of Guise</u> and Dryden's <u>Vindication</u>: A New Consideration." <u>ELN</u> 10 (March):208-12.
   Argues against Charles Hinnant (1968.35) that the play "must refer to contemporary politics" and that "therefore Dryden is . . . less than sincere in the <u>Vindication</u>" (where he claims that the play is unrelated to the <u>Exclusion</u> Crisis). Asserts that Dryden's publication of the play in 1682, regardless of when it was written, can bear no other interpretation. See 1973.30.

*9   BADY, DAVID M. "The Exact Balance of True Virtue: John Dryden and the Tradition of Epideictic Comparison." Ph.D. dissertation, Columbia University.
   Cited in Latt and Monk, 1976.30. Abstracted in <u>DAI</u> 33: 5712A-13A.

*10   BARDEN, THOMAS E. "Dryden's Aims in <u>Amphitryon</u>." <u>Costerus</u> 9: 1-8.
   Cited in Latt and Monk, 1976.30.

11   BIRRELL, T.A. "James Marius Corker and Dryden's Conversion."

ES 54 (October):461-68.
　　Gives an account of the priest who received Dryden's conversion. Suggests that it is significant that Corker was an English
Benedictine; suggests that if he had been received by a Jesuit or
a priest of the Secular Clergy Chapter there might have been
"grounds for doubts about his seriousness and sincerity."

12　BJÖRK, LENNART A. "The 'Inconsistencies' of Dryden's Criticism
　　　of Shakespeare." Anglia 91, no. 2:219-40.
　　　　Surveys critical opinion on the question of Dryden's critical
consistency. Discusses his comments on Shakespeare, reading them
in the light of their rhetorical contexts. Concludes that "Dryden
. . . is a practical critic. His essays on dramatic matters can
have no pretensions to be literary history."

*13　BOWLER, ELIZABETH A. "The Augustan Heroic Idiom in Dryden,
　　　Rowe, and Pope." Ph.D. dissertation, Bristol University.
　　　　Cited in Latt and Monk, 1976.30.

*14　BRERETON, JOHN C. "Heroic Praise: Dryden and the State
　　　Panegyric." Ph.D. dissertation, Rutgers University.
　　　　Cited in Latt and Monk, 1976.30. Abstracted in DAI 34:306A.

15　BROWN, CALVIN S. "John Dryden as Comparatist." Comparative
　　　Literature Studies 10 (June):112-24.
　　　　Argues that Dryden's critical method is that of the compara-
tivist, who sees literature as a unit, insists on reading it in its
original language, and is interested in sources and the relationships between literature and other arts. Notes particularly how
frequently Dryden proceeds by comparing two or more writers. Discusses Dryden's comments on translation; claims that they demonstrate his "lively and critical interest in the subject."

*16　CARVER, LARRY D. "Domineering Phantom: A Study in the Repre-
　　　sentations of the Father in Restoration Literature." Ph.D.
　　　dissertation, University of Rochester.
　　　　Cited in the 1973 MLA International Bibliography. Abstracted
in DAI 34:2550A.

*17　CASANAVE, DON S. "Shakespeare's The Tempest in a Restoration
　　　Context: A Study of Dryden's The Enchanted Island." Ph.D. dis-
　　　sertation, University of Michigan.
　　　　Cited in Latt and Monk, 1976.30. Abstracted in DAI 33:6303A.

18　CHAPPLE, J.A.V. Dryden's Earl of Shaftesbury: An Inaugural
　　　Lecture. Hull: University of Hull, 19 pp.
　　　　Examines Dryden's portrait of Achitophel; argues that it is
basically a literary fiction which has little significant resemblance to the historical Shaftesbury. Instead the figure stands
"for chaotic personal energies become incarnate in the state," and
for Whigs in general. Concludes by suggesting (admittedly without

evidence) that the portrait is an example of the near-simultaneous inspiration and composition Dryden hints at in the preface to The Rival Ladies.

19   COOK, DOROTHY. "Dryden's Adaptation of Shakespeare's Troilus
     and Cressida." Connecticut Review 7, no. 1 (October):66-72.
        Argues that Dryden's changes have turned a "darkly sardonic
     problem play" into "a heroic and moral drama that is concerned
     mainly with honor and its relationship to personal and public life."
     Contends that Dryden's main technique was to simplify character,
     issues, and structure, and to conform to the unities. Concludes
     that the theme of responsibility which Dryden emphasizes was appro-
     priate for his "era of irresponsibility."

*20   DEARING, VINTON A. "Concepts of Copy-Text Old and New."
      Library, 5th ser. 28 (December):281-93.
         Cited by George Hammerbacher in 1978.19.

*21   DEWITT, SUSAN VERA. "Ben Jonson and the English Verse Letter."
      Ph.D. dissertation, University of Washington.
         Cited in Latt and Monk, 1976.30. Abstracted in DAI 33:6868A.

*22   DIETZ, JONATHAN ERIC. "The Designs of Plot: The New Direction
      in Plot Resolution of Late Restoration Satiric Comedy." Ph.D.
      dissertation, University of Pennsylvania.
         Cited in Latt and Monk, 1976.30. Abstracted in DAI 33:3640A.

*23   EBBS, JOHN D. The Principle of Poetic Justice Illustrated in
      Restoration Tragedy. Salzburg: Institüt für englische Sprache
      und Literatur.
         Cited in the 1973 MLA International Bibliography.

24   ELKIN, P.K. The Augustan Defence of Satire. Oxford: Clarendon
     Press, 237 pp.
        Contains many scattered references to Dryden, especially the
     "Discourse . . . of Satire"; emphasizes the difficulty of defining
     and classifying satire.

*25   FOX, JAMES H. "The Actor-Audience Relationship in Restoration
      Comedy, with Particular Reference to the Aside." Ph.D. disser-
      tation, University of Michigan.
         Cited in the 1973 MLA International Bibliography. Abstracted
      in DAI 33:6308A.

*26   FROST, WILLIAM. "Dryden's Versions of Ovid." In Expression,
      Communication and Experience in Literature and Language. Pro-
      ceedings of the Twelfth Congress of the International Federation
      for Modern Languages Held at Cambridge University, 20 to 26
      August 1972. Edited by Ronald G. Popperwell. London: Modern
      Humanities Research Association, pp. 289-90.
         Cited in Latt and Monk, 1976.30.

27   GUIBBORY, ACHSAH. "Dryden's Views of History." PQ 52
      (April):187-204.
         Asserts that Dryden combines three views of history: the
      Graeco-Roman, in which nature is always the same, and history a
      series of cycles; the Christian, in which history is providential
      and teleologically oriented; and the modern, in which progress is
      the most significant factor. Argues that Dryden's "skepticism"
      allows him to moderate each of these views, but that it made his
      view of history ultimately very pessimistic (as in "To Sir Godfrey
      Kneller").

28   HARTH, PHILLIP. "Religion and Politics in Dryden's Poetry and
      Plays." MP 70 (February):236-42.
         A review-article on Volume 3 of the California Dryden
      (1969.52) and Anne Barbeau's The Intellectual Design of John
      Dryden's Heroic Plays (1970.10). Praises the edition but charges
      that the annotation of The Hind and the Panther is not sufficiently
      comprehensive. Faults the book for being too restrictive in its
      coverage of Dryden's political thought.

29   HINNANT, CHARLES H. "Dryden and Hogarth's Sigismunda." ECS
      6 (Summer):462-74.
         Notes that while Horace Walpole and Charles Churchill criti-
      cized Hogarth's painting and praised Dryden's treatment of the
      story in Fables, in the next century Wordsworth and Scott found
      fault with Dryden. Suggests that while Dryden's heroine embodies
      the "heroic ideal of fortitude and self-sufficiency," Hogarth's
      painting emphasizes the pathetic side of the story, and that this
      distinction accounts for different reactions in different periods.

30   _____. "The Duke of Guise and Dryden's Vindication: A New
      Consideration." ELN 10 (March):224-25.
         Defends his earlier essay (1968.35) against Laurence L.
      Bachorik (1973.8). Argues that The Duke of Guise is not solely,
      or primarily, a topical play which can be understood only in terms
      of the Exclusion Crisis. Also defends Dryden's Vindication of the
      play against Bachorik's charge of insincerity.

31   HOPKINS, D.W. "An Echo of La Fontaine in Dryden's 'Baucis and
      Philemon.'" N&Q, n.s. 20 (May):178-79.
         Argues that Dryden's description of the goose's movements in
      his translation of Ovid's fable (11. 137-38) is probably borrowed
      from La Fontaine's Baucis et Philémon (1685).

32   HUME, ROBERT D. "The Date of Dryden's Marriage A-la-Mode."
      HLB 21 (April):161-66.
         Argues in support of Charles Ward (in 1961.57) that the play
      was first performed in the fall of 1671, possibly in November.
      Bases his argument on the similarities of the tone and allusions
      of Dryden's prologues to the play with others known to date from
      the same time, shortly before the beginning of the Third Dutch War.

Furthermore The Rehearsal, which seems to contain swipes at the
play, is known to have been staged in mid-December.

33   ____. "Theory of Comedy in the Restoration." MP 70 (May):
        302-18.
        Surveys commonly held theories, both in the period and in
our own time. Finds much oversimplification. Argues that the
dominant theory--that comedy teaches by holding people up to ridi-
cule--does not conform to the practice of comic dramatists. Suggests that in fact writers like Dryden, reacting against farce,
were trying "to raise the social tone of comedy" and as a result
ridicule became less practicable a device. Suggests that the most
valid distinction in the period is between those comedies which
emphasized "action" (like Shadwell's) and those which emphasized
"discourse" (like Dryden's). Stresses that we must be aware of
the great diversity within Restoration comedy.

*34   JAQUITH, WILLIAM G. "Dryden's Tyrannick Love and All for Love:
        A Study of Comic and Tragic Dialects." Ph.D. dissertation,
        University of California at Los Angeles.
        Cited in Latt and Monk, 1976.30. Abstracted in DAI 34:
        3345A-46A.

35   JENSEN, H. JAMES. "Comparing the Arts in the Age of Baroque."
        ECS 6 (Spring):334-47.
        Argues that because the arts were all supposed to work through
senses and passions they were "interchangeable in the sense that any
one of them could project the same kind of imagery to produce the
same kind of passion." Relates this attitude to the process of
composition developed in classical rhetoric (inventio, dispositio,
elocutio). Looks at Dryden's Song for St. Cecilia's Day, Vivaldi's
Concerto for Two Trumpets in C, Rubens's "Le Coup de Lance," Fra
Andrea Pozzo's ceiling in Sant' Ignazio (Rome), Michelangelo's
"Last Judgment," and Rubens's "Large Judgment Day," showing how
each uses similar conventions to produce "the strong passions of
admiration and astonishment." See 1974.51.

*36   JOHNSON, DONALD R. "Plowshares, Politics, and Poetry: The
        Georgic Tradition from Dryden and Thomson." Ph.D. dissertation,
        University of Wisconsin.
        Cited in Latt and Monk, 1976.30. Abstracted in DAI 33:6314A.

37   KEARFUL, FRANK J. "'Tis Past Recovery': Tragic Consciousness
        in All for Love." MLQ 34 (September):227-46.
        Takes an affective view of the tragedy: sees it as an at-
tempt at "modification of the audience's consciousness." Analyzes
the play on this basis. Argues that the audience is conditioned
by its awareness that the play is an imitation of Shakespeare, and
that this knowledge emphasizes and assists the tragic theme of the
irrecoverability of the past. Concludes that "the tragic consciousness which the play has affectively induced" is a "perception of

the impossibility, as well as the tragic necessity, of enacting
our images of that which is 'past recovery.'"

38   KORSHIN, PAUL J. From Concord to Dissent: Major Themes in
      English Poetic Theory 1640-1700. Menston, Yorkshire: Scolar
      Press, 231 pp.
          "Dryden (I): The Major Strain of Public Poetry" (pp. 105-44)
      distinguishes four types of public poem in Dryden's work: histori-
      cal poems, prologues or epilogues, panegyrics, and satires.
      "Dryden (II): Toward the Poetics of Dissent" (pp. 175-215) deals
      with his late work which, in contrast to his poetry before 1682,
      turns inward to deal with individual problems, as Dryden's atten-
      tion shifts from politics to ethics and to the subject of poetry
      itself.

39   KUNZ, DON R. "Shadwell and His Critics: The Misuse of Dryden's
      MacFlecknoe." RECTR 12, no. 1 (May):14-27.
          Asserts that proper evaluation of Shadwell has been hampered
      by Dryden's characterization of him in MacFlecknoe. Argues that
      it is a satiric portrait which distorts the real Shadwell. Gives
      many examples of the resulting critical misreadings. Concludes
      that "Dryden's clever ironic, figurative jibes at Shadwell in a
      fictional world have been translated into blunt, prosaic indict-
      ments."

40   LANGBAINE, GERARD. An Account of the English Dramatick Poets.
      Preface by Arthur Freeman. New York: Garland.
          A facsimile reprint of 1691.1.

41   LEGOUIS, PIERRE. Aspects du XVIIe siècle. Paris: Didier, 277
      pp.
          Reprint of 1932.16; 1938.6; 1971.50 (with updated notes).

*42   LEMLY, JOHN WILLIAM. "Into Winter Quarters Gone: The Last
      Plays of Jonson and Dryden." Ph.D. dissertation, Yale University.
          Cited in Latt and Monk, 1976.30. Abstracted in DAI 34:324A.

*43   LEVISON, WILLIAM S. "Restoration Adaptations of Shakespeare as
      Baroque Literature." Ph.D. dissertation, University of Illinois.
          Cited in Latt and Monk, 1976.30. Abstracted in DAI 34:730A.

44   LEWALSKI, BARBARA KIEFER. Donne's Anniversaries and the Poetry
      of Praise: The Creation of a Symbolic Mode. Princeton:
      Princeton University Press, 395 pp.
          Discusses Dryden's use of Donne, especially Donne's
      Anniversaries. Sees verbal, thematic, and formal echoes in "Upon
      the Death of the Lord Hastings," "To . . . Anne Killigrew,"
      Eleonora, and "The Monument of a Fair Maiden Lady, who dy'd at
      Bath" (pp. 342-55).

*45   LEWIS, MINEKO S. "Humor Characterization in Restoration Comedy."

Ph.D. dissertation, University of Tennessee.
Cited in Latt and Monk, 1976.30. Abstracted in <u>DAI</u> 34:1247A.

46 LOFTIS, JOHN. <u>The Spanish Plays of Neoclassic England</u>. New
Haven and London: Yale University Press, 276 pp.
Stresses the extent of English interest in Spanish literature
during the late seventeenth century; points out several parallels
between the development and nature of English and Spanish Renaissance drama. Traces the English vogue of the "Spanish plot." Argues that the "important and distinctive plays" of this type and
period "can be traced to the [Spanish] comedia." Identifies Sir
Samuel Tuke's <u>The Adventures of the Five Hours</u> as the "decisive
play in establishing the vogue." Notes Dryden's disdain for the
play. Argues that Dryden's (and William Wycherley's) adaptations
of Spanish materials "reveal an intermediate stage" between Cavalier
plays and the comedy of manners. Shows how Dryden's plots differ
from earlier Spanish plots, despite the extent of his borrowing.
Takes up the issue of the resemblances between <u>The Indian Emperour</u>
and Calderón's <u>El Príncipe constante</u>; finds that they are not really
close, except in general ways. Demonstrates Dryden's knowledge and
use of dramatic treatments of the wars against the Moors which provide "firm evidence of his participation in an international literary culture." Looks at similarities among <u>The Conquest of Granada</u>,
Corneille's <u>Le Cid</u>, and Guillén de Castro's <u>Las mocedades del Cid</u>,
and at correspondences between Dryden's play and Mariana's <u>Historia
general de España</u>, a popular history. Cautions against "assuming
that Dryden intended a sustained satire on the heroic ideals held
by his characters [in <u>The Conquest of Granada</u>]," but admits that
the play "lacks the strength the Spanish play [<u>Las mocedades del
Cid</u>] gains from its folk origins." Concludes that Dryden's interest in Spanish materials is one aspect of his overall participation
in a broad, international intellectual literary tradition. But
stresses that he was essentially independent of his sources: "In
his work, Spanish materials are assimilated into the mainstream
of the Restoration dramatic tradition."

*47 LOOFBOUROW, JOHN W. "Robinson Crusoe's Island and the
Restoration <u>Tempest</u>." <u>Enlightenment Essays</u> 2:201-7.
Cited in Latt and Monk, 1976.30.

48 LOVE, HAROLD. "Dryden, Durfey, and the Standard of Comedy."
<u>SEL</u> 13 (Summer):422-36.
Looks at a controversy in the 1690s between Dryden, Thomas
Southerne, and William Congreve on one side and Thomas Durfey and
Charles Gildon on the other. Argues that Dryden's contentions in
his controversy show that he was developing a view of comedy in
which the justness of the overall design replaced genteel repartee
as the primary standard of success.

49 McCONN, GARTH A. "Dryden and Poetic Continuity: A Comparative
Study." <u>South Atlantic Quarterly</u> 72 (Spring):311-21.

Argues that Dryden's poetry is part of a continuous development from the Renaissance; that despite minor differences his attitudes toward poetry and its uses are essentially those of Sidney,
Donne, Jonson, and Herbert. Concludes that Dryden is "the bridge
between the dying exuberance of the 'former' age and the dawning
age of prose and reason."

50   McFARLAND, THOMAS. "Poetry and the Poem: The Structure of
      Poetic Content." In Literary Theory and Structure: Essays in
      Honor of William K. Wimsatt. Edited by Frank Brady, John Palmer
      and Martin Price. New Haven and London: Yale University Press,
      pp. 81-114.
          Examines the distinction between "poetry" and "poem." Sees
      "poetry" as the emotion or vision; "poem" as the artifact. Cites
      Religio Laici as a good example of a "poem" which seems to contain
      a minimum of "poetry." Concludes that there is a significant dis-
      tinction between "content" and "form," and that a "poem" does not
      necessarily contain "poetry." Reprinted: 1979.21.

*51   McHENRY, ROBERT W., Jr. "Anglican Rationalism, Right Reason,
      and John Dryden." Ph.D. dissertation, University of Michigan.
          Cited in Latt and Monk, 1976.30. Abstracted in DAI 33:5132A.

*52   _____. "Dryden's Religio Laici: An Augustan Drama of Ideas."
      Enlightenment Essays 4:60-64.
          Cited in Latt and Monk, 1976.30.

*53   McHENRY, ROBERT W., Jr., and DAVID LOUGEE, eds. Critics on
      Dryden. London: George Allen & Unwin; Miami: University of
      Miami Press.
          Cited by George Hammerbacher in 1978.19.

54   McINTOSH, WILLIAM. "Handel and the Muse." Cithara 12, no. 2:
      18-40.
          Describes the circumstances in which Dryden wrote Song for
      St. Cecilia's Day and Alexander's Feast, and those in which Handel
      set them to music. Reviews criticism on the structure of the poems;
      discusses Handel's settings, emphasizing how well the music fits
      the poem.

55   MARTIN, LESLIE HOWARD. "Aureng-Zebe and the Ritual of the
      Persian King." MP 71 (November):169-71.
          Suggests that the allusion to the Persian King, condemned
      but lodged in state (Act 4, scene 1), derives from William
      Cartwright's play The Royall Slave (1639), which in turn is based
      on the historical story of Shah Abbas the Great.

56   _____. "The Consistency of Dryden's Aureng-Zebe." SP 70
      (July):306-28.
          Asserts that Dryden does not reject the heroic mode in the
      play. Argues that although there are differences between this

play and Dryden's other heroic plays, its characteristics are not significantly different from those included in the tradition, especially as found in the works of Madeleine de Scudéry. Notes especially Aureng-Zebe's attributes: prudence, temperance, piety, and jealousy. Suggests that Dryden is restoring credit to the heroic mode; that he is "obstinately averse to perfunctory imitation, even . . . of himself."

57 _____. "The Source and Originality of Dryden's Melantha." PQ 52 (October):746-53.
    Argues that Melantha, the coquette of Marriage a-la-Mode, is derived from Berisa in Madeleine de Scudéry's Grand Cyrus, which also is the source of the main plot of Dryden's play. Notes verbal parallels, but also notes that there are sufficient differences between the two characters and works to support Dryden's claims to originality.

58 MAUPIN, LARRY M. "Dryden's Astraea Redux, 163-168." Expl 31 (April): note 64.
    Argues that in this passage Dryden compares General Monk to the human heart.

*59 MAZZEO, JOSEPH A. "Seventeenth-Century English Prose Style: The Quest for a Natural Style." Mosaic 6, no. 3:107-44.
    Cited in Latt and Monk, 1976.30.

60 MERRIMAN, JAMES DOUGLAS. The Flower of Kings: A Study of the Arthurian Legend in England between 1485 and 1835. Lawrence: University of Kansas Press, 318 pp.
    Briefly describes Dryden's King Arthur; claims that in it "Dryden pandered with cynical calculation to the debased tastes of the Restoration audience" (pp. 60-64).

61 MINER, EARL. "Problems and Possibilities of Literary History Today." Clio 2 (June):219-38.
    Deals with the "crisis" in modern literary history (the split between narrative and critical analysis). Notes that Dryden saw narrative (as in the "progress piece") as one of three elements in literary history, the other two being comparison/parallel and the concept of literary ages. Suggests that his variety of approaches can serve as a pattern for a modern method that combines analysis and narrative (as in Miner's own theory of modes).

62 _____. "Renaissance Contexts of Dryden's Criticism." Michigan Quarterly Review 12 (Spring):97-115.
    Discusses Dryden's resemblances to and differences from late sixteenth and early seventeenth-century critics, especially Sidney. Argues that in fact in every way but chronology, Dryden fits the general characteristics we associate with Renaissance criticism better than any who actually lived during that time. Notes the similar beliefs of Sidney and Dryden that poetry has mimetic and

moral ends; notes also that both see the poet as a kind of second
creator. Points out that one of Dryden's major new contributions
is his concept of literary periods. Suggests that Dryden had a
great advantage over Sidney in being born late enough to have a
sense of the achievements of English literature. Notes the great
variety of prose styles in both writers, suggesting that both had
a sense of the needs of decorum. Concludes that "Dryden's criticism shows by example that the study of literature may give us a
just and lively understanding of ourselves."

63   MYERS, WILLIAM. <u>Dryden</u>. London: Hutchinson, 191 pp.
          A rapid examination of the full body of Dryden's work. At-
      tempts to show "how completely and impressively he in fact learned
      to deploy a limited and perhaps debased poetic idiom in an examina-
      tion of the human problems created by the pressures of history."
      Sees three phases in Dryden's development: orthodoxy (to about
      1678), ambivalence toward monarchy (through the Exclusion Crisis)
      and, after the accession of James II, a phase in which he had "to
      [integrate] his faith in divine love and human awareness with a
      steady, thoroughly modern awareness of history's infinite capacity
      to violate every conceivable kind of value." Emphasizes the politi-
      cal contexts of Dryden's works, as well as their ongoing political
      implications. Concludes that Dryden "was a great reconciler of
      opposites," who combined an "attachment to established traditions"
      with an "openness to a future that denied them."

*64   NAGLER, ALOIS M. "Courtiers, Beaux, Wits and Cits." In <u>Essays</u>
      <u>on Drama and Theatre: Liber Amicorum Benjamin Hunningher</u>
      <u>Presented to Professor Dr. B. Hunningher on the Occasion of His</u>
      <u>Retirement from the Chair of Drama and Theatre Arts in the</u>
      <u>University of Amsterdam</u>. Edited by Erica Hunningher-Schilling.
      Amsterdam/Baarn: Moussault's Uitgeverij; Antwerp: Standaard
      Uitgeverig, pp. 108-28.
          Cited in the <u>1973 MLA International Bibliography</u>.

*65   NEWELL, ROSALIE. "<u>Troilus and Cressida, or Truth Found Too</u>
      <u>Late</u>: A Study of External and Internal Form in Dryden's Critical
      Theory and Dramatic Practice." Ph.D. dissertation, University
      of California at Los Angeles.
          Cited in Latt and Monk, 1976.30. Abstracted in <u>DAI</u> 33:5739A.

66   OLINDER, BRITTA. "<u>The Links of a Curious Chain</u>": Studies in
      <u>the Acts and Scenes of John Dryden's Tragedies and Tragi-</u>
      <u>Comedies</u>. Göteborg: Engelska Inst., Götesborgs Universitet,
      240 pp.
          Deals with the effects of Restoration theater practices upon
      the structure of the plays under discussion. Notes that Dryden
      was sometimes forced to violate his own theories to accomodate the
      needs of the theater. Concludes that the basic unit of structure
      in Dryden's plays is the scene. (Defines a scene as beginning
      whenever the composition of a group of characters on stage changes.)

Includes a table showing comparative lengths of acts and scenes
in each of the plays under discussion.

*67   O'NEILL, JOHN H. "An Art Beyond the Reach of Grace: English
       Pornographic Verse, 1660-1685." Ph.D. dissertation, University
       of Minnesota.
           Cited in the 1973 MLA International Bibliography. Abstracted
       in DAI 33:3662A-63A.

 68   OSBORN, JAMES M. "A Lost Portrait of Dryden." HLQ 36 (August):
       341-45.
           Describes a newly found portrait by John Riley, thought to
       have been lost, painted in 1683. Includes a black-and-white repro-
       duction.

*69   PERLBERG, CHARLEY W. "The Public Verse Panegyrics of John
       Dryden." Ph.D. dissertation, Northern Illinois University.
           Cited in Latt and Monk, 1976.30. Abstracted in DAI 34:1251A.

*70   RIVERS, ISABEL. The Poetry of Conservatism 1600-1745: A Study
       of Poets and Public Affairs from Jonson to Pope. Cambridge:
       Rivers Press.
           Cited in the 1973 MLA International Bibliography.

*71   RODNEY, CAROLINE C. "Dryden's Tragicomedy." Ph.D. disserta-
       tion, Cornell University.
           Cited in Latt and Monk, 1976.30. Abstracted in DAI 34:1253A.

 72   ROPER, ALAN. "A Critic's Apology for Editing Dryden's The
       History of the League." In The Editor as Critic and The Critic
       as Editor (Papers Read at a Clark Library Seminar November 13,
       1971). Introduction by Murray Krieger. Los Angeles: Clark
       Memorial Library, University of California, pp. 41-72.
           Discusses various textual problems and how he resolved them
       in the California Edition. Recounts the circumstances of the pub-
       lication and reception of Dryden's translation. Notes that it
       provides good material for reconstructing "the difficult process
       by which a style is made out of numerous choices of diction and
       syntax."

*73   RUDDICK, W. "John Dryden: Absalom and Achitophel, lines
       583-629." Critical Survey 6:26-31.
           Cited by George Hammerbacher in 1978.19.

*74   SCHAP, KEITH. "A Transformational Study of John Dryden's
       Metrical Practice." Ph.D. dissertation, Indiana University.
           Cited in Latt and Monk, 1976.30. Abstracted in DAI 33:
       5692A-93A.

*75   SCHULTZ, DIETER. "The Coquette's Progress From Satire to
       Sentimental Novel." Literatur und Wirklichkeit 6:77-89.

Cited in the Annual Bibliography of English Language and
Literature for 1973 (London: Modern Humanities Research Association).

76   SECRETAN, DOMINIQUE. Classicism. The Critical Idiom. London:
      Methuen, 85 pp.
         Discusses meanings of the term "classicism." Finds in Dryden
      fluctuations between a classic desire for order and a dynamic and
      exuberant modernism. Charges that Dryden scattered and squandered
      his talent.

77   SELDEN, R[AMAN]. "Hobbes, Dryden, and the Ranging Spaniel."
      N&Q, n.s. 20 (October):388-90.
         Points out that Dryden's two uses of the analogy between the
      "ranging spaniel" and "fancy" or "wit" differ. One (in the dedica-
      tion to The Rival Ladies) presents the spaniel as the least directed
      mode of mental "discursion," while the other (in the preface to
      Annus Mirabilis) identifies it with purpose and design.

78   SELDEN, RAMAN. "Juvenal and Restoration Modes of Translation."
      MLR 68 (July):481-93.
         Examines translations of Juvenal's Tenth Satire to show that
      despite the fashion for free translation, in practice "more scholar-
      ly and literalist attitudes were still influential." Contrasts
      Shadwell's and Dryden's handling of several passages to establish
      the extremes within which Restoration translators worked (Dryden
      is much freer than Shadwell, and uses a much greater variety of
      levels of style).

79   SHAWCROSS, JOHN T. "An Unnoticed Reaction to Dryden's The Hind
      and the Panther." ELN 11 (December):110-12.
         Quotes the preface to Robert Jenkin's An Historical Examina-
      tion of the Authority of General Councils (1685), collates the book,
      and briefly identifies the author.

*80   SLOMAN, JUDITH. "Dryden, Caliban, and Negative Capability."
      Transactions of the Samuel Johnson Society of the Northwest 6:
      45-57.
         Cited in Latt and Monk, 1976.30.

81   SPENCER, JEFFRY B. Heroic Nature: Ideal Landscape in English
      Poetry from Marvell to Thomson. Evanston, Ill.: Northwestern
      University Press, 349 pp.
         "Dryden's Decorative Landscapes: Harmonizing the Classical
      and the Baroque" (pp. 139-89) deals with visual aspects of Dryden's
      imagery, emphasizing The State of Innocence, the translation of
      Virgil, "To . . . Anne Killigrew," and "Palamon and Arcite." Finds
      in Dryden both baroque and classical elements, sometimes (as in
      Milton) in combination. Relates Dryden to such painters as Rubens,
      Annibale Caracci, and especially Nicholas Poussin. Concludes that
      Dryden "was the sensitive, responsive product of a visual age."

*82 SWEARINGEN, JAMES. "Time and the Character of the Wolf in The Hind and the Panther." Concerning Poetry 6, no. 2:45-52.
    Cited in Latt and Monk, 1976.30.

83 TOBIN, TERENCE. "Plays Presented in Scotland 1660-1700." RECTR 12, no. 1 (May):51-53, 59.
    Lists plays, with author and date of performance for each. Includes several plays by Dryden.

*84 TOMA, SANDA. "Remarks on Caliban's Identity." Analele universităţii bucureşti, limbi germanica 22:207-13.
    Cited by George Hammerbacher in 1978.19.

85 TRITT, CARLETON S. "The Title of All for Love." ELN 10 (June): 273-75.
    Argues that the sense of "well" in the subtitle (The World Well Lost) is not necessarily "justifiably," as it has commonly been taken to be. Suggests "completely," and, or, "decorously" as preferable meanings.

*86 TYSON, GERALD P. "Dryden's Dramatic Essay." Ariel 4, no. 1: 72-86.
    Cited in Latt and Monk, 1976.30.

*87 VERDURMEN, JOHN PETER. "Lee, Dryden and the Restoration Tragedy of Concernment." Ph.D. dissertation, Stanford University.
    Cited in Latt and Monk, 1976.30. Abstracted in DAI 33: 6887A-88A.

88 WAITH, EUGENE M. "Spectacles of State." SEL 13 (Spring): 316-30.
    Discusses the court masque's ways of paying tribute to the King, who was often in attendance. Links these to heroic drama and opera: draws major examples from The Conquest of Granada, Albion and Albanus, and King Arthur. Suggests that "the relatively static and formal nature of some heroic plays . . . testif[ies] to the close relationship between the forms."

89 WATSON, GEORGE. "Dryden and the Jacobites." TLS, 16 March, pp. 301-2.
    Sees Jacobite themes in the work of Dryden's last decade, especially in his translation of the Aeneid. Suggests that Dryden's reading of the epic may have had more in common with the modern ironic or ambiguous interpretations of the poem and its main character than with the straightforward reading of his own time. Sees in Dryden's translation an expression of "a stubborn and dedicated recusancy that he accepted years before . . . his exiled king." Also sees the secret moral of Don Sebastian as nonresistance.

90 _____. The Literary Critics. 2d ed. rev. Totowa, N.J.: Rowman & Littlefield.

A revision of 1964.53 (which is the second edition of 1962.49).

*91   WEST, MICHAEL. "Dryden and the Disintegration of Renaissance Heroic Ideals." Costerus 7:193-222.
       Cited in Latt and Monk, 1976.30.

92   _____. "Dryden's Ambivalence as a Translator of Heroic Themes." HLQ 36 (August):347-66.
       Argues that Dryden's ambivalence toward the heroic hardened into hostility in his later years. Discusses his translation of the Aeneid, emphasizing the "frankly anti-heroic sensibility of much of the commentary, and mock-heroic elements in the poem itself." Looks at Amphitryon (1690); sees it as "an exercise in debunking." Finds in the Fables (1700) "a cynical view of conventional heroic values."

93   _____. "Some Neglected Continental Analogues for Dryden's MacFlecknoe." SEL 13 (Summer):437-50.
       Argues that the synthetic element in the poem has been underemphasized. Links the poem to many examples of such forms as the mock encomium, the mock didactic poem, and the sessions poem (as well as the mock heroic and mock epic). Concludes that in MacFlecknoe "Dryden assumes a conscientiously and industriously European outlook."

*94   WILLIAMS, DAVID W. "The Funeral Elegies of John Dryden." Ph.D. dissertation, Yale University.
       Cited in Latt and Monk, 1976.30. Abstracted in DAI 33:5756A.

*95   ZAMFIRESCU, ION. "Urmaşii lui Shakespeare. Teatrul anglez al Restauraţiei. Intre baroc şi clasicism" [Shakespeare's Successors: The English Theater of the Restoration Between Baroque and Classicism]. In Panorama dramaturgiei universale [The Panorama of the Universal Dramaturgy]. Bucharest: Editura enciclopedica romana, pp. 225-40.
       In Rumanian. Cited in the Annual Bibliography of English Language and Literature for 1973 (London: Modern Humanities Research Association).

96   ZAMONSKI, JOHN A. "The Spiritual Nature of Carnal Love in Dryden's Assignation." Educational Theatre Journal 25:189-92.
       Summarizes the plot. Argues briefly that "the play strives to show that carnal love can be just as sacramental as spiritual love." Asserts that the play's theme—the value of "authentic love"—should make it attractive to modern audiences.

1974

1   ALSSID, MICHAEL W. Dryden's Rhymed Heroic Tragedies: A

Critical Study of the Plays and Their Place in Dryden's Poetry. 2 vols. Salzburg Studies in English Literature 7. Salzburg: Institüt für englische Sprache und Literatur, Universität Salzburg, 430 pp.

Attacks previous criticism for its hostility to the rhymed heroic tragedies. Argues that Dryden's concept of epic poetry is the crucial element in his idea of what heroic tragedy should be. Even his treatment of Aristotle suggests that he felt Aristotle's observations on drama were actually based on Homer. Deals with each of the rhymed heroic tragedies (The Indian Emperour, Tyrannic Love, The Conquest of Granada, Aureng-Zebe) individually, discussing their predominant themes and noting how they reflect Dryden's intellectual and political views. Discusses the language of the plays, suggesting that the rhymed heroic couplet helps introduce the spirit of epic poetry. Relates the tendency of characters to think aloud to the narrative voice in epic. Examines the plays' typical imagery; argues that Dryden "appeals increasingly to the thinking soul's power to create and to perceive not only concrete images but images suggested by abstractions." Relates the plays to Dryden's nondramatic poetry; suggests that writing them helped him develop his skill at couplet versification, contributed to his panegyric style, and was a factor in his association of satire with panegyric. Concludes that "Dryden's rhymed heroic tragedies provide what is probably the best illustration of the fusion of the extreme views, objects of admiration and objects of repugnance both occupying a single world, both joined in a stupendous struggle."

*2 BENTLEY, THOMAS R. "Money, God, and King: Economic Aspects of Restoration Comedy." Ph.D. dissertation, Memorial University of Newfoundland.
Cited in the 1974 MLA International Bibliography.

3 BLACK, JAMES. "Dryden on Shadwell's Theatre of Violence." Dalhousie Review 54 (Summer):298-311.
Argues that MacFlecknoe is related to Dryden's criticism in general and to the Dryden-Shadwell controversy over the nature of comedy in particular. Claims that the poem's object is not the man Shadwell but Shadwellian comedy, especially its tendencies toward cruelty and salaciousness.

*4 BRUCE, DONALD. Topics of Restoration Comedy. London: Gollancz; New York: St. Martin's, 189 pp.
Cited in "The Eighteenth Century: A Current Bibliography," PQ 54 (Fall):851-52, and abstracted there by J. Harold Wilson.

5 BUDICK, SANFORD. Poetry of Civilization: Mythopoeic Displacement in the Verse of Milton, Dryden, Pope, and Johnson. New Haven and London: Yale University Press, 194 pp.
Discusses the public aspects of some poems by the four authors. Sees, in each case, the poet in the role of keryx, or herald, who announces and prophesies the replacement of one myth

by another. "Dryden's Circle of Divine Power" (pp. 81-110) deals
with Absalom and Achitophel and The Medal. Sees "The Epilogue
Spoken to the King . . . at Oxford" (1681) as a kind of prologue
to Absalom and Achitophel, in which Dryden speaks, with the confidence of a "myth-displacing poet," directly to the King. Argues
that the opening lines of Absalom and Achitophel are severely critical of the King's adultery, thereby establishing the poet's crucial independence, and hence his authority. Asserts that the poem's
lack of narrative is intentional, making possible "a remarkable
union of myth and dialectic." Interprets the "Plot" as an example
of false myth, "gross and anarchic," without a "Lawfull Lord."
Sees The Medal as a structurally unified but mechanical attempt to
repeat the success of Absalom and Achitophel.

*6   CAMPBELL, DOWLING G. "Background and Applications of the Honor
      Code in Dryden's Four Spanish-Oriented Heroic Plays." Ph.D.
      dissertation, University of Missouri at Columbia.
          Cited in Latt and Monk, 1976.30. Abstracted in DAI 35:1041A.

7   CHAMBERS, A.B., and WILLIAM FROST, eds. The Works of John
     Dyrden. Volume IV: Poems 1693-1696. Vinton A. Dearing, textu-
     al editor. Berkeley, Los Angeles, and London: University of
     California Press, 832 pp.
         This volume also includes the "Discourse concerning the
     Original and Progress of Satire." The commentary (pp. 507-795)
     follows the format of volume 1 (1956.16). Textual notes and an
     appendix (Congreve's verses on Dryden's Persius) follow. Further
     volumes in the "California Dryden" to date: 1962.42 (8); 1966.32
     (9); 1969.52 (3); 1970.59 (10); 1971.58 (17); 1972.83 (2); 1974.54
     (18); 1976.41 (15); 1978.29 (11); 1979.30 (19).

*8   DILLARD, NANCY FREY. "The English Fabular Tradition: Chaucer,
      Spenser, Dryden." Ph.D. dissertation, University of Tennessee.
          Cited in Latt and Monk, 1976.30. Abstracted in DAI 34:7186A.

9   DILLON, GEORGE L. "Complexity and Change of Character in Neo-
     Classical Criticism." Journal of the History of Ideas 35
     (January-March):51-61.
         Discusses neoclassical ideas about dramatic character change.
     Includes Dryden among those who believed that characters should be
     distinctive and relatively unchanging. Notes however that toward
     the end of his career (in Don Sebastian) he seemed to change his
     principles, suggesting the shift toward "a more flexible and in-
     sightful psychological criticism" that was to come in the eighteenth
     century and after.

10   DOWNES, JOHN. Roscius Anglicanus. New York and London:
      Garland.
          Reprint of 1708.1 in facsimile with a preface by Arthur
      Freeman.

11   DUGGAN, MARGARET M.   "Mythic Components in Dryden's The Hind
     and the Panther." CL 26 (Spring):110-23.
         Discusses Dryden's Panther and Hind in terms of Ovid's treat-
     ments of the same animals in Metamorphoses. Suggests that seen
     with Ovid's version in mind the Panther is perhaps even "more mon-
     strous and dangerous" than the other animals in Dryden's poem.
     Notes that although the Hind is related on the whole to figures
     treated favorably by Ovid, some of those to whom she is connected
     introduce surprising complexities. Looks at the example of Ovid's
     story of Io, which seems to "contradict some essential parts of
     the Hind's makeup." Suggests however that "these apparent con-
     tradictions . . . all belong to the traditional claims of the Roman
     Catholic Church, and refer to the physicality of the church, the
     motherhood and purity of the church, and to the church's existence
     both in time and outside it."

12   EHRENPREIS, IRVIN.   "Meaning: Implicit and Explicit." In New
     Approaches to Eighteenth-Century Literature. Edited by Phillip
     Harth. Selected Papers from the English Institute. New York:
     Columbia University Press, pp. 117-55.
         Attacks the overreliance of critics on implicit allusions
     and echoes in their interpretations of Augustan literary works.
     Uses as a major example interpretations which depend on Paradise
     Lost to explain Absalom and Achitophel. Argues that a writer's
     explicit comments on his own work should be given primary emphasis.
     The essay appears in expanded form in the author's Literary Meaning
     and Augustan Values (Charlottesville: University Press of Virginia,
     1974), pp. 1-48. The Dryden material is essentially unchanged.

13   EMERSON, OLIVER FARRAR.   John Dryden and a British Academy.
     Folcroft, Pa.: Folcroft Library Editions.
         Reprint of 1921.4.

14   FARLEY-HILLS, DAVID.   The Benevolence of Laughter: Comic Poetry
     of the Commonwealth and Restoration. London: Macmillan;
     Totowa, N.J.: Rowman & Littlefield, 220 pp.
         "John Dryden" (pp. 99-131) portrays Dryden as a reluctant
     but nonetheless superb comic writer. Discusses the plays and trans-
     lations briefly before focussing on MacFlecknoe and Absalom and
     Achitophel. Claims that the former is comic because it treats the
     the disparity between "two imcompatible views of the poet"; that
     the latter is "a non-comic poem which makes use of comic devices."
     Sees it as moving "from the comic world of disorder to a world
     dominated by divine orderliness."

*15 FAULKNER, SUSAN N.   "The Concept of Decorum in Dryden's Works."
     Ph.D. dissertation, City University of New York.
         Cited in Latt and Monk, 1976.30. Abstracted in DAI 34:7229A.

16   FOLKENFLIK, ROBERT.   "Some Allusions to Dryden in The Battle of
     the Books." RLV 40, no. 4:355-58.

331

Notes and explains allusions to Shadwell's attack on The
Indian Queen and to Matthew Prior and Charles Montague's The Hind
and the Panther Transvers'd (1687.6). Concludes that these allusions help to suggest Swift's kinship to earlier satirists in the
Jonson-Shadwell tradition.

*17 FORRESTER, KENT. "Decay of the Literary Supernatural during
     the Age of Dryden." Enlightenment Essays 5, no. 1:57-64.
        Cited in the 1976 MLA International Bibliography.

 18 FROST, WILLIAM. "Dryden's Versions of Ovid." CL 26 (Summer):
     193-202.
        Attributes Dryden's success as a translator of Ovid to a
     compatibility between the two. Notes in particular that both poets
     seem to be writing "at a transition point between oral and written
     narration." Asserts that Dryden "dilates and enlarges" on "some-
     thing recurrently erotic, psychological, specific, realistic, and
     domestic" in Ovid. Claims also that "Ovid's inventiveness as a
     psychologist of ordinary life . . . endeared him to Dryden."

 19 FUJIMURA, THOMAS H. "The Personal Element in Dryden's Poetry."
     PMLA 89 (October):1007-23.
        Argues that in the last fifteen years of his life Dryden's
     poetry was strongly personal. His neoclassicism made it possible
     for him to generalize the personal element in his poetry, and there-
     by preserve the "vital myth of the poet as a leader of men." Sees
     in "To . . . Oldham" Dryden's apologia as a satirist; in "To . . .
     Anne Killigrew" his demonstration, as a Catholic, of his "increased
     moral sensitivity." "To . . . Congreve" reflects the frustrations
     and problems of his last decade but also his awareness of his own
     stature; Alexander's Feast, a "confident apologia," is his final
     self-vindication.

*20 GALIGANI, GIUSEPPI. Il Boccaccio nella cultura Inglesa a
     Anglo-Americana. Florence: Olschki.
        Cited in Latt and Monk, 1976.30.

 21 HATTON, THOMAS J. "Medieval Anticipations of Dryden's Stylistic
     Revolution: The Knight's Tale." Lang&S 7:261-70.
        Analyzes Dryden's version of "The Knight's Tale" to argue
     that his technique of "substituting abstract concept for metaphor"
     was common in medieval literature.

*22 HIRAI, TAKASHI. "Dryden's Transparency." In Essays Presented
     to Shiko Murakami on the Occasion of His Retirement from Osaka
     University. Tokyo: Eihosha.
        Cited in the 1974 MLA International Bibliography.

 23 HOLLIS, CHRISTOPHER. Dryden. New York: Haskell House.
        Reprint of 1933.7.

24   HOPKINS, D.W. "Dryden and Sandys's Ovid: A Note." N&Q, n.s.
     21 (March):104.
         Asserts that Dryden, in his translation of a line from Ovid's
     Metamorphoses, echoes Sir George Sandys's translation of the same
     line.

25   _____. "Two Hitherto Unrecorded Sources for Dryden's Ovid
     Translations." N&Q, n.s. 21 (November):419-21.
         Notes apparent borrowings from Charles Hopkins's Epistolary
     Poems (1694) and Peter Ker's ΛΟΓΟΜΑΧΙΑ: or the Conquest of
     Eloquence (1690).

26   JENSEN, H. JAMES. "A Note on Restoration Aesthetics." SEL 14
     (Summer):317-26.
         Discusses the period's preference for the "elan vital" as a
     higher criterion of excellence than conventional rhetorical values.
     Emphasizes Dryden's dichotomy between "lively" and "just" attributes
     of poetry, and his interest in literary qualities which appeal to
     the emotions and imagination.

*27 KIRWAN, NORMA J. "A Revised Edition of the Woodward and
     MacManaway Check List of English Plays 1641-1700." Ph.D. dis-
     sertation, University of Maryland.
         Cited in the 1974 MLA International Bibliography.

*28 KISHI, TETSUO. "Oseifukkoki Kigeki no 'Taikutsusa'" ['Dullness'
     in Restoration Comedy]. Eigo Seinen 119:762-63.
         Cited in the 1974 MLA International Bibliography.

*29 LAW, RICHARD A. "Admiration and Concernment in the Heroic
     Plays of John Dryden." Ph.D. dissertation, Temple University.
         Cited in Latt and Monk, 1976.30. Abstracted in DAI 35:
     3688A-89A.

*30 LAWLOR, NANCY KATHERINE. "His Flecknotique Majesty: A Study
     of Richard Flecknoe and His Critics." Ph.D. dissertation,
     Rutgers University.
         Cited in Latt and Monk, 1976.30. Abstracted in DAI 35:406A.

*31 LEVIN, MARK J. "Literature and Numismatics in England, 1650-
     1750." Ph.D, dissertation, University of Pennsylvania.
         Cited in Latt and Monk, 1976.30. Abstracted in DAI 35:
     2230A-31A.

*32 LEVY, ROBERT A. "Dryden's Translation of Chaucer: A Study of
     the Means of Re-Creating Literary Models." Ph.D. dissertation,
     University of Tennessee.
         Cited in Latt and Monk, 1976.30. Abstracted in DAI 34:
     5108A-09A.

*33 LYNN, MURRAY T. "The Concept of Enthusiasm in Some Major Poems

by John Dryden." Ph.D. dissertation, McMaster University.
Cited in the 1974 MLA International Bibliography. Abstracted
in DAI 35:6672A.

34   McFADDEN, GEORGE. "Political Satire in The Rehearsal." YES
      4:120-28.
         Argues that Henry Bennett, Earl of Arlington, was the main
target of the play. Uses contemporary evidence, including Dryden's
mild reaction. Points out that Arlington was Buckingham's chief
political rival. Asserts also that the play's Two Kings of
Brentford are Charles II and James II.

35   McHENRY, ROBERT W., Jr. "The Importance of Right Reason in
      Dryden's Conversion." Mosaic 7, no. 3:69-86.
         Suggests that a clue to Dryden's conversion may be found in
the nature of his attitudes toward "right reason." Notes that
while he follows Anglican apologists in Religio Laici, he is more
ambivalent than they in his attitude toward "right reason." In
The Hind and the Panther he makes no appeal to this tradition at
all: in fact it is clear that he has rejected it.

*36   McINTOSH, WILLIAM A. "The Harmonic Muse: Musical Currents in
      Literature 1450-1750." Ph.D. dissertation, University of
      Virginia.
         Cited in Latt and Monk, 1976.30. Abstracted in DAI 35:
3692A-93A.

37   MALEK, JAMES S. The Arts Compared: An Aspect of Eighteenth-
      Century British Aesthetics. Detroit: Wayne State University
      Press, 175 pp.
         Discusses Dryden's "Parallel betwixt Poetry and Painting"
(pp. 15-24). Sees Dryden as a pioneer in establishing a method-
ology for comparing arts, which in Dryden's case is the concept
of "rhetorical form," in which "poetic and pictorial kinds are
viewed as conventional means of producing predetermined effects."

38   MARESCA, THOMAS E. "The Context of Dryden's Absalom and
      Achitophel." ELH 41 (Fall):340-58.
         Discusses several of the poem's scriptural contexts, empha-
sizing its opening and closing passages. Argues that the opening
lines establish a dichotomy between law and grace: grace is associated with David and the "pious times, e'r Priest-craft did begin."
Notes the poem's emphasis on paternity, and its contrasts among the
sons of various of its figures. Sees the "godlike David" as a
creative force which passes on its "maker's image" both as father
and, at the end of the poem, as giver of the Word.

39   _____. Epic to Novel. Columbus: Ohio State University Press,
      248 pp.
         "Dryden" (pp. 3-75) discusses Absalom and Achitophel and
MacFlecknoe. Sees Absalom and Achitophel as a "synopsis of the

state of traditional epic poetry in the late seventeenth century";
also asserts that it is the last serious epic in English. Finds
in MacFlecknoe a parody of the epic form. Looks at commentaries
on the Aeneid which established the orthodox allegorical interpretation of the poem (as representing the "growth" or "ages" of
man). Argues that while Absalom and Achitophel adapts this theme,
MacFlecknoe, with its static structure and use of tautology, paro-
dies it.

40   MASON, H.A. "Dryden's 'Georgics' and Pope's 'Essay of Criti-
        cism.'" N&Q, n.s. 21 (July):252.
        Argues that 11. 496-97 of Pope's poem recall 11. 108-109 of
Dryden's translation of Book 3 of Virgil's.

41   MELL, DONALD C. A Poetics of Augustan Elegy: Studies of Poems
        by Dryden, Pope, Prior, Swift, Gray, and Johnson. Amsterdam:
        Rodopi, 116 pp.
        The second chapter (pp. 15-28) deals with "To the Memory of
Mr. Oldham." Comments on the poem's highly stylized nature; asserts
that Dryden achieves its necessary depersonalization (necessary because of Oldham's lack of poetic stature) through the use of allusions. Notes that the poem's roughness reflects the style of its
subject. Concludes that "Dryden's speaker expresses confidence in
art as an adequate compensation for time because he is under no
illusions about its truths or limitations."

42   MILHOUS, JUDITH, and ROBERT D. HUME. "Dating Play Premieres
        from Publication Data." HLB 22 (October):374-405.
        Determines as far as possible the normal lapse of time between
performance and publication during the Restoration, and tries to
account for anomalies. Warns of the imprecision of previously published data and guesswork. Includes several plays by Dryden. Or-
ganized by decades for the period 1660-1700.

43   MINER, EARL. The Restoration Mode from Milton to Dryden.
        Princeton: Princeton University Press, 611 pp.
        Begins with a discussion of the theory of "modes." Modes
arise from the similar perceptions of authors in a period, and
"the interrelations in those perceptions between the self, others,
and the world." Identifies three modes in the seventeenth century:
the "Metaphysical," the "Cavalier," and the "Restoration." The
"Restoration mode" lasted (overlapping the others) from about 1640
to 1700. It is the product of a general shift in the century's
poetry from private to public subjects, and from lyric to narrative. Sees Dryden as a major example of a poet in this mode:
like Milton, he was a public poet who saw himself as "dealing with
versions of historical truth." Links Dryden's style to this image
of himself; notes his heavy use of active verbs and clear connections between ideas. Closely examines poems which deal with contemporary events, emphasizing ways in which their forms reflect
their occasions. Discusses the satire of the period, finding

three functions for it: to give pleasure, to make "moral discrim-
inations and judgments," and to "provide a rhetoric" for poets to
use in dealing with other poetic situations (such as panegyric).
Stresses the originality of Dryden's satires. Looks at lyrics in
the "Restoration mode." Suggests that the "flowering" of Dryden's
lyrics in the 1690s is a sign of his political isolation. Concludes
by looking at Fables, stressing its variety and unity. Praises
Dryden's insight into the poets he used. Claims that the work is
the "finest poetic achievement in the century apart from Paradise
Lost."

*44   MOLINOFF, MARLENE S.   "The Via Media of John Dryden's Tragi-
      comedy." Ph.D. dissertation, George Washington University.
         Cited in Latt and Monk, 1976.30. Abstracted in DAI 35:
      1114A-15A.

 45   MOORE, ROBERT ETHERIDGE. Henry Purcell and the Restoration
      Theatre. Westport, Conn.: Greenwood.
         Reprint of 1961.38.

*46   NAKANO, NANCY YOSHIKO. "The Authority of Narrative Technique
      and Argument in Milton, Bunyan, Dryden, and John Reynolds."
      Ph.D. dissertation, University of California at Los Angeles.
         Cited in Latt and Monk, 1976.30. Abstracted in DAI 34:7199A.

*47   POPSON, JOSEPH JOHN. "The Collier Controversy: A Critical
      Basis for Understanding Drama of the Restoration Period." Ph.D.
      dissertation, University of Florida.
         Cited in Latt and Monk, 1976.30. Abstracted in DAI 35:
      3695A-96A.

*48   RANGNO, MELANIE COLLINS. "Nathaniel Lee's Plays of the Exclusion
      Crisis." Ph.D. dissertation, University of California at Los
      Angeles.
         Cited in Latt and Monk, 1976.30. Abstracted in DAI 34:4215A.

 49   REASKE, CHRISTOPHER. "A Shakespearean Backdrop for Dryden's
      MacFlecknoe?" SQ 25 (Summer):358.
         Suggests that Flecknoe's advice to Shadwell may echo several
      details in 1 Henry IV 2. 4. There are some verbal parallels, and
      both scenes use comic royal props and share an "attack on bad act-
      ing."

*50   REEDY, GERARD, S.J. "Restoration Interpretation." Ph.D. dis-
      sertation, University of Pennsylvania.
         Cited in Latt and Monk, 1976.30. Abstracted in DAI 34:5201A.

 51   REMPEL, W. JOHN. "The Sound of Trumpets." ECS 7 (Summer):
      489-93.
         Attacks H. James Jensen's "Comparing the Arts in the Age of
      Baroque" (1973.35) on points of detail, especially having to do
      with the nature of seventeenth-century musical instruments.

52 ROGERS, PAT. The Augustan Vision. London: Weidenfeld & Nicolson, 318 pp.

Credits Dryden with being an example to Augustan satirists. In Absalom and Achitophel he shows how a satirist can be at once partisan and detached; in MacFlecknoe he shows "the use of genial contempt." Concludes that Dryden "was the first English satirist who could remain elegant whilst preserving the sharpest cutting-edge."

53 ROPER, ALAN. "Characteristics of Dryden's Prose." ELH 41 (Winter):668-92.

Examines Dryden's translations of Maimbourg and Tacitus (as providing the most objective evidence) to discover what gives Dryden's prose the "spirit and vigour" Arnold attributed to it. Notes Dryden's consistent amplification, his substitution of sequence for simultaneity in narrative, and his preference for live metaphors over dead and half-dead ones. Applies these findings to Dryden's original prose and discovers the same characteristics there.

54 _____, ed. The Works of John Dryden. Volume XVIII. Prose: The History of the League, 1684. Vinton A. Dearing, textual editor. Berkeley, Los Angeles, and London: University of California Press, 577 pp.

The commentary (pp. 417-540) includes a long headnote on the context of Dryden's translation, which had not been published complete since the seventeenth century. The edition also includes notes on individual words and passages, textual notes, and two appendixes (a glossary, and "The Table" printed with the work in 1684). Further volumes in the "California Dryden" to date: 1956.16 (1); 1962.42 (8); 1966.32 (9); 1969.52 (3); 1970.59 (10); 1971.58 (17); 1972.83 (2); 1974.7 (4); 1976.41 (15); 1978.29 (11); 1979.30 (19).

*55 ROSS, CAROLYN C. "Dryden's Concept of Originality." Ph.D. dissertation, Ohio State University.

Cited in Latt and Monk, 1976.30. Abstracted in DAI 35: 2953A-54A.

*56 ROTH, FREDERIC HALL, Jr. "'Heaven's Center, Nature's Lap': A Study of the English Country-Estate Poem of the Seventeenth Century." Ph.D. dissertation, University of Virginia.

Cited in Latt and Monk, 1976.30. Abstracted in DAI 34: 5120A-21A.

*57 SAITO, BISHU. "Puritan no Iyarashisa" [Puritan Obnoxiousness]. Eigo Seinen 119:750-51.

Cited in the 1974 MLA International Bibliography.

58 SALTER, C.H. "Dryden and Addison." MLR 69 (January):29-39.

Gives many examples of Addison's borrowings, including verbal

borrowings, from Dryden's criticism. Concludes that Addison "is
a much less intelligent and original critic," and that "it was
Dryden, and not Addison, who broke with the formal canons of neo-
classical criticism, laid the foundations of Romantic aesthetics,
and did for criticism what Descartes did for philosophy."

*59   SAMUELS, MARILYN S. "The Age of Analogy: Theories of Knowledge
       and Their Influence on Major Eighteenth-Century English Litera-
       ture." Ph.D. dissertation, City University of New York.
           Cited in the 1974 MLA International Bibliography. Abstracted
   in DAI 34:4284A.

 60   SASLOW, EDWARD L. "Shaftesbury Cursed: Dryden's Revision of
       the Achitophel Lines [180-91]." SB 28:276-83.
           Argues, against Vinton A. Dearing (in 1972.83), that the
   original text jumped from what became 1. 151 to 1. 159, and from
   1. 166 to 1. 173. Dearing had argued that 11. 180-91 were a late
   addition; Saslow finds the events on which Dearing based his argument "individually unlikely, and next to impossible collectively."

*61   SHEA, PETER K. "Juvenal's Tenth Satire Englished: The Art of
       Translation, 1617-1802." Ph.D. dissertation, University of
       North Carolina.
           Cited in Latt and Monk, 1976.30. Abstracted in DAI 35:3769A.

 62   SMITH, DANE FARNSWORTH. The Critics in the Audience of the
       London Theatres from Buckingham to Sheridan: A Study of Neo-
       classicism in the Playhouse 1671-1779. Norwood, Pa.: Norwood
       Editions.
           Reprint of 1953.19.

 63   STAVES, SUSAN. "Why Was Dryden's Mr. Limberham Banned? A
       Problem in Restoration Theatre History." RECTR 13, no. 1 (May):
       1-11.
           Concludes that despite the various theories that have been
   put forward on insufficient evidence, we do not know why the play
   was stopped. Suggests as a possibility that the title character
   was taken to be, though not intended to be, a representation of
   the Earl of Lauderdale.

*64   STRINGER, GARY. "Ease and Control in Dryden's Prose Style."
       Southern Humanities Review 8:303-16.
           Cited in the 1974 MLA International Bibliography.

 65   WEST, MICHAEL D. "Shifting Concepts of Heroism in Dryden's
       Panegyrics." PLL 10 (Fall):378-93.
           Traces a shift in Dryden's panegyrics from extolling "heroic
   virtue" in Heroic Stanzas and Annus Mirabilis to praising "milder
   virtues," especially that of fortitude, in his later poems of
   praise. Sees the process as culminating in the debunking of the
   heroic in Alexander's Feast. Suggests that he had become aware

of the dangers of the charismatic hero who is, or feels himself
to be, an instrument of divine will.

*66   WOODS, THOMAS FRANCIS. "Dryden and the Prophetic Mode: An
       Examination of His Poetic Theory and Practice in Light of
       Seventeenth-Century Concepts of Prophecy." Ph.D. dissertation,
       Ohio State University.
            Cited in Latt and Monk, 1976.30. Abstracted in DAI 34:7254A.

1975

1   BROWER, REUBEN. Mirror on Mirror: Translation, Imitation,
     Parody. Harvard Studies in Comparative Literature. Cambridge,
     Mass.: Harvard University Press, 190 pp.
          Contains "Dryden's Epic Manner and Virgil" (1940.2) and
     "Verbal and Visual Translation of Myth: Neptune in Virgil, Rubens,
     Dryden" (1972.5).

2   BROWN, HAROLD CLIFFORD, Jr. "Etherege and Comic Shallowness."
     TSLL 16 (Winter):675-90.
          Briefly examines Dryden's comedies, contrasting them with
     those of Etherege, who is accused of "pathological shallowness."
     Claims that Dryden, on the other hand, writes of "misbehavior"
     rather than "libertinism," perhaps because of his respect for
     authority.

3   BUCK, JOHN DAWSON CARL. "The Ascetic's Banquet: The Morality
     of Alexander's Feast." TSLL 17 (Fall):573-89.
          Emphasizes the poem's "moral seriousness"; notes that
     Dryden's later occasional poems show a developing "awareness of
     the decadence of his own world." Argues that "the poem was written
     against the kind of emotional persuasion employed by Timotheus."
     Finds the figure of St. Cecilia "fraught with complexity and quali-
     fications" and the idea of "redemptive music" ultimately questioned,
     given the corruption of the times.

4   BYARS, JULIE ANNE. "The Tory-Poets: Anonymous?" N&Q, n.s. 22
     (June):259-62.
          Examines two literary attacks on Dryden, The Tory Poets
     (1682.2) and The Medal of John Bayes (1682.7), both of which have
     been attributed to Thomas Shadwell. Argues that they are not by
     the same author; points out that the author of The Tory Poets seems
     not to have known Dryden well and therefore is probably not Shadwell.

5   CANFIELD, J. DOUGLAS. "The Image of the Circle in Dryden's 'To
     My Honour'd Kinsman.'" PLL 11 (Spring):168-76.
          Discusses various meanings of the image, which is seen as
     central to the poem. Argues that ultimately it is a symbol of
     perfection, which also signifies "the cycle of human life." Sees
     also a memento mori and a reference to the wheel of fortune. Notes
     that the poem is itself concentric in structure.

6   _____ . "The Jewel of Great Price: Mutability and Constancy in Dryden's <u>All for Love</u>." <u>ELH</u> 42 (Spring):38-61.

Asserts that constancy operates in the play as a balancing motif to mutability. The theme is centered in the character of Cleopatra, and often expressed through the imagery of jewelry. Examines Renaissance literary treatments of the story; finds that the twin motifs of constancy and mutability are features of the tradition. Discusses Dryden's play, stressing its insistence on Cleopatra's constancy and Antony's vacillation. Concludes that ultimately Antony and Cleopatra are seen to have transcended their fate.

7   CAPELLAN, ANGEL. "John Dryden's Indebtedness to Pedro Calderón de la Barca in <u>An Evening's Love or the Mock-Astrologer</u>." <u>RLC</u> 49 (October-December):572-89.

Asserts that Dryden was familiar with Spanish drama, that he could read Spanish, and that he "liberally imitated and borrowed from the Spanish dramatists." Examines the texts of <u>An Evening's Love</u>, and Calderón's <u>Astrólogo fingido</u> (and T. Corneille's translation of it). Concludes that Dryden borrowed heavily from both, but that his play surpasses its sources in plot and characterization.

8   CLARK, JOHN R. "Anticlimax in Satire." <u>SCN</u> 33 (Spring):22-26.

Argues that anticlimax is "a most crucial satiric strategy." Looks at several examples in <u>MacFlecknoe</u>. Claims that anticlimax is the dominant structural principle of the poem in detail as well as in its overall structure.

*9   DAVIDOW, LAWRENCE LEE. "The English Verse Epistle from Jonson to Burns." Ph.D. dissertation, Princeton University.

Cited in the <u>1975 MLA International Bibliography</u>. Abstracted in <u>DAI</u> 36:2189A.

10   DAVIES, H. NEVILLE. "Davenant, Dryden, Lee, and Otway." In <u>English Drama (Excluding Shakespeare): Select Bibliographical Guides</u>. Edited by Stanley Wells. London: Oxford University Press, pp. 150-72.

Describes and evaluates the various available editions of the plays; gives a chronological listing of the plays themselves; provides a brief list of criticism.

11   _____ . "Dryden's <u>Rahmenerzählung</u>: The Form of 'An Essay of Dramatick Poesie.'" In <u>Fair Forms: Essays in English Literature from Spenser to Jane Austen</u>. Edited by Maren-Sofie Røstvig. Cambridge: D.S. Brewer; Totowa, N.J.: Rowman & Littlefield, pp. 119-46, 219-22.

Argues that the essay's structure derives from Boccaccio, Chaucer, and <u>The Cobler of Caunterburie</u> (1590), attributed to Robert Armin. The latter work includes a literary discussion set on a boat going down the Thames, and tales within the tale as in

Boccaccio and Chaucer. Argues that the essay also mocks each of the three unities, that it is designed to boost national morale, and that its use of Boccaccio establishes a parallel between Renaissance Florence and Restoration London. Suggests that the essay's specific references to Somerset House and Covent Garden evoke architecture in the Italian manner.

12 _____ . "'Laid Artfully Together': Stanzaic Design in Milton's 'On the Morning of Christ's Nativity.'" In Fair Forms: Essays in English Literature from Spenser to Jane Austen. Edited by Maren-Sofie Røstvig. Cambridge: D.S. Brewer: Totowa, N.J.: Rowman & Littlefield, pp. 85-117.
Finds strong echoes of Milton's ode in Dryden's "To . . . Anne Killigrew." Notes especially Dryden's fourth stanza, in which the fifteen lines numerologically represent the ladder of redemption, and support the association of Anne Killigrew with Christ. Argues that Dryden, like Milton, was viewing poetry and the present poem as a gift to Christ, but also saw poetry as having been profaned in his own time. Concludes that the comparison "provides insight into the way that Dryden read Milton."

13 DEARING, VINTON A.; SERGE E. BRUNET; JOHN H. HALL; and R. GILL TOMARELLI. "Dryden's Heroique Stanza's on Cromwell: A New Critical Text." PBSA 69, no. 4:502-26.
Bases the text on a study of manuscripts unrecorded and unused by the first volume of the "California Dryden" (1956.16). Includes a description of the manuscripts, the relevant early printings of the poem, and the text itself, with full annotation.

*14 DESHBANDHU, LALAJI SHARMA. "The Impact of India on English Poetry and Drama, 1660-1800." Ph.D. dissertation, Temple University.
Cited in the 1975 MLA International Bibliography. Abstracted in DAI 36:3683A-84A.

15 Drydeniana. (The Life and Times of Seven Major British Writers: Dryden, Pope, Swift, Richardson, Sterne, Johnson, Gibbon.) 14 vols. New York: Garland.
Includes facsimiles of 1668.1-2; 1673.1-2, 4-5; 1674.2; 1680.2; 1681.2-4; 1682.1-8; 1683.3-4; 1685.1; 1687.1, 3-4, 6; 1688.1-3; 1690.1-2; 1695.1-2; 1698.1, 3; 1699.2; 1700.1-3, 6.

*16 DUGGAN, MARGARET MARY. "Aspects of John Dryden's The Hind and the Panther." Ph.D. dissertation, Columbia University.
Cited in the 1975 MLA International Bibliography. Abstracted in DAI 35:6663A.

17 EMPSON, WILLIAM. "A Deist Tract by Dryden." EIC 25 (January): 74-100.
Asserts that a tract published in Charles Blount's The Oracles of Reason (1693) and signed by "A.W." is in fact by Dryden, as had

been stated in a deist collection of 1745. Argues that the tract
is not inconsistent with <u>Religio Laici</u> because the poem does not
really attack deism. Notes Dryden's friendly relationship with
Blount and the tract's reference to Sir Charles Wolseley, whose
work Dryden used as the basis for the "Deist's" point of view in
<u>Religio Laici</u>.

*18   ERICKSON, DON LOWELL. "'The Progress of Dulness': Imagery of
      'Nothing' and Negation in the Satires of Rochester, Dryden,
      Swift, and Pope." Ph.D. dissertation, Washington University
      (St. Louis).
          Cited in the <u>1975 MLA International Bibliography</u>. Abstracted
      in <u>DAI</u> 36:2217A-18A.

19   FROST, WILLIAM. "<u>Aureng-Zebe</u> in Context: Dryden, Shakespeare,
      Milton, and Racine." <u>JEGP</u> 74 (January):26-49.
          Reads the play in the light of <u>King Lear</u>, <u>Samson Agonistes</u>,
      and <u>Mithridate</u>. Argues that it has a design similar to Shakespeare's,
      a common interest with Milton's in marital dilemmas, and like
      Racine's it contains a father-son-princess triangle at the heart
      of its plot. Argues for the significant influence of each of these
      works on Dryden's play, and concludes by emphasizing <u>Aureng-Zebe</u>'s
      differences, especially in its treatment of the title character as
      an ethical hero, and its thematic focus on "the nature of kingship."

20   FUJIMURA, THOMAS H. "Dryden's Poetics: The Expressive Values
      in Poetry." <u>JEGP</u> 74 (April):195-208.
          Argues that we should be more aware of Dryden's concern for
      proper expression (as opposed to thought). Asserts that in his
      theory and practice diction and prosody are more important than
      figurative language. Considers his views on prosody; points out
      his emphasis on quantity and cadence, sound, and syntax. Notes
      that in fact the latter is not constrained by the heroic couplet
      or any other form, and is in fact quite flexible. Sees his major
      values in diction as aptness, decorum, and harmonious sound. Con-
      cludes that his language in poetry was influenced more by his aes-
      thetic ideas than by the stylistic goals of the Royal Society.

21   _____. "John Dryden and the Myth of the Golden Age." <u>PLL</u> 11
      (Spring):149-67.
          Examines Dryden's use of this myth (and of its opposite, the
      Iron Age) as an example of his general use of myth as a "literary
      strategy." Finds examples of the conventional myth in <u>Astraea
      Redux</u>, <u>Annus Mirabilis</u> and ("without much conviction") in <u>Threnodia
      Augustalis</u>. Sees also a version of this myth in Dryden's treatment
      of American and African primitives. The Iron Age myth can be found
      in <u>Astraea Redux</u>, <u>Absalom and Achitophel</u>, <u>The Medal</u>, and especially
      in works written after 1688, when Dryden's (and in his view the
      nation's) fortunes turned for the worse.

22   _____. "The Temper of John Dryden." <u>SP</u> 72 (July):348-66.

Attacks the idea of Dryden as a literary conservative; notes his innovations. Emphasizes his aggressiveness and self-confidence in public exchanges. Looks at his views of himself; notes that he identifies with Homer and Achilles. Points out also his heavy use of military and athletic metaphors.

23 GARRISON, JAMES D. <u>Dryden and the Tradition of Panegyric</u>. Berkeley, Los Angeles, and London: University of California Press, 277 pp.

Traces the development of "panegyric" as both a term and a form. Distinguishes it from the encomium: it is a poem of praise to a great person which is also occasional and, traditionally, oratorical. Points out that "Dryden's career bridges the gap between the serious Renaissance appreciation of panegyric and its comic inversion in the eighteenth century." Surveys Dryden's panegyrics (and poems using panegyric techniques) up to 1688, touching upon <u>Heroic Stanzas</u>, <u>Astraea Redux</u>, <u>To His Sacred Majesty</u>, <u>Absalom and Achitophel</u>, <u>Threnodia Augustalis</u>, <u>Brittania Redivivus</u>, and <u>Eleonora</u>. Emphasizes "Dryden's reassertion of the original, oratorical functions of the genre." Sees also, however, a general movement from celebration of public figures to disillusion with them, and after 1688 his poems of praise become more private, although he still uses aspects of the public form and "clings to the essential values of traditional panegyrics, reconciliation and peace." Concludes by noting that after Dryden's time panegyric became either satiric or a vehicle for "party polemics."

*24 GOTTLIEB, SIDNEY PAUL. "I. Textual and Contextual Revision in Herbert's <u>The Temple</u>. II. Criticism as Dialectics: Johnson and the Example of Dryden. III. 'Life and Death, Sanity and Insanity': A Reading of <u>Mrs. Dalloway</u>." Ph.D. dissertation, Rutgers University.

Cited in the <u>1975 MLA International Bibliography</u>. Abstracted in <u>DAI</u> 35:6666A.

25 GRACE, JOAN CARROLL. <u>Tragic Theory in the Critical Works of Thomas Rymer, John Dennis, and John Dryden</u>. London: Associated University Presses; Rutherford, N.J.: Fairleigh Dickinson University Press, 143 pp.

Describes (pp. 89–128) Dryden's theories about tragedy. Emphasizes his pragmatism. Finds him consistent in his belief in "form, structure, style" and in his belief that poetry should be didactic. Notes the changes in his notion of catharsis, which became more important to his view of tragedy, and his move from the "heroic" concept to "an attempt to adapt Shakespeare's drama to his own age."

*26 GUINNESS, G.N.A. "A Study of Eroticism in English Non-dramatic Poetry: 1580-1680." Ph.D. dissertation, London University (Westfield College).

Cited in the <u>Annual Bibliography of English Language and Literature</u> for 1975 (London: Modern Humanities Research Association).

*27   HACHIYA, AKIO. "Topographical Poetry no Keifu: Denham kara
       Shelley made" [The Structure of Topographical Poetry: Denham
       through Shelley]. In Gengo to Buntai: Highashida Chiaki Kyoju
       Kanreki Kinen Ronbushu [Present-Day Language and Literary Ex-
       pression: Lectures Collected in Honor of the Sixtieth Birthday
       of Chiaki Higashida]. Osaka: Osaka Kyoiku Tosho, pp. 69-80.
          Cited in the 1975 MLA International Bibliography.

 28   HARTH, PHILLIP. "Legends No Histories: The Case of Absalom
       and Achitophel." In Studies in Eighteenth Century Culture 4.
       Edited by Harold E. Pagliaro. Madison: University of Wisconsin
       Press for the American Society for Eighteenth Century Studies,
       pp. 13-29.
          Traces the development of the legend that Dryden wrote the
       poem at King Charles's request to influence the grand jury proceed-
       ings against Shaftesbury. Argues that this legend, which modern
       critics and historians have accepted as historical fact, is a pro-
       duct of the work of Robert Bell and W.D. Christie, nineteenth-
       century editors of Dryden. Asserts that Dryden could never have
       hoped to influence the jury directly, and that the poem must be
       viewed in the general context of Tory propaganda. Suggests that
       the legend has been accepted out of a desire to enhance Dryden's
       stature as a politically influential poet.

*29   KIRBY, W.L. "Some Modes and Techniques of Affirmation in
       Restoration Verse Satire." Ph.D. dissertation, London
       University (University College).
          Cited in the Annual Bibliography of English Language and
       Literature for 1975 (London: Modern Humanities Research Associa-
       tion).

 30   KLAWITER, MARILYN. "A Third Source for Cibber's The Comical
       Lovers." N&Q, n.s. 22 (November):488-89.
          Argues that An Evening's Love; or, The Mock Astrologer is a
       source, as well as two other plays by Dryden, Marriage a-la-Mode
       and Secret Love.

 31   LARSON, RICHARD LESLIE. Studies in Dryden's Dramatic Technique:
       The Uses of Scenes Depicting Persuasion and Accusation. Poetic
       Drama and Poetic Theory 9. Salzburg: Institut für englische
       Sprache und Literatur, Universität Salzburg, 320 pp.
          Examines Dryden's "regular use of confrontation scenes in
       which persuasion or accusation (or both) take place." Traces
       changes in Dryden's use of such scenes, and their relevance to his
       dramatic aims. Argues that Dryden found in such scenes an alterna-
       tive means of rousing emotion and pleasure, and of providing moral
       instruction, which did not involve frequent events and reversals
       in the action. Sees a change in emphasis, as Dryden moved from
       heroic plays through tragicomedy to tragedy, from "the delineation
       of heroism to the cultivation of strong feelings . . . for their
       own sake." Emphasizes throughout the theme of the hero overcoming

temptation, usually accompanied by persuasive appeal; praises
Dryden's skill at varying tone and feeling within a scene, and in
"arranging successive feelings within scenes." Notes that the
most frequent pattern in the scenes of persuasion is that of accusation reversed by counter-accusation and, finally, conversion.

32   LEAVIS, F.R. The Living Principle: "English" as a Discipline
      of Thought. New York: Oxford University Press.
           Contains "Antony and Cleopatra and All for Love" (1936.13),
      pp. 144-54.

33   LOVE, HAROLD. "State Affairs on the Restoration Stage, 1660-
      1675." RECTR 14, no. 1 (May):1-9.
           Includes a brief discussion of Dryden's Amboyna, described
      as "in the fullest sense a play of incitation, denying its audience
      even the most elementary form of dramatic release."

*34   McDONALD, MARGARET LAMB. "The Independent Woman in the
      Restoration Comedy of Manners." Ph.D. dissertation, University
      of Colorado.
           Cited in the Annual Bibliography of English Language and
      Literature for 1975 (London: Modern Humanities Research Associa-
      tion). Abstracted in DAI 36:2850A-51A. See 1976.35.

35   McKEON, MICHAEL. Politics and Poetry in Restoration England:
      The Case of Dryden's "Annus Mirabilis." Cambridge, Mass.:
      Harvard University Press, 344 pp.
           A detailed reading of Annus Mirabilis which is also concerned
      with how to read Restoration poetry. Complains that critics have
      tended to split the politics off from the poetry. Argues for a
      "rhetorical analysis" which would try to read each work as its
      original audience would have read it, taking into account the work's
      occasion and strategy. Contends, for example, that critics have
      failed to distinguish Dryden's rhetorical stances and his personal
      views. Gives a "first" and "second" reading of the poem. The
      first emphasizes Dryden's use of a "familial framework" in which
      the state is compared to a household. Argues that "the family
      . . . provides a conventionally acceptable perspective for under-
      standing civil structures as 'natural' unities." Ultimately the
      poem shows England as dependent upon unquestioning loyalty to its
      father/king. The second reading deals with the poem as prophecy.
      Notes that it not only uses the "conventional language of prophecy"
      but that it also implies a belief in the validity of prophecy that
      was typical of all major groups of the period. A conclusion re-
      turns to the topic of the proper way to deal with political poetry.

36   MARSHALL, GEOFFREY. Restoration Serious Drama. Norman:
      University of Oklahoma Press, 277 pp.
           Argues that the plays deal seriously with serious issues,
      and that to audiences of the period serious drama was akin to
      heroic and epic poetry. Emphasizes the plays' moral themes; finds

in them the values of "courage, wisdom, self-control, decorum, and
acceptance of moral obligation." Cites the character of Almanzor
in The Conquest of Granada: he is exemplary in that he must learn
to control his passion by means of his will. Sees in the plays an
emphasis on choice (as with the Emperor's dilemma in Aureng-Zebe
concerning Aureng-Zebe and Indamora); finds also a great interest
in role conflicts (Antony in All for Love). Suggests that the
plays often reflect contemporary political problems which result
from human forces out of control. Concludes that there was no
radical split between comedy and tragedy during the period: the
same themes and plot structures repeat in both.

37   MARTIN, LESLIE HOWARD. "All for Love and the Millenarian
     Tradition." CL 27 (Fall):289-306.
          Argues that the play is "pervasively millenarian and optimis-
     tic." Sees Dryden's positive treatment of Octavius Caesar (even
     though he does not appear in the play) as the key to this interpre-
     tation: he is "a providential power bent upon the lawful reinte-
     gration of a disordered world." Locates this view in the mainstream
     of ancient and modern attitudes toward the story. Examines Sir
     Charles Sedley's Antony and Cleopatra (1677), which takes a similar
     view but is an artistic failure. Suggests that Dryden learned from
     Sedley's mistakes, and kept Octavius out of the play to render him
     "so abstract as to seem godlike."

38   MASON, TOM. "Dryden's Version of the Wife of Bath's Tale."
     CQ 6, no. 3:240-56.
          Notes Dryden's enthusiasm for a poem which has not found
     favor with modern readers. Argues that the vigor, wit, and genial-
     ity of the translation (and especially its emphasis on the Crone's
     speech to the Knight) encourage us to see the "humour with which
     [Chaucer's poem] touches upon natural frailty and . . . the inward
     feelings of the human heart."

39   MILLER, RAYMOND D. Secondary Accent in Modern English Verse
     (Chaucer to Dryden). Norwood, Pa.: Norwood Editions.
          Reprint of 1904.6.

40   MINER, EARL. "Mr. Dryden and Mr. Rymer." PQ 54 (Winter):
     137-51.
          Examines the attitudes each had toward the other, "combining
     admiration with suspicion." Traces the course of their relations;
     emphasizes that Dryden "never wholly lost his respect for Rymer,
     never classed him with Milbourne or Blackmore." Describes Rymer's
     critical system; notes that he took from Dryden "his conception of
     a literary period or age" and "a total view of literature in which
     national versions and period achievements were . . . versions of
     the whole rather than wholly separate entities." Claims that Rymer
     is a Renaissance humanist, perhaps the last.

41   MORRIS, G.C.R. "Dryden, Hobbs, Tonson and the Death of Charles

II." N&Q, n.s. 22 (December):558-59.
Argues that the physician Thomas Hobbs was in attendance during the King's last illness, and that Dryden, not Jacob Tonson, added his name to a line of Threnodia Augustalis in the 1701 folio edition of Dryden's poems.

*42   NELSON, TIMOTHY G.A.   "The Rotten Orange: Fears of Marriage in Comedy from Shakespeare to Congreve." Southern Review (Adelaide, Australia) 8:205-26.
Cited in the 1975 MLA International Bibliography.

43   NICOLL, ALLARDYCE. Dryden as an Adapter of Shakespeare. New York: AMS Press.
Reprint of 1922.7.

*44   OKA, TEKUO. "'Blessed Saints' Ko" [Thoughts on 'Blessed Saints']. Eigo Seinen 120:568-70; 121:18-20.
Cited in the 1975 MLA International Bibliography.

*45   O'NEILL, JOHN H. "Sexuality, Deviance, and Moral Character in the Personal Satire of the Restoration." Eighteenth-Century Life 2:16-19.
Cited in the 1975 MLA International Bibliography.

46   PECHTER, EDWARD. Dryden's Classical Theory of Literature. Cambridge: Cambridge University Press, 233 pp.
Describes and discusses "the structure of Dryden's literary theory." Finds balance to be its central characteristic. Notes Dryden's ability to assimilate various traditions; suggests that he liked being a transitional figure. Points out his great importance as a model for later English criticism. Looks at the poetry, emphasizing its "ordered variety."

47   PERSSON, AGNES V. Comic Character in Restoration Drama. De Proprietaribus Litterarum, Series Practica 99. The Hague: Mouton, 151 pp.
Sees a dichotomy in Restoration comic characters between those who are aware of what is going on around them and those who are not. Draws several examples from Dryden's theory and practice, especially in Sir Martin Mar-all and Marriage a-la-Mode. Sees Sir Martin as a prime example of an ignorant fool.

*48   PROFFITT, BESSIE CLARE. "Classical Concentric Structure in Seventeenth- and Eighteenth-Century Literature." Ph.D. dissertation, Southern Illinois University.
Cited in the 1975 MLA International Bibliography. Abstracted in DAI 35:7919A-20A.

49   RODWAY, ALLEN. English Comedy: Its Role and Nature from Chaucer to the Present Day. Berkeley: University of California Press, 288 pp.

Attempts "to give the reader an appropriate base for that
personal 'adventure among masterpieces' which is the proper completion of criticism." Discusses MacFlecknoe and Absalom and
Achitophel, but concludes that the latter "cannot be said [to]
sparkle throughout." Finds its didactic aspect a hindrance to its
success as comedy.

*50   SAMPLE, CAROL BERNIECE. "The Problem of the Conclusion of
      Dryden's Absalom and Achitophel: A Rhetorical Study." Ph.D.
      dissertation, Texas Christian University.
            Cited in the 1975 MLA International Bibliography. Abstracted
      in DAI 36:3737A.

51   SASLOW, EDWARD L. "Dryden in 1684." MP 72 (February):248-55.
            Gives a chronology of "Dryden's literary activities from
      the fall of 1683 to the end of 1684"; claims that it is more ac-
      curate and complete than any previous accounts of this period.
      Argues that Dryden's letter to Laurence Hyde, Earl of Rochester,
      was written on 17 March 1684, instead of 1683 as Charles Ward had
      suggested (in 1942.12). Relates this letter, because of its chron-
      ological proximity, to one from Dryden to Jacob Tonson in August
      1684.

52   SIGWORTH, OLIVER. "A Way of Looking at Some Baroque Poems."
      In Studies in Eighteenth Century Culture 4. Edited by Harold
      E. Pagliaro. Madison: University of Wisconsin Press for the
      American Society for Eighteenth Century Studies, pp. 31-41.
            Argues that it is important to see "To . . . Anne Killigrew,"
      Eleonora, and Alexander's Feast "among other art objects of the
      age." Finds analogues in baroque art and music to which they can
      be compared. Suggests that standard modern critical approaches,
      especially if they are New Critical or involve a romantic emphasis
      on sincerity, are too narrow to do the poems justice.

53   STEINER, T.R. English Translation Theory 1650-1800. Assen
      and Amsterdam: Van Gorcum, 159 pp.
            Describes and summarizes Dryden's "rules" for translation
      as they developed. Sees a shift in emphasis from favoring close
      translation to a recognition of its limits, and finally to a be-
      lief that the translator's responsibility is to communicate the
      essence of the original. Asserts that Dryden is the "chief law-
      giver" for English translation through the nineteenth century.

*54   STRASBURG, RICHARD. "The Sensational Mode: A Sociology of
      Dulness in English Augustan Satire." Ph.D. dissertation,
      Emory University.
            Cited in the 1975 MLA International Bibliography. Abstracted
      in DAI 35:4458A.

*55   STRAULMAN, ANN. "Zempoalla, Lyndaraxa, and Nourmahal: Dryden's
      Heroic Female Villians." English Studies in Canada 1:31-45.
            Cited in the 1975 MLA International Bibliography.

56   VISSER, COLIN. "The Anatomy of the Early Restoration Stage: The Adventures of Five Hours and John Dryden's 'Spanish' Comedies." TN 29, no. 2:57-69; no. 3:114-19.

    Suggests that the success of Sir Samuel Tuke's The Adventures of Five Hours established a strong staging convention which in turn helped dictate the nature of "Spanish" comedy. Shows in detail the compatibility of The Rival Ladies, An Evening's Love, and The Assignation to the conjectural setting of Tuke's play at the Lincoln's Inn Fields Theatre. Concludes that the "whole apparatus of houses, balconies, doors, night gardens, walks, and arbours" which make up the basic setting of the form were strongly influenced by Davenant's staging of Tuke's play, especially his use of "proscenium walls containing doors surmounted by balconies."

57   WILLSON, ROBERT F., Jr. "Their Form Confounded": Studies in the Burlesque Play from Udall to Sheridan. The Hague and Paris: Mouton, 184 pp.

    "Bayes Versus the Critics: The Rehearsal and False Wit" (pp. 81-110) puts Buckingham's play into the context of the heroic drama it parodies. Sees Dryden's views of drama in Essay of Dramatic Poesy as consistent with his heroic plays, but charges that he fails to see "the impracticability of translating the imaginary realm of heroic poetry into the idiom of the stage." Uses The Indian Queen as an example of heroic drama at its most excessive. Deals at length with The Rehearsal. Argues that Bayes is not only a portrait of Dryden but of the "newly-arrived virtuoso." Shows also how Buckingham's Drawcansir is modeled on Dryden's Almanzor (in The Conquest of Granada).

58   WILSON, GAYLE EDWARD. "Dryden and the Emblem of Fortuna-Occasio." PLL 11 (Spring):199-203.

    Asserts that emblematic representations of Opportunity, such as that in Geoffrey Whitney's A Choice of Emblems (1586), are the source of images used in The Conquest of Granada (1) by Lyndaraxa (1. 1) and Almanzor (4. 1). Finds a similar example in Absalom and Achitophel (11. 256-61).

59   ZAMONSKI, JOHN A. An Annotated Bibliography of John Dryden: Texts and Studies, 1949-1973. New York and London: Garland, 160 pp.

    Includes brief descriptions and summaries of most items. Arranged by categories of Dryden's works.

*60 ZIMMER, R.K. "The Emergence of the 'New' Woman on the English Stage." Kentucky Philological Association Bulletin (1975): 25-31.

    Cited in the 1975 MLA International Bibliography.

<u>1976</u>

1   ALLEN, NED BLISS. <u>The Sources of John Dryden's Comedies</u>.
    Norwood, Pa.: Norwood Editions.
       Reprint of 1935.1.

2   AMIS, GEORGE T. "The Structure of the Augustan Couplet." <u>Genre</u>
    9 (Spring):37-58.
       Studies patterns of rhyme, meter, and syntax within the form.
Uses Pope's <u>The Rape of the Lock</u> as his major example, but finds
Dryden's couplets to be essentially similar to Pope's. Argues
that the Augustan couplet has essentially the same typical pattern
as the English decasyllabic couplet, "only more clearly marked or
more fully developed." Concludes by suggesting that since the
Augustan couplet tends "toward the aphoristic" (by virtue of its
basic pattern) the senses of individual couplets seem separable
from the sense of the whole. Links this lack of continuity to the
habits of summary and generalization which are typical of Augustan
writing.

*3   ANDERBERG, GARY T. "<u>Cleomenes</u> and Affective Tragedy." <u>Essays</u>
    <u>in Literature</u> (Macomb, Ill.) 3:41-51.
       Cited in the <u>1976 MLA International Bibliography</u>.

4   ARMISTEAD, J.M. "The Mythic Dimension of Dryden's <u>The Hind and</u>
    <u>the Panther</u>." <u>SEL</u> 16 (Summer):377-86.
       Argues that the poem is designed to convince the reader of
the validity of "the Roman Catholic myth." This myth is created
in two key passages, 1. 251-90 (in which Dryden describes the origin of beasts in men) and 2. 499-519 (the revelation of the Hind's
identity). Concludes that "once the reader has solved the riddle
of the Hind's identity . . . , he is committed for the moment to
read the poem in terms of the myth."

5   ATKINS, G. DOUGLAS. "The Ancients, the Moderns, and Gnosticism."
    In <u>Transactions of the Fourth International Congress on the</u>
    <u>Enlightenment</u>. Edited by Theodore Besterman. Studies on
    Voltaire and the Eighteenth Century 151. Oxford: Voltaire
    Foundation, pp. 149-66.
       Argues that Dryden, Swift, and Pope were not only not
Gnostics, but were hostile to "tendencies, aims, and desires that
may best be viewed as Gnostic." Identifies Gnosticism in Dryden's
time with the Puritans he attacks in <u>Absalom and Achitophel</u>, especially as they seem to him to want to replace religion with the
political state.

*6   BOISAUBIN, ELISABETH ANN. "Identity and Difference in English
    and French Comedy: 1659-1722." Ph.D. dissertation, Stanford
    University.
       Cited in the <u>1976 MLA International Bibliography</u>. Abstracted
in <u>DAI</u> 36:6073A-74A.

7   BOYS, RICHARD C., ed. Studies in the Literature of the Augustan
     Age: Essays Collected in Honor of Arthur Ellicott Case.
     Folcroft, Pa.: Folcroft Library Editions.
          Reprint of 1952.3; 1966.6. Includes 1931.17; 1938.19;
     1946.7.

*8   BRATTON, CLINTON WOODROW. "The Use of Marriage in the Comedies
     of Etherege, Wycherley, Dryden, and Congreve." Ph.D. disserta-
     tion, University of Colorado.
          Cited in the Annual Bibliography of English Language and
     Literature for 1976 (London: Modern Humanities Research Associa-
     tion). Abstracted in DAI 36:7431A-32A.

*9   BROWN, TERENCE. "Dryden as Puritan Cavalier in His 'Letter to
     Honor Dryden.'" Concerning Poetry 9, no. 2:35-39.
          Cited in the 1976 MLA International Bibliography.

*10 _____. "John Dryden's Poetry 1649-1662: A Critical Study."
     Ph.D. dissertation, Southern Illinois University.
          Cited in the 1976 MLA International Bibliography. Abstracted
     in DAI 36:8069A-70A.

*11 BRUNKHORST, MARTIN. "Aspekte der Oedipus-Adaptation bei Dryden
     und Lee." Germanisch-Romanische Monatsschrift NS 26:386-406.
          Cited in the 1976 MLA International Bibliography.

12   DALY, ROBERT. "Dryden's Ode to Anne Killigrew and the Communal
     Works of Poets." TSLL 18 (Summer):184-97.
          Claims to read the poem "on its own terms"; finds its subject
     to be the "continuing social and moral function" of poetry and its
     fulfillment in the work of individual poets. Cites several other
     examples of Dryden's apparently sincere encouragement of minor
     poets who shared his view of the ends of poetry.

13   DEANE, CECIL V. Dramatic Theory and the Rhymed Heroic Play.
     Norwood, Pa.: Norwood Editions.
          Reprint of 1931.5.

*14 DEMARIA, ROBERT, Jr. "Critical Worlds: A View of Literary
     Criticism as an Artistic and Literary Form." Ph.D. disserta-
     tion, Rutgers University.
          Cited in the 1976 MLA International Bibliography. Abstracted
     in DAI 36:6698A-99A.

15   DOBRÉE, BONAMY. Variety of Ways. Norwood, Pa.: Norwood
     Editions.
          Reprint of 1932.8.

16   DYSON, A.E., and JULIAN LOVELOCK. Masterful Images: English
     Poetry from Metaphysicals to Romantics. London: Macmillan;

New York: Harper & Row, 254 pp.
      The book is "intended primarily for those who are making a
serious study of poetry for the first time." "Beyond the Polemics:
The Opening of Dryden's Absalom and Achitophel" (pp. 71-96) considers whether the poem is primarily polemical or, transcending
its occasion, "a triumph of form." Outlines its historical circumstances. Asks why the poem begins with the King's infidelities,
even though they are contrary to its values; suggests that Dryden
needs to establish Monmouth's illegitimacy. Concludes that Dryden
"makes a virtue of the necessary and striking limitations imposed
upon him": that he in fact demonstrates his thesis "that freedom
is . . . a successful coming to terms with reality."

17   FISHER, ALAN S. "Daring to be Absurd: The Paradoxes of The
        Conquest of Granada." SP 73 (October):414-39.
      Describes the play's nature, and "the artistic and moral
satisfactions such an enterprise might offer." Claims that
Dryden's characters do not seem lifelike because he dramatizes
their "general predicaments . . . , not their identities as people."
Emphasizes the play's heavy use of paradox in speech and action:
cites Almanzor's "huffing" and the "moral precision" of a character
like Ozmyn, who is torn between obligations. Finds in the play's
improbably lucky ending a miraculous reward for Almanzor's daring--
even his daring to be absurd. Concludes that through this paradox
Dryden asserts the presence of the metaphysical, despite the grow-
ing confidence of the time in its own powers.

*18   FREEDMAN, WILLIAM. "The Elemental Motif in All for Love."
        Hebrew University Studies In Literature 4:175-91.
          Cited in the 1976 MLA International Bibliography.

19   FROST, WILLIAM. Dryden and Future Shock. English Literary
        Studies 5. Victoria, B.C.: University of Victoria, 102 pp.
          Contains three essays. "The Hind in Context" (pp. 7-55)
links Donne, Milton, Rochester, and Dryden as writers whose religious work often deals with the problems caused by the diversity
of possible faiths in seventeenth-century England. Cites Donne's
"Satire III," several works by Milton, Rochester's "Satire Against
Mankind," and The Hind and the Panther as key examples. Asks
whether we are meant to view the conflict between the Hind and the
Panther as between good and evil or merely between different degrees
of illumination. "The Bawdy Hand of the Dial is now upon the Prick
of Noon" (pp. 56-77) deals with sexually explicit poems, focussing
on their frequent conjunction of "almost incompatible elements,"
the ludicrous and the grand. One example is Dryden's "Prologue to
An Evening's Love." "What Happened to Heroism" (pp. 78-98) discusses works with a political dimension, in which the apparent intent seems at variance with popular interpretation. Cites (among
others) Shakespeare's Richard II, Marvell's "An Horatian Ode,"
Racine's Phèdre, and Dryden's All for Love and Absalom and
Achitophel.

20   GRANSDEN, K.W.   "Milton, Dryden, and the Comedy of the Fall."
     EIC 26 (April):116-33.
        Compares Paradise Lost and The State of Innocence to show the
     comic aspect of the Fall as presented by both writers. Argues, for
     example, that Dryden's treatment brings out "the absurdity of Adam's
     situation at the moment of the Fall," which Milton's grand style
     obscures. Points out that Dryden's Adam, unlike Milton's, articu-
     lates the seeming paradox of God's foreknowledge and Man's free
     will. Claims that Adam's ability, in Dryden's work, to reach this
     conclusion, coupled with the little good it does him, shows the
     absurdity of relying on reason.

21   GRIFFIN, DUSTIN.   "Dryden's 'Oldham' and the Perils of Writing."
     MLQ 37 (June):133-50.
        Sees more complexity and uncertainty in the poem than most
     critics have allowed it. Suggests that the poem hints at "an anx-
     ious, even fearful, lament for all poets, and for Dryden himself."
     Relates it to the uncertainty of Dryden's own career in the early
     1680s. Concludes that Dryden saw himself in Oldham, and saw that
     both had failed, though in different ways.

22   HOPKINS, D.W.   "Dryden and the Two Editions of Sandys's Ovid."
     N&Q, n.s. 23 (December):552-54.
        Asserts that in his own translations from Ovid's
     Metamorphoses, Dryden drew on both the 1626 and 1632 editions of
     Sandys's translation.

*23   _____.   "Dryden's 'Baucis and Philemon.'" CL 28 (Spring):135-43.
        Cited in the 1976 MLA International Bibliography.

24   _____.   "Dryden's Cave of Sleep and Garth's Dispensary." N&Q,
     n.s. 23 (May-June):243-45.
        Argues that Dryden's depiction of the Cave of Sleep in his
     translation of the story of Ceyx and Alcyone from Ovid's
     Metamorphoses is indebted to Sir Samuel Garth's The Dispensary.
     Notes also that Garth's later revision borrowed from Dryden's
     Ceyx, providing "an interesting example of reciprocal borrowing."

25   HUME, ROBERT D.   The Development of English Drama in the Late
     Seventeenth Century. Oxford: Clarendon Press, 540 pp.
        Surveys the fifty-year period following the Restoration in
     great detail, taking into account all the available plays. Com-
     plains that critics have based their arguments on the inadequate
     evidence of the same few plays, and that they have generally ignored
     the importance of the theatrical situation. Emphasizes the period's
     diversity. Argues that while both comic and serious drama are typi-
     fied by the use of stock characters and situations, the validity
     of the traditional categories (such as "comedy of manners" and
     "comedy of humours") does not hold up when all the plays are studied.
     Distinguishes multiple types of comedy and serious play, but stresses
     that the playwrights of the period wrote with pragmatic ends in mind:

their plays had to please. Gives a chronological account of developments, decade by decade; emphasizes the error of making sharp
generic or temporal distinctions among plays and types of plays
during the period. Makes many references to Dryden; frequently
uses examples from Dryden's plays and criticism.

26   JACK, IAN, and RICHARD LUCKETT. "Augustan Poetry." In English
      Poetry. Edited by Alan Sinfield. London: Sussex, pp. 94-113.
          Prints a transcript of an "unscripted reading." The speakers
      discuss the poetry of the period, ranging widely. Their comments
      on Dryden emphasize his role in the success of the heroic couplet.

27   JENSEN, H. JAMES. The Muse's Concord: Literature, Music, and
      the Visual Arts in the Baroque Age. Bloomington and London:
      Indiana University Press, 274 pp.
          Sees Dryden as a spokesman for the "imaginative force in
      art." Notes his resistance to neoclassic French criticism in Essay
      of Dramatic Poesy, and his emphasis on liveliness as an essential
      element in poetry. Cites his comments on Shakespeare in the same
      work (pp. 116-27). Looks at Song for St. Cecilia's Day to demon-
      strate the rhetorical nature of baroque art. Argues that the poem
      attempts to create "strong passions of admiration and astonishment."
      Notes how the poem's imagery, especially in the last stanza, sug-
      gests vast space and sound (pp. 177-91).

28   JONES, THORA BURNLEY, and BERNARD deBEAR NICOL. Neo-Classical
      Dramatic Criticism 1560-1770. Cambridge: Cambridge University
      Press, 195 pp.
          Summarizes Essay of Dramatic Poesy and "The Grounds of
      Criticism in Tragedy"; argues that Dryden belongs firmly to the
      neoclassic tradition. Suggests that he shifted his attention from
      dramatic to nondramatic poetry in reaction to the general move to-
      ward a greater naturalism which "was never for Dryden the ultimate
      aim of the highest poetry" (pp. 95-114).

*29   JUCOVY, LANDA ZIERLER. "The Poetry of Continuity: Dryden as
      an Historical Poet." Ph.D. dissertation, City University of
      New York.
          Cited in the 1976 MLA International Bibliography. Abstracted
      in DAI 37:1564A-65A.

30   LATT, DAVID J., and SAMUEL HOLT MONK. John Dryden: A Survey
      and Bibliography of Critical Studies, 1895-1974. Minneapolis:
      University of Minnesota Press, 214 pp.
          Revises and updates Monk's John Dryden: A List of Critical
      Studies Published from 1895 to 1948 (1950.17). The introduction
      (pp. 3-19) reviews the history of work on Dryden. The bibliography
      continues Monk's practice of starring extremely significant works.
      Gives frequent annotation of items, indicating thesis or topic.

*31   LESLIE, DONALD McLEOD, Jr. "The Rhetoric of Love Intrigue: A

Study of Seventeenth-Century French and English Tragedy."
Ph.D. dissertation, University of Oregon.
     Cited in the 1976 MLA International Bibliography. Abstracted
in DAI 37:1532A-33A.

32   LEWIS, C.S.   Rehabilitations. St. Clair Shores, Mich.:
     Scholarly Press.
          Reprint of 1939.11.

33   LINK, FREDERICK M.   English Drama, 1660-1800: A Guide to In-
     formation Sources. Detroit: Gale, 374 pp.
          Lists, with frequent descriptive or evaluative comments,
     "every substantial book and article dealing with English drama
     1660-1800 published through 1973 and most significant material pub-
     lished in 1974." Part 1 is organized topically, Part 2 by indi-
     vidual author. Contains fourteen pages on Dryden.

34   LOFTIS, JOHN; RICHARD SOUTHERN; MARION JONES; and A.H. SCOUTEN.
     The Revels History of Drama in English. Vol. 5, 1660-1750.
     London: Methuen, 362 pp.
          Treats Dryden individually as a comic playwright (pp. 174-78)
     and as a writer of serious plays (pp. 261-67). Describes, evalu-
     ates, and briefly summarizes each of his plays, emphasizing recur-
     ring themes such as sex and marriage, conflicting obligations,
     incest, and political struggle (Scouten). The general parts of
     the volume, which deal with "the social and literary context"
     (Loftis) and "theatres and actors" (Southern and Jones), draw fre-
     quent illustrations from Dryden.

35   McDONALD, MARGARET LAMB.   The Independent Woman in the Restora-
     tion Comedy of Manners. Poetic Drama and Poetic Theory 32.
     Salzburg: Institut für Englische Sprache und Literatur, 255 pp.
          Traces the development of independent female characters who
     are marked by a "discerning wit and a consciousness of their own
     precarious roles in a shifting soeicty." Finds Sir George
     Etherege's Harriet (in The Man of Mode) and William Congreve's
     Angelica (in Love for Love) and Millamant (in The Way of the World)
     to be the perfected examples. Deals with Dryden's Melantha (a "fe-
     male fop" in Marriage a-la-Mode), Isabella ("callous and self-
     centered" in The Wild Gallant), and Florimell in Secret Love; sees
     the latter as an early example of the independent woman. Compares
     the "proviso" scene in Secret Love with that in The Way of the World
     to argue the greater depth of Congreve's treatment.

*36   MARBURY, SILVINE SLINGLUFF.   "'Let Me be Horace': The Influence
      of Horace on Ben Jonson, John Dryden, and Alexander Pope." Ph.D.
      dissertation, City University of New York.
           Cited in the 1976 MLA International Bibliography. Abstracted
      in DAI 36:4513A-14A.

*37   MECHANIC, LESLIE BARBARA.   "John Dryden's Fables: A Study in

Political Subversion." Ph.D. dissertation, University of
Pennsylvania.
        Cited in the 1976 MLA International Bibliography. Abstracted
in DAI 36:5322A.

38   MILES, JOSEPHINE. Eras and Modes in English Poetry. Westport,
      Conn.: Greenwood Press.
          Reprint of 1957.28.

39   MILLER, RAYMOND. Secondary Accent in Modern English Verse
      (Chaucer to Dryden). Philadelphia: R. West.
          Reprint of 1904.6.

40   MINER, EARL. "Time, Sequence, and Plot in Restoration Litera-
      ture." In Studies in Eighteenth-Century Culture 5. Edited by
      Ronald C. Rosbottom. Madison: University of Wisconsin Press
      for the American Society for Eighteenth-Century Studies, pp.
      67-85.
          Stresses the importance of narrative during the period; notes
      that it did not have comparable significance in earlier periods of
      English literature. Discusses Dryden's works after 1688, especially
      the Fables. Sees two kinds of narrative structure within the Fables:
      those with plot, in which "the temporal order defined by the plot
      is one remote from the poet and reader alike," and those without
      plot, organized by "associative succession," which deal with mater-
      ial close in place and time to Dryden himself. Asserts that the
      ordering of the Fables as a whole depends primarily on the plotless
      poems; draws an analogy from imperial anthologies of Japanese court
      poetry beginning in A.D. 905. There, as with the Fables, the "larg-
      er narrative is based on sequence rather than plot." Concludes
      that sequence is more basic to narrative than plot.

41   _____, ed. The Works of John Dryden. Volume XV: Plays.
      Albion and Albianus, Don Sebastian, Amphitryon. George R.
      Guffey, textual editor. Berkeley, Los Angeles, and London:
      University of California Press, 579 pp.
          The commentary (pp. 319-495) follows the format of volume 8
      (1962.42). Textual notes and charts comparing Dryden's, Molière's,
      and Plautus's versions of Amphitryon follow. Further volumes in
      the "California Dryden" to date: 1956.16 (1); 1966.32 (9);
      1969.52 (3); 1970.59 (10); 1971.58 (17); 1972.83 (2); 1974.7 (4);
      1974.54 (18); 1978.29 (11); 1979.30 (19).

42   NICOLL, ALLARDYCE. Dryden and His Poetry. Norwood, Pa.:
      Norwood Editions.
          Reprint of 1923.3.

43   OKERLUND, A.N. "Dryden's Joke on the Courtiers: Marriage a la
      Mode." SCN 34 (Spring):5-7.
          Argues that the play does have a unified structure, despite
      its apparent division into comic and heroic plots. Suggests that

by delighting his audience with comedy, and forcing them to endure
a boring heroic plot, he was showing them their own "preference for
sexual intrigue over spiritual ideals." Concludes that Dryden in
this way both pleased his audience and imposed his own, differing,
moral code upon the play.

44 OLDMIXON, JOHN. The Arts of Logick and Rhetorick. Anglistica
and Americana 163. Hildesheim: Georg Olms Verlag, 450 pp.
    A facsimile reprint of 1728.1.

45 OLSON, ROBERT C. "Shadwell's Irish Pen." Expl 35, no. 1
(September):14-16.
    Interprets "Irish pen" (MacFlecknoe, 1. 202) to mean "dull
pen," as Ireland is part of the kingdom of Dulness described in
the poem by Flecknoe. Notes that Shadwell seemed not to understand
the joke.

*46 ORRELL, JOHN. "A New Witness of the Restoration Stage, 1660-
1669." Theatre Research International 2:16-28.
     Cited in the 1976 MLA International Bibliography.

*47 PÁLFFY, ISTVÁN. "Conventions and Innovations in XVIIth Century
English Comedy." Acta Litteraria Academiae Scientorum Hungaricae
18:378-90.
     Cited in the 1976 MLA International Bibliography.

48 POYET, ALBERT. "Les echos du Virtuoso et de sa dédicace dans
Mac Flecknoe." EA 29 (October-December):525-33.
    Lists and examines several close verbal parallels between
the poem and Shadwell's play and its preface-dedication to the
Duke of Newcastle.

*49 _____. "French Influence in Dryden's Discourse concerning the
Original and Progress of Satire." Caliban 13:25-29.
     Cited in the 1976 MLA International Bibliography.

50 RICKS, CHRISTOPHER. "Allusion: The Poet as Heir." In Studies
in the Eighteenth Century III: Papers Presented at the Third
David Nichol Smith Memorial Seminar, Canberra 1973. Edited by
R.F. Brissenden and J.C. Eade. Toronto: University of Toronto
Press, pp. 209-40.
    Asserts that "literary allusion is a way of dealing with the
predicaments and responsibilities of 'the poet as heir.'" Concerned
with Augustan poets' uses of each other, and with the problem of
their anxiety that they have been left nothing to do. Notes passages in which Dryden seems to acknowledge fear or jealousy of
earlier writers such as Virgil, Jonson, and Milton. Relates the
situation to patronage, especially royal patronage. Argues that
Dryden's "most creative allusions [are] those of which the quick
is paternity and inheritance."

51   ROBINSON, K.E.   "A Reading of Absalom and Achitophel." YES
      6:53-62.
          Argues that the poem's opening admits the King's "sexual
      incontinence in such a context that it is extenuated without being
      excused." The biblical parallel provides "an objective source"
      for this extenuation. This incontinence mirrors a national weak-
      ness which the popular affection for Monmouth epitomizes. The
      King's behavior at the poem's ending, however, shows a regeneration
      which merits his country's approval and obedience.

52   ROGERS, PAT. "Trade and Dominion: Annus Mirabilis and Windsor-
      Forest." DUJ, n.s. 38 (December):14-20.
          Argues that Dryden's poem was a major influence on Pope's.
      The two poems share a common theme--national renewal--and "nodal
      words, images, concepts," e.g., destruction and renewal, "the
      prosperity/trade/harmony cluster," and hunting. The poems are
      especially close in their endings, where the echoes become verbal
      as well as general.

53   SAMPSON, H. GRANT. "The Hero and the Structural Design of The
      Conquest of Granada." Wascana Review 11, no. 2 (Fall):69-79.
          Argues that the play's "structural formality" should be the
      critic's focus, not the character of Almanzor, who does not in fact
      dominate the action of the play. Distinguishes seven subsidiary
      actions, each with its own protagonist. Almanzor links these, but
      is not essential to any of them. Concludes that approaching the
      play through its formal structure better suits both Dryden's view
      of drama and drama's theatrical dimension.

54   SMALLWOOD, P.J. "A Dryden Allusion to Rymer's Rapin." N&Q,
      n.s. 23 (December):554.
          Suggests that Dryden's phrase "fineness of raillery" (in
      "Discourse . . . of Satire") is borrowed from Rymer's translation
      of Rapin's Reflexions sur l'Aristotle.

55   SMITH, DAVID NICHOL. John Dryden. Folcroft, Pa.: Folcroft
      Library Editions.
          Reprint of 1950.24.

56   TARBET, DAVID W. "Reason Dazzled: Perspective and Language
      in Dryden's Aureng-Zebe." Criticism 18 (Summer):256-72.
          Reads the play in the light of the significance of visual
      and linguistic distancing in Renaissance art. The play's ultimate
      theme is "the adequacy of language to life and character." True
      authority is associated with language, and characters fail when
      they try to move beyond language: they "cannot distance themselves
      from their wishes or interpret what they do." Reprinted: 1979.38.

57   TRACY, CLARENCE. "The Tragedy of All for Love." UTQ 45
      (Spring):186-99.
          Asserts that Dryden's purpose was "to give the play

intellectual and moral content that he could not find in
Shakespeare's Antony and Cleopatra." Dryden makes use of polari-
ties such as love/honor, Cleopatra/Octavia, and especially Egypt/
Rome to simplify and clarify the play's moral issues. Antony is
forced to choose between the political value of Roman virtus and
the human value of love for Cleopatra. His tragedy is that he
loses both.

58 VALLESE, TARQUINIO. Politics and Poetry (Political Influences
on English Poetry). Folcroft, Pa.: Folcroft Library Editions.
Reprint of 1937.16.

59 VIETH, DAVID M. "Dryden's MacFlecknoe: The Case Against
Editorial Confusion." HLB 24 (April):204-45.
Attacks the text and commentary for MacFlecknoe in the
California Edition (1972.83), especially its treatment of manuscript evidence. Charges that the treatment is incomplete, un-
systematic, insufficiently knowledgeable, and unacceptably full
of errors. Discusses the relationships among the manuscripts, and
the ultimate relationship between Dryden's original version and
the version published in 1684: concludes that they differed "in
eight or nine single-word readings at the most." Claims to have
undertaken "the most thorough examination ever devoted to the text
of a Restoration poem that circulated in manuscript"; suggests that
a pattern has been set that can be followed with profit on many
texts of the period with similar problems. Lists, in two appendixes, the texts of MacFlecknoe and the variants.

60 VISSER, COLIN. "John Dryden's Amboyna at Lincoln's Inn Fields,
1673." RECTR 15, no. 1 (May):1-11, 32.
Suggests that the play "was influenced by, and . . . might
well have been designed to exploit the settings for" Davenant's
operas The History of Sir Francis Drake and The Cruelty of the
Spaniards in Peru. Notes that Amboyna was one of the plays produced in what had been the theater of the Duke's Company after the
King's Company, for which Dryden wrote, was burned out of its own
house in 1672.

*61 WELSH, ANNE MARIE. "The Baroque Style of John Dryden's Plays."
Ph.D. dissertation, University of Rochester.
Cited in the 1976 MLA International Bibliography. Abstracted
in DAI 37:3655A-56A.

62 WILSON, F.P. Seventeenth-Century Prose. Westport, Conn.:
Greenwood.
Reprint of 1960.29.

63 WYLIE, LAURA J. Studies in the Evolution of English Criticism.
Folcroft, Pa.: Folcroft Library Editions.
Reprint of 1894.5.

64   ZWICKER, STEVEN N. "Politics and Panegyric: The Figural Mode
      from Marvell to Pope." In Literary Uses of Typology from the
      Late Middle Ages to the Present. Edited by Earl Miner.
      Princeton: Princeton University Press, pp. 115-46.
          Briefly sketches seventeenth-century political typology (the
      habit of understanding history "as prophecy, as a continuous reve-
      lation of God's power and providence"). Argues that during the
      period in question the use of typology at first flourished, then
      declined, at least as a political technique. Draws several exam-
      ples from Dryden, who used the mode with confidence in his early
      panegyrics, but whose Absalom and Achitophel demonstrates the
      weakening of typology as a viable system. In this poem the split
      between king and country makes typology difficult to apply. Con-
      cludes that the poems of Dryden's last decade no longer use typolo-
      gy as a "language of political argument."

                                1977

1   ADAMS, PERCY G. Graces of Harmony: Alliteration, Assonance,
      and Consonance in Eighteenth-Century British Poetry. Athens:
      Ohio University Press, 265 pp.
          "John Dryden's Heavenly Harmony" (pp. 57-86) credits him
      with being an influential pioneer in the use of regular sound ef-
      fects in English literature. Argues that his use of these devices
      became increasingly resourceful and functional as his career de-
      veloped.

2   ALSSID, MICHAEL W. "The Impossible Form of Art: Dryden,
      Purcell, and King Arthur." SLitI 10, no. 1 (Spring):125-44.
          Discusses the opera in the context of the period's search
      for a proper blending of music and words. Finds a tension between
      "meaning and form." Notes Dryden's apparent resistance to the
      genre, as suggested by his prefaces. Describes the work scene by
      scene. Concludes that the problem of making "music and drama in-
      dispensible one to the other" has never been solved.

3   ARMSTRONG, REBECCA. "The Great Chain of Being in Dryden's All
      for Love." In A Provision of Human Nature: Essays on Fielding
      and Others in Honor of Miriam Austin Locke. Edited by Donald
      Kay. University, Ala.: University of Alabama Press, pp. 133-
      43.
          Asserts that "the Great Chain of Being . . . unifies the
      natural imagery, structure, and thematic conclusion of the play."
      Notes the frequent reference to disturbances of nature; concludes
      that the main characters' deaths can be seen as a "final restora-
      tion of order."

4   BELL, ROBERT H. "Dryden's Aeneid as English Augustan Epic."
      Criticism 19 (Winter):34-50.
          Asserts that despite the attacks on it by modern readers

"Dryden's Aeneid is . . . in significant ways closer to Virgil's epic vision than our twentieth-century perspective." Argues that in fact Dryden recognized that "the emphasis in the Aeneid is upon the limits . . . of great endeavor." Concludes that his understanding of the poem's moral--"the virtue of patience and constancy"--is in keeping both with his age's values and with our own sense of the poem's complexity.

5   BUCHAN, HANNAH. "Absalom and Achitophel: A Patron's Name or a Patriot's?" YES 7:86-90.
        Suggests that the reading, at line 179, of "Patron's" for "Patriot's" in two of the four issues of the first edition is not a mistake but rather a reflection of Dryden's hesitation between the two words. Relates both to contexts in Paradise Lost; also considers the second edition's change of "Assum'd" to "Usurp'd" in the same line, and the Miltonic uses of these words.

6   CARVER, LARRY. "The Restoration Poets and their Fallen King." HLQ 40 (August):333-51.
        Traces the concept of King Charles II as "father of the country." Finds its origin in "the patriarchal theory of government" associated with Sir Robert Filmer. Draws examples from Dryden among many other poets. Concludes by showing how the "fiction of the father king" becomes untenable after the accession of William III.

7   COHEN, MURRAY. Sensible Words: Linguistic Practice in England 1640-1785. Baltimore: John Hopkins University Press, 213 pp.
        Briefly discusses Absalom and Achitophel (pp. 23-25) as an example of how literary language paralleled "a shift in linguistic emphasis from the lexical to the syntactic." Despite the morally ambiguous tone and wording of the poem's opening, by the end its language is plain and direct.

*8   COOPER, ROBERT M. "Dryden's Cyclical Treatment of Order and Will." McNeese Review 24:28-33.
        Cited in the 1978 MLA International Bibliography.

9   DEANE, CECIL V. Dramatic Theory and the Rhymed Heroic Play. Philadelphia: R. West.
        Reprint of 1931.5.

10   De QUEHEN, A.H. "A Parenthetical Allusion in Dryden's 'To Dr. Charleton.'" N&Q, n.s. 24 (December):544-45.
        Argues that 11. 29-31 recall Charleton's Natural History of Nutrition, Life, and Voluntary Motion (1659).

11   DOBRÉE, BONAMY. Variety of Ways. Philadelphia: R. West.
        Reprint of 1932.8.

*12 FINDLAY, GILBERT POWELL. "Dryden's Last Ten Years." Ph.D.

dissertation, University of Washington.
   Cited in the 1977 MLA International Bibliography. Abstracted
in DAI 38:1406A-07A.

13   FISHER, ALAN S. "Necessity and the Winter: The Tragedy of
     All for Love." PQ 56 (Spring):183-203.
   Emphasizes the importance of ideals, rather than characters,
as the sources of emotion in the play. Argues that the "very validity of heroic abstractions becomes a principal question with
which the whole play deals." Examines Dryden's own statements
about the play, especially the prologue, to suggest that he meant
by the "tragedy of wit" the failure of these abstractions when
brought down to the level of human experience. The conflict of
our emotions toward Octavia--positive on the abstract level, negative on the surface level--is at the heart of the play. Concludes
that the ultimate triumphant concept is that of necessity, but also
that Antony and Cleopatra are tragic (and heroic) because they
cling to the defeated heroic abstractions.

14   GARRISON, JAMES D. "A Quotation from Waller in Dryden's Love
     Triumphant." ELN 15 (December):27-29.
   Notes that the fourth act ends with a modified quotation
from Waller's "A Panegyric to My Lord Protector" (1655). Points
out that Dryden has radically altered the context of Waller's
lines, but nonetheless they are appropriately used.

15   GRANSDEN, K.W. "What Kind of Poem is Religio Laici?" SEL 17
     (Summer):397-406.
   Locates the antecedents of the poem in the Roman satires
which Dryden translated. Notes that Dryden preferred satires
which were designed to instruct rather than castigate: the mixture of styles he uses in Religio Laici derives from the tradition
of the diatribe, which was didactic. Compares Dryden's poem and
his translation of Juvenal's tenth satire, showing close parallels
between them; finds parallels also with Persius's third satire and
some passages from Lucretius.

*16 HAMMERBACHER, GEORGE. "A Survey of Dryden Studies: 1949-1974."
     Ph.D. dissertation, Temple University.
   Cited in the 1977 MLA International Bibliography. Abstracted
in DAI 37:7762A.

17   HOLLIS, CHRISTOPHER. Dryden. Norwood, Pa.: Norwood Editions.
     Reprint of 1933.7.

18   HOLMES, TAV. "Poppies in John Dryden's MacFlecknoe." N&Q,
     n.s. 24 (May-June):219.
   Argues that the poppy reference (ll. 126-27) "has the dual
significance of pointing out both Shadwell's ignorance and his relation to Christ." Notes that the poppy is a symbol for ignorance
and indifference as well as for Christ's passion.

19 HOPKINS, D.W. "Dryden's Use of Thomas Heywood's *Troia Britanica*." *N&Q*, n.s. 24 (May–June):218–19.
Shows that Dryden, in his translation (with Mulgrave) of Ovid's letter of Helen to Paris, uses Heywood's translation (1609) as a source.

20 HUME, ROBERT D. "Marital Discord in English Comedy from Dryden to Fielding." *MP* 74 (February):248–72.
Argues that the treatment of marital discord in comedies of the period both makes "serious social commentary" and helps illuminate "shifting ideological stances" which mask the change from seventeenth- to eighteenth-century comedy. Cites many plays, focussing finally on *Marriage a-la-Mode* (1671) and Fielding's *The Modern Husband* (1732). Both plays present unhappy marriages, but while Dryden's implies, ruefully, that "people must make the best of what they cannot change," Fielding implies that solutions are possible.

21 _____. "The Myth of the Rake in 'Restoration' Comedy." *SLitI* 10, no. 1 (Spring):25–55.
Contains no extended commentary on Dryden, but makes the point that *Marriage a-la-Mode* "provides the first serious presentation and analysis of libertine ideas in Caroline comedy." Notes also that the play finds these ideas unworkable.

*22 KAVENIK, FRANCES MARY-MICHELE. "The Restoration Repertory Theatre: 1659–1668." Ph.D. dissertation, University of Wisconsin.
Cited in the *Annual Bibliography of English Language and Literature* for 1977 (London: Modern Humanities Research Association). Abstracted in *DAI* 38:3516A.

23 KRUTCH, JOSEPH WOOD. "Pope and Our Contemporaries." In *Pope and His Contemporaries: Essays Presented to George Sherburn*. Edited by James L. Clifford and Louis A. Landa. New York: Octagon, pp. 251–59.
Reprint of 1949.9.

*24 LeMASTER, J.R. "Imagery in Dryden's *Conquest of Granada*." *New Laurel Review* 7, no. 2:21–33.
Cited in the *1978 MLA International Bibliography*.

25 LEWIS, C.S. *Rehabilitations*. Norwood, Pa.: Norwood Editions.
Reprint of 1939.11.

26 LUBBOCK, ALAN. *The Character of John Dryden*. Folcroft, Pa.: Folcroft Library Editions.
Reprint of 1925.10.

*27 MISHRA, J.B. "Private Freedom and Public Responsibility: A Study of Dryden's Heroic Heroes." *Visvabharati Quarterly*

42:207-22.
Cited in the 1979 MLA International Bibliography.

28   MURRAY, DOUGLAS. "The Musical Structure of Dryden's 'Song for
     St. Cecilia's Day.'" ECS 10 (Spring):326-34.
         Argues that the poem's eight stanzas produce the effect of
     the traditional musical modes, in order. Thus the first and last
     of the eight stanzas represent the basic Ionian mode, while the
     second represents the Dorian mode (solemnity), the third the
     Phrygian mode (belligerence), the fourth the Lydian mode (sensual-
     ity), the fifth the Mixolydian mode (tragedy, despair, and love),
     and the sixth the Aeolian mode (calm). Sees the seventh stanza as
     a bridge to the eighth, which with the first represents the stand-
     ard major octave.

29   NICOLL, ALLARDYCE. Dryden and His Poetry. Philadelphia: R.
     West.
         Reprint of 1923.3.

30   _____. Dryden as an Adapter of Shakespeare. Folcroft, Pa.:
     Folcroft Library Editions.
         Reprint of 1922.7.

*31 NORRIS, EMMA COBURN. "The Concept of the Audience in Neoclas-
     sical Criticism, 1650-1711." Ph.D. dissertation, Georgia State
     University.
         Cited in the 1977 MLA International Bibliography. Abstracted
     in DAI 38:1382A-83A.

32   NOVAK, MAXIMILLIAN E. "Margery Pinchwife's 'London Disease':
     Restoration Comedy and the Libertine Offensive of the 1670's."
     SLitI 10, no. 1 (Spring):1-23.
         Suggests that the libertinism of the 1670s in drama may have
     taken its cue from the court of Charles II. Finds three central
     debates dominating these plays: marriage vs. single life, country
     vs. city, and contemporary manners vs. those of "the last age."
     Discusses Mr. Limberham and especially Marriage a-la-Mode among
     many examples.

33   ODEN, RICHARD, ed. and introd. Dryden and Shadwell, the
     Literary Controversy and "MacFlecknoe" (1668-1678): Facsimile
     Reproductions. Delmar, N.Y.: Scholars' Facsimiles and Reprints,
     320 pp.
         Prints facsimiles of printed material by Dryden and Shadwell
     relevant to their quarrel; also prints in an appendix a facsimile
     of Rochester's "An Allusion to Horace," the Oldham MS. MacFlecknoe,
     the Yale MS. MacFlecknoe, and the 1682 first edition of MacFlecknoe.
     The introduction (pp. v-xxii) surveys the controversy, distinguish-
     ing its various issues. Concludes in agreement with Vieth (1976.59)
     that Shadwell's The Virtuoso was very likely the immediate occasion
     of the poem, and that it (MacFlecknoe) was written in 1676.

*34   ORRELL, JOHN. "A New Witness of the Restoration Stage, 1670-
      1680." Theatre Research International 2:86-97.
          Cited in the 1979 MLA International Bibliography.

35   PARTRIDGE, A. COOPER. "Form and Language in English Neo-
      Classical Poetry." In An English Miscellany Presented to W.
      S. Mackie. Edited by Brian S. Lee. Cape Town: Oxford
      University Press, pp. 131-48.
          Discusses the "linguistic implications" of neoclassic style,
      emphasizing the drive toward simplification of diction and syntax,
      and rationalization of poetic devices and figures. Draws the bulk
      of his examples from Dryden and Pope.

36   PETTI, ANTHONY G. English Literary Hands from Chaucer to
      Dryden. Cambridge, Mass.: Harvard University Press, 142 pp.
          Prints photographs of examples of authors' handwriting during
      the period to illustrate various styles and conventions. Includes
      selections from Dryden's fair copy of Heroic Stanzas (1659) and
      from a letter to Charles Montague (October 1699). Notes the con-
      sistency of Dryden's hand, even over a forty-year period (p. 125,
      with two plates).

37   QUAYLE, THOMAS. Poetic Diction, A Study of Eighteenth-Century
      Verse. Philadelphia: R. West.
          Reprint of 1924.11.

38   RICHETTI, JOHN J. "The Portrayal of Women in Restoration and
      Eighteenth-Century English Literature." In What Manner of
      Woman: Essays on English and American Life and Literature.
      Edited by Marlene Springer. New York: New York University
      Press, pp. 65-97.
          Draws several examples from Dryden. Asserts that Almahide
      and Lyndaraxa (in The Conquest of Granada) "both illustrate the
      compulsive center of female personality that the stereotype always
      enforces." Finds the characterization of Cleopatra and Octavia
      satisfying, however, as is that of Doralice in Marriage a-la-Mode.
      Criticizes the "Ode to . . . Anne Killigrew" for condescension.

39   SASLOW, EDWARD L. "Dryden's Authorship of the Defence of the
      Royal Papers." SEL 17 (Summer):387-95.
          Argues, in agreement with Charles Ward's biography of Dryden
      and against Edmond Malone and the editors of the California Dryden,
      that Dryden wrote the entire Defence. Primarily attacks Malone's
      arguments (accepted and extended by the California edition) against
      Dryden's authorship.

*40   SILLING, EDWARD. "Heads of an Answer to Rymer and the Develop-
      ment of Dryden's Critical Theory." Ph.D. dissertation,
      University of North Dakota.
          Cited in the 1977 MLA International Bibliography. Abstracted
      in DAI 38:290A.

41   SMITH, DAVID NICHOL. John Dryden. Norwood, Pa.: Norwood
     Editions.
          Reprint of 1950.24.

42   TIERNEY, JAMES E. "Biblical Allusion as Character Technique
     in Dryden's All for Love." ES 58 (August):312–18.
          Argues that Dryden makes unusually heavy use of biblical
     allusion in his presentation of Antony in Act 1. Suggests that by
     doing so he intends to move the audience to "a greater sense of
     heroic proportion" in Antony's character.

43   TILLYARD, E.M.W. Poetry Direct and Oblique. Westport, Conn.:
     Greenwood.
          Reprint of 1934.18.

44   TROWBRIDGE, HOYT. From Dryden to Jane Austen: Essays on
     English Critics and Writers 1660–1818. Albuquerque: University
     of New Mexico Press, 311 pp.
          Includes 1943.13 and 1946.18. Also includes "Perception,
     Imagination, and Feeling in Dryden's Criticism," written for this
     volume (pp. 32–77). This new essay examines Dryden's view on non-
     rational responses to literature. Distinguishes three kinds:
     perceptual, imaginative, and emotional. Concludes that Dryden's
     attitude toward literature is Horatian rather than Aristotelian:
     that he is essentially pragmatic or rhetorical. Argues that he
     believes that nonrational effects are valid as long as they "sup-
     port and enhance the realization of the author's itention." Argues
     further that Dryden's theories are essentially similar to those of
     Rymer and Rapin, but more flexible and thoughtful.

45   VIETH, DAVID M. "Divided Consciousness: The Trauma and
     Triumph of Restoration Culture." Tennessee Studies in Literature
     22:46–62.
          Argues that the drastic rate of cultural change in the years
     after the Restoration "brought pressure on poets . . . to function
     as specially sensitive registers of the public consciousness."
     Finds four types of response; uses examples from Dryden (among
     others) for each: works giving a "providential" view of events
     (Heroic Stanzas and Astraea Redux), works showing a "many-sided
     awareness" of events (the heroic plays and Absalom and Achitophel),
     works with a structure of "extremes without a clear middle term"
     ("To . . . Anne Killigrew" and Alexander's Feast), and works with
     "reversible meaning" (MacFlecknoe).

46   WALKER, ROBERT G. "A Possible Dryden Echo in Johnson's 'Life
     of Dryden.'" N&Q, n.s. 24 (July–August):308.
          Suggests that Johnson echoes Dryden's "Discourse . . . of
     Satire" when he writes of him "I know not how it will be proved
     that if he had written less he would have written better."

47   WEDGWOOD, C.V. Seventeenth-Century English Literature.

366

Folcroft, Pa.: Folcroft Library Editions.
Reprint of 1950.27.

48   WENDORF, RICHARD. "Dryden, Charles II, and the Interpretation
       of Historical Character." PQ 56 (Winter):82-103.
           Asserts that an analysis of Dryden's references to Charles
       II, and a comparison of them with those of others, shows "the es-
       sential justice of his portraits." Notes the breadth of possible
       characterization Dryden allows in his theory. Examines characters
       of Charles by Halifax, Buckingham (John Sheffield), Evelyn, Burnet,
       and Welwood, noting their essential similarity to each other and to
       Dryden's.

49   WILLIAMS, AUBREY. "Of 'One Faith': Authors and Auditors in the
       Restoration Theatre." SLitI 10, no. 1 (Spring):57-76.
           Complains that modern readers tend to ignore the implications
       of the shared Christian belief of writers and audience during the
       period. Argues, for example, that reason and faith were basically
       not seen as at odds during the period; discusses Tyrannic Love to
       support the point. Asserts that Christian belief is significant
       in all forms of Restoration drama, from plays with clearly reli-
       gious themes to "Providential" interruptions in a bawdy farce like
       Mr. Limberham. Implies that the tolerance of the time, on stage
       and off, derives in large part from the Christian recognition of
       human frailty.

50   WILLSON, ROBERT F., Jr. "Sh------ and Shakespeare in Dryden's
       MacFlecknoe." Names 25 (September):155-57.
           Suggests that the "mock-heroic wit" of the poem encourages
       us occasionally to read Shakespeare's name into Dryden's conven-
       tional abbreviation for Shadwell. Because only Shakespeare could
       have merited such "praise" as the poem gives, the distance between
       him and Shadwell is emphasized.

51   WYKES, DAVID. A Preface to Dryden. London and New York:
       Longman, 255 pp.
           Gives a general survey of Dryden's life and career, with a
       major emphasis on the poetry. Contains many photographic illus-
       trations and a section of short biographies of "persons important
       in Dryden's career." Is designed to "set out such facts, reason-
       able guesses, informed opinions, and personal reactions as might
       help a new reader." Is especially concerned with steering such
       readers away from clichés and oversimplifications about Dryden
       and his literary period.

52   WYLIE, LAURA J. Studies in the Evolution of English Criticism.
       Norwood, Pa.: Norwood Editions.
           Reprint of 1894.5.

53   YOTS, MICHAEL. "Dryden's All for Love on the Restoration
       Stage." RECTR 16, no. 1 (May):1-10.

Suggests that Dryden's having written the major parts with
specific actors and actresses in mind has led to some of the problems critics have had with the play. The relationship among the
four main characters (Antony, Cleopatra, Ventidius, Octavia) can
be understood by reference to plays in which the same pairs of
actors and actresses had been successful before.

1978

1   ATKINS, G. DOUGLAS. "Dryden's Religio Laici: A Reappraisal."
      SP 75 (July):347-70.
         Asserts, against current critical trends (see especially
      Phillip Harth, 1968.33), that the poem is not an Anglican apologet-
      ic. Notes that it is difficult to reconcile its argument with any
      faction of the Established Church, especially Latitudinarianism.
      Suggests that the title of the poem should lead us to classify it
      with other similarly titled poems of the period, as a poem describ-
      ing "the kind of faith acceptable to and characteristic of laymen,"
      not clergymen. Ultimately it opposes the "usurpation of God's
      authority" by church or man alike. Suggests that Dryden also fears,
      paradoxically, the human tendency to take too much power, and there-
      fore "his most cherished principles [appear] to demand for their
      logical completion Roman Catholicism."

2   _____. "Serapion's Function in All for Love." Ball State
      University Forum 19, no. 2 (Spring):35-37.
         Argues that Serapion, who has few speeches but who opens and
      closes the play, "indicates that the way of intrigue has triumphed."
      Furthermore by his function as a framing character (as well as his
      nature as a corrupt priest) he embodies the boundaries within and
      against which Antony and Cleopatra act.

*3 BAIRD, JOSEPH L. "God's Plenty." Maledicta 2:146-48.
      Cited in the 1978 MLA International Bibliography.

*4 BROWN, LAURA SCHAEFER. "English Drama 1660-1760: The Develop-
      ment of the Form and Its Relation to the Emergence of the Novel."
      Ph.D. dissertation, University of California at Berkeley.
         Cited in the 1978 MLA International Bibliography. Abstracted
      in DAI 39:891A-92A.

5   CANFIELD, J. DOUGLAS. "Anarchy and Style: What Dryden 'Grants'
      in Absalom and Achitophel." PLL 14 (Winter):83-87.
         Argues that the syntactic ambiguity (eight readings are pos-
      sible) of l. 795 ("Yet, grant our Lords the People Kings can make")
      is intentional, suggesting the anarchy which would follow if anyone
      but God were to make Kings.

6   CORMAN, BRIAN. "Toward a Generic Theory of Restoration Comedy:
      Some Preliminary Considerations." In Studies in Eighteenth-Century

Culture, 7. Edited by Roseann Runte. Madison: University of
Wisconsin Press for the American Society for Eighteenth-Century
Studies, pp. 423-32.
 Discusses various ways of describing and evaluating the form:
the "historical," the "dialectical," and the "constructional." The
first makes use of sources and influences, the second is concerned
with ends "derived from some external ideal," and the third (preferred) method, essentially generic, argues "from completed works
to the specific artistic ends and problems they presuppose." Draws
several examples from Dryden.

*7   CULLUM, GRAHAM. "Dryden: Public Order in Private Places."
     Critical Review (Canberra, Australia) 20:72-87.
      Cited in the 1978 MLA International Bibliography.

8   DANCHIN, PIERRE. The Prologues and Epilogues of the Restoration
     (1660-1700): A Tentative Check-List. Nancy: Université de
     Nancy, 226 pp.
      A chronological list of "the great majority" of the surviving
texts: there are over 1,000. Gives the date of the play's first
performance, the theater and company, the title and author of the
play, and publication and reprint information. Contains seventy-
four Dryden entries.

*9   DEVINE, MARIE EILEEN. "The Reconciling Vision: Experience and
     Imagination in Dryden's Fables." Ph.D. dissertation, Bryn Mawr
     College.
      Cited in the 1978 MLA International Bibliography. Abstracted
in DAI 38:5493A-94A.

10   EHRENPREIS, IRVIN. "Continuity and Coruscation: Dryden's
     Poetic Instincts." In John Dryden II. Los Angeles: Clark
     Memorial Library, University of California at Los Angeles,
     pp. 1-26.
      Discusses stylistic discontinuity in Dryden's work: sees it
as a habitual characteristic, especially in his later poetry. Suggests that Dryden's concern for decorum of style often leads to a
contrast of style and subject matter which may be clearly comic or,
in heroic drama or panegyric, apparently comic. Draws examples
from Tyrannic Love, Alexander's Feast, and the Aeneid. Suggests
that the increasing "breadth and ambiguity of Dryden's sympathies"
may reflect his lack of official status and consequent freedom after
1688--he was no longer required to defend positions he disagreed
with, nor had he "confidence in the established social order."
Concludes that Dryden was an "essentially dualistic genius."

*11 ELIAS, RICHARD LANE. "Dryden's Restoration Criticism." Ph.D.
     dissertation, Temple University.
      Cited in the 1978 MLA International Bibliography. Abstracted
in DAI 39:893A-94A.

12   FALLE, GEORGE. "'A solemne measure . . . a just proportion.'"
      In Familiar Colloquy: Essays Presented to Arthur Edward Barker.
      Edited by Patricia Brückman. Ottawa: Oberon Press, pp. 209-26.
          Half of the essay deals with Song for St. Cecilia's Day (the
      rest treats Milton's "At a Solemn Music"). Analyzes the poem's
      structure and techniques; relates them to the notion of Harmony
      and that notion's "practical imitation." Concludes that although
      the poem ends with the dissolution of human life "music reasserts
      its pre-eminence as the alpha and omega of God's harmony."

13   FUJIMURA, THOMAS H. The Restoration Comedy of Wit. Westport,
      Conn.: Greenwood.
          Reprint of 1952.11.

*14   GILES, MICHAEL ANTHONY. "The Transformation of the Pindarique
      Ode from Cowley to Gray." Ph.D. dissertation, University of
      Virginia.
          Cited in the 1978 MLA International Bibliography. Abstracted
      in DAI 38:5459A.

*15   GLASSMAN, SUSAN FLORA. "The Emancipated Woman in John Dryden's
      Comedies." Ph.D. dissertation, University of Rhode Island.
          Cited in the 1978 MLA International Bibliography. Abstracted
      in DAI 39:2953A.

16   GRIFFIN, DUSTIN. "Dryden's Charles: The Ending of Absalom and
      Achitophel." PQ 57 (Summer):359-82.
          Argues that the conclusion of the poem is witty, self-
      consciously theatrical, and makes a "serious political point" about
      "the need to keep Charles on the throne," not only in obedience to
      divine will but for reasons of political expediency. Relates the
      end of the poem to Charles's own political behavior at the time in
      question; notes that he used good timing, wit, and theatricality to
      great effect during the Exclusion Crisis.

*17   GUTCHESS, GARY HOMER. "Early English Life-Story Drama." Ph.D.
      dissertation, University of Notre Dame.
          Abstracted in DAI 39:2953A-54A.

18   HAMILTON, K.G. The Two Harmonies: Poetry and Prose in the
      Seventeenth Century. Westport, Conn.: Greenwood.
          Reprint of 1963.15.

19   HAMMERBACHER, GEORGE. "An Annotated Bibliography of John
      Dryden." MP 75 (February):283-92.
          Reviews John Zamonski's An Annotated Bibliography of John
      Dryden (1975.59). Provides citations Zamonski missed, including
      some also missing in Latt and Monk's John Dryden: A Survey and
      Bibliography (1976.30).

20   HAMMOND, P.F. "Dryden's Zimri and Juvenal." N&Q, n.s. 25

(February):26.
Suggests that Dryden's portrait of Zimri in Absalom and Achitophel was influenced by Juvenal's third satire 11. 73-80.

*21 HANEY, JANICE LOUISE. "Eighteenth-Century Lyrical Models and Lyrical Languages: Essays towards a Theoretical History of the Lyric." Ph.D. dissertation, Stanford University.
Cited in the 1978 MLA International Bibliography. Abstracted in DAI 39:3597A.

22 HOPKINS, D.W. "Dryden, Le Bossu, and Ovid's Speeches of Ajax and Ulysses." N&Q, n.s. 25 (February):30-31.
Argues that when Dryden uses the example of the speeches of Ulysses and Ajax in the Metamorphoses to remind his readers (in "The Grounds of Criticism in Tragedy") of the poet's capacity to "concern an audience by describing of a passion" he is directly borrowing the example from Le Bossu's Traité du Poème Épique (1675).

23 _____. "Dryden's Borrowings from a Poem by His Son Charles." N&Q, n.s. 25 (February):31-32.
Notes two possible borrowings (in Aeneid 4. 762 and "The Wife of Bath's Tale") from Charles Dryden's "On the Happiness of a Retired Life."

24 JOHNSON, JAMES WILLIAM. The Formation of English Neo-Classical Thought. Westport, Conn.: Greenwood.
Reprint of 1967.29.

25 KUNZE, MICHAEL. Die Funktion der bukolischen Klichees in der englischen Literatur von Spenser bis Pope und Philips. Munich: Fink, 165 pp.
A subchapter ("Die neue Interpretation der Antike: John Drydens Vergil-Übersetzung 1697," pp. 98-109) deals with Dryden's translation of the Eclogues. Sees there the age's typical reliance on stock pastoral phrases.

26 KUPERSMITH, WILLIAM. "Vice and Folly in Neoclassical Satire." Genre 11 (Spring):45-62.
Examines the neoclassic distinctions between Horatian satire (attacking folly) and Juvenalian satire (attacking vice) as established by Dryden in "Discourse . . . of Satire." Argues that although Dryden's distinction is erroneous, he in fact inherited a Renaissance commonplace. The bulk of the essay considers "the literary and political implications for the satirist of the 1720's and 1730's who adopted the Horatian pose."

27 LINDQUIST, CAROL A. "The Jonsonian Design in Dryden's MacFlecknoe." Dalhousie Review 58 (Spring):130-38.
Compares the poem with Jonson's "To the Memory of . . . Shakespeare." Argues that the poems "share . . . a common design."

They both have a three-part structure: the first part establishes
the critic's authority; the second measures the subject's stature
against his tradition; the third in a narrative conclusion provides
a final judgment.

*28   LOCK, F.P. "Drama from Etherege to Fielding." Southern Review
       (Adelaide, Australia) 11:188-204.
           Cited in the 1979 MLA International Bibliography.

29   LOFTIS, JOHN, and DAVID STUART RODES, eds. The Works of John
      Dryden. Volume XI: Plays. The Conquest of Granada, Marriage
      a-la-Mode, The Assignation. Vinton A. Dearing, textual editor.
      Berkeley, Los Angeles, and London: University of California
      Press, 647 pp.
          The commentary (pp. 407-543) follows the format of volume 8
      (1962.42). An essay on "The Actors" (pp. 545-57) and textual notes
      follow. Further volumes in the "California Dryden" to date:
      1956.16 (1); 1966.32 (9); 1969.52 (3); 1970.59 (10); 1971.58 (17);
      1972.83 (2); 1974.7 (4); 1974.54 (18); 1976.41 (15); 1979.30 (19).

30   LOVE, HAROLD. "Dryden's 'Unideal Vacancy.'" ECS 12 (Fall):
      74-89.
          Discusses Dryden's occasional "brilliant incoherencies":
      argues that they are not lapses but "a conscious and calculated
      feature of style, a specialized form of the conceit." Suggests
      that the Restoration audience's preference for and expectation of
      metaphorical literalism made the use of paradoxes recalling the
      earlier poetry of the century useful as a shock device, especially
      in heroic drama. Concludes that modern critics should not unthink-
      ingly associate Dryden with the linguistic tradition of Augustan
      writers and thinkers who valued clarity above all.

31   _____, and ROSALEEN LOVE. "A Cartesian Allusion in Dryden and
      Lee's Oedipus." N&Q, n.s. 25 (February):35-37.
          Sees an allusion to Descartes's Principia Philosophiae (1644)
      in the opening lines of the play. Argues that this strengthens
      Dryden's claim to authorship of the first act, since he appears
      to have known the Principia.

32   LUBBOCK, ALAN. The Character of John Dryden. Norwood, Pa.:
      Norwood Editions.
          Reprint of 1925.10.

33   McFADDEN, GEORGE. Dryden: The Public Writer 1660-1685.
      Princeton: Princeton University Press, 316 pp.
          Concentrates on the public aspects of Dryden's work during
      the period. Notes in particular the dramas and their prefatory
      material, in which Dryden establishes a rhetorical situation be-
      tween himself, the object of his dedication, and his general audi-
      ence. Argues that the plays are more involved with the shifting
      contexts of their times than has been generally suggested. Asserts

that prefatory material must be taken seriously: there is no evidence that these pieces were written in hope of financial reward, or were ever rewarded. Finds in them "not opportunism, but a constant regard for his own integrity and for a certain type of public man whom he genuinely admired: one who was a careful administrator, not too much a timeserver or a self-seeker, and above all a preserver of continuity in government." Relates the stock situation in Dryden's serious drama (an aging, threatened king and a young hero) to Charles II and James Stuart. Treats the works of the period chronologically; pays particular attention to Aureng-Zebe and Absalom and Achitophel, relating both to the Succession Crisis. In the play the hero is in the position of James; the poem is written with Charles in mind as the most important member of its audience.

34   MANLOVE, COLIN NICHOLAS. Literature and Reality, 1600-1800.
      London: Macmillan; New York: St. Martin's, 248 pp.
         "Dryden" (pp. 57-75) deals with Dryden's satire and with his
      version of Chaucer's "Nun's Priest's Tale." Concludes that Absalom
      and Achitophel finally fails because it is too partisan; MacFlecknoe
      because it is too detached. Praises however the portrait of Zimri
      in the former poem, but finds Pope's portrait of Atossa in Moral
      Essays more complex and human. Examines Dryden's changes in
      Chaucer's original tale; notes his emphasis on the work's moral
      and social possibilities.

35   MASON, H.A. "The Dream of Happiness." CQ 8, no. 1:11-55; 9,
      no. 3 (1980):218-71.
         Examines Dryden's version of Horace's Second Epode in the
      context of the continuing question of what is happiness. Finds
      echoes there of Milton's Paradise, traditional English hunting
      vocabulary, verbal and pictorial commonplaces about country life,
      and various passages from Ovid, Tasso, and Spenser.

36   MILNE, FRED L. "Dryden's Palamon and Arcite: Its Merits and
      Flaws as a Translation of Chaucer's Knight's Tale." Meta 23
      (September):200-10.
         Reads Dryden's work in the light of his principles of translation; argues that Dryden is attempting a "paraphrase" of Chaucer,
      a loose rendering which preserves the spirit of the original. Examines the changes Dryden made in Chaucer: notes that there are
      now three divisions instead of four (and indeed the number three
      becomes a motif), the versification shifts to closed couplets, and
      love becomes the tale's dominant theme. However Dryden has significantly altered Chaucer by linking Arcite's death to his moral
      inferiority to Palamon: in this Dryden violates his source and
      also his own theory of "paraphrase."

37   MINER, EARL. "Dryden's Admired Acquaintance, Mr. Milton."
      Milton Studies 11:3-27.
         Discusses what is known or can be reasonably guessed about

their personal and literary relationships. Is not convinced that
Milton had Dryden in mind in his prefatory note to Paradise Lost,
defending his use of blank verse. Looks at Dryden's use of Milton
in his poetry; notes that Dryden alluded to and echoes Paradise
Lost as he would a classic, only a few years after its publication.
Links MacFlecknoe and Paradise Lost, Absalom and Achitophel and
Paradise Regained, and "Ode on the Death of . . . Purcell" and
"Lycidas." Suggests that Dryden did not fail as a "son" of Milton
because he was wise enough not to compete in blank-verse epic, but
concludes that in the Fables he produced "the second greatest narrative of the seventeenth century."

38 MISHRA, J.B. John Dryden: His Theory and Practice in Drama.
    Series in English Language and Literature 2. New Delhi: Bahri,
    177 pp.
       Matches Dryden's ideas about drama with the plays, arranged
    by type. Sees Dryden ultimately as a transitional figure between
    the Renaissance and neoclassicism. Attributes his changing views
    to changes in what the theaters wanted; exphasizes his flexibility
    and critical independence. Criticizes him for ignoring, unlike
    Shakespeare or Thomas Hardy, "the vital spirit, the elements of
    human nature."

39 MYERS, WILLIAM. "Dryden's Shakespeare." In Augustan Worlds:
    New Essays in Eighteenth-Century Literature. Edited by J.C.
    Hilson, M.M.B. Jones, and J.R. Watson. New York: Barnes &
    Noble, pp. 15-27.
       Argues, against such critics as F.R. Leavis and L.C. Knights,
    that Dryden is essentially "Shakespearean": that his plays are
    much more complex and ambiguous both in language and theme than
    they initially seem. Discusses Dryden's attitude toward Shakespeare:
    argues that Dryden recognized the importance of ambiguity to
    Shakespeare's work, and that "he accommodated neoclassicism to
    Shakespeare and not the other way round."

40 NOVAK, MAXIMILLIAN E. "Criticism, Adaptation, Politics, and
    the Shakespearean Model of Dryden's All for Love." In Studies
    in Eighteenth-Century Culture 7. Edited by Roseann Runte.
    Madison: University of Wisconsin Press for the American Society
    for Eighteenth-Century Studies, pp. 375-87.
       Considers the extent to which Dryden's play is "the type of
    adaptation that attempts to consume the original." Emphasizes the
    original aspects of Dryden's version, especially its shift of the
    central theme to tragic love, and its removal of Shakespeare's
    bawdiness. Points out that Dryden clearly considered his age, and
    himself, superior to the Elizabethans, especially in moral refine-
    ment and artistic craft.

41 ORMSBY-LENNON, HUGH. "Radical Physicians and Conservative Poets
    in Restoration England: Dryden among the Doctors." In Studies
    in Eighteenth-Century Culture 7. Edited by Roseann Runte.

Madison: University of Wisconsin Press for the American
Society for Eighteenth-Century Studies, pp. 389-411.
        Considers Dryden's "theory of medicine" in his writings and
what we know of his practice. Finds him (typically for his time)
equivocal in his attitude toward the debate between the conservative Galenists and the reformist Neoterics. Gives much information
about the issues involved, emphasizing the common split between
theory and practice among contemporary physicians, who persisted
in using Galen's methods even while they were being increasingly
called into question.

42   OSBORN, JAMES M. "Dryden, Shadwell, and 'a late fall'n poet.'"
      In John Dryden II. Los Angeles: Clark Memorial Library,
      University of California at Los Angeles, pp. 27-52.
          Describes, prints, and annotates a lampoon on Dryden entitled
"Upon a late fall'n Poet" (1678) from a manuscript volume in the
Osborn Collection at Yale. Suggests that despite superficial rea-
sons for ascribing it to Shadwell, as its scribe had done, it was
by someone else, "perhaps an actor, associated with the King's
Company."

*43   PIRAGES, PHILLIP JOE. "The Formative Years of Restoration
      Comedy." Ph.D. dissertation, University of Michigan.
          Cited in the 1978 MLA International Bibliography. Abstracted
   in DAI 38:6748A.

*44   PROCTOR, BETTY JANE. "John Dryden and the Earl of Musgrave:
      A Study in the Literary Patronage of the Restoration." Ph.D.
      dissertation, Texas A&M University.
          Cited in the 1978 MLA International Bibliography. Abstracted
   in DAI 39:2300A.

45   PROUDFOOT, L. Dryden's "Aeneid" and Its Seventeenth Century
      Predecessors. Norwood, Pa.: Norwood Editions.
          Reprint of 1960.19.

46   ROTHSTEIN, ERIC. Restoration Tragedy. Westport, Conn.:
      Greenwood.
          Reprint of 1967.51.

47   ROUTH, JAMES E. The Rise of Classical English Criticism.
      Norwood, Pa.: Norwood Editions.
          Reprint of 1915.3.

48   SAINTSBURY, GEORGE. A History of English Prose Rhythm.
      Westport, Conn.: Greenwood.
          Reprint of 1912.6.

*49   SAMPSON, H. GRANT. "Three Styles of Augustanism." English
      Studies in Canada 4:154-78.
          Cited in the 1978 MLA International Bibliography.

50   SASLOW, EDWARD L.   "Dryden as Historiographer Royal, and the
      Authorship of His Majesties Declaration Defended." MP 75
      (February):261-72.
          Argues against the common attribution of the tract to
      Dryden. Finds the reasons given by R.G. Ham (1935.7) unpersuasive,
      and finds one piece of evidence--that Dryden did not know in 1684
      of a book that the author of the tract knew in 1681--decisive
      against Dryden's authorship.

51   SELDEN, RAMAN.   English Verse Satire, 1590-1765. London:
      Allen & Unwin, 193 pp.
          Discusses Dryden as a satirist (pp. 105-118). Emphasizes
      his "conservative eclecticism"; notes how his nondogmatic flexi-
      bility enables him to use a wide range of tones, depending upon
      circumstances. Credits him with enlarging the tradition of satire
      by his heavy use of epic materials and allusions.

52   SHAABER, M.A.   English Seventeenth-Century Imprints in the
      Libraries of the University of Pennsylvania. Millwood, N.Y.:
      Kraus, 186 pp.
          Includes a "substantial collection of the works of John
      Dryden."

53   SMITH, DANE FARNSWORTH.   The Critics in the Audience of the
      London Theatres from Buckingham to Sheridan: A Study of Neo-
      classicism in the Playhouse 1671-1779. Folcroft, Pa.: Folcroft
      Library Editions.
          Reprint of 1953.19.

54   SMITH, RUTH.   "The Argument and Contexts of Dryden's Alexander's
      Feast." SEL 18 (Summer):465-90.
          Asserts that critics have never satisfactorily explained the
      relation of the final stanza to the poem as a whole. Reads the
      poem stanza by stanza, emphasizing ironies and ambiguities, espe-
      cially in the presentation of Alexander. Sees him as ultimately
      humiliated by Timotheus, who is related to "megalomanial" villains
      in Dryden's plays. Sees the final stanza as offering to pagan
      chaos a Christian alternative of distanced calm. Sets the poem
      in the context of St. Cecilia's Day sermons, which often contrasted
      the beneficial power of church music to the harmful potential of
      secular music. Concludes that Alexander is comparable to figures
      in Dryden's plays in whom "physical strength [is] at variance with
      moral right."

*55   SWAIM, DONNA ELLIOTT.   "Milton's Immediate Influence on Dryden."
      Ph.D. dissertation, University of Arizona.
          Cited in the 1978 MLA International Bibliography. Abstracted
      in DAI 39:904A.

56   THOMAS, W.K.   The Crafting of Absalom and Achitophel: Dryden's
      "Pen for a Party." Waterloo, Ont.: Wilfrid Laurier University
      Press, 239 pp.

Reads through the poem, concentrating on its nature as a response to an immediate political situation. Sees Dryden's first problem as the character of Charles II: suggests that his view makes light of the King's promiscuity but also establishes his credentials as a trustworthy commentator. Looks at the portraits of Shaftesbury and Monmouth: finds the same balance there, but shows that ultimately Shaftesbury is made to seem dangerous and Monmouth stupid. Notes the emphasis on the factiousness of the Whig followers of Shaftesbury, and how their biblical names suggest that they are "potentially treasonable." Looks also at the portraits of Charles's followers: finds in them recurring images of gravity, constancy, and majesty. Argues that the poem's genre is Varronian satire, and that its structure is that of the classical oration.

57 VALLESE, TARQUINIO. Politics and Poetry (Political Influences on English Poetry). Philadelphia: R. West.
 Reprint of 1937.16.

58 VERDURMEN, J. PETER. "Dryden's Cymon and Iphigenia at Century's End: Ploughshares into Swords." RLV 44, no. 4:285-300.
 Relates Dryden's translation of Boccaccio's tale of Cymon and Iphigenia to "the oblique attack on the linked ideals of chivalry and heroism" in All for Love, Oedipus, Troilus and Cressida, and The Duke of Guise, all "transitional plays produced between 1675 and 1683." Points out that Dryden had to reverse the meaning of his original to make his "anti-heroic statement."

59 WEINBROT, HOWARD. Augustus Caesar in "Augustan" England: The Decline of a Classical Norm. Princeton: Princeton University Press, 281 pp.
 Compares Dryden's version of Tacitus with that of Thomas Gordon (1728-31); finds Dryden's relatively neutral toward Augustus while Gordon's is fervently anti-Augustan. Sees Dryden as one who believed that although Augustus was a tyrant, he was the best alternative. The developing trend in the English Augustan Age was to see him as a cautionary example, the destroyer of the republic. Discusses the "Discourse . . . of Satire," quoting Dryden on his valuation of Juvenal above Horace as a satirist. Notes that this conforms to eighteenth-century preferences. Finds it ironic that the age is named for "a man who would have been as welcome there as hemlock to a philosopher."

60 WEITZMAN, ARTHUR J. "An Overlooked Manuscript of Dryden's Absalom and Achitophel." PBSA 72, no. 3:338-44.
 Describes a manuscript in the Massachusetts Historical Society. Suggests that it "may have textual value because of its affinities to the first and second folio editions of 1681 . . . and its many unique variant readings." Suggests the manuscript's genealogy; lists its variants. Dates it tentatively in the late seventeenth century.

61   WEST, MICHAEL. "Dryden's MacFlecknoe and the Example of
     Duffett's Burlesque Dramas." SEL 18 (Summer):457-64.
        Suggests that Duffett's travesties of new plays, popular
     during the 1670s, influenced Dryden's poem. Points out several
     parallels. Also notes a possible allusion to such farces and
     travesties in Dryden's "Discourse . . . of Satire."

62   WOLFE, HUMBERT. Notes on English Verse Satire. Norwood, Pa.:
     Norwood Editions.
        Reprint of 1929.10.

                              1979

1   BARBEAU, ANNE T. "The Disembodied Rebels: Psychic Origins of
     Rebellion in Absalom and Achitophel." In Studies in Eighteenth-
     Century Culture 9. Edited by Roseann Runte. Madison:
     University of Wisconsin Press for the American Society for
     Eighteenth-Century Studies, pp. 489-501.
        Suggests that the rebels have "dissociated themselves from
     the bonds and obligations arising from their physical nature."
     Notes their denial of "such basic relationships as those of mind
     and body, of parent and child, of husband and wife." All place
     too much reliance in their unaided individual minds. Sees their
     condition as placing David's initial licentiousness in perspective:
     while he may be "overindulging his flesh" he never rejects his phy-
     sical nature. Analyzes the portraits of Absalom, Achitophel,
     Zimri, Shimei, and Corah to demonstrate the pervasiveness and sig-
     nificance of their "disembodied" nature.

2   BERRY, REGINALD. "Chaucer and 'Absalom and Achitophel.'"
     N&Q, n.s. 26 (December):522-23.
        Credits George Sewell (1720) with being the first to notice
     an echo of Troilus and Criseyde 5. 817 at Absalom and Achitophel,
     1. 30.

3   BLOOM, EDWARD A., and LILLIAN D. BLOOM. Satire's Persuasive
     Voice. Ithaca: Cornell University Press, 305 pp.
        Includes a discussion of Absalom and Achitophel as an exam-
     ple of the compatibility of rhetoric and satire. Reads through
     the poem, pointing out its use of conventional rhetorical strate-
     gies: "the construction is four-tiered, its aim persuasive and
     ethical, its narrative elements delicately balanced between con-
     firmation and refutation" (pp. 73-82).

*4   BORKAT, ROBERTA F. SARFATT. "Dryden's All for Love, the
     Critics, and the Idea of Tragedy." Moderna Språk (Stockholm,
     Sweden):209-20.
        Cited in the 1979 MLA International Bibliography.

*5   BROOKS, DAVID. "Dryden and Juvenal's Satire." Sydney Studies

in English 5:60-83.
Cited in the 1979 MLA International Bibliography.

6   CANFIELD, J. DOUGLAS.   "The Significance of the Restoration
    Rhymed Heroic Play."   ECS 13 (Fall):49-62.
        Argues that these plays are defenses of the ethos which had
    descended from the chivalric code; that they reaffirm "the binding
    force in words in the face of the omnipresent threat of betrayal."
    Sees the threats to the code as "nominalism," "Machiavel-Hobbism,"
    and "Epicureanism and atheism."   Discusses The Conquest of Granada
    to show how it fits this pattern.   Appends a "tentative" chrono-
    logical listing of Restoration rhymed heroic plays.

7   CASTLE, TERRY J.   "Lab'ring Bards: Birth Topoi and English
    Poetics 1660-1820."   JEGP 78 (April):193-208.
        Explores the traditional metaphor linking poet to child-
    bearer.   Sees its changing function over the period as typical of
    the shift from neoclassicism to romanticism.   Sees in MacFlecknoe
    an uneasiness with the metaphor; giving birth is associated with
    writing bad poems.   This association becomes conventional until
    the Romantics, "who restore the childbearing motif to favorable
    status."

8   CONLON, MICHAEL J.   "The Passage on Government in Dryden's
    Absalom and Achitophel."   JEGP 78 (January):17-32.
        Studies the passage in which the poem takes up the question
    of whether the people have the authority to change royal succes-
    sion (11. 755-810).   Argues that the speech is a partisan state-
    ment of the view that the exclusion of James would revive the
    commonwealth model of government.   Claims furthermore that the
    passage juxtaposes "Whig uses of an original and revocable covenant
    to the Fall of man and to the effects of Adam's forfeit on mankind."
    Shows similarities between the arguments in the passage and argu-
    ments against exclusion.   Concludes that by associating the con-
    stitution with the Ark, the passage "creates and supplies Charles
    II with an enabling myth and Absalom and Achitophel with a center
    of unity."

*9   DUICK, JEAN; JEAN HOWARD; and ANNE-MARIE IMBERT.   Le théâtre
    anglais de 1660 à 1880.   Paris: Presses universitaires de
    France, 252 pp.
        Cited in the Library of Congress Subject Catalog.

10   EADE, J.C.   "Don Alonzo 'Gravelled':   Astrology in An Evening's
    Love."   SCN 37 (Fall-Winter):80-81.
        Praises Dryden's discreet handling of astrological jargon.

11   ERSKINE-HILL, HOWARD.   "Augustans on Augustanism: England,
    1655-1759."   In Of Private Vices and Publick Benefits:
    Beiträge zur englischen Literatur des frühen 18.Jahrhunderts.
    Edited by Johann N. Schmidt.   Frankfurt: Lang, pp. 7-34.

Examines the "Augustan" writers' own uses of the term, and
the contexts in which they used it. Discovers a divergence among
contemporary writers on who was Augustan, but a general agreement
on what was Augustan. Makes several references to Dryden, and to
other writers on Dryden, friendly and hostile.

*12   _____. "Literature and the Jacobite Cause." Modern Language
        Studies 9, no. 3:15-28.
           Cited in the 1979 MLA International Bibliography.

*13   GOLLADAY, GERTRUDE LaDEAN. "The Rhetorical-Poetic Tradition
       in Dryden's Two Verse Essays." Ph.D. dissertation, Texas
       Christian University.
          Cited in the 1979 MLA International Bibliography. Abstracted
       in DAI 39:5525A.

 14   HOLLAND, PETER. The Ornament of Action: Text and Performance
       in Restoration Comedy. Cambridge: Cambridge University Press,
       296 pp.
          Deals with "the relationship of performance to play and of
       performance to published text." Mentions Dryden frequently; dis-
       cusses the staging of The Indian Emperour to illustrate the point
       that there is a "high proportion of acting within the scene" in
       tragedy relative to comedy. Discusses Dryden's career as one ex-
       ample of the close tie between author and actors. Uses critical
       statements by Dryden in a discussion of the difference between
       reading and watching a play.

 15   HOPKINS, D.W. "Dryden: Two Supplementary Notes." N&Q, n.s.
       26 (December):523.
          Suggests that a couplet from Charles Dryden's "On the
       Happyness of a Retir'd Life" derives from a couplet in The Conquest
       of Granada; also that Ulysses' crocodile tears in Metamorphoses 13
       lie behind Absalom's similar tears at Absalom and Achitophel, ll.
       717-18.

 16   HUGHES, LEO. A Century of English Farce. Westport, Conn.:
       Greenwood.
          Reprint of 1956.17.

 17   HUGHES, PETER. "Wars Within Doors: Erotic Heroism and the
       Implosion of Texts." ES 60 (August):402-21.
          Sees a shift, culminating in eighteenth-century literature,
       from military to "erotic" heroism. Relates this shift to the de-
       velopment of baroque styles, which represent a shift from outward
       to inward heroism. Discusses All for Love as a major example.

*18   IMBERT, ANNE-MARIE. "Histoire et 'spectacle total': Albion
       and Albianus de John Dryden." Confluents 5, no. 1:197-216.
          Cited in the 1979 MLA International Bibliography.

19 KENNELLY, LAURA B. "Dryden and Byron on Single Virtue." N&Q, n.s. 26 (June):231.
Draws a parallel between Byron's The Corsair 11. 1863-64 and Dryden's The Spanish Friar 5. 2. 573.

20 LALL, RAMA RANI. Satiric Fable in English: A Critical Study of the Animal Tales of Chaucer, Spenser, Dryden, and Orwell. New Delhi: New Statesman, 155 pp.
Discusses The Hind and the Panther (pp. 61-91). Describes the poem and explains some of its meaning, drawing heavily on other critics. Concludes that the poem's length and complexity are basically inappropriate for a satiric fable: "its richness of religious and political allusion is a hindrance to its enjoyment and appreciation."

21 McFARLAND, THOMAS. "Poetry and the Poem: The Structure of Poetic Content." In Literary Theory and Structure: Essays in Honor of William K. Wimsatt. Edited by Frank Brady, John Palmer, and Martin Price. Ann Arbor, Mich.: University Microfilms International, pp. 81-114.
Reprint of 1973.50.

*22 McKENZIE, ALAN. "The Articulated Evil of Augustan Humanism." Modern Language Studies 9, no. 3:150-60.
Cited in the 1979 MLA International Bibliography.

23 MARTIN, LOY D. "Changing the Past: Theories of Influence and Originality, 1680-1830." Dispositio 4 (Summer-Autumn):189-212.
Compares Augustan and Romantic views about how individual authors respond to the authority of the past. Argues that "between the end of the seventeenth century and the beginning of the nineteenth, the perceived relationship between writers and their predecessors changed from that of a metonymic confrontation or displacement to that of a metaphoric recapitulation or resemblance." Uses several examples from Essay of Dramatic Poesy as major examples of the Augustan view. Notes that Dryden's (and the Augustans') interest in genre (as a special form of literature in which one can compete with past writers) was not carried on by the Romantics. Concludes that modern communication is "more Augustan than Romantic," and implies that we can and should imitate the Romantics, whose use of abstraction "allows the metaphoric principle of resemblance (or universal co-expression of the whole) to replace the metonymic principle of emulation."

24 MILLER, RACHEL A. "Political Satire in the Malicorne-Melanex Scenes of The Duke of Guise." ELN 16 (March):212-18.
Identifies both Malicorne and Melanex with Shaftesbury: he is associated therefore with a "conjurer-devil [in] Puritan habit" who is also a rabble-rouser, and with a Papist (Papists were traditionally thought of as claiming supernatural powers).

25 MINER, EARL. "The Poetics of the Critical Act: Dryden's Dealings with Rivals and Predecessors." In Evidence in Literary

Scholarship: Essays in Memory of James Marshall Osborn. Edited
by René Wellek and Alvaro Ribeiro. Oxford: Clarendon Press,
pp. 45-62.
    Emphasizes Dryden's awareness of his audience; asserts that
"any poet understands himself most clearly by taking a relation to
contemporaries." Notes his unusual generosity to those he wrote
poems to or about. Compares his poem to Congreve and MacFlecknoe,
and relates both to Dryden's belief that in imitating character,
"there is a better or worse likeness to be taken: the better is
panegyric, if it be not false, and the worse is [satire]." Emphasizes his "Horatian affectivism," and notes that he became more
didactic after 1688, when his fortune collapsed. Relates the situation to modern theories of influence, as in Harold Bloom's Anxiety
of Influence; argues that in translation "the audience often matters
more than the author translated, just as rival contemporary poets
certainly account for more of a writer's concern than does a
predecessor."

*26   ORRELL, JOHN. "The London Court Stage in the Savoy Correspond-
       ence, 1613-1675." Theatre Research International 4:79-94.
       Cited in the 1979 MLA International Bibliography.

27   PRICE, CURTIS A. Music in the Restoration Theatre. Studies
      in Musicology 4. UMI Research Press, 323 pp.
          Discusses the period's occasional use of music to accentuate
      dramatic mood or action. Uses examples from All for Love, Aureng-
      Zebe, and Troilus and Cressida. Also quotes Dryden's statement in
      Essay of Dramatic Poesy that music between the acts is a "relief
      to us from the best Plots and language."

28   RADDADI, MONGI. Davenant's Adaptations of Shakespeare.
      Stockholm: Almqvist & Wiksell, 181 pp.
          Discusses the authorship of The Tempest, or the Enchanted
      Island, often attributed to Dryden. Concludes that Dryden's con-
      tribution was limited to minor changes in the play, and the pro-
      logue and epilogue.

29   ROBINSON, K. "Juvenal, Oldham and Dryden." N&Q, n.s. 26
      (December):518-20.
          Gives several examples in which Dryden, in translating
      Juvenal's Third Satire, seems to have borrowed from John Oldham's
      translation of the same work.

30   ROPER, ALAN, ed. The Works of John Dryden. Volume XIX. Prose:
      The Life of St. Francis Xavier, 1688. Vinton A. Dearing, textual
      editor. Berkeley, Los Angeles, and London: University of
      California Press, 530 pp.
          The commentary (pp. 445-512) follows the format of volume 18
      (1974.54). Textual notes and a glossary of place-names follow.
      Further volumes in the "California Dryden" to date: 1956.16 (1);
      1962.42 (8); 1966.32 (9); 1969.52 (3); 1970.59 (10); 1971.58 (17);
      1972.83 (2); 1974.7 (4); 1976.41 (15); 1978.29 (11).

*31 SALVAGGIO, RUTH ANN. "Dryden's Syntax: A Reappraisal of His Couplet Verse and His Public Poetry." Ph.D. dissertation, Rice University.

Cited in the <u>1979 MLA International Bibliography</u>. Abstracted in <u>DAI</u> 40:1485A.

32 SCHMIDT, JOHANN N. "Die Politik der Satire." In Of Private <u>Vices and Publick Benefits: Beiträge zur englischen Literatur des fruhen 18. Jahrhunderts</u>. Edited by Johann N. Schmidt. Frankfurt: Lang, pp. 35-61.

Discusses and categorizes typical political attitudes of English satirists from the seventeenth century to the present. Refers frequently to Dryden as an example of the conservative type.

33 SEIDEL, MICHAEL. <u>Satiric Inheritance: Rabelais to Sterne</u>. Princeton: Princeton University Press, 297 pp.

Deals at length with <u>Absalom and Achitophel</u> (pp. 144-68). Finds the poem "deeply concerned with the form and substance of transmission": relates it in this to <u>MacFlecknoe</u>. Looks at Dryden's adaptations of his biblical sources; argues that it is significant that his version is less violent and leaves out the figure of Solomon, thus focussing on David/Charles's problem with the succession. Emphasizes the poem's use of dichotomies, balancing between the timeless and the temporal, the sacred and the secular, satire and tragic irony.

34 SHERBO, ARTHUR. "The Dryden-Cambridge Translation of Plutarch's <u>Lives</u>." <u>EA</u> 32 (April-June):177-84.

Argues that Dryden edited the collection of translations, and chose the translators, the great majority of whom were connected with Cambridge University, and many of whom, like Dryden, attended Westminster School and Trinity College. Notes and discusses what is known about the translators.

35 SLOMAN, JUDITH. "The Opening and Closing Lines of 'To . . . Mrs. Anne Killigrew': Tradition and Allusion." <u>N&Q</u>, n.s. 26 (February):12-13.

Suggests that Dryden was echoing the "music, or cadence" of the opening of Sidney's <u>Astrophel and Stella</u>, and that Keats was imitating both in the opening of "Ode on a Grecian Urn." Suggests also that Virginia Woolf echoes the last lines of Dryden's poem in the last paragraph of "How Should One Read a Book" (in <u>The Second Common Reader</u>, 1932).

36 STAVES, SUSAN. <u>Player's Scepters: Fictions of Authority in the Restoration</u>. Lincoln: University of Nebraska Press, 379 pp.

Studies how, in late seventeenth-century England, "secular democratic myths of authority replaced religious and feudal myths." Examines the period's drama, among several other phenomena, for

evidence of this change and its implications. Uses The Conquest
of Granada as an example of how "heroic romance" treated "political arguments about authority and obligation." Suggests that in
the positive example of Almanzor, and the negative examples of
Boabdelin and Lyndaraxa, we see the qualities which define "the
mythical natural law sovereign" (pp. 66-70). Sees also in the
play some examples of conflicts of authority arising when parents
are arbitrary or a husband is irrational (pp. 126-29).

37   SWENEY, JOHN R. "An Unnoticed Dryden Document at Lambeth
      Palace." N&Q, n.s. 26 (February):11-12.
         Notes the existence of Archbishop Gilbert Sheldon's Fiat
      for granting Dryden a Lambeth M.A.

38   TARBET, DAVID W. "Reason Dazzled: Perspective and Language
      in Dryden's Aureng-Zebe." In Probability, Time, and Space in
      Eighteenth-Century Literature. Edited by Paula R. Backsheider.
      New York: AMS Press, pp. 187-205.
         Reprint of 1976.56.

*39   TERR, LEONARD BRIAN. "Tragic Satire from Jonson to Pope: The
      Vituperative and Elegiac Phases, and Their Relationships to the
      Neoclassical Pictorial Tradition." Ph.D. dissertation, Brown
      University.
         Cited in the 1979 MLA International Bibliography. Abstracted
      in DAI 39:6784A.

*40   VANCE, JOHN A. "Beneath the Physical Beauty: A Study of
      Indamora in John Dryden's Aureng-Zebe." Essays in Literature
      (Macomb, Ill.) 6:167-77.
         Cited in the 1979 MLA International Bibliography.

41   VERDURMEN, J. PETER. "Grasping for Permanence: Ideal Couples
      in The Country Wife and Aureng-Zebe." HLQ 42 (Autumn):329-47.
         Asserts that the two plays have the same basic "comic struc-
      ture." Finds in both "new" characters who must overcome older
      "blocking" characters. Both also have "kaleidoscopic amatory con-
      figurations," couples who "stand on the side of permanence," and
      "characters who are virtual appetites in motion." Finds in both
      a conflict between stasis and change. Argues that Dryden's solu-
      tion is the more final of the two. Concludes that "the comedy of
      wit and the rhymed heroic play should be regarded not as radically
      different kinds of drama, but rather as two strains of the same
      'comic' kind."

42   VIETH, DAVID M. "The Discovery of the Date of MacFlecknoe."
      In Evidence in Literary Scholarship: Essays in Memory of James
      Marshall Osborn. Edited by René Wellek and Alvaro Ribeiro.
      Oxford: Clarendon Press, pp. 63-87.
         Narrates the history of his investigations into the date of
      the poem's composition; repeats his argument that the poem was
      written in 1676 (see 1967.14), and clarifies it in the light of

subsequent confusion. Notes particularly that the poem refers to no events after the publication of Shadwell's The Virtuoso (July 1676), including some he "surely would have utilized if MacFlecknoe were not already in existence." Concludes that the poem was "the crowning literary achievement of 1676," which year was "the apex of the 'high Restoration.'"

43   _____. "Shadwell in Acrostic Land: The Reversible Meaning of Dryden's MacFlecknoe." In Studies in Eighteenth-Century Culture 9. Edited by Roseann Runte. Madison: University of Wisconsin Press for the American Society for Eighteenth-Century Studies, pp. 503-16.
    Surveys recent criticism of the peom: divides it into two schools, the "solemn" and the "facetious." Criticizes the former for overingenuity and the latter for shallowness. Argues that the poem is in fact "Absurd," accommodating "all the images and allusions Dryden could pack into its text." Relates it to other "absurdist" works of the period, such as Buckingham's The Rehearsal and Rochester's satirical poems. Declares that we are forced by the overwhelming multiplicity of ironic devices in the poem to take Flecknoe and Shadwell at face value as royalty in a fantasy-realm of dullness.

44   WASSERMAN, EARL. The Subtler Language. Westport, Conn.: Greenwood.
    Reprint of 1959.43 (which includes 1956.38).

*45   WEADON, MARK PRESTON. "The English Virgil: Dryden's Aeneis as an Augustan Epic." Ph.D. dissertation, University of Michigan.
    Cited in the 1979 MLA International Bibliography. Abstracted in DAI 40:878A-79A.

*46   WILLIAMS, ARTHUR SHELDON. "Politics and the Social Background of English Augustan Verse, 1688-1744." Ph.D. dissertation, Emory University.
    Cited in the 1979 MLA International Bibliography. Abstracted in DAI 40:1489A-90A.

47   WILSON, JOHN. Specimens of the British Critics. Delmar, N.Y.: Scholars' Facsimile Reprints.
    A facsimile reprint, which includes 1845.1.

48   WOODRUFF, JAMES F. "A Dryden Echo in Johnson's 'Drury-Lane Prologue.'" N&Q, n.s. 26 (February):33.
    Notes an echo of Dryden's "To my Dear Friend Mr. Congreve." Contrasts the pessimism about the stage in Johnson's prologue with Dryden's optimism.

*49   ZAPAL, ANDREA. "Dryden and the Politics of Translation." Ph.D. dissertation, University of Virginia.
    Cited in the 1979 MLA International Bibliography. Abstracted in DAI 39:4294A.

1980

1   ATKINS, G. DOUGLAS. The Faith of John Dryden: Change and
     Continuity. Lexington: University Press of Kentucky, 205 pp.
        Examines the evolution of Dryden's religious views, ranging
     over his entire career. Emphasizes the fluidity of his positions,
     but notes a consistent anticlericalism and distrust of religious
     individualism. Links Religio Laici with the tradition of "layman's
     faiths"; argues that it does not advocate or defend the doctrine
     of any church, including the Anglican. Sees a general movement in
     Dryden's religious views from a "modernist" position, possibly in-
     fluenced by scientific movements, to a "traditional" position.
     Suggests that this is reflected in the increasing moral emphasis
     of his work after 1677. Attempts to explain Dryden's conversion
     by reference to his hatred for individualism; argues that he would
     have found the Roman Catholic faith the closest available analogue
     to his own beliefs by 1685. Points out that Dryden's antipathy to
     the clergy could well have been overcome by the Catholic priest-
     hood's general avoidance of politics. Suggests that his conver-
     sion may also have been provoked by the "crisis of authority" in
     the Anglican Church set off by Martin Clifford's arguments for
     individual interpretation of scripture. The experience of writing
     Religio Laici may also have been a factor. Sees in "The Character
     of a Good Parson" (in Fables, 1700) "one of [Dryden's] very rare
     positive statements on churchmen." Concludes that we see here
     evidence that Dryden had finally moved "from individualistic advo-
     cate of the rights of the laity to a devout adherent of Catholi-
     cism."

*2   BEATTY, BERNARD. "Rival Fables: The Pilgrim's Progress and
     Dryden's The Hind and The Panther." In The Pilgrim's Progress:
     Critical and Historical Views. Edited by Vincent Nemey.
     Totowa, N.J.: Barnes & Noble, pp. 263-81.
        Cited in the 1980 MLA International Bibliography.

3   BROWN, LAURA S. "The Divided Plot: Tragicomic Form in the
     Restoration." ELH 47 (Spring):67-79.
        Discusses plays which are divided into disparate, equally
     important, tragic and comic plots. Argues that "sustained dis-
     junction is a primary end of this drama, and the best divided
     plays are those which seem to strive for formal collision." Sug-
     gests that the form derives from "Fletcherian tragicomedy" and
     the "Spanish" plays of the early Restoration: finds its appeal in
     its strong sense of decorum. Examines Marriage a-la-Mode to show
     how the two plots are at once distinct and similar, providing the
     play with both variety and coherence.

*4   DOWST, PATRICIA ELLEN. "Power as a Vital Force in the
     Theaters of Corneille and Dryden." Ph.D. dissertation,
     University of Pittsburgh.
        Cited in the 1980 MLA International Bibliography. Abstracted
     in DAI 40:4582A.

5 DUTHIE, ELIZABETH. "'A Memorial of My Own Principles':
   Dryden's 'To My Honor'd Kinsman.'" ELH 47 (Winter):682-704.
       Argues that the poem's structural looseness is functional;
   relates it not only to the demands of the epistle form but more
   importantly to the ideal of "integrity" which the poem holds up.
   Claims that "the poem has the same 'integrity' as its subject
   [John Driden, M.P., the poet's cousin]: its various topics are
   interrelated and analogous in the same way that Driden's activities
   are." Argues further that the poem is not politically neutral, but
   stands in strong opposition to William III. Concludes that it is
   not elegaic (as has been argued) but "works through the disguise
   of a politically neutral portrait to put forward a highly charged
   ideal which reflects praise on both poet and subject."

*6 EHRENPREIS, IRVIN. Acts of Implication: Suggestion and Covert
   Meaning in the Works of Dryden, Swift, Pope and Austen.
   Berkeley: University of California Press.
       Cited in the 1980 MLA International Bibliography.

7 FABIAN, BERNHARD. "Lukrez in England im siebzehnten und
   achtzehnten Jahrhundert: Einige Notizen." Wolfenbütteler
   Studien zur Aufklärung 6:107-30.
       Briefly discusses Dryden's translation of Lucretius: notes
   its relative freedom and Dryden's apparent feeling that he had a
   temperamental affinity with his original.

*8 FENSTERMAKER, JOHN J. "All for Love and Mrs. Inchbald."
   Research Studies (Pullman, Wash.) 48:40-49.
       Cited in the 1980 MLA International Bibliography.

9 GARRISON, JAMES D. "Dryden and the Birth of Hercules." SP
   77 (Spring):180-201.
       Contrasts Dryden's version of Jupiter's proclamation of his
   own divinity and the coming birth of Hercules (in Amphitryon) to
   those in Plautus (Amphitruo) and Molière (Amphitryon). Argues
   that Dryden "transforms the inherited prophecy from a more
   (Plautus) to a less (Molière) satisfactory justification of the
   ways of Jupiter to man into a severe indictment of the contemporary world." Relates Dryden's version of Jupiter's prophecy to
   his public poetry, noting his increasing pessimism about the future. Examines the play as a whole, focussing on its satiric
   dimension, in which "the ideals of justice and faith become the
   subjects of jest." Also points to material added by Dryden which
   emphasizes the characters' mercenary nature. Concludes that the
   play "is a perfect introduction to Dryden's later career."

10 HAGSTRUM, JEAN H. Sex and Sensibility: Ideal and Erotic Love
   from Milton to Mozart. Chicago: University of Chicago Press,
   364 pp.
       Deals as a whole with literary and linguistic developments
   during the Restoration and eighteenth century which reflect a
   domestication of emotions, especially those having to do with love

in its various forms. Examines Dryden's heroic plays and All for
Love (pp. 50-71), arguing that he "created within a belligerent
heroic world moved by delicate love, tender pity, and soft compassion." Suggests that characters like Almanzor, Aureng-Zebe,
and Antony, who exemplify these traits, provided important models
for the sentimental literature which followed. Concludes that
Dryden was a pioneer whose work combines sex and sensibility.
Briefly discusses his portrayal of Dido (pp. 108-11); notes that
while Dryden has "sexualized the original" his attitude toward
the character is relatively hostile.

11   HUGHES, DEREK. "Aphrodite katadyomene: Dryden's Cleopatra on
     the Cydnus." Comparative Drama 14 (Spring):35-45.
          Argues that in All for Love Dryden does not simply rewrite
     Shakespeare's version of Plutarch's account of the scene, but
     changes it to adapt to his view of Cleopatra "as a passive victim,
     misrepresented and finally destroyed by the visions of superhuman
     evil or superhuman eroticism that she incongruously inspires in
     those who surround her." Gives close verbal analysis of the rele-
     vant passages in Dryden, Shakespeare, and Plutarch.

*12 IRIE, KEITARO. In Search of Dryden's Language. Hiroshima:
     Keisuisha, 118 pp.
          Cited in the 1980 MLA International Bibliography.

13   JONES, EMRYS. "Dryden's Sigismunda." In English Renaissance
     Studies Presented to Dame Helen Gardner in Honour of Her
     Seventieth Birthday. Edited by John Carey. Oxford: Clarendon
     Press, pp. 279-90.
          Notes that the poem has two incongruous strains: one
     "coarse and indecent" and the other "noble and magnanimous." Ar-
     gues that this antithesis (also reflected in the poem's two-part
     structure) is central to the poem. Looks at Dryden's changes in
     Boccaccio's original: these sharpen the contrast between the
     first (physical) and the second (spiritual) sections. Concludes
     that the heroine, Sigismunda, is made more human and believable
     by this juxtaposition. Relates the poem to Dryden's recurrent
     treatment of "the incongruity of spirit in a world of bodies."

14   KROPF, C.R. "Unity and the Study of Eighteenth-Century
     Literature." The Eighteenth Century: Theory and Interpretation
     21 (Winter):25-40.
          Argues that "unity" (as generally defined by modern critics)
     is not a relevant or useful concept to apply to eighteenth-century
     literature. Discusses Eleonora as an example. Contends that the
     work can indeed be shown to be unified, even more unified than
     Gulliver's Travels, but cannot be shown to be good (pp. 28-30).

*15 LAMB, MARGARET. "All for Love and the Theatrical Arts." In
     The Analysis of Literary Texts: Current Trends in Methodology.
     Edited by Randolph D. Pope, Third and Fourth York College
     Colloquia. Ypsilanti, Mich.: Bilingual Press, pp. 236-43.

Cited in the <u>1980 MLA International Bibliography</u>.

*16   LEONARD, JOHN FRANCIS XAVIER. "The Changing Hind: A Critical
      Study of <u>The Hind and the Panther</u>." Ph.D. dissertation,
      Queen's University at Kingston (Canada).
           Cited in the <u>1980 MLA International Bibliography</u>. Abstracted
      in <u>DAI</u> 40:5875A.

17   LOFTIS, JOHN. "Political and Social Thought in the Drama."
      In <u>The London Theatre World 1660-1800</u>. Edited by Robert D.
      Hume. Carbondale: Southern Illinois University Press; London
      and Amsterdam: Feffer and Simons, pp. 253-85.
           Surveys what drama can tell us about political and social
      attitudes during the period. Follows Dryden's career as typical
      of the "Royalist and aristocratic bias of the Restoration theatre."
      Notes that his double tragicomic plots (as in <u>Marriage a-la-Mode</u>)
      allow him to combine wit and repartee with serious material in-
      volving characters of high rank without violating decorum. Credits
      Dryden with having the bravery to write with a Jacobite bias even
      after 1688, as in <u>Cleomenes</u> and the prologue to <u>The Prophetess</u> (pp.
      256-69).

18   MacLACHLAN, CHRISTOPHER. "Dryden, Truth, and Nature." <u>British
      Journal of Aesthetics</u> 20 (Spring):153-59.
           Associates the "nature" which Dryden believed must be imi-
      tated to convey "truth" with "the transcendent facts of Christian-
      ity." Notes the difference between this view of truth as trans-
      cending nature and the modern view of truth as conforming to nature.

*19   MARKLEY, ROBERT MOSS. "The Language of Comedy from Fletcher in
      Congreve, 1615-1700." Ph.D. dissertation, University of
      Pennsylvania.
           Cited in the <u>1980 MLA International Bibliography</u>. Abstracted
      in <u>DAI</u> 41:2615A.

*20   MEIER, THOMAS K. "The 'English' Augustans." <u>Literary Half-
      Yearly</u> 21, no. 2:98-108.
           Cited in the <u>1980 MLA International Bibliography</u>.

*21   OLINDER, BRITTA. "<u>All for Love</u>: The Only Play Dryden Wrote
      for Himself." <u>Moderna Språk</u> 74:23-36.
           Cited in the <u>1980 MLA International Bibliography</u>.

22   PRICE, CURTIS. "Music as Drama." In <u>The London Theatre World
      1660-1800</u>. Edited by Robert D. Hume. Carbondale: Southern
      Illinois University Press; London and Amsterdam: Feffer &
      Simons, pp. 210-35.
           Discusses how music was used in the drama of the period.
      Uses the Purcell-Dryden-Howard <u>Indian Queen</u> as a major example.
      Points out that the work is not really close to opera: the music
      is a means of heightening the drama. Treats several of its scenes
      in detail; emphasizes points at which the music communicates more

than does the poetry. Also briefly mentions The Duke of Guise as
an example of a tragedy with incidental music supporting the
action.

23   REISS, TIMOTHY. Tragedy and Truth: Studies in the Development
      of a Renaissance and Neoclassical Discourse. New Haven: Yale
      University Press, 344 pp.
          Treats All for Love as part of a discussion of the neoclas-
      sical shift away from Shakespearean tragedy. Notes the emphasis
      on nostalgia in Dryden's play: the transcendent love of Antony
      and Cleopatra, shown by Shakespeare, has been "reduced to a set of
      familial, social, political, and finally economic relationships."
      Concludes that the play ultimately sees love as a chaotic threat
      to the cold but effective order which Caesar brings to Egypt at
      the end of the play (pp. 206-18).

24   SASLOW, EDWARD L. "Angelic 'Fire-Works': The Background and
      Significance of The Hind and the Panther, II, 649-62." SEL 20
      (Summer):373-84.
          Argues (against Earl Miner in 1965.42) that the passage
      provides no justification for dating Dryden's conversion in July
      1685. Relates the passages to its context in the poem and in
      literary tradition. Argues that the heavenly display in the pas-
      sage is a signal of divine approval of both King James and the
      Hind's attempt to persuade the Panther that the Roman Catholic is
      the one true Church. Notes that the passage derives from Aeneid
      2. 680-98, where a similar device is used.

*25   SEWARD, JOSEPH ALVIN. "Dryden and Lucretius." Ph.D. disser-
      tation, West Virginia University.
          Cited in the 1980 MLA International Bibliography. Abstracted
      in DAI 41:1066A.

26   SHAHEEN, ABDEL-RAHMAN. "Dryden's Use of Earle's 'Trumpeter.'"
      N&Q, n.s. 27 (August):351-52.
          Links Dryden's portrait of Shaftesbury in The Medal to John
      Earle's character of "A Trumpeter" in Microcosmographia (1628).
      Notes also verbal parallels between Earle's character and the por-
      trait of Corah in Absalom and Achitophel.

*27   SHECKELS, THEODORE FRANCIS, Jr. "Dryden's Quest for Certainty,
      1669-1685." Ph.D. dissertation, Pennsylvania State University.
          Cited in the 1980 MLA International Bibliography. Abstracted
      in DAI 40:5879A.

*28   SHERWOOD, JOHN COLLINGWOOD. "The Sources of John Dryden's
      Critical Essays: An Essay of Dramatic Poesy, the Preface to
      Troilus and Cresida, the Preface to the Fables." Ph.D. disser-
      tation, Yale University.
          Cited in the 1980 MLA International Bibliography. Abstracted
      in DAI 40:5456A.

29   VISSER, COLIN. "Scenery and Technical Design." In The London
       Theatre World 1660–1800. Edited by Robert D. Hume. Carbondale:
       Southern Illinois University Press; London and Amsterdam: Feffer
       & Simons, pp. 66–118.
           Surveys the development of the technical resources of London
     theaters during the period, with many prints and drawings. Makes
     several scattered references to productions of plays by Dryden.

30   WALLACE, JOHN M. "John Dryden's Plays and the Conception of a
       Heroic Society." In Culture and Politics from Puritanism to
       the Enlightenment. Edited by Perez Zagorin. Berkeley:
       University of California Press, pp. 113–34.
           Argues that a belief in "natural obligation" is at the philo-
     sophic center of Dryden's plays. Relates this belief to Seneca's
     De beneficiis, in which the ideal ethical situation is seen as
     balancing generosity and gratitude. Links Dryden's "vision of a
     heroic society, united by bonds of natural obligation" to
     Clarendon's vision of England's "decline from a national ideal"
     and to the actual decline in responsible government during Dryden's
     time. Associates the theme of jealousy, also central to Dryden's
     plays, to the political jealousy and competitive self-interest
     Dryden saw around him. Discusses several plays, especially The
     Rival Ladies and Secret Love.

31   WILLIAMSON, GEORGE. The Donne Tradition. New York: Octagon.
           Reprint of 1930.17.

32   _____. The Proper Wit of Poetry. New York: Russell & Russell.
           Reprint of 1961.60.

                                    1981

1   BATES, RICHARD. "Dryden's 'Short Excursion' and Virgil."
       N&Q, n.s. 28 (June):216.
           Argues that Dryden was going back to Virgil (Georgics 4.
     283) rather than Ovid for the phrase (in Ceyx and Alcyone, 1.
     475).

2   DONNELLY, JEROME. "Fathers and Sons: The Normative Basis of
       Dryden's Absalom and Achitophel." PLL 17 (Fall):363–80.
           Argues that the poem both supports David/Charles as monarch
     and withholds support from him as man. Notes that "the theme of
     illegitimacy as the result of promiscuity dominates much of the
     poem." Links Dryden's view of the king to the Aristotelian theory
     that children inherit their parents' traits. Sees the father-son
     relationships of David and Absalom, and Achitophel and his son, as
     opposite extremes; sees the relationship of Barzillai and his son
     as the ideal. At the end of the poem, however, the king "assumes
     his proper roles as monarch and father."

3   GARRISON, JAMES D.   "The Universe of Dryden's Fables."   SEL 21
    (Summer):409-23.
        Argues that the poems are intentionally diverse and "atempor-
    al" in sequence, but share through their "radical metaphors . . .
    a common universe." Concentrates on fire imagery, which has a dual
    significance; it may represent erotic or vengeful fire, or it may
    represent purifying, ceremonial fire. Sees this dichotomy as rep-
    resenting the poles of passion and piety, while the images of fire
    in "recurrent transformations reflect a universe in ultimate equi-
    librium."

4   HUGHES, DEREK. Dryden's Heroic Plays. Lincoln: University of
    Nebraska Press, 206 pp.
        Argues that the plays are "humane, intelligent, and subtle
    studies of the disparity between Herculean aspiration and human
    reality." Examines Dryden's modifications of his sources: finds
    that he made his ideals more demanding and his heroes more fallible.
    Notes as a general theme the attitude that "all who seek divinity
    in the pursuit of passion are . . . merely strengthening their
    bondage to change and death." Reads The Indian Queen, The Indian
    Emperour, Tyrannic Love, The Conquest of Granada, and Aureng-Zebe.
    Relates the heroic plays to Dryden's later career, arguing that
    their themes are a continuing concern. An appendix discusses
    "sources and analogues" of the five heroic plays.

5   MELL, DONALD C., Jr. "Dryden and the Transformation of the
    Classical." PLL 17 (Spring):146-63.
        Argues that Dryden's cyclical view of history led to a belief
    that the classical tradition was dynamic rather than static; that
    it was a poet's role to "affirm the past in the present." Sees
    allusion as his main means of doing this. Looks at "To Sir Godfrey
    Kneller," "To the Earl of Roscommon," and "To the Memory of Mr.
    Oldham" to show how allusions can establish that both the subjects
    of the poems and the poems themselves are embodiments of the clas-
    sical ideal.

6   POYET, ALBERT. "Echoes of Ovid in Dryden's Absalom and
    Achitophel." N&Q, n.s. 28 (February):52-53.
        Cites three possible echoes.

7   REVERAND, CEDRIC D. "Dryden on Dryden in 'To Sir Godfrey
    Kneller.'" PLL 17 (Spring):164-80.
        Argues that the poem is self-directed, a "probing examination
    of Dryden's own accomplishments," particularly in the context of
    his loss of the laureateship. Concludes that it takes a double
    view of the status of art which recognizes that economic demands
    upon the artist can have harmful effects, but also that "individual
    accomplishments . . . can endure."

Index

All references are to entry numbers. Readers who are interested in individual works should consult not only the title of that work (under Dryden, John) but also the relevant broader category in the Dryden entry, such as "poetry" or "heroic plays," where studies that deal with large numbers of works, or with the subject as a whole, are indexed.

A., J., 1787.1
Adam, Donald G., 1963.1
Adams, Betty S., 1971.1
Adams, F., 1893.1
Adams, Henry Hitch, 1949.1;
 1951.1
Adams, J.Q., 1922.2
Adams, Percy G., 1967.1; 1977.1
Adams, Robert M., 1973.1
Addison, Joseph (as author),
 1693.1; 1711.1-2; 1712.1-2;
 (as subject), 1713.1; 1933.4;
 1974.58
Aden, John M., 1951.2; 1953.1;
 1954.1; 1955.1-3; 1959.1;
 1963.2; 1970.1
Adolph, Robert, 1968.1
Adrian, Daryl B., 1968.2
Ainger, Alfred, 1871.1
Albraugh, Ralph M., 1947.1
Albrecht, Louis, 1906.1
Alden, John, 1958.1
Alden, Raymond M., 1911.1
Alderson, William L., 1970.2
Alexander, John M., 1973.2
Alleman, Gillert Spencer, 1942.1
Allen, John D., 1957.1; 1968.3
Allen, Ned Bliss, 1935.1; 1957.2
Alssid, Michael W., 1959.2;
 1962.1; 1965.2; 1967.2-3;

 1974.1; 1977.2
Alvarez, A., 1959.3
Amarasinghe, Upali, 1962.2
Amis, George T., 1968.4; 1976.2
Amos, Flora Ross, 1920.1
Anala, Phillip Z., 1971.2
Anderberg, Gary T., 1973.3; 1976.3
Anderson, Augustus E., 1953.2
Angel, Marc D., 1967.3A
Anselment, Raymond A., 1966.1
Anthony, Geraldine M., 1963.3
Anthony, Sister Rose, 1937.2
Arber, Agnes, 1957.3
Archer, Stanley, 1965.3; 1966.2-3;
 1967.4; 1968.5; 1970.3;
 1971.3-4; 1973.4-5
Aristotle (as subject), 1903.7;
 1930.6; 1946.18
Armistead, J.M., 1973.6-7; 1976.4
Armstrong, Rebecca, 1977.3
Arnold, Claude, 1958.2
Arnold, Matthew, 1880.2-3
Arnoldt, Johannes, 1951.4
Arnott, James Fullarton, 1970.4
Arrowsmith, Joseph, 1673.3
Arthos, John, 1949.2
Ashby, Stanley R., 1927.1
Atkins, G. Douglas, 1970.5; 1971.5;
 1976.5; 1978.1-2; 1980.1
Atkins, J.W.H., 1951.5

Butler, Ian Christopher, 1970.19
Butt, John, 1950.4
Butterworth, Richard, 1916.1
Byars, Julie Anne, 1975.4
Bysshe, Edward (as author),
    1700.4; (as subject), 1923.2

C., B.L.R., 1896.2
Cable, Chester, 1948.4
Cable, William G., 1958.9
Calder-Marshall, Arthur, 1952.6
Calderón de la Barca, Pedro (as
    subject), 1947.13; 1948.18;
    1966.49; 1970.52; 1972.77;
    1973.46; 1975.7
Cameron, Allen Barry, 1968.16
Cameron, L.W., 1938.1; 1956.4
Cameron, William J., 1953.6;
    1957.10; 1960.4; 1972.6
Campbell, Dowling G., 1974.6
Campkin, Henry, 1851.2
Canfield, J. Douglas, 1975.5-6;
    1978.5; 1979.6
Capellan, Angel, 1975.7
Caracciolo, Peter, 1964.7;
    1969.12
Carnochan, W.B., 1972.7
Carroll, J.T., 1961.6
Carter, Albert Howard, 1951.9
Carver, George, 1946.2
Carver, Larry D., 1973.16; 1977.6
Casanave, Don S., 1973.17
Case, Arthur E., 1935.5
Casey, Lucian T., 1945.6
Casson, T.E., 1932.4
Castle, Terry J., 1979.7
Castrop, Helmut, 1971.14; 1972.8
Cazamian, Louis, 1924.6; 1952.7
Chalker, John, 1969.13
Chambers, A.B., 1959.8; 1974.7
Chapple, J.A.V., 1973.18
Charlanne, Louis, 1906.4
Charles II (as subject), 1946.3;
    1961.1; 1963.55; 1964.34;
    1972.72; 1977.6, 48; 1978.16
Chase, Lewis N., 1903.2
Chaucer, Geoffrey (as subject),
    1706.1; 1804.1; 1845.1;
    1857.1; 1879.3; 1892.5;
    1897.6; 1903.1, 5; 1908.4;
    1920.4; 1932.15; 1951.11;

1955.11; 1956.32; 1960.5;
    1965.28; 1967.39; 1968.6;
    1970.2; 1972.10, 14; 1974.32;
    1975.11; 1979.2. (See also
    "The Character of a Good
    Parson"; "The Cock and the
    Fox"; "The Flower and the
    Leaf"; "Palamon and Arcite";
    and "The Wife of Bath Her
    Tale")
Chernaik, Warren L., 1965.12
Chester, Allan Griffith, 1934.5
Chiasson, Elias J., 1961.7
Child, C.G., 1904.2
"Chitteldroog," 1868.1
Christie, W.D., 1868.2; 1870.1;
    1872.2
Churchill, George B., 1906.5
Cibber, Colley, 1740.1
Cibber, Theophilus, 1753.1
Cicero (as subject), 1954.3;
    1972.45
Clark, A.F.B., 1925.3
Clark, Sir George, 1934.6
Clark, John R., 1970.20; 1971.16;
    1975.8
Clark, William S., 1927.2; 1928.2;
    1930.1; 1932.5; 1937.4-5;
    1938.2
Clarke, Charles Cowden, 1871.2
Clarke, Sir Ernest, 1906.6
Cleveland, John (as subject),
    1958.18
Clifford, Martin, 1687.3
Clough, Arthur Hugh, 1851.3
Clough, Ben C., 1920.2
Cloyd, Emily L., 1972.9
Cohen, Murray, 1977.7
Cohen, Ralph, 1967.12
Colby, Elbridge, 1936.2
Cole, Elmer J., Jr., 1971.17
Coleridge, Samuel Taylor, 1817.1;
    1832.1; 1833.2
Collier, Jeremy (as author),
    1698.2; (as subject), 1910.1;
    1920.6; 1924.5; 1931.35;
    1937.2; 1958.26; 1974.47
Collins, George Stuart, 1892.2
Collins, John Churton, 1878.1;
    1895.2
Collins, W. Lucas, 1867.1

Compton, Gail H., 1969.14
Congleton, James E., 1961.8
Congreve, William (as author),
    1717.1; (as subject), 1700.6;
    1931.35; 1941.5; 1947.15;
    1954.2
Conington, John, 1861.1; 1872.3
Conlon, Michael J., 1969.15;
    1979.8
Connelly, William J., 1972.10
Cook, Dorothy, 1973.19
Cook, Richard I., 1961.9
Cooke, Arthur L., 1951.10; 1954.2
Cooper, Robert M., 1977.8
Cope, Jackson I., 1956.5; 1958.10;
    1969.16
Corder, Jim W., 1959.9; 1967.13
Corman, Brian, 1978.6
Corneille, Pierre (as subject),
    1911.2; 1925.3; 1938.6;
    1951.9; 1954.21; 1955.2;
    1956.29; 1961.30; 1962.24;
    1970.50; 1972.4; 1980.4
Cornelius, David K., 1956.6
Corney, Bolton, 1851.4; 1854.3
Corvesor, D., 1926.1
Coshow, Betty Gay, 1957.12
Couper, Ramsay W., 1904.3
Courthope, W.J., 1877.2; 1885.2;
    1903.3
Cowley, Abraham (as subject),
    1932.17; 1948.7, 17; 1951.22;
    1956.27; 1957.3, 8, 30, 32;
    1960.9; 1969.39
Craig, Hardin, 1921.2
Crane, R.S., 1930.2; 1943.2
Crawford, John W., 1971.18
Crider, J.R., 1965.14; 1970.21
Crinò, Anna Maria, 1957.13;
    1958.11; 1962.8; 1966.8;
    1971.19
Cross, Gustav, 1956.7
Crossley, James, 1851.5
Cubbage, Virginia C., 1944.1
Culioli, Antoine, 1960.5
Cullum, Graham, 1978.7
Cunningham, Hugh T., 1940.3
Cunningham, John E., 1966.9
Cunningham, Peter, 1850.2;
    1862.2; 1864.1
Current, Randall, D., 1972.11

D., E.A., 1882.1
D., S.N., 1931.4
Dacier, André (as subject),
    1955.22
Daiches, David, 1956.8; 1960.6
Daly, Robert, 1976.12
Danchin, Pierre, 1968.17; 1978.8
Daniel, Samuel (as subject),
    1925.16; 1928.4; 1929.4;
    1940.19
Danielsson, Bror, 1967.14
Darby, J.E., 1969.17
Davenant, Sir William (as subject),
    1920.7; 1928.2; 1934.7;
    1935.10; 1938.9; 1950.16;
    1970.12; 1979.28. (See also
    The Tempest)
Davenport, Warren W., 1970.22
Davidow, Lawrence Lee, 1975.9
Davie, Donald, 1952.9
Davies, Godfrey, 1946.3
Davies, H. Neville, 1963.8;
    1964.9; 1965.15; 1966.10;
    1967.15; 1968.18; 1975.10-12
Davies, Paul C., 1972.12
Davies, Thomas, 1784.2
Davis, Floyd H., Jr., 1972.13
Davis, Harold E., 1955.9
Davis, Ira B., 1961.10
Davison, Dennis, 1968.19
Day, Cyrus L., 1932.6; 1940.4
Day, E. Morton, 1899.1
Deane, Cecil V., 1931.5; 1935.6
Dearing, Bruce, 1956.9
Dearing, Vinton A., 1955.8;
    1956.16; 1959.10; 1962.9, 42;
    1966.32; 1969.18, 52; 1971.58;
    1972.83; 1973.20; 1974.7, 54;
    1975.13; 1978.29; 1979.30
DeArmond, Anna J., 1943.3
de Beer, E.S., 1932.7; 1933.3;
    1936.3-4; 1940.5-7; 1941.3;
    1956.10
Deighton, Kenneth, 1892.3
Delius, N., 1869.2
Demaria, Robert, Jr., 1976.14
Demmery, Morton, 1956.11
Dennis, John (as author), 1693.2;
    1704.1; 1711.3; 1713.1;
    1715.1; 1720.1; (as subject),
    1939.9; 1971.37

38; 1978.29; 1980.3
--The Medal, 1950.6; 1956.36;
   1958.11, 32; 1959.19; 1962.13,
   37; 1965.48; 1966.14, 29, 39;
   1970.16; 1971.24; 1972.73,
   83, 98, 100; 1974.5, 31;
   1980.26
--The Mistaken Husband, 1880.4;
   1940.13; 1962.51
--Mr. Limberham, 1940.6; 1948.20;
   1972.1; 1974.63; 1977.32, 49
--"The Monument of a Fair Maiden
   Lady, who dy'd at Bath,"
   1973.44
--Notes and Observations on the
   Empress of Morocco, 1966.11,
   33. (See also Settle)
--"Ode on the Marriage of . . .
   Mrs. Anastasia Stafford,"
   1930.10; 1931.4; 1967.40
--Oedipus, 1693.2; 1711.1;
   1729.1; 1910.2; 1945.7;
   1956.7; 1962.51; 1966.22;
   1972.33; 1976.11; 1978.31.
   (See also Lee)
--"Of Heroic Plays" (prefatory to
   The Conquest of Granada),
   1959.1
--"Palamon and Arcite," 1756.2;
   1914.9; 1952.29; 1968.43;
   1973.81; 1974.21; 1978.36.
   (See also Chaucer; Fables)
--"Parallel of Poetry and Painting," 1909.1; 1955.22; 1973.2;
   1974.37
--"Philemon and Baucis," 1967.8.
   (See also Fables; Ovid)
--Religio Laici, 1687.1; 1859.2-3;
   1934.3, 18; 1945.7; 1946.20;
   1949.10; 1952.12; 1961.4, 7,
   16; 1962.30; 1964.4, 51;
   1965.20, 64; 1966.5; 1967.11-
   13, 23; 1968.33, 62; 1969.53;
   1970.17, 28, 31, 37, 41;
   1971.26, 55; 1972.83; 1973.50,
   52; 1974.35; 1975.17; 1977.15;
   1978.1; 1980.1
--The Rival Ladies, 1917.1;
   1931.5; 1956.2; 1962.42;
   1965.33; 1967.26; 1975.56
--"Preface to The Rival Ladies,"

1973.77
--Secret Love, 1885.7; 1902.1;
   1925.11; 1945.7; 1948.20;
   1966.32; 1967.6; 1970.71;
   1972.37, 39, 54; 1976.35
--"The Secular Masque," 1956.9;
   1962.38
--"Sigismonda and Guiscardo,"
   1932.15; 1972.79; 1973.29;
   1980.13. (See also Boccaccio;
   Fables)
--Sir Martin Mar-all, 1885.6;
   1906.1; 1918.4; 1942.1;
   1945.7; 1946.13; 1961.56;
   1966.32; 1967.6, 43; 1975.47
--A Song for St. Cecilia's Day,
   1687, 1706.1; 1756.1; 1857.2;
   1934.4; 1955.28; 1956.11, 28;
   1961.20, 58; 1964.27; 1965.35;
   1967.19; 1969.43; 1972.3;
   1973.35, 54; 1976.27; 1977.28;
   1978.12
--The Spanish Friar, 1808.1;
   1839.1; 1931.20; 1932.1;
   1952.20; 1962.50; 1963.17;
   1979.19
--The State of Innocence, 1704.1;
   1721.1; 1845.1; 1900.3;
   1906.5; 1922.4; 1929.9;
   1931.19, 34, 39, 41; 1932.25;
   1935.11; 1942.3; 1952.2, 13-14;
   1954.11; 1961.31; 1964.20;
   1965.62; 1967.35; 1968.31, 47,
   51; 1971.32; 1973.81; 1976.20
--The Tempest, 1899.4; 1904.5;
   1906.6, 8; 1921.8; 1925.16;
   1926.5; 1927.15-16; 1928.3;
   1938.9; 1943.5; 1946.21;
   1947.6; 1959.16; 1965.40;
   1967.56; 1970.6, 59; 1972.61;
   1973.17, 47, 84; 1979.28.
   (See also Davenant; Shakespeare)
--"Theodore and Honoria," 1756.2.
   (See also Boccaccio; Fables)
--Threnodia Augustalis, 1934.18;
   1969.4; 1975.21
--To His Sacred Majesty, 1971.75;
   1972.72
--"To Honor Dryden," 1976.9
--"To My Dear Friend Mr. Congreve,"
   1960.10; 1966.29; 1974.19;

1979.25, 48
--"To My Honoured Friend, Dr.
Charleton," 1956.38;
1966.19-20; 1968.16; 1969.81;
1977.10
--"To My Honoured Kinsman, John
Driden," 1964.24; 1975.5;
1980.5
--"To Sir Godfrey Kneller,"
1862.2; 1971.56; 1981.5, 7
--"To the Earl of Roscommon,"
1981.5
--"To the Memory of Mr. Oldham,"
1689.1; 1965.39; 1966.24;
1970.20; 1972.65; 1974.19,
41; 1976.21; 1981.5
--"To the Pious Memory of . . .
Mrs. Anne Killigrew," 1786.2;
1787.1; 1912.5; 1942.7;
1947.16; 1948.24; 1959.14-15,
24; 1962.35; 1963.16;
1964.30; 1965.57; 1969.81;
1973.44, 81; 1974.19; 1975.12,
52; 1976.12; 1977.38. 1979.35
--Troilus and Cressida, 1904.11;
1949.7; 1958.24; 1962.27;
1964.36; 1969.3, 72; 1971.5,
11; 1973.19, 65. (See also
Shakespeare)
--Tyrannic Love, 1673.2; 1931.5;
1935.23; 1936.22; 1951.1;
1965.31, 47; 1966.44, 62;
1970.59; 1973.34; 1974.1;
1977.49; 1978.10
--"Upon the Death of the Lord
Hastings," 1947.16; 1950.26;
1955.3; 1964.42; 1966.41;
1970.78; 1973.44
--Virgil, The Works of, 1935.2;
1936.1; 1950.12; 1955.11;
1960.19; 1962.15; 1969.2, 84;
1972.20; 1973.89; 1979.45;
(Aeneis, attacks on), 1698.3;
1712.1; 1718.2; 1763.1;
1779.3; 1849.1; 1919.2; (compared with the original),
1874.1; 1951.26; 1980.10;
(concordance), 1969.70; (contemporary politics), 1972.6;
(diction), 1910.5; 1939.6;
(mock-heroic), 1969.37;

1973.92; (other translations,
compared with), 1955.24; 1963.6;
1967.3A; 1971.1; 1972.67;
(praise of), 1695.2; 1861.1;
1867.1; 1868.7; 1910.5; 1930.4;
1963.10; 1977.4; (publication),
1963.5; (text used by Dryden),
1963.27; (understanding of the
original by Dryden), 1747.1;
1805.1; 1867.1; 1935.6; 1969.28;
(visual elements), 1972.5;
1973.81; (word frequency list),
1971.66; (Eclogues), 1960.15;
1978.25; (Georgics), 1908.3;
1946.8; 1954.22; 1969.13;
1974.40. (See also Virgil)
--"The Wife of Bath Her Tale,"
1975.38; 1978.23. (See also
Chaucer; Fables)
--The Wild Gallant, 1940.13;
1942.1; 1947.5; 1950.2;
1954.2, 20; 1962.42; 1967.26;
1969.57; 1970.71; 1976.35
--and the baroque, 1932.20;
1972.25, 96; 1973.35, 43, 81;
1975.52; 1976.61
--bibliography, 1939.12; 1940.1;
1941.11; 1942.5; 1954.28;
1956.13; 1970.15; 1971.7, 44;
1975.10; 1976.33; 1977.16;
1978.19; (children's roles),
1972.19; (drama), 1699.1;
1934.16; 1940.12; 1945.8;
1949.4; 1974.27; (exhibitions),
1900.1; 1901.1; (miscellanies),
1935.5; (musical drama),
1972.32; (New Zealand libraries),
1960.4; (Ohio State University
Library), 1969.34; (Pennsylvania,
University of, Library), 1978.52;
(performances in Scotland),
1973.83; (poetry), 1720.2;
1958.1; (prologues and epilogues), 1978.8; (secondary
material), 1888.3; 1947.7;
1950.17; 1951.20; 1966.34;
1970.4, 15; 1971.7, 44;
1975.10, 59; 1976.30; 1978.19;
(tragedies), 1966.55; (works),
1918.3; 1930.19; 1931.30;
1940.8

--biography, 1714.1; 1736.1;
1760.1; 1764.1; 1779.2;
1800.1; 1808.3; 1812.1;
1854.2; 1855.3; 1865.1;
1870.1; 1881.6; 1885.3;
1888.5; 1933.7; 1937.17;
1940.21; 1954.30; 1956.13;
1961.57; 1962.3; 1963.21, 39;
1967.60; (anecdotes), 1728.3;
1740.1; 1745.1; 1753.1;
(attacks), 1936.16; (bap-
tism), 1937.12; 1943.10;
(birth date of), 1931.9,
12-13, 23-24; (Cambridge
University), 1872.2; (Collector of Customs), 1932.24;
(Eton College), 1937.10;
(financial circumstances),
1868.5; 1881.1; 1925.16;
1932.23; (funeral), 1700.5;
1714.1; 1786.1; 1888.4;
1894.4; 1904.3-4; 1949.12;
(Historiographer Royal),
1921.1; (Lambeth M.A.),
1979.37; (marriage), 1833.1;
(Northamptonshire), 1884.3;
1931.10; (Oxford University),
1934.9; 1937.3; (parents'
marriage), 1861.4; (pension),
1933.1; 1935.18; (Poet
Laureate); 1921.1; 1941.3;
1953.26; (professionalism),
1957.16; 1972.16; (Rose Alley
attack), 1714.1; 1901.3;
1939.15; 1940.22; (1684,
Dryden's activities during),
1975.51; (Swift, Jonathan),
1915.1; 1924.9; 1948.16;
1952.16
--classical influences, 1951.32;
1954.3; 1958.5; 1961.53;
1972.20-21, 38; 1973.76;
1981.5
--comedies, 1924.1, 5; 1926.4;
1935.1; 1937.9; 1940.15;
1952.11; 1954.14; 1958.14;
1959.9; 1963.31; 1968.10, 56;
1970.68, 70; 1971.13; 1972.2,
13, 36, 49, 64; 1973.21, 25,
45; 1974.2, 4, 28; 1975.34;
1976.8; 1978.6, 16. (See

also individual plays)
--criticism, 1899.2; 1900.2;
1915.3; 1930.7; 1940.26;
1941.15; 1943.2; 1951.5;
1952.26; 1955.18; 1956.8, 26;
1957.36; 1962.49; 1963.2, 51;
1967.28; 1968.42; 1969.32, 36,
46, 60; 1970.42; 1972.11, 24;
1973.63; 1975.46; 1976.28;
1978.11; (ancients vs. moderns),
1912.1; 1943.9; (as first
English criticism), 1779.2;
1855.2; 1931.8; 1950.24; (as
innovative), 1957.36; 1959.41;
(audience), 1977.31; (comedy),
1948.14; 1972.64; 1973.33, 48;
[consistency (and inconsistency)], 1913.4, 7; 1925.14;
1930.18; 1943.6; 1961.17;
1968.11; 1971.17; (contemporary
context), 1900.2; 1911.7;
1927.12; 1968.64; 1973.15, 62;
(development of), 1906.3;
1907.1; 1959.1; (English literature), 1924.10; 1928.18;
1930.17; 1957.30; 1966.54, 66;
(epic), 1938.18-19; 1944.8;
(fancy), 1945.4; 1959.1;
1973.77; (French influence),
1898.1; 1920.5; (functions of
drama), 1967.32; 1968.11;
1969.21; 1973.62; 1977.44;
(imagination), 1933.4; 1945.4;
1959.1; 1967.27; 1969.21;
1970.40; 1977.44; (imitation),
1960.2; 1963.22; 1966.59-60;
1968.11; (language), 1972.17,
76; 1975.20; (liveliness of),
1724.1; 1951.33; 1953.21;
(prosody), 1923.2; 1975.20;
(psychology), 1970.24; 1971.21;
1974.9; (responsibility of),
1941.12; (rhetoric), 1948.11;
1959.32; (rhyme in drama),
1668.1-2; 1961.15; ("rules"),
1911.1; 1934.8; 1946.15, 18;
1969.71; (shallowness of),
1724.1; 1839.1; (skepticism
of), 1940.17; 1957.36;
(sources of) (see also individual authors), 1881.3;

1961.15; 1971.31-32
Freedman, William, 1976.18
Freehafer, John, 1968.22; 1972.18
Freeman, Arthur, 1973.40; 1974.10
Freeman, Edmund, 1924.2
Freeman, Phyllis, 1948.8
French, A.L., 1968.23
French, David P., 1963.11
Fried, Gisela, 1965.18
Friedland, Louis S., 1911.4
Friedman, Lenemaja, 1972.19
Frost, William, 1946.5; 1951.12; 1955.11; 1969.23; 1971.33; 1972.20-21; 1973.26; 1974.7, 18; 1975.19; 1976.19
Frye, Prosser H., 1908.1
Fujimura, Thomas H., 1952.11; 1960.8; 1961.16; 1972.22; 1974.19; 1975.20-22
Fussell, Paul, 1954.7

G., J.A., 1868.4
G., W., 1745.1
Gagen, Jean Elizabeth, 1954.8; 1962.12
Gaines, Ervin J., 1954.9
Galigani, Guiseppi, 1974.20
Gallagher, Mary. See Thale, Mary
Gallaway, Francis, 1937.6; 1940.10
Galvin, Brother Ronan, 1971.34
Gamble, Giles Y., 1968.26
Gardner, William Bradford, 1948.9; 1950.8
Garnett, Richard, 1895.4
Garrison, James D., 1972.23; 1975.23; 1977.14; 1980.9; 1981.3
Garth, Sir Samuel (as subject), 1700.1, 6; 1976.24
Gatto, Louis C., 1966.16
Gaw, Allison, 1917.1
Geduld, Harry, 1969.24
Geis, Walter, 1950.9
Geist, Edward V., Jr., 1972.24
Genest, John, 1832.2
Gentleman, Francis, 1770.1
Gerevini, Silvano, 1966.17
Ghosh, J.C., 1929.5
Gibb, Carson, 1963.12

Gifford, William, 1802.1; 1817.2
Gildon, Charles, 1718.1; 1721.1
Gildon, Joseph, 1699.1
Giles, Michael Anthony, 1978.14
Gilfillan, G., 1855.3
Gillet, J.C., 1913.2
Gillow, Joseph, 1885.3
Giovannini, G., 1940.11
Gladstone, W.E., 1857.1
Glassman, Susan Flora, 1978.15
Glazier, George, 1931.10
Godwin, William, 1804.1
Goggin, L.P., 1964.15
Gohn, Ernest, 1948.10
Golden, Samuel A., 1962.13; 1966.18-20
Golladay, Gertrude LaDean, 1979.13
Goodman, Paul, 1954.10
Gosse, Sir Edmund, 1885.4
Gotch, J. Alfred., 1884.3
Gottesman, Lillian, 1969.25
Gottlieb, Sidney Paul, 1975.24
Gould, Robert, 1689.1
Gousseff, James W., 1963.13
Grace, Joan Carroll, 1970.35; 1975.25
Grace, John William, 1958.14
Granger, James, 1769.1
Gransden, K.W., 1976.20; 1977.15
Grant, Douglas, 1967.20
Granville-Barker, Harley, 1931.11
Gray, W. Forbes, 1914.1
Greany, Helen T., 1964.16
Green, Clarence C., 1934.8
Green, Thomas, 1810.1
Greene, Donald, 1952.12
Greene, Graham, 1942.4
Grierson, H.J.C., 1929.6; 1944.2
Griffin, Dustin, 1976.21; 1978.16
Griffin, Ernest G., 1959.13
Griffith, R.H., 1947.3
Griffith, Richard R., 1957.17
Grolier Club, 1900.1; 1901.1
Groom, Bernard, 1962.14
Grübner, Willy, 1912.2
Guffey, George Robert, 1970.59; 1976.41
Guibbory, Achsah, 1971.36; 1973.27
Guilhamet, Leon M., 1969.26
Guinness, G.N.A., 1975.26
Guite, Harold, 1971.37